I0010748

SwiftUI

for Masterminds

How to take advantage of Swift and SwiftUI
to create insanely great apps for
iPhones, iPads, and Macs

J.D Gauchat

www.jdgauchat.com

SwiftUI for Masterminds
Copyright © 2024 John D Gauchat
All Rights Reserved

No part of this publication may be reproduced, distributed, or transmitted in any form or by any means, including photocopying, recording, or other electronic or mechanical methods, without the prior written permission of the publisher, except in the case of brief quotations embodied in critical reviews and certain other noncommercial uses permitted by copyright law.

Companies, services, or product names used in this book are for identification purposes only. All trademarks and registered trademarks are the property of their respective owners.

Apple™, iPhone™, iPad™, Mac™, among others mentioned in this work, are trademarks of Apple Inc.

The information in this book is distributed without warranty. Although every precaution has been taken in the preparation of this work, neither the author nor the publisher shall have any liability to any person or entity with respect to any loss or damage caused or alleged to be caused directly or indirectly by the information contained in this work.

The source code for this book is available at **www.formasterminds.com**

Copyright Registration Number: 1165896

ISBN: 978-1-7779782-4-2

1st Edition 2020 John D Gauchat
2nd Edition 2022 John D Gauchat
3rd Edition 2022 John D Gauchat
4th Edition 2023 John D Gauchat
5th Edition 2024 John D Gauchat

Table of Contents

Chapter 7—Lists

Chapter 8—Navigation

Chapter 9—Concurrency

Chapter 10—Storage

Chapter 11—Graphics and Animations

Chapter 20—Internationalization

Chapter 21—App Store

Conventions

This book covers basic and advanced topics required to develop professional applications. Depending on your current level of knowledge and experience, you may find some of these topics easy or difficult to learn. To help you navigate through the book, we have labeled each section as described below.

Basic The Basic label represents topics you can ignore if you already know the basics of Swift and app development. If you are learning how to develop applications for Apple devices for the first time, these sections are required.

Medium The Medium label represents topics that are not required for every application. You may ignore the information presented in these sections until it is later applied in practical situations or you need it in your own applications.

Advanced The Advanced label represents topics that are only needed in advanced applications or API development. The information contained in these sections is not required for the development of most applications, but may be helpful if you want to improve your understanding of how Apple technologies work.

Examples

Every single topic covered in this book is explained with examples that you can try for yourself. We recommend that you open Xcode and try out the examples as you learn, but you can also download the codes and projects from our website to save time (**www.formasterminds.com**).

The examples in this book only apply the technologies you already know, so they don't always follow best practices. There are several programming patterns and best practices that you can follow. What applies to you depends on the characteristics of your application and what you want to accomplish with it. We recommend that you explore all the options presented in this book, but also experiment and try your own.

 IMPORTANT: Apple technologies are extensive, and one book cannot teach you everything. After each topic is introduced, you should read Apple's official specifications and search the Internet for more examples. You can find links to the specifications, additional information, tutorials, and videos on our website at **www.formasterminds.com**. Apple's official documentation is available at **developer.apple.com**. References to frameworks and APIs can be found at **developer.apple.com/documentation**.

Apple Intelligence
for Masterminds

www.formasterminds.com

Chapter 1
App Development

(Basic) **1.1 Overview**

Apple has been providing developers with tools to create apps for its devices since the launch of the first iPhone in 2007, but the Apple ecosystem has expanded considerably since then. Developers now have to take into account that users own many devices, including iPhones, iPads, Mac computers, the Apple Watch, Apple TV and the new Apple Vision Pro. Having all of these devices available with such a variety of features is great for users, but difficult for developers. Developing applications that work on multiple platforms is challenging and requires a steep learning curve. As a result, many applications were developed exclusively for one system or another. Apple engineers quickly realized that the tools were not up to the demands of modern developers and released SwiftUI in June 2019. SwiftUI is an abstraction layer that builds on previous tools to simplify the design of user interfaces and reshape the way developers build applications for Apple devices. With SwiftUI, we can easily develop applications that work seamlessly on all devices and any screen size.

(Basic) **Requirements**

Apple requires developers to build applications using software provided by the company, and this software only works on Apple computers. For this reason, the options are limited, but the good news is that the tools and accounts we need are provided by the company for free.

Mac Computer

This in theory could be any Mac computer, but the development software always requires the latest operating system (currently macOS Sequoia), so in practice we need a relatively new computer with a recommended 16 GB of memory.

Xcode

This is the software provided by Apple for development. The latest version is number 16. It's free and the package comes with everything we need to create our apps, including an editor, the SDK (Software Development Kit), and a device simulator.

Apple Developer Account

This is a basic account we can get for free. From this account, we can manage our membership, create certificates, app identifiers and other information we need to test and publish our apps.

Apple Membership

This is the membership required to publish our apps in the App Store. As of this writing, the cost of this membership is $99 US dollars per year.

Mobile Device

This could be any of the devices available in the market that support the current versions of Apple's mobile operating systems (currently iOS 18 and iPadOS 18). Testing our applications on a real device is not required but highly recommended.

In short, to develop applications for Apple devices, we need a Mac computer with the operating system required for the latest version of Xcode (currently macOS Sequoia), make sure we have an Apple ID to access our developer account (developer.apple.com), and install the latest version of Xcode (currently 16).

1.2 Xcode

Xcode is a universal IDE (Integrated Development Environment). It includes a very powerful editor with graphical tools that help us write our code, the SDKs (Software Development Kits) for creating software for iOS, iPadOS, macOS, watchOS, tvOS and visionOS, and compilers for C, C++, Objective-C and Swift. With Xcode, we can program software for any Apple platform using any of these tools and programming languages.

Xcode is available as an app in the Mac App Store. To download this application, we must open the App Store from Launchpad (the application organizer included with macOS) or double-click the App Store icon in the Applications folder in Finder (macOS' file explorer).

When we search for the term "Xcode" in the App Store, the window at the top displays the Xcode icon and a download button (Figure 1-1, number 1).

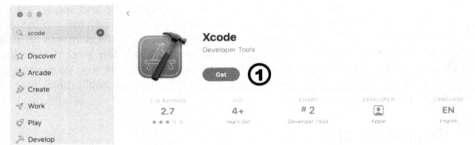

Figure 1-1: Xcode in the Mac App Store

 IMPORTANT: Xcode can also be downloaded from Apple's developer website (**https://developer.apple.com/download/**). This website not only includes the latest version of Xcode but also beta versions that we can test before they are released to the market.

After downloading Xcode, we can run the application from Launchpad or double-click the program in the Applications folder in Finder. Figure 1-2 shows Xcode's welcome screen.

Figure 1-2: Xcode's welcome screen

The welcome screen provides a list of recent projects on the right and buttons on the left to create a new project, clone a project stored in a repository, or open a project on our computer.

1.3 Development

Even though some simple projects can be developed without writing a single line of code, we always have to write our own code if we want to create useful applications, and for that we need programming languages, frameworks and APIs.

(Basic) **Programming Languages**

Many years ago, Apple introduced a language called Objective-C to create applications for its devices. Because of the technical level required to work with this language, the spectacular success of Apple's mobile devices did not impress developers as much as consumers. The demand for more and better applications grew rapidly, but the complicated nature of the system was not attractive to developers who were used to working with more traditional tools. To solve this problem, in 2014 the company introduced a new programming language called Swift. Swift offers a simpler syntax that developers are familiar with, while retaining the low-level features required to access all the functionality of Apple devices. Swift was developed to replace Objective-C and is therefore the recommended language for new developers.

(Basic) **Frameworks and APIs**

Programming languages provide all the elements required to interact with the system, but they are only a basic tool for data management. Because of the complexity of the information required to control sophisticated technologies and access every part of a system, it can take years to develop an application from scratch using only the instructions of a programming language. Simple things like printing graphics to the screen or saving data to files would become a nightmare if programmers had to rely solely on the tools provided by programming languages. For this reason, these languages are always accompanied by pre-programmed routines grouped into libraries and frameworks. Through a simple interface called API (Application Programming Interface), programmers can add amazing functionality to their applications with just a few lines of code. Apple provides all this functionality, including the frameworks and their APIs, in a set of tools called SDK (Software Development Kit) that comes with Xcode.

Frameworks and APIs are fundamental to app development. As developers, we need to learn and use these tools if we want to create useful applications, and that's why they will become the main topic of study in the following chapters.

(Basic) **Compiler**

Computers do not understand Swift or any other programming language. These languages were created for us to give instructions to machines that we can understand. Our code must be converted into elementary commands that work on an electronic level, turning multiple switches on and off to represent the abstraction that humans work with. The translation from the language that humans understand to the language that computers understand is done by a program called *compiler*.

Compilers have routines for translating instructions from programming languages into machine code. They are language and platform specific, which means that we need a specific compiler for each platform and programming language we want to use. There are several compilers available for Apple systems, but the one currently implemented in Xcode is called LLVM. LLVM is able to compile code written in Swift, C, C++, and Objective-C.

With the compiler, the machinery for creating an app is complete. Figure 1-3 below shows all the elements involved. There are three main sources of code that the compiler uses to build the application: our code in Swift, the frameworks required for our program, and a set of basic routines required to run the app (called Application Loop in Figure 1-3).

The process begins with Xcode. In this program, we write our code, access frameworks through their APIs, and configure the application to be compiled (built). By combining our code, the codes from the frameworks our app needs, and the basic routines (Application Loop), the compiler creates an executable program that can be run in a simulator, a device, or submitted to the App Store for distribution.

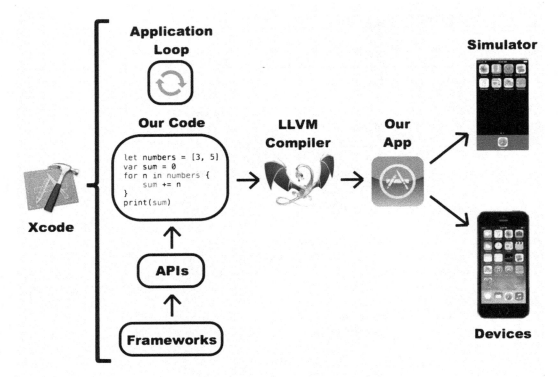

Figure 1-3: Building an App

 IMPORTANT: The Application Loop is a set of elementary routines common to every program that connect the application to the operating system and provide a loop (a code that executes itself over and over) to constantly check for events generated by the user or coming from the system. Although you never work directly with these routines, they are connected to your code to report the state of the application, as we will see in Chapter 14.

Chapter 2
Introduction to Swift

(Basic) **2.1 Computer Programming**

Computers cannot do anything without us writing a program. A program is a sequence of instructions that the computer must follow. We write the program using the instructions of a particular programming language, then a compiler translates those instructions into commands that the computer can understand, and when we tell the computer to run the program, the commands are executed one after another.

Instructions are always listed in sequential order, but programming languages offer different ways to organize the code and the data to be processed. Developing an app requires a deep understanding of these instructions and the combinations required to achieve the desired results. Since this can be daunting for beginners, Xcode includes a tool called Playground that can help us learn how to program and test our code.

(Basic) **Playground**

As the name suggests, Playground provides a place to experiment and play around with our code before using it in our applications. Although we could start an Xcode project to build an application right away, it's better to work with Playground first to learn how to code and how to use some of the basic frameworks included in the SDK. Playground files are created using the Playground option in the File menu at the top of the screen.

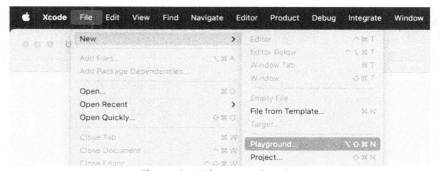

Figure 2-1: Playground option

A window opens with a list of icons for selecting the template to use. Templates are files with pre-programmed code to help us get started with our project. The currently available are called Blank (with only a few lines of code to start from scratch), Game (with basic code to program a video game), Map (with the code to display a map), and Single View (with the same code needed to create the user interface for an application).

Figure 2-2: Playground templates

After selecting the template, Xcode asks for the name of the Playground file and where we want to store it, and then shows the Playground's interface on the screen. Figure 2-3 below is what we see when we create a Blank template.

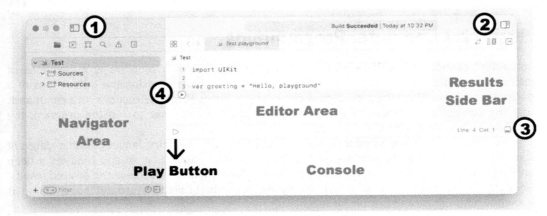

Figure 2-3: *Playground's interface*

Playground presents a simple interface with a toolbar at the top and four areas: the **Navigator Area** where we can see the resources included in our Playground project, the **Editor Area** where we write our code, the **Results Side Bar** on the right where the results produced by our code are displayed, and the **Console** at the bottom where we can read the errors produced by the code and print our own messages.

The interface includes buttons to open and remove some of these panels. The button in the upper left corner removes the Navigator Area (number 1), the one in the upper right corner controls a panel called Utilities Area with information about the selected resource (number 2), and the button in the lower right corner opens or removes the Console (number 3).

As illustrated in Figure 2-3, the Editor Area includes a button at the bottom of the panel to run and stop the code (Play Button). There is also a play button on the left side of the Editor Area that we can press if we want to execute parts of the code instead (number 4). When this button is pressed, the code is executed up to the line where the button is located.

Playground can run the code automatically or wait until we press the Play button. By default, the mode is set to Automatically Run, but we can hold down the Play button to bring up a menu that allows us to modify this behavior.

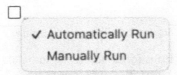

Figure 2-4: *Playground's running mode*

In the Editor Area, we can see the code we have programmed so far. When a new Playground file is created, Xcode offers a template that includes a few lines of code to get started. Listing 2-1, below, is the code currently being generated for the Blank template.

```
import UIKit

var greeting = "Hello, playground"
```

Listing 2-1: *Playground template*

A computer program is just text written with a specific syntax. Each line of text represents an instruction. Sometimes a single line includes several instructions, and therefore each line is usually called *statement*. Every statement is an order, or a group of orders, required for the computer to perform a task. In the code in Listing 2-1, the first statement uses the instruction **import** to include the pre-programmed codes from the UIKit framework, and the second statement uses the instruction **var** to store the text "Hello, playground" in memory.

If we press the Play Button to execute the code, we see the result inside the Results Side Bar. (In this case, the bar shows the text stored in memory by the **var** instruction.) When we move the mouse over the text on the bar, two small buttons show up, as illustrated below.

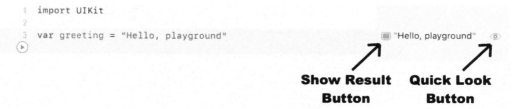

Figure 2-5: *Show Result and Quick Look buttons*

The button on the right is called *Quick Look*, and it shows a popup window with a visual representation of the result produced by the execution of the code, such as formatted text or an image. In this case, no visual effect is generated by the code, so we only see plain text.

Figure 2-6: *Quick Look window*

The button on the left is called *Show Result*, and what it does is to open a window within our code with a visual representation of the results of the execution of the code over time. In this case, nothing changes, so only the "Hello, playground" text is shown.

Figure 2-7: *Result window*

The code provided by Xcode for the Blank template is useless, but it shows the basic syntax of the Swift language and how to do elementary things in a program, such as importing frameworks to add functionality and storing data in memory. The reason why one of the statements is storing data in memory is because this is the most important task of a program. The main functions of a program are to store, retrieve, and process data. Working with data in the computer's memory is a delicate process that requires careful organization. If we are not cautious, data can be accidentally deleted, corrupted, or completely overwritten. To prevent this from happening, programming languages introduce the concept of variables.

(Basic) 2.2 Variables

Variables are names that represent values stored in memory. Once a variable is defined, its name remains the same, but the value in memory that it represents can change. In this way, we can store a value and retrieve it from memory without having to remember where in memory the value was stored. It is enough to mention the name of the variable we used to store the value to get it back or replace it with a new one.

When we use variables, the system takes care of managing the memory for us, but we still need to understand how memory works in order to know what kind of values we can store.

Memory

The computer's memory is like a giant honeycomb with successive cells that can be in two possible states: activated or deactivated. They are electronic switches whose on and off positions are determined by low and high energy levels.

Figure 2-8: Memory cells

Because of their two possible states, each cell is a small unit of information. One cell may represent two possible states (switch on or off), but by combining a sequence of cells we can represent more states. For example, if we combine two cells, we have four possible states.

Combination 1   Combination 2   Combination 3   Combination 4

Figure 2-9: Combining two cells

With these two cells, we can now represent up to four states (4 possible combinations). If we had used three cells instead, then the possible combinations would have been 8 (eight states). The number of combinations doubles every time we add another cell to the group. This can be extended to represent any number of states we want. Because of this characteristic, this system of switches is used to represent binary numbers, which are numbers expressed by only two digits: 0 and 1. An **on** switch represents the value **1** and an **off** switch represents the value **0**. Basic units were determined with the purpose of identifying parts of this endless series of digits. One cell was called a *bit* and a group of 8 bits was called a *Byte*. Figure 2-10, below, shows how a Byte looks like in memory, with some of its switches **on** representing the binary number 00011101.

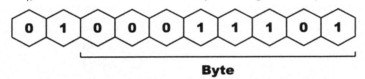

Byte

Figure 2-10: Representation of one Byte in memory

Numbers of one numeral system, such as the binary system, can be converted to any other numeral system, such as the decimal system. The binary system is the one a computer can understand because it translates directly into the electronic switches they are built with, but humans find it difficult to read, so we use other systems to express numbers, like the decimal system. For example, the possible combinations of 8 bits are 256, so a Byte can represent decimal numbers from 0 to 255. (If the Byte in our example is converted to the decimal system, we get the number 29).

To represent larger numbers, Bytes are combined into groups. For example, if we take two Bytes from memory, we get a binary number consisting of a total of 16 bits (16 zeros and ones). A binary number of 16 bits can represent decimal numbers from 0 to 65535 (a total of 65536 possible combinations). Each programming language declares its own data units to represent values of different sizes. These units are usually referred to as *primitive data types*.

Basic **Primitive Data Types**

Primitive data types are units of data defined by the programming language. They are always the same size, so when we store a value of one of these data types, the computer knows exactly how much memory to use. The following are the most basic data types provided by Swift.

▷ **Int**—This data type defines integer numbers, which are numbers with no fractional component. In 64 bits systems, the size of this data type is 8 Bytes and therefore it can store values from -9,223,372,036,854,775,808 to 9,223,372,036,854,775,807.

Although it is recommended to use the `Int` data type to store integers, some frameworks require very specific type of integers. For this reason, Swift also defines the following data types.

▷ **Int8**—This data type defines integer numbers of a size of 1 Byte (8 bits). Because of its size, it can store values from -128 to 127.

▷ **Int16**—This data type defines integer numbers of a size of 2 Bytes (16 bits). Because of its size, it can store values from -32,768 to 32,767.

▷ **Int32**—This data type defines integer numbers of a size of 4 Bytes (32 bits). Because of its size, it can store values from -2,147,483,648 to 2,147,483,647.

▷ **Int64**—This data type defines integer numbers of a size of 8 Bytes (64 bits). Because of its size, it can store values from -9,223,372,036,854,775,808 to 9,223,372,036,854, 775,807.

If we calculate the size of each type presented so far and determine the possible combinations of bits, we will discover that the maximum values don't match. For example, an `Int8` uses 1 Byte, which means it is composed of 8 bits, and it should be able to store numbers from 0 to 255 (256 possible combinations). The reason why an `Int8` has a positive limit of 127 is because it only uses 7 bits to store the value, the first bit on the left is reserved to indicate the sign (positive or negative). Although these limits are not restrictive, the language also provides the unsigned versions of these types in case we need to store larger positive values.

▷ **UInt**—This is the same as `Int` but for unsigned values. Because it does not reserve a bit for the sign, in 64-bit systems it can store values from 0 to 18,446,744,073,709, 551,615.

The specific data types for **UInt** are **UInt8**, **UInt16**, **UInt32**, and **UInt64**. These data types work exactly like the equivalents for `Int`, but they are intended to store only positive numbers.

Although all these data types are very useful, they are only good for storing binary values that can be used to represent integer numbers. Arithmetic operations also require the use of real numbers (e.g., 3.14 or 10.543). Computers cannot reproduce these types of values, but they can work with an approximation called *floating-point* numbers. The following are the most frequently used floating-point data types defined in the Swift language.

▷ **Float**—This data type defines 32 bits floating-point numbers with a precision of 6 digits.

▷ **Double**—This data type defines 64 bits floating-point numbers with a precision of at least 15 digits.

Floating-point types can handle large numbers using scientific notation, but because of their precision, it is recommended to declare a variable of type **Double** when performing calculations and use **Float** for minor tasks, such as storing coordinates to position graphics on the screen.

(Basic) Declaration and Initialization

If we want to store data in memory, the first thing we need to do is to select the right type from the data types provided by the language and then create a variable of that type. This action is called *Declaration*, and it is done using the **var** instruction and the syntax **var name: type**.

```
var mynumber: Int
```

Listing 2-2: Declaring variables

This example creates a variable called **mynumber** of type **Int**. When the system reads this statement, it reserves a space in memory of 8 Bytes long (64 bits) and assigns the name **mynumber** to that space. After the execution of this statement, we can use the variable **mynumber** to store in memory any integer value from -9,223,372,036,854,775,808 to 9,223,372,036,854,775,807.

 IMPORTANT: You can use any character you want to declare the name of a variable, except for spaces, mathematical symbols, and some Unicode characters. Also, the name cannot start with a number, and Swift distinguishes between lowercase and uppercase characters (**MyNumber** is considered a different variable than **mynumber**). You must also make sure that the name does not match any reserved word. If you declare a variable with an illegal name, Xcode will show you an error.

Memory is a reusable resource. The space in memory reserved for a variable may have been previously used by another variable, or a piece of code may have been stored in the same location. For this reason, after declaring a variable, we must always store a value in it to clear the space. This process is called *initialization*.

```
var mynumber: Int
mynumber = 5
```

Listing 2-3: Initializing variables

In this new example, we first declare the variable as we did before, and then initialize it with the value 5 (we store the number 5 in the space of memory reserved for this variable). To store the value, we use the = (equal) symbol and the syntax **name = value**, where **name** is the name of the variable and **value** is the value we want to store (once the variable was declared, we do not have to use the **var** instruction or specify its type anymore).

Most of the time, we know what the variable's initial value will be right away. In cases like this, Swift allows us to declare and initialize the variable in just one line of code.

```
var mynumber: Int = 5
```

Listing 2-4: Declaring and initializing variables in the same statement

 Do It Yourself: Create a Playground file using the Blank template. Replace all the statements in the template with the code in Listing 2-4 and press the Play button. You should see the value 5 in the Results Side Bar. Use this file to test the following examples.

Variables are called variables because their values are not constant. We can change them any time we want. To store a new value in the space of memory reserved for a variable, we must implement the same syntax used for initialization.

```
var mynumber: Int = 5
mynumber = 87
```

Listing 2-5: Assigning a new value to a variable

The process of storing a value in a variable is called *assignment*. In these terms, we can say that in the example in Listing 2-5 we "initialize the variable **mynumber** with the number 5 and then assign the value 87 to it". The value 87 replaces the value 5 in memory. After that second statement is executed, every time we read the **mynumber** variable from other statements in the code it will return the value 87 (unless another value is assigned to the variable later).

IMPORTANT: Once a variable is declared, the values stored in that variable must be of the same data type. If we declare a variable of type **Int**, we cannot store floating-point values in it later (e.g., 14.129).

Of course, we can create all the variables we want and of the data type we need.

```
var mynumber: Int = 5
var myfavorite: Float = 14.129
```

Listing 2-6: Declaring variables of different data types

The first statement in Listing 2-6 declares an integer variable and initializes it with the value 5. The second statement does the same but for a floating-point variable. When the data type of a value is easy to identify, Swift can infer it and the syntax may be simplified, as shown next.

```
var mynumber = 5
var myfavorite = 14.129
```

Listing 2-7: Declaring variables without specifying the data type

Swift infers the variable's data type from the value we are trying to assign to it. In this last example, the value 5 is clearly an integer and the value 14.129 is clearly a floating-point value, so Swift creates the variable **mynumber** of type **Int** and the variable **myfavorite** of type **Double** (Swift always selects the most comprehensive type).

 IMPORTANT: Xcode offers a simple tool you can use to see the data type assigned to a variable and get additional information. All you need to do is click on the name of the variable while holding down the Option key. This opens a popup window with the full declaration of the variable, including its data type, and any information we may need to identify the code's functionality. As we will see later, this not only applies to variables but also other instructions, including properties and methods.

An important feature of variables is that the value of one may be assigned to another.

```
var mynumber = 5
var myfavorite = mynumber
```

Listing 2-8: Assigning variables to variables

The second statement in Listing 2-8 reads the value of the variable **mynumber** and assigns it to the variable **myfavorite**. The data type of **myfavorite** is inferred to be **Int** (the same as that of **mynumber**). After executing this code, we have two integer variables, each with its own space in memory containing the value 5.

(Basic) Arithmetic Operators

Storing values in memory is what variables allow us to do, but those values do not have to be declared explicitly, they can also be the result of arithmetic operations. Swift supports the operations: **+** (addition), **−** (subtraction), ***** (multiplication), **/** (division) and **%** (remainder).

```
var mynumber = 5 + 10   // 15
```

Listing 2-9: Assigning the result of an operation to a variable

When the system reads the statement in Listing 2-9, it adds 10 to 5 and assigns the result to **mynumber** (15).

IMPORTANT: The text added at the end of the statement in Listing 2-9 is a comment that we use to show the value produced by the statement. Comments are ignored by the compiler but useful for programmers to remember vital information. They are introduced after the characters **//** (e.g., **// comment**) or in between the characters **/* */** (e.g., **/* comment */**). You can write the characters yourself or use Xcode's shortcut by selecting the lines of code you want to turn into a comment and press the keys Command and /.

Of course, we can perform not only addition but any operation we want.

```
var mynumber = 2 * 25    // 50
var anothernumber = 8 - 40 * 2   // -72
var myfraction = 5.0 / 2.0   // 2.5
```

Listing 2-10: Performing operations in variables of different type

The first two statements in Listing 2-10 are easy to read. They perform arithmetic operations over integer numbers that produce an integer value, so the variables **mynumber** and **anothernumber** will be of type **Int**. A problem arises when we work with operations that may produce floating-point numbers. That is why in the third statement, we explicitly declared the values as floating-point numbers by adding the decimal place (**.0**). This forces Swift to infer the variable's data type as **Double** and produce a result of that type.

When the compiler finds an operation with two or more numbers and has to infer the data type of the result, it converts the number of the less comprehensive type to the most comprehensive type. For example, when we declare an **Int** and a **Double** in the same operation (e.g., 5 + 2.0), the **Int** value is converted and processed as **Double**, and therefore the result will also be **Double**.

```
var myfraction1 = 5.0 / 2.0   // 2.5
var myfraction2 = 5 / 2.0   // 2.5
var myfraction3 = 5 / 2   // 2
```

Listing 2-11: Inferring the data type from an operation

This example declares and initializes three variables. In the first statement both numbers were declared as floating-point values, so the compiler infers a **Double** and creates the **myfraction1** variable of that data type. In the second statement, we have an integer value and a floating-point value. Because of the floating-point value, the compiler interprets the integer (5) as a **Double** (5.0) and creates the **myfraction2** variable of type **Double**. But in the last statement there is no clear floating-point value. Both numbers were declared as integers (with no fractional part). In this case, the compiler does not know what we want to do, so it interprets both numbers as integers and creates the **myfraction3** variable of type **Int**. When an operation produces a result that is expected to be an integer, any decimal part is discarded. In this example, the system gets rid of the decimal 5 from the result and only assigns the integer 2 to the variable. If we don't want to lose the decimal part, we must avoid inference and declare the data type explicitly as **Float** or **Double** (e.g. **var myfraction3: Double**).

Dividing integer numbers is pointless most of the time, except in some circumstances when we need to know the remainder. The remainder is the amount left over by a division between two numbers and it is calculated using the **%** symbol.

```
var remainder1 = 11 % 3   // 2
var remainder2 = 20 % 8   // 4
var remainder3 = 5 % 2   // 1
```

Listing 2-12: Calculating the remainder

Each statement in Listing 2-12 calculates the remainder that results from dividing the first number by the second number and assigns the result to the variable. For example, the first statement produces the remainder 2. The system divides 11 by 3 and finds a quotient of 3. Then, to get the remainder, it calculates 11 minus the multiplication of 3 times the quotient (**11 — (3 * 3) = 2**).

The second statement produces a remainder of 4 and the third statement produces a remainder of 1. This last statement is particularly useful because it allows us to determine whether a value is odd or even. When we calculate the reminder of an integer divided by 2, we get a result according to its parity. If the number is even, the remainder is 0, and if the number is odd, the remainder is 1 (or -1 for negative values).

Performing arithmetic operations becomes useful when instead of numbers we use variables.

```
var mynumber = 5
var total = mynumber + 10   // 15
```

Listing 2-13: *Adding numbers to variables*

This example declares the variable **mynumber** and initializes it with the value 5. In the next statement, the **total** variable is declared and initialized with the result of the addition of the current value of **mynumber** plus 10 (5 + 10).

In Listing 2-13, we used a new variable to store the result of the operation, but when the old value is not important anymore, we can store the result back into the same variable.

```
var mynumber = 5
mynumber = mynumber + 10   // 15
```

Listing 2-14: *Performing operations on the variable's current value*

In this example, the current value of **mynumber** is added to 10 and the result is assigned to the same variable. After the execution of the second statement, the value of **mynumber** is 15.

Working with values previously stored in a variable allows our program to evolve and adapt to new circumstances. For instance, we could add 1 to the current value of a variable and store the result in the same variable to create a counter. Every time the statement is executed, the value of the variable is incremented by one unit. Recurrent increments and decrements of the value of a variable are very important in computer programming. Because of this, Swift supports two operators that were specifically designed for this purpose.

- **+=** is a shorthand for **variable = variable + number**, where **number** is the value we want to add to the variable's current value.
- **-=** is a shorthand for **variable = variable – number**, where **number** is the value we want to subtract from the variable's current value.

With these operators, we can easily add or subtract a value to the current value of the variable and assign the result back to the same variable.

```
var mynumber = 5
mynumber += 4   // 9
```

Listing 2-15: *Modifying the value of a variable using incremental operators*

The process generated by the code in Listing 2-15 is simple. After the value 5 is assigned to the **mynumber** variable, the system reads the second statement, gets the current value of the variable, adds 4 to that value, and stores the result back in **mynumber** (9).

IMPORTANT: Swift also offers Overflow operators (**&+**, **&−**, **&***, **&/** and **&%**). These operators are useful when we think that an operation could produce a result that goes over the limit the data type can handle. For more information, visit our website and follow the links for this chapter.

Basic Constants

As we already mentioned, the memory of a computer is a sequence of switches. There are millions and millions of switches, one after another, with no clear delimitations. To be able to know where the space occupied by a variable starts and ends, the system uses addresses. These addresses are just consecutive numbers that correspond to each Byte of memory (8 bits). For example, if one Byte is at the address 000000, the next Byte will be at the address 000001, the next one at 000002, and so on. If we declare a variable of 4 Bytes, the system reserves the four consecutive Bytes and remembers where they are so as not to overwrite them with the value of another variable. The task is easy when working with primitive data types because their size is always the same, but the size of variables of more complex or custom data types depends on the values we assign to them. For example, the space in memory required to store the text "Hello" is smaller than the space required for the text "Hello World". Managing the memory for data of inconsistent sizes takes time and consumes more resources than working with fixed sizes. This is one of the reasons why Swift includes the concept of constants.

Constants are the same as variables, but their values cannot change. Once a constant is declared and initialized, we cannot change its value. Therefore, constants provide a secure way to store a value and help the system to manage memory. To declare them, we must use the same syntax for a variable but replace the keyword **var** with **let**.

```
let mynumber = 5
```

Listing 2-16: Declaring and initializing a constant

All the rules for variables also apply to constants; with the exception that we cannot assign a new value after the constant was already initialized. The **mynumber** constant declared in Listing 2-16 will always have the value 5.

IMPORTANT: When you should use constants or variables depends on your application. As a guide, you can use Apple's recommendations: If a stored value will not change in your code, always declare it as a constant with the **let** keyword. Use variables only to store values that must be able to change.

Basic 2.3 Swift Data Types

Besides primitive data types, Swift defines additional data types to allow us to work not only with numbers but also more complex values such as logical values (true or false), characters, and text.

Basic Characters

Because of their nature, computers cannot store decimal numbers, characters, or text. As we have seen in the previous section, the computer memory is only capable of storing 1s and 0s (switches on and off), but they can work with more complex values using tables that contain the information necessary to represent those values (numbers, letters, symbols, etc.). What the system stores in memory is not the character but the value corresponding to the index of the character on the table. For example, if we use the letter A, the value stored in memory will be the decimal number 65 (in its binary representation) because that's the position of the letter A on the table used by Swift to define these characters.

There are several standard tables of characters available. Swift is compliant with a table called Unicode. This is a comprehensive table that includes all characters from almost all languages in the world, as well as special characters such as emojis. Because of the wide range of characters, the amount of memory needed to store them varies from character to character. For this reason, Swift provides a data type called **Character** to store these values.

```
var myletter: Character = "A"
```

Listing 2-17: Declaring and initializing a Character *variable*

A character is declared using the **Character** data type and initialized with the value in double quotes. In Listing 2-17, we declare a variable called **myletter** with the value A.

In addition to the characters on the keyboard, Unicode allows us to store emojis and symbols. Xcode offers a handy tool to select the graphics we want. By pressing the combination of keys Control + Command + Space, we can open a popup window and select a graphic with a click of the mouse.

Figure 2-11: Emojis and symbols

(Basic) **Strings**

Individual characters are barely used in computer programming. Instead, we usually store strings of characters. The **String** type was created for this purpose.

```
let mytext: String = "My name is John"
```

Listing 2-18: Declaring and initializing a String *variable*

A string is a sequence of **Character** values. It is declared with the **String** type and the value in double quotes. These types of variables are very flexible; we may replace a string by another one of different length, concatenate two or more, or even modify parts of it. Concatenation is a common operation, and it is done with the **+** and **+=** operators.

```
var mytext = "My name is "
mytext = mytext + "John"   // "My name is John"
```

Listing 2-19: Concatenating strings

In Listing 2-19, the **mytext** variable is created with the value "My name is " and then the string "John" is added at the end of the current value to get the string "My name is John". The **+=** operator works in a similar way, and we can also combine them to get the string we want.

```
let name = "John"
var mytext = "My name is "
mytext += name    // "My name is John"
```

Listing 2-20: Concatenating strings with the + and += operators

With the **+** and **+=** operators we can concatenate strings with other strings. To concatenate strings with characters and numbers we must implement a procedure called *String Interpolation*. The variables are enclosed in the string between parentheses and prefixed with a backslash.

```
let age = 44
let mytext = "I am \(age) years old"   // "I am 44 years old"
```

Listing 2-21: Including variables in strings

In this code, we read the **age** variable and add its value to the string. The string "I am 44 years old" is then assigned to **mytext**. Using this tool, we can insert any value we want inside a string, including **Character** and **String** values, numbers, and arithmetic operations. In the following example, the value of **age** is multiplied by 12 and the result is included in the string.

```
let age = 44
let mytext = "I am \(age * 12) months old"   // "I am 528 months old"
```

Listing 2-22: Performing operations within strings

Sometimes we need to insert special characters into the string, like backslashes or quotes. Swift provides two ways to accomplish this. We can prefix the special character with another backslash or enclose the entire string in hash characters, as shown below.

```
let text1 = "This is \"my\" age"   // "This is "my" age"
let text2 = #"This is "my" age"#   // "This is "my" age"
```

Listing 2-23: Including special characters in a string

Another important feature of strings is the ability to create multiple lines of text. Again, Swift offers two alternatives: We can insert the special characters **\n** where we need a new line, or use triple quotes ("""), in which case the compiler will take into account the original format of the text and automatically insert the **\n** characters as needed.

```
let twolines = "This is the first line\nThis is the second line"
let multiline = """
This is the first line
This is the second line
"""
```

Listing 2-24: Generating multiple lines of text

The **twolines** constant defined in this example includes the characters **\n** between the sentences, prompting the compiler to generate two lines of text. When we click the Show Result button in the Results Side Bar, Xcode inserts a box below the code that displays the two lines of text on top of each other. Something similar happens with the value of **multiline**, although in this case the """ characters tell the compiler to add the **\n** characters at the end of each line.

(Basic) **Booleans**

Boolean variables can only store two values: **true** or **false**. These variables are particularly useful when we want to execute an instruction or a set of instructions only if a condition is met.

To declare a Boolean variable, we can specify the data type as **Bool** or let Swift infer it from the value, as in the following example.

```
var valid = true
```

Listing 2-25: Declaring a Boolean variable

The purpose of these types of variables is to simplify the process of identifying a condition. By using a Boolean variable instead of an integer, for example, we just need to check whether the value is equal to **true** or **false** to verify the condition. We will see some practical examples later.

Basic Optionals

As mentioned at the beginning of this chapter, after a variable is declared, we must specify its initial value. We cannot use a variable if it has not been initialized. This means that a variable always has a valid value. However, this is not always possible. Sometimes we do not have a value to assign to the variable, or we need to indicate the absence of a value because the current one becomes invalid. For these situations, Swift defines a modifier that turns any data type into an optional type. This means that the variable marked as optional can have a value or be empty. To declare an optional type, we add a question mark after the type's name.

```
var mynumber: Int?
```

Listing 2-26: Declaring an optional variable of type Int

New values are assigned to optionals as we do with normal variables.

```
var mynumber: Int?
mynumber = 5
```

Listing 2-27: Assigning new values to optional variables

The empty state is represented by the keyword **nil**. Therefore, when an optional variable is declared but not initialized, Swift assigns **nil** to the variable to indicate the absence of a value. Thus, if later we need to empty the variable, we can assign **nil** to it, as shown below.

```
var mynumber: Int?
mynumber = 5
mynumber = nil
```

Listing 2-28: Using nil *to empty an optional variable*

This example declares an optional integer, assigns the value 5 to it, and then declares the variable as empty with the keyword **nil**. Although optionals seem to work like regular variables, they do not expose their values. To read the value of an optional, we must unwrap it by adding an exclamation mark at the end of the name.

```
var mynumber: Int?
mynumber = 5
var total = mynumber! * 10   // 50
```

Listing 2-29: Unwrapping an optional variable

The last statement in Listing 2-29 unwraps **mynumber** to get its value, multiplies this value by 10, and assigns the result to the **total** variable. This is only necessary when we need to use the value. If we just want to assign an optional to another optional, the process is as always.

```
var mynumber: Int?
mynumber = 5
var total = mynumber
```

Listing 2-30: *Assigning an optional to another optional*

In this example, the system infers the type of the variable **total** to be an optional of type **Int** and assigns the value of **mynumber** to it. If we want to read the value of **total** later, we must unwrap it as we did with **mynumber** before.

 IMPORTANT: Before unwrapping an optional, we need to make sure it contains a value (it is not equal to **nil**). If we try to unwrap an empty optional, the app will return an error and crash. Later in this chapter we will learn how to use conditional statements to check this condition.

There are cases where we know that an optional variable will always have a value, but we do not know what the initial value is. For example, there could be a variable that receives a value from the system as soon as the application is executed. For such situations, Swift includes *Implicitly Unwrapped Optionals*. These are optional variables that are declared with an exclamation mark instead of a question mark. The system treats these variables as optionals until we use them in a statement, as in the following example.

```
var mynumber: Int!
mynumber = 5
var total = mynumber * 10   // 50
```

Listing 2-31: *Declaring Implicitly Unwrapped Optionals*

In this code, the **mynumber** variable was declared as an implicitly unwrapped optional and it was later initialized with the value 5. Note that it was not necessary to write the exclamation mark when reading its value anymore. The system unwraps the **mynumber** variable automatically to use its value in the multiplication (this is only available for implicitly unwrapped optionals).

(Basic) Tuples

A tuple is a variable that contains a group of one or more values of equal or different data type. It is useful when we need to store values that are somehow related to each other. Tuples are declared with their values and data types in parentheses and separated by comma.

```
var myname: (String, String) = ("John", "Doe")
```

Listing 2-32: *Declaring a tuple with two values*

In this example, the **myname** variable is a tuple that contains two **String** values. The values of this tuple are of the same type, but we can use any combination of values we want.

```
var myname = ("John", "Doe", 44)
```

Listing 2-33: *Declaring a tuple with values of different type*

To be able to read the values later, an index is automatically assigned to each of the values of the tuple. The first value will be at index 0, the second at index 1, and so on. Using the corresponding index and dot notation we can access the value we want to read.

```
var myname = ("John", "Doe", 44)
var mytext = "\(myname.0) is \(myname.2) years old" // "John is 44 years
old"
```

Listing 2-34: Reading the values of a tuple

In Listing 2-34, we read the values of the **myname** tuple at index 0 and 2 to include them in a new string and assign the string to **mytext**. The same syntax may be used to modify a value.

```
var myname = ("John", "Doe", 44)
myname.0 = "George"
var mytext = "\(myname.0) is \(myname.2) years old"
```

Listing 2-35: Modifying the value of a tuple

The second statement in Listing 2-35 assigns a new string to the first value of the tuple. The data type of the new value must be of the same as the old one or we will get an error. After the code is executed, the value of **mytext** is "George is 44 years old".

Indexes are a quick way to access the values of a tuple, but they do not help us remember what the values represent. To identify the values in a tuple, we can assign a name to each one of them. The name must be declared before the value and separated by a colon, as shown below.

```
var myname = (name: "John", surname: "Doe", age: 44)
var mytext = "\(myname.name) is \(myname.age) years old"
```

Listing 2-36: Declaring names for the values of a tuple

Swift also provides a way to copy the values of the tuple into independent variables.

```
var myname = ("John", "Doe", 44)
var (name, surname, age) = myname
var mytext = "\(name) \(surname) is \(age) years old"
```

Listing 2-37: Creating multiple variables from the values of a tuple

The names of the variables are declared between parentheses. The values are assigned to the variables in the same order they are declared in the tuple. If only some of the values are required, the rest may be ignored with an underscore, as shown next.

```
var myname = ("John", "Doe", 44)
var (name, _, age) = myname
var mytext = "\(name) is \(age) years old"
```

Listing 2-38: Ignoring some of the values of a tuple

Only the variables **name** and **age** are created in this last example. (Note the underscore in the place of the second variable.) The string assigned to **mytext** is "John is 44 years old".

Basic 2.4 Conditionals and Loops

Up to this point, we have written the instructions one after the other. In this programming pattern, the system executes each instruction once. It starts with the top statement and continues until it reaches the end of the list. The purpose of conditionals and loops is to break this sequential flow. Conditionals allow us to execute one or more statements only when a condition is met, and loops execute a group of statements repeatedly.

Basic If and Else

A simple but useful conditional statement is **if**. With **if**, we can check a condition and execute a group of statements only if the condition is met. The statements to be executed are specified after the condition between curly braces.

```
var age = 19
var message = "John is old"

if age < 21 {
    message = "John is young"
}
```

Listing 2-39: *Comparing two values with* if

Two variables are declared in this code. The **age** variable contains the value we want to check, and the **message** variable is the one we are going to modify depending on the state of the condition. The **if** statement compares the value of **age** with the number 21 using the character < (less than). This comparison returns the state of the condition (true or false). If the condition is true (the value of **age** is less than 21), the instruction between braces is executed, assigning a new value to the **message** variable, otherwise, the instruction is ignored and the execution continues with the instruction after the braces. In this case, the value of **age** is less than 21 and therefore the string "John is young" is assigned to the **message** variable.

> **IMPORTANT:** One or more lines of code enclosed in curly braces is called *block*. As illustrated by the example in Listing 2-39, the instructions inside a block are displaced to the right. The whitespace on the left is used to help us differentiate the statements in the block from the rest of the statements. This whitespace is automatically generated for you by Xcode, but you can add it yourself, when necessary, by pressing the Tab key on your keyboard.

The < character, used in the last example, is part of a group of operators called *Comparison Operators*. The following is the list of comparison operators available in Swift.

- **==** checks whether the value on the left is equal to the value on the right.
- **!=** checks whether the value on the left is different from the value on the right.
- **>** checks whether the value on the left is greater than the value on the right.
- **<** checks whether the value on the left is less than the value on the right.
- **>=** checks whether the value on the left is greater or equal than the value on the right.
- **<=** checks whether the value on the left is less or equal than the value on the right.

All of these operators are applied like the < operator in the previous example. For example, the following code modifies the value of **message** if the value of **age** is less than or equal to 21.

```
var age = 21
var message = "John is old"
if age <= 21 {
    message = "John is young"
}
```

Listing 2-40: *Comparing two values with the <= operator*

When only two results are required, we may define the condition using a Boolean. These values do not need to be compared to any value; they already return a state (true or false).

```
var underage = true
var message = "John is allowed"
if underage {
   message = "John is underage"
}
```

Listing 2-41: Conditions with Boolean values

This code checks whether the value of the **underage** variable is **true** or **false**. If it is **true** (which means the condition is true), a new string is assigned to **message**.

If what we want is to execute the statements when the value is **false**, Swift offers a logical operator to toggle the condition. All we need to do is to precede the condition with an exclamation mark.

```
var underage = true
var message = "John is underage"
if !underage {
   message = "John is allowed"
}
```

Listing 2-42: Using logical operators

The original value of the **underage** variable in the code of Listing 2-42 is **true**, so when the **if** statement toggles the condition, the resulting condition is false and therefore the value of the **message** variable is not modified.

The **exclamation mark** is part of a group of logical operators provided by Swift.

- **!** (logical NOT) toggles the state of the condition. If the condition is true, it returns false, and vice versa.
- **&&** (logical AND) checks two conditions and returns true if both are true.
- **||** (logical OR) checks two conditions and returns true if one or both are true.

Logical operators work with any kind of conditions, not only Booleans. To work with complex conditions, it is recommended to enclose them between parentheses.

```
var smart = true
var age = 19
var message = "John is underage or dumb"

if (age < 21) && smart {
   message = "John is allowed"
}
```

Listing 2-43: Using logical operators to check multiple conditions

The **if** statement in Listing 2-43 compares the value of the **age** variable with 21 and checks the value of the **smart** variable. If **age** is less than 21 and **smart** is **true**, then the overall condition is true, and a new string is assigned to **message**. If any of the individual conditions is false, then the overall condition is false, and the block of instructions is not executed. In this case, both conditions are true and therefore the string "John is allowed" is assigned to **message**.

 IMPORTANT: By using **&&** (AND) and **||** (OR) you can create a logical sequence of multiple conditions. The system evaluates one condition at a time from left to right and compares the results. If you want to make sure that the expressions are evaluated in the correct order, you can declare them within parentheses, as in **(true && false) || true**. The expression within the parentheses is evaluated first, and the result is then evaluated against the rest of the expression.

Although we can use comparison operators and logical operators in most of the data types available, optionals are slightly different. Their values are wrapped, so we cannot compare them with other values, or check their state as we do with Booleans. Optionals must be first compared against the **nil** keyword and then unwrapped before working with their values.

```
var count = 0
var myoptional: Int? = 5
if myoptional != nil {
    let uvalue = myoptional!
    count = count + uvalue   // 5
}
```

Listing 2-44: Checking whether an optional contains a value or not

This example presents the process we must follow to read the value of an optional variable. The optional is first compared to **nil**. If it is different from **nil** (which means it contains a value), the optional is unwrapped inside the block with an exclamation mark, its value is assigned to a constant, and then the constant is used to perform any operation necessary.

We must always make sure that an optional has a value before unwrapping it. For this reason, Swift introduces a convenient syntax that checks the optional and unwraps its value at the same time. It is called *Optional Binding*, and we can use it in an **if** statement, as shown below.

```
var count = 0
var myoptional: Int? = 5
if let uvalue = myoptional {
    count = count + uvalue   // 5
}
```

Listing 2-45: Using Optional Binding to unwrap an optional variable

This code is cleaner and easy to read. The optional is unwrapped as part of the condition. If it is different from **nil**, its value is assigned to the **uvalue** constant and the statements in the block are executed, otherwise, the statements inside the block are ignored.

As we will see later, variables and constants declared inside a block are only available to the code in the block. This also means that variables and constants declared in different blocks are independent (their values are stored in different locations in memory). An interesting consequence of this is that we can declare the constant for the Optional Binding with the same name as the variable, and they will be considered by Swift to be different.

```
var count = 0
var myoptional: Int? = 5
if let myoptional = myoptional {
    count = count + myoptional   // 5
}
```

Listing 2-46: Using the same name to unwrap a value

The **myoptional** constant declared by the **if** statement is only accessible by the code inside the block and therefore is different from the **myoptional** variable declared outside the block. The code can be simplified even more by only declaring the name of the constant, as shown next.

```
var count = 0
var myoptional: Int? = 5
if let myoptional {
    count = count + myoptional   // 5
}
```

Listing 2-47: Unwrapping an optional value of the same name

In this example, Swift looks for an optional variable called `myoptional`, unwraps the value, and assigns it to the constant. The result is the same as before, but the code has been simplified.

 IMPORTANT: The constants and variables declared inside and outside blocks have different scopes, which means they are independent and their values are stored in different locations in memory, even when they share the same name. We will learn more about the scope of variables in Chapter 3.

If we want to unwrap several optionals at the same time using Optional Binding, we must declare the expressions separated by comma. This also applies when we want to check for other conditions in the same statement. For instance, the following example unwraps an optional and only executes the code between braces if its value is equal to 5.

```
var count = 0
var myoptional: Int? = 5
if let uvalue = myoptional, uvalue == 5 {
    count = count + uvalue   // 5
}
```

Listing 2-48: Checking multiple conditions with Optional Binding

The `if` statement in Listing 2-48 unwraps the optional first and, if there is a value, compares it with the number 5. The statements in the block are executed only if both conditions are true (the variable `myoptional` contains a value and the value is equal to 5).

Sometimes, a group of instructions must be executed for each state of the condition. For this purpose, Swift includes the `if else` statement. The instructions are declared in two blocks. The first block is executed when the condition is true, and the second block when the condition is false.

```
var mynumber = 6
if mynumber % 2 == 0 {
    mynumber = mynumber + 2   // 8
} else {
    mynumber = mynumber + 1
}
```

Listing 2-49: Using `if else` to respond to both states of the condition

This is a simple example that checks whether a value is odd or even using the remainder operator. The condition gets the remainder of the division between the value of the `mynumber` variable and 2 and compares the result against 0. If true, it means that the value of `mynumber` is even, so the first block is executed. If the result is different from 0, it means that the value is odd and the condition is false, so the block corresponding to the `else` instruction is executed instead.

The `if` and `else` statements may be concatenated to check as many conditions as we need. In the following example, the first condition checks whether `age` is less than 21. If false, the second condition checks whether `age` is over 21. And if false, the final `else` block is executed.

```
var age = 19
var message = "The customer is "
if age < 21 {
    message += "underage"   // "The customer is underage"
} else if age > 21 {
    message += "allowed"
} else {
    message += "21 years old"
}
```

Listing 2-50: Concatenating `if else` instructions

If we are using the `if else` statements to assign a value to a variable, we can assign the statement directly to the variable, as shown below.

```
var age = 19
var message = if age < 21 {
    "Underage"   // "Underage"
} else {
    "Allowed"
}
```

Listing 2-51: Implementing `if else` *as an expression*

In this example, the system checks the condition first (`age < 21`) and then assigns the corresponding value to the variable. If we are working with simple values, as in this case, we can use a shortcut provided by Swift called *Ternary Operator*. A ternary operator is a construction composed by the condition and the two values we want to return for each case separated with the characters `?` and `:`, as shown below.

```
var age = 19
var message = age < 21 ? "Underage" : "Allowed"   // "Underage"
```

Listing 2-52: Implementing a ternary operator

The first value is returned if the condition is true, and the second value is returned if the condition is false. The advantage of using a ternary operator is that it reduces the size of the code significantly, but the result is the same as using an `if else` statement. In our example, the string "Underage" is assigned to the variable **message** because the value of **age** is less than 21.

Ternary operators can also be implemented to unwrap optionals. For instance, we can check whether an optional variable contains a value and assign it to another variable or give the variable a default value if the optional is empty.

```
var age: Int? = 19
var realage = age != nil ? age! : 0   // 19
```

Listing 2-53: Unwrapping an optional with a ternary operator

This code defines an optional variable called **age** with the value 19. Next, we unwrap it with a ternary operator and assign its value to a new variable called **realage**. If the optional contains a value, it is is assigned to the variable, otherwise, the value 0 is assigned instead.

Assigning values by default when the optional is empty is very common. To simplify our work, Swift offers the nil-coalescing operator, which is represented by the characters `??`. This operator works like the ternary operator implemented in Listing 2-53; it unwraps the optional and returns its value or returns another value if the optional is empty. In the following example, we create an empty optional called **age** and use the nil-coalescing operator to assign its value to the **maxage** variable or the value 100 if the optional is empty.

```
var age: Int?
var maxage = age ?? 100   // 100
```

Listing 2-54: Unwrapping an optional with the nil-coalescing operator

(Basic) **Switch**

We can keep adding `if` and `else` statements to check as many conditions as we need, but this pattern can make the code impossible to read and maintain. When multiple conditions need to be checked, it is better to use the **switch** instruction instead. This instruction compares a value to a list of values and executes the statements of the value that matches. The possible matches are listed between curly braces with the **case** keyword, as in the following example.

```
var age = 19
var message = ""
switch age {
   case 13:
      message = "Happy Bar Mitzvah!"
   case 16:
      message = "Sweet Sixteen!"
   case 21:
      message = "Welcome to Adulthood!"
   default:
      message = "Happy Birthday!"   // "Happy Birthday!"
}
```

Listing 2-55: Checking conditions with switch

The cases must be exhaustive. If we do not include a **case** statement for every possible value, we must add a **default** statement at the end that is executed when no match is found. In Listing 2-55, we compare the value of the **age** variable with a small set of values corresponding to special dates. If no **case** matches the value of the variable, the **default** statement is executed and the string "Happy Birthday!" is assigned to **message**.

When we need to execute the same set of instructions for more than one value, we can declare the values separated by comma.

```
var age = 6
var message = "You go to "
switch age {
   case 2, 3, 4:
      message += "Day Care"
   case 5, 6, 7, 8, 9, 10, 11:
      message += "Elementary School"   // "You go to Elementary School"
   case 12, 13, 14, 15, 16, 17:
      message += "High School"
   case 18, 19, 20, 21:
      message += "College"
   default:
      message += "Work"
}
```

Listing 2-56: Checking multiple conditions per case

The **switch** statement can also work with more complex data types, such as strings and tuples. In the case of tuples, **switch** provides additional options to build complex matching patterns. For example, the following code checks the second value of a tuple to determine the difference in age.

```
var message = ""
var ages = (10, 30)

switch ages {
   case (10, 20):
      message = "Too close"
   case (10, 30):
      message = "The right age"   // "The right age"
   case (10, 40):
      message = "Too far"
```

```
    default:
        message = "Way too far"
}
```

Listing 2-57: Matching a tuple in a switch *statement*

This example always compares the first value of the tuple against 10 but checks different matches for the second value. If a value does not matter, we can use an underscore to ignore it.

```
var message = ""
var ages = (10, 30)
switch ages {
    case (_, 20):
        message = "Too close"
    case (_, 30):
        message = "The right age"    // "The right age"
    case (_, 40):
        message = "Too far"
    default:
        message = "Way too far"
}
```

Listing 2-58: Matching only the second value of a tuple

An alternative offered by the **switch** statement to create complex matching patterns is to capture a value in a constant to be able to access it from the instructions of the **case**.

```
var message = ""
var ages = (10, 20)
switch ages {
    case (let x, 20):
        message = "Too close to \(x)"   // "Too close to 10"
    case (_, 30):
        message = "The right age"
    case (let x, 40):
        message = "Too far to \(x)"
    default:
        message = "Way too far"
}
```

Listing 2-59: Capturing values with constants

In this example, when the **switch** statement checks the first and third cases, it creates a constant called **x** and assigns it the first value, so that we can access and use that value from the statements within the case. (In this example, we simply add the value to a string, but we can compare it with an **if else** statement or do anything we need with the value.)

There is an even more complex matching pattern that involves the use of a clause called **where**. We can use this clause to check additional conditions. In the following example, we capture the values of the tuple and compare them.

```
var message = ""
var ages = (10, 20)
switch ages {
    case let (x, y) where x > y:
        message = "Too young"
    case let (x, y) where x == y:
        message = "The same age"
    case let (x, y) where x < y:
        message = "Too old"   // "Too old"
```

Chapter 2 - Introduction to Swift

```
    default:
        message = "Not found"
}
```

Listing 2-60: Comparing values with where

Every time the **switch** statement tries to match a **case** in this example, it creates a tuple and assigns the values of **ages** to it. The **where** clause compares the values and when the condition is true, it executes the statements within the **case**.

Like the **if else** statements, the **switch** statement can be used to assign a value to a variable depending on a condition. In the following example, we check the value of **age** and assign the appropriate message to the variable.

```
var age = 19
var message = switch age {
    case 13:
        "Happy Bar Mitzvah!"
    case 16:
        "Sweet Sixteen!"
    case 21:
        "Welcome to Adulthood!"
    default:
        "Happy Birthday!"   // "Happy Birthday!"
}
```

Listing 2-61: Implementing the switch *statement as an expression*

(Basic) **While and Repeat While**

The conditionals studied so far execute the statements only once, but sometimes the program requires executing a block of instructions several times until a condition is satisfied. An alternative offered by Swift to create these loops is the **while** statement (and its sibling **repeat while**).

The **while** statement checks a condition and executes the statements in the block while the condition is true. The following example initializes a variable with the value 0 and then checks its value in a **while** statement. If the value of the variable is less than 5, the statements inside the block are executed. After this, the condition is checked again. The loop keeps running until the condition is false (the value of the **counter** variable is equal or greater than 5).

```
var counter = 0
while counter < 5 {
    counter += 1
}
let finalNumber = counter   // 5
```

Listing 2-62: Using while *to create a loop*

If the first check of the condition returns false, the statements in the block are never executed. To execute the statements at least once, we must use **repeat while**.

```
var counter = 10
repeat {
    counter += 1
} while counter < 5
let finalNumber = counter   // 11
```

Listing 2-63: Using repeat while *to create a loop*

In this case, the initial value of the **counter** variable is declared as 10. This is greater than 5, but since we are using the **repeat while** instruction, the statements in the block are executed before the condition is checked, so the final value of **counter** will be 11. (Its value is incremented once and then the condition returns false, ending the loop.)

(Basic) **For In**

The purpose of the **for in** loop is to iterate over collections of values, like the strings of characters studied before. During the execution of a **for in** loop, the system reads the elements of the collection one by one in sequential order and assigns their values to a constant that can be used by the statements in the block. In this case, the condition that must be satisfied for the loop to be over is reaching the end of the collection.

The syntax of a **for in** loop is **for constant in collection {}**, where **constant** is the name of the constant that we are going to use to capture the value of each element in the collection, and **collection** is the name of the collection of values that we want to iterate over.

```
var mytext = "Hello"
var message = ""

for letter in mytext {
    message += message != "" ? "-" : ""
    message += "\(letter)"
}
```

Listing 2-64: *Using* `for in` *to iterate over the characters of a string*

The code in Listing 2-64 defines two **String** variables: **mytext** with the text "Hello" and **message** with an empty string. Next, we use a **for in** loop to iterate over the characters of the string in **mytext** and add each character to the current value of **message**. In each cycle of the loop, the **for in** instruction takes one character from the value of **mytext**, assigns it to the **letter** constant, and executes the statements in the block. The first statement uses a ternary operator to check whether the value of **message** is an empty string. If not, it adds the – character at the end of it, otherwise, it adds an empty string. Finally, the second statement adds the current value of **letter** to the end of **message**.

The code works as follows: in the first cycle, the character "H" is assigned to **letter**. Because at this moment **message** contains an empty string, nothing is added by the first statement in the block. Then, the second statement adds the value of **letter** to the current value of **message** and the next cycle is executed. In this new cycle, the character "e" is assigned to **letter**. This time, the **message** string already contains the letter "H", so the character "-" is added at the end by the first statement ("H-"), and then the second statement adds the letter "e" at the end of this new string ("H-e"). This process continues until all the characters in the **mytext** variable are processed. The final value of **message** is "H-e-l-l-o".

When the constant is not required inside the block, we can replace it with an underscore.

```
var mytext = "Hello"
var counter = 0

for _ in mytext {
    counter += 1
}
var message = "The string contains \(counter) letters"
```

Listing 2-65: *Iterating over a string without reading the characters*

In this example, we iterate over the value of **mytext** to count the number of characters in the string. The value of the **counter** variable is incremented by 1 in each cycle, giving a total of 5.

A **for in** instruction may include the **where** clause to perform the next cycle only when a condition is met. For instance, the following code checks the value of **letter** and only performs the cycle when the letter is not an L. In consequence, only the letters H, e, and o are counted.

```
var mytext = "Hello"
var counter = 0
for letter in mytext where letter != "l" {
    counter += 1
}
var message = "The string contains \(counter) letters"   // 3
```

Listing 2-66: Adding a condition to a loop

(Basic) ## Control Transfer Statements

Sometimes loops must be interrupted, independently of the state of the condition. Swift offers instructions to break the execution of loops and conditionals. The following are the most frequently used.

> **continue**—This instruction interrupts the current cycle and moves to the next. The system ignores the rest of the statements in the block after the instruction is executed.

> **break**—This instruction interrupts the loop. The rest of the statements in the block and any pending cycles are ignored after the instruction is executed.

The **continue** instruction is applied when we do not want to execute the rest of the statements in the block, but we want to keep the loop running. For instance, the following code counts the letters in a string but ignores the letters "l" (lowercase L).

```
var mytext = "Hello"
var counter = 0
for letter in mytext {
    if letter == "l" {
        continue
    }
    counter += 1
}
var message = "The string contains \(counter) letters"   // 3
```

Listing 2-67: Jumping to the next cycle of the loop

The **if** statement inside the **for in** loop of Listing 2-67 compares the value of **letter** with the letter "l". If the characters match, the instruction **continue** is executed, the last statement inside the loop is ignored, and the loop moves on to the next character in **mytext**. In consequence, the code counts all the characters that are different from "l" (H, e, and o).

Unlike the **continue** instruction, the **break** instruction interrupts the loop completely. The following example only counts the characters before the first letter "l".

```
var mytext = "Hello"
var counter = 0
for letter in mytext {
    if letter == "l" {
        break
    }
    counter += 1
}
var message = "The string contains \(counter) letters"   // 2
```

Listing 2-68: Interrupting the loop

Again, the **if** statement of Listing 2-68 compares the value of **letter** with the character "l", but this time it executes the **break** instruction when a match is found. If the character currently processed by the loop is "l", the **break** instruction is executed, and the loop is over, no matter how many characters are left in the string. In consequence, only the characters located before the first letter "l" are considered (H and e).

The **break** instruction is also useful to cancel the execution of a **switch** statement. The problem with the **switch** statement in Swift is that the cases must be exhaustive, which means that every possible value must be contemplated. When this is not possible or necessary, we can use the **break** instruction to ignore the values that do not apply. For example, we can declare the cases for the values we need and then break the execution in the **default** case for the rest of the values that we do not care about.

```
var age = 19
var message = ""
switch age {
   case 13:
      message = "Happy Bar Mitzvah!"
   case 16:
      message = "Sweet Sixteen!"
   case 21:
      message = "Welcome to Adulthood!"
   default:
      break
}
```

Listing 2-69: *Ignoring values in a* switch *statement*

After the execution of this code, the **message** variable is empty because there is no **case** that matches the value of the **age** variable and therefore the code in **default** is executed and the **break** instruction returns the control to the statements after the **switch**.

(Basic) **Guard**

The **guard** instruction is used to prevent the execution of the code that follows the statement. For example, we can break the execution of a loop when a condition is satisfied, as we do with an **if else** statement.

```
var mytext = "Hello"
var counter = 0
for letter in mytext {
   guard letter != "l" else {
      break
   }
   counter += 1
}
var message = "The string contains \(counter) letters"   // 2
```

Listing 2-70: *Interrupting a loop with* guard

The **guard** instruction works along with the **else** instruction and therefore it is very similar to the **if else** statement, but the code is only executed when the condition is false and the constant outlives the statement, so we can read its value outside the **else** block. In the example in Listing 2-70, the **for in** loop reads the characters of the string in **mytext** one by one, as before. If the characters are different from the letter "l", we increment the value of **counter** by 1, but when the value of **letter** is equal to "l", the condition of the **guard** instruction is false and therefore the **break** instruction is executed, interrupting the loop.

Basic **3.1 Programming Paradigms**

Programs would not be very useful if we could only write them as continuous instructions. Originally, this was the only way to write a program, but soon tools were built into programming languages that allowed the programmer to group instructions and execute them as needed. The way in which instructions are organized is called paradigm. Today, there are several paradigms available, but the most widely used is Object-Oriented Programming (OOP). This paradigm is based on the construction and integration of processing units called objects. Swift works with objects, but also implements other types of processing units, including structures, enumerations and protocols, to conform to a new paradigm called Protocol-Oriented Programming (POP). In this paradigm, protocols act like blueprints that define how the processing units behave.

 Do It Yourself: The examples in this chapter were designed to be tested in Playground. You need to create a Playground file with a Blank template and then replace the code with the example you want to try.

Basic **3.2 Functions**

The processing units that define the Swift paradigm (objects, structures, and enumerations) are capable of encapsulating data along with functionality. The data is stored in the same variables studied before, but the functionality is provided by functions. Functions are blocks of code delimited by curly braces and identified by a name. The difference between functions and the block of codes used in loops and conditional statements is that there is no condition to satisfy; the statements inside a function are executed every time the function is called. Functions are called by writing their names followed by parentheses. This call may be performed from anywhere in the code and every time necessary, which completely breaks the sequential processing of a program. Once a function is called, the execution of the program continues with the statements within the function and only returns to the section of the code that called the function once the execution of the function is over.

Basic **Declaration of Functions**

Functions are declared with the **func** keyword followed by a name, parentheses, and the code enclosed in curly braces.

```
func myfunction() {
   let mynumber = 5 * 2   // 10
}
myfunction()
```

Listing 3-1: *Declaring and calling functions*

The code in Listing 3-1 declares a function called **myfunction()**. The statements in a function are only processed when the function is called, so after the **myfunction()** function is declared, we call it with the **myfunction()** instruction. In this example, we multiply two values and assign the result to a constant, but of course a function can perform more complex tasks, as we will see later.

As we already mentioned, once the function is declared, we can call it any time necessary. For example, the following code runs a **while** loop that calls **myfunction()** a total of 5 times (the loop runs while **counter** is less than 5).

```
func myfunction() {
    let mynumber = 5 * 2   // 10
}
var counter = 0
while counter < 5 {
    myfunction()
    counter += 1
}
```

Listing 3-2: Calling functions from a loop

In this example, the function always performs the same operation, but functions can receive and process different values every time they are called. The type of values the function can receive and the names they are going to take are specified within the function's parentheses separated by a comma. When the function is executed, these parameters are turned into constants that we can read inside the function to get their values.

```
func doubleValue(number: Int) {
    let total = number * 2
    let message = "Result: \(total)"   // "Result: 10"
}
doubleValue(number: 5)
```

Listing 3-3: Sending values to a function

In this example, the value to be processed is sent to the function when it is called and received by the function's parameter. The parameters are declared within the function's parentheses with the same syntax used for constants and variables. We must write the name and the data type separated by a colon. In Listing 3-3, the function is declared with one parameter of type **Int** called **number**.

The call must include the name of the parameter and the value we want to send to the function. When the function of Listing 3-3 is called, the value between the parentheses of the call (5) is assigned to **number**, the value of this constant is multiplied by 2, and finally the result is included in a string with string interpolation.

Of course, we can include as many parameters as we need. The following example multiplies two values and creates a string with the result.

```
func multiply(number1: Int, number2: Int) {
    let result = number1 * number2
    let message = "The result is \(result)"   // "The result is 80"
}
multiply(number1: 20, number2: 4)
```

Listing 3-4: Sending multiple values to a function

Not only can functions be called at any time, but the values we pass to the function when we call it can be different. This makes functions reusable.

```
func doubleValue(number: Int) {
    let total = number * 2
    let message = "Result: \(total)"
}
doubleValue(number: 5)    // "Result: 10"
doubleValue(number: 25)   // "Result: 50"
```

Listing 3-5: Sending different values to a function

Chapter 3 - Swift Paradigm

The constants and variables declared inside a function, like **total** and **message**, are not accessible from other parts of the code. This means that a function can receive values, but the result produced by processing those values is trapped inside the function. To communicate the result of an operation to the rest of the code, functions can return a value using an instruction called **return**. The **return** instruction finishes the processing of the function, so we must declare it after all the required statements have been processed, as in the following example.

```
func doubleValue(number: Int) -> Int {
    let total = number * 2
    return total
}
let result = doubleValue(number: 25)
let message = "The result is \(result)"    // "The result is 50"
```

Listing 3-6: Returning a value from a function

When we create a function that returns a value, the data type of the value returned is specified in the declaration after the parentheses with the syntax **-> type**, where **type** is just the data type of the value that is going to be returned by the function. A function can only return values of the type specified in its definition. For instance, the function in Listing 3-6 can only return integer values because we declared the returned type as **-> Int**.

When a function returns a value, the system calls the function first and then the value returned is processed inside the statement that made the call. For example, in the code of Listing 3-6, we create the **result** variable and assign to it a call to the **doubleValue()** function. When the system processes this statement, the function is executed and then the value returned (50) is assigned to the **result** variable.

The values received and returned by a function may be of any available data type. The following example takes a string and returns a tuple with a string and an integer.

```
func sumCharacters(word: String) -> (String, Int) {
    var characters = ""
    var counter = 0
    for letter in word {
        characters += "\(letter) "
        counter += 1
    }
    return (characters, counter)
}
var (list, total) = sumCharacters(word: "Hello")
var message = "There are \(total) characters (\(list))"
```

Listing 3-7: Returning a tuple

The **sumCharacters()** function in Listing 3-7 receives a string (**word: String**) and returns a tuple composed of a string and an integer (**-> (String, Int)**). The function adds the characters to the **characters** variable and counts them with the **counter** variable, as we did before (see Listing 2-65). At the end, the tuple is returned, its values are assigned to the **list** and **total** variables, and then included in a string ("There are 5 characters (H e l l o)").

In addition to returning the result of an operation, the **return** instruction can also be used to interrupt the execution of a function. The **guard** instruction introduced in Chapter 2 is perfectly suited for such cases, as shown in the following example.

```
func doubleValue(number: Int) -> Int {
    guard number < 10 else {
        return number
    }
    return number * 2
}
```

```
let result = doubleValue(number: 25)
let message = "The result is \(result)"   // "The result is 25"
```

Listing 3-8: Interrupting the execution of a function with guard

The **doubleValue()** function in Listing 3-8 is similar to previous examples. It receives a number, multiplies it by 2, and returns the result, but this time we first check that the value received by the function is less than 10. If the value is equal or higher than 10, the **guard** instruction calls the **return** instruction with the value received by the function, otherwise, the statements of the function are executed as normal. In this case, the value sent to the function is 25, therefore the condition is false, and that value is returned.

Note that in the example in Listing 3-8, we simplified our code by performing the multiplication in the **return** instruction. The **return** instruction can take single values or expressions like this. The instruction solves the expression and returns the result. For this reason, we sometimes find functions with only one statement whose sole purpose is to return a value. In this case, we can omit the **return** keyword. For example, the following code sends the number 25 to the function, the function multiplies the value by 2 and returns it, as in the previous examples, but this time we did not need to declare the **return** keyword because there is only one statement inside the function and therefore the compiler knows what to return.

```
func doubleValue(number: Int) -> Int {
    number * 2
}
let result = doubleValue(number: 25)
let message = "The result is \(result)"   // "The result is 50"
```

Listing 3-9: Removing the return *keyword*

A related keyword is **inout**. This keyword is used to preserve a value after the function finishes processing. When a parameter is marked with **inout**, any changes performed on the value are stored in the original variable. This is useful when we call a function from another function, and we want the modifications introduced by the second function to persist.

```
func first() {
    var number = 25
    second(value: &number)
    print("The result is \(number)")   // "The result is 50"
}
func second(value: inout Int) {
    value = value * 2
}
first()
```

Listing 3-10: Modifying external variables from a function

This code defines two functions: **first()** and **second()**. The **second()** function receives an **inout** parameter called **value**, which means that any modification on its value is stored in the original variable. The **first()** function defines a variable called **number** and then executes the **second()** function with it, so when the **second()** function multiplies this value times 2, the result (50) is stored in **number**. At the end, we execute the **first()** function to start the process. Note that in the call to the **second()** function we include an ampersand before the variable's name (&). This tells the system that the variable is going to be modified by the function.

An important aspect of the definition of a function are the names of the parameters. For example, the function **doubleValue()** of previous examples includes a parameter called **number**. Every time we call this function, we must include the parameter's name (e.g., **doubleValue(number: 50)**). These names are called *argument labels*. Swift automatically generates argument labels for every parameter using their names. Sometimes the names assigned to the parameters of a function may be descriptive enough for the statements of the function but may be confusing when we perform the call. For cases like these, Swift allows us to define our own argument labels; we just need to declare them before the name of the parameter separated by a space.

```
func doubleValue(years number: Int) -> Int {
    number * 2
}
let result = doubleValue(years: 8)
let message = "The result is \(result)"   // "The results is 16"
```

Listing 3-11: *Declaring argument labels*

The **doubleValue()** function in Listing 3-11 declares an argument label called **years** for the **number** parameter. From now on, the name of the parameter (**number**) is the one used by the statements of the function to access the value received from the call, while the argument label (**years**) is the one used when calling the function.

If what we want instead is to remove an argument label, we can define it with an underscore.

```
func multiply(number1: Int, _ number2: Int) -> Int {
    number1 * number2
}
let result = multiply(number1: 25, 3)
let message = "The result is \(result)"   // "The result is 75"
```

Listing 3-12: *Removing argument labels*

In this example, we preserved the behavior by default for the first parameter and removed the argument label for the second parameter. Now the call only has to include the argument label of the first parameter (**multiply(number1: 25, 3)**).

The functions we have defined so far require that all values be specified in the call. We cannot omit any of the values expected by the function, but Swift allows us to declare a default value for a parameter to get around this requirement.

```
func sayhello(name: String = "Undefined") -> String {
    return "Your name is " + name
}
let message = sayhello()   // "Your name is Undefined"
```

Listing 3-13: *Declaring default values for parameters*

The code in Listing 3-13 declares the function **sayhello()** with one parameter of type **String** called **name** and with the string "Undefined" as the default value. When the function is called without a value, the string "Undefined" is assigned to **name**.

Medium Generic Functions

Although creating two or more functions with the same name is not allowed, we can do it if their parameters are not the same. This is called *Overloading* and allows us to define multiple functions with the same name to process different types of values.

```
func getDescription(value: Int) -> String {
    let message = "The value is \(value)"
    return message
}
func getDescription(value: String) -> String {
    let message = "The value is \(value)"
```

```
      return message
}
let result1 = getDescription(value: 3)    // "The value is 3"
let result2 = getDescription(value: "John")    // "The value is John"
```

Listing 3-14: Declaring different functions with the same name

The functions in Listing 3-14 have the same name, but one receives an integer and the other a string. We can say that the function that receives the string overloads the function that receives the integer. When we call the **getDescription()** function, the system selects which function is going to be executed depending on the value of the argument. (If we call the function with an integer, the first function is executed, but if we call it with a string, the second function is executed.)

The advantage of creating functions with the same name is that we only have to remember one name. We call them with the values we want and Swift makes sure that the correct function is executed. However, if the functions perform the same task and differ only in the type of value received, we end up with two or more pieces of code to maintain, which can lead to errors. In such cases, we can declare only one function with a generic data type.

Generic data types are placeholders for real data types. When the function is called, the generic data type is turned into the data type of the value received. If we send an integer, the generic data type turns into an **Int**, if we send a string, it becomes a **String**. To define a generic function, we must declare the generic data type using a custom name between angle brackets after the function's name, as in the following example.

```
func getDescription<T>(value: T) -> String {
   let message = "The value is \(value)"
   return message
}
let result1 = getDescription(value: 3.5)    // "The value is 3.5"
let result2 = getDescription(value: "George")    // "The value is George"
```

Listing 3-15: Defining generic functions

This function is a generic function. The generic data type was called **T** (this is a standard name for a generic data type, but we can use any name we want). The function performs the same task, and it has the same name than the two functions from the previous example, but now we have reduced the amount of code in our program. When the function is called, the **T** generic data type is converted into the data type received and the value is processed. (The first time the function is called in our example, **T** is turned into a **Double** and the second time into a **String**.)

In our example, we only use one parameter and therefore the function can only work with one data type, but we can declare two or more generic data types separated by commas (e.g., **<T, U>**).

 IMPORTANT: Although we can send any value of any type we want to a generic function, the operations we can perform on them are very limited due to the impossibility of the compiler to know the nature of the values received. For example, we can add two integers, but we cannot add two Boolean values. To solve these issues, we can constrain the generic data types with protocols. We will study how to define protocols and how to use them later in this chapter.

(Basic) Standard Functions

The advantage of functions is that we can call them from other parts of the code and they always perform the same operations. We don't even need to know how the function works, we just send the function the values we want to process and read the result. Because of this feature, functions can be shared, and programmers can implement pre-programmed functions provided by libraries and frameworks.

All the features of the Swift language we have implemented so far are included in a library called *Standard Library*. The Standard Library includes everything, from operators to primitive data types, as well as predefined functions. The following are some of the most frequently used.

▷ **print**(String)—This function prints a string on the Xcode's console.

▷ **abs**(Value)—This function returns the absolute value of an integer.

▷ **max**(Values)—This function compares two or more values and returns the largest.

▷ **min**(Values)—This function compares two or more values and returns the smallest.

There are also functions available to stop the execution of the application in case of an unrecoverable error.

▷ **fatalError**(String)—This function stops the execution of the application and prints a message on the console. The argument is a string with the message to be printed.

▷ **precondition**(Bool, String)—This function stops the execution of the application and prints a message on the console if a condition is false. The first argument is the condition to be checked and the second argument is the message we want to print.

Of all the functions in the Swift Standard Library, **print()** is probably the most useful. Its purpose is to print messages on the Xcode's console that may help us fix bugs in our code. In the following example, we use it to print the result of two operations.

```
let absolutenumber = abs(-25)
let minnumber = min(absolutenumber, 100)
print("The number is: \(minnumber)")   // "The number is: 25"
```

Listing 3-16: Printing values on the console with `print()`

The code in Listing 3-16 implements the **abs()** function to calculate the absolute value of -25, then gets the smallest value between **absolutenumber** and the number 100 with the **min()** function, and finally prints a message on the console with the result.

As we will see later, sequences and collections of values are very important in computer programming. The strings studied in Chapter 2 are a clear example. A string is a sequence of values of type **Character**. The Swift Standard Library includes a few functions to quickly create sequences of values our application may need to process information. The following are some of the most frequently used.

▷ **stride(from:** Value, **through:** Value, **by:** Value)—This function returns a collection of values from the value specified by the **from** argument to the value specified by the **through** argument in intervals specified by the **by** argument.

▷ **stride(from:** Value, **to:** Value, **by:** Value)—This function returns a collection of values from the value specified by the **from** argument to the value specified by the **through** argument in intervals specified by the **by** argument. The last value is not included.

▷ **repeatElement**(Value, **count:** Int)—This function returns a collection with the number of elements specified by the **count** argument and with the value specified by the first argument.

▷ **zip**(Collection, Collection)—This function returns a collection of tuples containing the values of the collections provided by the arguments in sequential order.

The following example applies some of these functions to create a list of tuples that contain a string and an integer.

```
let sequencetext = repeatElement("Hello", count: 5)
let sequencenumbers = stride(from: 0, to: 10, by: 2)
let finalsequence = zip(sequencetext, sequencenumbers)

for (text, number) in finalsequence {
    print("\(text) - \(number)")
}
```

Listing 3-17: Creating collections of values

The code in Listing 3-17 calls the **repeatElement()** function to create a collection of 5 elements, all of them with the string "Hello" ("Hello", "Hello", "Hello", "Hello", "Hello"). Next, the **stride()** function creates another collection with integers from 0 to 10, increased by 2, and without including the last one (0, 2, 4, 6, 8). Next, the **zip()** function merges these two collections in one collection of tuples (the first tuple contains the first value of the **sequencetext** collection along with the first value of the **sequencenumbers** collection, and so on). Finally, we use a **for in** loop to iterate over the values of the **finalsequence** collection and print them on the console ("Hello - 0", "Hello - 2", "Hello - 4", "Hello - 6", "Hello - 8").

(Basic) **Scope**

The conditionals and loops studied in Chapter 2 and the functions studied in this chapter have a thing in common; they all use blocks of code (statements between curly braces) to enclose their functionality. Blocks are independent processing units; they contain their own statements and variables. To preserve their independence and avoid conflicts between these units and the rest of the code, their variables and constants are isolated. Variables and constants declared inside a block are not accessible from other parts of the code; they can only be used inside the block in which they were created.

The space in the code where a variable is accessible is called *scope*. Swift defines two types of scopes: the global scope and the local scope (also referred to as global space and local space). The variables and constants outside a block have global scope, while those declared inside a block have local scope. The variables and constants with global scope are accessible from any part of the code, while those with local scope are only accessible from the statements inside the block in which they were created (and the statements from blocks created inside their block). We can declare variables in the global scope and then use them in a local scope, but not the other way around, as in the following example.

```
var multiplier = 1.2
var base = 0

while multiplier < 100 {
    let base = 10.0
    multiplier = multiplier * base
}
print("Base: \(base)")        // "Base: 0"
print("Total: \(multiplier)") // "Total: 120.0"
```

Listing 3-18: Using variables and constants of different scopes

This example declares two variables in the global space: **multiplier** and **base**. We use the **multiplier** variable in a **while** loop, but the **base** variable is replaced inside the loop with a constant of the same name. When we assign the value 10.0 to **base** inside the loop, this value is assigned to the **base** constant, not the **base** variable, but when later we print the value of **base**, the system reads this value from the variable in the global space, not the constant in the local space, because the global space doesn't have access to the **base** constant declared inside the loop.

Blocks of code, such as those used to create functions, conditionals, and loops, have their own scope and know the variables available to them. Because of this, we can create independent processing units that do not interfere with the operations of other units. This feature is so important in computer programming that Swift allows us to create these units by defining independent blocks called *closures*.

Closures are independent blocks of code with the syntax **{ (parameters) -> Type in statements }**. They are like functions (functions are closures with a name), but they are wrapped with braces and the **in** keyword is included to separate the data types from the statements.

Closures can be assigned to variables and executed using the name of the variable, as we do with functions. The name of the variable becomes the name of the closure, as shown next.

```
let multiplier = { (number: Int, times: Int) -> Int in
    let total = number * times
    return total
}
print("The result is \(multiplier(10, 5))")   // "The result is 50"
```

Listing 3-19: Assigning closures to variables

This example defines a closure and assigns it to the **multiplier** constant. After this, the name of the constant can be used to execute the closure. Note that the parameters of the closure and the return type are declared with the same syntax as functions (**(number: Int, times: Int) -> Int**), but the names of the parameters are not turned into argument labels and therefore they are ignored in the call.

An advantage of being able to assign closures to variables is the possibility to initialize the variables with the result of complex operations. The closure is assigned to the variable and executed right away adding parentheses at the end of the declaration. When the system reads the statement, it executes the closure and then assigns the value returned by the closure to the constant or variable.

```
let myaddition = { () -> Int in
    var total = 0
    let list = stride(from: 1, through: 9, by: 1)

    for number in list {
        total += number
    }
    return total
}()
print("The total is \(myaddition)")   // "The total is 45"
```

Listing 3-20: Initializing a variable with the value returned by a closure

The closure declared in Listing 3-20 doesn't receive any value and returns an integer (**() -> Int**). The code in the closure adds the values of a collection (1 to 9) and returns the result, but because we included the parentheses at the end of the definition, the value assigned to the **myaddition** constant is the one returned by the closure (45), not the closure itself.

If the closure does not receive any parameter, we can simplify the syntax by declaring the constant's data type to be the same than the data type of the value returned by the closure. Note that in this case, the **in** keyword can also be removed.

```
let myaddition: Int = {
    var total = 0
    let list = stride(from: 1, through: 9, by: 1)
```

```
    for number in list {
        total += number
    }
    return total
}()
print("The total is \(myaddition)")   // "The total is 45"
```

Listing 3-21: Simplifying a closure

Closures cannot only be assigned to constants and variables but also sent and returned from functions, as any other value. When a function receives a closure, the parameter's data type only has to include the data types the closure receives and returns, as in the following example.

```
let multiplier = { (number: Int, times: Int) -> Int in
    let total = number * times
    return total
}
func processclosure(myclosure: (Int, Int) -> Int) {
    let total = myclosure(10, 2)
    print("The total is: \(total)")   // "The total is: 20"
}
processclosure(myclosure: multiplier)
```

Listing 3-22: Sending a closure to a function

The first statement in Listing 3-22 defines a closure that multiplies two integers and returns the result. A function that receives a closure of this type is defined next. Note that the data type of the value received by the function was declared as **(Int, Int) -> Int**. This indicates to the compiler that the **processclosure()** function can receive a closure that in turn receives two integer values and returns another integer. When the **processclosure()** function is called in the last statement, the value of the **multiplier** variable is sent to the function. The function assigns the closure to the **myclosure** constant, and the closure is executed inside the function using this name and the values 10 and 2, producing the result 20.

The closure in the previous example was defined in the global space and was executed inside the **processclosure()** function, but we don't need to assign the closure to a variable, we can just define it in the call.

```
func processclosure(myclosure: (Int, Int) -> Int) {
    print("The total is: \(myclosure(10, 2))")   // "The total is: 20"
}
processclosure(myclosure: { (number: Int, times: Int) -> Int in
    return number * times
})
```

Listing 3-23: Assigning the closure to the function's argument

The code in Listing 3-23 works the same way as the previous example, but it was simplified by assigning the closure directly to the function's argument. This can be simplified even further by using a pattern called *Trailing Closures*. When the final argument of a function is a closure, we can declare the closure at the end of the call, as in the following example.

```
func processclosure(myclosure: (Int, Int) -> Int) {
    print("The total is: \(myclosure(10, 2))")   // "The total is: 20"
}
processclosure() { (number: Int, times: Int) -> Int in
    number * times
}
```

Listing 3-24: Using Trailing Closures

When we pass the closure this way, the call does not include the **myclosure** argument anymore. The closure declared after the parentheses is considered to be the last argument of the function and therefore the argument label is not necessary.

The code in Listing 3-24 works the same way as previous examples, the only advantage is the reduction in the amount of code we have to write. And that can be simplified even further. In the last example we already removed the **return** keyword. As explained before, when the content of a function (or in this case a closure) includes only one statement, the compiler implies that the value produced by that statement is the one to return and therefore the **return** keyword is not required anymore. But when we are passing the closure to a function, Swift can also infer the data types of the values received by the closure and therefore we don't have to declare that either. Instead, we can represent these values using shorthand argument names. These are special placeholders made up of the $ symbol and an index starting from 0. The first value received by the closure is represented by $0, the second value by $1, and so on.

```
func processclosure(myclosure: (Int, Int) -> Int) {
    print("The total is: \(myclosure(10, 2))")  // "The total is: 20"
}
processclosure() { $0 * $1 }
```

Listing 3-25: Inferring the closure's data types

Again, the code is the same, but now the closure is extremely simple. When it is executed from the **processclosure()** function, it receives the values 10 and 2, assigns them to the placeholders $0 and $1, multiplies their values and returns the result.

Basic 3.3 Structures

Structures are an essential part of the organizational paradigm proposed by Swift. They are custom data types that include not only data but also the code in charge of processing that data. When we define a structure, what we are doing is declaring a data type that may contain variables and constants (called *properties*) and functions (called *methods*). Later we can declare variables and constants of this type to store information with the characteristics defined by the structure. These values (called *instances*) will be unique, each one with its own properties and methods.

Basic Definition of Structures

To define a new structure, we must use the **struct** keyword and enclose the data and functionality in curly braces.

```
struct Item {
    var name: String = "Not defined"
    var price: Double = 0
}
```

Listing 3-26: Defining a structure

This example defines a structure called **Item** with two properties (variables): **name** and **price**. The definition is just delineating the elements of the data type (also called *members*), like a blueprint that will be later used to create the real structures. What we need to do to store values of this new data type is to declare a variable or a constant, as we did for any other data type before. In this case, the data type is the name of the structure and the initialization value is a special initializer with the syntax **Name()** (where **Name** is, again, the name of the structure).

```
struct Item {
    var name: String = "Not defined"
```

```
    var price: Double = 0
}
var purchase: Item = Item()
```

Listing 3-27: Declaring a variable of type Item

This code creates a variable of type **Item** that stores an instance of the **Item** structure containing the properties **name** and **price**. The instance is created by the **Item()** initializer and then assigned to the **purchase** variable.

In the example in Listing 3-27, the properties of a new instance always take the values declared in the structure's definition (**"Not Defined"** and **0**), but we can modify them as we do with any other variable. The only difference is that the properties are inside a structure, so every time we want to access them, we must mention the structure they belong to. The syntax implements dot notation, as in **variable.property**, where **variable** is the name of the variable that contains the instance of the structure and **property** is the name of the property we want to access.

```
struct Item {
    var name = "Not defined"
    var price = 0.0
}
var purchase = Item()
purchase.name = "Lamps"
purchase.price = 10.50

print("Product: \(purchase.name) $ \(purchase.price)")
```

Listing 3-28: Assigning new values to the properties of a structure

In this example, the properties of the **Item** structure and the **purchase** variable are declared as before, but this time we let Swift infer their data types. After the instance is created, new values are assigned to its properties using dot notation. Dot notation is not only used to assign new values but also to read the current ones. At the end, we read and print the values of the **name** and **price** properties on the console ("Product: Lamps $ 10.5").

 IMPORTANT: Note that we have stored the structure in a variable (**var**). This is to be able to assign new values to its properties later. When the values of the properties in a structure are modified, instead of modifying the properties of the instance, the system creates a new instance and assigns the new values to the properties of that instance. For this to be possible, the structure must be stored in a variable so it can be replaced by the new structure later.

Structures may be instantiated inside other structures, as many times as necessary. The dot notation is extended in these cases to reach every element in the hierarchy.

```
struct Price {
    var USD = 0.0
    var CAD = 0.0
}
struct Item {
    var name: String = "Not defined"
    var price: Price = Price()
}
var purchase = Item()
purchase.name = "Lamps"
purchase.price.USD = 10.50
```

Listing 3-29: Structures inside structures

Listing 3-29 defines two structures: **Price** and **Item**. The **Item** structure contains the same properties as before, but now the data type of the **price** property is **Price**, which means that instead of storing a single value, this property can now store a structure that in turn contains two properties: **USD** and **CAD**. When the **Item** structure is created and assigned to the **purchase** variable, the **Price** structure for the **price** property is also created with its values by default.

By concatenating the names of the variables and properties we can read and modify any value we want. For instance, the last statement in the code of Listing 3-29 accesses the **USD** property of the **price** structure inside the **purchase** structure to assign a price to the item in American Dollars (**purchase.price.USD = 10.50**).

In this example, the **price** structure is created during instantiation, but this is not usually the case. Sometimes the values of the properties containing structures are defined after the instance is created and therefore those properties must be declared as optionals. The problem with optionals is that we always need to check whether the variable or property has a value before we use it. To simplify this task, Swift introduces a tool called *Optional Chaining*.

Optional chaining makes it easy to access properties and methods in a hierarchical chain that contains optional components. As always, these components are accessed using dot notation, but a question mark is added to the names of the properties that have optional values. When the system finds an optional, it checks whether it contains a value and continues reading the expression only in case of success. Here is the same example, but with the **price** property turned into an optional.

```
struct Price {
    var USD = 0.0
    var CAD = 0.0
}
struct Item {
    var name: String = "Not defined"
    var price: Price?
}
var purchase = Item()
purchase.name = "Lamps"
purchase.price?.USD = 10.50   // nil
```

Listing 3-30: Accessing optional properties

The **price** property in this code is declared as an optional (its initial value is not defined). Every time we read this property, we must unwrap its value, but if we use Optional Chaining, we can just concatenate the values with dot notation and add a question mark after the name of the optional property (**purchase.price?.USD**). The system reads every component in the instruction from left to right and checks their values. If any of the optionals have no value, it returns **nil**, but when all the optionals have values, the instruction performs the task. (In this case, it would assign the number 10.50 to the **USD** property.)

Medium Key Paths

Besides using dot notation to read and write a property, we can use key paths. A key path is a reference to a property. The advantage of using key paths instead of dot notation is that they are stored in structures and therefore we can pass them to other parts of the code and then use them to access the values of the properties they are referencing without even knowing what those properties are. This can be useful when we need to interact with frameworks, or when we are extending code to include our own functionality.

Swift defines several structures to store key paths. For instance, a read-only key path is stored in an instance of a structure of type **KeyPath** and read-and-write key paths are stored in a structure of type **WritableKeyPath**.

The syntax to define a key path includes a backward slash and the name of the data type followed by the name of the property we want to reference. To access the value of a property using a key path, Swift uses a syntax that includes square brackets after the instance's name and the **keypath** keyword, as illustrated in the following example.

```
struct Item {
    let name: String
    let price: Double
}
var purchase: Item = Item(name: "Lamps", price: 27.50)
let keyPrice = \Item.price
print(purchase[keyPath: keyPrice])   // "27.5"
```

Listing 3-31: Creating key paths

This code defines a structure with two properties: **name** and **price**. Next, we create a key path to reference the **price** property. Because the properties are defined as constants, the key path is created of type **KeyPath** (a read-only key path). In the last statement, we use this key path to access the value of the **price** property of the **purchase** instance and print it on the console.

We can easily create a read-and-write key path by defining the structure's properties as variables. In the following example, we turn the **name** and **price** properties into variables and modify the value of **price** using our **keyPrice** key path.

```
struct Item {
    var name: String
    var price: Double
}
var purchase: Item = Item(name: "Lamps", price: 27.50)
let keyPrice = \Item.price
purchase[keyPath: keyPrice] = 30.00
print(purchase.price)
```

Listing 3-32: Using read and write key paths

(Basic) Methods

If we could only store properties, structures would be just complex data types, like tuples, but structures can also include code. This is done through functions. Functions inside structures are called *methods*, but the definition and functionality are the same.

The syntax to execute a method is **variable.method()**, where **variable** is the name of the variable that contains the instance of the structure and **method** is the name of the method we want to call inside that structure, as shown in the following example.

```
struct Item {
    var name = "Not defined"
    var price = 0.0

    func total(quantity: Double) -> Double {
        return quantity * price
    }
}
var purchase = Item()
purchase.name = "Lamp"
purchase.price = 10.50

print("Total: \(purchase.total(quantity: 2))")   // "Total: 21.0"
```

Listing 3-33: Defining methods

Chapter 3 - Swift Paradigm

In Listing 3-33, a method is declared as part of the definition of the **Item** structure. The method receives a value representing the number of items sold and calculates the total money spent in the transaction. We could have performed this operation outside the structure by reading the value of the **price** property, but having a method within the structure presents some advantages. First, we don't have to worry about how the method calculates the value; we just call the method with the right value and let it perform the task, no matter how complex it is. And second, we do not have to write the operation over and over again, because it is always part of the instance of the structure we are working with.

A method can read the values of the instance's properties but cannot assign new values to them. If we want a method to be able to modify the values of the properties of its own instance, we must prefix the **func** keyword with the **mutating** keyword, as shown below.

```
struct Item {
    var name = "Not defined"
    var price = 0.0

    mutating func changename(newname: String) {
        name = newname
    }
}
var purchase = Item()
purchase.changename(newname: "Lamps")

print("Product: \(purchase.name)")    // "Product: Lamps"
```

Listing 3-34: Assigning new values to properties from the methods in the structure

The **changename()** method of the **Item** structure in Listing 3-34 is declared as a mutating method so it can assign a new value to the **name** property. Therefore, we do not need to modify the **name** property directly, we can call this method with the value we want to store, and the method takes care of assigning the value to the property.

(Basic) Initialization

Every instance created from the structure's definition has the purpose to store and process specific data. For example, we can create multiple instances of our **Item** structure to store information about different products. Each product will have its own name and price, so the properties of each instance must be initialized with the proper values. The initialization of an instance is a very common task and it would be far too cumbersome if we had to assign the values one by one every time a new one is created. For this reason, Swift provides different alternatives to initialize the values of a structure. The one used by default is called *Memberwise Initializer*.

Memberwise initializers detect the properties of the structure and declare their names as argument labels. Using these argument labels, we can provide the values for initialization between the parentheses of the initializer. The following code implements a memberwise initializer to initialize an instance of the **Item** structure declared in previous examples.

```
struct Item {
    var name = "Not defined"
    var price = 0.0
}
var purchase = Item(name: "Lamp", price: 10.50)
print("Purchase: \(purchase.name) $ \(purchase.price)")
```

Listing 3-35: Initializing properties

Memberwise initializers reduce the amount of code and simplify initialization. Also, if we use the memberwise initializer, we don't need to assign values by default, as shown next.

```
struct Item {
   var name: String
   var price: Double
}
var purchase = Item(name: "Lamp", price: 10.50)
print("Purchase: \(purchase.name) $ \(purchase.price)")
```

Listing 3-36: Using memberwise initializers to provide the initial values of a structure

The two forms of initialization we have seen so far are not customizable enough. Some structures may have multiple properties that require initialization or even methods that must be executed right away to get the proper values for the instance to be ready. To add more alternatives, Swift provides a method called **init()**. The **init()** method is called as soon as the instance is created, so we can use it to initialize the properties any way we want.

```
struct Price {
   var USD: Double
   var CAD: Double

   init() {
      USD = 5
      CAD = USD * 1.29
   }
}
var myprice = Price()
```

Listing 3-37: Initializing properties from the init() *method*

When the instance is generated by the initializer, the properties are created first and then the **init()** method is executed. Inside this method we can perform any operation we need to get the properties' initial values. In the example of Listing 3-37, we assign an initial value of 5 to the **USD** property and then multiply this value by the corresponding exchange rate to get the value of the **CAD** property (the same price in Canadian dollars).

As well as with any other method or function, the **init()** method may include parameters. These parameters are used to specify initial values from the initializer.

```
struct Price {
   var USD: Double
   var CAD: Double

   init(americans: Double) {
      USD = americans
      CAD = USD * 1.29
   }
}
var myprice = Price(americans: 5)
```

Listing 3-38: Declaring the parameters to initialize the structure

This is similar to what Swift creates for us in the background when we use memberwise initializers, but the advantage of declaring the **init()** method ourselves is that we can specify only the parameters we need (as in the example in Listing 3-38) or even declare multiple **init()** methods to present several alternatives for initialization, as shown below.

```
struct Price {
   var USD: Double
   var CAD: Double

   init(americans: Double) {
      USD = americans
```

```
        CAD = USD * 1.29
    }
    init(canadians: Double) {
        CAD = canadians
        USD = CAD * 0.7752
    }
}
var myprice = Price(canadians: 5)
```

Listing 3-39: Declaring multiple init() *methods*

As explained before, Swift identifies each function by its name and parameters, so we can declare functions with the same name as long as they have different parameters. The example in Listing 3-39 declares two **init()** methods to initialize the instance of the structure. The first method receives a **Double** value with the name **americans** and the second method also receives a **Double** value but with the name **canadians**. The right method will be executed according to the argument included in the initializer. In this example, we use the argument **canadians** with the value 5, so the instance is initialized by the second **init()** method.

(Medium) ## Computed Properties

The properties we have declared up to this point are called *Stored Properties*. Their function is to store a value in memory. But there are other types of properties called *Computed Properties*. These properties do not store a value of their own, instead they have access to the rest of the properties of the structure and can perform operations to set and retrieve their values.

Two methods are available for computed properties to be able to set and retrieve a value: **get()** and **set()**. These methods are also called *getters* and *setters* and are declared in curly braces after the name of the property. Although both methods are useful, only the **get()** method is required.

```
struct Price {
    var USD: Double
    var ratetoCAD: Double

    var canadians: Double {
        get {
            return USD * ratetoCAD
        }
    }
}
var purchase = Price(USD: 11, ratetoCAD: 1.29)
print("Price in CAD: \(purchase.canadians)")   // "Price in CAD: 14.19"
```

Listing 3-40: Declaring computed properties

The structure defined in Listing 3-40 contains a stored property called **USD** to store the price in American dollars, a stored property called **ratetoCAD** to store the exchange rate for Canadian dollars, and a computed property called **canadians** that converts the US dollars into Canadian dollars and returns the result. Computed properties are like methods, they calculate the value every time the property is read. No matter if the value of the **ratetoCAD** property changes, the **canadians** property will always return the right price in Canadian dollars.

Computed properties with only a getter are called read-only properties because we can only read their values. When we declare a read-only property, we can omit the **get()** method. In addition, as we have seen before, when a block contains only one statement, it knows what to return, so we can omit the **return** keyword as well. The previous example can therefore be simplified as follows.

```
struct Price {
    var USD: Double
    var ratetoCAD: Double

    var canadians: Double {
        USD * ratetoCAD
    }
}
var purchase = Price(USD: 11, ratetoCAD: 1.29)
print(purchase.canadians)   // "14.190000000000001"
```

Listing 3-41: Defining read-only properties

By including the **set()** method for the **canadians** property we can, for example, set a new price using the same currency.

```
struct Price {
    var USD: Double
    var ratetoCAD: Double
    var ratetoUSD: Double

    var canadians: Double {
        get {
            USD * ratetoCAD
        }
        set {
            USD = newValue * ratetoUSD
        }
    }
}
var purchase = Price(USD: 11, ratetoCAD: 1.29, ratetoUSD: 0.7752)
purchase.canadians = 500
print("Price: \(purchase.USD)")   // "Price: 387.6"
```

Listing 3-42: Adding the set() method to set a new value

The new structure defined in Listing 3-42 can retrieve and set a price in Canadian dollars. When we set a new value for the **canadians** property, the value is stored in a constant called **newValue** (the constant is created automatically for us). Using this constant, we can process the new value and perform the operations we need. In this example, the value of **newValue** is multiplied by the exchange rate to get the price in American dollars. The price is always stored in American dollars but using the **canadians** property we can set it and retrieve it in Canadian dollars.

If we want to use a different name for the new value, we can specify it between parentheses. In the following example, the parameter was called **CAD** and used instead of **newValue** to calculate the value for the **USD** property.

```
struct Price {
    var USD: Double
    var ratetoCAD: Double
    var ratetoUSD: Double

    var canadians: Double {
        get {
            USD * ratetoCAD
        }
        set(CAD) {
            USD = CAD * ratetoUSD
        }
    }
}
```

```
var purchase = Price(USD: 11, ratetoCAD: 1.29, ratetoUSD: 0.7752)
```

Listing 3-43: Using a different name for the parameter of the `set()` *method*

Medium **Property Observers**

The properties of an instance of a structure may be modified at any moment by different processes, such as in response to user interaction or events triggered by the system. To inform an instance that one of its properties was modified, Swift introduces Property Observers.

Property Observers are special methods, similar to **get()** and **set()**, that we can include within a property to execute code before and after a value is assigned to it. The methods are called **willSet()** and **didSet()**, and are declared in braces after the property's name.

```
struct Price {
    var increment: Double = 0
    var oldprice: Double = 0

    var price: Double {
        willSet {
            increment = newValue - price
        }
        didSet {
            oldprice = oldValue
        }
    }
}
var product = Price(price: 15.95)
product.price = 20.75
print("New price: \(product.price)")    // "New price: 20.75"
print("Old price: \(product.oldprice)")  // "Old price: 15.95"
```

Listing 3-44: Adding observers to a store property

The **Price** structure in Listing 3-44 includes three properties: **increment**, **oldprice**, and **price**. We use the **price** property to store the value of an item, the **oldprice** property to store the previous price, and the **increment** property to store the difference between the old price and the new one. To set this last value, we declare property observers for the **price** property. Every time a new value is assigned to the property, the **willSet()** and **didSet()** methods are executed.

Swift automatically creates a parameter called **newValue** for the **willSet()** method to provide access to the value that is going to be assigned to the property, and a parameter called **oldValue** for the **didSet()** method to provide access to the property's old value after the new value was assigned. (We can change the names of these parameters as we did for the **set()** method in Listing 3-43.) In our example, when the **willSet()** method is executed, the current value of **price** is subtracted from **newValue** to get the difference, and the result is assigned to the **increment** property. And in the **didSet()** method, we assign the old price provided by **oldValue** to the **oldprice** property to have access to this price later.

Basic **Type Properties and Methods**

The properties and methods declared above are accessible on the instances created from the definition of the structure. This means that we must create an instance of the structure to be able to read and modify their values. But there are times when being able to execute properties and methods from the definition itself makes sense. We might need, for example, to get information related to all instances, or call methods to create instances with standard values. In Swift, this is possible by declaring type properties and methods. These are properties and methods accessible from the data type, not the instance created from that type.

Type properties and methods for structures are declared adding the **static** keyword to the definition. Once a property or method is declared with this keyword, they are only accessible from the definition itself. In the following example, we include a type property called **currencies** to inform how many currencies the structures can handle.

```
struct Price {
   var USD: Double
   var CAD: Double

   static let currencies = 2
}
print(Price.currencies)   // 2
```

Listing 3-45: Defining type properties

As illustrated by the code in Listing 3-45, there is no need to create an instance to access a type property or method. After the definition, the **currencies** property is read using the name of the structure and dot notation (**Price.currencies**). If we create an instance from this definition, the only properties accessible from the instance will be **USD** and **CAD**. The **currencies** property is a type property, only accessible from the type itself. The same happens with methods, as shown below.

```
struct Price {
   var USD: Double
   var CAD: Double

   static func reserved() -> Price {
      return Price(USD: 10.0, CAD: 11.0)
   }
}
var reservedprice = Price.reserved()
print("Price in USD: \(reservedprice.USD) CAD: \(reservedprice.CAD)")
```

Listing 3-46: Defining type methods

The structure in this example includes a type method called **reserved()**. The method creates and returns an instance of the **Price** structure with standard values. This is a common procedure and another way to create our own initializer. If we use the initializer by default, the values must be provided every time the instance is created, but with a type method all we need to do is to call the method on the type to get in return an instance configured with specific values. In our example, the values correspond to a reserved price. We call the **reserved()** method on the **Price** type, the method creates an instance of the **Price** structure with the values 10.0 and 11.0, and then this instance is assigned to the **reservedprice** variable. At the end, the values of both properties are printed on the console to confirm that their values were defined by the **reserved()** method. (Again, the method is not accessible from the instance, only from the data type.)

(Advanced) **Generic Structures**

At the beginning of this chapter, we explained how to create generic functions. These are functions that can process values of different data types. The function defines a placeholder for the data type and then adopts the data type of the value it receives. But generics data types are not exclusive to functions, we can also turn data types themselves, such as structures, into generic types. The advantage is that we can create independent processing units that can handle different types of values. To create a generic structure, we must declare the generic data type after the name of the structure and between angle brackets, as we did for functions.

```
struct MyStructure<T> {
   var myvalue:T

   func description() {
      print("The value is: \(myvalue)")   // "The value is: 5"
   }
}
let instance = MyStructure<Int>(myvalue: 5)
instance.description()
```

Listing 3-47: Defining generic structures

This example defines a generic structure called **MyStructure** with one generic type called **T**. The structure contains a generic property called **myvalue** and a method that prints a message with the value of the property. After the definition of the structure, we create an instance with an integer. The system replaces the **T** with the **Int** type, creates the instance, and assigns the value 5 to the **myvalue** property. In the last statement, we call the **description()** method to print it.

When we create an instance of a generic structure, the data type we want the structure to work with is included after the name and between angle brackets, but this is only required when the initialization doesn't include any value. For example, the following code creates an instance of the same structure but with a string and let Swift infer the generic data type from the value.

```
struct MyStructure<T> {
   var myvalue:T

   func description() {
      print("The value is: \(myvalue)")   // "The value is: Hello"
   }
}
let instance = MyStructure(myvalue: "Hello")
instance.description()
```

Listing 3-48: Using generic structures

 IMPORTANT: These are basic examples of how to create and work with generic data types. As with functions, generics only become useful when we constrain the data using protocols. We will learn more about generics in the following sections and study protocols at the end of this chapter.

Basic Primitive Type Structures

Including properties and methods inside a structure and then assigning an instance of that structure to a variable is a simple way to wrap data and functionality in a single portable unit of code. Structures are usually used this way, as practical wrappers of code, and Swift takes advantage of this feature extensively. In fact, all the primitive data types defined in Swift are structures. The syntax **variable: Int = value**, for example, is a shortcut provided by Swift for the initializer **variable = Int(value)**. Every time we assign a new value to a variable of a primitive data type, we are assigning a structure that contains that value. The following are the initializers of some of the primitive data types studied in Chapter 2.

▷ **Int(Value)**—This is the initializer of the **Int** data type. The argument is the value we want to assign to the instance. If no value is provided, the value 0 is assigned by default. Initializers for similar types are also available (**Int8()**, **Int16()**, **Int32()**, and **Int64()**).

▷ **UInt(Value)**—This is the initializer of the **UInt** data type. The argument is the value we want to assign to the instance. If no value is provided, the value assigned is 0. Initializers for similar types are also available (**UInt8()**, **UInt16()**, **UInt32()**, and **UInt64()**).

- **Float**(Value)—This is the initializer of the **Float** data type. The argument is the value we want to assign to the instance. If no value is provided, the value 0.0 is assigned by default.
- **Double**(Value)—This is the initializer of the **Double** data type. The argument is the value we want to assign to the instance. If no value is provided, the value assigned is 0.0.

The structures for these data types are defined in the Swift Standard Library. All we need to do to create an instance is to implement the initializer with the value we want to store.

```
var mynumber = Int(25)
var myprice = Double(4.99)
```

Listing 3-49: Initializing variables with standard initializers

This is the same as assigning the values directly to the variable (e.g., **var myprice = 4.99**), but these initializers become useful when the value we want to assign to the structure is of different type. The definitions of these structures include several initializers that convert the value to the right type. This is called *Casting*, and we can use it to turn a variable of one data type into another. For example, when we divide numbers, the system converts those numbers to the most comprehensive type and performs the operation, but variables are already of a specific type and therefore they must be explicitly converted before the operation is performed or we get an error. (The process does not really convert the variable; it just creates a new value of the right type.)

```
var number1: Int = 10
var number2: Double = 2.5
var total = Double(number1) / number2   // 4.0
```

Listing 3-50: Casting a variable

The variables **number1** and **number2** defined in Listing 3-50 are of type **Int** and **Double**. To perform a division between them we must cast one of them to the data type of the other (arithmetic operations cannot be performed on values of different data types). Using the **Double()** initializer, we create a new value of type **Double** from the value of **number1** and perform the operation. (The value 10.0 created by the initializer is divided by the value 2.5 of **number2** to get the result 4.0.) The process is described as "casting the **number1** variable to a **Double**".

These initializers are also useful when working with **String** values. Sometimes the characters of a string represent numbers that we need to process. The problem is that strings cannot be processed as numbers. We cannot include a string in an arithmetic operation without first converting the string into a value of a numeric data type. Fortunately, the initializers for numeric types such as **Int** and **Double** can convert a value of type **String** into a number. If the operation cannot be performed, the initializer returns **nil**, so we can treat it as an optional value. In the following example, we convert the string "45" into the integer 45 and add the value 15 to it.

```
var units = "45"

if let number = Int(units) {
    let total = number + 15
    print("The total is \(total)")   // "The total is 60"
}
```

Listing 3-51: Extracting numbers from strings

The structures defined for primitive data types also have their own properties and methods. This includes type properties and methods. For instance, the following are the most frequently used properties and methods provided by the structures that process integer values (e.g., `Int`).

▷ **min**—This type property returns the minimum value the data type can handle.

▷ **max**—This type property returns the maximum value the data type can handle.

▷ **random(in:** Range)—This type method returns a random number. The value is calculated from a range of integers provided by the **in** argument.

▷ **negate()**—This method inverts the sign of the value.

▷ **isMultiple(of:** Int)—This method returns **true** if the value is a multiple of the value provided by the **of** argument.

The **min** and **max** properties are particularly useful because they allow us to determine whether an operation might overflow a variable (produce a result greater or less than the minimum and maximum allowed).

```
var mynumber: Int8 = 120
let increment: Int8 = 10

if (Int8.max - mynumber) >= increment {    // (127 - 120) >= 10
    mynumber += increment
}
print(mynumber)    // "120"
```

Listing 3-52: Checking the maximum possible value for the Int8 *type*

This example takes advantage of the **max** property to make sure that incrementing the value of a variable will not overflow the variable (the result will not be greater than the maximum value the variable can handle). The code starts by defining a variable of type **Int8** to store the result of the operation and another to store the number we want to add. Then, we calculate how far the current value of **mynumber** is from the maximum value allowed by an **Int8** variable (**Int8.max — mynumber**) and compare this result with the value of **increment**. If the number of units we have left is greater or equal than the value of **increment**, we know that the operation can be performed without going over the limit. (In this example, the operation is not performed because the addition of 120 + 10 produces a result greater than the limit of 127 allowed by **Int8**.)

The type **Double** also includes its own selection of properties and methods. The following are the most frequently used.

▷ **pi**—This type property returns the value of the constant pi.

▷ **infinity**—This type property returns an infinite value.

▷ **random(in:** Range)—This type method returns a random number. The value is calculated from a range of values of type **Double** provided by the **in** argument.

▷ **negate()**—This method inverts the sign of the value.

▷ **squareRoot()**—This method returns the square root of the value.

▷ **remainder(dividingBy:** Double)—This method returns the remainder produced by dividing the value by the value specified by the **dividingBy** argument.

▷ **rounded(**FloatingPointRoundingRule)—This method returns the value rounded according to the rule specified by the argument. The argument is an enumeration with the values **awayFromZero, down, toNearestOrAwayFromZero, toNearestOrEven, towardZero** and **up**.

In this case, the most useful method is probably **rounded()**. With this method, we can round a floating-point value to the nearest integer.

```
var mynumber: Double = 2.890
mynumber = mynumber.rounded(.toNearestOrAwayFromZero)
print("The round number is \(mynumber)")   // "The round number is 3.0"
```

Listing 3-53: Rounding floating-point values

Of course, Boolean values are also structures. Among others, the **Bool** data type offers the following methods.

▷ **toggle()**—This method toggles the value. If the value is **true**, it becomes **false** and vice versa.

▷ **random()**—This type method returns a random **Bool** value.

The following example checks the current value of a variable and assigns the value **false** if it is **true**, or vice versa.

```
var valid: Bool = true
if valid {
    print("It is Valid")
    valid.toggle()
}
print(valid)   // false
```

Listing 3-54: Modifying the value of a Bool *variable*

(Basic) Range Structures

The **random()** method provided by some of the structures introduced above work with ranges of values (collections of values in sequential order). These are structures included in the Swift Standard Library that can manage open and closed ranges of values. For example, we can create a range from 1 to 5. If the range is open, it will include the values 1, 2, 3, and 4, but if the range is closed, it will include the values 1, 2, 3, 4, and 5. Swift includes two operators to generate ranges.

• ... (three dots) creates a range from the value on the left to the value on the right, including both values in the range (e.g., 1...5 creates a range that includes the values 1, 2, 3, 4 and 5). The value on the right can be omitted to create a one-sided range. A one-sided range goes from the value on the left to the maximum value allowed for the data type.

• ..< (two dots and the less than character) creates a range from the value on the left to the value before the value on the right (e.g., 1..<5 creates a range that includes the values 1, 2, 3 and 4).

When we declare a range using these operators, Swift creates the proper structure according to the operator. A structure of type **Range** is created for an open range and a structure of type **ClosedRange** is created for a closed range. These structures provide common properties and methods to work with the range. The following are the most frequently used.

▷ **lowerBound**—This property returns the range's lower value (the value on the left).

▷ **upperBound**—This property returns the range's upper value (the value on the right).

▷ **contains(Element)**—This method returns a Boolean value that determines if the value specified by the argument is within the range.

▷ **clamped(to: Range)**—This method compares the original range with the range specified by the **to** argument and returns a new range with the part of the ranges that overlap.

Chapter 3 - Swift Paradigm

▷ **reversed()**—This method returns a collection with the values in reversed order.

Ranges are useful in a variety of situations. For instance, if we need a loop with a fixed number of cycles, we can implement a **for in** loop with a range. The following example iterates over a closed range of integers from 0 to 10, generating a total of 11 cycles.

```
var total = 0
for value in 0...10 {
    total += value
}
print("The total is \(total)")   // "The total is 55"
```

Listing 3-55: *Using* for in *to iterate over a range*

We can also invert the range with the **reversed()** method.

```
var message = ""
var range = 0..<10
for item in range.reversed() {
    message += "\(item) "
}
print(message)   // "9 8 7 6 5 4 3 2 1 0 "
```

Listing 3-56: *Inverting a range*

This example creates a range from 0 to 9 with the **..<** operator and then calls the **reversed()** method to invert it. This method creates a collection with the values in reversed order, so we can read it with a **for in** loop. The statement inside the loop adds the values to the **message** string, and this string is printed on the console to confirm that the values were effectively reversed.

Ranges can also simplify **switch** statements that have to consider multiple values per case.

```
var age = 6
var message = "You have to go to "
switch age {
    case 2...4:
        message += "Day Care"
    case 5...11:
        message += "Elementary School"
    case 12...17:
        message += "High School"
    case 18..<22:
        message += "College"
    case 22...:
        message += "Work"
    default:
        message += "Breastfeeding"
}
print(message)   // "You have to go to Elementary School"
```

Listing 3-57: *Using range operators in a* switch *statement*

In this example, we compare the age with different ranges of values. If the value of **age** is within a range, the instructions for that **case** are executed. As illustrated by this example, we can also declare only one side of a range and let the system determine the other. The last **case** creates a one-sided closed range from the value 22 to the maximum value allowed for the data type.

As mentioned earlier, ranges are used by the **random()** method to get a random value. The following example generates a loop that calculates multiple random values from 1 to 10. The condition stops the loop when the number returned by the method is equal to 5. In the loop, we also increment the value of the **attempts** variable to calculate the number of cycles required for the **random()** method to return our number.

```
var mynumber: Int = 0
var attempts = 0

while mynumber != 5 {
    mynumber = Int.random(in: 1...10)
    attempts += 1
}
print("It took \(attempts) attempts to get the number 5")
```

Listing 3-58: *Calculating random numbers*

Basic · String Structures

As we have seen in Chapter 2, we can initialize a **String** structure by simply assigning a string (a text between double quotes) to a constant or a variable. This is another shortcut. In the background, instances are created from the **String** initializer.

▷ **String(Value)**—This initializer creates a string from the value provided by the argument. The **String** structure defines multiple versions of this initializer to create strings from different types of values, including other strings, characters, and numbers.

Once the string is created, we can manipulate it with the properties and methods provided by the **String** structure. The following are the most frequently used.

▷ **isEmpty**—This property returns a Boolean that indicates whether the value is an empty string. This is the same as comparing the string with an empty string (**string == ""**).

▷ **count**—This property returns the total number of characters in the string.

▷ **first**—This property returns the first character in the string.

▷ **last**—This property returns the last character in the string.

▷ **lowercased()**—This method returns a copy of the string in lowercase letters.

▷ **uppercased()**—This method returns a copy of the string in uppercase letters.

▷ **hasPrefix(String)**—This method returns a Boolean value that indicates whether the string begins with the text specified by the argument or not.

▷ **hasSuffix(String)**—This method returns a Boolean value that indicates whether the string ends with the text specified by the argument or not.

Most of the time, we will assign a string directly to a variable as we have done so far, but the **String()** initializer is useful when we need to convert values into strings. For instance, the following example converts the number 44 into a string and counts the number of digits.

```
var age = String(44)
var mytext = "Total digits \(age.count)"   // "Total digits 2"
```

Listing 3-59: *Converting a number into a string*

Swift strings are composed of Unicode characters, which occupy different amounts of memory. Because of this, it is not possible to establish the position of a character using integer values. The index of the first character is always 0, but the indexes of the consecutive characters depend on the size of their predecessors. Swift solves this problem by defining a data type called **Index**. This is a structure defined inside the **String** structure that was designed to manage string indexes. The **String** structure includes properties and methods to work with indexes and access the characters of a string. The following are the most frequently used.

- ▷ **startIndex**—This property returns the index of the first character of the string.
- ▷ **endIndex**—This property returns the index of one position after the last character of the string. It is useful to manipulate range of characters, as we will see later.
- ▷ **firstIndex(of: Character)**—This method returns the index where the character specified by the **of** argument appears for the first time in the string.
- ▷ **lastIndex(of: Character)**—This method returns the last index where the character specified by the **of** argument appears in the string.
- ▷ **insert(Character, at: Index)**—This method inserts into the string the character provided by the first argument at the position determined by the **at** argument.
- ▷ **insert(contentsOf: String, at: Index)**—This method inserts into the string the value of the **contentsOf** argument at the position determined by the **at** argument.
- ▷ **remove(at: Index)**—This method removes and returns the character at the position determined by the **at** argument.
- ▷ **prefix(Int)**—This method returns a string created from the first character of the original string to the maximum length determined by the argument.
- ▷ **prefix(through: Index)**—This method returns a string created from the first character of the original string to the character at the index indicated by the **through** argument.
- ▷ **prefix(upTo: Index)**—This method returns a string created from the first character of the original string to the character at the index indicated by the **upTo** argument, but without including this last character.
- ▷ **replaceSubrange(Range, with: String)**—This method replaces the characters in the position determined by the range provided as the first argument with the string provided by the **with** argument.
- ▷ **removeSubrange(Range)**—This method removes the characters in the positions determined by the range specified by the argument.

Strings are collection of values. To access a specific character in a string, we must declare the **Index** structure with the index of the character we want to read after the name of the variable and enclose it in square brackets, as in the following example.

```
var text = "Hello World"
if !text.isEmpty {
   let start = text.startIndex
   let firstChar = text[start]
   print("First character is \(firstChar)")   // "First character is H"
}
```

Listing 3-60: Processing the characters of a string

The first thing we do in this example is to check the value of the **isEmpty** property to make sure the string is not empty and there are characters to read (notice the **!** operator to invert the condition). Once we know that there are characters to work with, we get the index of the string's first character from the **startIndex** property and read the character in that position using square brackets.

If we want to access a character in a different position, we must increment the value returned by **startIndex**. The trick is that, since **Index** values are not integers, we cannot just add a number to them. Instead, we must use the methods provided by the **String** structure.

- **index(after:** Index)—This method increments the index specified by the **after** argument one unit and returns a new **Index** value with the result.
- **index(before:** Index)—This method decrements the index specified by the **before** argument one unit and returns a new **Index** value with the result.
- **index(Index, offsetBy:** Int)—This method increments the index specified by the first argument the amount of units specified by the **offsetBy** argument and returns a new **Index** value with the result.

The following example advances the initial index 6 positions to get a different character.

```
var text = "Hello World"
if text != "" {
    let start = text.startIndex
    let newIndex = text.index(start, offsetBy: 6)

    print("The character is \(text[newIndex])")   // "The character is W"
}
```

Listing 3-61: Calculating a specific index

The **index()** method applied in Listing 3-61 takes an integer to calculate the new index. The original index is incremented the number of units indicated by the integer and the new **Index** value is returned. With this index, we get the character at the position 6 (indexes start from 0).

If we wanted to get the previous index, we could have specified a negative number of units for the offset value, but another way to move forward and backward is to implement the other versions of the **index()** method. The following example gets the next index after the initial index and prints the corresponding character on the console.

```
var text = "John"
let start = text.startIndex
var next = text.index(after: start)

print("Second letter is \(text[next])")   // "Second letter is o"
```

Listing 3-62: Getting the next index

Once the right index is calculated, we can call some of the **String** methods to insert or remove characters. The **insert()** method, for instance, inserts a single character at the position indicated by the second argument. In the following example, we call it with the value of **endIndex** to add a character at the end of the string (**endindex** points to the position after the last character).

```
var text = "Hello World"
text.insert("!", at: text.endIndex)

print("New string is \(text)")   // "New string is Hello World!"
```

Listing 3-63: Inserting a character in a string

If we do not know where the character is located, we can find the index with the **firstIndex()** method. The value returned by this method is an optional containing the **Index** value of the first character that matches the argument or **nil** if no character is found. In the following example, we implement it to find the first space character and remove it with the **remove()** method.

```
var text = "Hello World"
var findIndex = text.firstIndex(of: " ")
```

```
if let index = findIndex {
   text.remove(at: index)
   print("New string is \(text)")  // "New string is HelloWorld"
}
```

Listing 3-64: Removing a character

If we want to work with groups of characters, we must implement ranges of **Index** values.

```
var text = "Hello World"
var start = text.startIndex
var findIndex = text.firstIndex(of: " ")

if let end = findIndex {
   print("First word is \(text[start..<end])")  //"First word is Hello"
}
```

Listing 3-65: Getting a range of characters

The **firstIndex()** method in Listing 3-65 looks for a space character and returns its index. With this value, we can create a range from the first character to the space character and get the first word. But we must be careful because the **end** index is pointing to the space character, not to the last character of the word. To get the word without the space, we create an open range with the **..<** operator, so the character on the right is not included.

We can also use ranges to replace or remove parts of the text. For this purpose, the **String** structure offers the methods **replaceSubrange()** and **removeSubrange()**.

```
var text = "Hello World"
var start = text.startIndex
var findIndex = text.firstIndex(of: " ")

if let end = findIndex {
   text.replaceSubrange(start..<end, with: "Goodbye")  // "Goodbye World"
}
findIndex = text.firstIndex(of: " ")
if let start = findIndex {
   text.removeSubrange(start...)  // "Goodbye"
}
```

Listing 3-66: Working with ranges of characters

The **replaceSubrange()** method in Listing 3-66 replaces the characters from the beginning of the string up to the character before the space character ("Hello") with the string "Goodbye", and the **removeSubrange()** method uses an open range to remove the characters of this sentence from the space character to the end of the string (" World"), getting the string "Goodbye". Note that after applying the methods over the same string, the indexes are lost and therefore they must be recalculated. That's why before calling the **removeSubrange()** method we search for the position of the space character once more and update the **findIndex** variable.

The rest of the methods provided by the **String** structure are straightforward. For instance, the following example implements two of them to check if a string contains the word "World" at the end and converts all the letters into uppercase letters.

```
let text = "Hello World"
if text.hasSuffix("World") {
   print(text.uppercased())  // "HELLO WORLD"
}
```

Listing 3-67: Implementing String methods

Basic # Array Structures

The strings studied before and the values we have created in previous examples with functions such as **stride()** or **repeatElement()** are collections of values. Collections do not represent a value; they are containers for other values. A value of type **String** does not contain the string "Hello", it contains a collection of variables of type **Character**, with the values H, e, l, l, and o. Swift includes several collections like this, some were defined to contain specific values, like **String**, and others are generic (they can store values of any data type we need). One of those collections is **Array**.

Arrays are collections that contain an ordered list of values. They are generic structures that have the capacity to store all the values we need of any data type we want, but with the condition that once a data type is selected, all the values must be of that same type. For example, if we create an array of type **Int**, we will only be able to store values of type **Int** in it. Swift offers multiple syntaxes to create an array, including the following initializers.

▷ **Array<Type>()**—This initializer returns an empty **Array** structure of the data type indicated by the value of **Type**.

▷ **Array(repeating:** Value, **count:** Int)—This initializer returns an **Array** structure with copies of the same value. The **repeating** argument determines the value to copy, and the **count** argument determines how many copies the array will contain.

A shortcut to create an array is declaring the data type between square brackets followed by parentheses (e.g., **var list = [Int]()**), but the most frequently used is declaring the array with initial values enclosed in square brackets and separated by comma.

```
var list: [Int] = [15, 25, 35]
```

Listing 3-68: Declaring arrays

As with any other variable, Swift can infer the data type from the values.

```
var list = [15, 25, 35]
```

Listing 3-69: Declaring arrays with type inference

The **list** array declared in this example is initialized with three integer values, 15, 25 and 35. The values of an array are usually called *elements* or *items*. On these terms, we can say that the code in Listing 3-69 declares an array of three elements of type **Int**.

An index is automatically assigned to each value starting from 0, and as with strings, we must specify the index of the value we want to read surrounded by square brackets.

```
var list = [15, 25, 35]
print(list[1])   // 25
```

Listing 3-70: Reading the array's elements

The last statement in Listing 3-70 prints the value of the second element of the **list** array on the console (the element at index 1). We can also use indexes to modify the values.

```
var list = [15, 25, 35]
list[0] = 400
print(list)   // [400, 25, 35]
```

Listing 3-71: Assigning a new value to an element

Assigning new values is only possible for elements that already exist in the array. If we try to access an element with an index that doesn't exist, we get an error. One way to add a new element, or several, is with the **+=** operator.

```
var list = [15, 25, 35]
list += [45, 55]
print(list)  // [15, 25, 35, 45, 55]
```
Listing 3-72: Adding new elements to an array

The **+=** operator adds an array at the end of another array. In Listing 3-72, we use it to add two more elements to the array declared in the first statement. The **+=** operator concatenates the two arrays and assigns the result back to the same variable. If we want to use two or more arrays to create a new one, we can apply the **+** operator.

```
var list1 = [15, 25, 35]
var list2 = [45, 55, 65]
var final = list1 + list2  // [15, 25, 35, 45, 55, 65]
```
Listing 3-73: Concatenating two arrays

It is possible to declare arrays of arrays. These types of arrays are called *Multidimensional Arrays*. Arrays inside arrays are listed separated by comma.

```
var list: [[Int]] = [[2, 45, 31], [5, 10], [81, 12]]
```
Listing 3-74: Creating multidimensional arrays

This example creates an array of arrays of integers. (Notice the declaration of the array inside another array **[[Int]]**.) To access the values, we must declare the indexes of each level in square brackets, one after another. The following example returns the first value (index 0) of the second array (index 1). The instruction looks for the array at index 1 and then gets the number at index 0.

```
var list: [[Int]] = [[2, 45, 31], [5, 10], [81, 12]]
print(list[1][0])  // 5
```
Listing 3-75: Reading values from a multidimensional array

To remove all the elements from an array, we can use one of the initializers introduced before or just assign to the variable square brackets without values.

```
var list = [15, 25, 35]
list = []
```
Listing 3-76: Removing the elements of an array

Arrays are collections of values and therefore we can iterate over their values with a **for in** loop, as we did with strings before.

```
var total = 0
let list = [15, 25, 35]

for value in list {
    total += value
}
```

```
print("The total is \(total)")  // "The total is 75"
```

Listing 3-77: Reading an array with a `for` `in` *loop*

The code in Listing 3-77 implements a `for` `in` loop to add the numbers in the **list** array to the **total** variable. At the end, we print the result. Although this is a legit way to do it, arrays offer multiple properties and methods to read and process their values. The following are the most frequently used properties.

▷ **count**—This property returns the total number of elements in the array.

▷ **isEmpty**—This property returns a Boolean value that indicates if the array is empty.

▷ **first**—This property returns the first element of the array or **nil** if the array is empty.

▷ **last**—This property returns the last element of the array or **nil** if the array is empty.

The following are some of the methods available to add elements to the array.

▷ **append(Element)**—This method adds the value specified by the argument at the end of the array.

▷ **insert(Element, at: Int)**—This method adds a new element to the array. The first argument is the value we want to assign to the new element, and the **at** argument represents the position of the array where we want to insert the element.

We also have various methods to remove elements from the array.

▷ **remove(at: Int)**—This method removes an element from the array at the index specified by the **at** argument.

▷ **removeFirst()**—This method removes the first element of the array. It returns the value of the element deleted.

▷ **removeLast()**—This method removes the last element of the array. It returns the value of the element deleted.

▷ **removeAll(where: Closure)**—This method removes the elements in the array that meet the condition established by the closure assigned to the **where** argument.

▷ **removeSubrange(Range)**—This method removes a range of elements from the array. The argument is a range of integers representing the indexes of the elements to remove.

▷ **dropFirst(Int)**—This method removes the number of elements specified by the argument from the beginning of the array. If no amount is declared, only the first element is removed.

▷ **dropLast(Int)**—This method removes the number of elements specified by the argument from the end of the array. If no amount is declared, only the last element is removed.

The following methods are used to sort the elements in the array.

▷ **sorted()**—This method returns an array with the elements of the array in ascending order.

▷ **sorted(by: Closure)**—This method returns an array with the elements of the array in the order determined by the closure provided to the **by** argument.

▷ **shuffled()**—This method returns an array with the elements of the array in random order.

▷ **reversed()**—This method returns an array with the elements of the array in reverse order.

▷ **swapAt**(Int, Int)—This method exchanges the values of the elements at the indexes specified by the arguments.

The following are methods used to retrieve specific elements from an array.

▷ **filter**(Closure)—This method filters an array and returns another array with the values that passed the filter. The argument is a closure that processes the elements and returns a Boolean value indicating whether the value passed the filter or not.

▷ **map**(Closure)—This method returns a new array containing the results of processing each of the values of the array.

▷ **compactMap**(Closure)—This method returns a new array containing the results of processing each of the values of the array, but ignores the values that produce a `nil` result.

▷ **reduce**(Value, Closure)—This method sends the values of the array to the closure one by one and returns the result of the operation. The first argument is the value that is going to be processed with the first value of the array.

▷ **contains**(where: Closure)—This method returns a Boolean that determines if the array contains an element that satisfies the condition in the closure.

▷ **allSatisfy**(Closure)—This method returns a Boolean value that determines if all the elements in the array comply with the requisites of a closure.

▷ **difference**(from: Array)—This method returns a `CollectionDifference` structure containing all the changes that have to be performed to synchronize the array with the array provided by the **from** argument. This method can work in conjunction with the `applying()` method to apply all the changes in the array at once.

▷ **randomElement**()—This method randomly selects an element from the array and returns it. If the array is empty, the value returned is `nil`.

▷ **replaceSubrange**(Range, with: Array)—This method replaces a range of elements with the elements of the array provided by the **with** argument. The first argument is a range of integers corresponding to the indexes of the elements we want to replace.

▷ **joined**(separator: String)—This method returns a string that includes all the values in an array of strings joined by the string specified by the **separator** argument.

And the following are some of the methods used to obtain information from the array.

▷ **count**(where: Closure)—This method returns an integer with the number of elements that satisfy the condition determined by the closure.

▷ **enumerated**()—This method is used to iterate over the elements of the array. It returns a tuple containing the index and the value of the current element.

▷ **min**()—This method compares the values of the elements and returns the smallest.

▷ **max**()—This method compares the values of the elements and returns the largest.

In the previous example, we have seen how to iterate over the elements of an array with the **for in** loop, but that iteration only returns the value of the element, not its index. An alternative is provided by the **enumerated()** method, designed to work with these types of loops. Each cycle returns a tuple with the index and the value of the current element.

```
let fruits = ["Banana", "Orange", "Apple"]
var message = "My fruits:"
```

```
for (myindex, myfruit) in fruits.enumerated() {
    message += " \(myindex + 1)-\(myfruit)"
}
print(message)   // "My fruits: 1-Banana 2-Orange 3-Apple"
```

Listing 3-78: Reading indexes and values of an array

This example uses the constants **myindex** and **myfruit** to capture the values produced by the **enumerated()** method and generates a string. Note that since the array's indexes start from 0, we added 1 to **myindex** to start counting from 1.

Another useful property is **count**. As mentioned before, we can access each element of the array with the index between square brackets. But trying to read a value in an index that has not yet been defined produces an error. To make sure that the index exists, we can check whether it is greater than 0 and less than the total amount of elements in the array using the **count** property.

```
let ages = [32, 540, 12, 27, 54]
let index = 3
if index > 0 && index < ages.count {
    print("The value is: \(ages[index])")   // "The value is: 27"
}
```

Listing 3-79: Checking whether an array contains a value in a specific index

The methods to add and remove elements from an array are straightforward. The following example illustrates how to implement them.

```
var fruits = ["Banana", "Orange"]
if !fruits.isEmpty {
    fruits.append("Apple")   // ["Banana", "Orange", "Apple"]
    fruits.removeFirst()   // "Banana"
    fruits.insert("Pear", at: 1)   // ["Orange", "Pear", "Apple"]
    fruits.insert(contentsOf: ["Cherry", "Peach"], at: 2)
    // ["Orange", "Pear", "Cherry", "Peach", "Apple"]
}
```

Listing 3-80: Adding and removing elements

 IMPORTANT: Every time an array is modified, its indexes are reassigned. If you remove the first element of an array of three elements, the index 0 is reassigned to the second element and the index 1 to the third element. The system makes sure that the indexes are always consecutive and start from 0.

A more complex method is **removeAll(where:)**. This method removes several elements at once, but only those that meet a condition. The condition is established by a closure that processes each of the values in the array and returns **true** or **false** depending on whether the value meets the condition or not. In the following example, we compare each value with the string "Orange" and therefore all the values "Orange" are removed from the array.

```
var fruits = ["Banana", "Orange", "Apple", "Orange"]
fruits.removeAll(where: { value in
    value == "Orange"
})
print(fruits)   // ["Banana", "Apple"]
```

Listing 3-81: Removing all the elements that meet a condition

Another method that requires a closure to process the values is **contains(where:)**. In the following example, we use this method to determine whether an array contains a value greater than 60 or not.

```
var list = [55, 12, 32, 5, 9]
let found = list.contains(where: { value in
   value > 60
})
print(found)   // false
```

Listing 3-82: Finding if an element meets a condition

We can also select a random value with the **randomElement()** method. This method selects a value from the array and returns an optional, so we must compare it against **nil** or use optional binding before processing it, as in the following example.

```
let fruits = ["Banana", "Orange", "Apple"]
if let randomValue = fruits.randomElement() {
   print("The selected value is: \(randomValue)")
}
```

Listing 3-83: Selecting a random value from an array

Another random operation is performed by the **shuffled()** method. With this method we can randomly sort the elements of an array.

```
var fruits = ["Banana", "Orange", "Apple"]
fruits = fruits.shuffled()
print(fruits)   // e.g., ["Orange", "Apple", "Banana"]
```

Listing 3-84: Changing the order of the elements of an array

Besides working with all the elements of an array, we can do it with a range of elements.

```
var fruits = ["Banana", "Orange", "Apple", "Cherry"]
var someFruits = fruits[0..<2]   // ["Banana", "Orange"]
print("The new selection has \(someFruits.count) fruits")
```

Listing 3-85: Reading a range of elements

This example gets the elements at the indexes 0 and 1 from the **fruits** array and assigns them to the new **someFruits** array. Now we have two arrays: **fruits** with 4 elements and **someFruits** with 2.

Arrays created from a range of indexes are of type **ArraySlice**. This is another collection type provided by Swift to store temporary arrays that are composed of elements taken from other arrays. We can iterate over these types of arrays with a loop or read its elements as we do with normal arrays, but if we want to assign them to other array variables or use them for persistent storage, we must cast them as **Array** types using the **Array()** initializer. The initializer takes the values in the **ArraySlice** variable and returns a normal array.

```
var fruits = ["Banana", "Orange", "Apple", "Cherry"]
var someFruits = fruits[0..<2]   // ["Banana", "Orange"]
var newArray = Array(someFruits)
```

Listing 3-86: Casting arrays of type ArraySlice

The **Array** structure also offers the methods **removeSubrange()** and **replace-Subrange()** to remove and replace a range of elements.

```
var fruits = ["Banana", "Orange", "Apple", "Banana", "Banana"]
fruits.removeSubrange(1...2)
```

```
fruits.replaceSubrange(0..<2, with: ["Cherry", "Cherry"])
print(fruits)   // "["Cherry", "Cherry", "Banana"]"
```

Listing 3-87: Removing and replacing elements

In Listing 3-87, we call the **removeSubrange()** method to remove the range of elements from index 1 to 2 (getting an array filled with the value "Banana"), and then we call the **replaceSubrange()** method to replace the elements from index 0 to 1 with another array filled with "Cherries". This is just to illustrate how the methods work, but it shows a recurrent situation in app development where sometimes we need to fill a collection with elements of the same value. When working with arrays, this is easy to achieve. The **Array** structure includes an initializer that takes two arguments, **repeating** and **count**, and generates an array with the number of elements indicated by **count** and the value indicated by **repeating**.

```
var fruits = ["Banana", "Orange", "Apple"]

let total = fruits.count
let newArray = Array(repeating: "Cherry", count: total)
fruits.replaceSubrange(0..<total, with: newArray)

print(fruits)   // "["Cherry", "Cherry", "Cherry"]"
```

Listing 3-88: Initializing an array with elements of the same value

In this example, we create an array with the same amount of elements as the **fruits** array and then use the **replaceSubrange()** method to replace every element with a new one.

The methods to remove and replace elements of an array are not selective enough; they affect the elements in a specific index or a range of indexes without considering their values. If we want to perform a more specific job, we can use the **filter()** method. This method takes a closure and sends each element to the closure for processing. If the closure returns **true**, the element is included in the new array, otherwise it is ignored, as shown below.

```
var fruits = ["Apple", "Grape", "Banana", "Grape"]
var filteredArray = fruits.filter({ $0 != "Grape" })
print(filteredArray)   // "["Apple", "Banana"]"
```

Listing 3-89: Filtering the values of an array

The **filter()** method sends the values one by one to the closure, the closure replaces the placeholder (**$0**) with the current value, compares it with the value "Grape", and returns a Boolean with the result. If the value is **true**, the element is included in **filteredArray**.

If what we need is to modify the elements of an array all at once, we can use the **map()** method. This method sends the values of the array one by one to a closure and returns another array with the results produced by the closure.

```
let list = [2, 4, 8, 16]
let half = list.map({ $0 / 2 })
print(half)   // "[1, 2, 4, 8]"
```

Listing 3-90: Mapping an array

The example in Listing 3-90 defines a list of integers and then calls the **map()** method on the array to divide each value by 2. The **map()** method sends the values of the array to the closure one by one, the closure replaces the placeholder (**$0**) with the current value, divides the number by 2, and returns the result. All the results are stored in a new array and that array is returned by the **map()** method when the process is over.

Of course, we can perform any kind of operations we want on the values in the closure. For instance, the following code converts the values into strings with the **String()** initializer.

Chapter 3 - Swift Paradigm

```
let list = [1, 2, 3, 4, 5]
let listtext = list.map({ String($0) })
print(listtext)  // "["1", "2", "3", "4", "5"]"
```

Listing 3-91: Converting the elements of an array into strings

When all we want to do is to initialize a new structure with the value received by the closure, instead of a closure, Swift allows us to provide the structure's initializer. The value received by the closure is sent to the initializer and a new structure of that type is returned.

```
let list = [1, 2, 3, 4, 5]
let listtext = list.map(String.init)
print(listtext)  // "["1", "2", "3", "4", "5"]"
```

Listing 3-92: Using a structure initializer with the map() method

This example produces the same result as before, but instead of using a closure, we use a reference to the **String** initializer. The **map()** method sends the value to the initializer, the initializer returns a new **String** structure with that value, and the process continues as before.

Another way to process all the values of an array at once is with the **reduce()** method. This method works like **map()**, but instead of storing the results in an array, it sends the result back to the closure to get only one value in return. For instance, the following code uses the **reduce()** method to get the result of the addition of all the numbers in an array.

```
let list = [2, 4, 8, 16]
let total = list.reduce(0, { $0 + $1 })
print(total)  // "30"
```

Listing 3-93: Reducing an array

The code in Listing 3-93 defines an array of integers and then calls the **reduce()** method on it. This method sends two values at a time to the closure. In the first cycle, the values sent to the closure are the ones provided by the first argument (**0**) and the first value of the array (**2**). In the second cycle, the values sent to the closure are the value returned by the closure in the first cycle (0 + 2 = **2**), and the second value of the array (**4**). The loop goes on until all the values of the array are processed.

When it comes to sorting the elements of an array, there are several options available. The most frequently used are **reversed()** and **sorted()** (and its variant **sorted(by:)**). The **reversed()** method takes the elements of an array and returns a new array with the same elements in reversed order. The value returned by the method is stored in a structure of type **ReversedCollection**. As we did before with the **ArraySlice** type, we can cast these values as **Array** structures with the **Array()** initializer.

```
var fruits = ["Apple", "Blueberry", "Banana"]
var array = Array(fruits.reversed())  // ["Banana", "Blueberry", "Apple"]
```

Listing 3-94: Reversing the elements of an array

The **sorted()** method sorts the array in ascending order and returns a new array.

```
var fruits = ["Blueberry", "Apple", "Banana"]
let basket = fruits.sorted()
print(basket)  // ["Apple", "Banana", "Blueberry"]
```

Listing 3-95: Sorting the elements of an array

If we want to sort the elements in a custom order, we can use the **sorted(by:)** method. This method takes a function or a closure that receives the value of two elements and returns **true** if the first element should appear before the second element, or **false** otherwise.

```
var fruits = ["Apple", "Raspberry", "Banana", "Grape"]
var newArray = fruits.sorted(by: { $0 > $1 })
print(newArray[0])   // "Raspberry"
```

Listing 3-96: Sorting the elements of an array in a custom order

When the **sorted()** method is executed, it performs a loop. On each cycle, two values of the **fruits** array are sent to the closure. The closure compares the values and returns **true** or **false** accordingly. This indicates to the **sorted()** method which value should appear before the other in the new array, effectively sorting the elements. Unlike the example we programmed for the **filter()** method before, this one does not compare the argument against a specific value. This allows us to order arrays of any data type. For example, we can use the closure to sort an array of integers.

```
var numbers = [55, 12, 32, 5, 9]
var newArray = numbers.sorted(by: { $0 < $1 })
print(newArray[0])   // 5
```

Listing 3-97: Sorting an array of integers

If we decide to work with specific data types, we can perform custom tasks. For example, we can count the characters in the strings and sort them according to their length.

```
var fruits = ["Apple", "Blueberry", "Banana", "Grape"]
var newArray = fruits.sorted(by: { $0.count < $1.count })
print(newArray)   // ["Apple", "Grape", "Banana", "Blueberry"]
```

Listing 3-98: Sorting strings according to the number of characters

Arrays also include two powerful methods to compare elements: **min()** and **max()**. These methods compare the values and return the smallest or largest, respectively.

```
let ages = [32, 540, 12, 27]
if let older = ages.max() {
    let digits = String(older)
    print("The maximum age is \(digits.count) digits long")
}
```

Listing 3-99: Getting the largest element

The code in Listing 3-99 takes the largest value from an array of integers and counts the number of digits in the value returned. Because the **max()** method returns an optional, we use optional binding to read the value. The rest of the code turns this value into a string and counts its characters to print the number of digits on the console.

Besides selecting the largest or smallest value with the **max()** and **min()** methods, we can also fetch values from the array using the **first** and **last** properties.

```
let ages = [32, 540, 12, 27]
if let firstAge = ages.first {
    print("The first person is \(firstAge) years old")   // 32
}
```

Listing 3-100: Getting the first value of an array

Chapter 3 - Swift Paradigm

The value returned by the **first** property is an optional, so we use optional binding to read it and store it in the **firstAge** constant. The **first** and **last** properties only get the first and last values, respectively. To search for any value in the array or its index, the **Array** structure offers the following methods.

- **firstIndex(of:** Element)—This method performs a search from the beginning of the array and returns the index of the first element that matches the value of the **of** argument.
- **lastIndex(of:** Element)—This method performs a search from the end of the array and returns the index of the first element that matches the value of the **of** argument.
- **firstIndex(where:** Closure)—This method returns the index of the first value that meets the condition in the closure assigned to the **where** argument.
- **lastIndex(where:** Closure)—This method returns the index of the last value that meets the condition in the closure assigned to the **where** argument.
- **first(where:** Closure)—This method returns the first value that meets the condition in the closure assigned to the **where** argument.
- **last(where:** Closure)—This method returns the last value that meets the condition in the closure assigned to the **where** argument.

If we only need the index of a particular element, we can use the **firstIndex(of:)** method. For instance, we can look for the first appearance of a number in an array and get the index.

```
let ages = [32, 540, 12, 27, 54]
if let index = ages.firstIndex(of: 540) {
  print("The value is at the position \(index)")   // 1
}
```

Listing 3-101: Getting the index of a specific value

If what we need instead is to get the index of a value that meets a condition, we can use methods like **firstIndex(where:)** or **lastIndex(where:)** depending on whether we want to search from the beginning or the end of the array. In the following example, we show how to look for the index of a value and the value itself with the **firstIndex(where:)** and **first(where:)** methods.

```
let ages = [32, 540, 12, 27, 54]
let firstIndex = ages.firstIndex(where: { value in value < 30 })
let firstValue = ages.first(where: { value in value < 30 })

if firstIndex != nil && firstValue != nil {
  print("First value is: \(firstValue!)")   // 12
  print("First value is at index: \(firstIndex!)")   // 2
}
```

Listing 3-102: Getting the index of a value that meets a condition

The **firstIndex(where:)** method reads every value of the array from the beginning and sends them to the closure assigned to the **where** argument. The closure takes the current value and compares it against the number 30, if the value is greater than 30, the closure returns **false**, otherwise it returns **true** and the index of that value is assigned to the **first** variable. The **first(where:)** method works exactly the same way, but it returns the value instead of the index. In this case, the first number in the array smaller than 30 is 12, which is at index 2.

The **Array** structure also includes methods to get the indexes of multiple elements and work with those values.

- **indices(where:** Closure)—This method returns a `RangeSet` value with a set of ranges that include all the indexes of the elements that match the condition determined by the closure provided by the **where** argument.

- **indices(of:** Value)—This method returns a `RangeSet` value with a set of ranges that include all the indexes of the elements that match the value provided by the **of** argument.

- **moveSubranges(**RangeSet, **to:** Index)—This method moves the elements at the indexes determined by the first argument to the position determined by the **to** argument.

- **removeSubranges(**RangeSet)—This method removes the elements in the indexes determined by the argument.

The `indices()` method returns a value of type `RangeSet`. This is a structure that stores a set of `Range` values with the indexes of the elements in the array (we will see Sets next). Using this method, we can retrieve the indexes of the values that match a condition and then use these values to read or modify the array, as in the following example.

```
var ages = [12, 32, 540, 27, 54]
let listIndexes = ages.indices(where: { $0 < 30 })

for value in ages[listIndexes] {
    print(value)
}
ages.removeSubranges(listIndexes)
print(ages)   // [32, 540, 54]
```

Listing 3-103: Working with a range of indexes

A `RangeSet` value can be used to read the elements of an array. When we use a `RangeSet` value instead of a single index to read an array, the system returns a collection called `DiscontiguousSlice` with all the values. In our example, we first implement the `indices()` method to get the indexes of the values that are less than 30 and then read these values with a `for in` loop (`ages[listIndexes]`). At the end, we remove the values in these indexes using the `removeSubranges()` method. The array now only contains values that are 30 or higher.

Basic Set Structures

If we store two elements in an array, one element automatically receives the index 0 and the other the index 1. This correlation between indexes and values never changes, allowing elements to be listed always in the right order and have elements with the same value at different indexes. But if we don't care about the order, we can create a set. Sets are like arrays, but they do not assign an index to their values, therefore there is no order and all the values are unique. Sets are created from the **Set** structure.

- **Set<Type>()**—This initializer returns an empty **Set** structure of the data type indicated by **Type**.

This initializer can be used to create an empty set (e.g., `let myset = Set<Int>()`), but we can also use square brackets, as we do with arrays. The difference with arrays is that we must specify that we are creating a set with the **Set** keyword, as shown below.

```
var ages: Set<Int> = []
```

Listing 3-104: Creating an empty set of integers

If we initialize the set with some values, Swift can infer its type from their data type, simplifying the declaration.

```
var ages: Set = [15, 25, 35, 45]
```

Listing 3-105: Creating a set of integers

To access and process the elements of a set, we can use a **for in** loop, as we did before with strings and arrays, but sets also provide their own properties and methods for this purpose.

▷ **count**—This property returns the number of elements in the set.

▷ **isEmpty**—This property returns a Boolean value that indicates whether the set is empty or not.

▷ **contains(Element)**—This method returns a Boolean value that indicates whether there is an element in the set with the value specified by the argument.

▷ **contains(where:** Closure)—This method returns a Boolean value that determines if the set contains an element that meets the condition in the closure.

▷ **min()**—This method compares the elements in the set and returns the smallest.

▷ **max()**—This method compares the elements in the set and returns the largest.

▷ **sorted()**—This method returns an array with the elements of the set in ascending order.

▷ **sorted(by:** Closure)—This method returns an array with the elements of the set in the order determined by the closure specified by the **by** argument.

▷ **randomElement()**—This method randomly selects an element from the set and returns it. If the set is empty, the value returned is **nil**.

▷ **shuffled()**—This method returns an array with the elements of the set in random order.

▷ **insert(Element)**—This method inserts a new element in the set with the value provided by the argument.

▷ **union(Collection)**—This method returns a new set created with the values of the original set plus the values provided by the argument (an array or another set).

▷ **subtract(Collection)**—This method returns a new set created by subtracting the elements provided by the argument to the original set.

▷ **intersection(Collection)**—This method returns a new set created with the values of the original set that match the values provided by the argument (an array or another set).

▷ **remove(Element)**—This method removes from the set the element with the value provided by the argument.

▷ **isSubset(of:** Set)—This method returns a Boolean value that indicates whether or not the set is a subset of the set specified by the **of** argument.

▷ **isSuperset(of:** Set)—This method returns a Boolean value that indicates whether or not the set is a superset of the set specified by the **of** argument.

▷ **isDisjoint(with:** Set)—This method returns a Boolean value that indicates whether or not the original set and the set specified by the **with** argument have elements in common.

Using these methods, we can easily access and modify the values of a set. For instance, we can implement the **contains()** method to search for a value.

```
var fruits: Set = ["Apple", "Orange", "Banana"]
if fruits.contains("Apple") {
   print("Apple exists!")
}
```

Listing 3-106: Using contains() *to find an element in a set*

To insert a new element, we just have to execute the **insert()** method.

```
var fruits: Set = ["Apple", "Orange", "Banana"]
if !fruits.contains("Grape") {
   fruits.insert("Grape")
}
print("The set has \(fruits.count) elements")  // 4
```

Listing 3-107: Inserting a new element in a set

In listing 3-107, we use the **contains()** method again to check if an element with the value "Grape" already exists in the set, but this is not really necessary. If the value is already part of the set, the **insert()** method does not perform any action.

To remove an element, we must call the **remove()** method.

```
var fruits: Set = ["Apple", "Orange", "Banana"]
if let removed = fruits.remove("Banana") {
   print("\(removed) was removed")   // "Banana was removed"
}
```

Listing 3-108: Removing an element from a set

The **remove()** method removes the element whose value matches the value of the argument and returns an optional with the value that have been removed or **nil** in case of failure. The code in Listing 3-108 gets the value returned by the method and prints a message if it was successfully removed.

Sets are collections without order. Every time we read a set, the order in which its values are returned is not guaranteed, but we can use the **sorted()** method to create an array with the values of the set in order. The following example sorts the elements of the **fruits** set in alphabetical order, creating a new array we call **orderFruits**.

```
var fruits: Set = ["Apple", "Orange", "Banana"]
var orderFruits = fruits.sorted()

if let lastItem = orderFruits.last {
   print(lastItem)   // "Orange"
}
```

Listing 3-109: Sorting the elements of a set

The rest of the methods available for sets are simple to use. The following example joins two sets with the **union()** method and then subtracts elements from the result with **subtract()**.

```
var fruits: Set = ["Apple", "Banana"]
var newSet = fruits.union(["Grapes"])   // "Banana", "Grapes", "Apple"
newSet.subtract(["Apple", "Banana"])   // "Grapes"
```

Listing 3-110: Combining sets

Chapter 3 - Swift Paradigm

The **Set** structure also offers methods to compare sets. We can determine if a set is a subset or a superset of another set with the **isSubset()** and **isSuperset()** methods, or check if two sets have elements in common with the **isDisjoint()** method. The following example implements the **isSubset()** method to check if the fruits in a basket come from the store. The code checks if the elements in the **basket** set are found in the **store** set and returns **true** in case of success.

```
var store: Set = ["Banana", "Apple", "Orange", "Pear"]
var basket: Set = ["Apple", "Orange"]

if basket.isSubset(of: store) {
    print("The fruits in the basket are from the store")
}
```

Listing 3-111: Comparing sets

(Basic) **Dictionary Structures**

There is only one way to access the elements of an array and that is through their numeric indexes. Dictionaries offer a better alternative. With dictionaries, we can define the indexes ourselves using any custom value we want. Each index, also known as *key*, must be explicitly declared along with its value. Swift offers multiple syntaxes to create a dictionary, including the following initializers.

▷ **Dictionary<Type1: Type2>()**—This initializer returns an empty **Dictionary** structure with the keys and values of the data type indicated by **Type1** and **Type2**.

▷ **Dictionary(grouping: Collection, by: Closure)**—This initializer returns a **Dictionary** structure with the values provided by the **grouping** argument grouped in arrays according to the keys returned by the closure provided by the **by** argument.

If the data types are explicitly defined, we can also declare a dictionary with a simplified syntax, as in **var list: [String: String] = Dictionary()**, or use square brackets with a colon, as in **var list: [String: String] = [:]**. The latest is also used to define a dictionary with initial values. In this case, the keys and values are separated by a colon and the items are separated by comma, as in the following example.

```
var list: [String: String] = ["First": "Apple", "Second": "Orange"]
```

Listing 3-112: Declaring a dictionary with initial values

The first value of each item is the key and the second is the value. Of course, Swift can also infer the data types.

```
var list = ["First": "Apple", "Second": "Orange"]
```

Listing 3-113: Declaring a dictionary with type inference

As with arrays, if we want to read or replace a value, we must declare the key (index) in square brackets after the name of the dictionary.

```
var list = ["First": "Apple", "Second": "Orange"]
list["Second"] = "Banana"
```

Listing 3-114: Assigning a new value to an element of a dictionary

The second statement in Listing 3-114 assigns a new value to the element identified with the "Second" key. Now, the dictionary contains two elements with the values "Apple" and "Banana". If the key used to assign the new value exists, the system updates the value, but if the key does not exist, a new element is created, as shown next.

```
var list = ["First": "Apple", "Second": "Orange"]
list["Third"] = "Banana"
print(list)  // "["Second": "Orange", "First": "Apple", "Third":
"Banana"]"
```

Listing 3-115: *Adding a new element to a dictionary*

In this example, the second statement assigns the value "Banana" to a key that does not exist, and therefore the system creates the new element with the specified key and value.

Dictionaries return optional values. If we try to read an element with a key that does not exist, the value returned is **nil**.

```
var list = ["First": "Apple", "Second": "Orange"]
print(list["Third"])  // nil
```

Listing 3-116: *Reading an element that does not exist*

The code in Listing 3-116 tries to read a value with the key "Third" in the **list** dictionary. Since a value with that key doesn't exist, the value **nil** is printed on the console. If the element exists and we want to read its value, we must unwrap it.

```
var list = ["First": "Apple", "Second": "Orange"]
if let first = list["First"], let second = list["Second"] {
    print("We have \(first) and \(second)")  // "We have Apple and Orange"
}
```

Listing 3-117: *Reading the value of an element in a dictionary*

Since dictionary elements are optionals, we can assign the value **nil** to remove them. The following example removes the element with the key "First".

```
var list = ["First": "Apple", "Second": "Orange"]
list["First"] = nil
```

Listing 3-118: *Removing an element from a dictionary*

As with arrays and sets, we can also iterate over the values of a dictionary with a **for in** loop. The value produced by each cycle of the loop is a tuple containing the element's key and value.

```
var fruits = ["First": "Apple", "Second": "Orange"]
var message = "My fruits:"
for (mykey, myfruit) in fruits {
    message += " \(mykey)-\(myfruit)"
}
print(message)  // "My fruits: First-Apple Second-Orange"
```

Listing 3-119: *Using* **for** *in to iterate over a dictionary*

The **for in** loop in Listing 3-119 reads the elements of the **fruits** dictionary one by one, assigns the index and the value to the **mykey** and **myfruit** constants, and adds their values to the **message** variable. At the end, we get a string with all the keys and values in the dictionary.

Of course, dictionaries may also contain arrays as values. The declaration is simple, the key is declared as always, and the single value is replaced by an array.

```
var fruits: [String: [String]] = ["A": ["Apple", "Apricot"], "B":
["Banana", "Blueberries"]]
```

Listing 3-120: Combining dictionaries with arrays

Reading the values of a dictionary like this is a bit more complicated. Because dictionaries return optionals, we cannot just specify the indexes as we do for multidimensional arrays (see Listing 3-75). The array returned by the dictionary must be unwrapped before reading the values.

```
var fruits: [String: [String]] = ["A": ["Apple", "Apricot"], "B":
["Banana", "Blueberries"]]
if let list = fruits["A"] {
    print(list[0])  // "Apple"
}
```

Listing 3-121: Reading arrays inside dictionaries

In this example, we create a dictionary with two values. The values are arrays of strings with a string as key. The code gets the array corresponding to the "A" key, unwraps it, and stores it in a constant. The **list** constant now contains the array assigned to the "A" key, and therefore when we read the element at index 0, we get the value "Apple".

What we have created in the last example is what the **Dictionary(grouping:, by:)** initializer does. It takes the values of a collection and groups them together in arrays according to the value of a key returned by the closure, as shown below.

```
let list = [15, 25, 38, 55, 42]
let group5 = Dictionary(grouping: list, by: {$0 % 5 == 0 ? "Yes" : "No"})
print(group5)  // "["No": [38, 42], "Yes": [15, 25, 55]]"
```

Listing 3-122: Grouping values by a key

The **Dictionary** initializer implemented in Listing 3-122 takes the values of the **list** array, sends them to the closure one by one, and creates a new dictionary with the keys returned by the closure. The closure receives the value and returns the strings "Yes" or "No" depending on whether the current value is multiple of 5. If the value is multiple of 5, it is included in an array with the "Yes" key, otherwise it is included in an array with the "No" key.

Dictionaries also include properties and methods to manage the values. The following are the most frequently used.

- ▷ **count**—This property returns the total number of elements in the dictionary.
- ▷ **isEmpty**—This property returns a Boolean value that indicates if the dictionary is empty.
- ▷ **keys**—This property returns a collection with the keys in the dictionary.
- ▷ **values**—This property returns a collection with the values in the dictionary.
- ▷ **sorted(by:** Closure**)**—This method returns an array of tuples with each element of the dictionary (key and value) in the order determined by the closure.
- ▷ **randomElement()**—This method randomly selects an element from the dictionary and returns a tuple with its key and value. If the dictionary is empty, the value returned is **nil**.
- ▷ **shuffled()**—This method returns an array of tuples containing the keys and values of each element of the dictionary in random order.

▷ **updateValue(Value, forKey:** Key**)**—This method updates the value of an element with the value and key specified by its arguments. If the key does not exist, the method creates a new element. If the key exists, it returns the previous value, otherwise, the value returned is `nil`.

▷ **removeValue(forKey:** Key**)**—This method removes the element with the key equal to the value of the **forKey** argument. It returns an optional containing the value of the deleted element or `nil` if no element with the specified key was found.

▷ **contains(where:** Closure**)**—This method returns a Boolean value that determines if the dictionary contains an element that meets the condition in the closure.

Some of the methods provided by the **Dictionary** structure are like those included in the **Array** and **Set** structures, but others are more specific. For example, the **updateValue()** and **removeValue()** methods require the element's key to be able to process the value.

```
var fruits = ["one": "Banana", "two": "Apple", "three": "Pear"]
fruits.updateValue("Banana", forKey: "three")   // "Pear"
fruits.removeValue(forKey: "one")   // "Banana"
print(fruits)   // "["three": "Banana", "two": "Apple"]"
```

Listing 3-123: Adding and removing elements from a dictionary

The **updateValue()** method updates the value of an element when there is already an element with that key or creates a new one if the key does not exist. This is the same as assigning a value directly to an element (see Listings 3-115 and 3-116), but the method returns the previous value, which can sometimes be useful.

Like sets, dictionaries are an unordered collection of values, but we can create an array with their elements in a specific order using the **sorted()** method. The method returns the values as tuples, with the element's key first and the value second.

```
var fruits = ["one": "Banana", "two": "Apple", "three": "Pear"]
var list = fruits.sorted(by: { $0.1 < $1.1 })
print(list)
```

Listing 3-124: Sorting the values of a dictionary

As with arrays, the **sorted(by:)** method sends to the closure two values at a time, but the values in a dictionary are sent as tuples containing the key and value of each element. For instance, the first values sent to the closure in Listing 3-124 are ("one", "Banana") and ("two", "Apple"). These values replace the placeholders **$0** and **$1**, so if we want to order the elements according to the names of the fruits, we must compare the values of the tuples at index 1 (**$0.1 < $1.1**). The array returned is a collection of tuples in alphabetical order, with every element containing the keys and values of the dictionary (**[(key: "two", value: "Apple"), (key: "one", value: "Banana"), (key: "three", value: "Pear")]**).

Earlier, we saw how to iterate over the elements of a dictionary with a **for in** loop (see Listing 3-119). The loop gets each element and generates a tuple with the key and value. But there are times when we only need the element's key or value. The **Dictionary** structure provides two properties for this purpose: **keys** and **values**. These properties return a collection containing only the keys or the values of the elements, respectively.

```
var fruits = ["one": "Banana", "two": "Apple", "three": "Pear"]
for key in fruits.keys {
   if key == "two" {
      print("We have an element with the key 'two'")
   }
}
```

```
}
```

Listing 3-125: Iterating over the dictionary's keys

The collections returned by the **keys** and **values** properties are structures of type **Keys** and **Values** defined inside the **Dictionary** structure. As we did before with other collection types, we can turn them into arrays with the **Array()** initializer.

```
var fruits = ["one": "Banana", "two": "Apple", "three": "Pear"]
let keys = Array(fruits.keys)
print(keys)
```

Listing 3-126: Reading the keys of a dictionary

(Basic) 3.4 Enumerations

Enumerations are a way to create data types with a limited set of values. An enumeration type is like the **Bool** type but with the possible values defined by the programmer. They are declared with the **enum** keyword, and the values are defined in braces with the **case** keyword.

```
enum Number {
    case one
    case two
    case three
}
```

Listing 3-127: Defining an enumeration type

This example defines an enumeration call **Number** with three possible values: **one, two,** and **three**. We can assign any names we want for the enumeration and its values. The values may also be declared just in one **case** statement separated by comma.

```
enum Number {
    case one, two, three
}
```

Listing 3-128: Declaring the enumeration values in one statement

An enumeration is a custom data type. As we did with structures, we must create a variable of this type and assign to that variable one of the possible values using dot notation.

```
enum Number {
    case one, two, three
}
var mynumber: Number = Number.one
```

Listing 3-129: Initializing an instance of an enumeration

Variables of this data type can only store the values allowed by the type (**one**, **two**, or **three**). To assign a value, we must use the name of the enumeration and dot notation. The **mynumber** variable declared in Listing 3-129 is of type **Number** and has the value **one**.

Once the data type of the variable was already defined, only the dot and the value are necessary to modify its value.

```
enum Number {
    case one, two, three
}
```

```
var mynumber = Number.one
mynumber = .two
```

Listing 3-130: Assigning a new value to a variable of type Number

In the last statement, we assign a new value to **mynumber**. The value **.two** may have been written as **Number.two**. Both syntaxes are valid, but Swift infers that the new value is of the same data type, so it is not necessary to declare the name anymore.

Like Booleans, enumeration types can be used as signals to indicate a state that can later be checked to decide whether a particular task should be performed. For this reason, they are often used with conditionals and loops. In the following example, the value of an enumeration variable is checked with a **switch** statement. This statement is especially useful when working with enumerations because the limited number of values makes it easier to define the cases.

```
enum Number {
    case one
    case two
    case three
}
var mynumber = Number.two
switch mynumber {
    case .one:
        print("The number is 1")
    case .two:
        print("The number is 2")   // "The number is 2"
    case .three:
        print("The number is 3")
}
```

Listing 3-131: Using switch *with an enumeration type*

In this example, the **Number** enumeration is defined and then the **mynumber** variable is declared with the value **two**. Next, a **switch** statement compares the value of this variable with the three possible values of its type and prints a message on the console.

(Medium) **Raw Values**

The cases of an enumeration can have values by default. These values are called *Raw Values*. Swift assigns values by default to every case, starting from 0, but we can assign our own.

```
enum Number: String {
    case one = "Number One"
    case two = "Number Two"
    case three = "Number Three"
}
var mynumber = Number.one
```

Listing 3-132: Assigning raw values to enumeration values

Enumerations behave like structures. We can define our own properties and methods inside an enumeration, and they also include initializers, properties, and methods by default. The most useful property is called **rawValue**, which allows us to read the raw value of each **case**.

```
enum Number: String {
    case one = "Number One"
    case two = "Number Two"
    case three = "Number Three"
}
```

Chapter 3 - Swift Paradigm

```
var mynumber = Number.one
print("The value is \(mynumber.rawValue)")   // "The value is Number One"
```

Listing 3-133: Reading raw values

Additionally, enumerations include an initializer to create an instance from a raw value. Instead of declaring the variable using the value's name (**one**, **two** or **three**), we can use the initializer and the raw value. The initializer includes the **rawValue** argument to specify the value used to create the instance.

```
enum Number: String {
    case one = "Number One"
    case two = "Number Two"
    case three = "Number Three"
}
var mynumber = Number(rawValue: "Number Two")

if mynumber == .two {
    print("Correct Value")   // "Correct Value"
}
```

Listing 3-134: Creating an enumeration from a raw value

We can read the **case** value or the raw value to identify an instance of an enumeration type. In Listing 3-134, we create an instance of **Number** with the raw value "Number Two" and then check that the variable contains the proper **case** value with an **if** statement.

What makes enumerations part of the programming paradigm proposed by Swift is not their capacity to store different types of values but the possibility to include custom methods and computed properties. The following example adds a method to our **Number** enumeration that prints a message depending on the instance's current value.

```
enum Number: Int {
    case one
    case two
    case three

    func getMessage() -> String {
        switch self {
        case .one:
            return "We are the best"
        case .two:
            return "We have to study more"
        case .three:
            return "This is just the beginning"
        }
    }
}
var mynumber = Number.two
print(mynumber.getMessage())   // "We have to study more"
```

Listing 3-135: Adding methods to an enumeration

When we need to check the current value of the instance from inside a method, we must use the **self** keyword. This keyword refers to the instance where the method is being executed (in our case, **mynumber**), and this is how we can check for the instance's current value and return the right message. (We will learn more about the **self** keyword later.)

Associated Values

Enumerations include the possibility to associate values to a case. These are values we can attach to a case when variables of that type are initialized. For instance, in the following example we create an enumeration that can store information about a character, but it differentiates between letters and numbers.

```
enum MyCharacters {
    case number(Int, String)
    case letter(Character, String)
}
var character = MyCharacters.number(1, "Number One")
switch character {
    case .number(let value, let description):
        print("\(description) - \(value)")   // "Number One - 1"
    case .letter(let letter, let description):
        print("\(description) - \(letter)")
}
```

Listing 3-136: Associating values

This example defines an enumeration called **MyCharacters** that includes two cases. The first case is called **number** and it takes two associated values: an integer and a string. The second case is called **letter** and it also takes two associated values: a character and a string. When we create a value of this type, we must select the **case** value, as always, but we must also specify the associated values. If the value of the enumeration is **number**, we must provide an integer and a string, and if the value is **letter**, we must provide a character and a string. The example in Listing 3-136 creates an instance with the value **number** and the associated values 1 and "Number One", and then checks the value with a **switch** statement. Note that in each **case** we test whether the value is **number** or **letter** and extract their associated values with constants between parentheses, similar to what we did with tuples before (see Listing 2-37).

If we need to check a single case, we can use an **if** or a **guard** statement and assign the value to the case we want to check.

```
enum MyCharacters {
    case number(Int, String)
    case letter(Character, String)
}
var character = MyCharacters.number(1, "Number One")

if case .number(let number, let text) = character {
    print("Number: \(number)")   // "Number: 1"
    print("Text: \(text)")   // "Text: Number One"
}
```

Listing 3-137: Reading associated values from an if statement

This syntax includes the **case** keyword and the necessary constants to receive the values. The statement is saying something like "Assign the value to this case, if not possible, return false". In our example, if the **character** variable doesn't contain a **MyCharacters** enumeration with the value **number**, the statement returns **false** and nothing is done, otherwise, the associated values in the **character** variable are assigned to the constants and printed on the console.

Basic **3.5 Objects**

Objects are data types that encapsulate data and functionality in the form of properties and methods, but unlike the structures and enumerations introduced before they are stored by reference, which means that more than one variable can reference the same object in memory.

Basic Definition of Objects

Like structures and enumerations, objects are defined first and then instances are created from their definition. The definitions of objects are called *Classes*, and what we called objects are the instances created from those classes. Classes are declared the same way as structures or enumerations, but instead of the **struct** or **enum** keywords we must use the **class** keyword.

```
class Employee {
    var name = "Undefined"
    var age = 0
}
```

Listing 3-138: Defining a class

This example defines a simple class called **Employee** with two properties: **name** and **age**. As always, this does not create anything, it is just defining a new custom data type. To store data in memory in this format, we must assign an instance of this class to a constant or variable.

```
class Employee {
    var name = "Undefined"
    var age = 0
}
let employee1 = Employee()
employee1.name = "John"
employee1.age = 32
```

Listing 3-139: Creating an object from a class

In Listing 3-139, the **Employee()** initializer creates a new instance of the class **Employee**. The words instance and object are synonyms, so we can say that in this example we have created a new object called **employee1** containing two properties, **name** and **age**.

Of course, we can also modify the values of the properties of an object from its methods, but unlike structures, we don't need to declared them as **mutating**.

```
class Employee {
    var name = "Undefined"
    var age = 0

    func changename(newname: String, newage: Int) {
        name = newname
        age = newage
    }
}
let employee1 = Employee()
employee1.changename(newname: "Martin", newage: 32)
print("Name: \(employee1.name)")  // "Name: Martin"
```

Listing 3-140: Modifying properties from the object's methods

In Listing 3-140, the **changename()** method is added to the **Employee** class to modify the values of the properties. After the instance is created, we call this method to assign the values "Martin" and 32 to the **name** and **age** properties, respectively.

 IMPORTANT: As well as structures, we can create all the objects we need from the same definition (class). Each object will have its own properties, methods, and values.

Basic   Type Properties and Methods

We have studied type properties and methods before with structures. These are properties and methods accessible from the data type, not the instances. They work in classes the same way as in structures, but instead of the **static** keyword we must use the **class** keyword to define them.

```
class Employee {
    var name = "Undefined"
    var age = 0

    class func description() {
        print("This class stores the name and age of an employee")
    }
}
Employee.description()
```

Listing 3-141: Declaring a type method for a class

This example defines an **Employee** class with two properties: **name** and **age**. The type method declared next is just describing the purpose of the class. Every time the **description()** method is executed on the class, a description is printed on the console. Again, we don't have to create an instance because the method is executed on the class itself.

 IMPORTANT: Classes can also use the **static** keyword to define type properties and methods. The difference between the **static** and **class** keywords is that properties and methods defined with the **static** keyword are immutable and those defined with the **class** keyword can be modified by subclasses. (We will learn about subclasses and inheritance later in this chapter.)

Basic   Reference Types

Structures and enumerations are value types. This means that every time we assign a variable of any of these data types to another variable, the value is copied. For example, if we create an instance of a structure and then assign that instance to another variable, we end up with two instances of the same structure in memory, as illustrated below.

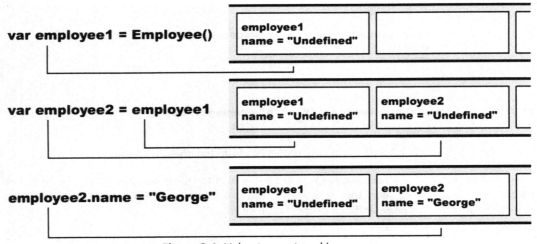

Figure 3-1: Value types stored in memory

Figure 3-1 shows how two different copies of the **Employee** structure, one referenced by the variable **employee1** and the other referenced by the variable **employee2**, are stored in memory.

Any modification to the values of one of the instances will not affect the other, because they occupy different spaces in memory.

 IMPORTANT: Structures and enumerations are copied because they conform to the `Copyable` protocol. If you need to create unique copies of values, you can declare the instance as noncopyable. We will learn more about protocols later. For more information about noncopyable types, visit our website and follow the links for this chapter.

Objects, on the other hand, are passed by reference. This means that when we assign an object to a constant or a variable, they store a reference to the object, not the object itself. In the following example, the object in **employee2** is the same as the object in **employee1**. Any change in the **name** property is reflected in the other because both variables point to the same object in memory (they reference the same instance).

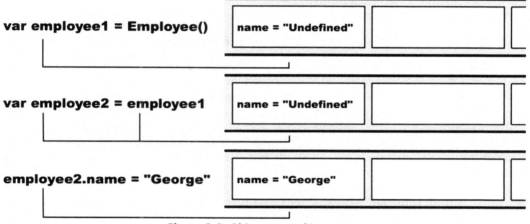

Figure 3-2: Objects stored in memory

Constants or variables that were assigned an object do not store the object; they store the value of the memory address where the object is located. When a constant or a variable containing this address is assigned to another constant or variable, only the address is copied, and therefore the object is not duplicated. This is the most important characteristic of objects, and what makes them suitable for situations in which data in memory must be accessed and shared by different parts of the code.

 IMPORTANT: Because constants and variables store a reference to an object (a memory address), two or more variables in your code may reference the same object. If you need to know whether this is the case, you can compare the variables with the operators **===** (identical to) and **!==** (not identical to) provided by Swift. If what you need is to know whether two objects contain different information, you can use the basic operators **==** and **!=**, but you can only do this when the objects conform to the **Equatable** protocol; a protocol that determines how the objects are compared. We will study protocols and the **Equatable** protocol later in this chapter.

(Basic) Self

Because the same object may be referenced by multiple constants or variables, every language that works with objects offers a way for the object to reference itself. In Swift, this is done automatically, but there are situations in which this reference must be declared explicitly. For this purpose, Swift defines a special keyword called **self**. We have introduced this keyword earlier to read the current value of an enumeration from inside the instance (see Listing 3-135). In structures and objects, the **self** keyword works the same way; it references the instance to which the values belong.

The most common situation requiring the use of this keyword is when the names of the parameters of a method are equal to the names of the properties of the object. If the names are the same, the system does not know whether we are trying to modify the property or the parameter. The **self** keyword clarifies the situation.

```
class Employee {
    var name = "Undefined"

    func changename(name: String) {
        self.name = name
    }
}
let employee1 = Employee()
employee1.changename(name: "Martin")
print("Name: \(employee1.name)")   // "Name: Martin"
```

Listing 3-142: Referencing the object with `self`

The **self** keyword in the **changename()** method of Listing 3-142 represents the object created from the **Employee** class and helps the system understand what we are trying to access when we use the word **name**. When we call the **changename()** method in the **employee1** object, the value of the **name** parameter is assigned to the object's **name** property (**self.name**).

The **self** keyword in this example is a reference to the object stored in the **employee1** variable. This would be the same as declaring **employee1.name**, but since we do not know the name of the variable that is going to store the instance when the class is defined, we must use **self** instead.

Another useful application of the **self** keyword is to reference the data type itself. The value generated by reading the **self** keyword on a data type is called *Metatype*. A metatype refers to the type itself, not an instance of it. For example, the value **Int.self** refers to the definition of the **Int** data type, not an integer number created from that type, as shown in the following example.

```
let reference = Int.self
let newnumber = reference.init(20)
print(newnumber)   // "20"
```

Listing 3-143: Referring to the data type with `self`

The code in Listing 3-143 stores a reference to the **Int** data type in a constant and then uses that constant to create an instance of **Int** with the value 20. Note that when working with metatypes we must call the **init()** method implicitly to create an instance. Metatypes are widely used to pass references of data types to methods and initializers of other types, as we will see in further chapters.

(Advanced) Memory Management

Since objects are stored by reference, they can be referenced by multiple variables at the same time. If a variable is no longer used, the object referenced by that variable cannot be deleted from memory because another variable could still be using it. This could result in memory being filled with objects that are no longer needed by the application. The solution offered by Apple is an automatic system that counts the number of variables that reference an object and does not remove the object from memory until all references have been cleared (all the variables have been deleted, set to **nil**, or are referencing another object). The system is called ARC (Automatic Reference Counting). ARC automatically deletes the objects when there is no longer a constant or a variable referencing that location in memory.

Ideally, this system works like magic: it counts how many references we create to the same object, and deletes that object when none of those references exist anymore. However, there are situations where we can create what is called a *Strong Reference Cycle*. This happens when two objects have a property that references the other object, as shown below.

```
class Employee {
    var name: String?
    var location: Department?
}
class Department {
    var area: String?
    var person: Employee?
}
var employee: Employee? = Employee()
var department: Department? = Department()
employee?.name = "John"
employee?.location = department
department?.area = "Mail"
department?.person = employee
```

Listing 3-144: Referencing one object from another

This example defines two classes: **Employee** and **Department**. Both classes contain a property that references an object of the other class (**location** and **person**). After the definition, objects of each class are created and stored in the **employee** and **department** variables. The reference in the **department** variable is assigned to the **location** property of the **employee** object, and the reference in the **employee** variable is assigned to the **person** property of the **department** object. After this, each object contains a reference to the other.

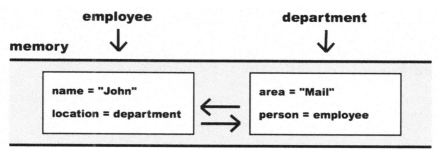

Figure 3-3: Objects referencing each other

At this point, each object is referenced by a variable and a property. The object of the **Employee** class is referenced by the **employee** variable and the **person** property, and the object of the **Department** class is referenced by the **department** variable and the **location** property. If, for some reason, we do not need to access these objects from our code anymore and erase or modify the values of the **employee** and **department** variables, ARC will not erase the objects from memory because their properties still have a reference that keeps them alive.

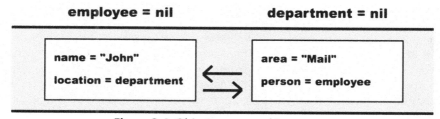

Figure 3-4: Objects preserved in memory

In this example, we assume that the value **nil** was assigned to the **employee** and **department** variables, and in consequence the objects are not accessible anymore, but they are preserved in memory because ARC has no way to know that they are no longer required.

Swift solves this problem by classifying the references into three categories: strong, weak, and unowned. Normal references are strong; they are always valid and the objects associated to them are preserved in memory for as long as they exist. These are the kind of references we have been using so far, and that is why the cycle created by our example is called Strong Reference Cycle. The solution to break this cycle is to define one of the references as **weak** or **unowned**. When ARC encounters one of these types of references to be the last reference to an object, the object is erased from memory as if the reference had never existed.

```
class Employee {
    var name: String?
    var location: Department?
}
class Department {
    var area: String?
    weak var person: Employee?
}
var employee: Employee? = Employee()
var department: Department? = Department()

employee?.name = "John"
employee?.location = department

department?.area = "Mail"
department?.person = employee
```

Listing 3-145: Assigning weak references

In the code of Listing 3-145, the **person** property was declared as **weak**. Now, when the references from the variables are erased, the object created from the **Employee** class is erased from memory because the only reference left is the weak reference from the **person** property. After this object disappears, the object created from the **Department** class does not have any other strong reference either, so it is also erased from memory.

The **unowned** reference works the same way, but it differs from the weak reference on the type of values it applies to. Weak references apply to variables with optional values (they can be empty at some point) and unowned references apply to non-optional values (they always have a value).

 IMPORTANT: Closures can create strong reference cycles if we try to access properties or methods defined outside the closure. If we need to reference properties or methods with **self** inside a closure, we can declare the reference to **self** as weak with the syntax **[weak self]** or **[unowned self]**. The expression must be declared before the closure's parameters. For more information on ARC and how to avoid strong reference cycles, visit our website and follow the links for this chapter.

Medium Inheritance

One of the main purposes of structures and objects is to define pieces of code that can be copied and shared. The code is defined once and then instances (copies) of that code are created every time they are required. This programming pattern works well when we define our own code but presents some limitations when working with code programmed by other developers and shared through libraries and frameworks. The programmers creating the code for us cannot anticipate how we are going to use it and all the possible variations required for every application. To provide a solution to this problem, classes incorporate inheritance. A class can inherit properties and methods from another class and then improve it by adding properties and methods of its own. This way, programmers can share classes and developers can adapt them to their needs.

To illustrate how inheritance works, the following examples present a situation in which a class must be expanded to contain additional information that was not initially contemplated.

```
class Employee {
    var name = "Undefined"
    var age = 0

    func createbadge() -> String {
        return "Employee \(name) \(age)"
    }
}
```

Listing 3-146: Defining a basic class

The **Employee** class declared in Listing 3-146 is a normal class, like those we have defined before. It has two properties and a method called **createbadge()** that returns a string with the values of the properties. This class would be enough to create objects that generate the string of text necessary to print a badge for every employee with his or her name and age. But for the sake of argument, let's say that some of the employees require a badge that also displays the department they work in. One option is to define another class with the same properties and methods and add what we need, but this produces redundant code, and it is difficult to do when the class was taken from a library (they are usually not accessible or too complex to modify or duplicate). The solution is to create a new class that inherits the characteristics of the basic class and adds its own properties and methods to satisfy the new requirements.

To indicate that a class inherits from another class, we must write the name of the basic class after the name of the new class separated by a colon.

```
class Employee {
    var name = "Undefined"
    var age = 0

    func createbadge() -> String {
        return "Employee \(name) \(age)"
    }
}
class OfficeEmployee: Employee {
    var department = "Undefined"
}
```

Listing 3-147: Inheriting properties and methods from another class

The **OfficeEmployee** class added to our code in Listing 3-147 only has one property called **department**, but it inherits the **name** and **age** properties, and also the **createbadge()** method from the **Employee** class. All these properties and methods are available in any of the objects created from the **OfficeEmployee** class, as shown below.

```
class Employee {
    var name = "Undefined"
    var age = 0

    func createbadge() -> String {
        return "Employee \(name) \(age)"
    }
}
class OfficeEmployee: Employee {
    var department = "Undefined"
}
let employee = OfficeEmployee()
```

```
employee.name = "George"
employee.age = 25
employee.department = "Mail"

var badge = employee.createbadge()
print("Badge: \(badge)")   // "Badge: Employee George 25"
```

Listing 3-148: Creating objects from a subclass

A class like **Employee** is called *Superclass*, and a class that inherits from another class like **OfficeEmployee** is called *Subclass*. In these terms, we can say that the **OfficeEmployee** class is a subclass that inherits the properties and methods of the **Employee** superclass. A class can inherit from a superclass that already inherited from another superclass in an infinite chain. When a property is accessed, or a method is called, the system looks for it on the object's class and, if it is not there, it keeps looking in the superclasses up the hierarchical chain until it finds it.

 IMPORTANT: Inheritance does not work the other way around. For example, considering the code in Listing 3-148, objects created from the class **OfficeEmployee** have access to the **department** property of this class and the properties and methods of the **Employee** class, but objects created from the **Employee** class do not have access to the **department** property.

Because of this hierarchical chain, sometimes a method does not have access to all the properties available to the object. For example, the **createbadge()** method called on the **employee** object created in Listing 3-148 have access to the properties declared on the **Employee** class but not those declared in the **OfficeEmployee** class. If we want the method to also print the value of the **department** property, we must implement it again in the **OfficeEmployee** class with the appropriate modifications. This is called *Overriding*. To override a method of a superclass, we prefix it with the **override** keyword.

```
class Employee {
    var name = "Undefined"
    var age = 0

    func createbadge() -> String {
        return "Employee \(name) \(age)"
    }
}
class OfficeEmployee: Employee {
    var department = "Undefined"

    override func createbadge() -> String {
        return "Employee \(department) \(name) \(age)"
    }
}
let employee = OfficeEmployee()
employee.name = "George"
employee.age = 25
employee.department = "Mail"
var badge = employee.createbadge()
print("Badge: \(badge)")   // "Badge: Employee Mail George 25"
```

Listing 3-149: Overriding an inherited method

The new **OfficeEmployee** subclass of Listing 3-149 overrides the **createbadge()** method of its superclass to generate a string that includes the value of the **department** property. Now, when the method is called from an object of this class, the system executes the one defined in **OfficeEmployee** (the old method from the superclass is ignored), and therefore the badge includes the values of the three properties.

Using inheritance, we have created a new class without modifying previous classes or duplicating any code. The **Employee** class can create objects to store the name and age of an employee and generate a badge with this information, and the **OfficeEmployee** class can create objects to store the name, age, and the department of the employee and generate a more complete badge with the values of all these properties.

When we call the **createbadge()** method on the **employee** object created from the **OfficeEmployee** class in Listing 3-149, the method executed is always the one defined in the **OfficeEmployee** class. If we want to execute the method on the superclass instead, we must use a special keyword called **super**. The **super** keyword is like the **self** keyword, but instead of representing the object, **super** represents the superclass. It is often used when we have overridden a method but we still need to execute the method on the superclass.

```
class Employee {
    var name = "Undefined"
    var age = 0

    func createbadge() -> String {
        return "Employee \(name) \(age)"
    }
}
class OfficeEmployee: Employee {
    var department = "Undefined"

    override func createbadge() -> String {
        let oldbadge = super.createbadge()
        return "\(oldbadge) \(department)"
    }
}
let employee = OfficeEmployee()
employee.name = "George"
employee.age = 25
employee.department = "Mail"

var badge = employee.createbadge()
print("Badge: \(badge)")   // "Badge: Employee George 25 Mail"
```

Listing 3-150: Calling a method on the superclass

This is the same as the previous example, but now, when the **createbadge()** method of an object created from the **OfficeEmployee** class is called, the method calls the **createbadge()** method of the superclass first and assigns the result to the **oldbadge** constant. The value of this constant is later added to the value of the **department** property to generate the string to return.

(Medium) Type Casting

Inheritance not only transfers functionality from one class to another but also connects the classes together. The superclasses and their subclasses are linked together in a hierarchical chain. Because of this, whenever we declare a variable of the type of the superclass, objects of the subclasses can be assigned to that variable too. This allows us to do things like creating arrays of objects that are of different classes but belong to the same hierarchy.

```
class Employee {
    var name = "Undefined"
    var age = 0
}
class OfficeEmployee: Employee {
    var deskNumber = 0
}
class WarehouseEmployee: Employee {
    var area = "Undefined"
}
```

```
var list: [Employee] = [OfficeEmployee(), WarehouseEmployee(),
OfficeEmployee()]
```

Listing 3-151: Creating an array of objects from different subclasses

This example defines a superclass called **Employee** and then two subclasses of **Employee** called **OfficeEmployee** and **WarehouseEmployee**. The purpose is to have the information for every employee in one class and then have classes for specific types of employee. Following this organization, we can create objects that contain the **name, age,** and **deskNumber** properties to represent employees working at the office and objects that contain the **name, age,** and **area** properties to represent employees working at the warehouse.

No matter the differences between one object and another, they all represent employees of the same company, so sooner or later we will have to include them in the same list. The class hierarchy allows us to do that. We can declare a collection of the data type of the superclass and then store objects of the subclasses in it, as we did in Listing 3-151 with the **list** array.

This is all good until we try to read the array. The array was declared of type **Employee,** so we can only access the properties defined in the **Employee** class. Also, there is no way to know what type of object each element is. We could have an **OfficeEmployee** object at index 0 and later replace it with a **WarehouseEmployee** object. The indexes do not provide any information to identify the objects. Swift solves these problems with the **is** and **as** operators.

▷ **is**—This operator returns a Boolean value indicating whether the value is of a certain data type.

▷ **as**—This operator converts a value of one class to another class when possible.

Identifying an object is easy with the **is** operator. This operator returns a Boolean value that we can use in an **if** statement to check the object's class.

```
var countOffice = 0
var countWarehouse = 0

for obj in list {
    if obj is OfficeEmployee {
        countOffice += 1
    } else if obj is WarehouseEmployee {
        countWarehouse += 1
    }
}
print("We have \(countOffice) employees working at the office")   // 2
print("We have \(countWarehouse) employees working at the warehouse") //1
```

Listing 3-152: Identifying the object's data type

In Listing 3-152, we create the **list** array again with objects from the same classes defined in the previous example, but this time we add a **for in** loop to iterate over the array and count how many objects of each class we have found. The **if** statement inside the loop implements the **is** operator to check if the current object stored in the **obj** constant is of type **OfficeEmployee** or **WarehouseEmployee** and increments the counter respectively (**countOffice** or **countWarehouse**).

Counting objects is not really what these operators are all about. The idea is to figure out the type with the **is** operator and then convert the object with the **as** operator to be able to access their properties and methods. The **as** operator converts a value of one type to another. The conversions are not always guaranteed, and that is why this operator comes in two more forms: **as!** and **as?**. These versions of the **as** operator work like optionals. The **as!** operator forces the conversion and returns an error if the conversion is not possible, and the **as?** operator tries to convert the object and returns an optional with the new object or **nil** in case of failure.

Chapter 3 - Swift Paradigm

```
for obj in list {
   if obj is OfficeEmployee {
      let temp = obj as! OfficeEmployee
      temp.deskNumber = 100
   } else if obj is WarehouseEmployee {
      let temp = obj as! WarehouseEmployee
      temp.area = "New Area"
   }
}
```

Listing 3-153: Casting an object

When we use the **as!** operator we are forcing the conversion, so we need to be sure that the conversion is possible, otherwise the app will crash. (This is the same that happens when we unwrap optionals with the exclamation mark.) In the code in Listing 3-153, we only use this operator after we have already checked with the **is** operator that the object is of the right class. Once the object is casted (converted) into its original data type, we can access its properties and methods. In this example, the objects returned by the **as!** operator are stored in the **temp** constant and then new values are assigned to the **deskNumber** and **area** properties.

Checking for the type before casting is redundant. To simplify the code, we can use the **as?** operator. Instead of forcing the conversion and crashing the app, this version of the **as** operator tries to perform the conversion and returns an optional with the result.

```
for obj in list {
   if let temp = obj as? OfficeEmployee {
      temp.deskNumber = 100
   } else if let temp = obj as? WarehouseEmployee {
      temp.area = "New Area"
   }
}
```

Listing 3-154: Casting an object with the as? operator

In this example, we use optional binding to cast the object and assign the result to the **temp** constant. First, we try to cast **obj** as an **OfficeEmployee** object. If we are successful, we assign the value 100 to the **deskNumber** property, but if the value returned is **nil**, then we try to cast the object to the **WarehouseEmployee** class and modify its **area** property.

Casting can also be performed on the fly if we are sure that the conversion is possible. The statement to cast the object is the same but it must be declared between parentheses.

```
let myarea = (list[1] as! WarehouseEmployee).area
print("The area of employee 1 is \(myarea)")   // "Undefined"
```

Listing 3-155: Casting an object on the fly

In this example, we do not assign the object to any variable; we just cast the element of the **list** array at index 1 as a **WarehouseEmployee** object inside the parentheses and then read the **area** property. The value of this property is stored in the **myarea** constant and then printed on the console.

 IMPORTANT: The **as!** operator is applied when the conversion is guaranteed to be successful, and the **as?** operator is used when we are not sure about the result. But we can also use the basic **as** operator when the Swift compiler can verify that the conversion will be successful, as when we are casting some primitive data types (e.g., **String** values into **NSString** objects).

The **as** operator works on objects that belong to the same class hierarchy. Because sometimes the objects that require casting are not in the same hierarchy, Swift defines several generic data types to represent values of any kind. The most frequently used are **Any** (structures), **AnyObject** (objects), and **AnyClass** (classes). By taking advantage of these generic types, we can create collections with values that are not associated with each other.

```
class Employee {
    var name = "Undefined"
}
class Department {
    var area = "Undefined"
}
var list: [AnyObject] = [Employee(), Department(), Department()]

for obj in list {
    if let temp = obj as? Employee {
        temp.name = ""
    } else if let temp = obj as? Department {
        temp.area = ""
    }
}
```

Listing 3-156: Working with objects of AnyObject *type*

The **list** array declared in Listing 3-156 is of type **AnyObject** and therefore it can contain objects of any data type. To populate the array, we created two simple and independent classes: **Employee** and **Department**. A few objects are created from these classes and included in the array. The objects are later casted by the **as?** operator inside a **for in** loop and their properties are modified following the same procedure used in previous examples.

(Basic) **Initialization**

So far, we have initialized the properties of classes in the definition. This is because classes, unlike structures, do not provide memberwise initializers. The properties of a class must be initialized explicitly in the definition or when they are instantiated with the **init()** method.

```
class Employee {
    var name: String
    var age: Int

    init(name: String, age: Int) {
        self.name = name
        self.age = age
    }
}
let employee1 = Employee(name: "George", age: 28)
```

Listing 3-157: Declaring a Designated Initializer

The **init()** method declared for the **Employee** class in Listing 3-157 initializes every property of the class with the values specified by the **Employee()** initializer. This type of initializer is called *Designated Initializer*. When we declare a Designated Initializer, we need to make sure that all the properties are initialized.

If we know that our code will not be able to provide all the values during initialization, we can also declare a Convenience Initializer. A Convenience Initializer is an initializer that offers a convenient way to initialize an object with values by default for some or all of its properties. It is declared with the **init()** method but preceded by the **convenience** keyword. A Convenience Initializer must call the Designated initializer with the corresponding values.

Chapter 3 - Swift Paradigm

```
class Employee {
   var name: String
   var age: Int

   init(name: String, age: Int) {
      self.name = name
      self.age = age
   }
   convenience init() {
      self.init(name: "Undefined", age: 0)
   }
}
let employee1 = Employee()
```

Listing 3-158: Declaring a Convenience Initializer

When we create an instance of **Employee**, the system detects the number and type of arguments we specify and executes the corresponding initializer. For example, if we provide the values for the **name** and the **age** parameters, the system executes the Designated Initializer because this is the initializer that contains the necessary parameters to receive those values, but if the initialization does not include any argument, the Convenience Initializer is executed instead and then the Designated Initializer is called with values by default ("Undefined" and 0).

Unlike structures, classes can inherit properties and methods from other classes, and this includes the **init()** method. When a subclass does not provide its own Designated Initializer, the initializer of its superclass is used instead.

```
class Employee {
   var name: String
   var age: Int

   init(name: String, age: Int) {
      self.name = name
      self.age = age
   }
}
class OfficeEmployee: Employee {
   var department: String = "Undefined"
}
let employee1 = OfficeEmployee(name: "George", age: 29)
```

Listing 3-159: Inheriting the Designated Initializer

The code in Listing 3-159 defines the subclass **OfficeEmployee** that inherits from the **Employee** class. The **OfficeEmployee** class does not provide any initializer, so the only initializer available is the one provided by its superclass. This initializer only initializes the properties **name** and **age**. The **department** property of **OfficeEmployee** is explicitly initialized with the value "Undefined". To provide an initializer that also includes this property, we must declare a new Designated Initializer in the **OfficeEmployee** class.

```
class Employee {
   var name: String
   var age: Int

   init(name: String, age: Int) {
      self.name = name
      self.age = age
   }
}
class OfficeEmployee: Employee {
   var department: String
```

```
    init(name: String, age: Int, department: String) {
        self.department = department

        super.init(name: name, age: age)
    }
}
let employee1 = OfficeEmployee(name: "John", age: 24, department: "Mail")
```

Listing 3-160: Declaring a Designated Initializer for the subclass

The Designated Initializer of a subclass must initialize the properties of its own class first and then call the initializer of its superclass. This is done by calling the **init()** method on **super**. The **super** keyword refers to the superclass, so when the system executes the **super.init()** statement in the code in Listing 3-160, the **init()** method of the superclass is executed and the **name** and **age** properties of this class are initialized.

IMPORTANT: There are different ways to combine Designated and Convenience initializers. The possibility of classes to inherit from other classes in an unlimited chain can turn initialization into a very complex process. This book does not explore all the possibilities provided by Swift for initialization. For more information, visit our website and follow the links for this chapter.

(Medium) Deinitialization

There is a counterpart of the initialization process called *Deinitialization*. Despite its name, this process is not directly related to the initialization process but rather to the ARC system. ARC, as we studied previously in this chapter, is an automatic system adopted by Swift to manage memory. Letting the system manage the memory and take care of removing the objects our program no longer needs presents a huge advantage, but it also means that we do not always know when an object is going to be removed. There are times when an object is using resources that must be released or information that needs to be stored. Whatever the task, Swift offers the **deinit** method to execute any last-minute instructions we need before the object is erased from memory.

```
class Item {
    var quantity = 0.0
    var name = "Not defined"
    var price = 0.0

    deinit {
        print("This instance was erased")
    }
}
var purchase: Item? = Item()
purchase = nil
```

Listing 3-161: Declaring a deinitializer

This example defines a simple class with a deinitializer. The object is created and assigned to an optional variable. Right after that, the **nil** value is assigned to the same variable to erase the reference and test the **deinit** method, which prints a message on the console.

(Medium) Access Control and Modifiers

Swift defines keywords (also called modifiers) that can be applied to entities (classes, structures, properties, methods, and more) to confer them special attributes. We have already seen the **mutating** and **override** keywords, but there are others, as described below.

▷ **lazy**—This keyword defines a property whose initial value is not assigned until the property is used for the first time.

▷ **final**—This keyword is used on a class when we don't want to allow the code to create subclasses of it. It must be declared before the **class** keyword.

The **lazy** keyword is often used when our code needs some time to determine the value of a property and we don't want the initialization of the structure or the class to be delayed. For example, we may have a property that stores a name that is retrieved from a server, which is a resource intensive task that we should only perform when the value is required.

```
class Employee {
    lazy var name: String = {
        // Loading name from a server
        print("Loading...")
        return "Undefined"
    }()
    var age = 0
}
let employee = Employee()
```

Listing 3-162: Defining lazy *properties*

The **Employee** class in Listing 3-162 defines two properties, **name** and **age**, but this time a closure is assigned to the **name** property to get the employee's name from a server. (We will see how to retrieve information from the web in Chapter 17) Because we declared this property as **lazy**, the closure will only be executed when we try to read it. If we execute the example as it is, we get nothing in return, but if we read the **name** property with a statement at the end, we will see the text "Loading..." printed on the console.

The Swift language also includes keywords to define the level of access for each entity in our code. Access control in Swift is based on modules and source files, but it also applies to single properties and methods. Source files are the files we create for our application, the properties and methods are the ones we have created for our structures and classes in previous examples, and modules are units of code that are related with each other. For instance, a single application and each of the frameworks included in it are considered modules. (We will introduce frameworks in Chapter 4) Considering this classification, Swift defines five keywords to determine accessibility.

▷ **open**—This keyword determines that an entity is accessible from the module it belongs to and other modules.

▷ **public**—This keyword determines that an entity is accessible from the module it belongs to and other modules. The difference between **public** and **open** is that we can't create subclasses of **public** classes outside the module in which they were defined. This also applies to methods and properties (e.g., **public** methods can't be overridden outside the module in which they were declared).

▷ **internal**—This keyword determines that an entity is accessible only inside the module in which it was created. This is the default access mode for applications. By default, every entity defined in our application is only accessible from inside the application.

▷ **private**—This keyword determines that an entity is accessible only from the context in which it was created (e.g., a **private** property in a class will only be accessible from methods of the same class).

▷ **fileprivate**—This keyword determines that an entity is accessible only from the file in which it was declared (e.g., a **fileprivate** property in a class will only be accessible by other entities defined inside the file in which it was declared).

As we will see later, most of these keywords apply to frameworks and are rarely used in single applications. By default, the properties and methods we include in our classes and structures are declared **internal**, which means that our classes and structures are only available from inside our application (module). Unless we are creating our own frameworks, this is all we need for our applications, and is the reason why we didn't have to specify any keyword when we defined our structures and classes before. All our classes and structures are accessible by the rest of the code inside our application, but if we want to have a level of control in our data types or avoid modifying values by mistake, we can declare some of them as **private**, as shown next.

```
class Employee {
    private var name = "Undefined"
    private var age = 0

    func showValues() {
        print("Name: \(name)")
        print("Age: \(age)")
    }
}
let employee = Employee()
employee.showValues()
```

Listing 3-163: *Declaring* `private` *properties*

The code in Listing 3-163 defines the **name** and **age** properties of our **Employee** class as **private** and adds a method called **showValues()** to access their values. Due to access control, these properties are only accessible by the method in the class. If we try to read their values from outside the object using dot notation, Xcode will return an error (e.g., **employee.name**).

If what we want is to be able to read the property from outside the object but not allow assigning new values to it, we can declare it with a public getter but a private setter.

```
class Employee {
    private var name = "Undefined"
    public private(set) var age = 0

    func setAge(newAge: Int) {
        age = newAge
    }
}
let employee = Employee()
employee.setAge(newAge: 25)
print(employee.age)
```

Listing 3-164: *Declaring a public getter and private setter*

The **age** property in the **Employee** class of Listing 3-164 was declared as public, so everyone can read its value, but with a private setter (**private(set)**), so only the methods inside the class can modify it. To change the value, we defined the **setAge()** method. The code creates an instance of the class and calls the method, but this time we can read the value of the **age** property and print it on the console because it was declared with a public getter.

Medium **Singletons**

As already mentioned, we can create as many objects as we want from a single class. These objets are independent from one another; they have their own properties and methods and process their own values. But sometimes our code needs only one object to be created from a class, so every piece of code have access to the same object and works on the same values. To guarantee that only one instance of a class is created and the instance is available from anywhere in our code, the class needs to implement two things: a type property to create the only instance available, and a private initializer that doesn't allow the code to create more, as shown in the following example.

```
@MainActor
class Employee {
    var name: String
    var age: Int

    static let shared = Employee(newName: "Undefined", newAge: 0)

    private init(newName: String, newAge: Int) {
        name = newName
        age = newAge
    }
}
let employee1 = Employee.shared
let employee2 = Employee.shared
employee1.name = "George"

print("\(employee1.name) - \(employee2.name)")   // "George - George"
```

Listing 3-165: *Defining a singleton*

The `Employee` class in this example defines a type property called `shared` and initializes it with an instance of the same class, so every time we read this property from anywhere in the code, we get the same `Employee` object in return. For instance, in this example, we define two constants called `employee1` and `employee2`, and initialize them with the instance returned by the `shared` property. Because this is the same object, when we modify a value in the `employee1` object, the same value is returned by the `employee2` object.

Because the purpose of this class is to only allow the creation of one instance (one object), we prefix the initializer with the `private` keyword. As a result, only the single instance created by the `shared` property is available. That is the reason why the object created from this class is called *Singleton*.

 IMPORTANT: Note that we have prefixed the definition of the class with the `@MainActor` modifier. This is to prevent the object in the `shared` property from being changed by different threads at the same time and causing an error called data race. The `@MainActor` modifier tells the system that objects of this class should only be used in the main thread. We will learn more about this modifier and other ways to avoid data races in Chapter 9.

(Basic) **3.6 Protocols**

The main characteristics of classes, and therefore objects, are the capacity to encapsulate data and functionality and the possibility to share and improve code through inheritance. This introduced an advantage over previous paradigms and turned the Object-Oriented Programming paradigm into the industry standard for a while. But that changed with the introduction of protocols in Swift. Protocols define properties and methods that structures can have in common. This means that Swift's structures not only can encapsulate data and functionality, just like objects, but by conforming to protocols they can also share code. Figure 3-5 illustrates the differences between these two paradigms.

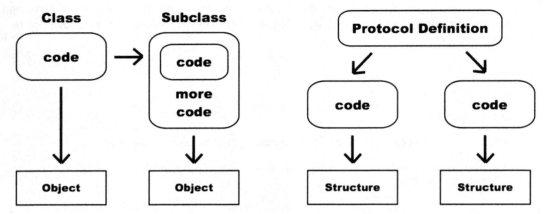

Figure 3-5: *Object-Oriented Programming versus Protocol-Oriented Programming*

In OOP, the code is implemented inside a class and then objects are created from that class. If we need to create objects with additional functionality, we must define a subclass that inherits the code from the superclass and adds some of its own. Protocols offer a slightly different approach. The properties and methods we want the structures to have in common are defined in the protocol and then implemented by the structures' definitions. This allows us to associate different structures together through a common pattern. The code implemented by each structure is unique, but they follow a blueprint set by the protocol. If we know that a structure conforms to a protocol, we can always be sure that besides its own definitions, it will also include the properties and methods defined by the protocol. In addition, protocols can be extended to provide their own implementations of the properties and methods we want the structures to have in common, allowing the paradigm to completely replace classes and objects.

 IMPORTANT: The Swift paradigm is built from the combination of structures and protocols, but protocols may also be adopted by enumerations and classes. For instance, many frameworks use protocols to offer a programming pattern called *Delegation*. We will study how classes conform to protocols and how to implement delegation later.

Basic Definition of Protocols

Protocols are defined with the **protocol** keyword followed by the name and the list of properties and methods between curly braces. No values or statements are assigned or declared inside a protocol, only the names and the corresponding data types. Because of this, methods are defined as always, but they omit the braces and the statements, and properties must include the **get** and **set** keywords between braces to indicate whether they are read-only properties, or we can read and assign values to them (see Listing 3-42 for an example of getters and setters). To indicate that the structure conforms to the protocol, we must include the protocol's name after the name of the structure separated by a colon, as shown in the following example.

```
protocol Printer {
   var name: String { get set }
   func printdescription()
}
struct Employees: Printer {
   var name: String
   var age: Int
   func printdescription() {
      print("Description: \(name) \(age)")   // "Description: John 32"
   }
}
```

```
let employee1 = Employees(name: "John", age: 32)
employee1.printdescription()
```

Listing 3-166: Defining protocols

A protocol tells the structure what properties and methods are required, but the structure must implement them. In the example of Listing 3-166, we define a protocol called **Printer** that includes the **name** property and the **printdescription()** method. The **Employees** structure defined next conforms to this protocol, and along with the protocol's property and method it also implements its own property called **age**. Although this property was not defined in the protocol, we can read it inside the **printdescription()** method and print its value.

The advantage of this practice is evident when structures of different types conform to the same protocol, as shown in the following example.

```
protocol Printer {
    var name: String { get set }
    func printdescription()
}
struct Employees: Printer {
    var name: String
    var age: Int

    func printdescription() {
        print("Description: \(name) \(age)")
    }
}
struct Offices: Printer {
    var name: String
    var employees: Int

    func printdescription() {
        print("Description: \(name) \(employees)") // "Description: Mail 2"
    }
}
let employee1 = Employees(name: "John", age: 32)
let office1 = Offices(name: "Mail", employees: 2)
office1.printdescription()
```

Listing 3-167: Defining multiple structures that conform to the same protocol

Although the structures created in Listing 3-167 from the **Employees** and **Offices** definitions are different (they have different properties), they both conform to the **Printer** protocol and provide their own implementation of the **printdescription()** method. The common functionality defined by the protocol ensures that no matter what type of structure we are working with, it will always have an implementation of **printdescription()**.

Protocols are also data types. This allows us to associate structures by the common functionality.

```
let employee1 = Employees(name: "John", age: 32)
let office1 = Offices(name: "Mail", employees: 2)
var list: [Printer] = [employee1, office1]
for element in list {
    element.printdescription()
}
```

Listing 3-168: Using protocols as data types

Listing 3-168 uses the same protocol and structures defined in the previous example, but this time it stores the instances in an array. The type of the array was defined as **Printer**, which means the array may contain structures of any type as long as they conform to the **Printer** protocol. Because of this, no matter the element's data type (**Employees** or **Offices**) we know that they always have an implementation of the **name** property and the **printdescription()** method.

When we process a structure or an object as a protocol type, we can only access the properties and methods defined by the protocol. If we need to access the instance's own properties and methods, we must cast it using the **as** operator as we did with classes before. The following example prints the value of the **age** property if the element of the array is of type **Employees**.

```
let employee1 = Employees(name: "John", age: 32)
let office1 = Offices(name: "Mail", employees: 2)

var list: [Printer] = [employee1, office1]
for element in list {
   if let employee = element as? Employees {
      print(employee.age)   // "32"
   }
   element.printdescription()
}
```

Listing 3-169: *Accessing the instance's own properties*

Because protocols are data types, we can use them to define variables, or return them from functions. The following example declares a function that returns a value of type **Printer**.

```
func getFile(type: Int) -> Printer {
   var data: Printer!
   if type == 1 {
      data = Employees(name: "John", age: 32)
   } else if type == 2 {
      data = Offices(name: "Mail", employees: 2)
   }
   return data
}
let file = getFile(type: 1)
file.printdescription()   // "Description: John 32"
```

Listing 3-170: *Returning values of a protocol type*

The **getFile()** function in Listing 3-170 creates an instance of a structure depending on the value received. If the **type** parameter is equal to 1, it returns an instance of **Employees**, but if the value is equal to 2, it returns an instance of **Offices**. But because the value returned by the function is of type **Printer** we know it will always include the **printdescription()** method.

(Advanced) **Generic Protocols**

Protocols can also define generic properties and methods, but they work slightly different than the generic types studied before. When we want to define a protocol with a generic property or method, we first must define the name of the generic type with the **associatedtype** keyword.

```
protocol Printer {
   associatedtype protype
   var name: protype { get set }
}
struct Employees: Printer {
   var name: String
}
```

```
let employee = Employees(name: "John")
print(employee.name)  // "John"
```

Listing 3-171: Defining generic protocols

This example defines a generic protocol called **Printer** and a structure that conforms to that protocol called **Employees**. The protocol defines a generic type with the name **protype** and then declares a property of that type. The property's real data type is defined by the structure or the class that conforms to the protocol. In this case, the **Employees** structure defines the **name** property as type **String**, and that's the type of values we can use in the instances of this structure, but we could have declared the property as type **Int** or any other necessary.

(Medium) ## Swift Protocols

The Swift language makes extensive use of protocols. Almost every API includes protocols that define common features and behavior. But there are also important protocols defined in the Swift Standard Library that we can use to improve our custom data types. The following are the most frequently used.

▷ **Equatable**—This protocol defines a data type which values can be compared with other values of the same type using the operators == and !=.

▷ **Comparable**—This protocol defines a data type which values can be compared with other values of the same type using the operators >, <, >=, and <=.

▷ **Numeric**—This protocol defines a data type that only works with values that can participate in arithmetic operations.

▷ **Hashable**—This protocol defines a data type that provides the hash value (unique identifier) required for the instance to be included in collections, such as sets and dictionaries.

▷ **CaseIterable**—This protocol defines a data type, usually an enumeration without associated values, that includes a property called **allCases** that contains the collection of all the cases included in the enumeration.

These protocols are responsible of elemental processes performed by the system and the Swift language. For example, when we compare two values with the == or != operators, the system checks whether the values conform to the **Equatable** protocol and then calls a type method in the data type to compare them and solve the condition (true or false, depending on whether the values are equal or not). Swift primitive data types conform to the **Equatable** protocol and implement its methods, but we can also implement them in our own data types to compare their values. For this purpose, we must declare that the data type conforms to the protocol and implement the methods required by it. The **Equatable** protocol requires only one method called == to check for equality. (The system infers that if two values are not equal, they are different, and therefore the method for the != operator is optional.) This method must have a name equal to the operator (==), receive the two values to compare, and return a Boolean value to communicate the result. For instance, we can make our **Employees** structure conform to the **Equatable** protocol and implement a method called == to be able to compare two different instances of the same structure.

```
struct Employees: Equatable {
    var name: String
    var age: Int

    static func == (value1: Employees, value2: Employees) -> Bool {
        return value1.age == value2.age
    }
}
```

```
let employee1 = Employees(name: "John", age: 32)
let employee2 = Employees(name: "George", age: 32)
let message = employee1 == employee2 ? "Equal" : "Different"
print(message)  // "Equal"
```

Listing 3-172: Conforming to the `Equatable` *protocol*

In this example, we use the **==** method to compare the values of the **age** properties and therefore the structures are going to be equal when the employees are the same age. In this case, both instances are created with the value 32 and therefore the value "Equal" is assigned to the **message** constant when we compare the objects with the ternary operator.

If what we want is to compare each of the properties in the structure, then we can omit the method. When we conform to the **Equatable** protocol, the compiler automatically generates the method for us to compare all the values of the structure (in this case, **name** and **age**).

```
struct Employees: Equatable {
   var name: String
   var age: Int
}
let employee1 = Employees(name: "John", age: 32)
let employee2 = Employees(name: "George", age: 32)
let message = employee1 == employee2 ? "Equal" : "Different"
print(message)  // "Different"
```

Listing 3-173: Letting the compiler create the protocol methods for us

Because we did not declare the **==** method in the example of Listing 3-173, the system creates the method for us and compares the values of all the properties. As a result, the system determines that the objects are different (the ages are the same, but the names are not).

Of course, we could have compared the properties directly (**employee1.name == employee2.name**) but being able to compare the objects instead simplifies the code and allows us to use our structures (or objects) in APIs that require the values to be comparable. For example, when we created a generic function earlier in this chapter, we could not perform any operations on the values (see Listing 3-15). Since the data type used in those functions is generic, Swift is incapable of knowing the capabilities of the data type and therefore Xcode returns an error if we try to perform operations on the values, but we can easily solve this problem by making the generic type conform to a protocol. This feature is called *Type Constraint* because it constrains the generic type to a data type with certain capabilities. For instance, the function in the following example receives two generic values, but only of a data type that conforms to the **Equatable** protocol, so they can be compared.

```
struct Employees: Equatable {
   var name: String
   var age: Int
}
func compareValues<T: Equatable>(value1: T, value2: T) -> String {
   let message = value1 == value2 ? "equal" : "different"
   return message
}
let employee1 = Employees(name: "George", age: 55)
let employee2 = Employees(name: "Robert", age: 55)

let result = compareValues(value1: employee1, value2: employee2)
print("The values are \(result)")  // "The values are different"
```

Listing 3-174: Adding a type constraint to a generic function

The conformance to the protocol is specified inside the angle brackets after the name of the generic type. The **compareValues()** function in Listing 3-174 declares the **T** type to conform to

Equatable and then compares the values with a ternary operator and returns the result. In this case, the ages of the employees are the same (55), but the names are different ("George" and "Robert"), and therefore the system considers the structures to be different.

Another protocol used as a type constraint is **Numeric**. This protocol determines that the data types of the values received by the function must support arithmetic operations.

```
func calculateResult<T: Numeric>(value1: T, value2: T) {
   print(value1 + value2)   // 7.5
}
calculateResult(value1: 3.5, value2: 4)
```

Listing 3-175: Using the Numeric *protocol to set a type constraint*

The **calculateResult()** function in this example is a generic function and therefore it can receive any value of any type, but because we set a type constraint with the **Numeric** protocol, the function can only receive values of data types that can participate in arithmetic operations.

Besides comparing for equality with the **Equatable** protocol, we can also compare magnitudes with the **Comparable** protocol. This protocol is like **Equatable**, but the system does not offer a default implementation of the type methods, we must implement them ourselves. The protocol requires four methods to represent the operations >, <, >= and <=. In the following example, we compare the ages of the employees.

```
struct Employees: Comparable {
   var name: String
   var age: Int

   static func > (value1: Employees, value2: Employees) -> Bool {
      return value1.age > value2.age
   }
   static func < (value1: Employees, value2: Employees) -> Bool {
      return value1.age < value2.age
   }
   static func >= (value1: Employees, value2: Employees) -> Bool {
      return value1.age >= value2.age
   }
   static func <= (value1: Employees, value2: Employees) -> Bool {
      return value1.age <= value2.age
   }
}
let employee1 = Employees(name: "George", age: 32)
let employee2 = Employees(name: "Robert", age: 55)

if employee1 > employee2 {
   print("\(employee1.name) is older")
} else {
   print("\(employee2.name) is older")   // "Robert is older"
}
```

Listing 3-176: Conforming to the Comparable *protocol*

When we compare two instances of the **Employees** structure, the system calls the corresponding type method and the method returns **true** or **false** depending on the values of the **age** property. Because in this example the value of **age** in the **employee1** structure is not greater than the value of **age** in the **employee2** structure, we get the message "Robert is older".

Another useful protocol is **Hashable**. Every time we include a structure or an object in a set or use them as the index of a dictionary, the system requires the data type to provide a hash value that can be used to uniquely identify each element. This is a random integer that is created based on the values of the properties. The purpose of the **Hashable** protocol is to define properties and methods to handle this value. Most of the data types defined by Swift conform to this protocol and that is why we do not have any problems when including these values in a set or as the index of dictionaries, but for custom structures and objects we must provide the hash value ourselves. Fortunately, if the values in our data type are already hashable, we do not need a specific property to be used to create the hash value, all we need to do is conform to the protocol and the system creates the value for us. The following example makes the **Employees** structure conform to the **Hashable** protocol, so we can include the instances in a set.

```
struct Employees: Hashable {
   var name: String
   var age: Int
}
let employee1 = Employees(name: "John", age: 32)
let employee2 = Employees(name: "Robert", age: 55)

let list: Set<Employees> = [employee1, employee2]
for item in list {
   print(item.name)
}
```

Listing 3-177: Conforming to the `Hashable` *protocol*

Hash values are random integers created based on the values of the properties. If we just conform to the protocol, the system uses the values of all the properties in the instance to create it (all the properties must be hashable), but we can specify which properties should be included by implementing the properties and methods defined by the protocol.

▷ **hashValue**—This property returns the hash value of the instance. It is of type **Int**.

▷ **hash(into:** inout Hasher)—This method defines the properties that are going to be included by the hasher to create the hash value.

To calculate the hash value, the Swift Standard Library includes a structure called **Hasher**. This is the structure received by the **hash(into:)** method and it contains a method called **combine()** to tell the hasher which properties should be used to create the value. The following example illustrates how to implement the **hash(into:)** method and call the **combine()** method on the hasher to create a hash value from the value of the **name** property.

```
struct Employees: Hashable {
   var name: String
   var age: Int

   func hash(into hasher: inout Hasher) {
      hasher.combine(name)
   }
}
let employee = Employees(name: "George", age: 32)
print(employee.hashValue)   // e.g., 7722685913545470055
```

Listing 3-178: Defining our own hash value

At the end of Listing 3-178, we print the value of the **hashValue** property. Since the resulting value is always an integer calculated randomly every time the app is executed, we won't notice any difference, but this procedure may be useful when managing sensitive information.

The last protocol from our list is called **CaseIterable**. This is a simple protocol that defines a property called **allCases** to store a collection with all the cases in an enumeration. Again, the system automatically initializes this property, so all we need to do is to declare that the enumeration conforms to the protocol. In the following example, we define an enumeration with three cases and then iterate through the collection in the **allCases** property to print the names.

```
enum Departments: CaseIterable {
   case mail
   case marketing
   case managing
}
var message = ""
for department in Departments.allCases {
   message += "\(department) "
}
print(message)  // "mail marketing managing "
```

Listing 3-179: Conforming to the `CaseIterable` *protocol*

(Medium) **Extensions**

Protocols only define the properties and methods that the data types will have in common, but they do not include any implementation. However, we can implement properties and methods that will be common to all the data types that conform to the protocol by taking advantage of a feature of the Swift language called *Extensions*. Extensions are special declarations that add functionality to an existing data type. We can use them with structures, enumerations, and classes, but they are particularly useful with protocols because this is the way protocols can provide their own functionality. The syntax includes the keyword **extension** followed by the name of the data type we want to extend. The following example recreates the **Printer** protocol introduced in previous examples but extends it with a method.

```
protocol Printer {
   var name: String { get set }
}
extension Printer {
   func printdescription() {
       print("The name is \(name)")
   }
}
struct Employees: Printer {
   var name: String
   var age: Int
}
struct Offices: Printer {
   var name: String
   var employees: Int
}
let employee = Employees(name: "John", age: 45)
let office = Offices(name: "Mail", employees: 2)

employee.printdescription()  // "The name is John"
office.printdescription()   // "The name is Mail"
```

Listing 3-180: Extending a protocol

In this example, we define a **Printer** protocol with just the **name** property and then extend it to include a common implementation of the **printdescription()** method. Now, the **Employees** and **Offices** structures in our example share the same implementation and produce the same result when their **printdescription()** methods are executed.

As we already mentioned, extensions are not only available for protocols but also for any other data type. We can use them to extend structures, enumerations, and classes. This is particularly useful when we do not have access to the definitions of the data types and need to add some functionality (like when they are part of a library or a framework). In the following example, we extend the **Int** structure to provide a method that prints a description of its value.

```
extension Int {
    func printdescription() {
        print("The number is \(self)")
    }
}
let number = 25
number.printdescription()   // "The number is 25"
```

Listing 3-181: Extending data types

The **Int** data type is a structure defined in the Swift Standard Library. We cannot modify its definition but we can extend it to add more functionality. In this example, we add a method called **printdescription()** to print a message with the current value. (Notice the use of the **self** keyword to refer to the instance.) This method is not included in the original definition, but it is now available in our code.

Of course, we can also extend our own data types if we consider it appropriate. The following example extends our **Employees** structure to add a new method.

```
struct Employees {
    var name: String
    var age: Int
}
extension Employees {
    func printbadge() {
        print("Name: \(name) Age: \(age)")
    }
}
let employee = Employees(name: "John", age: 50)
employee.printbadge()   // "Name: John Age: 50"
```

Listing 3-182: Extending custom data types

Extensions can also be conditional. For instance, if we have a generic structure, we can add an extension only for specific types of values. The condition is determined by the **where** clause. The clause works like an **if** statement, so the extension is only applied if the condition is met.

```
struct Employees<T> {
    var value: T
}
extension Employees where T == Int {
    func doubleValue() {
        print("\(value) times 2 = \(value * 2)")
    }
}
let employee = Employees(value: 25)
employee.doubleValue()   // "25 times 2 = 50"
```

Listing 3-183: Defining a conditional extension

In this example, we define a generic structure called **Employees** with a generic property called **value** and then define an extension for this structure with a method called **doubleValue()**, but this method will only be added to the instance if the data type used to create the instance is **Int**. At the end, we create an instance with the value 25 and call the method, which multiplies the value by 2 and prints a string with the result. This works because we created the instance with an integer, but if we try to use another type of value, Xcode will show an error.

Another useful implementation of extensions is the customization of string interpolation. We have introduced string interpolation in Chapter 2 and have been using it in almost every example to insert values in strings (e.g., `print("My name is \(name)")`). What we haven't mentioned is that these values are managed by a structure called **StringInterpolation** (a typealias of **DefaultStringInterpolation**) and that by extending this structure we can customize how the system processes the values. The **StringInterpolation** structure includes the following methods for this purpose.

> ▷ **appendInterpolation(**Value**)**—This method interpolates the value provided by the argument into the final string.

> ▷ **appendLiteral(**String**)**—This method adds the string provided by the argument to the interpolation.

To customize the interpolation, we extend the **StringInterpolation** structure with an overload of the **appendInterpolation()** method, process the value inside this method, and finally append the result to the interpolation with the **appendLiteral()** method.

```
extension String.StringInterpolation {
    mutating func appendInterpolation(celsius value: Double) {
        let fahrenheit = ((value * 9)/5) + 32
        appendLiteral(String(fahrenheit))
    }
}
print("Temperature in Fahrenheit \(celsius: 25)")
```

Listing 3-184: *Customizing string interpolation*

The **appendInterpolation()** method can take as many parameters as we need. In this example, we define only one parameter with the name **value** and a label called **celsius**. When we create a string with this label and a number, the method is executed. Within the method, we use a formula to turn Celsius degrees into Fahrenheit and then add the result to the interpolation with the **appendLiteral()** method to get the string "Temperature in Fahrenheit 77.0".

(Medium) **Delegates**

As we have already seen, an instance of a structure or an object can be assigned to the property of another instance. For example, we could have an instance of a structure called **Employees** with a property that contains an instance of a structure called **Offices** to store information about the office where the employee works. This opens the door to new programming patterns where the instances adopt different roles. The most useful pattern is called *Delegation*. A structure or object delegates responsibility for the execution of certain tasks to another structure or object.

```
struct Salary {
    func showMoney(name: String, money: Double) {
        print("The salary of \(name) is \(money)")
    }
}
struct Employees {
    var name: String
    var money: Double

    var delegate: Salary

    func generatereport() {
        delegate.showMoney(name: name, money: money)
    }
}
```

```
let salary = Salary()
var employee1 = Employees(name: "John", money: 45000, delegate: salary)
employee1.generatereport()   // "The salary of John is 45000.0"
```

Listing 3-185: Delegating tasks

The **Employees** structure in Listing 3-185 contains three properties. The properties **name** and **money** store the employee's data, but the **delegate** property stores the instance of the **Salary** structure in charge of printing that data. The code creates the **Salary** instance first and then uses this value to create the **Employees** instance. When we call the **generatereport()** method on the **employee1** structure at the end, the method calls the **showmoney()** method on **delegate**, effectively delegating the task of printing the data to this structure.

This pattern presents two problems. First, the structure that is delegating needs to know the data type of the structure that is going to become the delegate (in our example, the **delegate** property always has to be of type **Salary**). Following this approach, not every structure can be a delegate, only the ones specified in the definition. The second problem is related to how we know which are the properties and methods that the delegate must implement. If the structure is too complex or is taken from a library, we could forget to implement some methods or properties and get an error when the structure tries to access them. Both problems are solved by protocols. Instead of declaring a specific structure as the delegate, we define a protocol and declare the **delegate** property to be of that type, as shown in the following example.

```
protocol SalaryProtocol {
    func showMoney(name: String, money: Double)
}
struct Salary: SalaryProtocol {
    func showMoney(name: String, money: Double) {
        print("The salary of \(name) is \(money)")
    }
}
struct Employees {
    var name: String
    var money: Double
    var delegate: SalaryProtocol

    func generatereport() {
        delegate.showMoney(name: name, money: money)
    }
}
let salary = Salary()
let employee1 = Employees(name: "John", money: 45000, delegate: salary)

employee1.generatereport()   // "The salary of John is 45000.0"
```

Listing 3-186: Delegating with protocols

The **delegate** property of the **Employees** structure is now of type **SalaryProtocol**, which means that it can store any instance of any type providing that it conforms to the **SalaryProtocol** protocol. As illustrated by this example, the advantage of protocols is that we can use structures of different types to perform the task. It doesn't matter what type they are as long as they conform to the delegate's protocol and implement its properties and methods. For example, we could create two different structures to print the data of our last example and assign to the delegate one instance or another depending on what we want to achieve.

```
protocol SalaryProtocol {
    func showMoney(name: String, money: Double)
}
struct Salary: SalaryProtocol {
    func showMoney(name: String, money: Double) {
```

Chapter 3 - Swift Paradigm

```
        print("The salary of \(name) is \(money)")
    }
}
struct BasicSalary: SalaryProtocol {
    func showMoney(name: String, money: Double) {
        if money > 40000 {
            print("Salary is over the minimum")
        } else {
            print("The salary of \(name) is \(money)")
        }
    }
}
struct Employees {
    var name: String
    var money: Double
    var delegate: SalaryProtocol

    func generatereport() {
        delegate.showMoney(name: name, money: money)
    }
}
let salary = Salary()
var employee1 = Employees(name: "John", money: 45000, delegate: salary)
employee1.delegate = BasicSalary()
employee1.generatereport()   // "Salary is over the minimum"
```

Listing 3-187: *Using different delegates*

The **BasicSalary** structure added in Listing 3-187 conforms to **SalaryProtocol** and implements its **showMoney()** method, but unlike the **Salary** structure, it produces two different results depending on the employee's salary. The output produced by the execution of the **generatereport()** method on the **Employees** structure now depends on the type of structure we previously assigned to the **delegate** property.

Medium **3.7 Errors**

Errors are common in computer programming. Either our code or the code provided by libraries and frameworks may return errors. No matter how many precautions we take, we can't guarantee success and many problems may be found as our code tries to serve its purpose. For this reason, Swift introduces a systematic process to handle errors called *Error Handling*.

Medium **Throwing Errors**

When a method produces an error, it is said that it *throws* an error. Several frameworks provided by Apple are already programmed to throw errors, as we will see in further chapters, but we can also do it from our own structures and classes. To throw an error, we must use the **throw** and **throws** keywords. The **throw** keyword is used to throw the error and the **throws** keyword is specified in the method's declaration to indicate that the method can throw errors.

Because a method can throw multiple errors, we also must indicate the type of error found with values of an enumeration type. This is a custom enumeration that conforms to the **Error** protocol. For instance, let's consider the following example.

```
struct Stock {
    var totalLamps = 5
    mutating func sold(amount: Int) {
        totalLamps = totalLamps - amount
    }
}
var mystock = Stock()
```

```
mystock.sold(amount: 8)
print("Lamps in stock: \(mystock.totalLamps)")   // "Lamps in stock: -3"
```

Listing 3-188: Getting an error inside a method

The code in Listing 3-188 defines a structure called **Stock** that manages the stock of lamps available in the store. The class includes the **totalLamps** property to store the number of lamps we still have available and the **sold()** method to process the lamps sold. The method updates the stock by subtracting the number of lamps we have sold from the value of the **totalLamps** property. If the number of lamps sold is less than the number of lamps in stock, everything is fine, but when we sell more lamps than we have, as in this example, there is clearly a problem.

To throw an error from a method, we must define the types of errors available, add the **throws** keyword to the definition (between the arguments and the returning data types), detect the error, and throw it with the **throw** keyword.

```
enum Errors: Error {
    case OutOfStock
}
struct Stock {
    var totalLamps = 5
    mutating func sold(amount: Int) throws {
        if amount > totalLamps {
            throw Errors.OutOfStock
        } else {
            totalLamps = totalLamps - amount
        }
    }
}
var mystock = Stock()
```

Listing 3-189: Throwing errors

In this example, we declare an enumeration called **Errors** that conforms to the **Error** protocol and includes a case called **OutOfStock**. By declaring **sold()** as a throwing method with the **throws** keyword, we can now throw the **OutOfStock** error every time we try to sell more lamps than we have. If the lamps sold are more than the number of lamps in stock, the method throws the error, otherwise the stock is updated.

(Medium) **Handling Errors**

Now that we have a method that can throw errors, we must handle the errors when the method is executed. Swift includes the **try** keyword and the **do catch** statements for this purpose. The **do catch** statements create two blocks of code. If the statements inside the **do** block return an error, the statements in the **catch** block are executed. To execute a method that throws errors, we must call the method inside the **do** statement with the **try** keyword in front of it.

```
enum Errors: Error {
    case OutOfStock
}
struct Stock {
    var totalLamps = 5
    mutating func sold(amount: Int) throws {
        if amount > totalLamps {
            throw Errors.OutOfStock
        } else {
            totalLamps = totalLamps - amount
        }
    }
}
```

Chapter 3 - Swift Paradigm

```
var mystock = Stock()
do {
    try mystock.sold(amount: 8)
} catch Errors.OutOfStock {
    print("We do not have enough lamps")
}
```

Listing 3-190: Handling errors

This code expands the previous example to handle the error thrown by the **sold()** method. Because of the addition of the **try** keyword, the system tries to execute the **sold()** method in the **mystock** structure and check for errors. If the method returns the **OutOfStock** error, the statements inside the **catch** block are executed. This pattern allows us to respond every time there is an error and report it to the user or correct the situation without having to crash the app or produce unexpected results.

 IMPORTANT: You can add as many errors as you need to the **Errors** enumeration. The errors can be checked later with multiple **catch** statements. Also, you may add all the statements you need to the **do** block. The statements before **try** are always executed, while the statements after **try** are only executed if no error is found.

If the error is not one of the types we are expecting, we can print information about it. The information is stored in a constant called **error** that we can read inside the **catch** block.

```
enum Errors: String, Error {
    case OutOfStock = "Hello"
}
struct Stock {
    var totalLamps = 5
    mutating func sold(amount: Int) throws {
        if amount > totalLamps {
            throw Errors.OutOfStock
        } else {
            totalLamps = totalLamps - amount
        }
    }
}
var mystock = Stock()
do {
    try mystock.sold(amount: 8)
} catch {
    print(error)    // OutOfStock
}
```

Listing 3-191: Getting information about the error

On the other hand, if we do not care about the error, we can force the **try** keyword to return an optional with the syntax **try?**. If the method throws an error, the instruction returns **nil**, and therefore we can avoid the use of the **do catch** statements.

```
enum Errors: Error {
    case OutOfStock
}
struct Stock {
    var totalLamps = 5
    mutating func sold(amount: Int) throws {
        if amount > totalLamps {
            throw Errors.OutOfStock
```

```
      } else {
          totalLamps = totalLamps - amount
      }
    }
}
var mystock = Stock()
try? mystock.sold(amount: 8)    // nil
```

Listing 3-192: Catching errors with `try?`

The instruction at the end of Listing 3-192 returns the value **nil** if the method throws an error, or an optional with the value returned by the method if all goes well.

Sometimes, we know beforehand that a throwing method is not going to throw an error and therefore we want to avoid writing unnecessary code. In cases like this, we can use the syntax **try!**. For instance, the following code checks if there are enough lamps before calling the **sold()** method, so we know that the instruction will never throw the **OutOfStock** error.

```
enum Errors: Error {
    case OutOfStock
}
struct Stock {
    var totalLamps = 5
    mutating func sold(amount: Int) throws {
        if amount > totalLamps {
            throw Errors.OutOfStock
        } else {
            totalLamps = totalLamps - amount
        }
    }
}
var mystock = Stock()
if mystock.totalLamps > 3 {
    try! mystock.sold(amount: 3)
}
print("Lamps in stock: \(mystock.totalLamps)")
```

Listing 3-193: Ignoring the errors

(Medium) **Results**

Sometimes we need to return more than just an error. For this purpose, the Swift Standard Library defines the **Result** enumeration. This enumeration defines two cases with associated values to use in case of success or failure called **success()** and **failure()**. The **Result** enumeration is generic, which means that the data types of the associated values can be anything we want. For instance, in the following examples we define a **Result** enumeration of type **<Int, Errors>** to return an integer and the **OutOfStock** error defined in the previous example.

```
enum Errors: Error {
    case OutOfStock
}
struct Stock {
    var totalLamps = 5

    mutating func sold(amount: Int) -> Result<Int, Errors> {
        if amount > totalLamps {
            return .failure(.OutOfStock)
        } else {
            totalLamps = totalLamps - amount
```

```
            return .success(totalLamps)
      }
   }
}
var mystock = Stock()

let result = mystock.sold(amount: 3)
switch result {
   case .success(let stock):
      print("Lamps in stock: \(stock)")
   case .failure(let error):
      if error == .OutOfStock {
         print("Error: Out of Stock")
      } else {
         print("Error")
      }
}
```

Listing 3-194: Returning an error with a Result *enumeration*

The **sold()** method in Listing 3-194 now returns a **Result** value of type **<Int, Errors>**, so if an error occurs, the method can return a **failure()** value with the associated value **OutOfStock**, but if we have enough lamps to fulfill the order, we can return a **success()** value with the remaining number of lamps. The result can be processed by a **switch** statement. We check whether the value returned by the method is **failure()** or **success()**, get the associated value with a constant, and proceed accordingly. In this case, there are enough lamps available, so a message is printed on the console with the remaining stock.

Instead of using a **switch** statement, we can use the following method defined by the **Result** enumeration.

> ▷ **get()**—This method returns the associated value of the **success()** case or throws an error with the associated value of the **failure()** case.

The only purpose of the **get()** method is to simplify the code. Now, instead of a **switch** statement, we can use a **do catch**.

```
enum Errors: Error {
   case OutOfStock
}
struct Stock {
   var totalLamps = 5

   mutating func sold(amount: Int) -> Result<Int, Errors> {
      if amount > totalLamps {
         return .failure(.OutOfStock)
      } else {
         totalLamps = totalLamps - amount
         return .success(totalLamps)
      }
   }
}
var mystock = Stock()

let result = mystock.sold(amount: 2)
do {
   let stock = try result.get()
   print("Lamps in stock: \(stock)")
} catch Errors.OutOfStock {
   print("Error: Out of Stock")
}
```

Listing 3-195: Processing an error with the get() *method*

The result is the same, but now all we need to do is to call the `get()` method. If the method doesn't return an error, the remaining stock is printed on the console, otherwise, the `catch` block is performed, and an error is printed instead.

(Medium) **3.8 Property Wrappers**

Property wrappers are a tool provided by the Swift language that allows us to encapsulate functionality in a property. They are like the computed properties presented earlier (see Listing 3-40), but applicable to multiple properties. Like other Swift features, they are designed to simplify our code. For instance, we can define a property wrapper that limits the value of a property to a specific range. All properties declared with it will then only accept values between those limits.

A property wrapper is just a structure, but it must be preceded by the `@propertyWrapper` keyword and include a property with the name `wrappedValue` to process and store the property's value. The structure must also include an initializer for the `wrappedValue` property. The following example illustrates how to define a property wrapper that limits the value of a property to a minimum of 0 and a maximum of 255.

```
@propertyWrapper
struct ClampedValue {
    var storedValue: Int = 0
    var min: Int = 0
    var max: Int = 255

    var wrappedValue: Int {
        get {
            return storedValue
        }
        set {
            if newValue < min {
                storedValue = min
            } else if newValue > max {
                storedValue = max
            } else {
                storedValue = newValue
            }
        }
    }
    init(wrappedValue: Int) {
        self.wrappedValue = wrappedValue
    }
}
```

Listing 3-196: Defining a property wrapper

Listing 3-196 defines a property wrapper called `ClampedValue`. The structure contains three properties to store and control the value. The `storedValue` property stores the current value of the property, and the `min` and `max` properties determine the minimum and maximum values allowed for the properties defined with this property wrapper. There is also the required `wrappedValue` property, defined as a computed property with a getter and a setter. The getter returns the current value of the `storedValue` property, and the setter checks whether the new value is within the minimum and maximum allowed before storing it. If the new value exceeds any of these limits, the values of the `min` or `max` properties are assigned to the `storedValue` property accordingly.

The code in Listing 3-196 defines the property wrapper, but it doesn't define any property of this kind. Implementing a property wrapper is easy, we must declare the properties as we always do but preceded with the name of the property wrapper prefixed with the `@` character.

```
struct Price {
   @ClampedValue var firstPrice: Int
   @ClampedValue var secondPrice: Int

   func printMessage() {
      print("First Price: \(firstPrice)")   // "First Price: 0"
      print("Second Price: \(secondPrice)")   // "Second Price: 255"
   }
}
var purchase = Price(firstPrice: -42, secondPrice: 350)
purchase.printMessage()
```

Listing 3-197: Using a property wrapper

The **Price** structure in Listing 3-197 includes two properties that use the **ClampedValue** property wrapper, **firstPrice** and **secondPrice**, and a method to print their values. The instances of the structure are initialized with the values -42 and 350. Both values exceed the limits established by the property wrapper, so the value stored in each property is the limit they exceeded (0 for **firstPrice** and 255 for **secondPrice**).

(Medium) 3.9 Macros

Macros are a feature of the Swift programming language that frees developers from writing repetitive code. A macro automatically generates code and inserts it into our code before the application is compiled. All we have to do is include the macro, and then the system takes care of writing the code for us.

There are two types of macros: Freestanding macros and Attached macros. Freestanding macros insert code into an expression, such as those assigned to variables, while Attached macros modify a declaration, such as an enumeration, structure, or class. Freestanding macros are included in our code by prefixing the name with the # character, while Attached macros use the @ character. For example, below are some useful Freestanding macros defined by the Swift Standard Library.

▷ **#file**—This macro produces the name of the file.

▷ **#filePath**—This macro produces the path of the file.

▷ **#line**—This macro produces the line number in the code where the macro appears.

▷ **#function**—This macro produces the name of the function in which the macro appears.

The following example shows how to use these macros in our code.

```
func showMacros() {
   print("File Name \(#file)")   // "File Name MyPlayground.playground"
   print("File Path \(#filePath)")  // "File Name MyPlayground.playground"
   print("Line \(#line)")   // "Line 4"
   print("Function \(#function)")   // "Function showMacros()"
}
showMacros()
```

Listing 3-198: Implementing Freestanding macros

When the compiler finds a macro, the macro is executed, the code generated by the macro is inserted into our code, and then the application is compiled. For instance, when the compiler finds the `#file` macro, the macro gets the name of the file and adds it to the string in the `print()` function. After all the macros are processed, the code is compiled and executed.

 IMPORTANT: Macros are an advanced feature. They are included in Swift packages that can be shared with a team of developers or other programmers. You don't need to create your own macros to develop an application, but they are used extensively by Apple frameworks to simplify our work, as we will see in further chapters. If you want to know more about macros or learn how to create your own, visit our website and follow the links for this chapter.

Basic ## 4.1 Frameworks

The programming tools introduced in previous chapters are not enough to build professional applications. Creating an app requires accessing complex technologies and performing repetitive tasks that involve hundreds or even thousands of lines of code. Faced with this situation, developers have always implemented pre-programmed codes that perform common tasks. These pieces of code are organized according to their purpose in what we know as frameworks.

Frameworks are libraries (pre-programmed code) and APIs (Application Programming Interfaces) that we can use to add functionality to our applications. This includes managing databases, creating graphics on the screen, storing files, accessing resources on the web, sharing data online, and more. These frameworks are essential for building professional applications for Apple devices and are therefore part of the SDK (Software Development Kit) included with Xcode.

Do It Yourself: The examples in this chapter are designed for Playground. To see how they work, you need to create a Playground file with a Blank template, as in previous chapters, and then replace the code with the one you want to try.

Basic ## Importing Frameworks

The Swift Standard Library implemented in previous chapters is automatically loaded for us and available everywhere in our code, but when additional frameworks are required, we must tell the compiler what we need. This is done by adding the **import** instruction at the beginning of each file followed by the name of the framework we want to include (e.g., **import Foundation**). Once the framework is imported, it is included with our file, giving the code in that file access to all the structures, classes, functions, and any of the values defined by it.

Basic ## 4.2 Foundation

Foundation is one of the oldest frameworks provided by Apple. It was written in Objective-C and developed by Steve Jobs's second company NeXT. It was created to manage basic tasks and store data. The framework provides its own data types (structures and classes) to store any value we want, including numbers, strings, arrays and dictionaries, and a primary class called **NSObject** with basic functionality that every other class inherits from. Most of these definitions are now obsolete, replaced by Swift data types, but others remain useful, as we will see next.

Basic ## More Standard Functions

As we have seen in Chapter 3, the Swift Standard Library includes a few standard functions, such as **print()** and **abs()**, but others are provided by frameworks like Foundation. The following are some of the basic functions available when we import the Foundation framework.

▷ **pow(Float, Float)**—This function returns the result of raising the first value to the power of the second value. The arguments may be numbers of type **Float** or **Double**.

▷ **sqrt(Float)**—This function returns the square root of the value of its argument. The argument may be of type **Float** or **Double**.

▷ **log(Float)**—This function returns the natural logarithm of a value. Similar functions are **log2()**, **log10()**, **log1p()**, and **logb()**. It can take a value of type **Float** or **Double**.

- **sin(Float)**—This function returns the sine of a value. Similar functions are **asin()**, **sinh()**, and **asinh()**. The argument may be of type **Float** or **Double**.

- **cos(Float)**—This function returns the cosine of a value. Similar functions are **acos()**, **cosh()**, and **acosh()**. The argument may be of type **Float** or **Double**.

- **tan(Float)**—This function returns the tangent of a value. Similar functions are **atan()**, **atan2()**, **tanh()**, and **atanh()**. The argument may be of type **Float** or **Double**.

The application of these functions is simple, as shown in the following example.

```
import Foundation
let square = sqrt(4.0)
let power = pow(2.0, 2.0)
let maximum = max(square, power)
print("The maximum value is \(maximum)")   // "The maximum value is 4.0"
```

Listing 4-1: Applying math functions

The first thing we do in the code in Listing 4-1 is to import the Foundation framework. After this, we can implement any of the tools defined inside the framework, including the basic functions introduced above. This example gets the square root of 4.0, calculates 2.0 to the power of 2.0, and compares the results using the **max()** function from the Swift Standard Library.

Basic Strings

Foundation defines a class called **NSString** to store and manage strings of characters. The **String** structure offered by the Swift Standard Library for this same purpose adopts most of its functionality, turning the class obsolete, but because Swift coexists with old frameworks and data types, **NSString** objects are still required in some circumstances. The **NSString** class includes several Initializers to create these objects. The one usually implemented in Swift takes an argument called **string** with the string of characters we want to assign to the object.

```
import Foundation
var text: NSString = NSString(string: "Hello")
print(text)   // "Hello"
```

Listing 4-2: Creating an NSString object

If we already have a **String** value in our code, we can cast it into an **NSString** object with the **as** operator.

```
var text = "Hello World"
var newText = text as NSString
print(newText)   // "Hello World"
```

Listing 4-3: Casting a String value into an NSString object

A **String** structure can be turned into an **NSString** object with the **as** operator because they are interconnected. It is said that the **String** structure bridges with the **NSString** class. This means that we can access the functionality offered by the **NSString** class from a **String** structure, including the following properties and methods.

- **capitalized**—This property returns a string with the first letter of every word in uppercase.

▷ **length**—This property returns the number of characters in the string of an `NSString` object. (For `string` values, we should use the `count` property instead.)

▷ **localizedStringWithFormat(String, Values)**—This type method creates a string from the string provided by the first argument and the values provided by the second argument. The first argument is a template used to create the string, and the second argument is the list of values we want to include in the string separated by comma.

▷ **contains(String)**—This method returns a Boolean value that indicates whether or not the string specified by the argument was found inside the original string.

▷ **localizedStandardContains(String)**—This method returns a Boolean value that indicates whether or not the character or string specified by the argument is present in the string. It works like `contains()`, but the search is case-insensitive and local conventions, such as language, are taken into account.

▷ **components(separatedBy: String)**—This method divides the string by the separator specified by the **separatedBy** argument and returns an array with all the parts.

▷ **replacingOccurrences(of: String, with: String)**—This method returns a new string with all the strings that match the value specified by the **of** argument replaced by the string specified by the **with** argument.

▷ **trimmingCharacters(in: CharacterSet)**—This method erases the characters indicated by the **in** argument at the beginning and the end of the string and returns a new string with the result. The argument is a `CharacterSet` structure with type properties to select the type of characters to remove. The most frequently used are `whitespaces` (spaces) and `whitespacesAndNewlines` (spaces and new line characters).

▷ **compare(String, options: CompareOptions, range: Range?, locale: Locale?)**—This method compares the original string with the string provided by the first argument and returns an enumeration of type `ComparisonResult` with a value corresponding to the lexical order of the strings. The `orderedSame` value is returned when the strings are equal, the `orderedAscending` value is returned when the original string precedes the value of the first argument, and the `orderedDescending` value is returned when the original string follows the value of the first argument. The **options** argument is a property of the `CompareOptions` structure. The properties available are `caseInsensitive` (it considers lowercase and uppercase letters to be the same), `literal` (performs a Byte-to-Byte comparison), `diacriticInsensitive` (ignores diacritic marks such as the visual stress on vowels), `widthInsensitive` (ignores the width difference in characters that occurs in some languages), and `forcedOrdering` (the comparison is forced to return `orderedAscending` or `orderedDescending` values when the strings are equivalent but not strictly equal). The **range** argument defines a range that describes the portion of the original string we want to compare. Finally, the **locale** argument is a `Locale` structure that defines localization. Only the first argument is required.

▷ **caseInsensitiveCompare(String)**—This method compares the original string with the string provided by the argument. It works exactly like the `compare()` method but with the option `caseInsensitiveSearch` set by default.

▷ **range(of: String, options: CompareOptions, range: Range?, locale: Locale?)**—This method searches for the string specified by the first argument and returns a range to indicate where the string was found or `nil` in case of failure. The **options** argument is a property of the `CompareOptions` structure. The properties available for this method are the same we have for the `compare()` method, with the difference that we can specify three more: **backwards** (searches from the end of the string), **anchored** (matches characters only at the beginning or the end, not in the middle), and **regularExpression** (searches with a regular expression). The **range** argument defines a range that determines the portion of the original string where we want to search. Only the first argument is required.

As we already mentioned, the **String** structure is bridged to the **NSString** class and therefore we can call these methods from **String** values, but because they are defined in the **NSString** class, we still must import the Foundation framework to be able to use them. Some of them are like those offered by the **String** structure but allow us to perform additional operations on the values. For instance, we can incorporate values into strings with string interpolation, but the **localizedStringWithFormat()** method offers a different approach. This method takes a string with placeholders and replaces them with a list of values. The placeholders are declared with the **%** symbol followed by a character that represents the type of value we want to include. For example, if we want to replace the placeholder with an integer, we must use the characters **%d**.

```
var age = 44
var mytext = String.localizedStringWithFormat("My age is %d", age)
print(mytext)   // "My age is 44"
```

Listing 4-4: Creating a formatted string

There are different placeholders available. The most frequently used are **%d** for integers, **%f** for floating-point numbers, **%g** to remove redundant 0 (zeros), and **%@** for objects and structures. We can use any of these characters and as many times as necessary. This is like what we would get with string interpolation, but with this method we can also format the values. For instance, we can determine the number of digits a value will have by adding the amount before the letter.

```
let length = 12.3472
let total = 54
let decimals = String.localizedStringWithFormat("Decimals: %.2f", length)
let digits = String.localizedStringWithFormat("Digits: %.5d", total)
print(decimals)   // "Decimals: 12.35"
print(digits)   // "Digits: 00054"
```

Listing 4-5: Formatting numbers

The code in Listing 4-5 formats two numbers: a double and an integer. The double is processed with the %.2f placeholder, which means that the value is going to be rounded to two decimals after the point, and the integer is processed with the %.5d placeholder, which means that the number in the string is going to contain a total of five digits.

Other methods perform operations that are already available for **String** values, but they produce a more comprehensive result. For example, the **compare()** method compares strings like the == operator, but the returned value is not just **true** or **false**.

```
var fruit = "Orange"
var search = "Apple"
var result = fruit.compare(search)

switch result {
   case .orderedSame:
      print("Fruit and Search are equal")
   case .orderedDescending:
      print("Fruit follows Search")   // "Fruit follows Search"
   case .orderedAscending:
      print("Fruit precedes Search")
}
```

Listing 4-6: Comparing String values

The **compare()** method takes a string, compares it to the original string, and returns a **ComparisonResult** value to indicate the order. The **ComparisonResult** enumeration contains three values: **orderedSame**, **orderedDescending**, and **orderedAscending**. After comparing the values of the **fruit** and **search** variables in our example, the **result** variable contains one of these values according to the lexical order of the strings. In this case, the value "Orange" assigned to **fruit** is larger (follows alphabetically) the value "Apple" assigned to **search**, so the value returned is **orderedDescending** (the order is descending from **fruit** to **search**).

The **compare()** method implemented in Listing 4-6 and the == operator studied in Chapter 2 distinguish a lowercase string from an uppercase string. By adding an option to the **compare()** method, we can compare two strings without considering lowercase or uppercase letters.

```
var fruit = "Orange"
var search = "ORANGE"

var result = fruit.compare(search, options: .caseInsensitive)
switch result {
   case .orderedSame:
      print("The values are equal")   // "The values are equal"
   case .orderedDescending:
      print("Fruit follows Search")
   case .orderedAscending:
      print("Fruit precedes Search")
}
```

Listing 4-7: Comparing `String` *values with options*

The strings stored in the **fruit** and **search** variables in Listing 4-7 are different, but because of the **caseInsensitive** option, they are considered equal. This type of comparison is very common, which is why the class includes the **caseInsensitiveCompare()** method that all it does is calling the **compare()** method with the **caseInsensitive** option already set.

We can make a more precise comparison by specifying the range of characters we want to compare.

```
var phone = "905-525-6666"
var search = "905"

var start = phone.startIndex
var end = phone.firstIndex(of: "-")

if let endIndex = end {
   let result = phone.compare(search, options: .caseInsensitive, range:
start..<endIndex)
   if result == .orderedSame {
      print("The area code is the same")   // "The area code is the same"
   } else {
      print("The area code is different")
   }
}
```

Listing 4-8: Comparing only a range of characters

This example compares only the initial characters of a string to check the area code of a phone number. The code defines a range that goes from the first character of the **phone** variable to the position before the – character. This range is provided to the **compare()** method and in consequence the value of the **search** variable is compared against the first three characters.

We can also use ranges to search for strings using the **range()** method. This method searches for a string inside another string and returns a range that determines where the string was found.

```
var text = "The Suitcase is Black"
var search = "black   "
search = search.trimmingCharacters(in: .whitespacesAndNewlines)

var range = text.range(of: search, options: .caseInsensitive)
if let rangeToReplace = range {
   text.replaceSubrange(rangeToReplace, with: "Red")
}
print(text)   // "The Suitcase is Red"
```

Listing 4-9: *Searching and replacing characters in a string*

The **range()** method returns an optional value that contains the range where the string was found or **nil** in case of failure. In Listing 4-9, we search for the value of the **search** variable inside the **text** variable and check the optional value returned. When we have a range to work with (which means that the value was found) we use it to call the **replaceSubrange()** method of the **String** structure to replace the characters in the range with the word "Red" (see Listing 3-66). Note that because search values are usually provided by the user, we trim the value of the **search** variable with the **trimmingCharacters()** method to make sure that there are no space characters at the beginning or the end of the string (the two spaces after the word "black" are removed).

If what we want is to process the components of a string, like the area code and prefixes of a phone number, we can divide it with the **components(separatedBy:)** method. In the following example, we get the line number from a phone number by reading the last element of the array returned by the method.

```
let phone = "905-525-6666"
let elements = phone.components(separatedBy: "-")
print(elements.last!)   // "6666"
```

Listing 4-10: *Getting the components of a string*

Basic **Ranges**

Although Swift includes structures to store ranges of values, some frameworks programmed in Objective-C still implement an old Foundation class called **NSRange**. The **NSRange** class is slightly different than the **Range** structure. Instead of storing the initial and final values of the range, **NSRange** objects store the initial value and the length of the range. The following are some of the initializers provided by the **NSRange** class, as well as the initializers included in the **Range** structure to convert the values.

▷ **NSRange(Range)**—This initializer creates an **NSRange** object from a **Range** value.

▷ **NSRange(Range, in: String)**—This initializer creates an **NSRange** object to represent a **Range** structure with string indexes.

▷ **Range(NSRange)**—This initializer creates a **Range** structure from an **NSRange** value.

▷ **Range(NSRange, in: String)**—This initializer creates a **Range** structure to represent an **NSRange** object with string indexes.

The **NSRange** class includes two properties to retrieve the values: **location** and **length**. The following example initializes an **NSRange** object from a Swift range and prints its values.

```
import Foundation

let range = NSRange(4..<10)
print("Initial: \(range.location)")   // "Initial: 4"
```

```
print("Length: \(range.length)")   // "Length: 6"
```

Listing 4-11: Creating and reading an NSRange value

The initializer implemented in this example is for countable ranges. If we work with string indexes, we must use the initializer defined for strings. This is because the **String** structure works with Unicode characters while **NSString** objects work with a less comprehensive character encoding called *UTF-16*. Working with different character encodings means that the space the characters occupy in memory varies. A range that represents a series of characters in a **String** value may differ from a range that represents the same series of characters in an **NSString** value. The following example illustrates how to work with this initializer.

```
let text = "Hello World"
if let start = text.firstIndex(of: "W") {
    let newRange = NSRange(start..., in: text)
    print("Initial: \(newRange.location)")   // "Initial: 6"
    print("Length: \(newRange.length)")   // "Length: 5"
}
```

Listing 4-12: Converting a range of string indexes

Basic Numbers

Foundation offers a class called **NSNumber** to represent and store numbers. With the introduction of the Swift's primitive data types, the use of this class is no longer necessary, but there are a few old frameworks that still require these types of values. The class includes the following initializer.

▷ **NSNumber(value:** Value)—This initializer creates an **NSNumber** object with the value specified by the **value** argument. The argument may be a value of any of the data types available in Swift for numbers.

The class also provides properties to perform the opposite operation of retrieving Swift data types from **NSNumber** objects. The following are the most frequently used.

▷ **intValue**—This property returns an **Int** value with the object's number.

▷ **floatValue**—This property returns a **Float** value with the object's number.

▷ **doubleValue**—This property returns a **Double** value with the object's number.

The following example shows how to create **NSNumber** objects and how to get them back as Swift data types to perform operations.

```
import Foundation
var mynumber = NSNumber(value: 35)
var mydouble = mynumber.doubleValue * 2   // 70
```

Listing 4-13: Working with NSNumber objects

In addition to the data type, Foundation also provides the means to format numbers. Every time we print a number, all the digits are shown on the screen, including all the decimal digits. In Listing 4-5, we explained how to specify how many digits of a number we want to include in a string using placeholders (e.g., **%.2f**), but this is not customizable enough. To provide a better alternative, the framework includes the following formatting method that we can use with our Swift data types.

▷ **formatted(**FormatStyle)—This method formats the number according to the styles provided by the argument.

To format a number, we must call this method from the instance with the styles we want to apply to it. The styles are defined by a structure that conforms to the **FormatStyle** protocol. For numbers, the framework defines the **IntegerFormatStyle** and the **FloatingPointFormat-Style** structures. These structures include the following methods to style a number.

▷ **precision(**Precision**)**—This method defines the number of digits included in the integer and decimal parts of the number. The argument is a **Precision** structure, which includes the **integerLength(Int)** and **fractionLength(Int)** methods to specify the number of digits in the integer and decimal parts, and the **integerAnd-FractionLength(integer: Int, fraction: Int)** method to specify both.

▷ **rounded(rule:** FloatingPointRoundingRule**)**—This method rounds the number to the nearest value. The **rule** argument is an enumeration with the values **up**, **down**, **awayFromZero**, **toNearestOrAwayFromZero**, **toNearestOrEven**, and **towardZero**.

▷ **grouping(**Grouping**)**—This method determines if the digits of a number are going to be separated in groups (e.g., 9,000,000). The argument is a structure with the properties **automatic** (default) and **never**.

▷ **notation(**Notation**)**—This method determines the notation. The argument is a structure with the properties **automatic** (default), **compactName**, and **scientific**.

▷ **sign(strategy:** SignDisplayStrategy**)**—This method determines if the sign will be included (+ and -). The **strategy** argument is a **SignDisplayStrategy** structure, which includes the **automatic** (default) and **never** properties, and also the **always-(includingZero: Bool)** method to determine if the sign is displayed or not.

▷ **decimalSeparator(strategy:** DecimalSeparatorDisplayStrategy**)**—This method determines if a separator is going to be included after the number. The **strategy** argument is a structure with the properties **automatic** (default) and **always**.

The **FormatStyle** protocol defines the **number** property, which contains an instance of the **IntegerFormatStyle** or the **FloatingPointFormatStyle** structures, depending on the number's data type. From this instance, we can apply all the styles we want to a number.

```
let mynumber: Double = 32.56789
let text = mynumber.formatted(.number.precision(.fractionLength(2)))
print(text)  // "32.57"
```

Listing 4-14: Formatting a number

The styles are provided one by one with dot notation. We first get the styling structure from the **number** property. (In this case, the number is a **Double** so the value of the property is an instance of the **FloatingPointFormatStyle** structure.) Next, we call the **precision()** method, and send to this method the value returned by the **fractionLength()** method, which formats the number with 2 decimal digits. As a result, we get a string with the value "32.57" (the value is rounded up).

Styles can be concatenated, one after another, with dot notation. For instance, in the previous example, the number was rounded up by default, but we can change this behavior by applying the **rounded(rule:)** method, as shown below.

```
let mynumber: Double = 32.56789
let text =
mynumber.formatted(.number.precision(.fractionLength(2)).rounded(rule:
.down))
print(text)  // "32.56"
```

Listing 4-15: Rounding a number

In this example, the **rounded(rule:)** method is called after the number is formatted with 2 decimal digits, so the rest of the digits are rounded down.

The grouping, notation, and decimal separator styles usually apply to large numbers. For instance, by default, the digits of large numbers are separated in groups, as in 32,000,000, but we can change this behavior with the **grouping()** method.

```
let mynumber: Int = 32000000
let text = mynumber.formatted(.number.grouping(.never))
print(text)   // "32000000"
```

Listing 4-16: Disabling grouping

We can also show the sign in front of the number (+ or -). In the following example, we always show the sign except when the number is equal to 0.

```
let mynumber: Int = 32000000
let text =
mynumber.formatted(.number.sign(strategy: .always(includingZero: false)))
print(text)   // "+32,000,000"
```

Listing 4-17: Adding the sign

In addition to **number**, the **FormatStyle** protocol defines the **percent** property to style the number as a percentage, and the **currency(code:)** method to format monetary values. The **percent** property is a **Percent** structure that all it does is to add the % sign to the number.

```
let mynumber: Int = 32
let text = mynumber.formatted(.percent)
print(text)   // "32%"
```

Listing 4-18: Formatting the number as a percentage value

On the other hand, the **currency(code:)** method can produce a number with any format and currency symbol we want. The currency is defined by the string assigned to the **argument**. There are values for any currency available. For instance, the USD string is for American Dollars, the CAD string is for Canadian Dollars, EUR for Euros, and more. The following example gets the number expressed in Canadian dollars.

```
let mynumber: Double = 32.55
let text = mynumber.formatted(.currency(code: "CAD"))
print(text)   // "CA$32.55"
```

Listing 4-19: Formatting currency values

(Basic) **Dates**

Foundation defines multiple classes and structures to create and process dates, including **Date**, **Calendar**, **DateComponents**, **DateInterval**, **Locale**, and **TimeZone**. The data type in charge of creating the structure to store the actual date is **Date**. The following are some of the initializers.

▷ **Date()**—This initializer creates a **Date** structure with the current date.

▷ **Date(timeIntervalSinceNow:** TimeInterval)—This initializer creates a **Date** structure with a date calculated from the addition of the current date plus the time specified by the **timeIntervalSinceNow** argument. The argument is a value of type **TimeInterval** that indicates how many seconds the date is from the initial date.

▷ **Date(timeInterval:** TimeInterval, **since:** Date)—This initializer creates a **Date** structure with a date calculated from the addition of the date specified by the **since** argument plus the time specified by the **timeInterval** argument in seconds.

▷ **Date(timeIntervalSinceReferenceDate:** TimeInterval)—This initializer creates a **Date** structure with a date calculated from a reference date in the past plus the time interval in seconds specified by the argument.

The following example shows different ways to initialize a date.

```
import Foundation
var currentdate = Date()
var nextday = Date(timeIntervalSinceNow: 24 * 60 * 60)
var tendays = Date(timeInterval: -10 * 24 * 3600, since: nextday)
```

Listing 4-20: *Storing dates with* Date *structures*

If the initializer requires an interval, as those in the code in Listing 4-20, the value is specified in seconds. An easy way to calculate the seconds is by multiplying every component. For example, the date for the **nextday** object created in our example is calculated adding 1 day to the current date. The number of seconds in 1 day are calculated by multiplying the 24 hours of the day by the 60 minutes in an hour by the 60 seconds in a minute (24 * 60 * 60). For the **tendays** object, we apply the same technique. This initializer adds the interval to a specific date (**nextday**). The seconds are calculated by multiplying the components, albeit this time it multiplies the previous result by -10 to get a date 10 days before **nextday**. (We will see better ways to add components to a date next.)

 IMPORTANT: These methods require a value of type **Double** to declare the interval in seconds, but instead of **Double** the framework calls it **TimeInterval**. This is a typealias (an alternative name for an existing type). Once defined, aliases are used exactly like regular data types. To create your own type aliases, you can use the instruction **typealias** (e.g., **typealias Myinteger = Int**).

Besides the initializers, the class also includes type properties that return special dates. Some of these properties produce values that are useful to set limits and sort lists, as the following.

▷ **distantFuture**—This type property returns a **Date** structure with a value that represents a date in a distant future.

▷ **distantPast**—This type property returns a **Date** structure with a value that represents a date in a distant past.

The **Date** structure also includes properties and methods to calculate and compare dates. The following are the most frequently used.

▷ **timeIntervalSinceNow**—This property returns a **TimeInterval** value representing the difference in seconds between the date in the **Date** structure and the current date.

▷ **timeIntervalSinceReferenceDate**—This property returns a **TimeInterval** value representing the difference in seconds between the current date and a reference date in the past (In modern systems, this is January 1st, 2001). The structure also includes the **timeIntervalSince1970** property to return the interval between the current date and January 1st 1970.

▷ **compare(**Date**)**—This method compares the date in the **Date** structure with the date specified by the argument and returns an enumeration of type **Comparison-Result** with a value corresponding to the order of the dates. The possible values are orderedSame (the dates are the same), orderedAscending (the date is earlier than the value), and orderedDescending (the date is later than the value).

▷ **timeIntervalSince(Date)**—This method compares the date in the **Date** structure with the date specified by the argument and returns the interval between both dates in seconds.

▷ **addingTimeInterval(TimeInterval)**—This method adds the seconds specified by the argument to the date and returns a new **Date** structure with the result.

▷ **addTimeInterval(TimeInterval)**—This method adds the seconds specified by the argument to the date and stores the result in the same **Date** structure.

Comparing dates and calculating the intervals between dates is a constant requirement in app development. The following example compares the current date with a date calculated from a specific number of days. If the resulting date is later than the current date, the code prints a message on the console to show the time remaining in seconds.

```
var days = 7
var today = Date()
var event = Date(timeIntervalSinceNow: Double(days) * 24 * 3600)
if today.compare(event) == .orderedAscending {
    let interval = event.timeIntervalSince(today)
    print("We have to wait \(interval) seconds")
}
```

Listing 4-21: Comparing two dates

The dates in **Date** structures are not associated to any calendar. This means that to get the components in a date (year, month, day, etc.) we must decide first in the context of which calendar the date is going to be interpreted. The calendar for a date is defined by the **Calendar** structure. This structure provides properties and methods to process a date according to a specific calendar (Gregorian, Buddhist, Chinese, etc.). To initialize a **Calendar** structure, we have the following initializer and type property.

▷ **Calendar(identifier:** Identifier)—This initializer creates a **Calendar** structure with the calendar specified by the argument. The **identifier** argument is a property of a structure called **Identifier** defined inside the **Calendar** structure. The properties available are **gregorian, buddhist, chinese, coptic, ethiopicAmeteMihret, ethiopicAmeteAlem, hebrew, ISO8601, indian, islamic, islamicCivil, japanese, persian, republicOfChina, islamicTabular** and **islamicUmmAlQura**.

▷ **current**—This type property returns a structure with the current calendar set in the system.

A **Calendar** structure includes the following properties and methods to manage the calendar and to get and set new dates.

▷ **identifier**—This property returns the value that identifies the calendar.

▷ **locale**—This property sets or returns the **Locale** structure used by the **Calendar** structure to process dates. The value by default is the **Locale** structure set by the system.

▷ **timeZone**—This property sets or returns the **TimeZone** structure used by the **Calendar** structure to process dates. The value by default is the **TimeZone** structure set by the system.

▷ **dateComponents([Calendar.Component],** from: Date)—This method returns a **DateComponents** structure with the components indicated by the first argument from the date indicated by the **from** argument. The first argument is a set of enumeration values that represent the components we want to extract from the date. The values available are `era`, `year`, `yearForWeekOfYear`, `quarter`, `month`, `weekOfYear`, `weekOfMonth`, `weekday`, `weekdayOrdinal`, `day`, `hour`, `minute`, `second`, and `nanosecond`.

▷ **dateComponents(**[Calendar.Component], **from:** Date, **to:** Date)—This method returns a `DateComponents` structure with the components indicated by the first argument. These components represent the difference between the dates specified by the **from** and **to** arguments. The first argument is a set of enumeration values that represent each component. The values available are `era`, `year`, `yearForWeekOfYear`, `quarter`, `month`, `weekOfYear`, `weekOfMonth`, `weekday`, `weekdayOrdinal`, `day`, `hour`, `minute`, `second`, and `nanosecond`.

▷ **date(byAdding:** DateComponents, **to:** Date)—This method returns a `Date` structure with the value obtained by adding the components indicated by the **byAdding** argument to the date indicated by the **to** argument.

▷ **date(from:** DateComponents)—This method returns a date created from the components provided by the **from** argument.

The `Calendar` structure works along with the `DateComponents` structure to read and return components from a date. The instances created from the `DateComponents` structure include the properties `era`, `year`, `yearForWeekOfYear`, `quarter`, `month`, `weekOfYear`, `weekOfMonth`, `weekday`, `weekdayOrdinal`, `day`, `hour`, `minute`, `second`, and `nanosecond` to read and set the values of the components. The following example combines these tools to get the year of the current date.

```
var today = Date()
let calendar = Calendar.current
var components = calendar.dateComponents([.year], from: today)
print("The year is \(components.year!)")
```

Listing 4-22: Extracting components from a date

In Listing 4-22, we get a reference to the calendar set in the system from the **current** property and then use the **dateComponents()** method to get the year from the current date.

Several components may be retrieved at once by adding the corresponding values to the set. The following example gets the year, month, and day from the current date.

```
var today = Date()
let calendar = Calendar.current
var comp = calendar.dateComponents([.year, .month, .day], from: today)
print("Today \(comp.day!)-\(comp.month!)-\(comp.year!)")
```

Listing 4-23: Extracting multiple components from a date

`DateComponents` structures are used to retrieve the components of existing dates and to set the values for new dates. In the following example, a new `Date` structure is created from the values of a `DateComponents` structure.

```
let calendar = Calendar.current
var comp = DateComponents()
comp.year = 1970
comp.month = 8
comp.day = 21
var birthday = calendar.date(from: comp)   // "Aug 21, 1970, 12:00 AM"
```

Listing 4-24: Creating a new date from single components

Chapter 4 - Introduction to Frameworks

The **date(from:)** method of the **Calendar** structure returns a new date with the values provided by the **DateComponents** structure. The components which values are not explicitly defined take values by default (e.g., 12:00 AM).

Generating a new date requires a specific calendar. For example, in the code in Listing 4-24, the values of the components are declared with the format established by the Gregorian calendar. In this case, we rely on the calendar returned by the system, but if we want to use the same calendar no matter where the app is executed, we must set it ourselves from the **Calendar** initializer.

```
let id = Calendar.Identifier.gregorian
let calendar = Calendar(identifier: id)

var comp = DateComponents()
comp.year = 1970
comp.month = 8
comp.day = 13
var birthday = calendar.date(from: comp)   // "Aug 13, 1970 at 12:00 AM"
```

Listing 4-25: Using a Gregorian calendar

Declaring a specific calendar is not only recommended when creating new dates but also when calculating dates by adding components, as in the following example.

```
let id = Calendar.Identifier.gregorian
let calendar = Calendar(identifier: id)
var comp = DateComponents()
comp.day = 120

var today = Date()
var appointment = calendar.date(byAdding: comp, to: today)
```

Listing 4-26: Adding components to a date

The **date()** method implemented in Listing 4-26 adds components to a date and returns a new **Date** structure with the result. The component **day** was set to 120. The **date()** method takes this value, adds it to the date in the **today** structure, and returns the result.

A common task when working with multiple dates is getting the time between dates, such as the hours remaining for a process to complete or the days remaining for an event to begin. The **Calendar** structure includes a version of the **dateComponents()** method that allows us to compare two dates and get the difference expressed in a specific component.

```
let calendar = Calendar.current
var comp = DateComponents()
comp.year = 1970
comp.month = 8
comp.day = 21

var today = Date()
var birthdate = calendar.date(from: comp)

if let olddate = birthdate {
    let components = calendar.dateComponents([.day], from: olddate, to: today)
    print("Days between dates: \(components.day!)")
}
```

Listing 4-27: Comparing dates

This example calculates the days between a date of birth and the current date. The value returned by the **date()** method used to generate the date of birth returns an optional, so we unwrap it before calculating the difference. We assign this value to the **olddate** constant and then compare it with the current date. The number of days between dates is returned and printed on the console.

Another way to specify intervals between dates is with the **DateInterval** structure. This structure allows us to create an interval with **Date** values. The following are the initializers.

▷ **DateInterval(start:** Date, **end:** Date)—This initializer creates a **DateInterval** structure with the interval between the values provided by the **start** and **end** arguments.

▷ **DateInterval(start:** Date, **duration:** TimeInterval)—This initializer creates a **DateInterval** structure with an interval that starts at the date specified by the **start** argument and last as long as the time specified by the **duration** argument.

The **DateInterval** structure also offers the following properties and methods.

▷ **start**—This property sets or returns the initial **Date** of the interval.

▷ **end**—This property sets or returns the final **Date** of the interval.

▷ **duration**—This property sets or returns the duration of the interval in seconds.

▷ **contains(Date)**—This method returns a Boolean value that indicates whether the date specified by the argument is inside the interval or not.

▷ **intersects(DateInterval)**—This method returns a Boolean value that indicates if the interval intersects with the interval specified by the argument.

▷ **intersection(with:** DateInterval)—This method returns a **DateInterval** value with the interval in which the original interval and the one provided by the **with** argument overlap.

A typical use of the **DateInterval** structure is to create an interval from two dates and check if a specific date falls within the interval, as in the following example.

```
let calendar = Calendar.current
var components = DateComponents()
components.year = 1970
components.month = 8
components.day = 21
var birthday = calendar.date(from: components)

components.year = 2020
components.month = 8
components.day = 21
var future = calendar.date(from: components)
if birthday != nil && future != nil {
   let today = Date()
   let interval = DateInterval(start: birthday!, end: future!)
   if interval.contains(today) {
      print("You still have time")   // "You still have time"
   }
}
```

Listing 4-28: Finding a date in an interval

The code in Listing 4-28 creates two dates, **birthday** and **future**, and then generates an interval from one date to another. The **contains()** method is used next to check whether the current date is within the interval or not.

As with numbers, Foundation also provides the tools to format dates. The **Date** structure defines two versions of the **formatted()** method.

▷ **formatted(date:** DateStyle, **time:** TimeStyle)—This method formats the date with the styles specified by the arguments. The **date** argument defines the style for the date. It is a structure with the type properties **abbreviated, complete, long, numeric,** and **omitted.** And the **time** argument defines the style for the time. It is a structure with the type properties **complete, omitted, shortened,** and **standard.**

▷ **formatted(**FormatStyle**)**—This method formats the date with the styles specified by the argument.

If all we need is a standard format, we can call the **formatted(date:, time:)** method with the styles we want for the date and time. The method takes these values and returns a string with a date in the format defined by the current locale (the user's language and location).

```
let mydate = Date.now
let text = mydate.formatted(date: .abbreviated, time: .omitted)
print(text)  // "Jun 18, 2021"
```

Listing 4-29: Formatting dates

The code in Listing 4-29 gets the current date from the **now** property and then calls the method with the **abbreviated** and **omitted** values. This creates a string that contains an abbreviated date and no time ("Jun 18, 2021").

Standard styles include all the components of the date, but the **Date** structure includes an additional version of the **formatted()** method that takes a **FormatStyle** structure to format the date any way we want. The following are some of the methods included for customization.

▷ **day(**Day**)**—This method includes the day. The argument defines the style for the day. It is a structure with the properties **defaultDigits, ordinalOfDayInMonth,** and **twoDigits.**

▷ **month(**Month**)**—This method includes the month. The argument defines the style for the month. It is a structure with the properties **abbreviated, defaultDigits, narrow, twoDigits,** and **wide.**

▷ **year(**Year**)**—This method includes the year. The argument defines the style for the year. It is a structure with the properties **defaultDigits** and **twoDigits.**

▷ **hour(**Hour**)**—This method includes the hour. The argument defines the style for the hour. It is a structure with the properties **defaultDigitsNoAMPM** and **twoDigitsNoAMPM.**

▷ **minute(**Minute**)**—This method includes the minutes. The argument defines the style for the minutes. It is a structure with the properties **defaultDigits** and **twoDigits.**

▷ **second(**Second**)**—This method includes the seconds. The argument defines the style for the seconds. It is a structure with the properties **defaultDigits** and **twoDigits.**

▷ **weekday(**Weekday**)**—This method includes the weekday. The argument defines the style for the day. It is a structure with the properties **abbreviated, narrow, oneDigit, short, twoDigits,** and **wide.**

The **FormatStyle** structure includes the following properties to configure the parameters used to format the date.

▷ **calendar**—This property sets or returns the calendar used to format the date. It is of type **Calendar.**

▷ **locale**—This property sets or returns the locale used to format the date. It is of type **Locale.**

▷ **timeZone**—This property sets or return the time zone used to format the date. It is of type **TimeZone.**

Although we can create our own **FormatStyle** structure, the structure includes a type property called **dateTime** to return an instance with the calendar and standard values set by the device. If the configuration by default is enough, we can use this property to format the date.

```
let mydate = Date.now
let text = mydate.formatted(.dateTime.weekday(.wide))
print(text)   // "Friday"
```

Listing 4-30: Specifying a custom format

The code in Listing 4-30 calls the **weekday()** method from the **FormatStyle** structure returned by the **dateTime** property to get the day of the week. In this case, we call the method with the value **wide**, which returns the day's full name ("Friday"). Only one component is included in this example, but we can add more by concatenating the methods with dot notation, as we did before for numbers.

```
let mydate = Date.now
let text = mydate.formatted(.dateTime.day().hour().month(.wide))
print(text)   // "June 18, 6 PM"
```

Listing 4-31: Including multiple date components

In this code, we implement the **day()**, **month()**, and **hour()** methods. Note that the order in which the methods are called doesn't matter. The result is a string with a date that includes the month (full name), the day, and the hour ("June 18, 6 PM").

The date and time are always formatted with a standard format that depends on the user's locale (language and country). This is because the **formatted()** method processes dates according to local conventions, including the language, symbols, and more. This means that the components of a date are interpreted according to the conventions currently set on the device. For example, the same date will look like this "Tuesday, August 6, 2024" for a user in the United States and like this "2024年8月6日 星期二" for a user in China. How dates are processed is determined by an object of the **Locale** structure. Every device has a **Locale** structure assigned by default, and our code will work with it unless we determine otherwise. To get a reference to the current structure or create a new one, the **Locale** structure includes the following initializer and type property.

▷ **Locale(identifier:** String)—This initializer creates a **Locale** structure configured for the region specified by the argument. The argument is a string that represents a language and a region (e.g., en_US for the United States, zh_CN for China).

▷ **current**—This type property returns the **Locale** structure assigned by default to the device or defined by the user in the Settings app.

The **FormatStyle** structure includes the following method to format a date for a locale.

▷ **locale(**Locale)—This method specifies the locale to use by the formatter.

While it is recommended to use the **Locale** structure set by the system and keep the values by default, there are cases where our application must present the information with a specific configuration. For example, we may need to create an application that always displays dates in Chinese, regardless of where the user is located. We can do this by defining a **Locale** structure and then including the **locale()** method with this value in the formatter.

```
let mydate = Date.now
let chinaLocale = Locale(identifier: "zh_CN")
let text =
mydate.formatted(.dateTime.locale(chinaLocale).day().month().year())
```

```
print(text)   // "2024年6月18日"
```

Listing 4-32: Specifying a different locale

This example creates a new **Locale** structure with the zh_CN identifier, which corresponds to China and the Chinese language, and then formats the date with this locale and the **day()**, **month()**, and **year()** methods. The result is a string with the date in Chinese.

 IMPORTANT: The list of identifiers you can use to create a **Locale** structure is extensive. You can print the type property **availableIdentifiers** from the **Locale** structure to get an array with all the values available.

The date stored in a **Date** structure is not a date but the number of seconds between the date represented by the object and an arbitrary date in the past (January 1st, 2001). To process these values and get the actual date, the **Calendar** structure needs to know the user's time zone. Foundation includes the **TimeZone** structure to manage time zones. An object is assigned by default to the system containing the time zone where the device is located (that is why when we display a date it coincides with the date in our device), but we can define a different one as we did with the **Locale** structure. To get a reference to the current structure or create a new one, the **TimeZone** structure includes the following initializer and type property.

▷ **TimeZone(identifier: String)**—This initializer creates a **TimeZone** structure configured for the time zone determined by the value of the **identifier** argument. The argument is a string that represents the name of the time zone (e.g., "Europe/Paris", "Asia/Bangkok").

▷ **current**—This type property returns the **TimeZone** structure assigned by default to the device or defined by the user in the Settings app.

The **FormatStyle** structure does not include a method to provide a specific time zone to format the date. For this purpose, we must create a custom instance and then assign the time zone to the structure's **timeZone** property, as in the following example.

```
if let tokyoTimeZone = TimeZone(identifier: "Asia/Tokyo"), let
madridTimeZone = TimeZone(identifier: "Europe/Madrid") {
    let mydate = Date.now
    let mytime = mydate.formatted(.dateTime.hour().minute().second())

    var dateTimeStyle = Date.FormatStyle()
    dateTimeStyle.timeZone = tokyoTimeZone
    let tokyoTime =
mydate.formatted(dateTimeStyle.hour().minute().second())

    dateTimeStyle.timeZone = madridTimeZone
    let madridTime =
mydate.formatted(dateTimeStyle.hour().minute().second())

    print("My Time: \(mytime)")        // "My Time: 9:25:19 PM"
    print("Tokyo Time: \(tokyoTime)")  // "Tokyo Time: 10:25:19 AM"
    print("Madrid Time: \(madridTime)") // "Madrid Time: 3:25:19 AM"
}
```

Listing 4-33: Working with different time zones

The code in Listing 4-33 creates two **TimeZone** structures, one for Tokyo and another for Madrid. If successful, we initialize a **FormatStyle** structure and format the date twice, first for Tokyo and then for Madrid. Note that the **TimeZone** structure is assigned to the **timeZone** property of the **FormatStyle** structure before using it to format each date.

IMPORTANT: The list of names for the time zones is stored in a database. The **TimeZone** structure offers the **knownTimeZoneIdentifiers** type property that you can print to see all the values available.

(Medium) **Measurements**

Some applications require the use of units of measurement, such as pounds, miles, liters, and more. Defining our own units present some challenges, but Foundation includes the **Measurement** structure to simplify our work. This structure includes two properties, one for the value and another for the unit. The initializer requires these two values to create the structure.

▷ **Measurement(value: Double, unit: Unit)**—This initializer creates a **Measurement** structure with the values specified by the **value** and **unit** arguments. The **unit** argument is a property of a class that inherits from the **Dimension** class.

The value declared for the **Measurement** structure is a number that determines the magnitude, like 55 in 55 km, and the unit is a property of a subclass that inherits from the **Dimension** class and represents the unit of measurement, like km in 55 km. The **Dimension** class contains all the basic functionally required for measurement but is through its subclasses that the units of measurement are determined. Foundation offers multiple subclasses for this purpose. The following are the most frequently used.

▷ **UnitDuration**—This subclass defines the units of measurement for duration (time). It includes the following properties to represent the units: **seconds**, **minutes**, and **hours**, with **seconds** defined as the basic unit.

▷ **UnitLength**—This subclass defines the units of measurement for length. It includes the following properties to represent the units: **megameters**, **kilometers**, **hectometers**, **decameters**, **meters**, **decimeters**, **centimeters**, **millimeters**, **micrometers**, **nanometers**, **picometers**, **inches**, **feet**, **yards**, **miles**, **scandinavianMiles**, **lightyears**, **nauticalMiles**, **fathoms**, **furlongs**, **astronomicalUnits**, and **parsecs**, with **meters** defined as the basic unit.

▷ **UnitMass**—This subclass defines the units of measurement for mass. It includes the following properties to represent the units: **kilograms**, **grams**, **decigrams**, **centigrams**, **milligrams**, **micrograms**, **nanograms**, **picograms**, **ounces**, **pounds**, **stones**, **metricTons**, **shortTons**, **carats**, **ouncesTroy**, and **slugs**, with **kilograms** defined as the basic unit.

▷ **UnitVolume**—This subclass defines the units of measurement for volume. It includes the following properties to represent the units: **megaliters**, **kiloliters**, **liters**, **deciliters**, **centiliters**, **milliliters**, **cubicKilometers**, **cubicMeters**, **cubicDecimeters**, **cubicMillimeters**, **cubicInches**, **cubicFeet**, **cubicYards**, **cubicMiles**, **acreFeet**, **bushels**, **teaspoons**, **tablespoons**, **fluidOunces**, **cups**, **pints**, **quarts**, **gallons**, **imperialTeaspoons**, **imperialTablespoons**, **imperialFluidOunces**, **imperialPints**, **imperialQuarts**, **imperialGallons**, and **metricCups**, with **liters** defined as the basic unit.

The **Measurement** structure includes the following properties and methods to access the values and convert them to different units.

▷ **value**—This property sets or returns the structure's value. It is of type **Double**.

▷ **unit**—This property sets or returns the structure's unit of measurement. It is represented by a property of a subclass of the **Dimension** class.

▷ **convert(to: Unit)**—This method converts the values of the **Measurement** structure to the unit specified by the **to** argument.

▷ **converted(to:** Unit)—This method converts the values of the `Measurement` structure to the unit specified by the **to** argument and returns a new `Measurement` structure with the result.

The initialization of a **Measurement** structure is simple, we just need to provide the value for the magnitude and the property that represents the unit of measurement we want to use. The following example creates two structures to store a measurement of 30 centimeters and another of 5 pounds.

```
import Foundation
var length = Measurement(value: 30, unit: UnitLength.centimeters) //30.0 cm
var weight = Measurement(value: 5, unit: UnitMass.pounds)  // 5.0 lb
```

Listing 4-34: Initializing Measurement *structures*

If the measurements are of the same dimension (e.g., length), we can perform operations with their values. The **Measurement** structure allows the operations **+**, **−**, *****, **/**, and also the use of the comparison operators **==**, **!=**, **<**, **>**, **<=**, and **>=** to compare values. The following example adds two measurements in centimeters.

```
var length = Measurement(value: 200, unit: UnitLength.centimeters)
var width = Measurement(value: 800, unit: UnitLength.centimeters)
var total = length + width  // 1000.0 cm
```

Listing 4-35: Adding the values of two Measurement *structures*

If the units are different, the **Measurement** structure returned by the operation is defined with the dimension's basic unit. For example, if we are working with lengths, the basic unit is meters.

```
var length = Measurement(value: 300, unit: UnitLength.meters)
var width = Measurement(value: 2, unit: UnitLength.kilometers)
var total = length + width  // 2300.0 m
```

Listing 4-36: Adding two values of different units

The code in Listing 4-36 adds two lengths of different units (meters and kilometers). The system converts kilometers to meters and then performs the addition, returning a **Measurement** structure with a value in meters (the basic unit).

If we want everything to be performed in the same unit, we can convert a value to a different unit using the methods **convert()** or **converted()**. In the following example, we convert the unit of the **length** variable to kilometers and perform the addition again in kilometers.

```
var length = Measurement(value: 300, unit: UnitLength.meters)
var width = Measurement(value: 2, unit: UnitLength.kilometers)
length.convert(to: UnitLength.kilometers)
var total = length + width  // 2.3 km
```

Listing 4-37: Converting units

The values of a **Measurement** structure are printed as they are stored and with the units they represent, but this is usually not what we need to show to users. To prepare the value for display, the **Measurement** structure defines the **formatted()** method.

▷ **formatted(**FormatStyle)—This method formats the measurement with the styles specified by the argument.

This method requires a `FormatStyle` structure to format the value. The structure includes the following initializer and type method to create an instance for every type of unit.

▷ **FormatStyle(width:** UnitWidth, **locale:** Locale, **usage:** Measurement-FormatUnitUsage, **numberFormatStyle:** FloatingPointFormatStyle**)**—This initializer creates a `FormatStyle` structure with the format set by the arguments. The **width** argument specifies how the unit is going to be displayed. It is a structure with the properties **abbreviated**, **narrow**, and **wide**. The **locale** argument specifies the locale. The **usage** argument specifies the purpose of the measurement. The structure to declare this value includes properties for any type of measurement, including **asProvided** (UnitType), **food** (UnitEnergy), **general** (UnitType), **person**: (UnitLength), **personHeight** (UnitLength), **personWeight** (UnitMass), **road** (UnitLength), **weather** (UnitTemperature), and **workout** (UnitEnergy). Finally, the **numberFormatStyle** argument specifies the format of the value.

▷ **measurement(width:** UnitWidth, **usage:** Measurement-FormatUnit-Usage, **numberFormatStyle:** FloatingPointFormatStyle**)**—This method returns a `FormatStyle` structure with the format set by the arguments (the same required by the initializer).

The `FormatStyle` structure also includes an additional initializer and method specific to format temperatures.

▷ **FormatStyle(width:** UnitWidth, **locale:** Locale, **usage:** Measurement-FormatUnitUsage, **hidesScaleName:** Bool, **numberFormatStyle:** FloatingPointFormatStyle**)**—This initializer creates a `FormatStyle` structure with the format set by the arguments. The **width** argument specifies how the unit is going to be displayed. It is a structure with the properties **abbreviated**, **narrow**, and **wide**. The **locale** argument specifies the locale. The **usage** argument specifies the purpose of the measurement. The structure to declare this value includes properties for any type of measurement. The ones available at the moment are **asProvided** (UnitType), **food** (UnitEnergy), **general** (UnitType), **person** (UnitTemperature), **personHeight** (Unit-Length), **personWeight** (UnitMass), **road** (UnitLength), **weather** (UnitTemperature), and **workout** (UnitEnergy). The **hidesScaleName** argument determines if the name of the unit is going to be displayed, and the **numberFormatStyle** argument specifies the format of the value.

▷ **measurement(width:** UnitWidth, **locale:** Locale, **usage:** Measurement-FormatUnitUsage, **hidesScaleName:** Bool, **numberFormatStyle:** FloatingPointFormatStyle**)**—This method returns a `FormatStyle` structure with the format set by the arguments. The arguments are the same as the initializer.

Most of the arguments in these initializers and methods are optional. If an argument is not declared, the formatter uses values by default. For instance, if we just want to show the full name of the unit, we can implement the **measurement()** method with the **width** argument and the value **wide**.

```
let length = Measurement(value: 40, unit: UnitLength.kilometers)
let text = length.formatted(.measurement(width: .wide,
usage: .asProvided))
print(text)  // "40 kilometers"
```

Listing 4-38: Formatting a measurement

In this example, we have also included the **usage** argument with the **asProvided** value to tell the formatter to use the original units (kilometers). If this argument is not declared, the formatter uses the value by default, which formats the measurement with the configuration and locale set in the device. For example, if we specify the **road** value instead, the formatter will format the value to represent a distance using the device's locale, which for a device running in the United States means that the original value will be expressed in miles.

```
let length = Measurement(value: 40, unit: UnitLength.kilometers)
let text = length.formatted(.measurement(width: .wide, usage: .road))
print(text)   // "25 miles"
```

Listing 4-39: Formatting a measurement for a specific purpose

By default, the formatter rounds the number. That's why in this example the result of converting 40 kilometers to miles is 25, when it should've been 24.8548. If we want to specify a different format, we can add the **numberFormatStyle** argument and implement the methods provided by the `IntegerFormatStyle` and `FloatingPointFormatStyle` structures introduced before. For instance, we can specify a precision of 2 digits for the decimal part with the **fractionLength()** method, as shown below.

```
let length = Measurement(value: 40, unit: UnitLength.kilometers)
let text = length.formatted(.measurement(width: .wide, usage: .road,
numberFormatStyle: .number.precision(.fractionLength(2))))
print(text)   // "24.85 miles"
```

Listing 4-40: Formatting the measurement value

The **formatted()** method in this example includes the **width** argument to get the unit's full name, the **usage** argument to format the value to represent a distance, and the **numberFormatStyle** argument to format the value. The value is expressed in miles again, but with better accuracy.

If our application must always display a value with the same unit of measurement independently of the device's location, we can set a specific locale. The **formatted()** method doesn't include an **argument** to designate a locale, but the initializers included in the **FormatStyle** structure do. The following example formats the measurements in Chinese, no matter where the device is located.

```
let length = Measurement(value: 40, unit: UnitLength.kilometers)
let chinaLocale = Locale(identifier: "zh_CN")
var format = Measurement<UnitLength>.FormatStyle(width: .wide, locale:
chinaLocale, usage: .asProvided)
let text = length.formatted(format)
print(text)   // "40.00公里"
```

Listing 4-41: Formatting a measurement for a specific locale

The code in Listing 4-41 initializes a **FormatStyle** structure with the locale configured for China and then calls the **formatted()** method with this structure to format the value. Note that the **FormatStyle** structure is defined inside the **Measurement** structure, which is a generic structure and therefore we must specify the type of values the structure is going to process. In this case, we are working with units of length so we must specify the **UnitLength** data type.

(Medium) **Timer**

Timers are objects that perform an action after a specific period of time. There are two types of timers: repeating and non-repeating. Repeating timers perform the action and then reschedule themselves to do it again in an infinite loop. Non-repeating timers, on the other hand, perform the action one time and then invalidate themselves. Foundation defines the **Timer** class for this purpose. The class includes the following properties and methods to create and manage timers.

▷ **isValid**—This property returns a Boolean value that indicates if the timer can still be fired or it was invalidated.

▷ **timeInterval**—This property returns the time interval in seconds for repeating timers.

▷ **tolerance**—This property sets or returns a period of tolerance in seconds to provide the system with more flexibility. It is a value of type `TimeInterval`. The value by default is 0.

▷ **scheduledTimer(withTimeInterval:** TimeInterval, **repeats:** Bool, **block:** Closure)—This type method returns repeating and non-repeating timers depending on the values of its arguments. The **withTimeInterval** argument represents the seconds the timer must wait before performing the action, the **repeats** argument is a Boolean value that determines if the timer is repeating (`true`) or non-repeating (`false`), and the **block** argument is the closure to be execute when the time is up.

▷ **fire()**—This method fires the timer without considering the time remaining.

▷ **invalidate()**—This method invalidates the timer (stops the timer).

The `scheduledTimer()` method creates a timer according to the value of the arguments and automatically adds it to an internal loop that processes the timer when the time is up. The time is set in seconds with a `TimeInterval` value (a typealias of `Double`), and we can declare the closure as a trailing closure to simplify the code, as in the following example.

```
print("Wait 5 seconds...")
Timer.scheduledTimer(withTimeInterval: 5.0, repeats: false) { (timer) in
    print("The time is up")
}
```

Listing 4-42: Creating a non-repeating timer

The code in Listing 4-42 creates a non-repeating timer. It prints a message and then initializes a timer with the `scheduleTimer()` method. The timer is set to 5 seconds, non-repeating, and the closure just prints a message on the console. When we execute the code, the first message appears on the console and 5 seconds later the message "The time is up" is printed below.

The closure receives a reference to the `Timer` object that we can use to access the timer's properties or invalidate it. It was not required in the last example, but it may be useful when working with repeating timers, as in the following example.

```
import Foundation

nonisolated(unsafe) var counter = 0

func startTimer() {
    Timer.scheduledTimer(withTimeInterval: 1.0, repeats: true)
{ (timerref) in
        report(timer: timerref)
    }
}
func report(timer: Timer) {
    print("\(counter) times")
    counter += 1
    if counter > 10 {
        print("Finished")
        timer.invalidate()
    }
}
startTimer()
```

Listing 4-43: Creating a repeating timer

In this code, we define two functions. The **startTimer()** function schedules the timer, and the **report()** function is executed when the time is up. In this last function, we count how many times the code was executed with the **counter** variable and print a message on the console with the result. If the value is greater than 10, we print the text "Finished" and invalidate the timer, so the function is not executed anymore. (Repeating timers keep running indefinitely until they are invalidated.)

 IMPORTANT: Global variables can be modified from anywhere in the code, including different threads, which can produce a bug called data race. A data race is an error that occurs when two or more pieces of code try to modify a value at the same time. In this example, we know that the variable is only going to be modified from the closure assigned to the timer, so we prefix it with the **nonisolated(unsafe)** keyword to tell the system that we are going to take care of the issue ourselves. We will learn more about data races and how to avoid them in Chapter 9.

(Medium) 4.3 Regular Expressions

With the methods provided by Foundation and the **String** data type, we can modify a string, remove or insert a string from another one, and determine whether a string contains another string, or the characters match a specific pattern, such as an email address. For simple patterns, like finding a word at the beginning or the end of the string, these tools are more than enough, but determining if a string represents a phone number, an email address, or extracting the values of more complex structures like the content of a spreadsheet, requires looping through the characters one by one and comparing them with previous characters to recognize valid or invalid patterns. This process is generally cumbersome and error-prone. To simplify our work, Swift implements regular expressions.

A regular expression is a sequence of characters that represent the pattern we want to identify in a string. It consists of common characters that match the characters in the string one by one, and also special characters that describe specific patterns or matches. For example, the expression **/message/** matches any string that contains the word "message". However, if we add the special characters **\s+** at the end (**/message\s+/**), the regular expression matches a string containing the word "message" followed by one or more spaces.

To differentiate special characters from common characters, they are preceded by a backward slash, as in **\s** (the s represents a white space). There are dozens of special characters to represent anything we need. The following are the most frequently used.

- **\s** and **\t** match a whitespace. The **\s** character matches any whitespace character, and the **\t** character matches only tab characters.
- **\d** matches a digit (any number from 0 to 9).

To match a character from a group of characters, regular expressions include the following special characters.

- **[ ]** matches any character in the square brackets (e.g., **[abc]** matches the character **a** or **b** or **c**). It can also match a character in a range of consecutive characters. The range is defined with a hyphen, as in **[a-z]** to match a lowercase letter from **a** to **z**, or **[a-zA-Z]** to match a lowercase or uppercase letter from **a** to **z**.
- **[^]** matches any character different from those in the square brackets (e.g., **[^abc]** matches any character that is not **a** or **b** or **c**).
- **.** (dot) matches any character except a new line (new lines are represented by the special character **\n**).
- **|** (or) matches the character on the left or the right (e.g., **a|b** matches the character **a** or the character **b**).

These special characters match a single character. To specify quantity, regular expressions include the following.

- * specifies 0 or more occurrences of the previous character.
- + specifies 1 or more occurrences of the previous character.
- ? specifies 0 or 1 occurrences of the previous character.
- {min, max} specifies the minimum and maximum occurrences of the previous character (e.g., {3, 5} matches 3, 4, or 5 characters). If the maximum value is ignored, the expression matches the character at least the times specified by the minimum value (e.g., {2,} matches the character at least two times). And if only one value is declared, the expression matches the character exactly the times specified by the value (e.g., {2} matches the characters only two times).

There are also special characters to delineate the expression. The following are the most frequently used.

- ^ matches the beginning of the string.
- $ matches the end of the string.
- () define a subexpression (useful when we want to capture the value).

Regular expressions are defined by a combination of these special characters and also common characters, as we have seen before. For instance, if we have a string like "Name: John" and we want to know whether the string contains any name, we can match it against the regular expression /Name:\s+[a-zA-Z]+/. The slashes at the beginning and the end are the way to tell Swift that this is a regular expression. The string "Name:" matches exactly the same sequence of characters in the original string. The \s+ characters tell the system that the string "Name:" must be followed by one or more spaces. And the [a-zA-Z]+ characters indicate that after the space there should be one or more lowercase or uppercase letters. If the original string doesn't contain the string "Name:" followed by one or more spaces and one or more letters, we won't get a match.

To match the regular expression against a string, the Swift Standard Library includes the following methods.

▷ **firstMatch(of:** Regex)—This method finds the first sequence of characters in the string that match the regular expression specified by the **of** argument.

▷ **wholeMatch(of:** Regex)—This method matches the whole string against the regular expression.

▷ **prefixMatch(of:** Regex)—This method matches the beginning of the string against the regular expression.

▷ **matches(of:** Regex)—This method finds all the sequences of characters in the string that match the regular expression.

These methods take a value of type **Regex** (a structure defined to contain a regular expression) and return a value of type **Match** if a match is found or **nil** otherwise. The **Match** structure contains two properties: **output** with the strings that matched the regular expression, and **range** with a **Range** value that represents the range of the overall match.

For example, the following code processes the string and regular expression introduced before with the **firstMatch()** method to check if the string contains a name.

```
let message = "Name: John"
let regex = /Name:\s+[a-zA-Z]+/

if let match = message.firstMatch(of: regex) {
    let found = match.output
```

```
    print("Found: \(found)")   // "Found: Name: John"
}
```

Listing 4-44: Using regular expressions

This code defines a regular expression and assigns it to a constant. The compiler detects that the value is a regular expression and creates a **Regex** structure with it. Next, the **firstMatch()** method matches the string in **message** against the regular expression and returns a value with the result. In this case, the string contains the string "Name:" followed by one or more spaces and one or more letters, so the match is successful. The part of the string that matches the regular expression is assigned to the **output** property of the **Match** structure returned by the method, so we assign it to a constant and print it on the console.

 IMPORTANT: Declaring the regular expression between slashes, as we did in our example, allows Xcode to recognize it and provide feedback. If the expression is invalid, it is displayed in a single color, otherwise, the special characters are highlighted. This is the recommended notation in Swift, but the language provides others. For instance, we can create the **Regex** structure directly with the structure's initializer and the regular expression in quotes. Swift also allows us to declare the regular expression using different syntaxes, including an extended syntax that can be used to provide names and define the data types of the values we captured. For more information, visit our website and follow the links for this chapter.

The values returned in the **Match** structure depend on the expression. In the previous example, the **output** property returns a single string with the sequence of characters that match the regular expression, but we can define subexpressions to capture specific values. For instance, if we want to get back the name, we can define a subexpression with parentheses.

```
let message = "Name: John"
let regex = /Name:\s+([a-zA-Z]+)/

if let match = message.firstMatch(of: regex) {
   let found = match.output.1
   print("The name is: \(found)")   // "The name is: John"
}
```

Listing 4-45: Capturing values with subexpressions

In this example, the **output** property returns a tuple. The first element of the tuple is the string that matches the regular expression, as before, but the second value is the string that matches the expression between parentheses. (In this case, one or more letters after a space.)

The **firstMatch()** method finds the first sequence of characters that match the regular expression and returns that value. If we want to get all the matches in a string, we must implement the **matches()** method.

```
let message = "Name: John, Name: George, Name: David"
let regex = /Name:\s+([a-zA-Z]+)/

let matches = message.matches(of: regex)
if !matches.isEmpty {
   let names = matches.map({ value in
      return value.output.1
   })
   let list = names.joined(separator: ", ")
   print("Names are: \(list)")   // "Names are: John, George, David"
}
```

Listing 4-46: Capturing multiple values

The `matches()` method returns an array of `Match` structures. Again, we use a subexpression to capture the names, so we loop through the array with the `map()` function, return the name from each match, and then join them with the `joined()` method to get the list of names separated by comma.

The Swift Standard Library includes a few more methods to take advantage of regular expressions. The following are the most frequently used.

▷ **split(separator: Regex)**—This method divides a string by a separator and returns an array with the parts. The **separator** argument specifies the regular expression that matches the characters used to split the string.

▷ **replacing(Regex, with: String)**—This method replaces the sequence of characters that match the regular expression specified by the first argument with the string specified by the **with** argument.

The `split()` method is useful when we have to process long texts or a text file line by line. In the following example, we use triple quotes to tell the compiler to add the characters \n after each line of text to generate a new line (see Listing 2-24). This is how usually text documents are structured. To read each line, we define a regular expression with the special character \n and then call the `split()` method to get each line of text in an array.

```
let message = """
John
George
Martin
"""
let separator = /\n/
let lines = message.split(separator: separator)
print(lines)  // ["John", "George", "Martin"]
```
Listing 4-47: Processing multiple lines of text with a regular expression

The `replacing()` method could be implemented in a similar way, but instead of using the regular expression as a separator, we can use it to replace the sequence of characters with another one. For example, we can replace each new-line character in our string (\n) with a comma to get all the lines of text in a single string.

```
let message = """
John
George
Martin
"""
let separator = /\n/
let result = message.replacing(separator, with: ", ")
print(result)  // "John, George, Martin"
```
Listing 4-48: Replacing the characters that match a regular expression

 IMPORTANT: This introduction to regular expressions only scratches the surface. The topic is beyond the scope of this book. For more information, visit our website and follow the links for this chapter.

Basic 4.4 Core Graphics

Core Graphics is an old framework programmed in the C language. It was developed to provide a platform-independent two-dimensional drawing engine for Apple systems. The framework is composed of drawing tools and its own data types. Due to its characteristics, instead of being replaced, the framework was integrated with newer frameworks and, therefore, it remains in use.

(Basic) **Data Types**

What modern applications require the most from this old framework are its data types. In Swift, Core Graphics' data types are implemented as structures, with their own initializers, properties, and methods. They can store values that represent attributes of elements on the screen, such as position or size. For instance, the following is the structure used to specify coordinate values.

▷ **CGFloat**—This structure is used to store values of type `Double` for drawing purposes.

A more complex structure is `CGSize`, designed to store values that represent dimensions (width and height). This data type includes the following initializer and properties.

▷ **CGSize(width:** CGFloat, **height:** CGFloat)—This initializer creates a `CGSize` structure with the values specified by the **width** and **height** arguments. The structure defines initializers to create instances from values of type `Int`, `CGFloat`, and `Double`.

▷ **zero**—This type property returns a `CGSize` structure with its values set to zero.

▷ **width**—This property sets or returns the structure's width.

▷ **height**—This property sets or returns the structure's height.

Another structure included in the framework is `CGPoint`, which is used to define points in a two-dimensional coordinate system. It includes the following initializer and properties.

▷ **CGPoint(x:** CGFloat, **y:** CGFloat)—This initializer creates a `CGPoint` structure with the coordinates specified by the **x** and **y** arguments. The structure defines initializers to create instances from values of type `Int`, `CGFloat`, and `Double`.

▷ **zero**—This type property returns a `CGPoint` structure with its values set to zero.

▷ **x**—This property sets or returns the structure's x coordinate.

▷ **y**—This property sets or returns the structure's y coordinate.

There is also a more complex structure called `CGRect` that we can use to define and work with rectangles. This data type includes the following initializers and properties.

▷ **CGRect(origin:** CGPoint, **size:** CGSize)—This initializer creates a `CGRect` structure to store the origin and size of a rectangle. The **origin** argument is a `CGPoint` structure with the coordinates of the rectangle's origin, and the **size** argument is a `CGSize` structure with the rectangle's width and height.

▷ **CGRect(x:** CGFloat, **y:** CGFloat, **width:** CGFloat, **height:** CGFloat)—This initializer creates a `CGRect` structure to store the origin and size of a rectangle. The **x** and **y** arguments define the coordinates of the rectangle's origin, and the **width** and **height** arguments its size. The structure defines initializers to create instances from `Int`, `CGFloat`, and `Double` values.

▷ **zero**—This type property returns a `CGRect` structure with its values set to zero.

▷ **origin**—This property sets or returns a `CGPoint` structure with the coordinates of the rectangle's origin.

▷ **size**—This property sets or returns a `CGSize` structure with the width and height.

▷ **midX**—This property returns the value of the rectangle's **x** coordinate located at the horizontal center of the rectangle. The framework also include the `minX` and `maxX` properties to return the smallest and largest value in the x-coordinate for the rectangle.

▷ **midY**—This property returns the value of the rectangle's **y** coordinate located at the vertical center of the rectangle. The framework also include the `minY` and `maxY` properties to return the smallest and largest value in the y-coordinate for the rectangle.

The structures provided by Core Graphics are declared and initialized as any other structures in Swift, but we must import the Core Graphics framework first for the types to be recognized.

```
import CoreGraphics
var myfloat: CGFloat = 35
var mysize: CGSize = CGSize(width: 250, height: 250)
var mypoint: CGPoint = CGPoint(x: 20, y: 50)
var myrect: CGRect = CGRect(origin: mypoint, size: mysize)
```

Listing 4-49: Initializing Core Graphics' structures

The **CGSize** and **CGPoint** structures may be initialized with their member initializers, but the **CGRect** structure provides an additional initializer to create the instance from the values of its internal structures.

```
import CoreGraphics
var myrect = CGRect(x: 30, y: 20, width: 100, height: 200)
print("The origin is at \(myrect.origin.x) and \(myrect.origin.y)")
print("The size is \(myrect.size.width) by \(myrect.size.height)")
```

Listing 4-50: Using the CGRect convenience initializer

The **origin** and **size** properties of a **CGRect** value are **CGPoint** and **CGSize** structures, respectively, so they can be copied into other variables or properties as any other values.

```
import CoreGraphics
var myrect = CGRect(x: 30, y: 20, width: 100, height: 200)
var mypoint = myrect.origin
var mysize = myrect.size
print("The origin is at \(mypoint.x) and \(mypoint.y)")
print("The size is \(mysize.width) by \(mysize.height)")
```

Listing 4-51: Accessing the structures inside a CGRect structure

When we don't have initial values for the coordinates or the size, we can use the **zero** type property to create a structure with all the values initialized to 0.

```
import CoreGraphics
var myrect = CGRect.zero
print("The origin is at \(myrect.origin.x) and \(myrect.origin.y)")
print("The size is \(myrect.size.width) by \(myrect.size.height)")
```

Listing 4-52: Assigning empty structures to a CGRect variable

The **myrect** variable in Listing 4-52 is a **CGRect** structure with all its properties initialized with the value 0. Assigning the value of the **zero** property to a variable is the same as using the initializer **CGRect(x: 0, y: 0, width: 0, height: 0)**.

The **CGRect** structure also includes properties to calculate values from the coordinates and size. For example, the **midX** and **midY** properties return the coordinates at the center.

```
import CoreGraphics
var rect = CGRect(x: 0, y: 0, width: 100, height: 100)
print("The horizontal center is \(rect.midX)")   // 50.0
```

Listing 4-53: Calculating the coordinate at the center of the rectangle

Chapter 4 - Introduction to Frameworks

Chapter 5
SwiftUI Framework

Basic **5.1 Xcode**

Until now, we have been using a simplified interface known as Playground. Playground was created to make learning easier and allow developers to experiment with code. However, to develop fully functional applications, we need to transition to the main Xcode interface. This interface offers a comprehensive set of tools, including an editor, a canvas to display previews, resource management, configuration panels, and debugging tools. All these features are integrated into one workspace, enabling us to build our applications efficiently.

Basic **Projects**

Applications are built from several files and resources, including our own codes, frameworks, images, databases, and more. Xcode organizes this information in projects. An Xcode project includes all the information and resources necessary to create an application. The welcome window, illustrated in Figure 1-2, presents a button called *Create a new Xcode project* to initiate a project. When we click this button, a window appears to select the type of project we want to create.

Figure 5-1: *Selecting the type of project*

The project window includes options to create applications for every Apple device and operating system, including iOS for iPhones and iPads, macOS for Mac computers, watchOS for the Apple Watch, tvOS for Apple TV, and visionOS for Apple Vision Pro. With the introduction of SwiftUI, we can now create apps for each device using the same framework, and therefore there is an additional option called Multiplatform. A Multiplatform project is set up to create an application for iPhones, iPads and Mac computers using SwiftUI (although we can add more platforms later). All we need to do is to open the Multiplatform section and select the App option, as shown in Figure 5-1. Once this option is selected, we must configure the project, as shown below.

Figure 5-2: *Project configuration window*

The Product Name is the name of the project. By default, this is the name of our application, so we should enter a value that is appropriate to show to our users (we can change it later if needed). The next field is the Team's account. This is the developer account created with our Apple ID or our company's account. If we haven't yet registered our account with Xcode, we will see the Add Account button to add it. The next value is the Organization Identifier. Xcode uses this value to create a unique identifier for our app, so it is recommended to specify it with an inverted domain, as we have done in our example (com.formasterminds). Using the inverted domain ensures that only our app has this identifier. Next, there is a drop-down menu to select the Testing System. This is the system we want to use to test our application. Automatic tests are not usually necessary for small applications, but they are useful when developing large applications or working with a team. There are two options available: the traditional system called XCTest and a system specifically designed for Swift called Swift Testing. In the next drop-down menu, we can select the system we want to use to store information permanently on the device. There are two options available: SwiftData and Core Data. Code Data is a system that provides low-level tools for storing information in a database. SwiftData, on the other hand, is a modern system that simplifies working with a Code Data database for applications developed in SwiftUI. Selecting either of these options will generate sample code showing how to work with one system or the other. Finally, there is a checkbox at the bottom called Host in CloudKit to configure the application to automatically share information between devices.

As mentioned above, the option to specify the Team shows a list of developer accounts registered with Xcode. If we haven't yet inserted our account, we will see the Add Account button instead. Pressing this button opens Xcode preferences and a window to insert our Apple ID. (This is the same ID used to initialize our computer, but we can create a new one if necessary.)

Figure 5-3: *Registering our Apple account in Xcode*

Once we have entered our Apple ID, the Apple account is configured to work with our copy of Xcode and we can select it from the list. With the account selected and all the information inserted in the form, we can now click Next to select the folder where we want our project to be saved. Xcode creates a folder for each project, so all we have to do is select the destination folder where we want to save all our projects and everything else will be created for us.

Do It Yourself: Open Xcode. In the welcome screen, click on the option Create New Project (Figure 1-2). You can also go to the File menu at the top of the screen and select the options New/Project. After this, you should see the window to create the project (Figure 5-1). Select the Multiplatform tab, click on the App icon, and press Next. Now you should see a form like the one in Figure 5-2. In Product Name, Insert the name of your application. In the Team option, select your developer account or press the Add Account button to add it to Xcode. In Organization Identifier insert the inverted domain of your website. Select None for the Testing System and Storage options (see Figure 5-2). Press Next and select a folder where to store the project.

IMPORTANT: Although it's not mandatory, you should get your own domain and website. Apple not only recommends the use of an inverted domain to generate the Bundle Identifier, but at the time of submitting your app to the App Store you will be asked to provide the web page used for promotion and where the users should go for support (see Chapter 21).

Chapter 5 - SwiftUI Framework

Once the project is created, Xcode generates some files according to the selected template and presents the main interface on the screen. Figure 5-4 shows what this interface looks like.

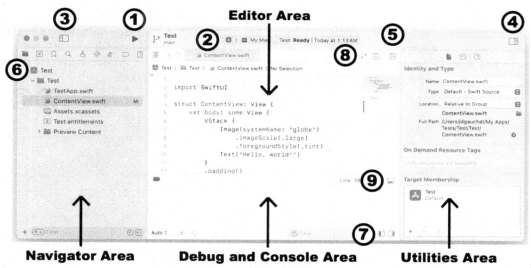

Figure 5-4: *Xcode's interface*

Like the Playground interface, the Xcode's main window is organized in several areas. There is a toolbar at the top, an area to edit the files at the center called *Editor Area*, and three removable panels on the sides called *Navigator Area*, *Debug and Console Area*, and *Utilities Area*.

Toolbar

This is the area at the top with buttons to control the appearance of the interface, and a display to show warnings, errors, and the status of the app. It provides buttons to run and stop the app (number 1), a drop-down list to select the device or the simulator where we want to run the app (number 2), a button that opens a popup window with tools to create the user interface (number 5), and two buttons to show or hide the removable panels (number 3 and number 4).

Navigator Area

This is a removable area that provides information about the files that comprise the application and tools for debugging (identify and remove errors in the code). From here, we can select the files to edit, create groups to organize them, add resources, check for errors, and more. In addition to the files, this area shows an option at the top to configure the app (number 6).

Editor Area

This is the only non-removable area and is the one where we will do much of the work. The content of files and configuration panels are displayed here. Although the Editor Area cannot be removed, it includes buttons at the top to split the area into multiple editors or panels, as we will see later (number 8).

Debug and Console Area

This is a removable area with two sections. The section on the left provides information for debugging, while the section on the right displays the results of the execution of our code, including warnings and errors. The panel can be shown or hidden from the button at the top-right corner (number 9), and each section can be shown or hidden from the buttons at the bottom-right corner (number 7).

Utilities Area

This is a removable area that provides additional information about the app and tools to edit the interface.

Editor Area

The Editor Area is the only non-removable area in the interface. By default, this area always displays the content of the selected file, but we can modify the layout from the buttons in the upper right corner (Figure 5-4, number 8). The button on the right adds more editor panels to the area (Figure 5-5, number 2). New editors are placed on the right side of previous editors, but we can place them below by pressing and holding the Option key. Figure 5-5, below, shows what we see when we press the Add Editor button. Two editors are shown side by side.

Figure 5-5: Multiple editors in the Editor Area

These inner panels are useful when we need to edit two or more files at the same time. We can divide each editor as many times as we want, resize them by dragging the lines between them, and close them by pressing the X button in the upper left corner.

On the other hand, the button on the left (Figure 5-5, number 1) shows a popup menu with options to expand the editor, as shown below.

Figure 5-6: Adjust Editor Options

In SwiftUI, the most useful options are the Canvas, the Layout, and the Minimap. The Canvas option displays a panel where we can see a preview of the views as they are created, the Layout option allows us to place the preview on the right or at the bottom of the code, and the Minimap option shows a visual representation of our code that we can use for reference and navigation.

Figure 5-7: Editor panel

Chapter 5 - SwiftUI Framework

In addition to the previews offered by the Canvas, there are two other ways to run and test our application: the simulator and a real device. The buttons to select these options, run and stop the application, are located on the toolbar (Figure 5-4, number 1 and number 2).

Applications always run on a specific destination and can have different configurations called *Schemes*. The destination could be multiple things, from real devices to windows or simulators, and the scheme defines things like the region where the device is located, or the human language used by the app to display the information on the screen. To set the scheme and destination, Xcode's toolbar includes two buttons (Figure 5-4, number 2). If we click on the button on the left (the one with our app's name), a menu appears with options to edit the current scheme, create a new one, or select the one we want to use.

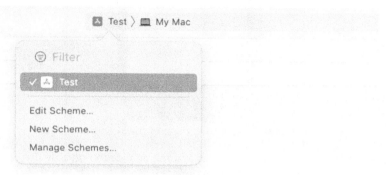

Figure 5-8: Scheme menu

On the other hand, the button on the right allows us to select the destination. The Multiplatform template includes a target configured to create an application for iPhones, iPads, and Mac computers. Therefore, when we want to run our application, all we need to do is to click this button to open the drop-down list (Figure 5-4, number 2) and select a simulator or a device.

Figure 5-9: Options available to run the app

After the destination is selected, we can press the Play button to run the application (Figure 5-4, number 1). If we use a simulator, a new window opens where we can see our app and interact with it, as shown below.

Figure 5-10: App running in the simulator

The simulator works out of the box, but to run the application on a device, we must connect the device to the computer with a USB cable, select it from the list, and then open the Settings app on the device, select the Privacy & Security option, open the Developer Mode option at the bottom, and turn Developer Mode on, as shown below.

Figure 5-11: Developer mode

 Do It Yourself: If you haven't done it yet, create a Multiplatform project with the App template following the steps described above. From the toolbar, select an iPhone simulator (Figure 5-9). Press the Play button to run the app (Figure 5-4, number 1). You should see the simulator on the screen with an icon and the text "Hello World" at the center (Figure 5-10).

 IMPORTANT: The option to select the simulator or the device (Figure 5-9) is also used by Xcode to determine the tools available to program the application. Some tools are available for some systems and not for others. Therefore, you should always select the system for which you are developing the application. For example, if you are developing an application for iOS, you should select an iPhone or iPad simulator, but if you are developing an application for Mac computers, you should select the My Mac option. We will learn how to create applications for Mac computers in Chapter 19.

The app's configuration is stored on a target. The target includes things like the app's name and version, the systems it will support, and the capabilities the app will have, such as access to the camera or iCloud servers. The option to change these values is available in the Navigator Area (Figure 5-4, number 6). Once we click on it, a series of panels are displayed in the Editor Area (Figure 5-12, number 1).

Figure 5-12: Target configuration

From the General panel we can change basic aspects of the application such as the devices the app will support, the app's name, version, available orientations for iPhones and iPads, and the deployment target (the versions of the operating systems that the app supports). In the Signing & Capabilities panel we can set up the signing certificates required for distribution (usually set up automatically by Xcode) or assign capabilities to the app, such as access to the camera or iCloud servers. Another useful panel is called *Info*. Here we can find a list of configuration values and insert new ones.

Key		Type	Value	
Bundle version string (short)	⇕	String	$(MARKETING_VERSION)	
Bundle identifier	⇕	String	$(PRODUCT_BUNDLE_IDENTIFIER)	
⌄ Supported interface orientations (iPad)	⇕	Array	(4 items)	
Item 0		String	Portrait (bottom home button)	⇕
Item 1		String	Portrait (top home button)	⇕
Item 2		String	Landscape (left home button)	⇕
Item 3		String	Landscape (right home button)	⇕
Bundle name	⇕	String	$(PRODUCT_NAME)	
InfoDictionary version	⇕	String	6.0	
Localization native development region	⇕	String	$(DEVELOPMENT_LANGUAGE)	⇕
Executable file	⇕	String	$(EXECUTABLE_NAME)	

Figure 5-13: App configuration

The information in this panel is stored in a plist file. A plist file has a format that allows us to store keys and values. The keys represent configuration options, and the values are the settings we want for our application. These configuration options include those declared in other panels, such as the available orientations set in the General panel, and also custom options, such as the image to display when the app starts, as we will see later.

Basic **SwiftUI Files**

The Multiplatform App template includes two Swift files: one with the code to initialize the app (TestApp.swift in our example) and another to define the user interface (ContentView.swift). Figure 5-14, below, shows the Navigator Area with all the items created by the template.

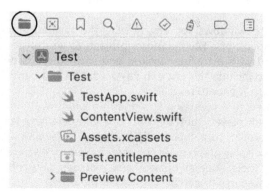

Figure 5-14: Files created by the Multiplatform App template

The first file is named after the application and includes the "App" suffix to indicate that the code it contains is in charge of initializing the app (TestApp in our example). The following is the code generated by the template for this file.

```
import SwiftUI

@main
struct TestApp: App {
    var body: some Scene {
        WindowGroup {
            ContentView()
        }
    }
}
```

Listing 5-1: Initializing the app

Everything in SwiftUI is created within the definition of a structure. As illustrated by the code in Listing 5-1, the initial configuration of the application is defined inside a structure that conforms to the **App** protocol. This is a protocol declared in the SwiftUI framework to define the structure and behavior of an application. The protocol's only requirement is the definition of a computed property called **body** that determines the app's content and returns a Scene (window).

The **App** structure must be preceded by the **@main** attribute, which indicates the app's point of entry. When the app is launched, the system looks for a structure that conforms to the **App** protocol and is preceded by the **@main** attribute, creates an instance of that structure, and then executes the code in the **body** property.

In Apple devices, we can open multiple instances of an app. For instance, in iPads and Mac computers, we can open two or more copies of the same app to process different information, such as two windows of the Text editor to process two different documents. To manage these instances, the system implements Scenes. A Scene is a structure that conforms to the **Scene** protocol. This is a SwiftUI protocol defined to manage the app's interface and adapt it to every platform. Although we can create our own Scenes by defining a structure that conforms to this protocol, SwiftUI includes several structures to create standard Scenes for every system. The currently available are **WindowGroup**, **Window**, **DocumentGroup**, **Settings**, and **MenuBarExtra**. Some of these structures are designed to create Scenes for Mac computers, as we will see later, and others are more generic. For example, the **WindowGroup** structure can manage multiple windows for iPhones, iPads and Macs, and therefore it is the one recommended for most projects. The following is the structure's initializer.

▷ **WindowGroup(**Text, **id:** String, **content:** Closure**)**—This initializer creates a Scene to manage all the windows of an instance of the application. The first argument defines the window's title, the **id** argument specifies the window's identifier, and the **content** argument is a closure that defines what the windows are going to display.

Because it can create windows for any device, the **WindowGroup** structure is the one implemented in the template of a Multiplatform project, as we can see in Listing 5-1. Note that the argument is declared with a trailing closure, and since there is only one statement in the block, we did not need to include the **return** keyword. This is a common practice in SwiftUI to simplify the code and make it easy to read.

The **WindowGroup** structure creates a Scene with a window. Windows determine the space where the graphics are displayed, but they do not generate any visible content. The user's interface is built from similar containers called *Views*. These views are rectangular areas of custom size, designed to display graphics on the screen. Some views are used as containers while others present graphical tools, such as buttons and switches, and content, such as images and text. The views are organized in a hierarchy, one within the other.

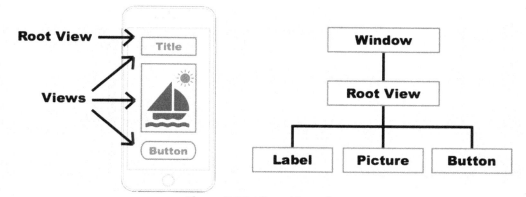

Figure 5-15: *Views hierarchy*

SwiftUI views are defined by structures. In the example provided by the App template, the closure assigned to the **WindowGroup** structure initializes and returns a structure called **ContentView**. This is a custom structure included by the template to define the initial view. (The initial view represents the initial content the user sees on the screen when the app is launched.) The structure is defined in the ContentView.swift file, as shown below.

```
import SwiftUI

struct ContentView: View {
    var body: some View {
        VStack {
            Image(systemName: "globe")
                .imageScale(.large)
                .foregroundStyle(.tint)
            Text("Hello, world!")
        }
        .padding()
    }
}
```

Listing 5-2: *Defining a structure that conforms to the* View *protocol*

As the code in Listing 5-2 shows, a structure that defines a SwiftUI view must conform to the **View** protocol. This is another protocol defined in the SwiftUI framework whose only requirement is the implementation of a computed property called **body** that returns at least one view. Inside the closure assigned to this property is where we declare all the views we need to design the user interface, as we will see later.

When the system processes a **View** structure, it creates a view called *root view*, and then determines its size from the size of its container. This container can be the window or another view. For instance, the **ContentView** view created by the App template is assigned as the window's root view by the **WindowGroup** structure, and therefore its size is going to be determined by the size of the window.

The views defined in the **body** property follow a different path. They determine their size from the size of the container, but then they propose that size to their content and it is the content that finally decides which size the view is going to take.

We can see this at work when we preview the interface produced by the **ContentView** structure on the canvas or the simulator. The structure creates a white view that occupies the entire screen and then two small views inside, one with an icon and another with the text "Hello World!", as shown below.

Figure 5-16: Views created by the App template on the Canvas

Canvas

SwiftUI files include the definition of two structures, one to declare the view and another to create the preview on the canvas. This second structure is produced by a Freestanding macro called #Preview, as shown below.

```
#Preview {
    ContentView()
}
```

Listing 5-3: Defining the preview for the canvas

The #Preview macro is similar to those introduced in Chapter 3 (see Macros), with the difference that it can take some attributes to configure the preview.

▷ **#Preview(**String?, **traits:** PreviewTrait, **body:** Closure**)**—This macro produces a preview of the view on the canvas. The first argument assigns a label to the preview (the canvas can display multiple previews at a time), and the **traits** argument configures the preview. This last argument is a structure with properties to configure the orientation, including `defaultLayout`, `landscapeLeft`, `landscapeRight`, `portrait` and `portraitUpsideDown`, another property called `sizeThatFits-Layout` to set the size of the preview to the size of the views, and also a method useful when developing apps for Mac computers to set a specific size for the view (`fixed-Layout(width: CGFloat, height: CGFloat)`). Finally, the **body** argument takes a closure with the view we want to preview.

The minimum requirement to create a preview is the initializer for the view (see Listing 5-3), but we can also add a name and a trait, as in the following example.

```
#Preview("My iPhone", traits: .landscapeLeft) {
    ContentView()
}
#Preview("My Second iPhone") {
    ContentView()
}
```

Listing 5-4: Generating multiple previews

This example defines two previews, one to display the device in landscape orientation and another to display the device in the orientation by default (portrait). The canvas displays one preview at a time, but if more than one is available, it includes buttons at the top to select them.

Figure 5-17: Preview buttons

The configuration options provided by the #Preview macro are limited to orientation and size, but we can also change other aspects of the preview and configure the canvas using the buttons at the bottom of the area.

Figure 5-18: Preview configuration

There is the Live button (number 1) to start a live preview (enabled by default), the Selectable button (number 2) to disable live preview and enable selection, the Variants button (number 3) to show the app in multiple configurations, such as portrait and landscape orientation, the Settings button (number 4) to set the device's configuration, such as the color scheme and orientation, the Preview Device button (number 5) to select the device to represent on the canvas, and the Zoom buttons (number 6) to change the size of the preview.

Do It Yourself: Click on the ContentView.swift file. You should see the code from Listings 5-2 and 5-3 in the Editor Area. If you don't see the canvas, click on the Adjust Editor button in the upper right corner (Figure 5-5, number 1) and select the Canvas option (Figure 5-6). If you want to see what the interface looks like in a different device, select the target and the desired device from the toolbar (Figure 5-9) or the Preview Device button (Figure 5-18, number 5). You should see something like Figure 5-16. To test the application on a device, connect the device to a USB port. The system will ask you for your pin to pair the device with the computer and then you will be able to select it from the Preview Device button (Figure 5-18, number 5). Once the device is selected, every change you introduce to your application will appear on the device's screen.

(Advanced) **Opaque Types**

The value produced by the **body** property is a view (a structure that conforms to the **View** protocol), but because the views assigned to the property may be different each time, it is declared as an opaque type (**some View**). Opaque types are data types that hide the value's data type from the programmer. They are usually required when working with generic data types, like the generic structures introduced before (see Listing 3-47). For example, the **reversed()** method included in **Array** structures returns a **ReversedCollection** structure, and this structure is generic, so the definition of the type depends on the type of values we are processing. An array of strings will generate a structure of type **ReversedCollection-<Array<String>>** and an array of integers will return a structure of type **Reversed-Collection<Array<Int>>**, as in the following example.

```
func reverseit(mylist: [Int]) -> ReversedCollection<Array<Int>> {
    let reversed = mylist.reversed()
    return reversed
}
let reversedlist = reverseit(mylist: [1, 2, 3, 4, 5])
```

```
print(Array(reversedlist))   // "[5, 4, 3, 2, 1]"
```

Listing 5-5: Returning values of complex data types

The code in Listing 5-5 defines a function called **reverseit()** that receives an array of integers and returns a **ReversedCollection** value with the values in reverse order, and then casts the collection returned by the function into an array and print it on the console.

This code runs fine and there are no issues with it, until we decide to work with different value types, such as strings. Instead of **ReversedCollection<Array<Int>>**, the return data type would have to be defined as **ReversedCollection<Array<String>>**. Although in this case it may seem easy to switch types, the generic data types used to create SwiftUI views can be complex and replacing them repeatedly in generic properties and methods can be time consuming and error prone. But if we know that the values we want to return conform to the same protocol, we can declare the return type as opaque and let the compiler figure out the data type for us. When the compiler finds an opaque type, it takes care of determining the real data type of the value and process it as such.

Opaque types are declared with the **some** keyword followed by the name of the protocol to which the type conforms. For example, collections such as the one returned by the **reversed()** method, conform to a protocol called **Collection**, so we can define the return type as **some Collection** and let the compiler figure out the real data type.

```
func reverseit(mylist: [String]) -> some Collection {
    let reversed = mylist.reversed()
    return reversed
}
let reversedlist = reverseit(mylist: ["One", "Two", "Three", "Four",
"Five"])
print(Array(reversedlist))   // "["Five", "Four", "Three", "Two", "One"]"
```

Listing 5-6: Returning opaque types

This example defines the same **reverseit()** function as before, but this time the function receives an array of strings and returns the opaque type **some Collection**. The value returned by the function is of type **some Collection**, but the compiler recognizes that the value's data type is **ReversedCollection<Array<String>>** and process it as such, which means that we are still able to turn it into an **Array** and print it on the console.

 IMPORTANT: Functions, methods and closures that return an opaque type must always return a value of a specific type. When the compiler finds an opaque type, it determines the value's real data type from the value returned. If we, for instance, use an **if else** statement to select the view we want to assign to the **body** property, the compiler won't be able to determine the right data type of the value returned and will show an error. Possible solutions are to wrap the views in a **Group** view (as we will see in Listing 5-82), or implement the **@ViewBuilder** property wrapper (as we will see in Listing 5-91).

(Basic) 5.2 User Interface

The user interface is the most important aspect of an application. In SwiftUI, the interface is declared in the definition of a structure, one view at a time, and then the compiler takes care of generating the code necessary to display it on the screen and adapt it to every device.

All SwiftUI views are defined by structures, including those defined by the developer and the system. The framework includes several structures to produce standard views. For instance, the **Image** and **Text** structures implemented in the example defined by the App template create views to display images and text, respectively. These are the most basic views in SwiftUI, but there are many more, including some to contain other views and many to display graphics.

Text View

The `Text` structure takes a string and returns a view that displays the text on the screen. The structure defines multiple initializers. The following are the most frequently used.

▷ **Text(String)**—This initializer creates a `Text` view with the text defined by the argument.

▷ **Text(Date, style:** DateStyle**)**—This initializer creates a `Text` view to present a date. The first argument defines the date, and the **style** argument is a structure that determines the format. The structure includes the type properties **date, offset, relative, time,** and **timer** to define this value.

Since text is the primary means of communication, `Text` views are implemented all the time in SwiftUI applications, and that is why the `ContentView` view generated by the App template includes one. The `Text` view included in the template is created with a `String` value to display the text "Hello World!" on the screen (see Listing 5-2), but a `Text` view can also include values using string interpolation.

```
import SwiftUI
struct ContentView: View {
    let number: Float = 30.87512

    var body: some View {
        Text("My Number: \(number)")
    }
}
```

Listing 5-7: Displaying values with a Text *view*

This example displays the value as it is, but we can use the `formatted()` method to format the value, as we did in Chapter 4. For instance, we can turn the number into currency to represent US Dollars.

```
struct ContentView: View {
    let number: Float = 30.87512

    var body: some View {
        Text("My Number: \(number.formatted(.currency(code: "USD")))")
    }
}
```

Listing 5-8: Formatting a value for a Text *view*

My Number: $30.88

Figure 5-19: Text *view with formatted values*

Of course, we can include and format other types of values. For instance, we can use the `formatted()` method on a `Date` value to show a date.

```
struct ContentView: View {
    let today = Date()
```

```
var body: some View {
    Text(today.formatted(date: .abbreviated, time: .omitted))
}
}
```

Listing 5-9: Displaying a date with a Text *view*

13 Jun 2023

Figure 5-20: Date displayed with a Text *view*

The **Text** structure defines a specific initializer to show dates. The initializer includes an argument that takes a **DateStyle** structure to format the date. The formats available are not as comprehensive as those provided by the **formatted()** method, but the advantage of using this formatter is that some of the styles available can update the values as they change. For instance, one of the type properties included by the **DateStyle** structure is called **timer**. This formatter displays the date as a counter that starts counting from the current date.

```
struct ContentView: View {
    let today = Date()

    var body: some View {
        Text(today, style: .timer)
    }
}
```

Listing 5-10: Displaying a timer with a Text *view*

 Do It Yourself: Update the **ContentView** view in your ContentView.swift file with the example you want to try. If the canvas is not visible, click on the Adjust Editor button and select the Canvas option. You should see the text produced by the **Text** view on the canvas (Figure 5-16). The last example should display a counter on the screen counting up from 0.

(Basic) Modifiers

Views are presented with attributes by default, such as a standard font and color, but the **View** protocol defines methods to modify their aspect. These methods are called *Modifiers*, and they are executed right after the instance is created, as in the following example.

```
struct ContentView: View {
    var body: some View {
        Text("Hello World")
            .font(.largeTitle)
    }
}
```

Listing 5-11: Applying modifiers to a view

When the system reads the **body** property of the example in Listing 5-11 to build the interface, it creates an instance of the **Text** structure with the string "Hello World", and then calls the **font()** method on this structure. This method creates a new view with the **largeTitle** attribute applied to the text and returns that view. As a result, the **body** property produces a view with a large title. If we open the canvas, we can see the change in real time.

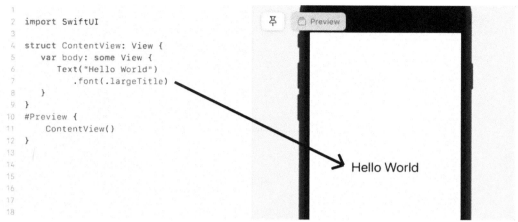

```
1
2    import SwiftUI
3
4    struct ContentView: View {
5        var body: some View {
6            Text("Hello World")
7                .font(.largeTitle)
8        }
9    }
10   #Preview {
11       ContentView()
12   }
13
14
15
16
17
18
```

Figure 5-21: *Modifier applied to a* Text *view*

The code and the canvas are interconnected. If we add a modifier to a view, as we did in Listing 5-11, the changes automatically appear on the canvas, but we can also edit the views from the canvas. By default, the canvas is in Live Preview mode, but we can change it to Selectable mode by pressing the Selectable button at the bottom (see Figure 5-22, number 1). To edit a view, we must click on it from the canvas (Figure 5-22, number 2) and then open the Attributes Inspector panel in the Utilities Area (Figure 5-4, number 4). The panel shows a list of all the attributes we can change for the selected view (Figure 5-22, number 3).

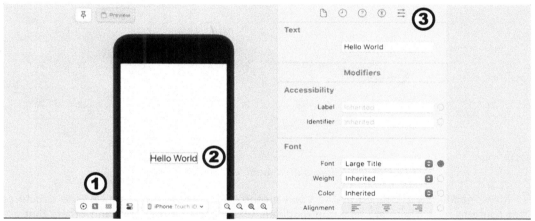

Figure 5-22: *View's attributes*

The Attributes Inspector panel shows the attributes currently assigned to the view. In our example, the option Large Title is already selected because we added the **font()** modifier in Listing 5-11. If we remove this modifier, the panel is updated to show the current values. The same happens the other way around. if we change any value on this panel, the change is reflected on the canvas and the corresponding modifier is added to the code.

Another way to modify our views is with a context menu. If we move the mouse over a view in the code and click on it while holding down the Control key, we will see a menu with multiple options to modify the view. One of those options is called *Show SwiftUI Inspector*, which opens a panel with all the same options we can find in the Attributes Inspector panel. Changing the options in this window produces the same effect as before.

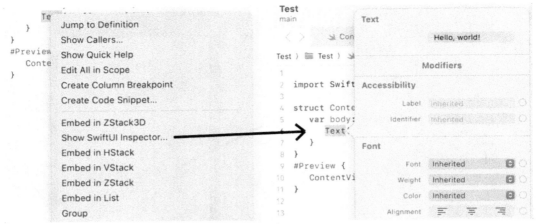

Figure 5-23: View's context menu

Additionally, Xcode offers a library with a list of views and modifiers that we can incorporate to our interface by dragging and dropping them into our code. The library is accessible from the Library button in the toolbar (Figure 5-4, number 5), and the lists of views and modifiers are selected from the buttons at the top of the window. The first button presents a list with all the views we can add to the interface and the second button opens a list with all the modifiers available. We can also use the search bar at the top of the window for a quick search. Figure 5-24, below, illustrates how to add a modifier from this library to change the color of the text.

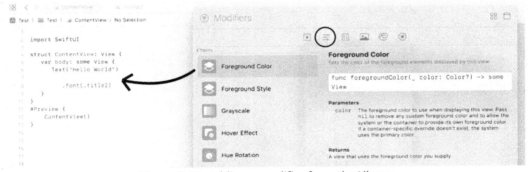

Figure 5-24: Adding a modifier from the Library

Most modifiers are defined by the **View** protocol and then implemented by the structures that conform to it. There are common modifiers that apply to most views and others that are more specific. The following are some of the modifiers used to determine the size of the view.

▷ **frame(width:** CGFloat?, **height:** CGFloat?, **alignment:** Alignment)—This modifier assigns a new size and alignment to the view. The **alignment** argument determines the alignment of the view's content. It is a structure of type **Alignment** with the type properties **bottom, bottomLeading, bottomTrailing, center, leading, top, topLeading, topTrailing**, and **trailing**.

▷ **frame(minWidth:** CGFloat?, **idealWidth:** CGFloat?, **maxWidth:** CGFloat?, **minHeight:** CGFloat?, **idealHeight:** CGFloat?, **maxHeight:** CGFloat?, **alignment:** Alignment)—This modifier assigns a minimum and a maximum size to the view. We can also define an ideal width and height that will be taken into consideration when the space must be distributed among the views. The **alignment** argument determines the alignment of the view's content. It is a structure of type **Alignment** with the type properties **bottom, bottomLeading, bottomTrailing, center, leading, top, topLeading, topTrailing**, and **trailing**.

▷ **padding(CGFloat)**—This modifier adds a padding between the view's content and its frame. The argument determines the width of the padding. We can provide a **CGFloat** value to specify the padding for all sides. (If we do not specify a value, the system assigns a standard padding that adapts to each device.) The modifier can also take an **EdgeInsets** value to specify a padding for each side, or a set of **Edge** values along with a **CGFloat** value to declare which sides we want to modify and how much (**padding([Edge], CGFloat)**). The **Edge** type is an enumeration with the values **bottom**, **leading**, **top**, **trailing**, **horizontal** (left and right), and **vertical** (top and bottom).

The screen of a device is composed of a grid of hundreds of dots called *pixels*, ordered in rows and columns. The number of pixels varies from one device to another. To compensate for the disparities between devices, Apple adopted the concept of points (sometimes called *logical pixels*). The goal is to have a unit of measurement that is independent of the device and the density of the pixels on the screen. A point occupies a square of one or more pixels, depending on the device. For instance, the screen of an iPhone 15 has a grid of 1170 pixels by 2532 pixels, but the views are positioned and sized according to the grid in points (390 by 844). Using this reference, we can determine the appropriate size of a view for every device. In the following example, we implement the **frame()** modifier to give the **Text** view a size of approximately two thirds the width of the screen (250 points).

```
struct ContentView: View {
    var body: some View {
        Text("Hello World!")
            .frame(width: 250, height: 100, alignment: .leading)
    }
}
```

Listing 5-12: Assigning a fixed size to a view

In this example, we take advantage of the **alignment** argument provided by the initializer to align the text to the left. Note that the value does not specify the side. Instead, the side is represented by the **leading** value. There are two values available, **leading** and **trailing**. These values represent the left or the right side of the view depending on the language. For instance, if the language set on the device is left-to-right, like English, the **leading** value is associated to the left side of the view and the **trailing** value to the right.

Figure 5-25: View with a fixed size and the content aligned to the left (leading)

 Do It Yourself: Update the **ContentView** view with the code in Listing 5-12. Press the Selectable button to activate the Selectable mode on the canvas. Click on the **Text** view in the canvas to select it. You should see a blue rectangle indicating the area occupied by the view, as illustrated in Figure 5-25.

The arguments in the **frame()** modifier are optional. We can declare only the width or the height, and the rest of the arguments will be defined by the view and its content. This is particularly useful when we want to turn one side of the view flexible. Flexible views are defined with the **maxWidth** and **maxHeight** arguments. For instance, we can apply the **maxWidth**

argument to extend the view to the left and right side of the window, and let the content determine the height.

```
struct ContentView: View {
    var body: some View {
        Text("Hello World!")
            .frame(minWidth: 0, maxWidth: .infinity)
    }
}
```

Listing 5-13: Creating flexible containers

The value **infinity** is a type property defined in the **CGFloat** structure that asks the system to expand the view to occupy all the space available in its container. In our example, we applied this value to the **maxWidth** argument, so the **Text** view extends to the edges of the screen.

Figure 5-26: Flexible view

 IMPORTANT: Note that for a flexible view to work properly it is recommended to always declare the minimum size as well. If you are declaring a flexible width, you should set the **minWidth** argument, and if you are declaring a flexible height, you should also include the **minHeight** argument.

Another way to specify a custom size is with the **padding()** modifier. The padding is inserted between the content and the edges of the view. There are different ways to determine the padding's thickness. For instance, if we don't specify any value, the system assigns one by default, depending on the device, but we can also provide a **CGFloat** value to declare a specific thickness in points.

```
struct ContentView: View {
    var body: some View {
        Text("Hello World")
            .padding(25)
    }
}
```

Listing 5-14: Adding padding to a view

The code in Listing 5-14 assigns a padding of 25 points to the **Text** view. The padding is applied between the text and the view's frame, as shown below.

Figure 5-27: View with padding

The **View** protocol defines a structure called **EdgeInsets** that we can use to specify a width for each side of the view.

▷ **EdgeInsets(top:** CGFloat, **leading:** CGFloat, **bottom:** CGFloat, **trailing:** CGFloat)—This initializer returns an **EdgeInsets** structure with the values specified by the arguments.

Chapter 5 - SwiftUI Framework

The following example implements this structure to assign a padding of 40 points only to the left and right sides.

```
struct ContentView: View {
    var body: some View {
        Text("Hello World")
            .padding(EdgeInsets(top: 0.0, leading: 40.0, bottom: 0.0,
trailing: 40.0))
    }
}
```

Listing 5-15: Assigning a specific padding for each side

Figure 5-28: Padding only on the sides

The code in Listing 5-15 assigns padding to specific sides of the view. Another way to achieve the same is with the values of an enumeration provided by SwiftUI called **Edge**. This enumeration includes the values **bottom, leading, top**, and **trailing** to represent each side. We must declare a set with the values that represent the sides we want to modify and a second argument with the thickness we want to assign to the padding. The following example adds a padding of 50 points at the view's top and bottom.

```
struct ContentView: View {
    var body: some View {
        Text("Hello World")
            .padding([.top, .bottom], 50)
    }
}
```

Listing 5-16: Assigning padding with Edge values

Figure 5-29: Padding at the top and bottom

In addition to the view, we can also style its content. For instance, the **View** protocol defines modifiers that are especially useful with **Text** views. The following are the most frequently used.

▷ **font(Font)**—This modifier assigns a font to the text. The argument is a **Font** structure that provides type properties and methods to select the font we want.

▷ **bold(Bool)**—This modifier assigns the bold style to the text. The argument is a Boolean value to dynamically enable or disable the modifier.

▷ **italic(Bool)**—This modifier assigns the italic style to the text. The argument is a Boolean value to dynamically enable or disable the modifier.

▷ **fontWeight(Weight)**—This modifier assigns a weight to the text. The argument is a structure with the type properties **black, bold, heavy, light, medium, regular, semibold, thin**, and **ultraLight**.

▷ **textCase(**Case**)**—This modifier transforms the text to lowercase or uppercase letters. The argument is an enumeration with the values `lowercase` and `uppercase`.

▷ **dynamicTypeSize(**DynamicTypeSize**)**—This modifier sets the dynamic type size to apply to the text. The argument is an enumeration with the values `large`, `medium`, `small`, `xLarge`, `xSmall`, `xxLarge`, and `xxxLarge`. It can be declared as a range of values to determine the minimum and maximum size allowed.

▷ **underline(**Bool, **color:** Color**)**—This modifier underlines the text. The first argument is a Boolean value that indicates if the style is applied to the text or not, and the second argument defines the color of the line.

▷ **strikethrough(**Bool, **color:** Color**)**—This modifier draws a line through the text. The first argument is a Boolean value that indicates if the style is applied to the text or not, and the second argument defines the color of the line.

▷ **shadow(color:** Color, **radius:** CGFloat, **x:** CGFloat, **y:** CGFloat**)**—This modifier assigns a shadow to the text. The arguments define the color of the shadow, its size, and the horizontal and vertical offsets.

The most important aspect of a text is the font. The system defines standard fonts and sizes to show the text produced by a `Text` view, but we can specify our own with the `font()` modifier. The `font()` modifier assigns the font to the view, but the font is defined by an instance of a structure included in the SwiftUI framework called `Font`. With this structure, we can create custom and dynamic fonts. Custom fonts are fonts provided by the system or the developer, and dynamic fonts are the fonts Apple recommends using because they adapt to the font size selected by the user from Settings.

The easiest to implement are dynamic fonts. They are defined by type properties provided by the `Font` structure, so all we have to do is to apply the `font()` modifier with the property that represents the font type we want to assign to the text. We have done this before with the `largeTitle` property (see Listing 5-11), but the structure also includes the properties `title`, `title2`, `title3`, `headline`, `subheadline`, `body`, `callout`, `caption`, `caption2`, and `footnote` to define different styles and sizes.

```
struct ContentView: View {
    var body: some View {
        Text("Hello World")
            .font(.body)
    }
}
```

Listing 5-17: Assigning dynamic font types

The **body** property produces a font similar to the standard font provided by the system. Figure 5-30, below, shows some of the fonts returned by these properties compared to the system's standard font.

Hello World	Hello World	Hello World	Hello World
Standard / Body	**footnote**	**title**	**headline**

Figure 5-30: Dynamic font types

 Do It Yourself: Dynamic fonts have a predefine size, but they change according to the size set by the user from Settings. If you want to see how your text looks like in different sizes, press the Settings button at the bottom of the canvas (Figure 5-18, number 4), activate the Dynamic Type option, and select the size you want to apply.

Although it is recommended to use dynamic fonts so the interface automatically adapts to the size set by the user, the **Font** structure also includes the following type methods to implement the font defined by the system or to load custom fonts.

▷ **system(size:** CGFloat)—This type method returns the system font with the size defined by the **size** argument.

▷ **custom(**String, **size:** CGFloat)—This type method returns a font of the type specified by the first argument and with the size specified by the **size** argument.

With the **system()** method, we can get the standard font provided by the system but of any size we want. The font and size defined by this method are not affected by the choices the user makes from Settings.

```
struct ContentView: View {
    var body: some View {
        Text("Hello World")
            .font(Font.system(size: 50))
    }
}
```

Listing 5-18: Using the system font

This example displays a text with a size of 50 points that always remains at that size no matter the changes performed by the user, but the font type is the one defined by the system. If we want to use a custom font, we have to implement the **custom()** method.

Operating systems come with a set of standard fonts. If the font we want to use is already included in the system, we just need to specify its name and size, as in the following example.

```
struct ContentView: View {
    var body: some View {
        Text("Hello World")
            .font(Font.custom("Georgia", size: 50))
    }
}
```

Listing 5-19: Using standard fonts

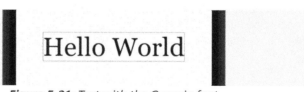

Figure 5-31: Text with the Georgia font

If the font we want to include is not provided by the system, we must copy the file into the project. Including the file in our project is easy; we must drag it from Finder to the Navigator Area, as shown below.

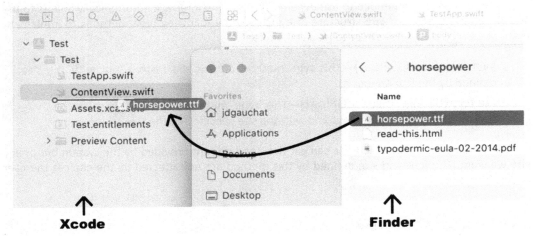

Figure 5-32: Dragging files from Finder to our Xcode's project

When we drop the files in our Xcode project, a window asks for information about the destination and the target. To copy the files to the project folder (recommended), we must select the *Copy files to destination* option form the drop-down menu, and to add the file to a target, we must check the box next to the name of the target below, as shown in Figure 5-33.

Choose options for adding these files:

Action: Copy files to destination

Targets: ☑ 🅰 Test

Cancel   Finish

Figure 5-33: Options to add files to the project

This adds the font file to our project, but to be able to use the font, we must modify the app's configuration from the Info panel (see Figure 5-13). Every option on the list includes a + button. By pressing any of these buttons, we can add a new key (Figure 5-34, number 1). The key we need in this case is called "Fonts provided by application". This key already includes an item (Item 0), so all we need to do to add a font is to press the arrow on the left to expose the item (Figure 5-34, number 2) and then replace its value with the name of the file that contains our font (Figure 5-34, number 3).

Figure 5-34: Custom fonts declared in the Info panel

In this example, we include the horsepower.ttf file, which defines a font called *Horse Power*. Now, we can use this font from our application.

```
struct ContentView: View {
   var body: some View {
      Text("Hello World")
         .font(Font.custom("Horsepower-Regular", size: 50))
   }
}
```

Listing 5-20: Using custom fonts

Figure 5-35: Text with a custom font

 Do It Yourself: Download the horsepower.ttf file from our website or provide your own. Drag the file from Finder to the project's Navigator Area (Figure 5-32). Make sure to check the option "Copy files to destination" and the target (Figure 5-33). Go to the app's settings (Figure 5-4, number 6), open the Info panel, click on the + button in any of the rows, and select the key "Fonts provided by the application". Click on the arrow at the option's left hand side to reveal the items. You should see the item 0 with no value. Click on the value field to change it. Copy and paste the name of your font's file, including the extension. Modify the **ContentView** view with the code in Listing 5-20. You should see the text styled with the new font in the canvas.

 IMPORTANT: The names we have to provide to the **custom()** method are the PostScript names. To find the PostScript name of the font you want to add to your project, open the Font Book application from the Applications folder, go to the View menu, and select the option Show Font Info. Click on the font. The PostScript name is shown in the panel on the right.

Applying the rest of the modifiers available for **Text** views is straightforward, as shown next.

```
struct ContentView: View {
   var body: some View {
      Text("Hello World")
         .font(.largeTitle)
         .underline()
         .fontWeight(.heavy)
         .shadow(radius: 1, x: 1, y: 1)
   }
}
```

Listing 5-21: Applying multiple styles to a text

The structure in Listing 5-21 defines a **Text** view with a **largeTitle** font, a weight of type **heavy**, a shadow, and underlines the text with the **underline()** modifier. In this example, we define the **radius, x**, and **y** arguments of the **shadow()** modifier to 1 to cast a subtle shadow that extends to the right and bottom of the text.

 Hello World

Figure 5-36: Multiple styles applied to a text

`Text` views can be provided as the content of other `Text` views, which allows us to assign different styles to each portion of the text, as shown below.

```
struct ContentView: View {
    var body: some View {
        Text("Hello \(Text("World").underline())")
            .font(.largeTitle)
    }
}
```

Listing 5-22: *Nesting* Text *views*

In this example, we applied the `largeTitle` and `underline()` modifier, but because the `underline()` modifier was applied to the second `Text` view, only the text in this view is underlined.

Figure 5-37: Nested Text *views with different styles*

The `Font` structure also includes the following modifiers to style the font.

▷ **bold()**—This modifier adds the bold style to the font.

▷ **italic()**—This modifier adds the italic style to the font.

▷ **weight(**Weight**)**—This modifier assigns a weight to the font. The argument is a structure of type **Weight** with the properties **black, bold, heavy, light, medium, regular, semibold, thin**, and **ultraLight**.

Because these modifiers are defined by the **Font** structure, they are applied to the font, not the view. For instance, we can apply the `weight()` modifier to the **Font** structure returned by the `largeTitle` property to get a bold text.

```
struct ContentView: View {
    var body: some View {
        Text("Hello World")
            .font(.largeTitle.weight(.semibold))
    }
}
```

Listing 5-23: Styling the font

Figure 5-38: Semibold text

By default, `Text` views can show multiple lines of text, but we can implement modifiers provided by the `View` protocol to set a limit on the number of lines allowed or to format the text.

▷ **lineLimit(**Int**)**—This modifier determines how many lines the text can contain. The argument is an optional that indicates the number of lines we want. By default, the value is set to **nil**, which means the view will extend to include the number of lines necessary to show the whole text.

> **multilineTextAlignment(**TextAlignment**)**—This modifier defines the alignment of multiline text. The argument is an enumeration with the values **center**, **leading** (default), and **trailing**.

> **lineSpacing(**CGFloat**)**—This modifier determines the space between lines.

> **truncationMode(**TruncationMode**)**—This modifier determines how the text is truncated when it doesn't fit inside the view's frame. The argument is an enumeration with the values **head**, **middle**, and **tail** (default).

> **textSelection(**TextSelectability**)**—This modifier determines if the text is selectable by the user (the user can copy the text and paste it somewhere else). The argument is a structure with the type properties **enabled** and **disabled**.

> **privacySensitive()**—This modifier indicates that the view contains sensitive information. It is used to prevent the system from exposing private data.

The following example displays a text aligned to the center and with a space of 5 points between lines.

```
struct ContentView: View {
    var body: some View {
        Text("Monsters are real, and ghosts are real too. They live inside
us, and sometimes, they win. Stephen King.")
            .padding()
            .multilineTextAlignment(.center)
            .lineSpacing(5)
            .textSelection(.enabled)
    }
}
```

Listing 5-24: Formatting text

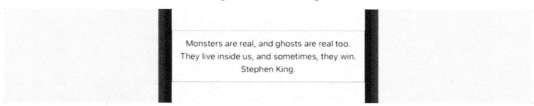

Figure 5-39: Multiline text

If we limit the number of lines, we must consider how the text is going to be displayed to the user when it is too long or does not fit within the view. By default, the system truncates the text and adds ellipsis at the end to indicate that part of the text is missing, but we can move the ellipsis to the beginning or the middle with the **truncationMode()** modifier.

```
struct ContentView: View {
    var body: some View {
        Text("Monsters are real, and ghosts are real too. They live inside
us, and sometimes, they win. Stephen King.")
            .padding()
            .lineLimit(1)
            .truncationMode(.middle)
    }
}
```

Listing 5-25: Truncating text

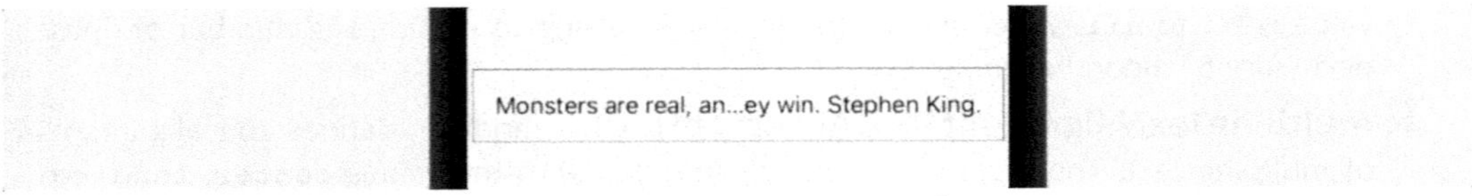

Monsters are real, an...ey win. Stephen King.

Figure 5-40: Truncation mode

(Basic) **Color View**

Some modifiers can change the colors of the view and the content. Colors in SwiftUI are defined by a **Color** view. The following are some of the structure's initializers.

▷ **Color(**RGBColorSpace, **red:** Double, **green:** Double, **blue:** Double, **opacity:** Double)—This initializer returns a **Color** view with the color and opacity defined by the arguments. The first argument defines the color system used to interpret the values. It is an enumeration with the values **sRGB**, **sRGBLinear**, and **displayP3**. If ignored, the application will use the default color system set on the device. The **red**, **green**, and **blue** arguments determine the levels of red, green, and blue with values from 0.0 (no color) to 1.0 (full color). And the **opacity** argument determines the level of opacity with a value from 0.0 (transparent) to 1.0 (opaque). The opacity may be ignored.

▷ **Color(**RGBColorSpace, **white:** Double, **opacity:** Double)—This initializer returns a **Color** view with the color defined by the arguments. The first argument defines the color system used to interpret the values. It is an enumeration with the values **sRGB**, **sRGBLinear**, and **displayP3**. If ignored, the application will use the default color system set on the device. The **white** argument determines the level of white with a value from 0.0 to 1.0 (black to white), and the **opacity** argument determines the level of opacity with a value from 0.0 (transparent) to 1.0 (opaque). The opacity may be ignored.

▷ **Color(hue:** Double, **saturation:** Double, **brightness:** Double)—This initializer returns a **Color** view with the color defined by the arguments. The arguments determine the level of hue, saturation, and brightness of the color with values from 0.0 to 1.0.

The **Color** structure also offers an extensive list of type properties that return a **Color** view with a predefined color that adapts to the interface mode (light or dark). The properties available are **black**, **blue**, **brown**, **cyan**, **gray**, **green**, **indigo**, **mint**, **orange**, **pink**, **purple**, **red**, **teal**, **white**, and **yellow**. There is also a property to make the element transparent called **clear**, a property to get the color by default called **accentColor**, and two properties called **primary** and **secondary** that return predefined colors that also change depending on the mode set for the interface (light or dark).

Most of the time, **Color** views are used to define a color for the content of other views, but they are standalone views and therefore can be included in the interface like the rest.

```
struct ContentView: View {
    var body: some View {
        Color(red: 0.9, green: 0.5, blue: 0.2)
            .frame(width: 250, height: 100)
    }
}
```

Listing 5-26: Implementing Color *views*

Figure 5-41: Color *view*

The code in Listing 5-26 creates an orange **Color** view with a size of 250 by 100 points. In this case, the **Color** initializer specifies values from 0.0 to 1.0 to determine the levels of red, green and blue, but RGB colors (Red, Green, Blue) are usually defined with integer values from 0 to 255. If we want to work with these values, we can divide the number by 255. For instance, the following initializer assigns an RGB color with the values 100, 228, 255 (cyan).

```
struct ContentView: View {
    var body: some View {
        Color(red: 100/255, green: 228/255, blue: 255/255)
            .frame(width: 250, height: 100)
    }
}
```

Listing 5-27: Defining the color with RGB values

The colors defined by the initializers are static, that is, they are always the same regardless of the appearance of the interface (light or dark), but we can assign dynamic colors with the properties of the structure. Dynamic colors adapt to the appearance. The following example creates a **Color** view with the **red** property. In dark mode, this color will look slightly different than in light mode.

```
struct ContentView: View {
    var body: some View {
        Color.red
            .frame(width: 250, height: 100)
    }
}
```

Listing 5-28: Assigning a dynamic color

In addition to the SwiftUI files, the App template includes a file called Assets.xcassets (see Figure 5-14). This is a tool called Asset Catalog that provides easy access to resources, including images, icons, colors, and more. When selected, Xcode shows a visual interface in the Editor Area to manage and configure the content. The interface includes two columns: the column on the left presents a list of sets of resources, such as images and colors, and the column on the right displays the content of the selected set, as shown below.

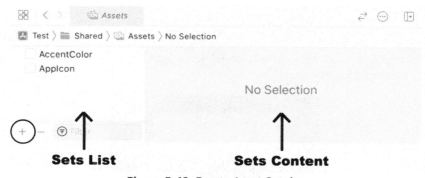

Figure 5-42: Empty Asset Catalog

The type properties provided by the `Color` structure, like the `red` property implemented in Listing 5-28, define colors that adapt to the appearance (light or dark). With the Asset Catalog, we can define our own sets of adaptive colors. The set is added from the Editor menu (**Add New Asset / Color Set**), or by pressing the + button at the lower left corner (circled in Figure 5-42). Once we select the Color Set option, Xcode creates a set with two placeholders for the colors, one for the color to show in Any appearance, and another for the Dark mode.

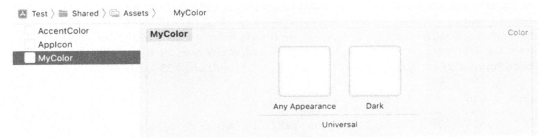

Figure 5-43: *Colors for Light and Dark appearances*

The name of the set is the name we use to reference the color from code. In this example, we call it *MyColor*. To assign the color, we must select the placeholder we want to change and define the color from the Attributes Inspector panel. For instance, in the following example we change the color for the dark appearance to orange.

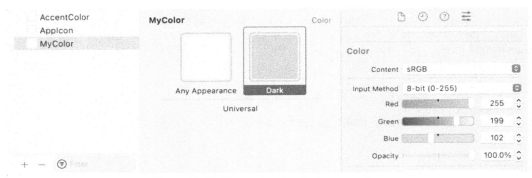

Figure 5-44: *New color for Dark appearance*

Once the set is defined, we can assign it to a view, as shown next.

```
struct ContentView: View {
    var body: some View {
        Color("MyColor")
            .frame(width: 250, height: 100)
    }
}
```

Listing 5-29: *Assigning a custom color*

In this example, the `Color` view will be white in light appearance, but orange when the appearance is changed to dark.

Figure 5-45: *Custom color in Dark appearance*

Chapter 5 - SwiftUI Framework

Do It Yourself: Click on the Assets item in the Navigator Area to open the Asset Catalog. Click on the + button and select the option Color Set (Figure 5-42). Click on the set to select it, open the Attributes Inspector panel and change its name to MyColor (Figure 5-43). Click on the squares that represent the colors in the Editor Area and set a different color for each one of them from the Attributes Inspector panel. Modify the **ContentView** view with the code in Listing 5-29. To change the appearance, click on the Settings button (Figure 5-18, number 4), activate Color Scheme and select the Dark Appearance option. You should see something like Figure 5-45.

The Asset Catalog includes two predefined sets called *AccentColor* and *AppIcon*. The AppIcon set defines the icons we must provide to represent the application. (Icons are the little images the user taps or clicks to launch the app.) On the other hand, the AccentColor set defines the color used by some views, such as buttons and other controls, to style their content. The color by default is blue, but we can modify this set to define a new one. In the example below, we change the accent color to green. From now on, all the controls that use the accent color will be green.

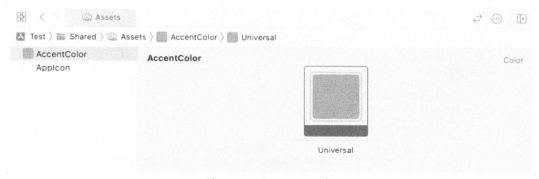

Figure 5-46: *Accent color*

As we already mentioned, the most common application of **Color** views is to define the colors of other views. The following are some of the modifiers that implement **Color** views to define the color of the views or are useful when working with colors.

▷ **foregroundColor(**Color**)**—This modifier assigns a color to the view's content.

▷ **border(**Color, **width:** CGFloat**)**—This modifier assigns a border to the view. The first argument determines the border's color and the **width** argument determines its width.

▷ **background(**View, **alignment:** Alignment**)**—This modifier assigns a view as the view's background. The first argument is a SwiftUI view, including **Color** views, and the **alignment** argument determines how the view is going to be aligned within the bounds of the parent view.

▷ **foregroundStyle(**ShapeStyle**)**—This modifier assigns a style to the view's content. The argument is a value that conforms to the **ShapeStyle** protocol, such as the **Color** structure for colors, the **AngularGradient** and **LinearGradient** structures for gradients, and the **Material** structure for materials.

▷ **overlay(**View, **alignment:** Alignment**)**—This modifier displays a view in front of the view that is being modified. The first argument is a SwiftUI view, including **Color** views, and the **alignment** argument determines how the view is going to be aligned within the bounds of the view we are modifying.

Using these modifiers, we can apply colors to different parts of the view. For instance, the **foregroundColor()** modifier assigns a color to the view's content. In the following example, we use it to change the color of the text in a **Text** view.

```
struct ContentView: View {
    var body: some View {
        Text("Hello World")
            .font(.largeTitle)
            .foregroundColor(Color.red)
    }
}
```

Listing 5-30: Assigning a color to the text of a Text *view*

Figure 5-47: Text in different color

Besides changing the color of the text, we can assign a color to the view's background. The **background()** modifier can take any view, but it is usually applied with a **Color** view.

```
struct ContentView: View {
    var body: some View {
        Text("Hello World")
            .font(.largeTitle)
            .background(Color.gray)
    }
}
```

Listing 5-31: Assigning a background color to a Text *view*

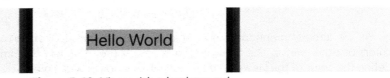

Figure 5-48: View with a background

The area occupied by the view is determined by a rectangular frame. In **Text** views, the size of this rectangle is determined by the size of the text. If we want to extend the background, we can set the frame's size with the **frame()** modifier or add a padding with the **padding()** modifier, as we do in the following example.

```
struct ContentView: View {
    var body: some View {
        Text("Hello World")
            .font(.largeTitle)
            .padding(20)
            .background(Color.gray)
    }
}
```

Listing 5-32: Assigning a background color to a view with a padding

Note that the padding was applied before the background. This is important because the order of the modifiers matters. Every time a modifier is executed, a new view is created with the characteristics of the previous view plus the changes requested by the modifier. For example, the code in Listing 5-32 creates a **Text** view with the text "Hello World", then the **font()** modifier creates a new view with a larger font, after that the **padding()** modifier creates another view with the characteristics of the previous one but with a padding of 20 points, which expands the

Chapter 5 - SwiftUI Framework

view's frame 20 points on each side, and finally the **background()** modifier creates another view with a background that covers the whole area occupied by the previous view, which includes the padding. If we had declared the background before the padding, the background color would have been applied to the view generated by the **font()** modifier, which didn't include the padding, as illustrated below.

Figure 5-49: Background applied before and after the padding

In addition to the background, we can assign a border to the view with the **border()** modifier. This modifier takes a view that represents the style of the border (usually a **Color** view) and the width, and adds a border with those characteristics.

```
struct ContentView: View {
    var body: some View {
        Text("Hello World")
            .font(.largeTitle)
            .padding(20)
            .background(Color.gray)
            .border(Color.yellow, width: 10)
    }
}
```

Listing 5-33: Assigning a border to the view

Figure 5-50: Background and border applied to the view

 IMPORTANT: The border is applied to the frame occupied by the view. If we want to add a border to a view with a different shape, like a circle, we must create an overlay with a shape view. We will learn more about overlays next and how to add a border with shape views in Chapter 11.

The **overlay()** modifier works like the **background()** modifier, but instead of displaying the view in the background, it displays it in the foreground. For example, the following code adds a translucent yellow view in front of the view created in the previous example.

```
struct ContentView: View {
    var body: some View {
        Text("Hello World")
            .font(.largeTitle)
            .padding(20)
            .background(Color.gray)
            .overlay(
                Color(red: 1, green: 1, blue: 0.3, opacity: 0.2)
                    .frame(width: 160, height: 40)
            )
    }
}
```

Listing 5-34: Displaying a view in front of another view

Figure 5-51: Overlay

The `Color` view also includes the following property and method to apply simple effects to the views.

▷ **gradient**—This property applies a gentle gradient to the color.

▷ **opacity**(Double)—This method defines the color's opacity. The argument takes values from 0.0 (fully transparent) to 1.0 (fully opaque).

The `gradient` property returns a gentle gradient generated from the original color. It can be applied anywhere a `Color` view is implemented. For instance, in the following example, we apply it to the background of our `Text` view.

```
struct ContentView: View {
    var body: some View {
        Text("Hello World")
            .font(.largeTitle)
            .padding(20)
            .background(Color.gray.gradient)
    }
}
```

Listing 5-35: Applying a predefined gradient to a view

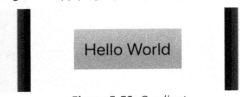

Figure 5-52: Gradient

The `Color` structure also includes a type method to blend two colors.

▷ **mix(with:** Color, **by:** Double, **in:** Gradient.ColorSpace)—This type method mixes the original color with the color specified by the **with** argument and returns a `Color` view with the result. The **by** argument specifies the amount of blending (0.0 to 1.0), and the **in** argument determines the color space used to blend the colors (`.perpetual` by default)

In the following example, we define the background color of the text view with a 50% blend between red and blue.

```
struct ContentView: View {
    var body: some View {
        Text("Hello World")
            .font(.largeTitle)
            .padding(20)
            .background(Color.blue.mix(with: Color.red, by: 0.5))
    }
}
```

Listing 5-36: Blending colors

Chapter 5 - SwiftUI Framework

(Basic) **Materials**

Modern interfaces make extensive use of blur effects and transparency. Although we can set the opacity of a `Color` view to make it translucent, as we did in Listing 5-34, the SwiftUI framework offers a better alternative with Materials. Materials apply a blur effect to the background of a view that resembles the visual effect caused by frosted glass. SwiftUI includes the `Material` structure to create these materials, and this structure defines the following type properties to produce standard effects: `ultraThinMaterial`, `thinMaterial`, `regularMaterial`, `thickMaterial`, and `ultraThickMaterial`.

Materials are applied to the view with the `background()` modifier. The translucent effect they produce is useful when the view appears on top of other views, but we can test it with a single view, as shown below.

```
struct ContentView: View {
    var body: some View {
        Text("Hello World")
            .font(.largeTitle)
            .background(.thickMaterial)
    }
}
```

Listing 5-37: Applying a material

Because we only have one view and the root view is white, the effect is barely visible, but materials become useful when working with multiple views and images, as we will see later.

Figure 5-53: Material applied to a view

Materials can also be applied to the view's content with the `foregroundStyle()` modifier, as in the following example.

```
struct ContentView: View {
    var body: some View {
        Text("Hello World")
            .font(.largeTitle)
            .background(.red)
            .foregroundStyle(.thickMaterial)
    }
}
```

Listing 5-38: Applying a material to the view's content

Figure 5-54: Material applied to the text

Images

Images are used for everything in modern applications, from backgrounds and patterns to the creation of customized controls. But before incorporating images into our projects, we must consider that they are stored in files with a resolution in pixels, while the user interface is defined in points. As we already mentioned, the screens of Apple devices have different resolutions and scales. In some devices, one point represents one pixel and in others more. At this moment, three scales have been defined: 1x, 2x, and 3x. The 1x scale defines one point as one pixel, the 2x scale defines 1 point as a square of 2 pixels, and the 3x scale defines one point as a square of three pixels. For this reason, every time we want to show images in our interface, we must consider the conversion between pixels and points. For example, if we have an image of 300 pixels wide and 400 pixels tall, in a device with a scale of 1x the image will almost fill the screen, but in a device with a scale of 2x the image will look half its size. The image is occupying the same space, 300 by 400 pixels, but because of the higher resolution the pixels represent a smaller area on the screen in devices with scales of 2x or 3x, as shown below.

Figure 5-55: Same image in devices with different scale

One solution to this problem is to scale up a small image in devices with higher resolution or scale down a big image in devices with lower resolution. For example, we can expand an image of 300 x 400 pixels to 600 x 800 pixels and make it look like the same size in a screen with a scale of 2x (a space of 300 x 400 points represents 600 x 800 pixels at this scale), or we could start with an image of 600 x 800 pixels and reduce it to 300 x 400 pixels for devices with half the scale. One way or another, we have a problem. If we expand a small image to fill the screen, it loses quality, and if we reduce it, it occupies unnecessary space in memory because the image is never shown in its original resolution. Fortunately, there is a more efficient solution. It requires us to include in our project three versions of the same image, one for every scale. Considering the image of our example, we will need one picture of the husky in a size of 300 x 400 pixels for devices with a scale of 1x, another of 600 x 800 pixels for devices with a scale of 2x, and a third one of 900 x 1200 for devices with a scale of 3x. Now, the images can be shown in the same size and with the same quality no matter the device or the scale.

Figure 5-56: Different images for specific scales

Providing the same image in different resolutions solves the problem but introduces some complications. We must create three versions of the same image and then select which one is going to be shown depending on the scale of the device. To help us select the right image, Apple systems detect the scale that corresponds to the image by reading a suffix on the file's name. What we need to do is to provide three files with the same name but with suffixes that determine the scale for which they were designed. The file containing the image for the 1x scale (300 x 400 pixels in our example) only requires the name and the extension (e.g., **husky.png**), the name of the file with the image for the 2x scale (600 x 800) must include the suffix @2x (e.g., **husky@2x.png**), and the name of the file with the image for the 3x scale (900 x 1200) must include the suffix @3x (e.g., **husky@3x.png**). Every time the interface requires an image, the system reads the suffixes and loads the one corresponding to the scale of the screen.

 IMPORTANT: We have created an app that can take an image of a scale of 3x and reduce it to create the versions for the rest of the scales. It can also help you generate the icons for your app and apply effects (We will see how to add icons to the project in Chapter 21). The application is available at **www.jdgauchat.com/easyconverter/**.

There are two ways to incorporate images into our project. We can drag the files to the Navigator Area, as we did before for the font type (see Figure 5-32), or add the images to the Asset Catalog. The latter is the preferred option because it simplifies the management of a large number of images. The images are added to the Asset Catalog and then referenced from code by name. This is similar to what we have done to create custom colors (see Figure 5-43). We create an Image Set and then fill the placeholders with the images we want to add to the project.

New sets are added from the + button in the lower left corner (circled in Figure 5-42) or the Editor menu at the top of the screen. If we open the Editor menu and click on the option Add New Asset / *Image Set*, a new empty set is created.

Figure 5-57: *New set of images*

The name of the set is the name we are going to use to get the image from code. Xcode calls the new set *Image* but we can click on it and change it, as we did for colors. Once the set is created, we can drag the files from Finder to the corresponding squares. For example, the file husky.png mentioned before goes inside the 1x square, the file husky@2x.png goes inside the 2x square, and the file husky@3x.png goes inside the 3x square. Figure 5-58, below, shows the Editor Area after the images of a husky are dragged from Finder to the Asset Catalog and the name of the set is changed to "husky".

Figure 5-58: *The husky set is ready*

Although we can add all of our images one by one, as we did in this example, the process soon becomes tedious. An easy way to create a new set is to drag the three images for the set to the Asset Catalog. Xcode creates a new set with the images and assigns their names as the name of the set. The creation and configuration of the set is done automatically when we drag the files and drop them inside the Asset Catalog. In fact, we can drag several files at the same time and Xcode takes care of extracting the information and creating all the sets for us.

In addition to the image for every scale, we can also add versions for different devices and appearances. By default, the set of images is assigned to a Universal device, which means that the images of the set are going to be displayed on all devices, but we can add to the set images for a specific device by selecting the options in the Attributes Inspector panel.

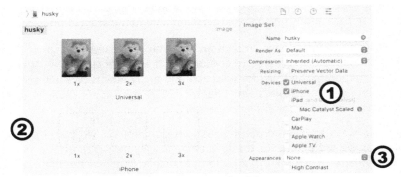

Figure 5-59: *Images for iPhones*

When a set is selected, the Attributes Inspector panel shows the list of properties assigned to the set, including Devices and Appearance (Figure 5-59, number 1 and 2). If we check the box of a device or select a different value for the appearance (Dark or Light), the interface adds placeholders where we can drag and drop the images for that specific attribute. For instance, in Figure 5-59, we checked the box for iPhones and now we have three placeholders to add images for that specific device (number 2). After the images are incorporated into the Asset Catalog, we can load the image from our code using its name and the system will pick the right version according to the characteristics of the device in which the app is running.

 IMPORTANT: The Multiplatform App template includes an additional Asset Catalog to incorporate images into the project that are only going to be used for previews during development. The item is called Preview Assets and it is inside a group called Preview Content. The resources added to this Asset Catalog are available during development but not included in the app's final build.

Once the images are included in the Assets Catalog, we can show them in our application. SwiftUI includes the **Image** view for this purpose. The following are some of the view's initializers.

▷ **Image**(ImageResource)—This initializer creates an **Image** view with the image indicated by the argument. The argument is a reference to the **ImageResource** structure that represents the image in the Asset Catalog or a string with the name of the set.

▷ **Image(systemName:** String, **variableValue:** Double)—This initializer creates an **Image** view with an SF symbol. The **systemName** argument is the name of the symbol, and the **variableValue** argument is a value between 0.0 and 1.0 that determines the symbol's appearance.

▷ **Image(uiImage:** UIImage)—This initializer creates an **Image** view from a **UIImage** object.

An **Image** view can load and display any image in the Asset Catalog. All we need is to specify its name. For instance, the following example creates an **Image** view with an image we put in the Asset Catalog called "Toronto".

```
struct ContentView: View {
   var body: some View {
      Image("Toronto")
   }
}
```

Listing 5-39: Displaying an image

When an image is added to the Asset Catalog, Xcode creates an `ImageResource` structure to represent it, and this structure is assigned to a static property that we can reference to load the image. Note that the name of the property is defined after the name of the set, but in lowercase letters, as shown below.

```
struct ContentView: View {
   var body: some View {
      Image(.toronto)
   }
}
```

Listing 5-40: Loading an image from the `ImageResource` structure

 Do It Yourself: Download the Toronto.jpg image from our website or provide your own. Drag the files to the Asset Catalog in your project. Modify the **ContentView** view with the code in Listing 5-40. You should see a picture of Toronto on the canvas.

By default, **Image** views are the size of their content. If the image is larger than the window, as in this case, the view will extend beyond the limits of the screen.

Figure 5-60: Image view larger than the screen

The image is independent of the view. If we resize the view with the `frame()` modifier, the image remains at its original size. To fit the image to the space provided by the view, we need to apply the following modifiers.

▷ **clipped()**—This modifier clips the image to the view's frame.

▷ **resizable(capInsets:** EdgeInsets, **resizingMode:** Image.ResizingMode)—
   This modifier resizes the image to fit the view frame. The **capInsets** argument specifies the portion of the image that shouldn't be resized, and the **resizingMode** argument specifies how the image is resized to fit the available space. It is an enumeration with the values **stretch** (default) and **tile**.

- **aspectRatio(CGSize, contentMode:** ContentMode)—This modifier changes the image's aspect ratio to the values specified by the first argument and resizes the image according to the mode specified by the **contentMode** argument. This argument is an enumeration of type **ContentMode** with the values **fill** and **fit**. If we want to use the original aspect ratio, we can declare the first argument as **nil** or just ignore it.
- **scaledToFit()**—This modifier scales the image to fit within the view. It works like the **aspectRatio()** modifier with the aspect ratio set to **nil** and the mode to **fit**.
- **scaledToFill()**—This modifier scales the image to fill the view. It works like the **aspectRatio()** modifier with the aspect ratio set to **nil** and the mode to **fill**.

There are several types of transformations we can perform on an image using these modifiers. An alternative is to clip the image to the frame of the view with the `clipped()` modifier.

```
struct ContentView: View {
    var body: some View {
        Image(.toronto)
            .frame(width: 250, height: 100)
            .clipped()
    }
}
```

Listing 5-41: Clipping the image

The `clipped()` modifier creates a new view that only shows the part of the image that is within the view's frame.

Figure 5-61: Image clipped

This reduces the size of the visible image, but the image is still presented in its original size, independent of the size of the view. To adapt the size of the image to the size of the view, we have to make the image flexible with the `resizable()` modifier.

```
struct ContentView: View {
    var body: some View {
        Image(.toronto)
            .resizable()
            .frame(width: 250, height: 100)
    }
}
```

Listing 5-42: Resizing the image

If we only need to resize the image to fit the available space, we don't need to specify an argument. By default, the `resizable()` modifier creates a view that stretches the image.

Figure 5-62: Image resized

IMPORTANT: As we already mentioned, modifiers return a new view and therefore the order in which they are applied matters. The `resizable()` modifier applied in Listing 5-42 is implemented by the **Image** structure and therefore it must be applied first. If we try to declared this modifier after the `frame()` modifier, we will get an error because the `frame()` modifier does not return an **Image** view, it returns a view of type **some View**.

In the previous example, we didn't need to clip the image because the `resizable()` modifier resizes the image to fit the view, but that creates a different problem. The image is squashed. If we want to resize the image but keep its original aspect ratio, we must define the content mode with the `aspectRatio()` modifier. The available values are `fit` (Aspect Fit) and `fill` (Aspect Fill).

```
struct ContentView: View {
    var body: some View {
        Image(.toronto)
            .resizable()
            .aspectRatio(contentMode: .fit)
            .frame(width: 250, height: 100)
    }
}
```
***Listing 5-43:** Resizing an image to fit the view*

In this example, we create an **Image** view with the same image as before, but this time we resize it with the `resizable()` modifier and make it fit within the space available preserving its original aspect ratio with the `aspectRatio()` modifier. The same effect can be achieved with the `scaledToFit()` modifier.

```
struct ContentView: View {
    var body: some View {
        Image(.toronto)
            .resizable()
            .scaledToFit()
            .frame(width: 250, height: 100)
    }
}
```
***Listing 5-44:** Resizing the image to fit within the view with the* `scaledToFit()` *modifier*

There are two modes available: `fit` and `fill` (`scaledToFit()` and `scaledToFill()`) Figure 5-63, below, shows what happens when we apply these content modes to the image of our example.

***Figure 5-63:** Aspect fit (left) and aspect fill (right)*

In `fit` mode, the image is resized to fit the view but some parts of the frame remain empty (Figure 5-63, left), while in `fill` mode, the image is resized to fill the view but some parts of the image are displayed outside the area occupied by the view (Figure 5-63, right). If we want to use the **fill** mode to fill the view but don't want the image to extend beyond the boundaries of the view, we can clip it with the **clipped()** modifier.

```
struct ContentView: View {
    var body: some View {
        Image(.toronto)
            .resizable()
            .scaledToFill()
            .frame(width: 250, height: 100)
            .clipped()
    }
}
```

Listing 5-45: *Resizing and clipping the image to fill the view*

Figure 5-64: *Clipped image*

Often, the user interface must include a view with an image that adapts to the space available. An easy way to achieve this is to make the image resizable and set its mode to **fit**.

```
struct ContentView: View {
    var body: some View {
        Image(.toronto)
            .resizable()
            .scaledToFit()
    }
}
```

Listing 5-46: *Resizing image to fill the container*

When the size of the frame is not declared, the view works along with the content to set its size. At first, the view takes all the space available in its container, but then it asks the image what size to take. Because the image mode was set to **fit**, the image allows the view to extend as much as it can but adjusts the view's height to its own height to preserve the original aspect ratio. The result is shown below.

Figure 5-65: *Flexible* Image *view*

Of course, we can also apply common modifiers to an **Image** view. Some modify the view, others the image. The following example adds a padding and a shadow to our image.

```
struct ContentView: View {
    var body: some View {
        Image("Toronto")
            .resizable()
            .scaledToFit()
            .shadow(color: Color.black, radius: 10, x: 10, y: 10)
            .padding(30)
    }
}
```

***Listing 5-47:** Applying style modifiers to an* Image *view*

***Figure 5-66:** Image view with common modifiers*

The **View** protocol also defines modifiers that are particularly useful with **Image** views. The following are the most frequently used.

▷ **blur(radius:** CGFloat, **opaque:** Bool)—This modifier applies a blur effect to the view. The **radius** argument determines how diffuse the blur effect is, and the **opaque** argument determines whether the blur effect is going to be opaque or transparent.

▷ **colorMultiply(**Color)—This modifier multiplies the colors of the view by a specific color. The result is that the original colors of the view tend to the color defined by the argument.

▷ **grayscale(**Double)—This modifier adds a grayscale effect to the view. The argument is a value between 0.0 (colorful) to 1.0 (grayscale).

▷ **contrast(**Double)—This modifier applies contrast to the view.

▷ **opacity(**Double)—This modifier defines the view's opacity. The argument takes values from 0.0 (fully transparent) to 1.0 (fully opaque).

▷ **scaleEffect(**CGSize)—This modifier changes the horizontal and vertical scales of the view to the values specified by the argument. The modifier only affects the view's content.

The implementation of these modifiers is straightforward. The following example scales the image to half its size and makes it blurry.

```
struct ContentView: View {
    var body: some View {
        Image(.toronto)
            .resizable()
            .scaledToFit()
            .padding()
            .scaleEffect(CGSize(width: 0.5, height: 0.5))
            .blur(radius: 5)
```

```
        }
}
```

Listing 5-48: Applying visual effects to an `Image` *view*

The size of the view remains the same, but the size of the image is reduced by half with the `scaleEffect()` modifier.

Figure 5-67: Visual effects applied to an image

In addition to the modifiers available to specify the size of the view and scale the image, we can also adapt it to the font size selected by the user from Settings, as we did before with Dynamic fonts (see Listing 5-17). For this purpose, SwiftUI includes the following property wrapper.

▷ **@ScaledMetric(relativeTo:** TextStyle)—This property wrapper scales a value according to the font size selected by the user from the Settings app. The **relativeTo** argument is an enumeration value that determines the dynamic font type of reference. The values available are **body**, **callout**, **caption1**, **caption2**, **footnote**, **headline**, **subheadline**, **largeTitle**, **extraLargeTitle**, **extraLargeTitle2**, **title1**, **title2**, and **title3**. If the argument is ignored, the value is scaled relative to the style set by the system.

As mentioned in Chapter 3, property wrappers create properties with predefined functionality that can store and process values. In this case, the **@ScaledMetric** property wrapper increments or decrements a base value according to the font size selected by the user from the Settings app. This is particularly useful with images. For instance, we can define a property with a value of 100 and use it to set the size of an **Image** view with the **frame()** modifier.

```
struct ContentView: View {
    @ScaledMetric var customSize: CGFloat = 100

    var body: some View {
        Image(.toronto)
            .resizable()
            .frame(width: customSize, height: customSize)
    }
}
```

Listing 5-49: Scaling an image to the selected font size

 Do It Yourself: Update the `ContentView` view with the code in Listing 5-49. You should see the image with the size determined by the base value (100) and the dynamic font type set by the system. Click the Settings button at the bottom of the canvas (Figure 5-18, number 4), activate the Dynamic Type option, and select the size you want to test. You should see that the size of the image changes depending on the selected font size.

Apple systems provide predefined images we can use in our applications. We have introduced emojis in Chapter 2 (see Figure 2-11). Emojis can be included in strings and displayed on the screen with a **Text** view, as any other character. Their purpose is to convey information or mood, so they don't scale well and should only be used along with text to establish an emotional connection with the user or between users. To incorporate icons that represent functionality, Apple recommends using symbols designed specifically for this purpose called *SF Symbols*. These symbols are scalable, come in different versions, and adapt to the current font, so that they can be easily integrated into the rest of the interface.

There are a variety of symbols for any need our application might have. To help us find the symbols we want, Apple offers a free application called SF Symbols, which we can download from **developer.apple.com** (Develop/Downloads/Release/Applications). The application includes options to search for symbols by name or category.

Figure 5-68: *SF Symbols app*

Symbols are displayed with an **Image** view using the initializer **Image(systemName:)**, as in the following example.

```
struct ContentView: View {
    var body: some View {
        Image(systemName: "envelope")
    }
}
```

Listing 5-50: *Displaying SF symbols*

SF symbols were designed to work with text and therefore their size and style can be determined by a **Font** structure, as shown below.

```
struct ContentView: View {
    var body: some View {
        Image(systemName: "envelope")
            .font(Font.system(size: 100).weight(.semibold))
    }
}
```

Listing 5-51: *Styling a symbol*

In the example of Listing 5-51, we apply the **font()** modifier with the system font, a size of 100 points, and a weight of type **semibold**. Note that we declare the modifiers all in one line, but we could have defined the **Font** in a constant and use that constant to apply it to the **Image** view, as in the following example.

```
struct ContentView: View {
    let myfont = Font.system(size: 100)

    var body: some View {
        Image(systemName: "envelope")
            .font(myfont.weight(.semibold))
    }
}
```

Listing 5-52: Storing the font in a constant

The code in Listing 5-52 initializes a **Font** structure with the system's font and a size of 100, and then modifies an **Image** view with this font and a weight of type **semibold**. This is the same as before, but makes our code easier to read. No matter how our code is organized, the view always shows the symbol of an envelope on the screen.

Figure 5-69: SF Symbol

SF Symbols come in different versions. For instance, the symbol with the name "envelope" implemented in our example has a version with a circle around it, another with a badge, and more. These are called *Variants* and are specified after the symbol's name using dot notation, as in envelope.circle, or envelope.fill. All the variants of a symbol can be found in the SF Symbol application, but the framework also includes the following modifier to specify a variant.

▷ **symbolVariant(**SymbolVariants**)**—This modifier assigns a variant to a symbol. The argument is a structure with the type properties **none**, **circle**, **square**, **rectangle**, **fill**, and **slash**.

The image is created as before, but now the modifier determines the symbol's variant.

```
struct ContentView: View {
    var body: some View {
        Image(systemName: "envelope")
            .font(Font.system(size: 100))
            .symbolVariant(.fill)
    }
}
```

Listing 5-53: Assigning a variant to a symbol

This is the same as creating the **Image** view with the "envelope.fill" string, but selecting the variant from a modifier allows us to modify the symbol and animate the changes according to changes in the state of the view, as we will see later.

Figure 5-70: A variant of an SF Symbol

SF Symbols are displayed in the color and size of the font, but some symbols can include up to three more colors, and all of them can be scaled up or down. SwiftUI includes the following modifiers for this purpose.

▷ **symbolRenderingMode**(SymbolRenderingMode)—This modifier sets the symbol's rendering mode. The argument is a structure with the type properties **hierarchical**, **monochrome** (default), **multicolor**, and **palette**.

▷ **imageScale**(Scale)—This modifier sets the symbol's scale. The size is determined from the size of the font and the scale specified by the argument. The argument is an enumeration with the values **small**, **medium**, and **large**.

The **symbolRenderingMode()** modifier can set up four different color modes. By default, the **monochrome** mode is selected, which means that the symbol is displayed in only one color (the color of the font or the view), but there are others available. The **hierarchical** mode defines a set of colors from a base color, the **multicolor** mode shows the symbol with its original colors, and the **palette** mode shows the symbol with custom colors.

Not all the symbols are multicolor. We can find multicolor symbols by selecting the Multicolor category in the SF Symbol app. For instance, in the following example we show the mic.badge.plus, which has two colors.

```
struct ContentView: View {
    var body: some View {
        Image(systemName: "mic.badge.plus")
            .font(Font.system(size: 100))
            .symbolRenderingMode(.multicolor)
    }
}
```

Listing 5-54: Displaying multicolor symbols

Figure 5-71: Multicolor symbol

The microphone is displayed with the color by default (the font color or the foreground color assigned to the view), and the badge is green. These are the symbol's original colors, but we can change them by specifying the **hierarchical** or **palette** modes. The colors for these modes are specified by the **foregroundStyle()** modifier, as in the following example.

```
struct ContentView: View {
    var body: some View {
        Image(systemName: "mic.badge.plus")
            .font(Font.system(size: 100))
            .symbolRenderingMode(.palette)
            .foregroundStyle(.red, .blue)
    }
}
```

Listing 5-55: Displaying a multicolor symbol with custom colors

The colors are declared with the **foregroundStyle()** modifier separated by comma. In this example, the symbol requires two colors, one for the microphone and another for the badge, but some symbols may use more. The result is shown below.

Figure 5-72: Multicolor symbol with custom colors

Some SF Symbols may have variable colors to represent different states. For example, some symbols contain graphics that resemble radio waves and change color to represent different signal levels. To implement these symbols, we must initialize the `Image` view with the `variableValue` argument. The value of this argument determines the variety of the symbol that will be displayed. The value required to jump from one state to another depends on the number of states the symbol can take. In the following example, we display a symbol with 5 states.

```
struct ContentView: View {
    var body: some View {
        Image(systemName: "dot.radiowaves.forward", variableValue: 0.8)
            .font(.largeTitle)
    }
}
```

Listing 5-56: Displaying a variable SF Symbol

The value of the **variableValue** argument must be below the threshold for each state. The symbol implemented in the view of Listing 5-56 have 5 states and therefore we just have to find a value that is below the threshold for the state we want to display. Below are the possible values for this symbol and all the states it can take.

Figure 5-73: Variable SF Symbol

Although we can combine `Text` views with symbols to build the interface, as we will see later, SwiftUI includes a view called `Label` to show a text along with an image. This is specially useful with SF Symbols because they can automatically adapt to the size and style of the text. The structure includes the following initializers and modifier to create these views.

- ▷ **Label**(String, **systemImage:** String)—This initializer creates a label with the text specified by the first argument and the SF Symbol specified by the **systemImage** argument.

- ▷ **Label**(String, **image:** String)—This initializer creates a label with the text specified by the first argument and the image specified by the **image** argument.

- ▷ **labelStyle**(LabelStyle)—This modifier configures the label. The argument is a structure that conforms to the `LabelStyle` protocol, which defines type properties to tell the label what to include. The properties available are `automatic` (default), `iconOnly`, `titleAndIcon`, and `titleOnly`.

A `Label` view determines the text and the image to be shown, but we can use the `font()` modifier to specify the characteristics of the font, as shown below.

```
struct ContentView: View {
    var body: some View {
        Label("Hello", systemImage: "envelope.circle")
            .font(.largeTitle)
            .labelStyle(.titleAndIcon)
            .imageScale(.large)
    }
}
```

Listing 5-57: Displaying a text with an SF Symbol

Note that in this example we implement the **imageScale()** modifier to make the symbol slightly larger than the text. The result is shown below.

Figure 5-74: Label with an SF Symbol

 IMPORTANT: SF Symbols can also be animated. There are a variety of options available. We will learn how to apply animations and effects to views and SF Symbols in Chapter 11.

(Basic) **Event Modifiers**

In addition to the modifiers to change the styles and format of the views, SwiftUI includes modifiers to respond to events. These events can be produced by the user, such as when the user touches the screen with a finger, or by the system, such as when information is received from a network. There are multiple modifiers available to process events, some are generic, others more specific. The most important for views and the user interface are **onAppear()** and **onDisappear()**, used to perform a task when a view appears or disappears from the screen.

 ▷ **onAppear(perform:** Closure)—This modifier executes the closure specified by the **perform** argument when the view appears on the screen.

 ▷ **onDisappear(perform:** Closure)—This modifier executes the closure specified by the **perform** argument when the view disappears from the screen.

These modifiers are applied like any other, but they are executed when the system detects the event to which they respond. For instance, in the following example we print a message on the console with the **onAppear()** modifier, but the text is not printed until the view appears on the screen.

```
struct ContentView: View {
    let fontSize: CGFloat = 100

    var body: some View {
        Image(systemName: "envelope.circle")
            .font(Font.system(size: fontSize))
            .onAppear(perform: {
                print("Current font size: \(self.fontSize)")
            })
```

```
    }
}
```

Listing 5-58: Performing a task when the view appears

 IMPORTANT: In addition to the **onAppear()** and **onDisappear()** modifiers, SwiftUI includes other event modifiers, such as gesture modifiers to perform a task when a gesture is detected. We will see some practical examples of these modifiers in later chapters and study gesture modifiers in Chapter 12.

(Medium) # Custom Modifiers

Interfaces with single views, like those we have created so far, are the exception. User interfaces are created from the combination of multiple views. This means that more often than not we will find ourselves applying the same modifiers over and over again. In cases like this, we can avoid repetition by implementing custom modifiers. Custom modifiers encapsulate multiple modifiers in a single structure that we can apply later to the views with the **modifier()** modifier. The structure must conform to the **ViewModifier** protocol and implement a method called **body** that receives a parameter of type **Content**. The parameter represents the view we want to modify and, therefore, it is to this parameter that we apply the actual modifiers, as shown below.

```
import SwiftUI
struct MyModifiers: ViewModifier {
    func body(content: Content) -> some View {
        content
            .font(Font.system(size: 100).weight(.semibold))
            .foregroundColor(Color.blue)
    }
}
struct ContentView: View {
    var body: some View {
        Image(systemName: "envelope.circle")
            .modifier(MyModifiers())
    }
}
```

Listing 5-59: Applying custom modifiers

In this example, we define a structure that conforms to the **ViewModifier** protocol and then apply the **font()** and **foregroundColor()** modifiers to the **content** parameter of the **body** method. This defines a custom modifier called **MyModifiers** that then we can apply to the views in our interface. The result is the same as applying the modifiers directly to the views, but it makes our code less repetitive.

Figure 5-75: Custom modifiers applied to a view

As any other structure, the **ViewModifier** structure can include properties, and those properties may get different values every time the modifier is applied. For example, we can include a property to store a **CGFloat** value, so every time the custom modifier is applied, we can select the size to be assigned to the font.

```
struct MyModifiers: ViewModifier {
    var size: CGFloat

    func body(content: Content) -> some View {
        content
            .font(Font.system(size: size).weight(.semibold))
            .foregroundColor(Color.blue)
    }
}
struct ContentView: View {
    var body: some View {
        Image(systemName: "envelope.circle")
            .modifier(MyModifiers(size: 50))
    }
}
```

Listing 5-60: Customizing a custom modifier

Basic ## 5.3 Layout

The closure assigned to the **body** property must return only one view. So far we haven't had any problems because all our examples have returned only a **Text** view or an **Image** view, but a useful user interface requires the implementation of multiple views. Some serve as containers, others display content, and there are multiple views for processing user input. Therefore, to create a user interface, we need to be able to group multiple views into a single view and arrange them on the screen. The solution proposed by SwiftUI is to work with stacks.

Basic Stacks

Views can be arranged in three different ways: horizontally, vertically, or overlapping. SwiftUI defines the following views to create these stacks.

▷ **VStack(alignment:** HorizontalAlignment, **spacing:** CGFloat?, **content:** Closure)—This view creates a vertical stack to arrange a group of views vertically. The **alignment** argument determines the horizontal alignment of the views. It is a structure with the type properties **center**, **leading**, and **trailing**. The **spacing** argument determines the space between the views, and the **content** argument is a closure that defines the list of views we want to show in the stack.

▷ **HStack(alignment:** VerticalAlignment, **spacing:** CGFloat?, **content:** Closure)—This view creates a horizontal stack to arrange a group of views horizontally. The **alignment** argument determines the vertical alignment of the views. It is a structure with the type properties **bottom**, **center**, **firstTextBaseline**, **lastTextBaseline**, and **top**. The **spacing** argument determines the space between the views, and the **content** argument is a closure that defines the list of views we want to show in the stack.

▷ **ZStack(alignment:** Alignment, **content:** Closure)—This view creates a stack that overlays a group of views. The **alignment** argument determines the horizontal and vertical alignment of the views. It is a structure with the type properties **bottom**, **bottomLeading**, **bottomTrailing**, **center**, **leading**, **top**, **topLeading**, **topTrailing**, and **trailing**. The **content** argument is a closure that defines the list of views we want to show in the stack.

Stacks are created with values by default. For instance, a **VStack** aligns its views to the center and with a standard space in between. If that's all we need, we just have to declare its content.

```
struct ContentView: View {
    var body: some View {
        VStack {
            Text("City")
            Text("New York")
        }
    }
}
```

Listing 5-61: Creating a vertical stack of views

The closure assigned to the **content** argument is a **Content** closure. **Content** closures are processed by a property wrapper called **@ViewBuilder** which job is to construct views from closures. This means that all we need to do to create the content of a stack is to list the views one after another, and the compiler takes care of creating the code to present them on the screen in that same order.

In Listing 5-61, we include two **Text** views inside a **VStack** view. The **Text** views take the size of their content and are displayed one on top of the other, and the **VStack** view takes the width of its largest child and the height from the sum of the heights of its children.

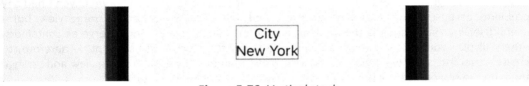

Figure 5-76: Vertical stack

By default, the views inside a **VStack** are aligned to the center, but we can change that with the **alignment** argument. In addition to **center**, the argument can take the values **leading** and **trailing**, which mean left and right when the device is configured with a left-to-right language.

```
struct ContentView: View {
    var body: some View {
        VStack(alignment: .leading) {
            Text("City")
            Text("New York")
        }
    }
}
```

Listing 5-62: Aligning views in a vertical stack

Another value defined by default is the space between the views. If we don't specify any value, the views are placed on top of each other with a standard space in between. There are multiple ways to include a space between the views. One is with the **padding()** modifier introduced before. But if the stack contains multiple views, we will have to assign the modifier to each one of them. An easier way to do this is to declare the **spacing** argument.

```
struct ContentView: View {
    var body: some View {
        VStack(alignment: .leading, spacing: 20) {
            Text("City")
            Text("New York")
        }
    }
}
```

Listing 5-63: Adding a space between the views

The space is added only between the views, not at the top or the bottom. The purpose is to separate the views, as shown below.

Figure 5-77: *Vertical stack aligned to the left with a space of 20 points in between*

The **HStack** view works in a similar way. The views are declared as before, one after another, and the compiler takes care of creating the code to display them side by side.

```
struct ContentView: View {
    var body: some View {
        HStack {
            Image(systemName: "cloud")
                .font(.system(size: 80))
            Text("New York")
        }
    }
}
```

Listing 5-64: *Creating a horizontal stack of views*

By default, the views in a horizontal stack are aligned to the center and positioned with a standard space in between (usually 8 points).

Figure 5-78: *Horizontal stack aligned to the center*

An **HStack** view includes the same arguments as a **VStack** for alignment and spacing, but the **alignment** argument specifies the vertical alignment. This is useful when the stack is composed of views of different heights, as in our example. The height of the stack is determined by the height of its tallest view and the rest of the views are aligned according to the argument's value. Figure 5-79, below, shows all the possible vertical alignments. In this example, we reduced the width of the stack to force the **Text** view to display the text in two lines, which allows us to show how the **firstTextBaseline** and the **lastTextBaseline** alignments work.

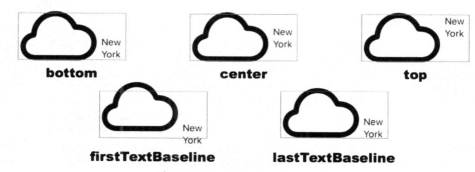

Figure 5-79: HStack *alignments*

In addition to vertical and horizontal stacks, SwiftUI also provides the `ZStack` view for overlaying views. The views appear on the screen in front of each other in the same order in which they are declared in the stack.

```
struct ContentView: View {
    var body: some View {
        ZStack(alignment: .center) {
            Image(systemName: "cloud")
                .font(.system(size: 80))
            Text("New York")
                .font(.body.bold())
                .foregroundColor(.gray)
        }
    }
}
```

Listing 5-65: Creating a `ZStack`

Figure 5-80: Views in a `ZStack`

If we ignore the **alignment** argument, the views are aligned to the center, but there are other alignments available. The values are **bottom**, **bottomLeading**, **bottomTrailing**, **center**, **leading**, **top**, **topLeading**, **topTrailing**, and **trailing**.

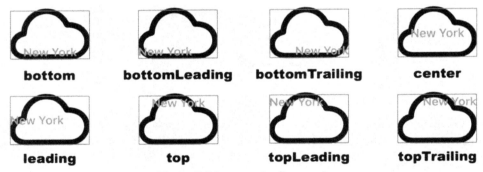

Figure 5-81: `ZStack` alignments

When views overlap, like those included in a `ZStack` view, the system determines the order in which they appear on the screen from the order in the code. The first view is drawn first, then the second view is drawn in front of it, and so on. The `View` protocol defines the following modifier to change this order.

▷ **zIndex**(Double)—This modifier sets the order of the view in the Z axis (the axis perpendicular to the screen).

By default, all the views are assigned the index 0, which means they are all at the same level, and that is why the system draws the views according to the order in which they are declared in the code, but we can move a view to the back by assigning a negative Z index or to the front with a value greater than 0. When views have different indexes, they are drawn in the order determined by those values, starting from the view with the smallest index. In the following example, we include the same `Image` view and `Text` view used before, but because we set an index of -1 for the `Text` view, it is drawn in the back.

Chapter 5 - SwiftUI Framework

```
struct ContentView: View {
    var body: some View {
        ZStack {
            Image(systemName: "cloud")
                .font(.system(size: 80))
            Text("New York")
                .padding(8)
                .background(Color.yellow)
                .zIndex(-1)
        }
    }
}
```

Listing 5-66: *Setting the Z index of a view*

The **Text** view in Listing 5-66 includes a yellow background, so we can see its position in the Z axis. The **Image** view should be drawn first, and then the **Text** view should cover most of the image, but because we set an index of -1 for the **Text** view, it is drawn in the back.

Figure 5-82: *Custom Z index*

When we group views with a stack, we can apply style modifiers to all the views at the same time by assigning them to the stack instead of the individual views. For instance, if we want to assign the same color to the **Text** view and the **Image** view of the previous example, we can apply the **foregroundColor()** modifier to the **ZStack** view.

```
struct ContentView: View {
    var body: some View {
        ZStack(alignment: .center) {
            Image(systemName: "cloud")
                .font(.system(size: 80))
            Text("New York")
                .font(.body.bold())
        }.foregroundColor(Color.red)
    }
}
```

Listing 5-67: *Assigning modifiers to the stack and its content*

Figure 5-83: *Modifier applied to the container*

Stacks can be combined and nested as required by the interface. For instance, we can incorporate a **VStack** inside the previous **HStack** to include more text next to the image.

```
struct ContentView: View {
    var body: some View {
        HStack {
            Image(systemName: "cloud")
```

```
            .font(.system(size: 80))
        VStack(alignment: .leading) {
            Text("City")
                .foregroundColor(.gray)
            Text("New York")
                .font(.title)
        }
    }
  }
}
```

Listing 5-68: Nesting stacks

The code in Listing 5-68 defines a **Vstack** view inside an **HStack** view. The **VStack** includes two **Text** views aligned to the left and with different styles.

Figure 5-84: Nested stacks

 IMPORTANT: To include a view in a stack, you can write the code yourself or get Xcode to do it for you by selecting the option from the context menu. We've already used this menu to add modifiers to a **Text** view (see Figure 5-23). To open the menu, hold down the Control key and click on the view. You will find options to embed the view in an **HStack**, a **VStack** or a **ZStack**.

The alignment options available for **VStack** and **HStack** views align the views in the perpendicular axis. A vertical stack can align the views horizontally, and a horizontal stack can align the views vertically. To align the views on the same axis, we must add a flexible space. SwiftUI includes the **Spacer** view for this purpose.

▷ **Spacer(minLength:** CGFloat)—This initializer creates a **Spacer** view that generates a flexible space. The **minLength** argument determines the minimum size in points the space can take. If the argument is not declared, the minimum length is 0.

A **Spacer** view can be implemented any time we need to add a flexible space. It provides a more customizable way to align the views or extend them to the sides of its container. For instance, in the following example we add a flexible space between the image and the **VStack** of our view to move the views to the left and right side of their container.

```
struct ContentView: View {
    var body: some View {
        HStack {
            Image(systemName: "cloud")
                .font(.system(size: 80))
            Spacer()
            VStack(alignment: .leading) {
                Text("City")
                    .foregroundColor(.gray)
                Text("New York")
                    .font(.title)
            }
        }
    }
}
```

Chapter 5 - SwiftUI Framework

}

Listing 5-69: Aligning the views with a flexible space

The system calculates the widths of the image and the stack, and then assigns the rest of the space available to the **Spacer** view in the middle.

Figure 5-85: Flexible space between views

A **Spacer** view can be positioned anywhere on the list, not only between views. This is useful when we want the views to be at the top or the bottom of the screen. For instance, we can embed the **HStack** of previous examples in a **VStack** and add a **Spacer** at the bottom to move our views to the top of the screen.

```
struct ContentView: View {
    var body: some View {
        VStack {
            HStack {
                Image(systemName: "cloud")
                    .font(.system(size: 80))
                VStack(alignment: .leading) {
                    Text("City")
                        .foregroundColor(.gray)
                    Text("New York")
                        .font(.title)
                }
                Spacer()
            }
            Spacer()
        }
    }
}
```

Listing 5-70: Aligning the views to the left and the top

In this example, we use two **Spacer** views, one at the end of the **HStack** to move the views to the left, and another at the end of the main **VStack** to move the **HStack** to the top. This **Spacer** view takes all the space available at the bottom, moving the rest of the views up.

Figure 5-86: Views at the top of the screen

Basic **Safe Area**

The system defines a layout guide called *Safe Area* where we can place the content of our interface. This is the area determined by the space remaining in the window after all the toolbars and special views are displayed by the system (including the island at the top of modern iPhones). That's the reason why there is a space between the view of our previous example and the top of the screen (see Figure 5-86). The white bar at the top is the space occupied by the system's toolbar. Although it is recommended to always build the interface inside the safe area, the **View** protocol provides the following modifier to ignore it.

▷ **ignoresSafeArea(**SafeAreaRegions, **edges:** Edge**)**—This modifier expands the view outside the safe area. The first argument determines the safe areas that are ignored. It is a structure with the type properties **all**, **container**, and **keyboard**. The **edges** argument is a value or a set of values that indicates the sides to be ignored. This is an enumeration with the values **all**, **bottom**, **leading**, **top**, and **trailing**.

There are two safe areas, one called **container** that determines the space available inside the window after all the navigation bars and toolbars are displayed, and another called **keyboard** that determines the remaining space after the virtual keyboard becomes visible.

Figure 5-87: Safe areas

For instance, if we want the interface of our previous example to always extend to the edges of the screen, we can apply the modifier to the **VStack** view with the value **all**.

```
struct ContentView: View {
    var body: some View {
        VStack {
            HStack {
                Image(systemName: "cloud")
                    .font(.system(size: 80))
                VStack(alignment: .leading) {
                    Text("City")
                        .foregroundColor(.gray)
                    Text("New York")
                        .font(.title)
                }
                Spacer()
            }
```

```
            Spacer()
      }.ignoresSafeArea(.all)
   }
}
```

Listing 5-71: Ignoring the safe area

Figure 5-88: *Views ignoring the safe area*

In this example, we ignore all the safe areas and, therefore, our views extend to the edges of the screen, but we can ignore only the container safe area but not the keyboard, so when the virtual keyboard opens, it doesn't overlap the views.

```
struct ContentView: View {
   var body: some View {
      VStack {
         Spacer()
         HStack {
            Image(systemName: "cloud")
               .font(.system(size: 80))
            VStack(alignment: .leading) {
               Text("City")
                  .foregroundColor(.gray)
               Text("New York")
                  .font(.title)
            }
            Spacer()
         }
      }.ignoresSafeArea(.container, edges: .bottom)
   }
}
```

Listing 5-72: Ignoring only the container safe area at the bottom

In this example, we move the **Spacer** view to the top of the vertical stack to push the content down. We ignore the safe area again, so the content is placed right at the bottom of the screen, but because we ignore only the **container** safe area at the bottom, if later we add an element that opens the keyboard, the views will move up to remain visible.

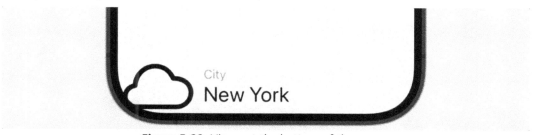

Figure 5-89: *Views at the bottom of the screen*

SwiftUI includes a modifier to expand the safe area. The modifier changes the safe area inset to include additional space.

▷ **safeAreaInset(edge:** Axis, **alignment:** Alignment, **spacing:** CGFloat?, **content:** Closure)—This modifier expands the safe area with a custom view. The **edge** argument determines the side we want to modify. It is specified with the values `leading` and `trailing`, provided by the `HorizontalEdge` enumeration, or the values `bottom` and `top`, provided by the `VerticalEdge` enumeration. The **alignment** argument determines the alignment of the views inside the area. It is specified with the type properties `center`, `leading`, and `trailing`, provided by the `Horizontal-Alignment` structure, or the type properties `bottom`, `center`, `firstTextBaseline`, `lastTextBaseline`, and `top`, provided by the `VerticalAlignment` structure. The **spacing** argument determines the space between the views inside the area. And finally, the **content** argument is a closure that returns the views to show inside the area.

This modifier may be used to make sure that important views at the edge of the screen are always visible, or to create our own navigation bars, as shown next.

```
struct ContentView: View {
    var body: some View {
        VStack {
            Spacer()
            HStack {
                Image(systemName: "cloud")
                    .font(.system(size: 80))
                VStack(alignment: .leading) {
                    Text("City")
                        .foregroundColor(.gray)
                    Text("New York")
                        .font(.title)
                }
                Spacer()
            }
        }
        .safeAreaInset(edge: .bottom, content: {
            HStack {
                Spacer()
                Text("Important")
                    .padding()
                Spacer()
            }.background(.yellow)
        })
    }
}
```

Listing 5-73: Expanding the safe area

In this example, we add an `HStack` view at the bottom of the safe area. This creates a yellow bar at the bottom of the screen with the text "Important", but because this view is part of the safe area, the rest of the content is shown on top.

Figure 5-90: Views expanding the safe area

Stacks divide the space equally among the views, but we must decide what to do when there is not enough room to show them all. By default, the system assigns a fixed size to images and reduces the size of **Text** views to make them fit, as shown below.

```
struct ContentView: View {
    var body: some View {
        HStack {
            Text("Manchester")
                .font(.title)
                .lineLimit(1)
            Image(systemName: "cloud")
                .font(.system(size: 80))
            Text("New York City")
                .font(.title)
                .lineLimit(1)
        }
    }
}
```

Listing 5-74: Arranging the views with priorities by default

This example creates an **HStack** with three views: a text, an image, and another text. In a small iPhone in portrait mode, where there is no room to display them all, the system preserves the image's original size but compresses the **Text** views to make them fit in the remaining space.

Figure 5-91: Priorities by default

Because the **Text** views are limited to only one line, the system truncates the texts. If what we want is to show one of the texts in full, we must assign a higher priority to it. The **View** protocol defines the following modifiers for this purpose.

▷ **layoutPriority(Double)**—This modifier sets the view's priority. A higher priority determines that the view will get as much space as possible. The value by default is 0.

▷ **fixedSize(horizontal: Bool, vertical: Bool)**—This modifier fixes the view to its ideal horizontal or vertical size. If no arguments are specified, the size is fixed on both dimensions.

All the views have a priority of 0 by default. If we want the system to reserve more space for a view, we must declare its priority higher than 0, as in the following example.

```
struct ContentView: View {
    var body: some View {
        HStack {
            Text("Manchester")
                .font(.title)
                .lineLimit(1)
            Image(systemName: "cloud")
                .font(.system(size: 80))
            Text("New York City")
                .font(.title)
                .lineLimit(1)
```

```
            .layoutPriority(1)
        }
    }
}
```

Listing 5-75: Assigning a higher priority to a view

The code in Listing 5-75 assigns a priority of 1 to the second **Text** view. Now the system calculates the space required by this view first and therefore the text is shown in full.

Figure 5-92: Custom priorities

When we assign a higher priority to a view and there is no space to show them all, the system lays out the views with lower priority first, gives them the minimum possible size, and then assigns the remaining space to the view with the higher priority. So, if there is still no room to show the entire view, its content is clipped. If what we want is to force the view to take the size of its content no matter what, we must apply the **fixedSize()** modifier.

```
struct ContentView: View {
    var body: some View {
        HStack {
            Text("Manchester")
                .font(.title)
                .lineLimit(1)
                .fixedSize()
            Image(systemName: "cloud")
                .font(.system(size: 80))
            Text("New York City")
                .font(.title)
                .lineLimit(1)
                .layoutPriority(1)
        }
    }
}
```

Listing 5-76: Defining a view with a fixed size

This is the same code as before, but now we assign the **fixedSize()** modifier to the first **Text** view. In consequence, this view is going to adopt the size of its content and the "Manchester" text will be shown in full, regardless of the priority of the rest of the views.

Figure 5-93: View with a fixed size

Medium Alignment Guides

There are two possible alignments, horizontal and vertical. Horizontal stacks align the views vertically and vertical stacks align the views horizontally. This is because SwiftUI expects the views in the stack to be of different sizes and therefore it needs to know how they are going to be aligned in the perpendicular axis. Usually, this is enough to build a simple interface, but professional applications require more control. The **View** protocol defines the following modifier to customize alignment.

> ▷ **alignmentGuide(**Alignment, **computeValue:** Closure**)**—This modifier defines the values of the horizontal or vertical alignment. The first argument determines the type of alignment we want to customize. It is defined with the type properties **center**, **leading**, and **trailing** from the **HorizontalAlignment** structure, or the type properties **bottom, center, firstTextBaseline, lastTextBaseline**, and **top** from the **VerticalAlignment** structure. The **computeValue** argument is a closure that receives the current dimensions of the view and returns a **CGFloat** with the new value for the alignment.

The following example aligns three images of different sizes. They are all 100 points wide, but the signbus image is 200 points tall, the signplane image is 170 points tall, and the signphone image is 220 points tall. (The images are available on our website.)

```
struct ContentView: View {
    var body: some View {
        HStack(alignment: .center) {
            Image(.signbus)
            Image(.signplane)
            Image(.signphone)
        }.border(Color.blue, width: 2)
    }
}
```

Listing 5-77: Aligning images to the center with standard values

A stack view determines a common point of alignment according to its alignment type and the dimensions of the views. For instance, if the alignment of a vertical stack is **center**, the stack gets the position of the **center** alignment of each view and from that value it calculates a common point of alignment (usually the point of alignment of its tallest view) and then repositions all the views to match that common point.

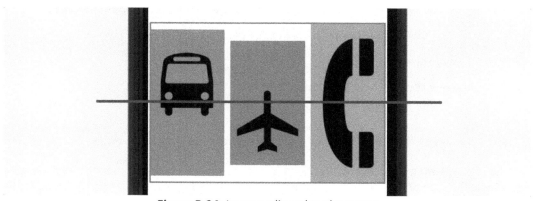

Figure 5-94: Images aligned to the center

Figure 5-94 shows our three images aligned to the center. In this example, we applied a blue border to the stack to make it easy to see the changes produced by the alignment and added a red line on top of the picture to visualize the common point of alignment chose by the stack.

 Do It Yourself: Download the signbus, signplane and signphone images from our website and add them to the Asset Catalog. Update the **ContentView** view with the code in Listing 5-77. You should see something similar to Figure 5-94.

The alignment values are determined by the stack's coordinates system, starting from the top-left corner. The value at the top is 0 and the value at the bottom of the view depends on the children's height. Every view has an alignment guide with values that determine their points of alignment. The value associated with the **top** alignment is 0, the value associated with the **bottom** alignment is equal to the view's height, and the value associated with the **center** alignment is the height divided by two (the formula is: **top** + (**bottom** - **top**) / 2).

The views return these alignment guides by default, but we can change them with the modifier introduced above. For instance, the wheels of the bus in our example are below the common point of alignment (see Figure 5-94, above). This image is 200 points tall, so the center alignment returned by the image is at 100 points, but the wheels are 18 points below.

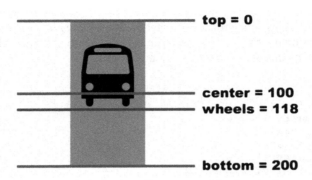

Figure 5-95: *Alignment guides for the bus*

As illustrated in Figure 5-95, the **center** alignment by default for the bus is 100 points (half its height), but the wheels are positioned at 118 points. If we want to center the image at this point, we must add 18 points to the image's natural center, as shown below.

```
struct ContentView: View {
    var body: some View {
        HStack(alignment: .center) {
            Image(.signbus)
                .alignmentGuide(VerticalAlignment.center, computeValue:
{ dimension in
                    return dimension[VerticalAlignment.center] + 18
                })
            Image(.signplane)
            Image(.signphone)
        }.border(Color.blue, width: 2)
    }
}
```

Listing 5-78: *Aligning an image to the center with custom values*

The **alignmentGuide()** modifier requires two values. The first one is a value that represents the type of alignment we want to modify. In this case, we are aligning the views to the center, so we modify the **VerticalAlignment.center** type. The second value is a closure that must return the new value for this type of alignment. The closure receives a value of type **ViewDimensions**. This is a structure with two properties, **width** and **height**, to return the current width and height of the image, and also includes the definition of a subscript, which allows us to get the values for each alignment guide using square brackets and the alignment as the key. In the example of Listing 5-78, we get the current value of the **Vertical-Alignment.center** key for the view, add 18 to it and return the result. From that moment on, the **center** alignment for this view will return 118 instead of 100, so the view is aligned 18 points higher.

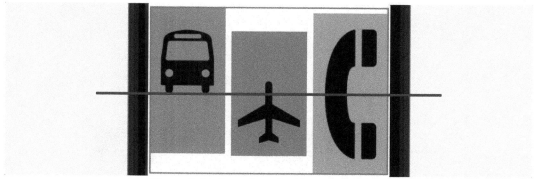

Figure 5-96: *Bus aligned with custom values*

If we want to align all the images by the bottom of the graphic, we must modify the alignment guide for each **Image** view.

```
struct ContentView: View {
    var body: some View {
        HStack(alignment: .center) {
            Image(.signbus)
                .alignmentGuide(VerticalAlignment.center) { dimension in
                    dimension[VerticalAlignment.center] + 18 }
            Image(.signplane)
                .alignmentGuide(VerticalAlignment.center) { dimension in
                    dimension[VerticalAlignment.center] + 68 }
            Image(.signphone)
                .alignmentGuide(VerticalAlignment.center) { dimension in
                    dimension[VerticalAlignment.center] + 89 }
        }.border(Color.blue, width: 2)
    }
}
```

Listing 5-79: *Aligning all images to the center with custom values*

The code in Listing 5-79 declares the closures as trailing closures and omits the **return** keyword to simplify the code, but the process is the same. The image of the bus is 200 points tall, its default center is at 100 points, but the base of the bus is at 118 points, so we add 18 points to the current center alignment (118 - 100). The image of the plane is 170 points tall, its default center is at 85 points, but the base of the plane is at 153 points, so we add 68 points to the current center alignment (153 - 85). And we do the same for the phone. The image is 220 points tall, its default center is at 110 points, but the base of the phone is at 199 points, so we add 89 points to the current center alignment (199 - 110). As a result, we get all the images aligned by the baseline of the graphics.

Figure 5-97: Images aligned by the baselines

So far, we have modified the alignment guides of views that belong to the same stack. If our interface requires us to align views from different containers (stacks), we must define custom alignment types. Custom alignment types are defined as extensions of the alignment structures (**VerticalAlignment** and **HorizontalAlignment**). We worked with extensions before in Chapter 3. They add functionality to an existing data type (see Listing 3-180). In this case, we need an extension to add a custom alignment guide. For this purpose, the extension must include an enumeration that conforms to the **AlignmentID** protocol, which requires the implementation of a method called **defaultValue** to return the alignment's default value. The extension must also include a type property which sole purpose is to simplify the declaration of the alignment, as shown in the following example.

```
import SwiftUI

extension VerticalAlignment {
    enum BusAlignment: AlignmentID {
        static func defaultValue(in dimension: ViewDimensions) -> CGFloat {
            return dimension[VerticalAlignment.center]
        }
    }
    static let alignBus = VerticalAlignment(BusAlignment.self)
}
struct ContentView: View {
    var body: some View {
        HStack(alignment: .alignBus) {
            VStack {
                Image(.signbus)
            }
            VStack(alignment: .leading) {
                Text("Transportation")
                Text("Bus").font(.largeTitle)
            }
        }.border(Color.blue, width: 2)
    }
}
```

Listing 5-80: Defining custom alignment guides

This code defines an extension for the **VerticalAlignment** structure. We call the enumeration **BusAlignment** because we use it to align the image of the bus. Its default value was defined as the current value of the **center** alignment. After this, we define a type property called **alignBus** that returns an alignment of this type. Note that the value provided to the **VerticalAlignment**'s initializer is a reference to the definition of the **BusAlignment** enumeration, not an instance of it (see Listing 3-143).

Chapter 5 - SwiftUI Framework

Our `ContentView` view includes two `VStack` views embedded in an `HStack` view, one with the image of the bus and another with two `Text` views. The custom `alignBus` alignment defined at the beginning is assigned to the `HStack`, and therefore the `VStack` views are aligned to the center.

Figure 5-98: Views aligned with custom alignment guides

The red line drawn in front of the picture in Figure 5-98 shows the common point of alignment. The `HStack` calls the `defaultValue` method for each `VStack` view, gets in return the value of their current `center` alignment, and therefore it aligns the `VStack` views to the center.

Of course, we can change this alignment by modifying the alignment guides of the views. For instance, if we want to position the word "Bus" in line with the bus's window, we must move the `alignBus` alignment for those views. The alignment for the bus image has to be at the center of the bus's window and the alignment for the text has to be at the center of the word.

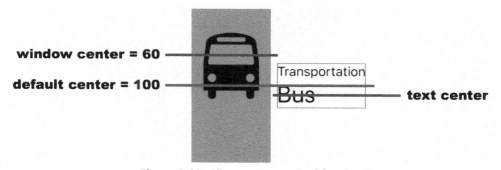

Figure 5-99: Alignments required for the views

The `center` alignment of the image of the bus is at the position 100, and the center of the bus's window is at the position 60, so to move the alignment point to the center of the window we must subtract 40 to this view's `center` alignment. For the text is simpler, we just have to return the value of the current `center` alignment, as in the following example.

```
import SwiftUI

extension VerticalAlignment {
   enum BusAlignment: AlignmentID {
      static func defaultValue(in dimension: ViewDimensions) -> CGFloat {
         return dimension[VerticalAlignment.center]
      }
   }
   static let alignBus = VerticalAlignment(BusAlignment.self)
}
struct ContentView: View {
   var body: some View {
      HStack(alignment: .alignBus) {
```

```
        VStack {
            Image(.signbus)
                .alignmentGuide(.alignBus) { dimension in
dimension[VerticalAlignment.center] - 40 }
            }
            VStack(alignment: .leading) {
                Text("Transportation")
                Text("Bus")
                    .font(.largeTitle)
                    .alignmentGuide(.alignBus) { dimension in
dimension[VerticalAlignment.center] }
            }
        }.border(Color.blue, width: 2)
    }
}
```

Listing 5-81: *Aligning views with custom alignment guides*

The definition of the custom alignment is the same as before, but now we modify the values for each view we want to move with the **alignmentGuide()** modifier. The alignment for the image of the bus is moved 40 points up the center line, and the alignment for the **Text** view is moved to its center alignment, so we get the views right where we want them.

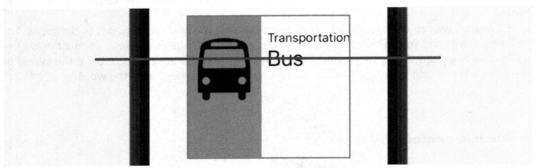

Figure 5-100: *Views with a custom alignment*

(Basic) **Groups**

Stack views create a structure of type **TupleView** to organize their content. This structure can manage up to 10 views and therefore that's the maximum number of views a stack can contain. Although it is not common to find this issue in a professional application, if necessary, we can avoid it by using **Group** views.

▷ **Group(content:** Closure)—This initializer creates a **Group** view that contains the views defined by the closure assigned to the argument.

The purpose of **Group** views is to group views together. We can use them to split large lists of views into groups of 10 or less to avoid the issue mentioned above, but also for other purposes, such as applying styles to several views at the same time, as in the following example.

```
struct ContentView: View {
    var body: some View {
        VStack {
            Group {
                Text("This is the list of")
                Text("Cities")
            }.foregroundColor(Color.gray)
```

```
        Group {
            Text("Manchester")
            Text("Viena")
        }.font(.largeTitle)
    }
  }
}
```

Listing 5-82: Arranging the views in groups

Each **Group** view defined in Listing 5-82 contains two **Text** views. To style these views, we apply modifiers to the **Group** views, not their content, so all the views within a group are affected by the same modifier.

Figure 5-101: Modifiers applied to groups of views

The closure assigned to the **body** property can only return one view, so the compiler is able to determine the data type of the view and process the value correctly. If we try to use an `if else` instruction to return different views depending on a condition, we will get an error. But we can use a **Group** view to solve this issue. The solution is to insert the conditional statement inside a **Group** view and return that view instead.

Usually, the views to be displayed are selected depending on the current state. We will learn how to work with view states in the next chapter, but we can test it with a simple condition, as shown below.

```
struct ContentView: View {
    let valid = true

    var body: some View {
        Group {
            if valid {
                Image(systemName: "keyboard")
            } else {
                Text("The state is invalid")
            }
        }
    }
}
```

Listing 5-83: Assigning different views to the body property

This code defines a Boolean constant to select the view. If the constant is **true**, we show an **Image** view with an SF Symbol, otherwise, we show a **Text** view. Therefore, the view displayed on the screen is selected at run time, depending on the value of the **valid** constant, but because we embedded the views in a **Group** view, the compiler can identify the value returned and therefore the code is functional. (We will learn how to make this selection dynamic in Chapter 6).

Grids

We can embed one stack into another as many times as needed to achieve the design we are after, but SwiftUI defines an additional container view called `Grid` for this purpose. A `Grid` view can distribute static content in multiple rows and columns. The following is the view's initializer.

▷ **Grid(alignment:** Alignment, **horizontalSpacing:** CGFloat, **verticalSpacing:** CGFloat, **content:** Closure)—This initializer creates a `Grid` view to define a grid-like layout. The **alignment** argument specifies the alignment of the content. It is a structure with the type properties `leading`, `center` (default), and `trailing`. The **horizontalSpacing** and **verticalSpacing** arguments define the space between cells. And the **content** argument provides the content for the grid.

The rows of the grid are defined by the `GridRow` structure.

▷ **GridRow(alignment:** VerticalAlignment, **content:** Closure)—This initializer creates a row for a grid. The **alignment** argument specifies the vertical alignment of the content. It is a structure with the type properties `top`, `center`, `bottom`, `firstText-Baseline`, and `lastTextBaseline`. And the **content** argument provides the content for the row.

SwiftUI also includes the following modifiers to configure the rows.

▷ **gridCellColumns(**Int)—This modifier specifies the number of columns the cell should occupy.

▷ **gridColumnAlignment(**HorizontalAlignment)—This modifier overrides the horizontal alignment for a row. The argument is a structure with the type properties `leading`, `center`, and `trailing`.

▷ **gridCellUnsizedAxes(**Axis)—This modifier returns a row that doesn't ask the grid for additional space in the axis specified by the argument. The argument is a structure with the type properties `horizontal` and `vertical`.

By default, the content of a grid is aligned to the center with a standard space between cells (usually 8 points). If that's what we want, all we need to do is to declare the grid's content. The rows are defined by `GridRow` structures and the columns are determined by the views inside these structures, as shown below.

```
struct ContentView: View {
    var body: some View {
        Grid {
            GridRow {
                Image(systemName: "message")
                    .frame(width: 100, height: 100)
                Image(systemName: "mic")
                    .frame(width: 100, height: 100)
            }.background(.red)
            GridRow {
                Image(systemName: "phone")
                    .frame(width: 100, height: 100)
                Image(systemName: "envelope")
                    .frame(width: 100, height: 100)
            }.background(.blue)
        }.font(.largeTitle)
    }
}
```

Listing 5-84: Defining a grid layout

This example creates a grid with two rows and two columns. The rows are defined by two `GridRow` structures and the columns by the views inside them. (In this case, two `Image` views per row displaying SF Symbols.)

Figure 5-102: Grid

If we specify a different number of columns per row, the grid will generate empty columns to fill the gap. However, we can also use the `gridCellColumns()` modifier to make a row occupy multiple columns, as in the following example.

```
struct ContentView: View {
    var body: some View {
        Grid(verticalSpacing: 5) {
            GridRow {
                Text("Send us a Message")
            }.gridCellColumns(2)
            GridRow {
                Image(systemName: "phone")
                    .frame(width: 100, height: 100)
                Image(systemName: "envelope")
                    .frame(width: 100, height: 100)
            }.background(.blue)
        }.font(.title2)
    }
}
```

Listing 5-85: Defining a multicolumn cell

In this example, the first row includes only one cell defined by a `Text` view, but because we apply the `gridCellColumns()` modifier with the value 2, the view occupies two columns.

Figure 5-103: Multicolumn cell

If what we want is for a cell to occupy two or more rows, we need to embed a grid within another grid, as shown below.

```
struct ContentView: View {
    var body: some View {
        Grid {
            GridRow {
                Image(systemName: "phone")
                    .frame(width: 100, height: 100)
                    .background(.blue)
                Grid(alignment: .leading) {
                    GridRow {
                        Text("My Name")
                    }
                    GridRow {
                        Text("My Number")
                    }
                }
            }
        }.font(.title2)
    }
}
```

Listing 5-86: Embedding a grid within another grid

In this example, the grid contains two columns, the one on the left with an image and the one on the right with another grid, which in turn contains two rows. Therefore, the two cells on the right share the same row with the cell on the left.

Figure 5-104: Multiple grids

(Basic) Custom Views

The code required to define the user interface can grow considerably as we build our application. When we reach a certain level of complexity, we must think about refactoring (reorganizing our code). The pattern proposed by SwiftUI involves breaking down the views into smaller pieces. For instance, we can define the second grid in our previous example as a separate view, so the code will be easier to read and maintain. This is so common that Xcode provides a tool to automatically create the new view for us. The option is available when we hold down the Control key and click on the structure's name.

```
            }
        }.font(.│     Embed in ZStack3D
    }                Show SwiftUI Inspector...
}                    Extract Subview
#Preview {           Embed in HStack
    ContentView      Embed in VStack
}                    Embed in ZStack
```

Figure 5-105: Extract Subview option

Chapter 5 - SwiftUI Framework

Once we select the Extract Subview option, a new view is created and placed at the bottom of the file. The view is assigned the name `ExtractedView`, but we can change it to one that better represents our view.

```
import SwiftUI

struct ContentView: View {
    var body: some View {
        Grid {
            GridRow {
                Image(systemName: "phone")
                    .frame(width: 100, height: 100)
                    .background(.blue)
                ExtractedView()
            }
        }.font(.title2)
    }
}
struct ExtractedView: View {
    var body: some View {
        Grid(alignment: .leading) {
            GridRow {
                Text("My Name")
            }
            GridRow {
                Text("My Number")
            }
        }
    }
}
```

Listing 5-87: Extracting views

The new view also conforms to the `View` protocol and implements the `body` property, as any other SwiftUI view. Once defined, we initialize it and the system takes care of creating the views and place them in the right location.

The views created with the Extract Subview option are defined in the same file, but in some cases it is better to move them to a separate file. The options for creating new files are available in the File menu at the top of the screen. The File/New/Empty File option creates an empty Swift file, and the File/New/File from Template... option creates a file with sample code. Xcode provides two templates for creating these files, one for Swift code and another for SwiftUI views. They are available on the iOS tab under the names Swift File and SwiftUI View.

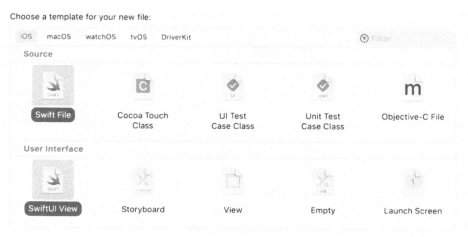

Figure 5-106: Swift files

Although the options to create the Swift templates have different names, they are both Swift files and are created with the same extension (.swift). The only difference between the two is the code included by Xcode. A Swift file only includes an **import** statement for the **Foundation** framework, while a SwiftUI View file includes a **View** structure with a simple view and the **#Preview** macro to create the preview on the canvas. The **View** structure takes the name assigned to the file. For instance, if we want to create a SwiftUI View file to store the **ExtractedView** structure from the previous example, we must call the file ExtractedView.swift, so Xcode creates the structures with the right name.

 IMPORTANT: Note that every file must import the frameworks it needs to work. For instance, if we store a view in a separate file, we must import the SwiftUI framework again with the **import** statement or the SwiftUI views won't be recognized.

(Medium) **Custom Layout**

With stacks and grids we can organize our views as needed and create any structure we want, but sometimes that's not enough. To provide more options, SwiftUI includes custom layouts. Custom layouts allow us to specify the exact position of each view in a container. They are created using structures that conform to the **Layout** protocol. The following are the two methods required by the protocol.

▷ **sizeThatFits(proposal:** ProposedViewSize, **subviews:** Subviews, **cache:** Cache)—This method is called on the layout structure when the system needs to know the size of the container view. The method must calculate the size and return a **CGSize** value with the container's width and height. The **proposal** argument is a structure that determines the proposed size for the container. The structure defines three type properties to return a proposal: **zero**, **infinity**, and **unspecified**. The **subviews** argument is a collection of structures that represent each view in the container. And the **cache** argument is a storage space to share the calculated values between methods.

▷ **placeSubviews(bounds:** CGRect, **proposal:** ProposedViewSize, **subviews:** Subviews, **cache:** Cache)—This method is called on the layout structure when the system needs to know the position of each view inside the container. The **bounds** argument is the bounds of the container. The **proposal** argument is a structure that determines the proposed size for the container. The structure defines three type properties to return a proposal: **zero**, **infinity**, and **unspecified**. The **subviews** argument is a collection of structures that represent each view in the container. And the **cache** argument is a storage space to share the calculated values between methods.

The **sizeThatFits()** method receives a collection of **LayoutSubview** structures. This is a proxy between our code and the views we need to allocate inside the container. To provide information about the views, the **LayoutSubview** structure includes the following properties and methods.

▷ **spacing**—This property returns a **ViewSpacing** structure with values that determine the space preferred by the view between itself and other views. The structure defines the **distance(to: ViewSpacing, along: Axis)** method to return a **CGFloat** value with the preferred spacing between two views.

▷ **priority**—This property returns a **Double** value with the view's layout priority.

▷ **sizeThatFits(**ProposedViewSize)—This method returns a **CGSize** value with the size of the view the structure is representing. The argument is a structure that determines the proposed size we want to read. The structure defines three type properties to represent a proposal: **zero**, **infinity**, and **unspecified**.

▷ **dimensions(proposal:** ProposedViewSize)—This method returns a `View-Dimensions` structure with the view's size and alignment guides. The **proposal** argument is a structure that determines the proposed size we want to read. The structure defines three type properties to represent a proposal: `zero`, `infinity`, and `unspecified`.

On the other hand, the `placeSubviews()` method is called in the layout structure when the system needs to know the position of each view within the container. This method receives similar values to allow us to calculate the right position for each view. To assign the position to the view, the `LayoutSubview` structure includes the following method.

▷ **place(at:** CGPoint, **anchor:** UnitPoint, **proposal:** ProposedViewSize)—This method sets the position of the view. The **at** argument specifies the position in x and y coordinates. The **anchor** argument determines what point within the view is positioned at those coordinates. It is a structure returned by the type properties `bottom`, `bottomLeading`, `bottomTrailing`, `center`, `leading`, `top`, `topLeading` (default), `topTrailing`, `trailing`, and `zero`. And the **proposal** argument is the proposed size for which we want to set the position.

To define a custom layout, all we need to do is to define a structure that conforms to the `Layout` protocol and implement the protocol methods. In the `sizeThatFits()` method, we must use the size of each view to calculate the size of the container, and in the `placeSubviews()` method, we must calculate and assign the position of each view. The following example shows a possible implementation.

```
import SwiftUI

struct ContentView: View {
    var body: some View {
        MyLayout {
            Group {
                Text("First")
                    .padding(10)
                    .background(.red)
                Text("Second")
                    .padding(10)
                    .background(.red)
                Text("Third")
                    .padding(10)
                    .background(.red)
            }.font(.title)
        }
    }
}
struct MyLayout: Layout {
    func sizeThatFits(proposal: ProposedViewSize, subviews: Subviews,
cache: inout ()) -> CGSize {
        var totalWidth: CGFloat = 0
        var totalHeight: CGFloat = 0

        for (index, view) in subviews.enumerated() {
            if index > 0 {
                totalHeight += 10
            }
            let viewSize = view.sizeThatFits(.unspecified)
            totalWidth += viewSize.width + CGFloat(30 * index)
            totalHeight += viewSize.height
        }
        return CGSize(width: totalWidth, height: totalHeight)
    }
```

```
func placeSubviews(in bounds: CGRect, proposal: ProposedViewSize,
subviews: Subviews, cache: inout ()) {
    var posX: CGFloat = bounds.origin.x
    var posY: CGFloat = bounds.origin.y

    for (index, view) in subviews.enumerated() {
        if index > 0 {
            posY += 10
            posX += 30
        }
        view.place(at: CGPoint(x: posX, y: posY),
proposal: .unspecified)
        posY += view.sizeThatFits(.unspecified).height
    }
}
}
```

Listing 5-88: *Defining a custom layout*

In this example, we define a layout structure called **MyLayout** and use it in the **ContentView** view to create the interface. The content of the layout structure must be embedded in a container view, such as a **Group** view or a **ForEach** view for dynamic lists. (We will learn how to implement the **ForEach** view in Chapter 7). In this case, we use a **Group** view to show three **Text** views, so the work of the layout structure is to determine the position of these three views.

We begin by calculating the size of the container in the **sizeThatFits()** method. For this purpose, we define two variables to store the width and height and then create a **for in** loop to get the size of each view and add it to the total. Because the views will be vertically separated by 10 points, we add this value to the **totalHeight** variable for the second and third views (when the view's index is greater than 0). Then, we get the view's size with the **sizeThatFits()** method and add the view's width and height to the total. To calculate the container's height, we add the height of each view, but for the width we add the width plus 30 points per view because we are going to displace each view 30 points to the right from the previous one. And finally, the total values are returned in a **CGSize** structure.

Note that the **sizeThatFits()** method returns a proposed size. Views can take any size they want, but first they receive a proposal from the container, so we can calculate the size of the view according to the size proposed by the container. There are three types of proposals: **zero**, **infinity**, and **unspecified**. The **zero** proposal returns the minimum size the view can take (in our case, it is 20 by 20 points because of the padding), the **infinity** proposal returns the maximum size the view can take, and the **unspecified** proposal returns the view's ideal size (the size determined by the size of the content, padding, and border). In our example, we always returned the size we want for the **unspecified** proposal, but we can do it for each proposal by checking the value of the method's **proposal** argument.

In the **placeSubviews()** method, we must calculate the position of each view. The process is similar than before; we loop through the subviews collection and get the size of each view, but this time use it to calculate their positions. The position of the view is calculated from the container's position, returned by the **bounds** argument. To those values, we add the vertical and horizontal displacements for the second and third views, and assign the final values back to the views with the **place()** method. The result is shown below.

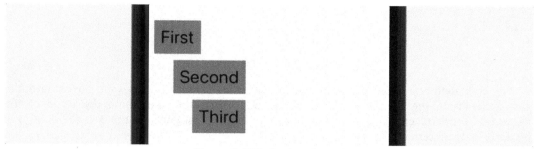

Figure 5-107: *Custom layout*

Although we can present different interfaces with conditional statements, this requires the system to recreate the views. SwiftUI includes the `AnyLayout` structure to create a wrapper that makes it easy to swap layouts without recreating the views. As we will see later, this allows us to implement complex features such as view identification and animations.

To show how we can switch layouts with the `AnyLayout` structure, we are going to use the custom layout defined in the previous example along with layouts provided by the system. SwiftUI includes the following structures to define horizontal and vertical layouts.

▷ **VStackLayout(alignment:** HorizontalAlignment, **spacing:** CGFloat?)—This structure creates a layout that arranges a group of views vertically. The **alignment** argument determines the horizontal alignment of the views. It is a structure with the type properties **center**, **leading**, and **trailing**. And the **spacing** argument determines the space between the views.

▷ **HStackLayout(alignment:** VerticalAlignment, **spacing:** CGFloat?)—This structure creates a layout that arranges a group of views horizontally. The **alignment** argument determines the vertical alignment of the views. It is a structure with the type properties **bottom**, **center**, **firstTextBaseline**, **lastTextBaseline**, and **top**. And the **spacing** argument determines the space between the views.

These structures work like the `VStack` and `HStack` structures, but they conform to the `Layout` protocol and are therefore used to define a layout. For instance, we can use a `VStackLayout` structure to replace our custom layout when the value of a property changes. To switch between layouts, we need to assign them to a property, as shown below.

```
struct ContentView: View {
   var selected: Bool = true

   var body: some View {
      let SelectedLayout = selected ? AnyLayout(MyLayout()) :
AnyLayout(VStackLayout(alignment: .leading))

      VStack(alignment: .leading) {
         SelectedLayout {
            Group {
               Text("First")
                  .padding(10)
                  .background(.red)
               Text("Second")
                  .padding(10)
                  .background(.red)
               Text("Third")
                  .padding(10)
                  .background(.red)
            }
         }
         Spacer()
      }.padding()
```

```
        .font(.title)
   }
}
```

Listing 5-89: Selecting a layout

This code defines a property of type `Bool` to select the layout and stores the current layout in a variable inside the closure assigned to the `body` property. Every time the value of the `selected` property changes, the corresponding layout is assigned to the `SelectedLayout` property with a ternary operator (see Listing 2-52), and then the layout is applied to the interface. When the value of the property is `true`, we show the custom layout, otherwise, we show the views with a standard `VStackLayout` aligned to the left.

Figure 5-108: Custom and Standard layouts

 Do It Yourself: Replace the code in your ContentView.swift file with the code in Listing 5-88. Remember to keep the `#Preview` macro at the bottom to be able to see the preview on the canvas. You should see the interface illustrated in Figure 5-107. Update the `ContentView` view with the code in Listing 5-89. Modify the value of the `selected` property (`true` or `false`) to see how the layouts are applied (Figure 5-108). We will learn how to perform this changes dynamically in Chapter 6 and how to animate the changes in Chapter 11.

(Medium) Generic Views

Views are of different data types, so if we want to pass different views around from a property or a method, we must wrap them in container views, such as the `Group` view introduced before. Although this is allowed, SwiftUI includes a structure called `AnyView` that we can use for that purpose.

▷ **AnyView**(View)—This initializer creates an `AnyView` view to contain the views specified by the argument. The argument can be a single view or a hierarchy of views.

In the following example, we check a condition in a method and return an `AnyView` view with the content for the `body` property.

```
struct ContentView: View {
   var body: some View {
      getView()
   }
   func getView() -> AnyView {
      let valid = true
      var myView: AnyView!

      if valid {
         myView = AnyView(Image(systemName: "keyboard"))
      } else {
```

```
            myView = AnyView(Text("The state is invalid"))
        }
        return myView
    }
}
```

Listing 5-90: Wrapping views in an `AnyView` *view*

The **ContentView** structure in Listing 5-90 includes a method called **getView()** that returns a structure of type **AnyView**. This structure is defined according to the value of a Boolean property. If the value is **true**, we create an **Image** view, otherwise, we create a **Text** view, but both views are inside an **AnyView** view, so we always return the same type of view. When the content of the **body** property is processed, the method is called, and the view returned by the method is displayed on the screen.

The **AnyView** view is a wrapper we can use to pass different views around. The problem is that the views lose their identity. The system considers the views wrapped in an **AnyView** view to be the same, which affects performance. A better alternative is processing the views before they are returned by the method with the **@ViewBuilder** property wrapper. We have introduced this property wrapper before. It is used to construct the views returned by **Content** closures (e.g., the closures assigned to the **body** property), but we can also use it with our custom methods to be able to return different views without having to use a wrapper view, as in the following example.

```
struct ContentView: View {
    var body: some View {
        getView()
    }
    @ViewBuilder
    func getView() -> some View {
        let valid = false

        if valid {
            Image(systemName: "keyboard")
        } else {
            Text("The state is invalid")
        }
    }
}
```

Listing 5-91: Constructing views with the `@ViewBuilder` *property wrapper*

The code in Listing 5-91 applies the **@ViewBuilder** property wrapper to the **getView()** method, so now we can use this method as a **Content** closure and produce any type of view we want without using a wrapper.

When the views returned by a method are dynamically selected, as we did in the previous examples, we may not always be able to provide one. For cases like this, SwiftUI includes the **EmptyView** view.

▷ **EmptyView()**—This initializer creates an **EmptyView** view with no content and no size.

The **EmptyView** view works like the rest, but it doesn't provide any content and it has no size, so it doesn't affect the interface. The following example creates an empty view when a condition is not met.

```
struct ContentView: View {
    var body: some View {
        VStack {
            Text("View Title")
            getView()
        }
    }
    @ViewBuilder
    func getView() -> some View {
        let valid = false

        if valid {
            Image(systemName: "keyboard")
        } else {
            EmptyView()
        }
    }
}
```

Listing 5-92: Returning an empty view

Medium 5.4 Environment

The environment is a data structure that belongs to the application and can store values for the application and the views. It is like an external storage that can be accessed from anywhere in our code. SwiftUI defines a structure called `EnvironmentValues` to store these values and the following property wrapper to read them.

▷ **@Environment(**KeyPath**)**—This property wrapper creates a binding with an environment property or an object stored in the environment. The argument is the key path of the property we want to read or a reference to the data type of the object we want to access.

The `EnvironmentValues` structure includes many properties to store the configuration of the system, the app and the views. The following are the most frequently used.

▷ **colorScheme**—This property sets or returns the interface appearance. It is an enumeration of type `ColorScheme` with the values `light` and `dark`.

▷ **dynamicTypeSize**—This property sets or returns the size for dynamic content (It simulates the size set by the user from the Settings app). It is an enumeration with the values `large`, `medium`, `small`, `xLarge`, `xSmall`, `xxLarge`, and `xxxLarge`.

▷ **font**—This property sets or returns the font by default. It is a value of type `Font`.

▷ **accessibilityEnabled**—This property sets or returns a Boolean value that determines whether any accessibility service has been enabled on the device.

▷ **layoutDirection**—This property sets or returns the layout's direction. It is an enumeration of type `LayoutDirection` with the values `leftToRight` and `rightToLeft`.

▷ **calendar**—This property sets or returns the calendar used by the views to process dates. It is a value of type `Calendar`.

▷ **locale**—This property sets or returns the locale used by the views to process local data, such as language, currency, etc. It is a value of type `Locale`.

▷ **timeZone**—This property sets or returns the time zone used by the views to calculate dates and times. It is a value of type `TimeZone`.

To read these values, we need to create a property using the `@Environment` property wrapper and specify the property's key path (see Chapter 3, Listing 3-31). For instance, in the following example, we read the `colorScheme` property to get the current color scheme.

```
struct ContentView: View {
   @Environment(\.colorScheme) var mode

   var body: some View {
      Image(systemName: "trash")
         .font(Font.system(size: 100))
         .foregroundColor(mode == .dark ? Color.yellow : Color.blue)
         .symbolVariant(mode == .dark ? .fill : .circle)
   }
}
```

Listing 5-93: Responding to updates in the states of the environment

In Listing 5-93, we define a property called **mode** to read the environment's **colorScheme** property, and then assign different values to the modifiers of a **Text** view depending on the current appearance (**dark** or **light**). The `@Environment` property wrapper creates a binding between the **mode** property and the **colorScheme** property in the environment, so it can respond to changes. When the user changes the appearance from Settings, the value of the **colorScheme** property in the environment changes, this changes the value of the **mode** property in our view, and the view is updated according to the new state. Note that we check the value of the **mode** property in the modifiers with a ternary operator, as we did before, so SwiftUI can effectively process the changes. If the appearance is **light**, we display a blue trash can with a circle around it, otherwise, we display the can's **fill** variant in yellow.

Figure 5-109: States in light and dark appearances

Do It Yourself: Update the **ContentView** view with the code in Listing 5-93. You should see the blue trash can (Figure 5-109, left). Press the Settings button at the bottom of the canvas and activate the Dark appearance option in the Color Scheme section (Figure 5-18, number 4). You should see the yellow trash can (Figure 5-109, right).

The values and objects stored in the environment can be modified or more data can be added. Below are the modifiers provided by SwiftUI for this purpose.

▷ **environment(KeyPath, Value)**—This modifier sets a new value for a property in the environment. The first argument is a key path to the property we want to modify, and the second argument is the value we want to assign to that property.

▷ **environment(Object)**—This modifier assigns an object to the environment. The argument is a reference to the object we want to share with the views.

Changing system values is useful when working with previews. The implementation is straightforward. We must apply the `environment()` modifier to the view with the key path of the property we want to modify and provide the new value, as shown below.

```
struct ContentView: View {
    var body: some View {
        Text("Hello World")
            .foregroundColor(Color("MyColor"))
    }
}
#Preview {
    ContentView()
        .environment(\.colorScheme, .dark)
}
```

Listing 5-94: *Activating dark mode*

In this example, we assign a custom color called MyColor to the **Text** view, and then set the appearance for the preview to dark. The example assumes that we have added a Color Set to the Asset Catalog called MyColor and assigned different colors to the Any and Dark appearances, as we did before (see Figure 5-44). The **environment()** modifier assigns the value **dark** to the environment's **colorScheme** property, changing the view's appearance to dark, so the preview displays the text in the color we have selected for that appearance.

 Do It Yourself: Create a Color Set in the Asset Catalog with the name MyColor and assign different colors for the Any and Dark appearances, as we did in the example in Figure 5-44. Update the ContentView.swift file with the code in Listing 5-94. On the canvas, you should see the text in the color selected for the dark appearance. Remove the **environment()** modifier. Now, you should see the text in the color selected for Any.

In addition to the values defined by the system, we can store our own. One way to do it is to create an extension for the **EnvironmentValues** structure and use it to add new properties. To simplify the creation of these properties, SwiftUI includes the following macro.

▷ **@Entry**—This macro produces the code necessary to create properties for the environment and similar systems used to share information between the operating system, the app and the views.

In the following example, we create an environment property to store a string, then read its value from the view and show it on the screen.

```
import SwiftUI

extension EnvironmentValues {
    @Entry var myValue: String = "Default value"
}
struct ContentView: View {
    @Environment(\.myValue) var value

    var body: some View {
        Text(value)
            .font(Font.system(size: 20))
    }
}
#Preview {
    ContentView()
}
```

Listing 5-95: *Adding custom properties to the environment*

 IMPORTANT: Besides reading and storing properties, the environment can be used to access the user's data and respond to changes in the state of the app. We will learn how to work with this feature next.

Chapter 5 - SwiftUI Framework

Chapter 6
Declarative User Interface

(Basic) **6.1 States**

In the previous chapter, we introduced the main feature of SwiftUI, its declarative syntax. With SwiftUI, we can declare the views as we want them to appear on the screen and leave it to the system to create the code necessary to show them. However, declarative syntax is not just about organizing the views, but also about how they are updated when the state of the app changes. For example, we can have an interface like the one in Figure 6-1 below, with a `Text` view that displays a title, an input field where the user can type a new title, and a button to replace the old title with the new one. The `Text` view with the original title represents the initial state of our interface. The state is updated with each character the user types in the input field (Figure 6-1, left), and when the button is pressed, the interface enters a new state in which the title inserted by the user has replaced the original title and the color of the text has changed (Figure 6-1, right).

Figure 6-1: *User Interface*

Every time there is a change in a state, the views must be updated to reflect it. In previous systems, this required the code to keep the data and the interface synchronized, but in a declarative syntax all we have to do is to declare what the configuration of the views should be in each state and the system takes care of generating all the code necessary to show those changes on the screen.

The possible states the interface can go through are determined by the information stored by the app. For example, the characters inserted by the user in the input field and the color used in our example are values stored by the app. Every time these values change, the app is in a new state and therefore the interface is updated to reflect it. Establishing this dependency between the app's data and the interface demands a lot of code, but SwiftUI keeps it simple using property wrappers.

(Basic) **@State**

As mentioned in Chapter 3, property wrappers allow us to define properties that can perform tasks with the values assigned to them. SwiftUI implements property wrappers extensively to store values and report the changes to the views. The one designed to store the states of a single view is called `@State`. This property wrapper stores a value in a structure of type `State` and notifies the system when that value changes, so the views are automatically updated to reflect the change on the screen.

The property wrapper `@State` is designed to store the states of a single view. Therefore, we should declare the properties of this type as part of the view structure and as `private`, so that access is restricted to the structure in which they are declared.

```
struct ContentView: View {
    @State private var title: String = "Default Title"
```

```
var body: some View {
   VStack {
      Text(title)
         .padding(10)
      Button(action: {
         title = "My New Title"
      }, label: {
         Text("Change Title")
      })
      Spacer()
   }.padding()
  }
}
```

Listing 6-1: Defining a state

The code in Listing 6-1 declares a @**State** property called **title** of type **String**. The property is initialized with the value "Default Title". In the body of the view, we show this value with a **Text** view inside a vertical stack, and include a **Button** view below it to change it. We will study **Button** views later, but for now we just need to know that a **Button** view displays a label and performs an action when the user clicks or taps on it. To represent the label, we use a **Text** view with the text "Change Title" so the user knows what the button is for, and to define the action, we provide a closure that changes the value of the **title** property to "My New Title" so when the button is pressed the title is modified.

The **title** property created with the @**State** property wrapper is used in two places, first in the **Text** view to show the current value to the user, and then in the action for the **Button** view to modify its value. In consequence, when the button is pressed, the value of the **title** property changes, the @**State** property wrapper notifies the system that the state of the app has changed, and the content of the **body** property is refreshed to display the new value on the screen.

Default Title

Change Title

My New Title

Change Title

Figure 6-2: Initial state (left) and state after the button is pressed (right)

 Do It Yourself: Create a Multiplatform project. Update the **ContentView** view with the code in Listing 6-1. Make sure that Live Preview is activated on the canvas (Figure 5-18, number 1). Press the Change Title button to assign the string to the **Text** view. You should see something similar to Figure 6-2, right.

This whole process is automatic. We don't have to assign the new value to the **Text** view or tell the view that a new value is available, that's all handled by the @**State** property wrapper. And we can include all the @**State** properties we need to store any state of the interface. For instance, the following example adds a **Bool** type @**State** property to our view to assign a different text to the **title** property each time the button is pressed.

```
struct ContentView: View {
   @State private var title: String = "Valid"
   @State private var isValid: Bool = true

   var body: some View {
      VStack {
         Text(title)
            .padding(10)
         Button(action: {
            isValid.toggle()
            title = isValid ? "Valid" : "Invalid"
```

Chapter 6 - Declarative User Interface

```
        }, label: { Text("Change Validation") })
        Spacer()
    }.padding()
  }
}
```

Listing 6-2: Defining multiple states

The **isValid** property stores a Boolean value that determines the current validation state, so that we can display the corresponding text on the screen. The string to be assigned to the **title** property is selected with a ternary operator. Using a ternary operator to set the state of a view is the recommended practice because it allows the system to determine all the possible states the view can respond to and produce a smooth transition from one state to another. If the value of the **isValid** property is **true**, we assign the word "Valid" to the **title** property, otherwise the text "Invalid" is assigned instead. Each time the button is pressed, the value of the **isValid** property changes so that the view displays different text on the screen (see Listing 3-54 for more information about the **toggle()** method).

 IMPORTANT: There are two states in the example of Listing 6-2, and both change at the same time, but the system takes into consideration these situations and makes sure that the interface is updated only when necessary.

A **@State** property creates a dependency between itself and the view and therefore the view is updated every time its value changes. It is said that the view is *bound* to the property. The binding we have used so far is unidirectional. If the property is modified, the view is updated. But there are views which values are modified by the user and therefore they must be able to store values back into the property without the code's intervention. For this purpose, SwiftUI allows us to define a bidirectional binding. Bidirectional bindings are declared by prefixing the name of the property with the **$** sign.

The views that usually require bidirectional binding are control views, such as those that create switches the user can turn on and off, or input fields to insert text. The following example implements a **TextField** view to illustrate this feature. A **TextField** view creates an input field. The values required by its initializer are a string with the text we want to show as placeholder and the binding property we are going to use to store the value inserted by the user. (We will learn more about **TextField** views and other control views later.)

```
struct ContentView: View {
    @State private var title: String = "Default Title"
    @State private var titleInput: String = ""

    var body: some View {
        VStack {
            Text(title)
                .padding(10)
            TextField("Insert Title", text: $titleInput)
                .textFieldStyle(.roundedBorder)
            Button(action: {
                title = titleInput
                titleInput = ""
            }, label: { Text("Change Title") })
            Spacer()
        }.padding()
    }
}
```

Listing 6-3: Defining bidirectional binding

In this example, we add to the view the **@State** property we need to store the text inserted by the user, and then define a **TextField** view between the title and the button. The

TextField view was initialized with the placeholder "Insert Title", and the new **titleInput** property was provided as the binding property for the view (**$titleInput**). This creates a permanent connection between the **TextField** view and the property, so every time the user types or removes a character in the input field, the new value is assigned to the property.

In the action for the **Button** view, we introduced two modifications. First, we assign the value of the **titleInput** property to the **title** property. This effectively updates the title of the view with the text inserted by the user. And second, we assign an empty string to the **titleInput** property to clear the input field and leave it ready for the user to start typing again.

 Do It Yourself: Update the **ContentView** view with the code in Listing 6-3. Click on the text field and insert a text. Press the Change Title button. You should see your text appear on the screen.

Basic @Binding

@State properties belong to the structure in which they are declared, and should only be accessible from the code within that structure (which is why we declare them **private**), but as we saw in Chapter 5, when our views grow significantly, it is advisable to split them into independent structures. The problem with organizing the views this way is that the additional structures lose the reference to the **@State** properties, so we are no longer able to read or change their values. The solution is to create a bidirectional connection between the **@State** properties defined in one view and the code in the other. For this purpose, SwiftUI includes the **Binding** structure and the **@Binding** property wrapper.

The following view is the same as in previous examples, but this time we move the **Text** and **TextField** views to a separate view called **HeaderView**. This additional view contains two **@Binding** properties for accessing the **@State** properties in the **ContentView** structure, so we always work with the same states.

```
struct ContentView: View {
    @State private var title: String = "Default Title"
    @State private var titleInput: String = ""

    var body: some View {
        VStack {
            HeaderView(title: title, titleInput: $titleInput)
            Button(action: {
                title = titleInput
                titleInput = ""
            }, label: { Text("Change Title") })
            Spacer()
        }.padding()
    }
}
struct HeaderView: View {
    var title: String
    @Binding var titleInput: String

    var body: some View {
        VStack {
            Text(title)
                .padding(10)
            TextField("Insert Title", text: $titleInput)
                .textFieldStyle(.roundedBorder)
        }
    }
}
```

Listing 6-4: Using @Binding properties

A **@Binding** property always receives its value from a **@State** property, so we don't have to assign a default value to it, but the connection created between them is bidirectional, so we always have to remember to prefix the **@State** properties with the **$** sign to connect them with the **@Binding** properties (HeaderView(title: title, titleInput: $titleInput)).

Because of the bidirectional binding established between the **@Binding** property and the **@State** property, the value entered by the user is stored in one place, and each time the button is pressed, the changes are recognized by the system, the **body** property of the **HeaderView** structure is processed again, and the new value is displayed on the screen.

 Do It Yourself: Update the ContentView.swift file with the code in Listing 6-4. Remember to keep the **#Preview** macro at the bottom to be able to see the preview on the canvas. Insert a text in the text field, and press the Change Title button. Everything should work as before.

(Medium) Binding Structures

As we mentioned earlier, property wrappers are defined as structures and therefore they contain their own properties. SwiftUI allows access to the underlying structure of a property wrapper by prefixing the property's name with an underscore (e.g., **_title**). Once we gain access to the structure, we can work with its properties. The structure that defines the **@State** property wrapper is called **State**. This is a generic structure and therefore it can process values of any type. The following are the properties defined by this structure to store the state values.

▷ **wrappedValue**—This property returns the value managed by the **@State** property.

▷ **projectedValue**—This property returns a structure of type **Binding** that creates the bidirectional binding with the view.

The **wrappedValue** property stores the value we assign to the **@State** property, like the "Default Title" string assigned to the **title** property in the last example. The **projectedValue** property stores a structure of type **Binding** that creates the bidirectional binding we need to store a value back to the property. If we read the **@State** property directly (e.g., **title**), the value returned is the one stored in the **wrappedValue** property, and if we prefix the property's name with a **$** sign (e.g., **$title**), we access the **Binding** structure stored in the **projectedValue** property. This is how SwiftUI proposes we work with **@State** properties, but in theory we can also access the properties directly, as in the following example.

```
struct ContentView: View {
    @State private var title: String = "Default Title"
    @State private var titleInput: String = ""

    var body: some View {
        VStack {
            Text(_title.wrappedValue)
                .padding(10)
            TextField("Insert Title", text: _titleInput.projectedValue)
                .textFieldStyle(.roundedBorder)
            Button(action: {
                _title.wrappedValue = _titleInput.wrappedValue
                _titleInput.wrappedValue = ""
            }, label: { Text("Change Title") })
            Spacer()
        }.padding()
    }
}
```

Listing 6-5: *Accessing the properties of a* State *structure*

Chapter 6 - Declarative User Interface

This is the same example as before, but instead of using the SwiftUI shortcuts, we read the **wrappedValue** and **projectedValue** properties of the **State** structure directly. Of course, this is not necessary, but may be required sometimes to overcome SwiftUI's shortcomings. For instance, SwiftUI doesn't allow us to access and work with **@State** properties outside the closure assigned to the **body** property, but we can replace one **State** structure by another. For this purpose, we can use the following initializers provided by the **State** structure.

▷ **State(initialValue:** Value**)**—This initializer creates a **State** property with the value specified by the **initialValue** argument.

▷ **State(wrappedValue:** Value**)**—This initializer creates a **State** property with the wrapped value specified by the **wrappedValue** argument.

For example, if we want to assign an initial value to the input field of our previous example, we can add an initializer to the **ContentView** structure and use it to assign a new **State** structure to the property.

```
init() {
    _titleInput = State(initialValue: "Hello World")
}
```

Listing 6-6: *Initializing* @State *properties*

 Do It Yourself: Update the **ContentView** view with the code in Listing 6-5. Add the initializer in Listing 6-6 to the **ContentView** structure (below the **@State** properties). You should see the input field initialized with "Hello World".

 IMPORTANT: Accessing the content of binding properties this way is only recommended when there are no other options. When possible, we should use the property wrappers provided by SwiftUI and initialize a **@State** property with the **onAppear()** modifier introduced in Chapter 5 (see Listing 5-58) or by storing the states in an observable object, as we will see later.

We can access the values of a **@Binding** property the same way we do with a **@State** property. If we just read the property, as we did in Listing 6-5, the value returned is the value stored in it, and if we prefix the name with a **$** sign, the value returned is the **Binding** structure the property wrapper uses to establish the bidirectional binding with the view. But if we prefix the name of the **@Binding** property with an underscore (e.g., **_title**), the value returned is not a **State** structure but another **Binding** structure. This is because a **@Binding** property wrapper is defined by a structure of type **Binding**. Of course, the structure also includes properties to access the values.

▷ **wrappedValue**—This property returns the value managed by the **@Binding** property.

▷ **projectedValue**—This property returns a structure of type **Binding** that creates the bidirectional binding with the view.

As we did with the **State** structure, we can access and work with the values stored in the **Binding** structure. For instance, the following example implements a separate view again to manage the title and the input field, as we did in Listing 6-4. When the **HeaderView** is initialized, we get the value stored in the **Binding** structure from the **wrappedValue** property, count the total number of characters in the string, and display the result along with the title.

```
struct ContentView: View {
    @State private var title: String = "Default Title"
    @State private var titleInput: String = ""
```

```
   var body: some View {
      VStack {
         HeaderView(title: $title, titleInput: $titleInput)
         Button(action: {
            title = titleInput
            titleInput = ""
         }, label: { Text("Change Title") })
         Spacer()
      }.padding()
   }
}
struct HeaderView: View {
   @Binding var title: String
   @Binding var titleInput: String
   let counter: Int

   init(title: Binding<String>, titleInput: Binding<String>) {
      _title = title
      _titleInput = titleInput

      let sentence = _title.wrappedValue
      counter = sentence.count
   }
   var body: some View {
      VStack {
         Text("\(title) (\(counter))")
            .padding(10)
         TextField("Insert Title", text: $titleInput)
            .textFieldStyle(.roundedBorder)
      }
   }
}
```

Listing 6-7: Accessing the values of a `@Binding` *property*

In the **HeaderView** view of Listing 6-7, we define a property called **counter** and initialize it with the number of characters in the string returned by the **wrappedValue** property. Because the **@Binding** property doesn't have an initial value, we must also initialize it with the value received from the **ContentView** view (**_title = title**). Note that the value received by the **HeaderView** structure is a **Binding** structure that can manage values of type **String**, so the data type for the argument must be declared as **Binding<String>**.

Once the values are initialized, we can display them in the view. The title now shows the text inserted by the user along with the number of characters in the string.

Hello (5)

Insert Title

Change Title

Figure 6-3: Title defined with the values of the `@Binding` *property*

 Do It Yourself: Update the ContentView.swift file with the code in Listing 6-7. Insert a title. You should see the title with the number of characters on the right, as show in Figure 6-3.

The **@Binding** property of the **HeaderView** view is connected to the **@State** property of the **ContentView** view and therefore it receives its value from this property, but there are times when instances of structures like these are created independently and therefore, they require a binding value. To define this value, we can create the **Binding** structure ourselves with the following initializer.

> ▷ **Binding(get:** Closure, **set:** Closure)—This initializer creates a **Binding** structure. The **get** argument is a closure that returns the current value, and the **set** argument is a closure that receives a new value for storage or processing.

There are many circumstances in which we may need a **Binding** value. For instance, if we want to create a preview of the **HeaderView**, we must provide values for the **title** and **titleInput** properties. The following example illustrates how to create new **Binding** structures to provide these values and how to define the preview for this view.

```
#Preview("Header") {
    let constantTitle = Binding<String>(
        get: { return "My Preview Title"},
        set: { value in
            print(value)
        })
    let constantInput = Binding<String>(
        get: { return ""},
        set: { value in
            print(value)
        })
    return HeaderView(title: constantTitle, titleInput: constantInput)
}
```

Listing 6-8: Creating a Binding *structure*

The initializer for the **Binding** structure includes a getter and a setter. The getter returns the current value and the setter receives the values assigned to the structure. In this example, we always return a string, and since we are not assigning new values to the structure, we just print the value on the console. The instances are assigned to the constants **constantTitle** and **constantInput** and then sent to the **HeaderView** structure, so the view has the values to show on the canvas.

There is not much use for the **Binding** structure of this example other than providing the values required by the **HeaderView** structure. In cases like this, we can simplify the code with the **constant()** method. This type method creates and returns a **Binding** structure with an immutable value, so we don't have to create the structures ourselves.

```
#Preview("Header") {
    HeaderView(title: .constant("My Preview Title"),
titleInput: .constant(""))
}
```

Listing 6-9: Creating a Binding *structure with an immutable value*

Although we can create **Binding** properties or use the **constant()** method to provide the **Binding** values for a preview, sometimes it is better to create new state properties. For cases like this, SwiftUI includes the following macro.

> ▷ **@Previewable**—This macro makes state properties available for previews.

The following example shows how to create state properties for a preview. The process is the same as before, but we must prefixed the property with the **@Previewable** macro.

```
#Preview("Header") {
    @Previewable @State var title: String = "Default Title"
    @Previewable @State var titleInput: String = ""
    HeaderView(title: $title, titleInput: $titleInput)
}
```

Listing 6-10: Defining a state property for a preview

Chapter 6 - Declarative User Interface

6.2 Control Views

Controls are visual tools the user interacts with to change the state of the interface, select options, and insert, modify or delete information. We have implemented some of them already, like the **Button** view and the **TextField** view used in previous sections. To define a useful interface, we need to learn more about these views and the rest of the control views provided by SwiftUI.

Basic   Button View

As we have already seen, the **Button** view creates a simple control that performs an action when clicked or tapped. The following are some of the structure's initializers.

▷ **Button**(String, **action:** Closure)—This initializer creates a **Button** view. The first argument is a string that defines the button's label, and the **action** argument is a closure with the code to be executed when the button is pressed.

▷ **Button**(**action:** Closure, **label:** Closure)—This initializer creates a **Button** view. The **action** argument is a closure with the code to be executed when the button is pressed, and the **label** argument is a closure that returns the views used to create the label.

▷ **Button**(String, **role:** ButtonRole?, **action:** Closure)—This initializer creates a **Button** view. The first argument is a string that defines the button's label. The **role** argument is a structure with type properties to describe the purpose of the button. There are two properties available: **cancel** and **destructive**. And the **action** argument is a closure with the code to be executed when the button is pressed.

We have already implemented the second initializer to create our buttons, but if we only want to use a string for the label, we can simplify the code using the first initializer and a trailing closure for the action.

```
struct ContentView: View {
    @State private var colorActive: Bool = false

    var body: some View {
        VStack(spacing: 10) {
            Text("Default Title")
                .padding()
                .background(colorActive ? Color.green : Color.clear)
            Button("Change Color") {
                colorActive.toggle()
            }
            Spacer()
        }.padding()
    }
}
```

Listing 6-11: Implementing Button *views*

This example includes a **Text** view and a **Button** view in a **VStack**. The **Text** view displays always the same string with a background color defined by the **colorActive** property. If the value of this property is **true**, we assign the **green** color to the background, otherwise the color assigned is **clear** (transparent). When the button is pressed, we toggle the value of this property, the **body** property is evaluated again, and the background of the text changes to the next color.

Figure 6-4: Button view

 Do It Yourself: Create a Multiplatform project. Update the `ContentView` view with the code in Listing 6-11. Press the Change Color button. You should see the background color for the text change (Figure 6-4, right).

If we want to separate the views from the actions performed by the controls, we can move the statements to a function. For instance, we can add a function to the `ContentView` structure to toggle the value of the `colorActive` property and then call this function from the action of the button. The application works the same way, but the code is better organized.

```
struct ContentView: View {
    @State private var colorActive: Bool = false

    var body: some View {
        VStack(spacing: 10) {
            Text("Default Title")
                .padding()
                .background(colorActive ? Color.green : Color.clear)
            Button("Change Color") {
                changeColor()
            }
            Spacer()
        }.padding()
    }
    func changeColor() {
        colorActive.toggle()
    }
}
```

Listing 6-12: Using functions to organize the code

If the only action performed by the button is to call a method, we can simplify the definition of the view by declaring the **action** argument and specifying the name of the method as the action to perform, as shown below.

```
Button("Change Color", action: changeColor)
```

Listing 6-13: Referencing a method

Declaring the name of a method with parentheses executes the method right away, but declaring only the name provides a reference to the method that the system can use later to execute it.

 Do It Yourself: Update the `ContentView` view with the code in Listing 6-12. The application should work the same as before. Replace the **Button** view with the **Button** view in Listing 6-13. Press the button to confirm the action is performed.

In previous examples, we used a ternary operator to select the value for the **background()** modifier depending on the value of the **colorActive** property. This is the recommended practice, so SwiftUI can identify the views and effectively manage the transition between one state to another, but we can also use **if else** statements to respond to changes. For example, sometimes, controls like buttons are used to show or hide a view in the interface.

```
struct ContentView: View {
    @State private var showInfo = false

    var body: some View {
        VStack(spacing: 10) {
            Button("Show Information") {
                showInfo.toggle()
            }.padding()
            if showInfo {
                Text("This is the information")
            }
            Spacer()
        }
    }
}
```

Listing 6-14: Adding and removing views from the interface

The button in this example toggles the value of a **@State** property called **showInfo**. Below the button, we check the current value of the property. If the value is **true**, we show a **Text** view, otherwise, we do nothing. Therefore, when the button is pressed, the value of the **showInfo** property changes, the content of the **body** property is drawn again, and the **Text** view appears or disappears, depending on the current value of the property.

Show Information

Show Information

This is the information

Figure 6-5: Dynamic interface

The **if else** statements can also be used to select whether or not to perform the action for the button, but SwiftUI provides the following modifier to disable the button altogether if that is what we are looking for.

▷ **disabled(**Bool**)**—This modifier determines whether the control responds to the user interaction or not.

The following example applies this modifier to disable the button after it is pressed, so the user can perform the action only once.

```
struct ContentView: View {
    @State private var color = Color.clear
    @State private var buttonDisabled = false

    var body: some View {
        VStack(spacing: 10) {
            Text("Default Title")
                .padding()
                .background(color)
            Button("Change Color") {
                color = Color.green
                buttonDisabled = true
            }
            .disabled(buttonDisabled)
            Spacer()
        }.padding()
    }
}
```

Listing 6-15: Disabling a button

This view includes two **@State** properties, one to keep track of the color, and another to indicate whether the button is enabled or not. When the button is pressed, the action assigns the value **true** to the **buttonDisabled** property and the button stops working, so the user can press it only once.

Figure 6-6: *Button disabled*

As we have seen before, the initializers for the **Button** view can include the **label** argument to define the label with any view we want. This argument is very flexible and it can include views like **Text** views and **Image** views. Images in buttons are displayed in the original rendering mode, which means they are showing in the original colors, but there is another mode available that creates a mask with the image and show it in the app's accent color or the foreground color assigned to the control. To select the rendering mode, the **Image** view includes the following modifier.

▷ **renderingMode(**TemplateRenderingMode**)**—This modifier defines the rendering mode for an **Image** view. The argument is an enumeration with the values **original** and **template**.

The following example defines a button with an image and a text. The **renderingMode()** modifier is applied to the **Image** view to show the image as a template.

```
struct ContentView: View {
    @State private var expanded: Bool = false

    var body: some View {
        VStack(spacing: 10) {
            Text("Default Title")
                .frame(minWidth: 0, maxWidth: expanded ? .infinity : 150,
maxHeight: 50)
                .background(Color.yellow)
            Button(action: {
                expanded.toggle()
            }, label: {
                VStack {
                    Image(expanded ? .contract : .expand)
                        .renderingMode(.template)
                    Text(expanded ? "Contract" : "Expand")
                }
            })
            Spacer()
        }.padding()
    }
}
```

Listing 6-16: *Defining the label of a button with an* Image *view*

The view in Listing 6-16 includes a **@State** property called **expanded** to control the width of the **Text** view. If the value of the property is **true**, we give the view an infinite width with the **infinity** value, otherwise, we make it 150 points wide. Every time the user presses the button, the value of the **expanded** property is toggled with the **toggle()** method and therefore the width of the **Text** view changes.

Figure 6-7: Button with template image

 Do It Yourself: Download the expand.png and contract.png images from our website and add them to the Asset Catalog. Update the **ContentView** view with the code in Listing 6-16 and press the Expand button. You should see the interfaces in Figure 6-7. Remove the **renderingMode()** modifier. You should see the images in their original colors.

We can also assign standard styles for the buttons with the following modifiers.

▷ **buttonStyle(**ButtonStyle**)**—This modifier defines the style of the button. The argument is a structure that conforms to the **ButtonStyle** protocol.

▷ **controlSize(**ControlSize**)**—This modifier defines the scale of the button. The argument is an enumeration with the values **large**, **mini**, **regular**, and **small**.

The SwiftUI framework includes the **PrimitiveButtonStyle** protocol to provide standard styles. For this purpose, the protocol defines the type properties **automatic**, **bordered**, **borderedProminent**, **borderless**, and **plain**. These styles fulfill different purposes. For instance, the **bordered** style creates a button with a gray background to represent secondary actions, and the **borderedProminent** style creates a button with the app's accent color to represent primary actions, such as the possibility to save or submit the data. For instance, the following view includes two buttons, one to cancel the process and another to send the information to a server.

```
struct ContentView: View {
    var body: some View {
        VStack(spacing: 10) {
            HStack {
                Button("Cancel") {
                    print("Cancel Action")
                }.buttonStyle(.bordered)
                Spacer()
                Button("Send") {
                    print("Send Information")
                }.buttonStyle(.borderedProminent)
            }
            Spacer()
        }.padding()
    }
}
```

Listing 6-17: Styling buttons

Prominent buttons should be used only to represent primary actions. In this example, the Cancel button is bordered, which tells the user that this is a secondary action, but the Send button is prominent, which means that an important task is going to be performed when the button is pressed.

Figure 6-8: Buttons with standard styles

When the purpose of the button is to cancel a process, as in this case, or delete an item, we can assign that specific role to the button from the **Button**'s initializer. This allows the system to style the button according to the role and the device where the app is running. For instance, in mobile devices, a button with the **destructive** role is shown in red.

```
Button("Delete", role: .destructive) {
    print("Delete Action")
}.buttonStyle(.bordered)
```

Listing 6-18: Assigning a role

Figure 6-9: Destructive button

 Do It Yourself: Update the **ContentView** view with the code in Listing 6-17. You should see the button as illustrated in Figure 6-8. Replace the Cancel button with the **Button** view in Listing 6-18. You should see the destructive button as illustrated in Figure 6-9.

These styles were designed to look good with SF Symbols. The advantage of using SF Symbols instead of our own images is that they are scaled to the size of the font assigned to the button. This, along with the possibility of scaling the button itself with the **controlSize()** modifier, allows us to create buttons of different sizes.

```
struct ContentView: View {
    var body: some View {
        VStack(spacing: 10) {
            Button(action: {
                print("Delete item")
            }, label: {
                HStack {
                    Image(systemName: "mail")
                        .imageScale(.large)
                    Text("Send")
                }
            })
            .buttonStyle(.borderedProminent)
            .font(.largeTitle)
            .controlSize(.large)
            Spacer()
        }.padding()
    }
}
```

Listing 6-19: Scaling buttons

Chapter 6 - Declarative User Interface

In this example, we implement the **imageScale()** modifier to scale the SF Symbol, the **font()** modifier to assign a large font to the button, and the **controlSize()** modifier to scale the button. The result is shown below.

Figure 6-10: Button of custom size

If we want to define a style that deviates from those provided by the system, we must create our own **ButtonStyle** structure. The protocol's only requirement is for the structure to implement the following method.

▷ **makeBody(configuration:** Configuration)—This method defines and returns a view that replaces the body of the button. The **configuration** argument is a value of type **Configuration** that contains information about the button.

This method receives a value of type **Configuration**, a typealias of **ButtonStyle-Configuration**, which contains properties that return information about the button. The following are the properties available.

▷ **isPressed**—This property returns a Boolean value that indicates whether the button was pressed or not.

▷ **label**—This property returns the view or views that define the button's current label.

The following example defines a button that expands when pressed. The styles include a padding and a green border. To apply these styles, we must create a structure that conforms to the **ButtonStyle** protocol, implement the **makeBody()** method, and return from this method the view we want to assign to the body of the button.

The views that make up the body of the button are provided by the **label** property of the **Configuration** structure, so we can read and modify the value of this property to apply the new styles, as shown below.

```
import SwiftUI
struct MyStyle: ButtonStyle {
    func makeBody(configuration: MyStyle.Configuration) -> some View {
        let pressed = configuration.isPressed
        return configuration.label
            .padding()
            .border(Color.green, width: 5)
            .scaleEffect(pressed ? 1.2 : 1.0)
    }
}
struct ContentView: View {
    @State private var color = Color.gray

    var body: some View {
        VStack {
            Text("Default Title")
                .padding()
                .foregroundColor(color)
            Button("Change Color") {
                color = Color.green
            }.buttonStyle(MyStyle())
```

```
            Spacer()
        }.padding()
    }
}
```

Listing 6-20: Defining custom styles for the button

In Listing 6-20, we define a structure called **MyStyle** and implement the required **makeBody()** method. This method gets the current configuration of the button from the type properties and then proceeds to modify and return the label. First, we read the value of the **isPressed** property to know if the button was pressed or not, and then apply the new styles to the **label** property. This property returns a copy of the views that create the button's current label, and therefore by modifying its value we are effectively modifying the label. In this case, we apply a padding, a border, and then assign a scale depending on the value of the **isPressed** property. If the value is **true**, which means the button is being pressed, we assign a scale of 1.2 to expand it, but if the value is **false**, we bring the scale back to 1.

In the view, we create an instance of this structure and assign it to the **Button** view with the **buttonStyle()** modifier. The result is shown below.

Figure 6-11: Button with custom styles

 Do It Yourself: Update the ContentView.swift file with the code in Listing 6-20. Press the button. You should see the button expanding, as show in Figure 6-11, right. The button is automatically animated by SwiftUI. We will learn how to customize animations and create our own in Chapter 11.

Basic TextField View

The **TextField** view is another control we have introduced before. The view creates an input field the user can interact with to insert a value (a line of text). The following is one of the many initializers included by the structure.

▷ **TextField(**LocalizedStringKey, **text:** Binding, **selection:** Binding, **axis:** Axis**)** —This initializer creates an input field. The first argument defines the field's placeholder, the **text** argument is the binding property of type **String** used to store the value inserted by the user, the **selection** argument is a binding property of type **TextSelection**, a structure used to store the range of the selection, and the **axis** argument defines the axis in which the content will scroll when it exceeds the bound of the view. It is an enumeration with the values **horizontal** and **vertical**.

The framework defines a few modifiers for **TextField** views. The following are the most frequently used.

▷ **textFieldStyle(**TextFieldStyle**)**—This modifier defines the style of the text field. The argument is a structure that conforms to the **TextFieldStyle** protocol. The framework includes several structures to provide standard styles. These structures define the type properties **automatic**, **plain**, **roundedBorder**, and **squareBorder**.

- ▷ **autocorrectionDisabled(**Bool**)**—This modifier enables or disables the system's autocorrection feature. By default, the value is **true** (disabled).

- ▷ **textInputAutocapitalization(**TextInputAutocapitalization?**)**—This modifier defines the capitalization type used to format the text. The argument is a structure, which includes the type properties **characters**, **never**, **sentences** (default), and **words**.

- ▷ **keyboardType(**UIKeyboardType**)**—This modifier defines the type of keyboard the system is going to open when the input field is selected. The argument is an enumeration with the values **default**, **asciiCapable**, **numbersAndPunctuation**, **URL**, **numberPad**, **phonePad**, **namePhonePad**, **emailAddress**, **decimalPad**, **twitter**, **webSearch**, **asciiCapableNumberPad**, and **alphabet**.

We have already seen how to include a simple **TextField** view to get input from the user, but have only applied a few modifiers. The following example shows how to style the view and how to capitalize words.

```
struct ContentView: View {
    @State private var title: String = "Default Title"
    @State private var titleInput: String = ""

    var body: some View {
        VStack(spacing: 15) {
            Text(title)
                .lineLimit(1)
                .padding()
                .background(Color.yellow)
            TextField("Insert Title", text: $titleInput)
                .textFieldStyle(.roundedBorder)
                .textInputAutocapitalization(.words)
            Button("Save") {
                title = titleInput
                titleInput = ""
            }
            Spacer()
        }.padding()
    }
}
```

Listing 6-21: Configuring a text field

The style applied to the **TextField** view in Listing 6-21 is called **roundedBorder**. This adds a border to the input field that makes the area occupied by the view visible, as shown below.

Figure 6-12: Text field with a rounded border

 Do It Yourself: Update the **ContentView** view with the code in Listing 6-21. Insert a text in the input field and press the Save button. You should see something like Figure 6-12.

In addition to having a button, the user normally expects to be able to save the value by pressing the Done button on the keyboard. The framework includes the following modifiers for this purpose.

- ▷ **onSubmit(of:** SubmitTriggers, Closure)—This modifier performs an action when a trigger is fired (e.g., the keyboard's Done/Return button is pressed). The **of** argument determines the trigger to which the modifier responds. This structure includes the properties `search` and `text`. The second argument is the closure we want to execute.
- ▷ **submitLabel(**SubmitLabel)—This modifier specifies the label to use for the Done button in the virtual keyboard. The argument is a structure with the type properties `continue`, `done`, `go`, `join`, `next`, `return`, `route`, `search`, and `send`.
- ▷ **submitScope(**Bool)—This modifier determines whether the view will submit when is triggered.

The closure assigned to the `onSubmit()` modifier is executed when the focus is on the view (e.g., the user is editing the input field). If we apply it to a `TextField` view, the **of** argument can be omitted, as in the following example.

```
struct ContentView: View {
    @State private var title: String = "Default Title"
    @State private var titleInput: String = ""

    var body: some View {
        VStack(spacing: 15) {
            Text(title)
                .lineLimit(1)
                .padding()
                .background(Color.yellow)
            TextField("Insert Title", text: $titleInput)
                .textFieldStyle(.roundedBorder)
                .submitLabel(.continue)
                .onSubmit {
                    assignTitle()
                }
            HStack {
                Spacer()
                Button("Save") {
                    assignTitle()
                }
            }
            Spacer()
        }.padding()
    }
    func assignTitle() {
        title = titleInput
        titleInput = ""
    }
}
```

Listing 6-22: Responding to the Done button

The code in Listing 6-22 implements the `submitLabel()` modifier to change the title of the Done button to "Continue", and then adds a method to the structure called `assignTitle()` that performs the same action as before. The method is called from two places, the closure assigned to the `onSubmit()` modifier and the action of the `Button` view, so the operation is performed either when the button on the interface is pressed or when the keyboard's Done/Return button is pressed. The value inserted in the text field is always stored in the `title` property, regardless of the action the user decides to perform.

 Do It Yourself: Update the `ContentView` structure with the code in Listing 6-22 and run the app on the iPhone simulator. Click on the input field, insert a text, and press the Continue key on the keyboard. (To activate the virtual keyboard on the simulator, open the I/O menu, click on Keyboard, and select the option Toggle Software Keyboard.) The text should be assigned to the title, as before.

When a view that can take input or process feedback from the user is selected, it is said that the view is in focus. SwiftUI includes several tools to process this state. We can process a task when a view gains focus, determine if the focus is on a view, or remove focus from a view. There are two property wrappers available for this purpose: `@FocusState` and `@FocusedBinding`. `@FocusState` stores a value that determines where the focus is at the moment, and `@FocusedBinding` is used to pass the state to other views. To manage the state, the framework includes the following modifiers.

▷ **focused**(Binding, **equals:** Hashable)—This modifier stores the current state of the view in the binding property. The first argument is a reference to the `@FocusState` property, and the equals argument is the Hashable value used to identify the view.

▷ **focusable**(Bool)—This modifier determines if focus can be set on the view.

To track the state of the views, we need a `@FocusState` property of a hashable data type that provides values we can use to identify the views. In the following example, the property is created with the values of an enumeration. We have defined two values, `name` and `surname`, to track the focus state of two input fields and change the background color when the user starts typing on them.

```swift
import SwiftUI

enum FocusName: Hashable {
    case name
    case surname
}
struct ContentView: View {
    @FocusState var focusName: FocusName?
    @State private var title: String = "Default Name"
    @State private var nameInput: String = ""
    @State private var surnameInput: String = ""

    var body: some View {
        VStack(spacing: 10) {
            Text(title)
                .lineLimit(1)
                .padding()
                .background(Color.yellow)
            TextField("Insert Name", text: $nameInput)
                .textFieldStyle(.roundedBorder)
                .padding(4)
                .background(focusName == .name ? Color(white: 0.9) : .white)
                .focused($focusName, equals: .name)
            TextField("Insert Surname", text: $surnameInput)
                .textFieldStyle(.roundedBorder)
                .padding(4)
                .background(focusName == .surname ? Color(white:
0.9) : .white)
                .focused($focusName, equals: .surname)
            HStack {
                Spacer()
                Button("Save") {
                    title = nameInput + " " + surnameInput
                }
            }
            Spacer()
        }.padding()
    }
}
```

Listing 6-23: Responding to changes in focus

The initial value of the @FocusState property is nil, which means no view is focused. When the user taps on a text field, the focus moves to that view and the value that identifies the view is assigned to the property. By comparing this value with the values in the enumeration, we know which TextField view is focused and can change the background color accordingly. Note that the roundedBorder style adds a border and a white background to the text field, so only the background of the padding is visible in this example.

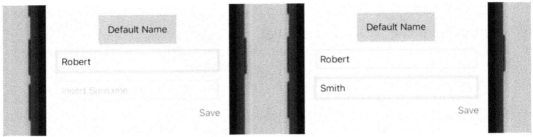

Figure 6-13: *Focus*

In mobile devices, the virtual keyboard opens when a view that can process the input gains focus (e.g., TextField view). The keyboard remains open as long as the focus is on a view that can process the input. This means that to close it, we must remove focus from the view. In SwiftUI this is achieved by assigning the value nil to the @FocusState property, as shown below.

```
Button("Save") {
    title = nameInput + " " + surnameInput
    focusName = nil
}
```

Listing 6-24: *Closing the keyboard*

The Button view in Listing 6-24 replaces the Button view defined in Listing 6-23. Now, every time the Save button is pressed, the values are processed and the keyboard is closed.

 Do It Yourself: Update the ContentView.swift file with the code in Listing 6-23 and run the application on the iPhone simulator. Click on an input field. You should see the background color changing to gray, as illustrated in Figure 6-13. Replace the Button view with the view in Listing 6-24. Run the application again. Insert values in both fields and press the Save button. The values should be assigned to the title and the virtual keyboard should be closed.

In previous examples, we didn't check whether the user inserted a value or not, but usually applications must prevent the user from saving invalid or empty values. There are different ways we can control this. One alternative is to check the values before storing them. We allow users to type whatever they want but only store the values accepted by the app.

```
Button("Save") {
    let tempName = nameInput.trimmingCharacters(in: .whitespaces)
    let tempSurname = surnameInput.trimmingCharacters(in: .whitespaces)

    if !tempName.isEmpty && !tempSurname.isEmpty {
        title = tempName + " " + tempSurname
        focusName = nil
    }
}
```

Listing 6-25: *Checking the values before storing*

Chapter 6 - Declarative User Interface

In this example, we first trim the **nameInput** and **surnameInput** properties to remove spaces at the beginning and the end (see Strings in Chapter 4) and then check that the resulting values are not empty before assigning them to the **title** property. The Save button is still enabled, but the values are not stored until the user inserts a text in both fields.

 Do It Yourself: Update the **Button** view in the **ContentView** view with the code in Listing 6-25. You shouldn't be able to modify the title until you have inserted a name and a surname.

Another alternative is to disable the button with the **disabled()** modifier if the values inserted by the user are not what the application is expecting.

```
Button("Save") {
    let tempName = nameInput.trimmingCharacters(in: .whitespaces)
    let tempSurname = surnameInput.trimmingCharacters(in: .whitespaces)

    if !tempName.isEmpty && !tempSurname.isEmpty {
        title = tempName + " " + tempSurname
        focusName = nil
    }
}
.disabled(nameInput.isEmpty || surnameInput.isEmpty)
```

Listing 6-26: Disabling the button

In this example, we implement the **disabled()** modifier introduced before to disable the button until the user types a text in both fields. If one text field or both are empty, the button doesn't work.

 Do It Yourself: Update the **Button** view with the code in Listing 6-26. You shouldn't be able to press the Save button until you have inserted a name and a surname.

Besides checking whether the properties contain a valid value, we can also limit what the user can type on the fields. For instance, we could only accept numbers or a specific amount of characters. For this, we need to check whether the value inserted by the user is valid or not every time the state of the view changes. The framework includes the following modifier for this purpose.

▷ **onChange(of:** State, **initial:** Bool, Closure)—This modifier executes a closure when a state changes. The **of** argument is the property that stores the value to be checked, the **initial** argument is a boolean value that specifies whether the check should also be performed when the view appears, and the last argument is the closure to be executed when the system reports a change in the value. The closure can receive two values, one representing the property's old value and another representing the new one.

This modifier can only check one state, so we should apply it to every view we want to control. For instance, we can use it in the **TextField** views of our example to limit the number of characters the user is allowed to type. If the user goes over the limit, we remove the extra characters and assign the result back to the property, as shown below.

```
TextField("Insert Name", text: $nameInput)
    .textFieldStyle(.roundedBorder)
    .padding(4)
    .background(focusName == .name ? Color(white: 0.9) : .white)
    .focused($focusName, equals: .name)
    .onChange(of: nameInput, initial: false) { old, value in
        if value.count > 10 {
```

```
              nameInput = String(value.prefix(10))
        }
    }
TextField("Insert Surname", text: $surnameInput)
    .textFieldStyle(.roundedBorder)
    .padding(4)
    .background(focusName == .surname ? Color(white: 0.9) : .white)
    .focused($focusName, equals: .surname)
    .onChange(of: surnameInput, initial: false) { old, value in
        if value.count > 15 {
           surnameInput = String(value.prefix(15))
        }
    }
```

Listing 6-27: Controlling user's input

In the code of Listing 6-27, we check for changes in the properties that store the state of the text fields. When the user types or removes a character, the value of the corresponding property changes, and the closure assigned to the `onChange()` modifier is executed. The closure receives the value of the property. Using this value, we can check whether the text inserted by the user is valid or not and respond accordingly. In this example, we count the number of characters in the string and if the value exceeds the limit, we subtract the beginning of the text with the `prefix()` method and assign the result back to the property, which updates the views and deletes the extra characters from the text field. As a result, when the number of characters exceeds the limit, the user cannot add more characters to the field.

 Do It Yourself: Update the `TextField` views in your project with the code in Listing 6-27. Run the application on the iPhone simulator. Insert a name and a surname. You shouldn't be able to add more than 10 characters for the name and 15 characters for the surname.

Of course, we can specify other conditions besides the number of characters. The following example creates a small application that accepts only integers.

```
struct ContentView: View {
    @State private var title = "Default Name"
    @State private var numberInput = ""

    var body: some View {
        VStack(spacing: 10) {
            Text(title)
                .padding()
                .background(Color.yellow)
            TextField("Insert Number", text: $numberInput)
                .textFieldStyle(.roundedBorder)
                .padding(4)
                .keyboardType(.numbersAndPunctuation)
                .onChange(of: numberInput, initial: false) { old, value in
                    if !value.isEmpty && Int(value) == nil {
                        numberInput = old
                    }
                }
            }
            HStack {
                Spacer()
                Button("Save") {
                    title = numberInput
                    numberInput = ""
                }
            }
            Spacer()
        }.padding()
```

```
        }
}
```

Listing 6-28: Accepting only integer numbers

As before, the view contains a **TextField** with the **onChange()** modifier. The difference is in how we check the validity of the input. In this case, we need to make sure that the text field is not empty, and then see if we can convert it into an integer, which means that the user have only entered numbers. If this is not possible, we use the old value received by the closure and assign it to the **numberInput** property, returning the text field to its previous state.

Note that we have also implemented the **keyboardType()** modifier to show the appropriate keyboard for the input we are expecting from the user (in this case, numbers).

 Do It Yourself: Update the ContentView.swift file with the code in Listing 6-28. Run the application on the iPhone simulator. You should only be able to type numbers.

By default, a **TextField** view only displays one line of text, but we can allow the view to expand to include more with the **lineLimit()** modifier. (The same modifier implemented before to expand **Text** views.) In addition to applying the modifier to set the number of lines we want, we also need to ask the view to scroll the content in the vertical axis, as shown below.

```
struct ContentView: View {
    @State private var text: String = ""

    var body: some View {
        TextField("Insert Text", text: $text, axis: .vertical)
            .textFieldStyle(.roundedBorder)
            .padding(20)
            .lineLimit(5)
    }
}
```

Listing 6-29: Defining a multiline text field

In this example, the **TextView** view expands until it reaches a height of 5 lines and then the text scrolls vertically to allow the user to keep typing. If we want to give the view a minimum and a maximum size, we can declare the modifier with a range, as in **lineLimit(3...5)**.

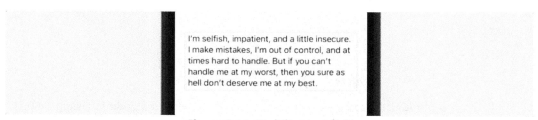

Figure 6-14: Multiline text field

The **TextField** structure can also use a binding property to work with the text selected by the user. The value stored in the property is a **TextSelection** structure. The structure includes the **indices** property to return an enumeration with two cases: **multiSelection()** for multiple selection and **selection()** for single selection. The cases have associated values to return the range of characters covered by the selection.

To get the text selected by the user, we need to define a **@State** property to store the **TextSelection** structure, use this property to create the **TextField** view, and then define a function that retrieves the selected text using the range of values returned by the **indices** property, as shown below.

```
struct ContentView: View {
    @State private var text = ""
    @State private var selected: TextSelection? = nil

    var body: some View {
        VStack {
            TextField("Insert Text", text: $text, selection: $selected,
axis: .vertical)
                .textFieldStyle(.roundedBorder)
                .padding(20)
                .lineLimit(5)
            Text(getSelection() ?? "")
            Spacer()
        }
    }
    func getSelection() -> String? {
        if let indices = selected?.indices {
            if case .selection(let range) = indices {
                let substring = text[range]
                return String(substring)
            }
        }
        return nil
    }
}
```

Listing 6-30: *Selecting text*

When the user selects characters in the text field, the **TextField** view automatically assigns a range to the **selected** property that determines the position of these characters. Once we have this range, we can retrieve and process the selected text. In this example, we define a function for this purpose. The **getSelection()** function ensures that a text has been selected by checking the value of the **selected** property and then reads the value associated with the **selection()** case to get the range (see Listing 3-137). Using this range, we get the substring from the **text** property and return it. The selected text is displayed on the screen with a **Text** view, as shown below.

Figure 6-15: *Text selected by the user*

Do It Yourself: Update the **ContentView** view with the code in Listing 6-30. Run the application. Write a text and double-click on a word to select it. You should see the word below the text field, as shown in Figure 6-15.

Basic SecureField View

SwiftUI also includes a view to create a secure text field. The view replaces the characters inserted by the user with dots to hide sensitive information, such as passwords.

▷ **SecureField(String, text: Binding)**—This initializer creates a secure input field. The first argument defines the placeholder, and the **text** argument is the binding property that stores the value inserted by the user.

The implementation is the same as with **TextField** views, and we can also apply some of the same modifiers, as shown below.

```
struct ContentView: View {
    @State private var pass: String = ""

    var body: some View {
        VStack(spacing: 15) {
            Text(pass)
                .padding()
            SecureField("Insert Password", text: $pass)
                .textFieldStyle(.roundedBorder)
            Spacer()
        }.padding()
    }
}
```

Listing 6-31: *Using a secure text field*

The **SecureField** view looks the same as the **TextField** view. The only difference is that the characters are hidden.

Figure 6-16: *Secure text field*

Do It Yourself: Update the **ContentView** view with the code in Listing 6-31. Insert characters in the input field. You should see the characters being replaced by black dots, as illustrated in Figure 6-16.

(Basic) TextEditor View

SwiftUI includes an additional view to allow the user to insert multiple lines of text called **TextEditor**. The following is the view's initializer.

▷ **TextEditor(text:** Binding, **selection:** Binding)—This initializer creates a text editor. The **text** argument is the binding property that stores the text inserted by the user, and the **selection** argument is a binding property of type **TextSelection**, a structure used to store the range of the selection.

This view can take some of the modifiers we have already applied to **TextField** and **Text** views to format the text. For instance, we can tell the view how to align the text, the space we want between lines, and whether the view should check for errors.

```
struct ContentView: View {
    @State private var text: String = ""

    var body: some View {
        TextEditor(text: $text)
            .multilineTextAlignment(.leading)
            .lineSpacing(10)
            .autocorrectionDisabled(true)
            .padding(8)
    }
}
```

```
}
```

Listing 6-32: Implementing a text editor

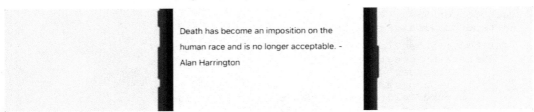

Death has become an imposition on the
human race and is no longer acceptable. -
Alan Harrington

Figure 6-17: Text editor

 IMPORTANT: The `TextEditor` view also allows the user to select a text. The selection works in the same way as with the `TextField` view. We need a binding property to store a `TextSelection` structure and then process this value, as we did in Listing 6-30.

(Basic) Toggle View

The `Toggle` view creates a control to switch between two states. By default, it is displayed as a user-friendly toggle switch on mobile devices and as a checkbox on Macs. The view includes the following initializer.

▷ **Toggle(**String, **isOn:** Binding**)**—This initializer creates a `Toggle` view. The first argument defines the label, and the **isOn** argument is the binding property that stores the current state. The view also includes an initializer to define the label with the views returned by a closure (`Toggle(isOn: Binding, label: Closure)`).

The view requires a binding property to store the current value. In the following example, we provide a `@State` property and use the value of this property to select the proper label.

```
struct ContentView: View {
    @State private var currentState: Bool = true

    var body: some View {
        VStack {
            Toggle(isOn: $currentState, label: {
                Text(currentState ? "On" : "Off")
            })
            Spacer()
        }.padding()
    }
}
```

Listing 6-33: Implementing a Toggle

The code in Listing 6-33 uses a ternary operator to check the value of the **currentState** property and display the corresponding text ("On" or "Off"). By default, we set the value of the property to **true**, so the switch is activated and the "On" label is displayed on the screen, but if we tap the switch, it is turned off, the view is updated, and the "Off" label is shown instead.

 On  Off

Figure 6-18: Switch on and off

The closure assigned to the **label** argument can include a second view to define a subtitle, as in the following example.

```
struct ContentView: View {
   @State private var currentState: Bool = true

   var body: some View {
      VStack {
         Toggle(isOn: $currentState, label: {
            Text(currentState ? "On" : "Off")
            Text("Enable or Disable")
         })
         Spacer()
      }.padding()
   }
}
```

Listing 6-34: Including a subtitle

Figure 6-19: Switch with a title and subtitle

The **Toggle** view creates a horizontal stack to contain the label and the control with a flexible space in between, in consequence, the view occupies all the horizontal space available in its container and the label and the control are displaced to the sides. If we want to have absolute control on the position and size of the views, we can apply the **fixedSize()** modifier introduced before to reduce the view's size, or hide the label with the following modifier.

▷ **labelsHidden()**—This modifier hides the labels assigned to controls.

This modifier works with several controls, but it is particularly useful with switches. The following example shows how to implement it to define a custom label for the control.

```
struct ContentView: View {
   @State private var currentState: Bool = true

   var body: some View {
      HStack {
         Toggle("", isOn: $currentState)
            .labelsHidden()
         Text(currentState ? "On" : "Off")
            .padding()
            .background(Color(currentState ? .yellow : .gray))
      }.padding()
   }
}
```

Listing 6-35: Defining a custom label for the Toggle *view*

The view is now of the size of the control and centered on the screen. The label is not shown anymore, so we declare it with an empty string, but include a **Text** view on the side to display the current value.

Figure 6-20: Custom size and label for the switch

Like **Button** views, **Toggle** views also implement a modifier to define the style of the control.

> **toggleStyle(ToggleStyle)**—This modifier defines the style of the toggle. The argument is a structure that conforms to the **ToggleStyle** protocol. To create standard structures, the framework includes the properties **automatic**, **button**, **checkbox**, and **switch**.

The value by default is **automatic**, which means the style of the control is going to be selected by the system. If we want to always apply the same style, we can assign the values **switch** or **checkbox** (only available for Macs). These values are used to specify standard styles, but the framework also includes the value **button** to create a completely different type of control. When we assign this style to the view, the system shows a toggle button to represent the on and off states. When the button is in the on state, it is highlighted, otherwise it is shown as a standard button.

```
struct ContentView: View {
    @State private var currentState: Bool = true

    var body: some View {
        HStack {
            Toggle(isOn: $currentState, label: {
                Label("Send", systemImage: "mail")
            })
            .toggleStyle(.button)
        }.padding()
    }
}
```

Listing 6-36: Implementing a toggle button

Figure 6-21: Toggle button in the on and off state

The styles offered by the framework are limited, but we can create our own. All we have to do is to define a structure that conforms to the **ToggleStyle** protocol. The protocol's requirement is for the structure to implement the following method.

> **makeBody(configuration: Configuration)**—This method defines and returns a view that replaces the body of the toggle. The **configuration** argument is a value of type **Configuration** that contains information about the control.

This method receives a value of type **Configuration**, a typealias of **ToggleStyle-Configuration**, which contains the following properties to return information about the control.

> **isOn**—This property returns a Boolean value that indicates if the toggle is on or off.

> **label**—This property returns the view that defines the toggle's label.

The **isOn** property is a binding property that creates a bidirectional binding with the view and therefore we can read and modify its value to activate or deactivate the control. In the following example, we create a **Toggle** view that looks like a checkbox. When the control is tapped, the graphic changes color indicating the current state (gray deactivated and green activated).

```
import SwiftUI

struct MyStyle: ToggleStyle {
    func makeBody(configuration: MyStyle.Configuration) -> some View {
        HStack(alignment: .center) {
            configuration.label
            Spacer()
            Image(systemName: "checkmark.rectangle.fill")
                .font(.largeTitle)
                .foregroundColor(configuration.isOn ? Color.green :
Color.gray)
                .onTapGesture {
                    configuration.$isOn.wrappedValue.toggle()
                }
        }
    }
}
struct ContentView: View {
    @State private var currentState: Bool = false

    var body: some View {
        VStack {
            HStack {
                Toggle("Enabled", isOn: $currentState)
                    .toggleStyle(MyStyle())
            }
            Spacer()
        }.padding()
    }
}
```

Listing 6-37: Defining a custom `Toggle` *view*

There are a few things we must consider before customizing a **Toggle** view. First, the **label** property of the **Configuration** structure contains a copy of the view that represents the control's current label, so if we want to keep this label, we must include the value of this property in the new content. Second, a **Toggle** view is designed with an **HStack** view and a **Spacer** view between the label and the control. If we want to preserve the standard design, we must use this arrangement. And third, we are responsible of responding to user interaction and update the state of the control, so we must check for a gesture and change the state by modifying the value of the **isOn** property when the gesture is performed by the user.

In the code in Listing 6-37, we define a structure called **MyStyle** and implement the required **makeBody()** method to provide the new design for the **Toggle** view. To preserve the standard design, we wrap the views with an **HStack** view and separate the label and the control with a **Spacer** view. We first read the value of the **label** property to include the current label, then declare the **Spacer** view, and finally define an **Image** view that presents an SF Symbol that looks like a checkbox. To turn this **Image** view into a control, we define its size with a **font()** modifier, apply the **foregroundColor()** modifier to change the color of the symbol depending on the current value of the **isOn** property, and finally, use the **onTapGesture()** modifier to detect when the user taps on the **Image** view. We will learn more about gesture modifiers in Chapter 12. For now, all we need to now is that this modifier executes a closure every time the view is tapped by the user. In this closure, we access the binding value of the **isOn** property and toggle its value by applying the **toggle()** modifier to the Boolean value stored in its **wrappedValue** property. (In this case, the setter of the binding value is private, so we access it from the **wrappedValue** property, as explained before in this chapter.) This modifies the current value of the property, which changes the state of the control, turning it on and off.

Figure 6-22: Custom style for the `Toggle` *view*

(Basic) **Slider View**

A `Slider` view creates a control that allows the user to select a value from a range of values. It is displayed as a horizontal bar with a knob that moves to the position corresponding to the selected value. The structure includes the following initializer.

▷ **Slider(value:** Binding, **in:** Range, **step:** Float, **onEditingChanged:** Closure**)** —This initializer creates a **Slider** view. The **value** argument is the binding property we want to use to store the current value, the **in** argument is a range that specifies the minimum and maximum values the user can choose from, the **step** argument indicates the number by which the current value will be incremented or decremented, and the **onEditingChanged** argument is a closure that is executed when the user starts or finishes moving the slider.

To create a slider, we must provide at least a **@State** property to store the value and a range to determine the minimum and maximum values allowed.

```
struct ContentView: View {
    @State private var currentValue: Float = 5

    var body: some View {
        VStack {
            Text("Current Value: \
(currentValue.formatted(.number.precision(.fractionLength(0))))")
            Slider(value: $currentValue, in: 0...10, step: 1.0)
            Spacer()
        }.padding()
    }
}
```

Listing 6-38: Creating a slider

The code in Listing 6-38 creates a slider from the value 0 to 10 and displays the current value with a **Text** view. The **Slider** view takes values of type **Float** or **Double**, and therefore it allows us to select a floating-point value, but we can specify that we want the user to be able to select only integers by declaring the **step** argument with the value 1.0, as we did in this example. (Note that we had to format the value for the **Text** view with the **formatted()** method introduced in Chapter 4 to display it as an integer.) Because the **currentValue** property was initialized with the number 5, the initial position of the knob is right in the middle.

Current Value: 5

Figure 6-23: Slider for integer values

The **Slider**'s initializer also includes the **onEditingChanged** argument, which takes a closure that receives a Boolean value to indicate whether the user started or finished moving the slider. We can use it to highlight the value that is been edited, as in the following example.

```
struct ContentView: View {
    @State private var currentValue: Float = 5
    @State private var textActive: Bool = false

    var body: some View {
        VStack {
            Text("Current Value: \
(currentValue.formatted(.number.precision(.fractionLength(0))))")
                .padding()
                .background(textActive ? Color.yellow : Color.clear)
            Slider(value: $currentValue, in: 0...10, step: 1.0,
onEditingChanged: { self.textActive = $0 })
            Spacer()
        }.padding()
    }
}
```

Listing 6-39: Responding to the slider state

The view in Listing 6-39 includes a new **@State** property called **textActive**. The closure assigned to the **onEditingChanged** argument assigns the value **true** to this property when the user begins moving the slider and the value **false** when the user releases the knob. The **background()** modifier of the **Text** view reads the value of this property to assign a different background color to the view depending on the current state. Because of this, the text that displays the slider's current value has a yellow background while the user is moving the slider, and no color otherwise.

Current Value: 2   Current Value: 8

Figure 6-24: Slider states

(Basic) ProgressView View

SwiftUI includes the **ProgressView** view to create a progress bar. The view was designed to show the progress of a task over time.

▷ **ProgressView(**String, **value:** Binding, **total:** Double**)**—This initializer creates a progress bar. The first argument specifies the label, the **value** argument indicates the current progress, and the **total** argument specifies the value that determines the completion of the process. (By default, the values go from 0.0 to 1.0).

The implementation of this view is straightforward. All we need is a property with the value that represents the current progress.

```
struct ContentView: View {
    @State private var currentValue: Float = 5

    var body: some View {
        VStack {
            ProgressView(value: currentValue, total: 10)
            Spacer()
        }.padding()
    }
```

```
}
```

Listing 6-40: Showing progress

This `ProgressView` view goes from 0.0 to 10.0 and starts at the value 5 (the initial value assigned to the `currentValue` property), so the progress is set in the middle.

Figure 6-25: Progress bar

The `ProgressView` view was designed to show the progress of a task over time, such as the amount of data currently downloaded from a server or how far we are from finishing a process. We will learn how to perform some of these tasks later, but for now we can test it with a `Slider` view, as shown below.

```
struct ContentView: View {
    @State private var currentValue: Float = 5

    var body: some View {
        VStack {
            ProgressView(value: currentValue, total: 10)
            Slider(value: $currentValue, in: 0...10)
            Spacer()
        }.padding()
    }
}
```

Listing 6-41: Simulating progress

In this example, we set the same values for the `Slider` and the `ProgressView`. They go from 0 to 10, so every time we move the slider, the progress bar shows the same value.

Figure 6-26: Progress bar at work

The `ProgressView` structure includes the following modifier to define the style of the progress bar.

▷ **progressViewStyle**(ProgressViewStyle)—This modifier specifies the style of a `ProgressView` view. The argument is a structure that conforms to the `ProgressViewStyle` protocol. The framework defines the properties **automatic**, **circular**, and **linear** to create standard views.

The style by default is **automatic**, which means that the view is going to be shown as a linear progress bar, but we can specify the **circular** value to create an activity indicator. This is a spinning wheel that indicates that a task is in progress, but unlike progress bars, this type of indicator has no implicit limitations, so we don't need to specify any values, as shown below.

```
struct ContentView: View {
    @State private var currentValue: Float = 5
```

```
    var body: some View {
        VStack {
            ProgressView()
                .progressViewStyle(.circular)
            Spacer()
        }.padding()
    }
}
```

Listing 6-42: Showing an activity indicator

Figure 6-27: Activity indicator

(Basic) **Stepper View**

The **Stepper** view creates a control with two buttons to increment or decrement a value. The structure provides multiple initializers with several combinations of arguments for configuration. The following are the most frequently used.

▷ **Stepper**(String, **value:** Binding, **in:** Range, **step:** Float, **onEditingChanged:** Closure)—This initializer creates a **Stepper** view. The first argument defines the label, the **value** argument is the binding property we want to use to store the current value, the **in** argument is a range that determines the minimum and maximum values allowed, the **step** argument is a **Float** or a **Double** (depending on the binding property) that determines the amount by which the value is going to be incremented or decremented, and the **onEditingChanged** argument is a closure that is executed when the user begins and ends editing the value.

▷ **Stepper**(String, **onIncrement:** Closure?, **onDecrement:** Closure?, **onEditingChanged:** Closure)—This initializer creates a **Stepper** view. The first argument defines the label, the **onIncrement** argument is a closure that is executed when the user taps on the + button, the **onDecrement** argument is a closure that is executed when the user taps on the - button, and the **onEditingChanged** argument is a closure that is executed when the user begins and ends editing the value.

To implement a **Stepper** view, we need a **@State** property to store the current value and define the range of values we want the user to choose from.

```
struct ContentView: View {
    @State private var currentValue: Float = 0

    var body: some View {
        VStack {
            Text("Current Value: \
(currentValue.formatted(.number.precision(.fractionLength(0))))")
            Stepper("Counter", value: $currentValue, in: 0...100)
            Spacer()
        }.padding()
    }
}
```

Listing 6-43: Creating a stepper

The **Stepper** view works with floating-point values of type **Float** or **Double**, so we format the value to display only integers. The result is shown below.

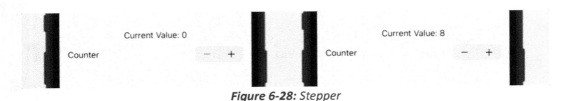

Figure 6-28: Stepper

By default, the value is incremented or decremented by one unit, but we can change that with the **step** argument. The following example defines a **Stepper** view that increments or decrements the value by 5 units.

```
struct ContentView: View {
    @State private var currentValue: Double = 0

    var body: some View {
        VStack {
            Text("Current Value: \
(currentValue.formatted(.number.precision(.fractionLength(0))))")
            Stepper("Counter", value: $currentValue, in: 0...100, step: 5)
            Spacer()
        }.padding()
    }
}
```

Listing 6-44: Defining the steps of a stepper

Like the **Toggle** view, the **Stepper** view is implemented with a horizontal stack and a flexible space between the label and the control. If we want to provide our own label and define a custom position for the control, we need to apply the **labelsHidden()** modifier, as we did in Listing 6-35. The following example defines a custom label and creates the view with the **onIncrement** and **onDecrement** arguments to display an arrow on the screen that tells the user whether the last value was incremented or decremented.

```
struct ContentView: View {
    @State private var currentValue: Float = 0
    @State private var goingUp: Bool = true

    var body: some View {
        VStack {
            HStack {
                Text("Current Value: \
(currentValue.formatted(.number.precision(.fractionLength(0))))")
                Image(systemName: goingUp ? "arrow.up" : "arrow.down")
                    .foregroundColor(goingUp ? Color.green : Color.red)
                Stepper("", onIncrement: {
                    currentValue += 5
                    goingUp = true
                }, onDecrement: {
                    currentValue -= 5
                    goingUp = false
                }).labelsHidden()
            }
            Spacer()
        }.padding()
    }
}
```

Listing 6-45: Modifying the interface when the value is incremented or decremented

In this example, we define two **@State** properties: **currentValue** to store the current value of the stepper, and a Boolean property called **goingUp** to indicate whether the last value was

Chapter 6 - Declarative User Interface

incremented or decremented. The views are included in an **HStack** to show them side by side. The first one is the same **Text** view used before to display the stepper's current value. After this view, we include an **Image** view that checks the **goingUp** property to show an SF Symbol of an arrow pointing up or down, depending on the property's value. The same property is used to determine the color of the arrows. Finally, we define the **Stepper** view with the **onIncrement** and **onDecrement** arguments. In the closures assigned to these arguments, we increment or decrement the value by 5 and change the value of the **goingUp** property to indicate whether the last value was incremented or decremented. As a result, the user can see a green arrow pointing up when the + button is pressed and a red arrow pointing down when the - button is pressed.

Figure 6-29: Custom stepper

(Basic) **GroupBox View**

SwiftUI includes a view called **GroupBox** to create a box around the views. The view is defined with a background color and round corners to visually group views and controls. The following is one of the view's initializers.

▷ **GroupBox**(String, **content:** Closure)—This initializer creates a **GroupBox** view. The first argument defines the label to show at the top of the box, and the **content** argument is the closure that defines the views contained by the group.

The view is styled by default with a background color, so all we need to do is to implement it and provide the closure with all the views we want to include inside the box.

```
struct ContentView: View {
    @State private var setting1: Bool = true
    @State private var setting2: Bool = true
    @State private var setting3: Bool = true

    var body: some View {
        GroupBox("Settings") {
            VStack(spacing: 10) {
                Toggle("Autocorrection", isOn: $setting1)
                Toggle("Capitalization", isOn: $setting2)
                Toggle("Editable", isOn: $setting3)
            }
        }.padding()
    }
}
```

Listing 6-46: Defining a group of views

Figure 6-30: Group box

6.3 Model

Professional applications consist of multiple views, all representing screens through which the user can navigate. These views must access the same data and respond to any change in the state of the application. Therefore, the application must provide a unique source of data that can be accessed and modified by all the views. This data source is usually referred to as the Model or Data Model.

The model is part of the basic organization of an application. In this paradigm, a group of structures or objects define the model (the app's data and states) and the views connect to the model to present the data on the screen and update it with the user's input.

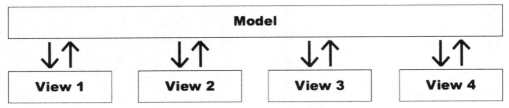

Figure 6-31: Data model

This organization cannot be created with **@State** properties. The **@State** property wrapper used in previous examples can only store values that control the states of a single view. What we need is an object that can be passed to the views and report any changes to the system. To define this object, SwiftUI includes the following Attached macro.

▷ **@Observable**—This macro adds to a class the code necessary to allow the properties to store and manage the states of the application.

With this macro, we can turn any class into an observable object, which means we can use the object's properties to store and manage the states of the application. Below you can see an example of the definition of this class. We call it **ApplicationData**, but it can take any name we want. Note that the **@Observable** macro is defined in the Observation framework, so we need to import that framework for the macro to be available, and the class must be defined as a singleton, so we can only create one instance of it and access it from anywhere in the code (see Listing 3-165).

```
import SwiftUI
import Observation
@Observable class ApplicationData: @unchecked Sendable {
    var title: String = "Default Title"
    var titleInput: String = ""

    static let shared: ApplicationData = ApplicationData()
    private init() {}
}
```

Listing 6-47: Storing our data in an observable object

This model includes two properties. We have a property called **title** to store the title of a book, and another called **titleInput** to allow the user to type a new one. But since we are modifying the class with the **@Observable** macro, we don't need to declare the **@State** properties in the views anymore. The macro takes care of generating the code needed for the properties of the class to store the states and report the changes to the system.

 IMPORTANT: The values in our model can be processed by new and old frameworks. This can lead to a problem called a data race, where different codes try to access and modify a value at the same time. As we will see later, we need to make sure that it is safe to send values from and to different structures and classes. In our example, we tell the compiler that it is safe to send the values in the model to other processes by conforming to the **Sendable** protocol, and that the values used by the model are also safe by prefixing the protocol with the **@unchecked** macro. This is fine for the examples in this book, but your models may require the implementation of other concurrent tools to ensure that no data race occurs. We will learn more about concurrency and data races in Chapter 9.

Once we have the model, we must get the instance from the **shared** property and pass it to the views. For simple applications, we can just assign the instance to a property of the view, as in the following example.

```
struct ContentView: View {
    var appData = ApplicationData.shared

    var body: some View {
        VStack(spacing: 8) {
            Text(appData.title)
                .padding(10)
            Button(action: {
                appData.title = "New Title"
            }, label: { Text("Save") })
            Spacer()
        }.padding()
    }
}
```

Listing 6-48: Initializing the observable object

This is similar to what we have done before, but instead of reading and storing the values in **@State** properties, we do it in the properties of the **ApplicationData** object. The view includes a **Text** view that reads the **title** property in the model and shows its value on the screen, and a button that assigns a new string to the property. When the button is pressed, the string "New Title" is assigned to the **title** property, the property reports the change to the system, and the system updates the view to show the new value on the screen.

 Do It Yourself: The classes defined to store the data are a central part of our application and can be large, so it makes sense to store them in a separate Swift file. Create a Multiplatform project. Open the File menu at the top of the screen and click on the New/Empty File options to create a new Swift file. Assign the name ApplicationData.swift to the file and copy the code in Listing 6-47. Update the **ContentView** view with the code in Listing 6-48. You should see a title and a button on the screen. Press the button. The title should change.

In this example, we display the **title** property and change its value when the button is pressed, but as we have already seen, there are controls that allow users to provide input and insert new values. In such cases, we need to create a bidirectional binding so that every time the user interacts with the control, the new value is stored in the corresponding property and the interface is updated. For this to work, we need to declare the observable object as bindable using the following property wrapper.

▷ **@Bindable**—This property wrapper creates a bidirectional binding between the property and the observable object.

In the code below, we add a **TextField** view to the previous example to demonstrate how to create a bidirectional binding with the observable object.

```
struct ContentView: View {
    @Bindable var appData = ApplicationData.shared

    var body: some View {
        VStack(spacing: 8) {
            Text(appData.title)
                .padding(10)
            TextField("Insert Title", text: $appData.titleInput)
                .textFieldStyle(.roundedBorder)
            Button(action: {
                appData.title = appData.titleInput
                appData.titleInput = ""
            }, label: { Text("Save") })
            Spacer()
        }.padding()
    }
}
```

Listing 6-49: *Creating a bidirectional binding with the observable object*

As always, we must prefix the property with the dollar sign to tell the **TextField** view were to store the value inserted by the user. Because we modify the **appData** property with **@Bindable**, this value is received by the observable object and stored in the model. When the button is pressed, we perform the same procedure as before. The characters inserted by the user are assigned to the **title** property and the interface is updated to show them on the screen.

 Do It Yourself: Update the **ContentView** view with the code in Listing 6-49. You should see a title, a text field, and a button. Insert a new text on the text field and press the button. The text should replace the title.

In the model of Listing 6-47, we define two properties, **title** to store the actual information and **titleInput** to receive input from the user. Other views added later to our application may need to access the **title** property to show its value to the user, but the **titleInput** property is only required by the view that contains the **TextField** view. This means that we are storing the private state of a view in the app's model. Although there is nothing wrong with this approach, it is recommended to use the model to store the app's data but manage the states of the views from within the views. There are different patterns we can implement to organize our application. One approach is to define **@State** properties for each view, as we did before, but another alternative is to create additional observable objects. For instance, we can remove the **titleInput** property from our model and define an observable object for the view to manage the user's input, as shown below.

```
import SwiftUI
import Observation

@Observable class ViewData {
    var titleInput: String = ""
}
struct ContentView: View {
    @Bindable var viewData = ViewData()
    var appData = ApplicationData.shared

    var body: some View {
        VStack(spacing: 8) {
            Text(appData.title)
                .padding(10)
            TextField("Insert Title", text: $viewData.titleInput)
                .textFieldStyle(.roundedBorder)
            Button(action: {
                appData.title = viewData.titleInput
```

Chapter 6 - Declarative User Interface

```
            viewData.titleInput = ""
        }, label: { Text("Save") })
        Spacer()
    }.padding()
  }
}
```

Listing 6-50: Defining an observable object for a view

Everything is the same as before, but we have defined an additional observable object for the **ContentView** view called **ViewData**. Now the characters inserted by the user are stored in the **titleInput** property of this object and therefore the model and the view's state are separated. When the user presses the Save button, we assign the value of the **titleInput** property to the **title** property so that the new title is stored in the model.

 Do It Yourself: Remove the **titleInput** property from the **Application-Data** class. Update the ContentView.swift file with the code in Listing 6-50. Everything should work as before, but now the state of the view is managed by the view itself and not the model.

One of the advantages of using an observable object to manage the states of a view instead of **@State** properties is that it is easy to initialize the properties of the object dynamically. For instance, we can assign the current title stored in the model to the **titleInput** property as soon as **ContentView** is initialized, so the user can see the previous value on the screen.

```
init() {
    viewData.titleInput = appData.title
}
```

Listing 6-51: Initializing the view's observable object

The initializer assigns the value of the model's **title** property to the **titleInput** property of the **viewData** object, so the **TextField** view shows the current value when the view appears.

Figure 6-32: Text field initialized with the value in the model

 Do It Yourself: Add the initializer from Listing 6-51 to the **ContentView** structure (over the definition of the **body** property). The string assigned to the **title** property in the model should appear inside the text field, as shown in Figure 6-32.

Another way to initialize properties of an observable object or **@State** properties is with the **onAppear()** modifier. As we have seen before, this modifier executes a closure when the view appears on the screen. For instance, we can assign it to the **VStack** view of our **ContentView** view to initialize the **titleInput** property as soon as the view is shown on the screen.

```
.onAppear {
    viewData.titleInput = appData.title
}
```

Listing 6-52: Initializing the view's observable object when the view appears

Do It Yourself: Remove the initializer introduced in Listing 6-51 from the `ContentView` structure. Add the `onAppear()` modifier of Listing 6-52 to the `VStack` view (below the `padding()` modifier). The result should be the same.

Although observable objects are great for building our app's model and managing the states of a view, the view does not always need to be updated when every value change. If we have a property in the observable object that does not require the view to be updated every time its value changes, we can implement the following Attached macro.

▷ **@ObservationIgnored**—This macro produces code that disables observation for a property.

For instance, we can add a property to the observable object used by the view in our example to count how many times a button is pressed.

```
import SwiftUI
import Observation
@Observable class ViewData {
   var titleInput: String = ""
   @ObservationIgnored var counter: Int = 0
}
struct ContentView: View {
   @Bindable var viewData = ViewData()
   var appData = ApplicationData.shared

   var body: some View {
      VStack(spacing: 8) {
         Text("\(appData.title) - \(viewData.counter)")
            .padding(10)
         TextField("Insert Title", text: $viewData.titleInput)
            .textFieldStyle(.roundedBorder)
         Button(action: {
            appData.title = viewData.titleInput
            viewData.titleInput = ""
         }, label: { Text("Save") })
         Button(action: {
            viewData.counter += 1
            print("Counter: \(viewData.counter)")
         }, label: { Text("Increment Counter") })
         Spacer()
      }.padding()
   }
}
```

Listing 6-53: Disabling observation for a property in an observable object

The view now includes two buttons, one to update the `Text` view with the text inserted by the user, as before, and another to increment the value of a property in the observable object called `counter`. When the latter is pressed, we add 1 to the current value of the property, but because it was modified with the `@ObservationIgnored` macro, the view is not updated.

 Do It Yourself: Update the ContentView.swift file with the code in Listing 6-53. Press the Increment Counter button. The value on the screen should not be modified. Insert a text in the text field or press the Save button. The text on the screen should be updated, including the value of the `counter` property.

Sometimes it is necessary to update the views when a new value is assigned to a non-observable property or when the system cannot recognize a change in the model. In such cases, we can assign a new identity to the view. For this purpose, SwiftUI provides the following modifier.

▷ **id(**Value**)**—This modifier associates the view with a custom identifier. The argument is the **Hashable** value we want to use to identify the view.

Views are identified by a unique value so that the system can process and display them on the screen. The **id()** modifier associates the view with a custom value and can therefore be used to change the view's identity. Each time the identity of the view changes, the system thinks it is a new view and updates the interface to show it. For example, we can apply the **id()** modifier with a unique value to the **Text** view from the previous example and then change this identifier to manually update the view when the value of **counter** changes.

```
struct ContentView: View {
    @Bindable var viewData = ViewData()
    @State private var textID: UUID = UUID()
    var appData = ApplicationData.shared

    var body: some View {
        VStack(spacing: 8) {
            Text("\(appData.title) - \(viewData.counter)")
                .padding(10)
                .id(textID)
            TextField("Insert Title", text: $viewData.titleInput)
                .textFieldStyle(.roundedBorder)
            Button(action: {
                appData.title = viewData.titleInput
                viewData.titleInput = ""
            }, label: { Text("Save") })
            Button(action: {
                viewData.counter += 1
                textID = UUID()
            }, label: { Text("Increment Counter") })
            Spacer()
        }.padding()
    }
}
```

Listing 6-54: *Updating the views manually*

There are many ways to get a unique value to identify a view, such as calculating a random number or using the current date, but they are not reliable. To make sure that we always have a unique and different value, we can use the **UUID** structure provided by the Foundation framework. The **UUID** structure guarantees that every time it is created it returns a unique value, so it is perfect to identify items in the interface and the model, as we will see later. In the example in Listing 6-54, we define a new **@State** property to store this value and use it to identify the **Text** view. When we assign a new **UUID** value to the property, the system assumes that there is a new **Text** view and updates the interface.

Basic Accessing the Model

Our application can have a view that presents a menu, another view that displays a list of items, and another that displays information about the item selected by the user. All of these views must access the same data, and therefore they must all contain a reference to the model. However, passing this reference from one view to another until we reach the one that needs the values can be cumbersome and error-prone. A better alternative is to pass a reference of the model to the environment and then read it from the environment when we need it.

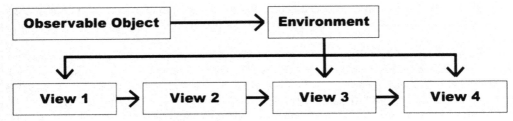

Figure 6-33: Accessing the model through the environment

As mentioned earlier, the environment is a general-purpose container that stores information about the application and the views, but it can also store custom data, including references to observable objects. In the example in Figure 6-33, an instance of the observable object is added to the environment, which is then accessed only by the views that need it.

The observable object is added to the environment with the **environment()** modifier and it is accessible from properties defined with the **@Environment** property wrapper. The only thing we must consider is that the **environment()** modifier assigns the object to the environment of a view's hierarchy, so we must apply it to the initial view for all the views on the interface to have access to it. The following code shows the modifications we need to introduce to the **App** structure to add the **ApplicationData** object to the environment of the initial view of our application (the **ContentView** view).

```
import SwiftUI

@main
struct TestApp: App {
   @State private var appData = ApplicationData.shared

   var body: some Scene {
      WindowGroup {
         ContentView()
            .environment(appData)
      }
   }
}
```

Listing 6-55: Assigning the observable object to the view's environment

The instance of the **ApplicationData** class must be stored in a **@State** property. Once we have this object, we apply the **environment()** modifier to the **ContentView** view to inject the object into the environment. Accessing this object from the views is easy. All we need to do is to create a property with the **@Environment** property wrapper, as shown below.

```
import SwiftUI
import Observation

@Observable class ViewData {
   var titleInput: String = ""
}
struct ContentView: View {
   @Bindable var viewData = ViewData()
   @Environment(ApplicationData.self) private var appData

   var body: some View {
      VStack(spacing: 8) {
         Text(appData.title)
            .padding(10)
         TextField("Insert Title", text: $viewData.titleInput)
            .textFieldStyle(.roundedBorder)
         Button(action: {
            appData.title = viewData.titleInput
```

```
                viewData.titleInput = ""
          }, label: { Text("Save") })
          Spacer()
      }.padding()
   }
}
#Preview {
   ContentView()
      .environment(ApplicationData.shared)
}
```

Listing 6-56: Getting a reference to the observable object from the environment

Using the `@Environment` property wrapper, we can access the model from any view in our interface. However, this does not apply to views that belong to a different hierarchy, such as the `ContentView` view created for the preview. This view has its own hierarchy and environment, and therefore we need to create an additional instance of the model and inject it into the view's own environment for the preview to work.

 Do It Yourself: Update the `App` structure with the code in Listing 6-55, and the ContentView.swift file with the code in Listing 6-56. The application works as before, but now the values are taken from the observable object through the environment and therefore they are available to all the views that belong to the `ContentView`'s hierarchy. We will learn how to add more views to this hierarchy in Chapter 8.

If we want the environment property to be able to handle bidirectional binding properties, we need to convert it to a bindable property using the `@Bindable` property wrapper. For example, if we store the user input in a property in the model, as we did with the model in Listing 6-47, we can make the property bindable by creating a new property inside the body with the same name.

```
import SwiftUI
import Observation

struct ContentView: View {
   @Environment(ApplicationData.self) private var appData

   var body: some View {
      @Bindable var appData = appData

      VStack(spacing: 8) {
         Text(appData.title)
            .padding(10)
         TextField("Insert Title", text: $appData.titleInput)
            .textFieldStyle(.roundedBorder)
         Button(action: {
            appData.title = appData.titleInput
            appData.titleInput = ""
         }, label: { Text("Save") })
         Spacer()
      }.padding()
   }
}
```

Listing 6-57: Turning the environment property into a bindable property

In this example, we turn the `appData` property into a bindable property inside the body. Every time the view is updated, this property is created and the controls in the view can now read and write the `titleInput` property in the model.

Do It Yourself: Update the ContentView.swift file with the code in Listing 6-57, and the ApplicationData.swift file with the model in Listing 6-47. The application should work as before, but now we are able to manage bidirectional binding properties from the model.

7.1 Lists of Views

One of the main characteristics of computer systems is their ability to process sequential data. Due to their elementary structure, made up of sequences of switches on and off, computers excel at organizing information into lists of values, and this is the perfect format for displaying data to users. We can implement this type of organization with vertical and horizontal stacks, but SwiftUI provides additional tools to create dynamic lists of views and edit their content.

Basic) **ForEach View**

The simplest tool provided by SwiftUI to create a list of views is the **ForEach** view. This view generates a loop that iterates through the values of a collection and creates a new view for each one of them. The structure includes the following initializer.

▷ **ForEach**(Data, **id:** KeyPath, **content:** Closure)—This initializer creates a **ForEach** view. The first argument is the collection of values the loop is going to iterate through, the **id** argument is the key path to the unique identifier for each value, and the **content** argument is the closure that creates the views in each cycle.

A **ForEach** view needs two values: the collection from which is going to get the data to build the list of views, and a key path that determines the value used to identify the views. This is important because the system needs to identify the views to remove them or add new ones when the collection is updated. If the collection is made of standard Swift values like **Int** or **String**, assigning an identifier is easy; these data types conform to the **Hashable** protocol and therefore they have a hash value that identifies each instance (see Listing 3-177). To use this hash value as the identifier, we must specify the key path **\.self**, as in the following example.

```
struct ContentView: View {
    var body: some View {
        VStack {
            ForEach(1...5, id: \.self) { value in
                Text("Value: \(value)")
            }
            Spacer()
        }
    }
}
```

Listing 7-1: Creating a list of views dynamically

The **ForEach** view adds the content to its container, so we must declare it inside a container view like a **VStack** or an **HStack**, as we did in Listing 7-1. In this example, the loop is defined with a range of integers from 1 to 5, and the views are identified by the hash value (**\.self**). The **ForEach** view loops through the values in the range and sends them to the closure one by one. The closure receives each value and then creates a **Text** view with it to show it on the screen.

Figure 7-1: List of views generated by a ForEach *loop*

In this example, the values are presented on the screen with a **VStack** and the configuration by default (center alignment and a width determined by the widest view). Although we can use all the views at our disposal to present each value and apply any styles we want, there is a standard design that users immediately recognize in which the values are separated by a line. SwiftUI includes the following view to create this line.

▷ **Divider()**—This initializer creates a **Divider** view. The view displays a line to separate content.

The **Divider** view is like any other view. If we want to position the line generated by this view below the value, we must embed the **Text** view and the **Divider** view in a **VStack**.

```
struct ContentView: View {
    let listCities: [String] = ["Paris", "Toronto", "Dublin"]

    var body: some View {
        VStack {
            ForEach(listCities, id: \.self) { value in
                VStack {
                    Text(value)
                    Divider()
                }
            }
            Spacer()
        }
    }
}
```

Listing 7-2: Creating a list with a standard design

The **ForEach** view in Listing 7-2 creates a list of views from an array of strings. The structure defines the array with the name of three cities and then implements the **ForEach** view to create the list. Note that **String** values are hashable, so we can also identify them by the hash value with **\.self**.

Paris

Toronto

Dublin

Figure 7-2: List of views with a standard design

Values of primitive data types like integers and strings conform to the **Hashable** protocol and therefore we can use their hash value to identify the views, as we did in these examples. But when working with data stored by the user in our model, it is better to provide a unique identifier that is stored along with the data and therefore is always the same. For this purpose, SwiftUI offers the **Identifiable** protocol. The protocol requires the structure to define a property called **id** to store a unique identifier for each instance, and this is how we prepare the values in our model to work with list of views. For example, the following model creates a structure to store information about a book that includes an **id** property with the unique identifier for each book.

```
import SwiftUI
import Observation
```

```
struct Book: Identifiable, Hashable {
    let id = UUID()
    var title: String
    var author: String
    var cover: String
    var year: Int
    var selected: Bool

    var displayYear: String {
        get {
            return String(year)
        }
    }
}
@Observable class ApplicationData: @unchecked Sendable {
    var userData: [Book] = []

    static let shared: ApplicationData = ApplicationData()
    private init() {
        userData = [
            Book(title: "Steve Jobs", author: "Walter Isaacson", cover:
"book1", year: 2011, selected: false),
            Book(title: "HTML5 for Masterminds", author: "J.D Gauchat",
cover: "book2", year: 2017, selected: false),
            Book(title: "The Road Ahead", author: "Bill Gates", cover:
"book3", year: 1995, selected: false),
            Book(title: "The C Programming Language", author: "Brian W.
Kernighan", cover: "book4", year: 1988, selected: false),
            Book(title: "Being Digital", author: "Nicholas Negroponte",
cover: "book5", year: 1996, selected: false),
            Book(title: "Only the Paranoid Survive", author: "Andrew S.
Grove", cover: "book6", year: 1999, selected: false),
            Book(title: "Accidental Empires", author: "Robert X. Cringely",
cover: "book7", year: 1996, selected: false),
            Book(title: "Bobby Fischer Teaches Chess", author: "Bobby
Fischer", cover: "book8", year: 1982, selected: false),
            Book(title: "New Guide to Science", author: "Isaac Asimov",
cover: "book9", year: 1993, selected: false),
            Book(title: "Christine", author: "Stephen King", cover:
"book10", year: 1983, selected: false),
            Book(title: "IT", author: "Stephen King", cover: "book11", year:
1987, selected: false),
            Book(title: "Ending Aging", author: "Aubrey de Grey", cover:
"book12", year: 2007, selected: false)
        ]
    }
}
```

Listing 7-3: Defining a model to work with lists of views

The **Book** structure is the actual model. It contains the **id** property with a unique value to identify the book, as well as properties to store the title, the author, the name of the image for the cover, the year the book was published, a boolean property that indicates whether the book is currently selected or not, and a computed property that converts the year to a string so it can be displayed by a **Text** view. Note that in this case, we have decided to use a **UUID** value to create the book's identifier. We have used this structure before (see Chapter 6, Listing 6-54). The **UUID** structure guarantees that every time it is created it returns a unique value, so it is perfect to identify items in the model.

Because the model to store the user's data is defined by the **Book** structure, all we need for the observable object is a property to store an array of these structures. In this example, we called this property **userData**, and initialize it with a total of 12 books to test the application.

IMPORTANT: The `Book` structure also conforms to the `Hashable` protocol. When a structure conforms to this protocol, the system creates a unique identifier that is used later to identify the instances of the structure within collections. Conformance to this protocol is required for navigation, as we will see in Chapter 8.

Once we have the model, we need to pass a reference to the views. As we saw in Chapter 6, it is best to inject the instance into the environment and then access it from the views using the `@Environment` property wrapper (see Listings 6-55 and 6-56). The following are the changes we need to introduce to the `App` structure.

```
import SwiftUI
@main
struct TestApp: App {
    @State private var appData = ApplicationData.shared

    var body: some Scene {
        WindowGroup {
            ContentView()
                .environment(appData)
        }
    }
}
```

Listing 7-4: Injecting the model into the environment

The `Identifiable` protocol defines an associated type called `ID`, which the system can use to identify the items. This associated type represents the data type assigned to the `id` property in our model and it is used by the `ForEach` view to identify the views, so we only need to declare the collection and the list of views is automatically created from these values.

```
struct ContentView: View {
    @Environment(ApplicationData.self) private var appData

    var body: some View {
        VStack {
            ForEach(appData.userData) { book in
                VStack {
                    HStack(alignment: .top) {
                        Image(book.cover)
                            .resizable()
                            .scaledToFit()
                            .frame(width: 80, height: 100)
                        VStack(alignment: .leading, spacing: 2) {
                            Text(book.title)
                                .bold()
                            Text(book.author)
                            Text(book.displayYear)
                                .font(.caption)
                        }.padding(.top, 5)
                        Spacer()
                    }
                    Divider()
                }
            }
            Spacer()
        }
    }
}
#Preview {
    ContentView()
```

```
        .environment(ApplicationData.shared)
}
```

Listing 7-5: Creating a list of views with data from the model

The **ForEach** view reads the array with all the books from the **userData** property of our observable object and sends the items one by one to the closure. The items are instances of the **Book** structure, each with the information of a book, so we use the values of the structure's properties to create the views.

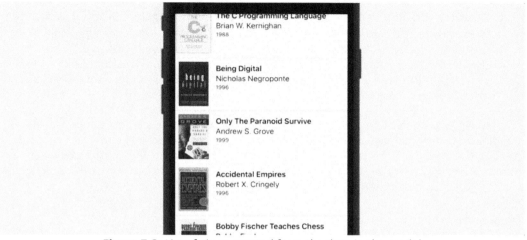

Figure 7-3: List of views created from the data in the model

Do It Yourself: Create a Multiplatform project. Download the book covers from our website and add them to the Asset Catalog. (You can use the Asset Catalog for development included by the template, as explained in Chapter 5.) Create a Swift file called ApplicationData.swift for the model in Listing 7-3. Update the **App** structure with the code in Listing 7-4. Update the **ContentView** view with the code in Listing 7-5. Run the application. You should see a list of books, as illustrated in Figure 7-3.

(Basic) ScrollView View

The **ApplicationData** class defined in Listing 7-3 stores 12 books in the model for testing purposes. This creates a long list of books that extends beyond the edge of the screen and is therefore not completely visible to the user. For a list to actually display all the content available in the model, it must be scrollable. To convert a static list of views into a scrollable one, SwiftUI includes the **ScrollView** view. The following is the structure's initializer.

▷ **ScrollView**(Axis, **showsIndicators:** Bool, **content:** Closure)—This initializer creates a container view the user can scroll. The first argument is an enumeration of type **Axis** that indicates the axis in which the views are going to scroll. The values available are **horizontal** and **vertical** (default). The **showsIndicators** argument is a Boolean value that determines if the view is going to display the scroll indicators or not, and the **content** argument is the closure that defines the scrollable content.

The **ScrollView** structure just creates a scrollable view, but the content is still generated by a vertical or a horizontal stack. SwiftUI defines the following views for this purpose.

▷ **LazyVStack(alignment:** HorizontalAlignment, **spacing:** CGFloat?, **pinned-Views:** PinnedScrollableViews, **content:** Closures)—This initializer creates a lazy vertical stack. The **alignment** argument determines the horizontal alignment of the views. It is a structure with the type properties **center**, **leading**, and **trailing**. The **spacing** argument determines the space between the views. The **pinnedViews** argument is a structure that determines which views will be momentarily pinned to the bounds of the scroll view while the content is scrolling. The structure defines the type properties **sectionFooters** and **sectionHeaders**. And the **content** argument is the closure that defines the list of views we want to show in the stack.

▷ **LazyHStack(alignment:** VerticalAlignment, **spacing:** CGFloat?, **pinned-Views:** PinnedScrollableViews, **content:** Closure)—This initializer creates a lazy horizontal stack. The arguments are the same as the lazy vertical stack, except for the **alignment** argument, which defines the vertical alignment of the views. It is a structure with the type properties **bottom**, **center**, **firstTextBaseline**, **lastTextBaseline**, and **top**.

Lazy stacks are similar to the normal stacks created by the **VStack** and **HStack** views, with the difference that the views in a lazy stack are created as needed. The system takes care of creating the views only before they are about to be rendered on the screen, consuming less resources and improving performance. Other than the use of lazy stacks, the list is defined as before, but embedded in a **ScrollView** view.

```
struct ContentView: View {
    @Environment(ApplicationData.self) private var appData

    var body: some View {
        ScrollView {
            LazyVStack {
                ForEach(appData.userData) { book in
                    VStack {
                        HStack(alignment: .top) {
                            Image(book.cover)
                                .resizable()
                                .scaledToFit()
                                .frame(width: 80, height: 100)
                            VStack(alignment: .leading, spacing: 2) {
                                Text(book.title).bold()
                                Text(book.author)
                                Text(book.displayYear).font(.caption)
                            }.padding(.top, 5)
                            Spacer()
                        }.padding([.leading, .trailing], 10)
                        .padding([.top, .bottom], 5)
                        Divider()
                    }
                }
            }
        }
    }
}
```

Listing 7-6: Creating a scrollable list of views

By default, the axis of the view is set to vertical, the indicators are shown, and the content adapts to the size of the view, so all we need to do in our example is to replace the **VStack** views implemented before with a **LazyVStack** and embed the list in a **SrollView** view. Now the user can scroll the list of books.

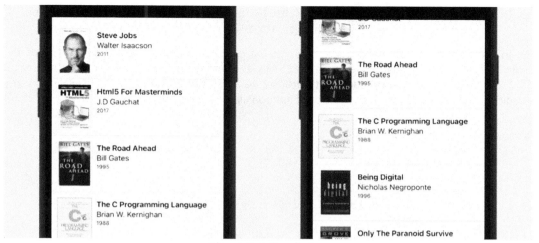

Figure 7-4: Scroll view

 IMPORTANT: The lazy vertical stack is used to create each row on the list, but the views inside a row are organized with normal stacks. This is because we need the system to create the rows only when they are needed, but the views that define the content of each row are always required.

The `View` protocol includes the following modifiers to configure the scroll view.

▷ **scrollDisabled(**Bool**)**—This modifier disables or enables scrolling.

▷ **scrollDismissesKeyboard(**ScrollDismissesKeyboardMode**)**—This modifier determines the behavior of the keyboard when the drag gesture begins. The argument is a structure with the type properties **automatic, immediately, interactively**, and **never** (default).

▷ **scrollBounceBehavior(**ScrollBounceBehavior, **axes:** Axis**)**—This modifier determines whether the scroll view bounces back when the user scrolls to the beginning or the end. The first argument determines the bounce behavior. It is a structure with the properties **automatic, always**, and **basedOnSize** (Only if the content exceeds the boundaries of the view). The **axes** argument is a set of values that determine the axis to which this behavior is applied. It is an enumeration with the values **horizontal** and **vertical**.

▷ **scrollContentBackground(**Visibility**)**—This modifier shows or hides the scroll view's background. It is useful when working with lists and tables that automatically add a background to the view. The argument is an enumeration with the values **automatic, visible**, and **hidden**.

▷ **scrollClipDisabled(**Bool**)**—This modifier determines whether or not the scroll view should clip the content that exceeds its boundaries.

And the following are the modifiers available to control the scroll indicators.

▷ **scrollIndicators(**ScrollIndicatorVisibility, **axes:** Axis**)**—This modifier sets the visibility of the scroll indicators. The first argument is a structure with the type properties **automatic, hidden, never**, and **visible** to define the visibility of the scroll indicators, and the **axes** argument defines the axis we want to affect. It is an enumeration with the values **vertical** and **horizontal**. (If the argument is ignored, the visibility is applied to both axes.)

▷ **scrollIndicatorsFlash(onAppear:** Bool**)**—This modifier determines if the indicators are going to flash when the view appears.

▷ **scrollIndicatorsFlash(trigger:** Value)—This modifier determines if the indicators are going to flash when a value changes. The **trigger** argument is the value to check.

In the following example, we show how some of these modifiers work. At the top of the `ScrollView` view, we have added a `TextField` view so that the user can enter text. Tapping on this text field opens the keyboard, but because we apply the `scrollDismissesKeyboard()` modifier to the view, the keyboard is closed as soon as the user scrolls the view.

```
struct ContentView: View {
    @Environment(ApplicationData.self) private var appData
    @State private var title: String = ""

    var body: some View {
        VStack {
            TextField("Title", text: $title)
                .padding()
            ScrollView {
                LazyVStack {
                    ForEach(appData.userData) { book in
                        VStack {
                            HStack(alignment: .top) {
                                Image(book.cover)
                                    .resizable()
                                    .scaledToFit()
                                    .frame(width: 80, height: 100)
                                VStack(alignment: .leading, spacing: 2) {
                                    Text(book.title).bold()
                                    Text(book.author)
                                    Text(book.displayYear).font(.caption)
                                }.padding(.top, 5)
                                Spacer()
                            }.padding([.leading, .trailing], 10)
                                .padding([.top, .bottom], 5)
                            Divider()
                        }
                    }
                }
            }
            .scrollDismissesKeyboard(.immediately)
            .scrollIndicatorsFlash(onAppear: true)
        }
    }
}
```

Listing 7-7: Configuring the scroll view

 Do It Yourself: Update the `ContentView` view with the code in Listing 7-7. When the view appears, the scroll indicators should flash, and after typing a few characters in the input field, you should be able to scroll the view to close the keyboard.

The content of a **ScrollView** view has to be inside a vertical or a horizontal stack, depending on the axis. If we want to scroll the list of books horizontally, we must embed the **ForEach** view of our example in a **LazyHStack** view, as shown next.

```
struct ContentView: View {
    @Environment(ApplicationData.self) private var appData

    var body: some View {
        ScrollView(.horizontal, showsIndicators: false) {
            LazyHStack(spacing: 0) {
```

```
            ForEach(appData.userData) { book in
                CellBook(book: book)
            }
        }
    }
}
}
struct CellBook: View {
    let book: Book

    var body: some View {
        VStack {
            Image(book.cover)
                .resizable()
                .scaledToFit()
                .frame(width: 80, height: 100)
            Text(book.title)
                .font(.caption)
        }.padding(10)
        .frame(width: 100, height: 150)
    }
}
```

Listing 7-8: Scrolling the list of views horizontally

In this example, we tell the `ScrollView` view to create a horizontal view without indicators, and then place the views inside a `LazyHStack` to display the list horizontally. Note that we have also moved the code that creates the views for each item to a separate view called `CellBook` (These views represent the cells or rows on the list). Moving the view that creates the rows to a separate view is not required but recommended because it improves the workflow and simplifies our code. The only thing we need to remember is that the view we use to build the row doesn't have access to the values processed by the loop, so we must pass the data this view needs to display its content (the `Book` structure in our example).

The application works the same way as before, but because of the changes we have introduced to the main view, the books are displayed side by side.

Figure 7-5: Horizontal scroll view

The cells in this example have a fixed size to match the look we were looking for in this application, but we can also resize the cells to fit the available space within the scroll view. For this purpose, the `View` protocol defines the following modifiers.

▷ **containerRelativeFrame(**Axis, **count:** Int, **span:** Int, **spacing:** CGFloat, **alignment:** Alignment)—This modifier defines the size of the view relative to the size of its container. The first argument defines the axis according to which the size of the view is calculated. It is a set of enumeration values. The available values are **horizontal** and **vertical**. The **count** argument determines how many columns or rows of views to create for the available space (one by default). The **span** argument determines how many columns or rows the view should take up (one by default). The **spacing** argument determines the amount of spacing between columns or rows. And the **alignment** argument specifies how the views should be aligned. It is an enumeration with the values **topLeading**, **top**, **topTrailing**, **leading**, **center** (default), **trailing**, **bottomLeading**, **bottom**, and **bottomTrailing**.

- **safeAreaPadding(Edges, Size)**—This modifier sets a margin between the safe area and the content of the scroll view. The first argument determines the edges to affected by the padding. It is a set of enumeration values. The available values are **top**, **bottom**, **leading** and **trailing**.

- **contentMargins(Size, for: Placement)**—This modifier adds a margin to the content of a scroll view. The first argument determines the size of the padding, and the **for** argument is a structure that determines whether the scroll indicators are affected. The structure includes the properties **automatic**, **scrollContent** and **scrollIndicators**.

Resizing the view to fit the available space within the scroll view is easy. All we need to do is apply the **containerRelativeFrame()** modifier to the view that generates the content for the scroll view, as shown in the following example.

```
struct ContentView: View {
    @Environment(ApplicationData.self) private var appData

    var body: some View {
        ScrollView(.horizontal, showsIndicators: false) {
            LazyHStack(spacing: 0) {
                ForEach(appData.userData) { book in
                    CellBook(book: book)
                        .containerRelativeFrame(.horizontal)
                }
            }
        }
    }
}
struct CellBook: View {
    let book: Book

    var body: some View {
        VStack {
            Image(book.cover)
                .resizable()
                .scaledToFit()
            Text(book.title)
                .font(.body)
        }.padding(10)
    }
}
```

Listing 7-9: Adapting the size of the views to the container

In this case, we want each view to be the size of the scroll view, so we only need to specify the axis to create the columns and the **containerRelativeFrame()** modifier takes care of everything. Note that for the view to adapt to the available space, we had to remove the **frame()** modifiers that were applied to the views inside the **CellBook** view. The result is shown below.

Figure 7-6: *The view fits the available space*

Scroll views calculate the speed of the gesture performed by the user and the deceleration rate to determine how the content should be scrolled. By altering these parameters, we can change the scrolling behavior. Below are the modifiers provided for this purpose.

▷ **scrollTargetBehavior(**ScrollTargetBehavior**)**—This modifier defines the scroll view's behavior. The argument is a structure that conforms to the **ScrollTarget-Behavior** protocol. SwiftUI includes two structures to define common behaviors called **paging** and **viewAligned**.

▷ **scrollTargetLayout(isEnabled:** Bool**)**—This modifier configures a view to become a scrolling target. The **isEnabled** argument determines if the views are considered scrolling targets or not.

The **ScrollTargetBehavior** protocol includes two properties called **paging** and **viewAligned** that return standard structures to define common behaviors. The structure returned by the **paging** property defines a scrolling behavior that calculates the deceleration rate based on the size of the views and the container, allowing the user to scroll view by view (page by page) instead of doing so continuously. If we apply the **scrollTargetBehavior()** modifier with the **.paging** value to the **ScrollView** view of our example, we can scroll through the books one by one.

```
struct ContentView: View {
   @Environment(ApplicationData.self) private var appData

   var body: some View {
      ScrollView(.horizontal, showsIndicators: false) {
         LazyHStack(spacing: 0) {
            ForEach(appData.userData) { book in
               CellBook(book: book)
                  .containerRelativeFrame(.horizontal)
            }
         }
      }
      .scrollTargetBehavior(.paging)
   }
}
```

Listing 7-10: *Scrolling the content page by page*

On the other hand, the structure returned by the **viewAligned** property aligns the scrolling to individual views. This means that we can tell the scroll view how to scroll its views and when to decelerate. This behavior is usually required when two or more views fit in the space within the container. For instance, if we apply the **containerRelativeFrame()** modifier with a count value of 2 and a span of 1 (one view per column), the scroll view displays two views at a time.

```
struct ContentView: View {
    @Environment(ApplicationData.self) private var appData

    var body: some View {
        ScrollView(.horizontal, showsIndicators: false) {
            LazyHStack(spacing: 0) {
                ForEach(appData.userData) { book in
                    CellBook(book: book)
                        .containerRelativeFrame(.horizontal, count: 2, span: 1,
spacing: 0)
                }
            }
        }
        .scrollTargetBehavior(.paging)
    }
}
```

Listing 7-11: Scrolling two views at a time

Now, we can see two books per page, and every time we drag the books to one side or the other, the scroll view displays the next two.

Figure 7-7: Two views per page

If instead we want to scroll one view at a time, we need to define a **viewAligned** behavior and tell the scroll view when to stop. This is accomplished by using the **scrollTargetLayout()** modifier. This modifier identifies each view as a scroll target, so the scroll view will align the content to the container one view at a time.

```
struct ContentView: View {
    @Environment(ApplicationData.self) private var appData

    var body: some View {
        ScrollView(.horizontal, showsIndicators: false) {
            LazyHStack(spacing: 0) {
                ForEach(appData.userData) { book in
                    CellBook(book: book)
                        .containerRelativeFrame(.horizontal, count: 2, span: 1,
spacing: 0)
                }
            }
            .scrollTargetLayout()
        }
        .scrollTargetBehavior(.viewAligned)
    }
}
```

Listing 7-12: Defining each view as a scroll target

Figure 7-8: *Views defined as scroll targets*

In addition to determining the scroll behavior, we can also programmatically scroll to a specific part of the content. To keep track of the scroll's position, SwiftUI includes the `ScrollPosition` structure.

▷ **ScrollPosition(idType:** Type**)**—This initializer creates a structure to store the scrolling position of a `ScrollView` view. The **idType** argument is the data type of the value used to track the position.

The `ScrollPosition` structure includes the following property and method to control the scrolling.

▷ **viewID**—This property returns a hashable value that represents the identifier of the view in the visible position.

▷ **scrollTo(edge:** Edge**)**—This method scrolls the content of the `ScrollView` view to the position indicated by the argument. The **edge** argument is an enumeration that determines the side to which the content should scroll. The possible values are **top**, **bottom**, **leading** and **trailing**. There are also methods to scroll to a specific point in the view, like `scrollTo(x: CGFloat, y: CGFloat)`.

SwiftUI also includes the following modifier to configure the system and programmatically controlled the `ScrollView` view.

▷ **scrollPosition(**Binding, **anchor:** UnitPoint?**)**—This modifier associates a binding property to the `ScrollView` view to store the content's position. The first argument is a binding property of type `ScrollPosition` that stores information about the current visible view, and the **anchor** argument determines what view is going to be used as a reference for alignment. Possible values are **top**, **bottom**, **leading** and **trailing**.

The `scrollPosition()` modifier requires a binding property to store the `ScrollPosition` structure used to control the current position. The `ScrollPosition` structure must be initialized with the data type used to identify each view in the `ScrollView` view. In our example, we can use the `UUID` data type assigned to the `id` property of our model or the associated type `ID` provided by the `Identifiable` protocol. As mentioned earlier, the associated type `ID` represents the data type of the `id` property in our model, so we can use it to represent the model's identifiers, as in the example below.

```
struct ContentView: View {
    @Environment(ApplicationData.self) private var appData
    @State private var position = ScrollPosition(idType: Book.ID.self)

    var body: some View {
        ScrollView(.horizontal, showsIndicators: false) {
            LazyHStack(spacing: 0) {
                ForEach(appData.userData) { book in
```

```
            CellBook(book: book)
                .containerRelativeFrame(.horizontal, count: 2, span: 1,
spacing: 0)
            }
            Button("< Back") {
                position.scrollTo(edge: .top)
            }
            .padding([.leading, .trailing], 50)
        }
        .scrollTargetLayout()
    }
    .scrollPosition($position)
    .scrollTargetBehavior(.viewAligned)

    .onChange(of: position, initial: true, {
        if let selected = position.viewID as? UUID {
            if let book = appData.userData.first(where: { $0.id ==
selected }) {
                print(book.title)
            }
        }
    })
   }
}
```

Listing 7-13: *Scrolling the content programmatically*

In this example, we create a `@State` property called `position` to store the `Scroll-Position` structure and then assign it to the `ScrollView` view with the `scrollPosition()` modifier. At the end of the list, we include a button that calls the `scrollTo()` method to allow the user to scroll back to the first book. To show how to read the values in the `ScrollPosition` structure, we have also implemented the `onChange()` modifier. Every time the user scrolls the list, the identifier of the prominent view is assigned to the `position` property, so we can read and process this value. To get the book's identifier, we cast the value returned by the `viewID` property of the `ScrollPosition` structure into a `UUID` value. If there is a value, we search for the book with that identifier and print the title on the console.

Figure 7-9: *Button to scroll the list to the beginning*

Do It Yourself: Update the `ContentView` view with the code in Listing 7-13. Run the application on the iPhone simulator or the canvas. You should see the list of books as before. Scroll the list to the end. You should see the title of the visible book printed on the console and a Back button at the end. Press this button to go back to the beginning of the list.

Another thing we can do with the views in a scroll view is to determine how they appear on the screen when they become visible to the user. In other words, how they transition from one state to another. To customize a transition, SwiftUI includes the following modifier.

▷ **scrollTransition**(ScrollTransitionConfiguration, **axis:** Axis, **transition:** Closure)—This modifier applies a visual effect to the transition of a view. The first argument determines how the transition will be applied. It is a structure with the properties `identity` (doesn't change the appearance of the view), `animated` (animates the transition when the view becomes visible), and `interactive` (interpolates the effect as the view becomes visible), and the methods `animated-(Animation)` to apply a custom animation, and `interactive(timingCurve: UnitCurve)` to define a custom timing curve. The **axis** argument determines if the effect will be applied to the horizontal or vertical axis (`horizontal` or `vertical`). And the **transition** argument is the closure that defines the transition.

The transition effect is defined by a closure. This closure receives two values: an `EmptyVisualEffect` structure that defines a basic visual effect to which we can apply our custom effects, and a `ScrollTransitionPhase` enumeration that defines the current state of the view. The enumeration includes the values `identity` (the view is in the visible area), `topLeading` (the view is at the top or leading edge of the visible area), and `bottomTrailing` (the view is at the bottom or the trailing edge of the visible area). The enumeration also includes a Boolean property called `isIdentity` which indicates whether the view is visible, and the property `value` to return a value indicating the position of the view (-1.0 if the view is at the top of leading edge of the visible area, 0.0 if it is visible, and 1.0 if it is at the bottom or the trailing edge of the visible area).

Adding a visual effect to a transition is simple. We need to apply the `scrollTransition()` modifier to the view and then add the visual effect to the base effect received by the closure. Visual effects are created using common view modifiers. For example, we can implement some of the modifiers introduced in Chapter 5, such as `opacity()`, `blur()`, and `grayscale()`, to change the characteristics of the views, and also others we will introduce in Chapter 11, such as `offset()`, `rotationEffect()`, and `rotation3DEffect()`, to perform transformations. The following example shows how to apply opacity to the views outside the visible area.

```
struct ContentView: View {
   @Environment(ApplicationData.self) private var appData

   var body: some View {
      ScrollView(.horizontal, showsIndicators: false) {
         LazyHStack(spacing: 0) {
            ForEach(appData.userData) { book in
               CellBook(book: book)
                  .containerRelativeFrame(.horizontal)
                  .scrollTransition(axis: .horizontal) { effect, phase in
                     effect.opacity(phase.isIdentity ? 1 : 0)
                  }
            }
         }
         .scrollTargetLayout()
      }
      .scrollTargetBehavior(.paging)
   }
}
```

Listing 7-14: Applying a visual effect to the transition

The system executes the closure passed to the `scrollTransition()` modifier for each view. Therefore, when applying the effect, we must determine the current state of the view. If the view is in the visible area, the `isIdentity` property of the `ScrollTransitionPhase` enumeration received by the closure returns `true`, otherwise `false`. By checking this value, we can apply different visual effects to the views that are inside or outside the visible area. In this example, we use a ternary operator to assign an opacity of 1 (fully opaque) to the visible view and an opacity of 0 (fully transparent) to the views outside the visible area. This creates an effect where views gradually appear on the screen as they scroll into the visible area, and fade out as they leave the area.

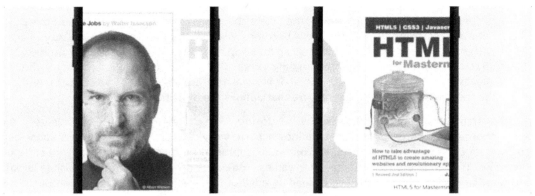

Figure 7-10: Visual effect applied to the transition

Many effects can be applied to the same transition. For instance, in the following example we change the opacity as before but also add a scaling effect with the `scaleEffect()` modifier.

```
.scrollTransition(axis: .horizontal) { effect, phase in
    effect
        .opacity(phase.isIdentity ? 1 : 0)
        .scaleEffect(phase.isIdentity ? 1 : 0.5)
}
```

Listing 7-15: Applying multiple visual effects to the transition

The `scaleEffect()` modifier takes a value representing the scale we want to assign to the view. A value of 1 represents the normal scale and values below or above 1 represent smaller or larger scales. In our example, when the view is visible, it has a scale of 1, but when it enters or leaves the visible area, the scale is reduced to 0.5.

 Do It Yourself: Update the `ContentView` view with the code in Listing 7-14 and scroll through the books. You should see the books fade in and out as they enter and leave the visible area. Update the `scrollTransition()` modifier with the code in Listing 7-15 and scroll through the books again. You should see the books getting larger and smaller as they enter or leave the visible area. We will learn more about the `scaleEffect()` modifier and how to create animations in Chapter 11.

Another way to control scrolling programmatically is to use the `ScrollViewReader` view. This view creates a container that determines the position of the elements in the list. The `ScrollViewReader` view works with all types of lists, including those created by the `List` view, as we will see later. The following is the view's initializer.

▷ **ScrollViewReader(content:** Closure)—This initializer creates a container view to allow programmatic scrolling on a `ScrollView` view. The **content** argument is a closure with the `ScrollView` view or the `List` view we want to control.

The `ScrollViewReader` view creates a structure of type `ScrollViewProxy` with the information required to scroll the list of views to a specific row. For this purpose, the `ScrollViewProxy` structure includes the following method.

▷ **scrollTo(**Value, **anchor:** UnitPoint?**)**—This method scrolls the list of views to the view identified with the value specified by the first argument. The **anchor** argument determines the position of the view after the scrolling is over. It is a structure that we can create from the type properties **bottom**, **bottomLeading**, **bottomTrailing**, **center**, **leading**, **top**, **topLeading**, **topTrailing**, **trailing**, and **zero**.

The procedure for scrolling the views with this method is similar to what we did before, but instead of using a modifier, we need to wrap the view in a **ScrollViewReader** view and use the **ScrollViewProxy** structure received by the closure to call the **scrollTo()** method with the identifier of the row we want to scroll to, as in the following example.

```
struct ContentView: View {
   @Environment(ApplicationData.self) private var appData

   var body: some View {
      ScrollViewReader { proxy in
         ScrollView(.horizontal, showsIndicators: false) {
            LazyHStack(spacing: 0) {
               ForEach(appData.userData) { book in
                  CellBook(book: book)
                     .containerRelativeFrame(.horizontal)
               }
               Button("< Back") {
                  if let firstIdentifier = appData.userData.first?.id {
                     proxy.scrollTo(firstIdentifier, anchor: .top)
                  }
               }.padding()
            }
            .scrollTargetLayout()
         }
         .scrollTargetBehavior(.viewAligned)
      }
   }
}
```

Listing 7-16: Scrolling the list programmatically

This example creates a horizontal scrollable list of books, but this time the **ScrollView** view is embedded in a **ScrollViewReader** view so we can control it from code. Below the **ForEach** view, we include a **Button** view to let the user scroll the list to the beginning. For this purpose, we get the first item in the **userData** array, read the **id** property, and call the **scrollTo()** method on the proxy with this value. As a result, when the user scrolls the list to the end, a button appears, and if pressed, it scrolls the list back to the beginning.

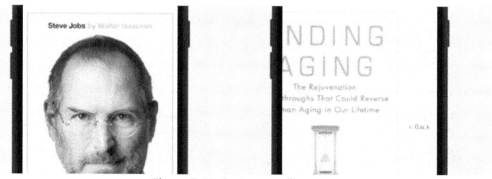

Figure 7-11: Custom scrolling

Do It Yourself: Update the `ContentView` view with the code in Listing 7-16. Scroll down the list to the end. You should see the Back button, as shown in Figure 7-11 (right). Press the button to scroll the list back to the top.

SwiftUI also includes modifiers to perform actions when the condition of the `ScrollView` view changes. The following allows us to check for content visibility.

▷ **onScrollVisibilityChange(threshold:** Double, **action:** Closure)—This modifier performs an action when the view moves on and off screen. The **threshold** argument determines the portion of the view that must enter or exit the screen for the action to be performed (0.0 to 1.0), and the **action** argument is the closure with the action we want to perform.

The **onScrollVisibilityChange()** modifier executes a closure when the view becomes visible or moves out of the visible area. The **threshold** argument specifies how much of the view must appear or disappear for the action to be performed. In the example below, we add an image to the end of the list and apply this modifier to it. The closure will print a message on the console each time the image appears or disappears from the screen.

```
struct ContentView: View {
    @Environment(ApplicationData.self) private var appData

    var body: some View {
        ScrollView(.horizontal, showsIndicators: false) {
            LazyHStack(spacing: 0) {
                ForEach(appData.userData) { book in
                    CellBook(book: book)
                        .containerRelativeFrame(.horizontal)
                }
                Image("nocover")
                    .resizable()
                    .scaledToFit()
                    .padding(10)
                    .containerRelativeFrame(.horizontal)
                    .onScrollVisibilityChange(threshold: 0.5, { visible in
                        if visible {
                            print("Visible!")
                        } else {
                            print("Gone")
                        }
                    })
            }
            .scrollTargetLayout()
        }
        .scrollTargetBehavior(.viewAligned)
    }
}
```

Listing 7-17: Performing an action when a view becomes visible

There is also a modifier we can use to perform an action when a specific state of the `ScrollView` view changes.

▷ **onScrollGeometryChange(for:** Type, **of:** Closure, **action:** Closure)—This modifier performs an action when the condition of the `ScrollView` view changes. The **for** argument is the data type of the value we want to check, the **of** argument is the closure that checks the current state and produces the value to be used in the action, and the **action** argument is the closure that performs the action with the value produce by the previous closure.

This modifier works in two steps. First, the closure assigned to the **of** argument checks the current state of the `ScrollView` view and turn those values into a value we can use, and then the closure assigned to the **action** argument is executed to work with this value. (The **for** argument just determines the data type of the value we are going to pass from one closure to the other.) The **of** closure receives a `ScrollGeometry` structure that represents the current state of the `ScrollView` view. This structure includes many properties to return these values. The **bound** property returns the position and size of the visible content, the `contentInsets` property returns the content's insets, the `containerSize` property returns the size of the visible portion of the content, the `contentOffset` property returns the content's x and y offsets, the `contentSize` property returns the total size of the content, and the `visibleRect` property returns the size and position of the visible portion of the content. For instance, in the following example we read the horizontal offset from the `contentOffset` property and the horizontal size from the `containerSize` property to determine the current page and display it on the screen.

```
struct ContentView: View {
    @Environment(ApplicationData.self) private var appData
    @State private var pageNumber: Int = 1

    var body: some View {
        ZStack {
            ScrollView(.horizontal, showsIndicators: false) {
                LazyHStack(spacing: 0) {
                    ForEach(appData.userData) { book in
                        CellBook(book: book)
                            .containerRelativeFrame(.horizontal)
                    }
                }
                .scrollTargetLayout()
            }
            .scrollTargetBehavior(.viewAligned)
            .onScrollGeometryChange(for: Int.self, of: { geometry in
                let ave = geometry.contentOffset.x / geometry.containerSize.width
                let pages = Int(ave.rounded()) + 1
                return pages
            }, action: { oldValue, newValue in
                pageNumber = newValue
            })
            VStack {
                Text(String(pageNumber))
                    .padding(10)
                    .background(.thinMaterial)
                    .padding(5)
                Spacer()
            }
        }
    }
}
```

Listing 7-18: Responding to the current state of the `ScrollView` *view*

Figure 7-12: Interface responds to the current state

Basic **Lazy Grids**

The horizontal and vertical stack views presented earlier can only contain one item per row or column. If we want to include more, we need to create a grid. SwiftUI defines the following views for this purpose.

▷ **LazyVGrid(columns:** [GridItem], **alignment:** HorizontalAlignment, **spacing:** CGFloat?, **pinnedViews:** PinnedScrollableViews, **content:** Closure)—This view creates a grid of views. The **columns** argument is an array of GridItem structures that determine how the items are arranged on the grid. The **alignment** argument determines how the items are aligned inside the container. It is a structure with the type properties **center**, **leading**, and **trailing**. The **spacing** argument determines the space between views. The **pinnedViews** argument is a structure that determines which views will be momentarily pinned to the bounds of the scroll view while the content is scrolling. And the **content** argument is the closure that provides the list of views.

▷ **LazyHGrid(rows:** [GridItem], **alignment:** VerticalAlignment, **spacing:** CGFloat?, **pinnedViews:** PinnedScrollableViews, **content:** Closure)—This view is similar to the **LazyVGrid** view, but the items are arranged horizontally and the **alignment** argument determines the vertical alignment instead of the horizontal alignment. This is a structure with the type properties **bottom, center, firstText-Baseline, lastTextBaseline**, and **top**.

The **LazyVGrid** and **LazyHGrid** views create a grid of views arranged in rows and columns, but the size and quantity of views in a row or a column is determined by instances of the **GridItem** structure.

▷ **Griditem(Size, spacing:** CGFloat?, **alignment:** Alignment?)—This structure defines the size, padding, and alignment of each item on the grid. The first argument is an enumeration that includes three associated values: **adaptive(minimum: CGFloat, maximum: CGFloat), fixed(CGFloat)**, and **flexible(minimum: CGFloat, maximum: CGFloat)**. The **spacing** argument defines the space around the item. And the **alignment** argument defines the item's alignment. It is a structure with the type properties **bottom, bottomLeading, bottomTrailing, center, leading, top, topLeading, topTrailing**, and **trailing**.

With a **GridItem** structure we can specify the number of views we want to display per row or column, or if we want the grid to determine the number of items to show depending on the space available. For this purpose, the structure can take three different associated values. The **fixed()** and **flexible()** values define a fixed or flexible size for a single view, and the **adaptive()** value defines a flexible size for multiple views. For instance, if we want to create a vertical grid with a specific number of items per row and a fixed size, we must create an array of `GridItem` structures with the `fixed()` value. The number of instances of the `GridItem` structure included in the array determine the number of items per row, as shown below.

```
struct ContentView: View {
   @Environment(ApplicationData.self) private var appData

   let guides = [
      GridItem(.fixed(75)),
      GridItem(.fixed(75)),
      GridItem(.fixed(75))
   ]
   var body: some View {
      ScrollView {
         LazyVGrid(columns: guides) {
            ForEach(appData.userData) { book in
               Image(book.cover)
                  .resizable()
                  .scaledToFit()
            }
         }
      }.padding()
   }
}
```

Listing 7-19: Creating a grid with a fixed number of items

In this example, we define an array of three `GridItem` structures, all with a fixed size of 75 points, and use it to define a vertical grid of books. Because we use a fixed size, and include three instances of the structure, the `LazyVGrid` view creates a grid with three books per row, of a size of 75 points each, no matter the space available.

Figure 7-13: Fixed grid

In the previous example, the views are always 75 points wide. If what we want is to create three items per row but expand the items to occupy all the space available, we can turn the items flexible with the `flexible()` value.

```
let guides = [
   GridItem(.flexible(minimum: 75), alignment: .top),
   GridItem(.flexible(minimum: 75), alignment: .top),
   GridItem(.flexible(minimum: 75), alignment: .top)
]
```

Listing 7-20: Defining flexible items

The `flexible()` value still represents one single item, so we still must include three `GridItem` structures in the array to include three items per row, but because we are not declaring a fixed size, the items expand to occupy all the space available in the container, as shown below. (Note that we have also aligned the items to the top with the **alignment** argument.)

Figure 7-14: Flexible grid

The `flexible()` value represents a single item, so the number of items per row is always the same. If what we want is to display as many items as possible per row but keeping the same proportions and space between views, we can use the `adaptive()` value.

```
let guides = [
    GridItem(.adaptive(minimum: 75))
]
```

Listing 7-21: Defining adaptive items

The `adaptive()` value represents multiple items, so we only need to declare one. This item tells the grid to include as many items per row as possible but they must be at least 75 points wide. The `LazyVGrid` view calculates the number of items that fit inside a row according to the space available. If there is any space left, it expands the items to keep the same space in between.

Figure 7-15: Adaptive grid

Do It Yourself: Update the `ContentView` view with the code in Listing 7-19. You can remove the `CellBook` structure included in the previous example. You should see the grid of books illustrated in Figure 7-13. Update the `guides` array with the examples in Listings 7-20 and 7-21. Test different values to understand how the grid adapts and how the layout values work.

(Basic) **7.2 List View**

Presenting information in a scrollable list of rows and columns is a common requirement of any application. For this reason, SwiftUI includes an additional container to create a scrollable list of views called `List`. Like a `LazyVStack` view, a `List` view creates a vertical list with a single column of items, but the items are automatically separated by a line, and the view includes built-in functionality to select, add, or remove content. The following are some of the initializers.

▷ **List**(Data, **rowContent:** Closure)—This initializer creates a list of views. The first argument is the collection of values to create the rows. These values must conform to the **Identifiable** protocol and implement the **id** property to provide a unique identifier. The **rowContent** argument is a closure that defines the views used to create the rows.

▷ **List**(Data, **id:** KeyPath, **rowContent:** Closure)—This initializer creates a list of views. The first argument is the collection of values to create the rows, the **id** argument is the key path to the unique identifier of each value, and the **rowContent** argument is a closure that defines the views used to create the rows.

▷ **List**(Data, **selection:** Binding, **rowContent:** Closure)—This initializer creates a list of views. The first argument is the collection of values to create the rows, the **selection** argument is a binding property that stores one or a set of identifiers to recognize the selected rows, and the **rowContent** argument is a closure that defines the views used to create the rows.

The syntax to implement a **List** view is the same we have used before for the **ForEach** view. The view requires a reference to the collection of data to be shown and a closure with the views that define the content for each row.

```
struct ContentView: View {
   @Environment(ApplicationData.self) private var appData

   var body: some View {
      List(appData.userData) { book in
         CellBook(book: book)
      }
   }
}
struct CellBook: View {
   let book: Book

   var body: some View {
      HStack(alignment: .top) {
         Image(book.cover)
            .resizable()
            .scaledToFit()
            .frame(width: 80, height: 100)
         VStack(alignment: .leading, spacing: 2) {
            Text(book.title).bold()
            Text(book.author)
            Text(book.displayYear).font(.caption)
            Spacer()
         }.padding(.top, 5)
         Spacer()
      }
   }
}
```

Listing 7-22: Creating a list of views with the List *view*

Like the **ForEach** view, the **List** view in Listing 7-22 reads the values in the model and creates the rows with the views defined by the closure.

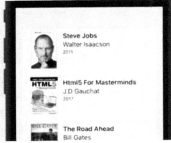

Figure 7-16: List of rows created by a `List` *view*

 Do It Yourself: Update the ContentView.swift file with the code in Listing 7-22. This example assumes that you have implemented the model introduced in Listing 7-3 and have injected the **ApplicationData** object into the environment, as we did in Listing 7-4. You should see a scrollable list of books, as illustrated in Figure 7-16.

 IMPORTANT: If you scroll down the list, you will see that the views go all to the top, behind the status bar. This is because **List** views were designed to work with the navigation bars provided by **NavigationStack** views. We will learn how to use these views and navigate between views in the next chapter.

In mobile devices, the list is shown with a style that generates a padding around the views and includes a background color. The **View** protocol defines the following modifier to customize the style.

▷ **listStyle(**ListStyle**)**—This modifier assigns a style to the **List** view. The argument is a structure that conforms to the **ListStyle** protocol. SwiftUI defines multiple styling structures, and these structures include the type properties **automatic**, **plain**, **inset**, **grouped**, **insetGrouped**, and **sidebar** to apply standard styles.

The style set by default in mobile devices is called **insetGrouped**, but we can change it with the **listStyle()** modifier. The **plain** style displays the views with not background or padding, the **inset** style adds padding to the list, the **insetGrouped** style adds a background and a padding around the views, and the **sidebar** style adds a background to the whole list. The following example applies a plain styling to the list.

```
struct ContentView: View {
    @Environment(ApplicationData.self) private var appData

    var body: some View {
        List(appData.userData) { book in
            CellBook(book: book)
        }.listStyle(.plain)
    }
}
```

Listing 7-23: Creating a plain list

The result is similar to what we achieved with the **ForEach** and **Divider** views before (see Listing 7-2), but now the list has an inset on the left side that gives it a distinctive look.

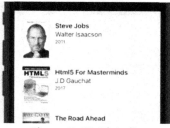

Figure 7-17: Plain list

The **View** protocol includes the following modifiers to customize the list.

▷ **listRowBackground(**View**)**—This modifier defines the background view for the row. The argument is a SwiftUI view, such as **Color**.

▷ **listRowInsets(**EdgeInsets**)**—This modifier defines the insets for the rows (padding).

▷ **listRowSeparator(**Visibility, **edges:** VerticalEdge**)**—This modifier configures the row separators. The first argument determines if the separators are visible or hidden. It is an enumeration with the values **automatic**, **hidden**, and **visible**. And the **edges** argument defines which separators are affected. It is a structure with the type properties **all**, **bottom**, and **top**.

▷ **listRowSeparatorTint(**Color?, **edges:** VerticalEdge**)**—This modifier defines the separators' color. The first argument specifies the new color, and the **edges** argument determines which separator is affected. It is a structure with the type properties **all**, **bottom**, and **top**.

▷ **listItemTint(**Color?**)**—This modifier defines a new tint color for the row. It overwrites the app's accent color (see Figure 5-46).

These modifiers are applied to the rows, but by modifying the rows we can change the style of the entire list. For instance, we can remove the padding assigned to the rows by the **plain** style with the **listRowInsets()** modifier.

```
struct ContentView: View {
   @Environment(ApplicationData.self) private var appData

   var body: some View {
      List(appData.userData) { book in
         CellBook(book: book)
            .listRowInsets(EdgeInsets(top: 0, leading: 0, bottom: 10,
trailing: 0))
            .listRowBackground(Color(white: 0.95))
            .listRowSeparator(.hidden)
      }.listStyle(.plain)
   }
}
```

Listing 7-24: Customizing the rows

In this example, we remove the insets on the sides, but assign an inset of 10 points to the bottom of each row. To show how other modifiers work, we have also assigned a background color and removed the separators. The result is shown below.

Figure 7-18: *Custom list*

The `listRowBackground()` modifier applied in Listing 7-24 changes the background color of each row, so they all look the same. If we want to apply alternate backgrounds, we need to identify each row and then apply a color accordingly. For our example, we can use the index of the book in the `userData` array. This value is unique for every book stored in the array, so we can use it to know which view we are working with.

```
struct ContentView: View {
    @Environment(ApplicationData.self) private var appData
    let colors = [.white, Color(white: 0.95)]

    var body: some View {
        List(appData.userData) { book in
            let index = appData.userData.firstIndex(where: { $0.id ==
book.id }) ?? 0

            CellBook(book: book)
                .listRowBackground(index % 2 == 0 ? colors[0] : colors[1])
                .listRowSeparator(.hidden)
        }.listStyle(.plain)
    }
}
```

Listing 7-25: *Assigning alternate backgrounds*

The view in Listing 7-25 defines a property called `colors` with the two colors we want to assign to the views (white and gray). In the closure assigned to the `List` view, we get the index of the book with the `firstIndex()` method. The method looks for an item in the array which `id` property has the same value than the `id` property of the current book, and returns the index of the item if found, or `nil` otherwise. To make sure that we always get a value, we use the nil-coalescing operator (`??`) to return the index 0 if no value is found. The `listRowBackground()` applies the remainder operator to the index value to select the color (see Chapter 2, Listing 2-49). If the value is even, the first color is assigned to the background (white), and if the index is odd, the second value is assigned instead (gray).

Figure 7-19: *Alternate backgrounds*

The **List** view was designed to work along with the **ForEach** view to mix static and dynamic content. The advantage is that we can create a list of rows with the data from the model and at the same time include other rows with static content to incorporate additional information or for styling purposes, as in the following example.

```
struct ContentView: View {
   @Environment(ApplicationData.self) private var appData

   var body: some View {
      List {
         HStack {
            Image(systemName: "book.circle")
               .font(.largeTitle)
            Spacer()
            Text("My Favorite Books")
               .font(.headline)
         }.frame(height: 50)
         ForEach(appData.userData) { book in
            CellBook(book: book)
         }
      }.listStyle(.plain)
   }
}
```

Listing 7-26: *Mixing static and dynamic content in a list*

A **List** view takes a list of views, one or more **ForEach** loops, or a combination of both, and includes every view in a row. In Listing 7-26, we create one static view with an SF Symbol and some text, and then a **ForEach** view to list the data in the model. The static content is shown along with the dynamic content and even scrolls with the rest of the rows, as shown below.

Figure 7-20: *Static and dynamic content*

(Basic) Sections

A list can be organized into sections. Sections help the user identify values that have something in common. SwiftUI includes the **Section** view to create these sections.

▷ **Section(content:** Closure)—This initializer creates a **Section** view to group related content. The **content** argument is the closure that defines the rows for the section.

▷ **Section(content:** Closure, **header:** View, **footer:** View)—This initializer creates a **Section** view to group related content. The **content** argument is the closure that defines the rows for the section, the **header** argument is a view or a group of views that define the section's header, and the **footer** argument is a view or a group of views that define the section's footer.

▷ **Section(String, isExpanded:** Binding, **content:** Closure)—This initializer creates a **Section** view to group related content. The first argument defines the text for the header, the **isExpanded** argument is a Boolean binding property that determines whether the section is expanded or not, and the **content** argument is the closure that defines the rows for the section.

The text assigned to the section's header is displayed at the top of the section with a style that matches the style of the list, but we can make it more prominent with the following modifier.

▷ **headerProminence(**Prominence)—This modifier defines the prominence of the section's title. The argument is an enumeration with the values **increased** and **standard**.

Although a section may contain no header or footer, in most situations it is better to provide a visual cue of where a section begins and ends. The following example creates two sections with a prominent header defined by a **Text** view.

```
struct ContentView: View {
    @Environment(ApplicationData.self) private var appData

    var body: some View {
        List {
            Section(header: Text("Statistics")) {
                HStack {
                    Text("Total Books:")
                    Spacer()
                    Text(String(appData.userData.count))
                }
            }.headerProminence(.increased)
            Section(header: Text("My Books")) {
                ForEach(appData.userData) { book in
                    CellBook(book: book)
                }
            }.headerProminence(.increased)
        }
    }
}
```

Listing 7-27: Dividing the content into sections

This example creates two sections, one to show the total number of books in the model and another to list the books.

Figure 7-21: Sections with headers

If the style of the list is **plain** or **inset**, the sections show separators at the top and bottom. The **View** protocol includes the following modifiers to configure these lines.

▷ **listSectionSeparator(**Visibility, **edges:** VerticalEdge)—This modifier configures the sections separators. The first argument determines if the separators are visible or hidden. It is an enumeration with the values **automatic**, **hidden**, and **visible**. And the **edges** argument defines which separators are affected. It is a structure with the type properties **all**, **bottom**, and **top**.

▷ **listSectionSeparatorTint(**Color?, **edges:** VerticalEdge)—This modifier defines the color of the separators. The first argument specifies the new color, and the **edges** argument determines which separators are affected. It is a structure with the type properties **all**, **bottom**, and **top**.

These modifiers work in a similar way to those for rows. We can remove the top and bottom lines, or both, and change their colors. For example, in the following view, we remove the top line, change the color of the bottom line for the first section, and completely remove the lines for the second section.

```
struct ContentView: View {
    @Environment(ApplicationData.self) private var appData

    var body: some View {
        List {
            Section(header: Text("Statistics")) {
                HStack {
                    Text("Total Books:")
                    Spacer()
                    Text(String(appData.userData.count))
                }
            }.listSectionSeparator(.hidden, edges: .top)
            .listSectionSeparatorTint(.blue)

            Section(header: Text("My Books")) {
                ForEach(appData.userData) { book in
                    CellBook(book: book)
                }
            }.listSectionSeparator(.hidden)
        }.listStyle(.plain)
    }
}
```

Listing 7-28: Configuring the section separators

Figure 7-22: Section separators

By default, the height of headers and rows is determined by their content, but the environment includes two properties to modify those values.

▷ **defaultMinListHeaderHeight**—This property defines the minimum height for the headers. It is a value of type **CGFloat**.

▷ **defaultMinListRowHeight**—This property defines the minimum height for the rows. It is a value of type `CGFloat`.

To change the values of these properties, we must apply the `environment()` modifier to the `List` view (see Listing 5-93). These properties are useful when the content of the headers or the rows is variable. For instance, we can assign a minimum size to the rows of our previous example so the row in the first section is of the same height as the rows with the books.

```
struct ContentView: View {
    @Environment(ApplicationData.self) private var appData

    var body: some View {
        List {
            Section(header: Text("Statistics")) {
                HStack {
                    Text("Total Books:")
                    Spacer()
                    Text(String(appData.userData.count))
                }
            }
            Section(header: Text("My Books")) {
                ForEach(appData.userData) { book in
                    CellBook(book: book)
                }
            }
        }.environment(\.defaultMinListRowHeight, 100)
    }
}
```

Listing 7-29: Configuring the list from the environment

Figure 7-23: Same height for all the rows

So far, we have used sections to group different types of content. The first section of our example contains information about the model and the second section contains the list of books. However, sections are also useful when we need to divide content into groups, such as movies into categories, or when we want to arrange items alphabetically. For this purpose, we must prepare the data according to the organization we want to present to the user. An alternative is to define a computed property in the view that returns the items in the order required to organize them into sections. For example, we can define a property that returns the list of books in alphabetical order.

```
struct ContentView: View {
    @Environment(ApplicationData.self) private var appData

    var orderList: [(key: String, value: [Book])] {
        let listGroup: [String: [Book]] = Dictionary(grouping:
appData.userData, by: { value in
```

```
            let index = value.title.startIndex
            let initial = value.title[index]
            return String(initial)
        })
        return listGroup.sorted(by: { $0.key < $1.key })
    }
    var body: some View {
        List {
            ForEach(orderList, id: \.key) { sections in
                Section(header: Text(sections.key)) {
                    ForEach(sections.value) { book in
                        CellBook(book: book)
                    }
                }.headerProminence(.increased)
            }
        }
    }
}
```

Listing 7-30: Providing an ordered list of values

Before defining the **body** property, the view in Listing 7-30 defines a computed property that returns an array of tuples with the books organized by the title's first letter. First, the closure applies the **Dictionary(grouping:, by:)** initializer to create a dictionary from the values of the **userData** array (the list of books in the model). The way this initializer works is that for every value in the array, it executes a closure and then groups the results by the values returned by the closure (see Listing 3-122). In this example, we get the index of the first character in the book's title with the **startIndex** property. Then, we use that index to extract the first character. And finally, we turn it into a string and return it. This creates an array with tuples which first value is a letter of the alphabet and the second value is an array with all the books which titles begin with that letter (**[(key: String, value: [Book])]**). After this array is created, we sort the values alphabetically with the **sorted()** method and return it, so every time the views read the **orderList** property, they get an array of tuples with the books sorted alphabetically.

The values of the tuples were identified with the labels **key** and **value**, so we can use these labels to read them and create our list. In this example, we define a **List** view with two **ForEach** loops inside, one to create the sections for each letter and another to list the books inside the sections. The first **ForEach** loop reads the content of the **orderList** property and creates a section with the value identified by the **key** label (the letter). Inside the section, another **ForEach** loop iterates through the array identified with the **value** label to create the list of books. As a result, we get a list of books organized alphabetically into sections.

Figure 7-24: Alphabetical sections

Edit Mode

List views also provide tools to work with the values on the list. The following are the modifiers available to remove and sort views.

▷ **onDelete(perform:** Closure)—This modifier executes the closure specified by the **perform** argument when the user tries to remove a row. The closure receives an **IndexSet** value with integers representing the indexes of the rows the user wants to delete.

▷ **deleteDisabled(**Bool)—This modifier enables or disables the possibility for the user to delete a row.

▷ **onMove(perform:** Closure)—This modifier executes the closure specified by the **perform** argument when the user tries to move a row to a different position on the list. The closure receives an **IndexSet** value with integers representing the indexes of the rows the user is moving, and an integer representing the index where the rows should be moved.

▷ **moveDisabled(**Bool)—This modifier enables or disables the possibility for the user to move a row.

These modifiers produce a value of type **IndexSet** that contains a set of integers representing the indexes of the values to be modified in the collection. To modify an array from these values, the Swift Standard Library defines the following methods.

▷ **remove(atOffsets:** IndexSet)—This method removes the items in the array with the indexes provided by the **atOffsets** argument.

▷ **move(fromOffsets:** IndexSet, **toOffset:** Int)—This method moves the items of the array in the indexes specified by the **fromOffsets** argument to the index determined by the **toOffset** argument.

The **onDelete()** and **onMove()** modifiers identify the items by the indexes in the array. The closure assigned to these modifiers receives a set with the indexes of the items to be deleted or moved, so all we need to do to perform the task requested by the user is to call the **remove()** or **move()** methods with these values.

There are different ways to allow the user to modify the list. For instance, if we apply the **onDelete()** modifier to the list, the system automatically activates a feature that lets the user drag the rows to the left to expose a Delete button. When this button is pressed, the closure assigned to the modifier is executed and we can proceed accordingly, as shown below.

```
struct ContentView: View {
    @Environment(ApplicationData.self) private var appData

    var body: some View {
        List {
            ForEach(appData.userData) { book in
                CellBook(book: book)
            }.onDelete { indexes in
                appData.userData.remove(atOffsets: indexes)
            }
        }
    }
}
```

Listing 7-31: Deleting rows

Note that the modifiers are implemented by the **ForEach** view, so we need to create the list with this view. In the example of Listing 7-31, we use the **onDelete()** modifier. The closure assigned to the modifier receives an **IndexSet** value with the index of the row to be deleted and calls the **remove()** method on the **userData** array to remove the item from the model. Now the user can delete the book by dragging the row to the left and pressing the Delete button.

Figure 7-25: Automatic delete feature

 Do It Yourself: Update the `ContentView` view with the code in Listing 7-31. Drag a row to the left and press the Delete button, as shown in Figure 7-25. The row should be removed from the list.

In addition to the possibility to drag a row to delete it, **List** views also include a set of tools that allow the user to select, remove, and move rows. The tools are displayed to the user when the list is in edit mode. The easiest way to activate this mode is with the **EditButton** view. This view creates a button that activates and deactivates the edit mode when pressed.

```
struct ContentView: View {
   @Environment(ApplicationData.self) private var appData

   var body: some View {
      VStack {
         EditButton()
         List {
            ForEach(appData.userData) { book in
               CellBook(book: book)
            }.onDelete { indexes in
               appData.userData.remove(atOffsets: indexes)
            }
         }.listStyle(.plain)
      }
   }
}
```

Listing 7-32: Activating the edit mode

The view in Listing 7-32 embeds the **List** view in a **VStack** view to add an **EditButton** at the top. When the button is pressed, the system activates the edit mode and the tools are shown according to the modifiers we have applied. For instance, in our example, we included the **onDelete()** modifier, so the view exposes buttons to let the user delete the row.

Figure 7-26: Edit button

The tool to move rows is included when the **onMove()** modifier is applied to the **ForEach** view, as in the following example.

```
struct ContentView: View {
    @Environment(ApplicationData.self) private var appData

    var body: some View {
        VStack {
            EditButton()
            List {
                ForEach(appData.userData) { book in
                    CellBook(book: book)
                }.onDelete { indexes in
                    appData.userData.remove(atOffsets: indexes)
                }
                .onMove { source, destination in
                    appData.userData.move(fromOffsets: source, toOffset:
destination)
                }
            }.listStyle(.plain)
        }
    }
}
```

Listing 7-33: Moving rows

The system detects that we have implemented the **onMove()** modifier and automatically provides the tools for the user to move the rows and reorganize the list. After the user drops a row in a new position, the modifier sends the indexes of the rows and the new location to the closure, and here is where we have the chance to call the **move()** method to perform the change in the **userData** array, so the next time the list is redrawn, the rows remain in the position selected by the user.

Figure 7-27: Move buttons

 Do It Yourself: Update the **ContentView** view with the code in Listing 7-33. Press the Edit button. Use the tools to remove a row or move it to a different position. You should see the interface illustrated in Figure 7-27.

The edit mode also allows the user to select one or more rows. For single selection, the mode is enabled by default. All we need to do is to initialize the **List** view with the **selection** argument. The argument takes a binding property to store the identifier of the selected row, which we can use later to process the item, as shown below.

```
struct ContentView: View {
    @Environment(ApplicationData.self) private var appData
    @State private var selectedRow: Book.ID? = nil

    var body: some View {
        VStack {
            HStack {
                Spacer()
```

```
                Button(action: {
                    removeSelected()
                }, label: {
                    Image(systemName: "trash")
                }).disabled(selectedRow == nil ? true : false)
            }.padding()

            List(selection: $selectedRow) {
                ForEach(appData.userData) { book in
                    CellBook(book: book)
                }
            }.listStyle(.plain)
        }
    }
    func removeSelected() {
        if let index = appData.userData.firstIndex(where: { $0.id ==
selectedRow }) {
            appData.userData.remove(at: index)
            selectedRow = nil
        }
    }
}
}
```

Listing 7-34: Selecting a row

When working with structures that conform to the **Identifiable** protocol, the **List** view automatically identifies the views with the values assigned to the **id** property. Therefore, the **@State** property must be of the same data type as the **id** property. To ensure this, we can declare the property with the associated type **ID**. As explained earlier, this associated type is defined by the **Identifiable** protocol and represents the data type assigned to the **id** property (see Listing 7-13). By using **ID** instead of the property's data type, we ensure that the **@State** property stores the correct values, even if we decide to change the data type of the **id** property later.

If the user selects an item, the **List** view assigns the value of the item's **id** property to the **selectedRow** property, so we can do whatever we want with it. In our example, we add a **Button** view at the top that calls a method to remove the selected book. The method gets the index of the selected item in the **userData** array, calls the **remove()** method to remove it, and assigns the value **nil** to the **selectedRow** property to cancel the selection. Note that we have applied the **disabled()** modifier to the button to only enable it when a book has been selected.

Figure 7-28: Single selection

To process multiple values, we can store the identifiers in an **IndexSet** structure and apply the same methods used above to move and remove rows. The **IndexSet** structure provides the following method for this purpose.

▷ **insert(Int)**—This method adds the index specified by the argument to the set.

In the following example, we modify the **@State** property to take a **Set** of **UUID** values instead of just one (**Set<Book.ID>**) so the user can select multiple rows, and create an **IndexSet** structure with the indexes of the selected rows to remove the values from the model.

```
struct ContentView: View {
    @Environment(ApplicationData.self) private var appData
    @State private var selectedRows: Set<Book.ID> = []

    var body: some View {
        VStack {
            HStack {
                EditButton()
                Spacer()
                Button(action: {
                    removeSelected()
                }, label: {
                    Image(systemName: "trash")
                }).disabled(selectedRows.count == 0 ? true : false)
            }.padding()

            List(selection: $selectedRows) {
                ForEach(appData.userData) { book in
                    CellBook(book: book)
                }
            }.listStyle(.plain)
        }
    }
    func removeSelected() {
        var indexes = IndexSet()
        for item in selectedRows {
            if let index = appData.userData.firstIndex(where: { $0.id ==
item }) {
                indexes.insert(index)
            }
        }
        appData.userData.remove(atOffsets: indexes)
        selectedRows = []
    }
}
```

Listing 7-35: *Selecting multiple rows*

The view now includes two views at the top: the **EditButton** view to activate or deactivate the edit mode, and the trash can button to remove the books selected by the user. When the user activates the edit mode, checkboxes appear on the left to select the rows. If the user selects a row, the **List** view adds the value of the **id** property to the **selectedRows** property, so we can call our **removeSelected()** method again to remove the books. In this case, the method creates an empty **IndexSet** structure and then iterates through the values in the **selectedRows** property to find the index of each book and add it to the set. Once all the indexes are found, we call the **remove()** method on the **userData** array to erase the books, and then clean the **selectedRows** property to allow the user to start the process again.

Figure 7-29: *Selected rows*

Do It Yourself: Update the `ContentView` view with the code in Listing 7-35. Press the Edit button. Select a row and click the button on the right. The row should be removed, as shown in Figure 7-29.

If we want to disable the edit mode after removing the books or after any other action, we need to control the mode programmatically. For this purpose, the environment provides the following property.

▷ **editMode**—This property defines the state of the edit mode for the view. It is a binding property of type **EditMode**, an enumeration with the values **active**, **inactive**, and **transient**. The enumeration also includes the **isEditing** property to return a Boolean value that indicates whether the view is in edit mode or not.

To manage the mode, we need a binding property with a Boolean value that stores the state of the edit mode (active or inactive), we must set the mode according to the value of this property with the **environment()** modifier, as we did before for other environment properties, and we also need to create a button to toggle this value, as shown below.

```
struct ContentView: View {
   @Environment(ApplicationData.self) private var appData
   @State private var selectedRows: Set<Book.ID> = []
   @State private var editActive: Bool = false

   var body: some View {
      VStack {
         HStack {
            Button(editActive ? "Done" : "Edit") {
               editActive.toggle()
            }
            Spacer()
            Button(action: {
               removeSelected()
            }, label: {
               Image(systemName: "trash")
            }).disabled(selectedRows.count == 0 ? true : false)
         }.padding()

         List(selection: $selectedRows) {
            ForEach(appData.userData) { book in
               CellBook(book: book)
            }
         }.listStyle(.plain)
         .environment(\.editMode, .constant(editActive ?
EditMode.active : EditMode.inactive))
      }
   }
   func removeSelected() {
      var indexes = IndexSet()
      for item in selectedRows {
         if let index = appData.userData.firstIndex(where: { $0.id ==
item }) {
            indexes.insert(index)
         }
      }
      appData.userData.remove(atOffsets: indexes)
      selectedRows = []
      editActive = false
   }
}
```

Listing 7-36: Customizing the edit mode

This code defines a **@State** property called **editActive** to keep track of the edit mode and replaces the **EditButton** view with a regular **Button** view. If the value of the property is **true**, it means that the mode is active, otherwise inactive, so we use it to select the mode, to deactivate it after the selected books are deleted, and to set the title for the button ("Done" if **true**, "Edit" if **false**). Note that the environment's **editMode** property is a binding property and therefore we had to use the **constant()** method to provide a binding value of type **EditMode** (see Listing 6-9).

The result is the same as before, but the process is now customized and therefore we can change the edit mode from code anytime we want by assigning the value **true** or **false** to the **editActive** property.

 Do It Yourself: Update the **ContentView** view with the code in Listing 7-36. Press the Edit button. Select a row and click the Remove button. The row should be removed, as before, but now the edit mode is automatically deactivated.

The selection process can also be customized, but it requires us to keep track of the selected rows ourselves and detect the selection with the **onTapGesture()** modifier. We have implemented this modifier before to detect when an image was tapped by the user (see Listing 6-37). The modifier executes a closure when the user taps the view. In this case, we need to apply it to every **CellBook** view to assign the value of the **id** property of the selected book to a binding property, as shown below.

```
struct ContentView: View {
    @Environment(ApplicationData.self) private var appData
    @State private var selectedRow: Book.ID? = nil

    var body: some View {
        List {
            ForEach(appData.userData) { book in
                CellBook(selected: $selectedRow, book: book)
                    .background(.white)
                    .onTapGesture {
                        if selectedRow == book.id {
                            selectedRow = nil
                        } else {
                            selectedRow = book.id
                        }
                    }
            }
        }.listStyle(.plain)
    }
}
struct CellBook: View {
    @Binding var selected: Book.ID?
    let book: Book

    var body: some View {
        HStack(alignment: .top) {
            Image(book.cover)
                .resizable()
                .scaledToFit()
                .frame(width: 80, height: 100)
            VStack(alignment: .leading, spacing: 2) {
                Text(book.title).bold()
                Text(book.author)
                Text(book.displayYear).font(.caption)
                Spacer()
            }.padding(.top, 5)
            Spacer()
```

```
        if selected == book.id {
            Image(systemName: "checkmark")
                .foregroundColor(Color.green)
                .frame(width: 25, height: 25)
        }
      }
    }
  }
}
```

Listing 7-37: Customizing the selection

In this example, we allow the selection of one row at a time. If the user taps on a row, the **onTapGesture()** modifier checks whether the book's id was already stored in the **@State** property. If it was, it deselects the row by assigning the value **nil** to the property, otherwise, the value of the book's **id** property is assigned to the **@State** property to indicate that the row was selected. To show the selection to the user, we connect the **@State** property with a **@Binding** property in the **CellBook** view and then show an image if the value of this property is equal to the book's identifier. As a result, a checkmark is shown on the row selected by the user.

Figure 7-30: Custom selection

 Do It Yourself: Update the **ContentView** and **CellBook** views with the code in Listing 7-37. Click on a row. You should see the checkmark shown in Figure 7-30. Of course, you can add a button to perform a task on the selected item, like removing the selected book from the model, as we did before.

 IMPORTANT: Note that we have applied the **background()** modifier to the **CellBook** view with a white color. This modifier generates a **Color** view that occupies the whole area, providing a surface for the **onTapGesture()** to detect the taps. This allows the user to select the row by tapping anywhere, not only on its content. SwiftUI also provides the **contentShape()** modifier for this purpose. We will learn more about this modifier and gesture recognizers in Chapter 12.

In the previous examples, the selection was stored in a **@State** property in the view. If for any reason the view is removed, the selection is removed with it. If we need to keep the selection active or access it from other views, we can save it in the model. The **Book** structure in our model already includes the **selected** property to store this value, so all we need is to change the value of this property every time the user taps on a row, as shown below.

```
struct ContentView: View {
    @Environment(ApplicationData.self) private var appData

    var body: some View {
        @Bindable var appData = appData

        List {
            ForEach($appData.userData) { $book in
```

```
            CellBook(book: book)
                .background(.white)
                .onTapGesture {
                    book.selected.toggle()
                }
            }
        }.listStyle(.plain)
    }
}
struct CellBook: View {
    let book: Book

    var body: some View {
        HStack(alignment: .top) {
            Image(book.cover)
                .resizable()
                .scaledToFit()
                .frame(width: 80, height: 100)
            VStack(alignment: .leading, spacing: 2) {
                Text(book.title).bold()
                Text(book.author)
                Text(book.displayYear).font(.caption)
                Spacer()
            }.padding(.top, 5)
            Spacer()
            if book.selected {
                Image(systemName: "checkmark")
                    .foregroundColor(Color.green)
                    .frame(width: 25, height: 25)
            }
        }
    }
}
```

Listing 7-38: Storing the selection in the model

Although we can access and modify the **Book** structures in the model through the array index, the **List** and **ForEach** views can take a binding value, which allows us to modify the model directly. To use this feature, we turn the app structure into a bindable property with the **@Bindable** macro so that we can change its values (see Chapter 6, Listing 6-57). In this example, the value of the **selected** property is toggled each time the user taps on a row. If the value is **true**, it becomes **false** and vice versa. The result is the same as before, but now we can select multiple books and each **Book** structure knows whether the book has been selected or not.

(Basic) Swipe Actions

The Delete button displayed by the list when the user swipes a row to the left is called *Swipe Action*. The swipe action that defines the Delete button is provided by the **List** view, but we can define our own with the following modifier.

▷ **swipeActions(edge:** HorizontalEdge, **allowsFullSwipe:** Bool, **content:** Closure)—This modifier defines swipe actions for a row on a list. The **edge** argument determines the side of the row where the buttons are going to be placed (left or right). It is an enumeration with the values **leading** and **trailing**. The **allowsFullSwipe** argument determines whether the first action is executed when the user swipes the row all the way to the side. And the **content** argument is a closure that provides the **Button** views that represent the swipe actions.

By default, the swipe action is created on the trailing side and it allows the user to perform the first action with a full swipe, so if that configuration is good for our application, all we need to do is to define the closure with the **Button** views we want to include.

```
struct ContentView: View {
   @Environment(ApplicationData.self) private var appData

   var body: some View {
      List {
         ForEach(appData.userData) { book in
            CellBook(book: book)
               .swipeActions {
                  Button(role: .destructive, action: {
                     removeBook(book: book)
                  }, label: {
                     Image(systemName: "trash")
                  })
               }
         }
      }.listStyle(.plain)
   }
   func removeBook(book: Book) {
      var indexes = IndexSet()
      if let index = appData.userData.firstIndex(where: { $0.id ==
book.id }) {
         indexes.insert(index)
      }
      appData.userData.remove(atOffsets: indexes)
   }
}
```

Listing 7-39: Defining custom swipe actions

In this example, we include a button with the **destructive** role and a label created with an **Image** view and the SF Symbol of a trash can. If the user swipes the row and presses the button, the closure calls a method to remove the book from the model, as before.

Figure 7-31: Custom swipe action

(Basic) **Custom Buttons**

In addition to the buttons generated by the system, we can include our own. Of course, when we use custom buttons to perform tasks on the list, there is no need to implement the methods defined for the edit mode. The following example illustrates how to include a remove button for each row.

```
struct ContentView: View {
   @Environment(ApplicationData.self) private var appData

   var body: some View {
      List {
         ForEach(appData.userData) { book in
            CellBook(book: book)
```

```
            }
        }.listStyle(.plain)
    }
}
struct CellBook: View {
    @Environment(ApplicationData.self) private var appData
    let book: Book

    var body: some View {
        HStack(alignment: .top) {
            Image(book.cover)
                .resizable()
                .scaledToFit()
                .frame(width: 80, height: 100)
            VStack(alignment: .leading, spacing: 2) {
                Text(book.title).bold()
                Text(book.author)
                Text(book.displayYear).font(.caption)
                Spacer()
            }.padding(.top, 5)
            Spacer()

            Button(action: {
                removeBook(book: book)
            }, label: {
                Image(systemName: "trash")
                    .foregroundColor(.red)
                    .frame(width: 30, height: 30)
            }).padding(.top, 5)
            .buttonStyle(.plain)
        }
    }
    func removeBook(book: Book) {
        if let index = appData.userData.firstIndex(where: { $0.id ==
book.id }) {
            appData.userData.remove(at: index)
        }
    }
}
```

Listing 7-40: Implementing a custom button to delete the rows

The buttons created by the **Button** view pass to the row the responsibility of responding to the user tapping the screen. To get the button to respond, we must define it as a plain button with the **plain** style. The action and the label are defined as always. In this example, we create a button on the right hand side of each row to delete it. The label is an SF Symbol of a trash can, and the action calls the **removeBook()** method implemented before.

Figure 7-32: Custom button to remove a row

(Basic) Refreshable

There is a useful feature, usually provided by modern applications, that allows the user to refresh the data by scrolling down the list. If the user continues to scroll down after reaching the top of the list, a spinning wheel appears to indicate that the system is refreshing the data. The `View` protocol includes the following modifier to add this feature to a `List` view.

▷ **refreshable(action:** Closure)—This modifier adds a refreshable control to a list. The **action** argument is the closure to be executed when the user performs the action.

To add this feature to the list, we must implement the modifier on the `List` view and provide a closure with the task we want to perform, as in the following example.

```
struct ContentView: View {
    @Environment(ApplicationData.self) private var appData

    var body: some View {
        List {
            ForEach(appData.userData) { book in
                CellBook(book: book)
            }
        }.listStyle(.plain)
        .refreshable {
            print("Loading values")
        }
    }
}
```
Listing 7-41: Refreshing the list

When the user scrolls down the list, the closure is executed to perform the task. In this example, we print a message on the console, but the task usually involves accessing a server or a database to download and process information. (We will learn how to perform these processes later.)

Figure 7-33: Refresh control

 Do It Yourself: Update the `ContentView` view with the code in Listing 7-41. Drag the list down. You should see a spinning wheel to indicate the list is refreshing its content. This example assumes that you are using the `CellBook` view defined in Listing 7-22.

 IMPORTANT: The task is performed asynchronously, which means that the statement in the closure are executed in the background, while the app keeps performing other tasks, such as refreshing the interface. We will learn more about concurrent and asynchronous tasks in Chapter 9.

Outline List

In addition to the list of views we have created so far, SwiftUI also provides tools to create hierarchical lists. These are list of views in which some rows can expand or collapse to display or hide other rows. The main views, also called *parents*, work as containers for other views, called *children*, that the user can see by tapping on the top view's accessory. The **List** view provides the following initializer to create these lists.

▷ **List(Data, children:** KeyPath, **rowContent:** Closure**)**—This initializer creates a hierarchical list. The first argument is the data used to create the views, the **children** argument is a key path to the property that contains the data to create the children views, and the **rowContent** argument is the closure with the views to create each row.

We don't need anything new to create these types of lists, all the functionality is provided by the **List** view, but the information in the model must be organized accordingly. For example, the following model includes a structure to store the items, which in turn contains a property with another array of instances of the same structure to store the items that will be displayed when the parent item is expanded.

```
import SwiftUI
import Observation
struct MainItems: Identifiable {
    var id = UUID()
    var name: String!
    var options: [MainItems]!
}
@Observable class ApplicationData: @unchecked Sendable {
    var items: [MainItems] = []

    static let shared: ApplicationData = ApplicationData()
    private init() {
        items = [
            MainItems(name: "Food", options: [
                MainItems(name: "Oatmeal", options: nil),
                MainItems(name: "Bagels", options: nil),
                MainItems(name: "Brownies", options: nil),
                MainItems(name: "Cheese", options: [
                    MainItems(name: "Roquefort", options: nil),
                    MainItems(name: "Mozzarella", options: nil),
                    MainItems(name: "Cheddar", options: nil)
                ]),
                MainItems(name: "Cookies", options: nil),
                MainItems(name: "Donuts", options: nil)
            ]),
            MainItems(name: "Beverages", options: [
                MainItems(name: "Coffee", options: nil),
                MainItems(name: "Juice", options: nil),
                MainItems(name: "Lemonade", options: nil)
            ])
        ]
    }
}
```

Listing 7-42: Defining the model to create a hierarchical list

The **MainItems** structure includes the **name** property to store the item's name, and the **options** property to store the children (also defined by **MainItems** structures). In this example, we define two parent items called "Food" and "Beverages", each with their own children assigned to the **options** property. There is also one item called "Cheese" with three children, creating an additional hierarchy. To represent it, all we need is a **List** view with the **children** argument.

```
struct ContentView: View {
   var appData = ApplicationData.shared

   var body: some View {
      List(appData.items, children: \.options) { item in
         Text(item.name)
      }
   }
}
```

Listing 7-43: Displaying a hierarchical list

When the user taps on the "Food" or "Beverages" items, all the items stored in the **options** property are displayed, and the same happens whit the "Cheese" item.

Figure 7-34: Hierarchical list

The **List** view implements another view in the background called **OutlineGroup** to create the hierarchical list of views, but we can declare this view ourselves to create more complex hierarchies. The **OutlineGroup** view includes the following initializer.

▷ **OutlineGroup(**Data, **children:** KeyPath, **content:** Closure**)**—This view creates a hierarchical list. The first argument is the data used to create the views, the **children** argument is a key path to the property that contains the data to create the children view, and the **content** argument is the closure with the views for each row.

For example, we can include this view inside a **Section** view to divide the hierarchy in sections.

```
struct ContentView: View {
   var appData = ApplicationData.shared

   var body: some View {
      List {
         ForEach(appData.items) { section in
            Section(header: Text(section.name)) {
               OutlineGroup(section.options ?? [], children: \.options)
{ item in
                  Text(item.name)
               }
            }
         }
      }
   }
}
```

Listing 7-44: Implementing an OutlineGroup view

In this example, we create the list with a **ForEach** view and the values of the **items** property. This property contains two items, "Food" and "Beverages", that we use to create the sections with a **Section** view. To display the content of the sections, we use an **OutlineGroup** view. This view takes the values in the **options** property of each item and creates an outline list.

Figure 7-35: Custom hierarchy

Do It Yourself: Create a Multiplatform project. Create a Swift file called ApplicationData.swift for the model in Listing 7-42. Update the **ContentView** view with the code in Listing 7-43. You should see the interface illustrated in Figure 7-34. Update the **ContentView** view again with the code in Listing 7-44. Now you should see the interface illustrated in Figure 7-35.

(Basic) 7.3 Tables

List views were designed for the small screen of mobile devices like iPhones and Apple Watches. iPads and Macs have a larger screen and therefore more space to display content. If we only need one column of values, we can use a **List** view, as we have done so far, but to present more columns SwiftUI includes the **Table** view.

▷ **Table(Data, selection:** Binding, **sortOrder:** Binding, **columns:** Closure)— This initializer creates a **Table** view with the configuration specified by the arguments. The first argument is the data used to fill the table, the **selection** argument is a binding value with the identifiers of the selected rows, the **sortOrder** argument is a binding value with the sort descriptors used to sort the values on the table, and the **columns** argument provides the views to create the columns.

▷ **Table(of:** Type, **selection:** Binding, **sortOrder:** Binding, **columns:** Closure, **rows:** Closure)—This initializer creates a **Table** view with the configuration specified by the arguments. The first argument is a reference to the data type of the data we want to show, the **selection** argument is a binding value with the identifiers of the selected rows, the **sortOrder** argument is a binding value with the sort descriptors used to sort the values on the table, the **columns** argument provides the views to create the columns, and the **rows** argument provides the views to create the rows.

The columns are defined by the **TableColumn** view.

▷ **TableColumn(String, value:** KeyPath, **content:** Closure)—This initializer defines a column for a table. The first argument specifies the column's title, the **value** argument is a key path to the property that provides the values for the column, and the **content** argument defines the views to display by the column.

▷ **TableRow(Value)**—This initializer defines the rows of a table. The argument provides the value of a row for each column of the table.

By default, the columns are flexible, which means that the width is determined by the number of columns in the table and the space available, but the **TableColumn** structure includes the following modifiers to specify a custom width.

- ▹ **width(CGFloat?)**—This modifier defines a fixed width for the column.
- ▹ **width(min:** CGFloat?, **ideal:** CGFloat?, **max:** CGFloat?)—This modifier defines a flexible column but with constraints.

As always, we need a model with some data to test the app. The following includes a structure with a few properties to provide the values for the columns, an observable property to provide the values to the views, and some data for testing.

```
import SwiftUI
import Observation
struct ConsumableItem: Identifiable {
   let id = UUID()
   var name: String
   var category: String
   var calories: Int
   var included: Bool
}
@Observable class ApplicationData: @unchecked Sendable {
   var listOfItems: [ConsumableItem] = []

   static let shared: ApplicationData = ApplicationData()
   private init() {
      listOfItems = [
         ConsumableItem(name: "Bagels", category: "Baked", calories: 250,
included: false),
         ConsumableItem(name: "Brownies", category: "Baked", calories:
466, included: false),
         ConsumableItem(name: "Butter", category: "Dairy", calories: 717,
included: false),
         ConsumableItem(name: "Cheese", category: "Dairy", calories: 402,
included: false),
         ConsumableItem(name: "Juice", category: "Beverages", calories:
23, included: false),
         ConsumableItem(name: "Lemonade", category: "Beverages",
calories: 40, included: false)
      ]
   }
}
```

Listing 7-45: Defining a model to test tables

The `Table` structure includes multiple initializers, each one with a different combination of arguments, so we can only implement those we need. Something similar happens with the `TableColumn` view. For instance, if the value presented by the column is a string, we can just specify the key path for the property and the view takes cares of creating the `Text` view to show the value. If not, we must provide a closure to the **content** argument, format the value, and create the view we want to use to show it.

The following example shows a possible implementation. The `Table` view is defined only with the data source (the `listOfItems` property) and a closure to create the columns. Some columns use a key path to provide the value and the last one a closure with a `Text` view.

```
struct ContentView: View {
   @Environment(ApplicationData.self) private var appData

   var body: some View {
      Table(appData.listOfItems) {
         TableColumn("Name", value: \.name)
         TableColumn("Category", value: \.category)
         TableColumn("Calories") { item in
            Text("\(item.calories)")
```

```
            }.width(100)
        }
    }
}
```

Listing 7-46: Creating a table with multiple columns

In this example, the first and second columns access the values of the `name` and `category` properties with key paths, but we use a closure for the `calories` property because its value is an integer that we must convert into a string.

This example assigns a width of 100 points to the Calories column with the `width()` modifier and keeps the rest of the columns flexible. On iPads and Macs, the system creates the Calories column with a size of 100 points and distributes the rest of the space between the first two columns, while on iPhones only the first column is displayed.

iPad **iPhone**

Figure 7-36: Table in iPads and iPhones

 Do It Yourself: Create a Multiplatform project. Create a Swift file called ApplicationData.swift for the model in Listing 7-45 and update the `ContentView` view with the code in Listing 7-46. Remember to inject an instance of the `ApplicationData` class into the environment and the preview, as we did in Listing 7-4. Run the application on the iPad simulator or the Mac (My Mac). You should see a table with three columns, as shown in Figure 7-36, left. Run the application again on the iPhone simulator. You should see only one column, as illustrated in Figure 7-36, right.

The `Table` view creates the columns from the `TableColumn` views provided by the closure and the rows from the values in the model, but we can also define the rows manually. This is useful when we want to insert static rows into the table. For this purpose, we must implement the initializer that allows us to provide the **of** and **rows** arguments. The **of** argument tells the table the data type of the values we want to display, and the **rows** argument provides the values for the rows, as shown below.

```
struct ContentView: View {
    @Environment(ApplicationData.self) private var appData

    var body: some View {
        Table(of: ConsumableItem.self, columns: {
            TableColumn("Name", value: \.name)
            TableColumn("Category", value: \.category)
            TableColumn("Calories") { item in
                Text("\(item.calories)")
            }.width(100)
        }, rows: {
            TableRow(ConsumableItem(name: "STANDARD", category: "",
calories: 0, included: false))
```

```
        ForEach(appData.listOfItems)
    })
  }
}
```

Listing 7-47: *Defining the rows manually*

In this example, a row with the text "STANDARD" is defined manually at the top and the remaining rows are generated with a `ForEach` loop from the values in the model.

Figure 7-37: *Static rows*

On iPads and Macs, tables include a feature that allows the user to sort the items by tapping or clicking on the column's title. For instance, if we tap on the header of the Name column in our example, the items will be sorted by name. The feature is added to the table when we include the **sortOrder** argument in the initializer. The argument takes a binding property with an array of values that determine the properties which values we want to sort. Foundation defines the `KeyPathComparator` structure for this purpose.

▷ **KeyPathComparator(**KeyPath, **order:** SortOrder**)**—This initializer defines a sort comparator for a property. The first argument is the key path of the property whose values we want to sort, and the **order** argument determines if the items will be sorted in ascending or descending order. It is an enumeration with the values `forward` and `reverse`.

The `KeyPathComparator` structure determines the values to sort, but we are responsible for sorting the values in the model. For this purpose, the Swift Standard Library includes the following method.

▷ **sorted(using:** Comparator**)**—This method returns a collection with the items sorted according to the sort comparator provided by the **using** argument.

The following example defines an array of `KeyPathComparator` structures to sort the items in the model by name and calories, and implements a computed property to sort the values in place, so every time the model is updated, the view is recreated, and the values are sorted again.

```
struct ContentView: View {
    @Environment(ApplicationData.self) private var appData
    @State private var sort = [KeyPathComparator(\ConsumableItem.name),
KeyPathComparator(\ConsumableItem.calories)]

    var sortedItems: [ConsumableItem] {
        let list = appData.listOfItems.sorted(using: sort)
        return list
    }
    var body: some View {
```

```
    Table(sortedItems, sortOrder: $sort) {
        TableColumn("Name", value: \.name)
        TableColumn("Category", value: \.category)
        TableColumn("Calories", value: \.calories) { item in
            Text("\(item.calories)")
        }.width(100)
    }
  }
}
```

Listing 7-48: Sorting the values by column

Table views require the sort comparators to be stored in a binding property so they can select which one to use according to the action performed by the user. In this example, we define a **@State** property with two sort comparators to allow the user to sort the items by name and calories. Next, we define a computed property called **sortedItems** that sorts the items according to these sort comparators and returns the list of values for the view.

Note that we have added a key path to the Calories column. The value is produced by the closure, but the key path is still required to tell the table which column to sort.

Do It Yourself: Update the **ContentView** view with the code in Listing 7-48. Run the application on the iPad simulator or the Mac (My Mac). Click on the header of the Name and Calories columns. You should see the items sorted by name or calories, respectively.

Tables also allow the user to select one or multiple rows. The process is the same used before for **List** views. We must provide a binding property to store the identifiers of the items selected by the user and assign that property to the table. For single selection, everything works out of the box, but iPads without a keyboard require the edit mode to be enabled. In the following example, we include an **EditButton** view to allow the user to enable this mode and also a **Text** view below to show the names of the items selected by the user.

```
struct ContentView: View {
    @Environment(ApplicationData.self) private var appData
    @State private var selectedItems: Set<ConsumableItem.ID> = []

    var body: some View {
        VStack {
            EditButton()
            Table(appData.listOfItems, selection: $selectedItems) {
                TableColumn("Name", value: \.name)
                TableColumn("Category", value: \.category)
                TableColumn("Calories") { item in
                    Text("\(item.calories)")
                }.width(100)
            }
            Text(listSelected())
                .padding()
        }
    }
    func listSelected() -> String {
        let list: [String] = selectedItems.map({ id in
            let item = appData.listOfItems.first(where: { $0.id == id })
            return item?.name ?? ""
        })
        return String(list.sorted().joined(separator: " "))
    }
}
```

Listing 7-49: Allowing the user to select items in a table

If we want to select just one item, we can tap on it, but selecting multiple items is only available if we have a keyboard or press the button created by the `EditButton` view. To show the names of the selected items, we created a method that maps the identifiers, gets the items from the `listOfItems` array, returns the value of the `name` property, and then sorts and joins the values to create a string with all the names.

In this example, we display the selected names on the screen, but of course we can add buttons to the interface to process the values as needed. A useful tool provided by tables for this purpose are context menus. With context menus, the user can right-click a selected row or rows and perform an action. SwiftUI includes the following modifier to create the menu.

▷ **contextMenu(forSelectionType:** Type, **menu:** Closure)—This modifier assigns a context menu to an item or multiple items of a view. The **forSelectionType** argument specifies the data type of the values we want to associate with the menu, and the **menu** argument provides the options for the menu.

The closure assigned to the **menu** argument receives a copy of the set with the values selected by the user. By checking these values, we can configure the menu with options for when the user right-clicks on a single row, on multiple selected rows, or the table's empty area. All we need to do to configure the menu is to count how many items are in the array, as shown below.

```
struct ContentView: View {
    @Environment(ApplicationData.self) private var appData
    @State private var selectedItems: Set<ConsumableItem.ID> = []

    var body: some View {
        Table(appData.listOfItems, selection: $selectedItems) {
            TableColumn("Name", value: \.name)
            TableColumn("Category", value: \.category)
            TableColumn("Calories") { item in
                Text("\(item.calories)")
            }.width(100)
        }
        .contextMenu(forSelectionType: ConsumableItem.ID.self, menu:
{ selected in
            if selected.count <= 0  {
                Button("Create New Item") {
                    let newItem = ConsumableItem(name: "Test", category:
"Test", calories: 0, included: false)
                    appData.listOfItems.append(newItem)
                }
            } else if selected.count == 1 {
                Button("Remove Item") {
                    appData.listOfItems.removeAll(where: { item in
                        item.id == selected.first
                    })
                }
            } else {
                Button("Remove Selected Items") {
                    appData.listOfItems.removeAll(where: { item in
                        selected.contains(item.id)
                    })
                }
            }
        })
    }
}
```

Listing 7-50: Using a context menu to process a row

If there are no items in the set, which means that the user right-clicked on an empty area of the table, we show a button to add a new item to the model. If there is only one item in the set, we offer a button to remove the value from the model, and if there are multiple items, the option removes them all. The context menu is created by the same `contextMenu()` modifier, but it adapts based on where the user right-clicks (taps and holds on iPads).

 Do It Yourself: Update the `ContentView` view with the code in Listing 7-50. Run the application on the iPad simulator or the Mac (My Mac). Right click on a row (Click and hold on the iPad simulator). Select the "Remove Item" option. The item should be removed. Select two or more rows and repeat the process to remove them. Do the same but in the table's empty area below and select the option "Create New Item". You should see a new item with the name "Test" at the bottom of the list. In this example, we always add the same item with the name "Test". Later we will learn how to open additional views to allow the user to insert custom values.

In addition to `Text` views, tables can show other views, from images to control views. For instance, we can include a `Toggle` view, which is presented as a checkbox on the Mac, to allow the user to check or uncheck the items.

```
struct ContentView: View {
    @Environment(ApplicationData.self) private var appData

    var body: some View {
        Table(appData.listOfItems) {
            TableColumn("Name", value: \.name)
            TableColumn("Category", value: \.category)
            TableColumn("Calories") { item in
                Text("\(item.calories)")
            }.width(100)
            TableColumn("Included") { item in
                Toggle("", isOn: itemBinding(id: item.id).included)
                    .labelsHidden()
            }.width(100)
        }
    }
    func itemBinding(id: UUID) -> Binding<ConsumableItem> {
        @Bindable var appData = appData

        let index = appData.listOfItems.firstIndex(where: { $0.id ==
id }) ?? 0
        return $appData.listOfItems[index]
    }
}
```

Listing 7-51: Defining the content of a column with a `Toggle` view

The `Toggle` view needs a bidirectional binding value to read and store the current value. The easiest way to provide this value is with a method. We call the method with the item's id, use this identifier to get the index of the item in the array, and return the item as a `Binding` value of type `ConsumableItem`. This creates the bidirectional connection between the `Toggle` view and the `ConsumableItem` structure, so every time the user clicks on the switch or the checkbox, the new value is stored directly into the item's `included` property.

Figure 7-38: *Column of* `Toggle` *views*

The `KeyPathComparator` structure implemented before to sort the values conforms to the `SortComparator` protocol. This protocol defines the tools required to sort the values. The sort comparator implemented by this structure can compare and sort values of common data types like `String` and `Int` values, but it cannot sort custom data types or special values like Booleans. For instance, if we want to sort the Included column from our previous example, we must define our own `SortComparator` structure and implement the following property and method required by the protocol.

▷ **order**—This property defines the order of the values. It is a **SortOrder** enumeration with the values **forward** and **reverse**.

▷ **compare(lhs:** Value, **rhs:** Value)—This method compares two values at a time and returns an enumeration value of type **ComparisonResult** to determine the order. The values available are **orderedAscending**, **orderedDescending**, and **orderedSame**.

In addition, we need to define a typealias with the name `Compared` of the data type of the values we want to compare, as shown below.

```
struct CompareBool: SortComparator {
    typealias Compared = Bool
    var order: SortOrder = .forward

    func compare(_ lhs: Bool, _ rhs: Bool) -> ComparisonResult {
        if lhs && !rhs {
            return order
== .forward ? .orderedAscending : .orderedDescending
        } else if !lhs && rhs {
            return order
== .forward ? .orderedDescending : .orderedAscending
        } else {
            return .orderedSame
        }
    }
}
```

Listing 7-52: *Defining a custom sort comparator*

The `order` property determines the order of the values (ascending or descending). In this example, we provide an initial value, but the property is updated every time the user clicks on the column's header. In the `compare()` method, we compare the values received by the method and return a `ComparisonResult` value depending on the value of that property. We return `orderedAscending`, if the property is equal to `forward`, the first value is `true`, and the second value `false`. On the other hand, if the value of the `order` property is `reverse`, the value returned is `orderedDescending`. And we do the opposite if the values receive by the method are inverted (`false` for the first one, and `true` for the second one). This shows the On switches at the top and the Off switches at the bottom (or vice versa, depending on the order selected by the user).

Now that we have a comparator for Boolean values, we must apply it to the table. The `TableColumn` view includes the following initializer to apply a custom sort comparator.

▷ **TableColumn(**String, **value:** KeyPath, **comparator:** StandardComparator, **content:** Closure**)**—This initializer defines a column for a table. The first argument specifies the column's title, the **value** argument is the key path of the property that provides the values for the column, the comparator is a custom **SortComparator** structure to sort the values, and the **content** argument defines the views to display by the column.

This initializer is applied as the previous ones, with the difference that now we must include an instance of our `CompareBool` structure to tell the table how to sort the values.

```
struct ContentView: View {
    @Environment(ApplicationData.self) private var appData
    @State private var sort = [KeyPathComparator(\ConsumableItem.name)]

    var sortedItems: [ConsumableItem] {
        let list = appData.listOfItems.sorted(using: sort)
        return list
    }
    var body: some View {
        Table(sortedItems, sortOrder: $sort) {
            TableColumn("Name", value: \.name)
            TableColumn("Category", value: \.category)
            TableColumn("Calories") { item in
                Text("\(item.calories)")
            }.width(100)
            TableColumn("Included", value: \.included, comparator:
CompareBool()) { item in
                Toggle("", isOn: itemBinding(id: item.id).included)
                    .labelsHidden()
            }.width(100)
        }
    }
    func itemBinding(id: UUID) -> Binding<ConsumableItem> {
        @Bindable var appData = appData

        let index = appData.listOfItems.firstIndex(where: { $0.id ==
id }) ?? 0
        return $appData.listOfItems[index]
    }
}
```

Listing 7-53: Sorting Boolean values on a table

 Do It Yourself: Add the structure in Listing 7-52 to the ApplicationData.swift file. Update the ContentView.swift file with the code in Listing 7-53. Run the application and turn some of the switches on. Click on the column's title. You should see the items sorted by the condition of the switches.

Tables can also display data in a hierarchical structure and reveal the information as needed. For this purpose, SwiftUI provides the following view.

▷ **DisclosureTableRow(**Value, **isExpanded:** Binding?, **content:** Closure**)**—This initializer creates a view that displays rows containing other rows in a hierarchical structure. The first argument is the value containing the data for the rows, the **isExpanded** argument is a binding property that allows the rows to be expanded or collapsed programmatically, and the **content** argument is the closure that provides the rows to be displayed when the main row is expanded.

The purpose of the `DisclosureTableRow` view is to disclose rows that represent the same data but belong to a different hierarchy. For example, if we have a list of employees, some of whom are managers and some subordinates, we can use a `DisclosureTableRow` view to show the subordinate employees only when needed. The following is the model for this example.

```
import SwiftUI
import Observation

struct Employees: Identifiable {
   let id = UUID()
   var name: String
   var position: String
   var subordinates: [Employees]
}
@Observable class ApplicationData: @unchecked Sendable {
   var listOfEmployees: [Employees] = []

   static let shared: ApplicationData = ApplicationData()
   private init() {
      let employee1 = Employees(name: "Sander", position: "Subordinate",
subordinates: [])
      let employee2 = Employees(name: "Annie", position: "Subordinate",
subordinates: [])
      let employee3 = Employees(name: "Charlie", position: "Subordinate",
subordinates: [])
      let employee4 = Employees(name: "Sebastian", position:
"Subordinate", subordinates: [])
      let employee5 = Employees(name: "Bill", position: "Subordinate",
subordinates: [])

      listOfEmployees.append(Employees(name: "Robert", position:
"Manager", subordinates: [employee1, employee2, employee3]))
      listOfEmployees.append(Employees(name: "Anna", position: "Manager",
subordinates: [employee4, employee5]))
   }
}
```

Listing 7-54: Defining a model with hierarchical data

This model defines the `Employees` structure to store the information about each employee in the company. The structure includes a property called `subordinates` to store the list of employees who are under the supervision of a manager. For testing purposes, we have created five employees who are subordinates to two managers. To display this information, we need to create the rows manually, as shown below.

```
struct ContentView: View {
   @Environment(ApplicationData.self) private var appData

   var body: some View {
      Table(of: Employees.self, columns: {
         TableColumn("Name", value: \.name)
         TableColumn("Position ", value: \.position)
      }, rows: {
         ForEach(appData.listOfEmployees) { employee in
            if employee.subordinates.isEmpty {
               TableRow(employee)
            } else {
               DisclosureTableRow(employee) {
                  ForEach(employee.subordinates)
               }
            }
         }
      })
```

```
            }
        }
```

Listing 7-55: Disclosing hierarchical data

In this example, we have a `ForEach` loop that goes through each employee in the `listOfEmployees` array and then determines whether or not the employee is a manager by checking the number of subordinates. If the `subordinates` property is empty, we show the employee's data, otherwise a `DisclosureTableRow` view is created to list the subordinates.

Figure 7-39: Hierarchical data

 Do It Yourself: Create a Multiplatform project. Create a Swift file called ApplicationData.swift for the model in Listing 7-54. Update the `ContentView` view with the code in Listing 7-55. Remember to inject an instance of the `ApplicationData` class into the environment and the preview, as we did in Listing 7-4. Click on each manager's row to disclose the subordinates.

Basic 7.4 Pickers

SwiftUI also provides pickers to present lists of values. A picker can show the values in a graphic that simulates a wheel, in a list, or as a series of buttons, depending on the platform and the configuration. The framework includes two views for this purpose, one to create a general-purpose list, and another to generate a list of dates and times.

Basic Picker View

The `Picker` view creates a general-purpose picker to show a list of values. The structure includes the following initializer.

> **Picker(**String, **selection:** Binding, **content:** Closure**)**—This initializer creates a `Picker` view with the label defined by the first argument. The **selection** argument is a binding property that stores the value selected by the user, and the closure assigned to the **content** argument provides the list of views required to present the values.

A `Picker` view needs a binding property to store the value currently selected by the user and a list of views to present the values available. The list of views can be created manually, one view per line, or dynamically with a `ForEach` view, as in the following example.

```
struct ContentView: View {
   @State private var selectedValue: String = "No Value"
   let listCities: [String] = ["Paris", "Toronto", "Dublin"]

   var body: some View {
      VStack {
```

```
        Text(selectedValue)
        Picker("Cities:", selection: $selectedValue) {
            ForEach(listCities, id: \.self) { value in
                Text(value)
            }
        }
        Spacer()
    }.padding()
    }
}
```

Listing 7-56: *Defining a picker*

By default, the picker is shown with a style of type `menu`. This creates a drop down menu on the Mac, and a button that opens a context menu when tapped in mobile devices. The label is not included on mobile devices at the moment, so if we test the application on an iPhone or iPad simulator, only the content of the picker is shown on the screen.

Figure 7-40: *Menu picker*

The value of the binding property is used to store the value selected by the user and also to initialize the picker. If the property contains a value, and the value is available in the model, the picker is shown with that value selected. There are several ways to provide this initial value. For instance, we can assign it to the `@State` property when the property is declared, or we can select it later when the views appear with the `onAppear()` modifier, as shown below.

```
struct ContentView: View {
    @State private var selectedValue: String = "No Value"
    let listCities: [String] = ["Paris", "Toronto", "Dublin"]

    var body: some View {
        VStack {
            Text(selectedValue)
            Picker("Cities:", selection: $selectedValue) {
                ForEach(listCities, id: \.self) { value in
                    Text(value)
                }
            }
            Spacer()
        }.padding()
        .onAppear {
            selectedValue = listCities[1]
        }
    }
}
```

Listing 7-57: *Selecting an initial value*

In this example, we initialize the **selectedValue** property with the second value in the **listCities** array and therefore this is the initial value selected by the **Picker** view.

Do It Yourself: Create a Multiplatform project. Update the `ContentView` view with the code in Listing 7-56. Press the button. You should see a context menu, as shown in Figure 7-40. Update the view with the code in Listing 7-57. Press the button again. You should see a context menu with the Toronto option already selected.

The picker identifies the items by the value displayed to the user (in our example, the name of the cities). If we want to use a different value to identify each view, we can specify it with the `tag()` modifier.

▷ **tag(**Value**)**—This modifier assigns an identifier to the view. The argument is a `Hashable` value, usually defined with an integer.

For example, we can use the indexes of the array instead of the values. When the user selects an item, we get the name of the city and display it on the screen. For this purpose, we can use the `indices` property provided by the Swift Standard Library to return a `Range` value with the indexes of a collection.

```
struct ContentView: View {
    @State private var selectedValue: Int = 0
    let listCities: [String] = ["Paris", "Toronto", "Dublin"]

    var body: some View {
        VStack {
            Text(listCities[selectedValue])
            Picker("Cities:", selection: $selectedValue) {
                ForEach(listCities.indices, id: \.self) { value in
                    Text(listCities[value])
                        .tag(value)
                }
            }
            Spacer()
        }.padding()
    }
}
```

Listing 7-58: Listing values by index

Because we are now working with the indexes of the array instead of the values, we define the `selectedValue` property of type `Int`. To get the index of each value, we define the `ForEach` view with the `Range` returned by the `indices` property of the `listCities` array, and then assign the index to each value with the `tag()` modifier. When a value is selected, the picker assigns the value of the `tag()` modifier to the `selectedValue` property, and therefore we can use this property to get the name of the city from the array.

 Do It Yourself: Update the `ContentView` view with the code in Listing 7-58. The application should work as before, but now the values processed by the picker are integers instead of strings.

The `Picker` view adopts a design according to the device and the conditions in which it is presented, but we can force the picker to adopt the design we want with the following modifier.

▷ **pickerStyle(**Style**)**—This modifier sets the style of the picker. The argument is a structure that conforms to the `PickerStyle` protocol. The system defines a few structures with predefined styles. To declare these values, the structures include the type properties `automatic`, `menu`, `segmented`, and `wheel`.

The `automatic` style allows the picker to adapt the design to the device and conditions, and the `menu` style creates a context menu, as we have seen in the previous examples. But there are two additional styles. The **wheel** style displays the values in a virtual wheel the user can rotate to make a pick, and the **segmented** style defines a unique picker where the values are turned into buttons. The latter is frequently used to allow the user to select a value from a limited set of options, as illustrated by the following example.

```
struct ContentView: View {
   @State private var selectedValue: String = "No Value"
   let listCities: [String] = ["Paris", "Toronto", "Dublin"]

   var body: some View {
      VStack {
         Text(selectedValue)
         Picker("Cities:", selection: $selectedValue) {
            ForEach(listCities, id: \.self) { value in
               Text(value)
            }
         }.pickerStyle(.segmented)
         Spacer()
      }.padding()
   }
}
```

Listing 7-59: *Implementing a segmented picker*

The implementation of the picker is the same, but by applying a custom style we change the way the values are presented to the user. Below are the pickers we see when the style is set to **wheel** or **segmented**.

Figure 7-41: *Wheel and segmented pickers*

 Do It Yourself: Update the **ContentView** view with the code in Listing 7-59. You should be able to click on the buttons to select a different city. Assign the **wheel** value to the **pickerStyle()** modifier. You should be able to drag a wheel up or down to select a value.

(Basic) **Date Picker**

SwiftUI includes two picker views designed to simplify the creation of pickers that allow the user to select a date or a time: **DatePicker** for a single date and **MultiDatePicker** for multiple dates. The following are the most frequently used initializers.

▷ **DatePicker(**String, **selection:** Binding, **in:** Range, **displayedComponents:** Components**)**—This initializer creates a **DatePicker** view with the label defined by the first argument. The **selection** argument is a binding property of type **Date** that stores the date selected by the user, the **in** argument defines the range of dates the user can choose from, and the **displayComponents** argument is a structure of type **DatePickerComponents** that defines the type of values managed by the picker. The structure includes two type properties for this purpose: **date** and **hourAndMinute**.

▷ **MultiDatePicker(**String, **selection:** Binding, **in:** Range**)**—This initializer creates a **MultiDatePicker** view with the label defined by the first argument. The **selection** argument is a binding property to a set of **DateComponents** values with the dates selected by the user, and the **in** argument defines the range of dates the user can choose from.

To define a **DatePicker** view, we must provide a binding property to store the value selected by the user and tell the picker the type of values we want to show. If we want to allow the user to select dates, we must specify the **date** value for the **displayedComponents** argument. For times, it is the **time** value. But if we want the user to be able to select both, we must ignore the argument altogether, as we do in the following example.

```
struct ContentView: View {
   @State private var selectedDate: Date = Date()

   var body: some View {
      VStack {
         DatePicker("Date:", selection: $selectedDate)
         Spacer()
      }.padding()
   }
}
```

Listing 7-60: *Defining a* DatePicker *to select a date*

The **@State** property used to store the selected value was initialized with the current date (**Date()**) and therefore the picker shows it as the selected date and time, but we can initialize this value with any date we want. The picker is presented with the style by default, which in mobile devices shows buttons to open a calendar to select the date and a spinning wheel to select the time.

Figure 7-42: *Picker for dates*

 Do It Yourself: Update the **ContentView** view with the code in Listing 7-60. You should see the interface in Figure 7-42, left. Add the **displayComponents** argument to the **DatePicker** view initializer with the value **date** or **hourandminute** to allow users to select only dates or times. You can also include the **labelsHidden()** modifier to remove the label.

By default, the **DatePicker** view presents a list with all the dates from a distant date in the past to a distant date in the future. To limit the list of values the user can select from, we must provide a range of dates. The range can be closed (from one date to another), or open. The following example shows a list of dates from the current date to a distant date in the future using an open range.

```
struct ContentView: View {
   @State private var selectedDate: Date = Date()

   var body: some View {
      VStack {
         DatePicker("Date:", selection: $selectedDate, in: Date()...,
displayedComponents: .date)
         Spacer()
```

```
      }.padding()
   }
}
```

Listing 7-61: Limiting the `DatePicker` *to a range of values*

In this example, we limit the picker with a range of dates (`Date()...`) and therefore the user is not allowed to select a date before the current date. A range `...Date()` does the opposite, it only allows the user to select a date from the past. But we can also provide specific dates by creating custom `Date` structures, as we did in Chapter 4 (see Listing 4-24).

A `DatePicker` view adopts a design according to the device and the conditions in which it is presented, but it includes the following modifier to specify the style we want.

▷ **datePickerStyle(**Style**)**—This modifier sets the style of the picker. The argument is a structure that conforms to the **DatePickerStyle** protocol. To provide standard styles, the system defines a few structures with the type properties **automatic**, **compact**, **graphical**, and **wheel**.

By default, the **DatePicker** view is configured with the **compact** style, which shows a button the user must press to reveal a calendar to select a date or a spinning wheel to select a time. But we can also show the calendar right away with the **graphical** style, or a spinning wheel with the **wheel** style, as we do in the following example.

```
struct ContentView: View {
    @State private var selectedDate: Date = Date()

    var body: some View {
        VStack {
            Text("Date: \(selectedDate.formatted(.dateTime.day().month()))")
            DatePicker("Date:", selection: $selectedDate,
displayedComponents: .date)
                .labelsHidden()
                .datePickerStyle(.wheel)
            Spacer()
        }.padding()
    }
}
```

Listing 7-62: Presenting a picker with a spinning wheel

In addition to assigning the wheel style to the picker, the view in Listing 7-62 also includes a **Text** view to show the day and month selected by the user. The result is shown below.

Figure 7-43: Wheel picker

To allow the user to select multiple dates, we must create the picker with a **MultiDatePicker** view and a binding property that stores a set of **DateComponents** values.

```
struct ContentView: View {
    @State private var selectedDates: Set<DateComponents> = []
    @State private var mydates: String = ""

    var body: some View {
        VStack {
            MultiDatePicker("Dates:", selection: $selectedDates)
            Spacer()
            Text(mydates)
        }.padding()
        .onChange(of: selectedDates, initial: false) { old, values in
            let days = values.map({ value in String(value.day!) })
            mydates = days.joined(separator: ",")
        }
    }
}
```

Listing 7-63: Picking multiple dates

A **MultiDatePicker** view works like the **DatePicker** view, but the selected values are stored in an array. In this example, we apply the **onChange()** modifier to show the days selected by the user in a **Text** view at the bottom of the screen.

Figure 7-44: Multiple date picker

 Do It Yourself: Update the **ContentView** view with the code in Listing 7-63. Run the application on the iPhone simulator and select a few dates. You should see the days displayed at the bottom (Figure 7-44).

(Basic) **7.5 Forms**

Most applications include views with a list of options users can select to set the configuration of the app, the style of the interface, or the type of information they want to see. We can create these screens with a list of controls in a **VStack**, as we have done before, but SwiftUI provides a view specifically designed for this purpose called **Form**.

(Basic) **Form View**

A **Form** view is a container that organizes the views in a list, like the **List** view, but adapts the controls to the device and the platform in which the app is running. Creating a form in SwiftUI is easy, we just have to include the controls one after another inside the **Form** view.

```
struct ContentView: View {
    @State private var setActive: Bool = false
    @State private var setShowPictures: Bool = false
    @State private var setTotal: Int = 10

    var body: some View {
        Form {
```

```
            Toggle("Active", isOn: $setActive)
            Toggle("Show Pictures", isOn: $setShowPictures)
            HStack {
                Text("Total")
                Spacer()
                Text(String(setTotal))
                Stepper("", value: $setTotal, in: 0...10)
                    .labelsHidden()
            }
        }
    }
}
```

Listing 7-64: Defining a form

The **Form** view adds padding on the sides of the controls and presents the list with a **grouped** style.

Figure 7-45: Simple form

Most views allow us to specify a string that the **Form** view can use to create the label for the control, but in some cases, we may need to hide the label and specify our own, as we did for the **Stepper** view in the previous example. To create custom labels, SwiftUI includes the **LabeledContent** view. This view attaches a label to another view. The following is the most frequently used initializer.

▷ **LabeledContent**(String, **content:** Closure)—This initializer attaches a label to a view. The first argument specifies the label and the **content** argument provides the views.

With this view, we can better organize our previous example and provide a custom label for the **Stepper** view.

```
struct ContentView: View {
    @State private var setActive: Bool = false
    @State private var setShowPictures: Bool = false
    @State private var setTotal: Int = 10

    var body: some View {
        Form {
            Toggle("Active", isOn: $setActive)
            Toggle("Show Pictures", isOn: $setShowPictures)
            LabeledContent("Total") {
                Text(String(setTotal))
                Stepper("", value: $setTotal, in: 0...10)
                    .labelsHidden()
            }
        }
    }
}
```

Listing 7-65: Defining a custom label for a form

A **Form** view works like a **List** view, so we can separate the content in sections.

```
struct ContentView: View {
    @State private var setActive: Bool = false
    @State private var setShowPictures: Bool = false
    @State private var setTotal: Int = 10

    var body: some View {
        Form {
            Section(header: Text("Options"), footer: Text("Activate the
options you want to see")) {
                Toggle("Active", isOn: $setActive)
                Toggle("Show Pictures", isOn: $setShowPictures)
            }
            Section(header: Text("Values"), footer: Text("Insert the number
of items to display")) {
                LabeledContent("Total") {
                    Text(String(setTotal))
                    Stepper("", value: $setTotal, in: 0...10)
                        .labelsHidden()
                }
            }
        }
    }
}
```

Listing 7-66: Styling a form

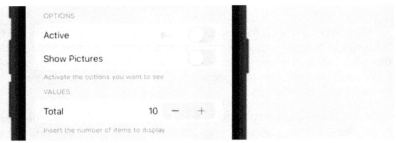

Figure 7-46: Form with a standard design

 Do It Yourself: Create a Multiplatform project. Update the **ContentView** view with the code in Listing 7-66. You should see the interface in Figure 7-46. Add controls to the **Form** view and create more sections to see how they look like.

 IMPORTANT: In these examples, we have stored the values locally with **@State** properties. This means that the values inserted by the user are going to be available only for this view. To make them available to the rest of the app, we must store them in the model with observable properties, or send them to other views, as we will see in the next chapter.

(Basic) Disclosure Group

Some forms are extensive and hard to read. SwiftUI includes the **DisclosureGroup** view to expand and collapse controls to make it easy for the user to work with them. This is similar to the **OutlineGroup** view implemented before to create hierarchical lists, but the **DisclosureGroup** view works with non hierarchical information, such as the one we find in a form.

▷ **DisclosureGroup(**String, **isExpanded:** Binding, **content:** Closure**)**—This initializer creates a **DisclosureGroup** view to hide or show content. The first argument is the view's label, the **isExpanded** argument is a binding property of type **Bool** that determines whether the view is expanded or collapsed, and the **content** argument is the closure that provides the views we want to show or hide.

With this view, we can organize the two sections of our form in expandable lists.

```
struct ContentView: View {
    @State private var setActive: Bool = false
    @State private var setShowPictures: Bool = false
    @State private var setTotal: Int = 10
    var body: some View {
        Form {
            DisclosureGroup("Controls") {
                Toggle("Active", isOn: $setActive)
                Toggle("Show Pictures", isOn: $setShowPictures)
            }
            DisclosureGroup("Values") {
                HStack {
                    Text("Total")
                    Spacer()
                    Text(String(setTotal))
                    Stepper("", value: $setTotal, in: 0...10)
                        .labelsHidden()
                }
            }
        }
    }
}
```

Listing 7-67: Disclosing controls

When the views are collapsed, all we see is the view's label. If we tap on these labels or the disclosure indicator, the content is expanded and we can interact with the controls.

Figure 7-47: Disclosure groups

Medium 7.6 Custom Containers

In addition to the predefined containers we have seen so far, we can also create our own. With custom containers, we can change the design of the views and also dynamically adapt it to the state of the app. To create a custom container, we need to define a structure that conforms to the View protocol, include a @ViewBuilder property to store and construct the views inside the container, and then read and design the views with a ForEach or a Group view. For this purpose, the ForEach and Group views include the following initializers.

▷ **ForEach(subviews:** Views, **content:** Closure)—This initializer creates a ForEach view that can iterate over the views constructed by a @ViewBuilder property wrapper. The **subviews** argument is the @ViewBuilder property that provides the views, and the **content** argument is the closure used to process the views.

▷ **Group(subviews:** Views, **transform:** Closure)—This initializer creates a group of views from the views constructed by a @ViewBuilder property wrapper. The **subviews** argument is the @ViewBuilder property that provides the views, and the **content** argument is the closure used to process the views.

The structure that defines the custom container must be generic to be able to process any type of views. In the following example, we define a structure for a custom container that creates a simple list of vertical views.

```
import SwiftUI
struct BoxListView<Content: View>: View {
    @ViewBuilder var content: Content

    var body: some View {
        VStack {
            ForEach(subviews: content) { subview in
                HStack {
                    subview
                        .padding()
                }
                .frame(minWidth: 0, maxWidth: .infinity)
                .border(.red, width: 5)
                .padding(5)
            }
        }
    }
}
#Preview {
    BoxListView {
        Text("Test")
    }
}
```

Listing 7-68: Defining a custom container

The **BoxListView** view takes a list of views and then implements a **ForEach** view to process and style the views. Now we can use this container in our interface, as shown below.

```
struct ContentView: View {
    var body: some View {
        BoxListView {
            Text("First")
            Text("Second")
            Text("Third")
        }
    }
}
```

Listing 7-69: Implementing a custom container

In this example, we include three **Text** views, but we can also use a normal **ForEach** view to define the views from a collection of data, as we did before with **List** views.

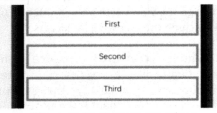

Figure 7-48: Custom container

 Do It Yourself: Create a Multiplatform project. Create a Swift file called BoxListView.swift for the custom container in Listing 7-68. Update the **ContentView** view with the code in Listing 7-69. Select an iPhone simulator. You should see a list of views, as shown in Figure 7-48.

Chapter 7 - Lists

The **BoxListView** container processes the views one by one and always assigns the same style to each one of them, but there are ways to select a different design depending on the situation. One alternative is to use a **Group** view. This view creates a collection with the views in the container, so we can process them any way we want, as shown below.

```
struct BoxListView<Content: View>: View {
   @ViewBuilder var content: Content

   var body: some View {
      VStack {
         Group(subviews: content) { subviews in
            let color = subviews.count > 2 ? Color.red : Color.blue
            ForEach(subviews) { subview in
               HStack {
                  subview
                     .padding()
               }
               .frame(minWidth: 0, maxWidth: .infinity)
               .border(color, width: 5)
               .padding(5)
            }
         }
      }
   }
}
```

Listing 7-70: Applying different styles to the views in a custom container

In this example, we count the number of views in the collection. If the number is greater than 2, we assign the color red to the border, otherwise the border will be blue. Another alternative to modify the views according to the state of the container or the app is to use Container Values. These are values stored in the system, like the Environment values, but specific to work with custom containers. One of the main functions is to allow us to build container specific modifiers.

Container values are managed by the system from an instance of a structure called **ContainerValues**. To add new values, we must create an extension of this structure and define the properties with the **@Entry** macro, as we did for environment properties (see Listing 5-95).

```
extension ContainerValues {
   @Entry var showBorder: Bool = true
}
```

Listing 7-71: Adding a container value

The extension in Listing 7-71 creates a new container value called **showBorder** with the value **true**. To change this value later, SwiftUI includes the following method.

▷ **containerValue**(WritableKeyPath, Value)—This method sets the value of a container value. The first argument is the property's key path and the second argument is the value we want to assign to the property.

The best way to change a container value is to create a view modifier. For this purpose, we need to create an extension of the **View** protocol and define a new method, as shown below.

```
extension View {
   func showBorder(_ show: Bool) -> some View {
      containerValue(\.showBorder, show)
   }
}
```

Listing 7-72: Modifying a container value

Once we have the container values, we can use them in our custom container. To provide access to these values, the structure used to create container views include the following property.

▷ **containerValues**—This property returns the `ContainerValues` structure associated with the view.

In the following example, we modify our custom container to adapt the views to the value of the `showBorder` property. If this container value is `true`, we show a border of 5 points, otherwise the width of the border is 0.

```
struct BoxListView<Content: View>: View {
    @ViewBuilder var content: Content

    var body: some View {
        VStack {
            ForEach(subviews: content) { subview in
                let values = subview.containerValues

                HStack {
                    subview
                        .padding()
                }
                .frame(minWidth: 0, maxWidth: .infinity)
                .border(.red, width: values.showBorder ? 5 : 0)
                .padding(5)
            }
        }
    }
}
```
Listing 7-73: Using container values

Now that we have a container value and a custom container that can process the views according to that value, we can use it in our interface. In this case, all we need to do is to apply the new modifier to the view which value we want to change.

```
struct ContentView: View {
    var body: some View {
        BoxListView {
            Text("First")
            Text("Second")
                .showBorder(false)
            Text("Third")
        }
    }
}
```
Listing 7-74: Changing the container value of a view

In this example, we assign the `showBorder()` modifier to the second view. The first and third views in the custom container now include a border, but the second doesn't.

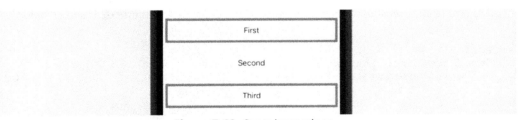

Figure 7-49: Container values

Chapter 7 - Lists

Basic ## 8.1 Multiple Views

The **ContentView** view we used in previous examples defines the interface for the initial screen, but applications that require only one view and a simple interface are hard to find. Because of the size of the screen, applications for mobile devices require multiple views that replace each other in response to the user. Professional applications consist of multiple views connected in predetermined paths that the user can follow to navigate through the content. Figure 8-1 below shows how these views work together to expand the user interface.

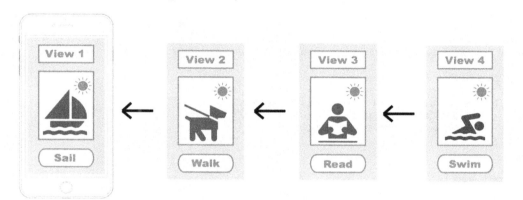

Figure 8-1: Multiple views to expand the interface

Basic ## Navigation Stack

The **ContentView** view included in the Multiplatform template represents the app's initial view, but we are responsible for creating the rest. The way these additional views are defined is always the same, we declare a structure that conforms to the **View** protocol and implement the **body** property, but there are different mechanisms to present them to the user. The one recommended by Apple creates a transition by moving the views from right to left, as illustrated in Figure 8-1. If the user wants to go back to the previous view, the current view is removed with a transition in the opposite direction. To create this navigation system, SwiftUI defines the **NavigationStack** view. The following is the structure's initializer.

▷ **NavigationStack(path:** Binding, **root:** Closure)—This initializer creates a navigation stack to manage the views the user can navigate through. The **path** argument is the binding property that stores the navigation path the user has followed, and the **root** argument is a closure that returns the root view (the first view presented by the navigation stack).

A **NavigationStack** view incorporates a navigation bar at the top of the interface to provide tools for navigation. The following are the modifiers available to configure this bar.

▷ **navigationTitle(**Text)—This modifier defines the title to show in the navigation bar. There is also a version of this modifier that takes a binding property to assign a title dynamically (**navigationTitle(Binding)**).

- **navigationBarTitleDisplayMode(**TitleDisplayMode**)**—This modifier determines the display mode for the title. The argument is an enumeration with the values **automatic** (the same mode as the previous view), **inline** (adapts to the size of the bar), and **large** (expands the bar to show a large title).
- **navigationBarBackButtonHidden(**Bool**)**—This modifier hides the Back button that is automatically generated by the **NavigationStack** view to navigate to previous views.
- **statusBarHidden(**Bool**)**—This modifier hides the status bar for all the views in the navigation hierarchy.

A **NavigationStack** view creates a stack of views with the views opened by the user. Therefore, to start this navigation hierarchy we need to embed the content of our app's initial view in a **NavigationStack** view, as we do in the following example.

```
struct ContentView: View {
    @Environment(ApplicationData.self) private var appData

    var body: some View {
        NavigationStack {
            List(appData.userData) { book in
                CellBook(book: book)
            }.navigationTitle(Text("Books"))
        }
    }
}
struct CellBook: View {
    let book: Book

    var body: some View {
        HStack(alignment: .top) {
            Image(book.cover)
                .resizable()
                .scaledToFit()
                .frame(width: 80, height: 100)
            VStack(alignment: .leading, spacing: 2) {
                Text(book.title).bold()
                Text(book.author)
                Text(book.displayYear).font(.caption)
                Spacer()
            }.padding(.top, 5)
            Spacer()
        }
    }
}
```

Listing 8-1: Initiating a navigation stack

This is the same application created in Chapter 7 to present a list of books, with the difference that now the list is embedded in a **NavigationStack** view and therefore the interface includes a navigation bar at the top with the title provided by the **navigationTitle()** modifier.

The size of the navigation bar created by the **NavigationStack** view depends on the title mode. By default, the mode is defined as **automatic** and therefore all the views in the navigation hierarchy show a large title, but if we scroll the list down, the size of the navigation bar and the title is automatically reduced to make room for the content.

Figure 8-2: Navigation stack

Do It Yourself: Create a Multiplatform project. For this application to work, you need to create a Swift file called ApplicationData.swift with the model in Chapter 7, Listing 7-3 and inject an instance of the **ApplicationData** class into the environment and the previews, as we did in Chapter 7, Listing 7-4. Update the **ContentView** view with the code in Listing 8-1. Download the book covers from our website and add them to the Asset Catalog. You should see an interface similar to Figure 8-2. Scroll the list down to see how the size of the navigation bar changes.

IMPORTANT: Note that the modifiers are applied to the content. For instance, the **navigationTitle()** modifier in our example is applied to the **List** view, not the **NavigationStack** view. This is because the rest of the views added to the stack are not going to be embedded in a **NavigationStack** view. This view is only required for the initial view to start building the stack. (This will become clear later.)

By default, the navigation bar shows a large title, but we can change that behavior by assigning the **inline** mode instead. This is particularly useful when the list is implemented with a style that doesn't include any backgrounds or padding, as in the following example.

```
struct ContentView: View {
   @Environment(ApplicationData.self) private var appData

   var body: some View {
      NavigationStack {
         List(appData.userData) { book in
            CellBook(book: book)
         }
         .listStyle(.plain)
         .navigationTitle(Text("Books"))
         .navigationBarTitleDisplayMode(.inline)
      }
   }
}
```

Listing 8-2: Setting the title mode

Now the title is shown in a standard size and with a predefined style, and all the views in the hierarchy will inherit this mode.

Figure 8-3: Inline mode

(Basic) **Toolbar**

Besides the title, the navigation bar can contain other elements, including images and buttons. SwiftUI provides the following modifiers to add items and configure the navigation bar.

▷ **toolbar(id:** String, **content:** Closure)—This modifier adds elements to a toolbar or navigation bar. The **id** argument is an optional identifier used by the system to store the toolbar's last configuration, and the closure assigned to the **content** argument defines the views we want to include.

▷ **toolbar(**Visibility, **for:** ToolbarPlacement)—This modifier shows or hides the bars. The first argument is an enumeration with the values **automatic**, **visible**, and **hidden**, and the **for** argument is a list of values representing the bars we want to modify, separated by comma. To specify the bars, the structure defines the type properties **automatic**, **bottomBar**, **navigationBar**, **tabBar**, and **windowToolbar**.

▷ **toolbarBackgroundVisibility(**Visibility, **for:** ToolbarPlacement)—This modifier determines the visibility of the toolbar's background. The first argument is an enumeration with the values **automatic**, **visible** and **hidden**, and the **for** argument is a structure that determines the toolbar that is going to be affected. The properties available are **automatic**, **bottomBar**, **navigationBar**, **tabBar**, and **windowToolbar**.

▷ **toolbar(removing:** ToolbarDefaultItemKind)—This modifier removes items added to the toolbar by the system. The **removing** argument is a structure that determines the item to be removed. There are two properties available: **sidebarToggle** to remove the toggle button added to the sidebar by the **NavigationSplitView** view, and **title** to remove the title and subtitle.

▷ **toolbarRole(**ToolbarRole)—This modifier defines the purpose of the content of the toolbar. The argument is a structure with the type properties **browser**, **editor**, **navigationStack**, and **automatic**.

Items can be added to the left or right side of the toolbar, and to different toolbars, including the navigation bar generated by the **NavigationStack** view, a toolbar at the bottom of the screen, and a toolbar on top of the keyboard. For this reason, SwiftUI includes the **ToolbarItem** view to define the items.

▷ **ToolbarItem(id:** String, **placement:** ToolbarItemPlacement, **content:** Closure)—This view defines an item for a toolbar. The **id** argument is an optional identifier used by the system to store the item's configuration. The **placement** argument is a structure that determines the place and the toolbar where the item will be located. The structure includes type properties to define standard configurations for every system. The properties available are **automatic**, **bottomBar**, **cancellation-**

Action, confirmationAction, destructiveAction, keyboard, navigation, navigationBarLeading, navigationBarTrailing, primaryAction, secondaryAction, principal, and status. The closure assigned to the content argument defines the view we want to include in the toolbar.

As we already mentioned, the toolbar() modifier can add items to any toolbar in our interface. For instance, we can use it to add a button to the navigation bar of our example.

```
struct ContentView: View {
   @Environment(ApplicationData.self) private var appData

   var body: some View {
      NavigationStack {
         List(appData.userData) { book in
            CellBook(book: book)
         }
         .navigationTitle(Text("Books"))
         .toolbar {
            ToolbarItem(placement: .navigationBarTrailing) {
               Button(action: {
                  print("Delete Element")
               }, label: { Image(systemName: "trash") })
            }
         }
      }
   }
}
```

Listing 8-3: Adding a button to the navigation bar

The modifier is applied to the views inside the **NavigationStack** view and then the items are defined inside the closure. In this case, we include one **ToolbarItem** view with the placement **navigationBarTrailing** to position the item on the right side of the navigation bar. The item is defined with a **Button** view and an SF Symbol. The result is shown below.

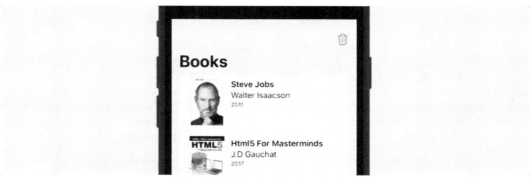

Figure 8-4: Navigation bar button

The **ToolbarItem** view defines a single item. If we want to define multiple items at once, we can use a **ToolbarItemGroup** view.

▷ **ToolbarItemGroup(placement:** ToolbarItemPlacement, **content:** Closure**)**
—This view defines multiple items for a toolbar. The **placement** argument is a structure that determines the place and the toolbar where the items will be located. The structure includes type properties to define standard configurations for every system. The properties available are **automatic**, **bottomBar**, **cancellationAction**, **confirmationAction**, **destructiveAction**, **keyboard**, **navigation**, **navigationBarLeading**, **navigationBarTrailing**, **primaryAction**,

secondaryAction, **principal**, and **status**. The closure assigned to the **content** argument defines the views we want to include.

The button in the previous example prints a message on the console, but of course we can perform more meaningful tasks. For instance, we can add buttons to the navigation bar to scroll the list of books to the top or to the bottom, as shown below.

```
struct ContentView: View {
    @Environment(ApplicationData.self) private var appData

    var body: some View {
        NavigationStack {
            ScrollViewReader { proxy in
                List(appData.userData) { book in
                    CellBook(book: book)
                        .id(book.id)
                }
                .navigationTitle(Text("Books"))
                .toolbar {
                    ToolbarItemGroup(placement: .navigationBarTrailing) {
                        Button(action: {
                            if let firstIndex = appData.userData.first?.id {
                                proxy.scrollTo(firstIndex, anchor: .bottom)
                            }
                        }, label: { Image(systemName: "arrow.up.doc") })
                        Button(action: {
                            if let lastIndex = appData.userData.last?.id {
                                proxy.scrollTo(lastIndex, anchor: .bottom)
                            }
                        }, label: { Image(systemName: "arrow.down.doc") })
                    }
                }
            }
        }
    }
}
```

Listing 8-4: Adding multiple buttons

To be able to scroll the list programmatically, we embed the **List** view in a **ScrollViewReader** view (see Chapter 7, Listing 7-16). Using a **ToolbarItemGroup** view, we include two buttons at the right side of the navigation bar. The first button gets the identifier of the first book in the **userData** array and scrolls the list to the beginning, and the second button gets the identifier of the last book in the array and scrolls the list to the end.

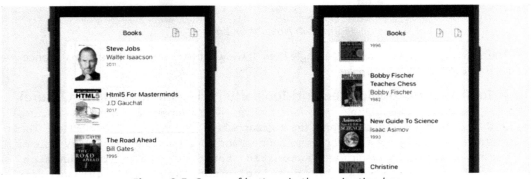

Figure 8-5: Group of buttons in the navigation bar

Chapter 8 - Navigation

As we have already mentioned, in addition to the navigation bar, the buttons may be added to a toolbar at the bottom of the screen or on top of the keyboard. These toolbars are automatically incorporated into the interface when a button is assigned to them. For instance, to show a toolbar at the bottom of the screen, all we need to do is to define a `ToolbarItem` view with the `bottomBar` placement value, as shown below.

```
struct ContentView: View {
    @Environment(ApplicationData.self) private var appData

    var body: some View {
        NavigationStack {
            List(appData.userData) { book in
                CellBook(book: book)
            }
            .navigationTitle(Text("Books"))
            .toolbar(.hidden, for: .navigationBar)
            .toolbar {
                ToolbarItem(placement: .bottomBar) {
                    HStack {
                        Button("Show") {
                            print("Show Values")
                        }
                    }.frame(minWidth: 0, maxWidth: .infinity,
alignment: .trailing)
                }
            }
        }
    }
}
```

Listing 8-5: Adding buttons to the bottom toolbar

Buttons added to the bottom toolbar are displayed at the center. That's the reason why in our example we have defined the button inside an `HStack` view, so it could be placed on the right and share the bar with other buttons, if necessary. Note that we have also implemented the other version of the `toolbar()` modifier to hide the navigation bar.

Figure 8-6: Bottom toolbar

Although we can position the buttons on the left or right side of the navigation bar with placement values like `navigationBarLeading` and `navigationBarTrailing`, the `ToolbarItemPlacement` structure also allows us to specify the intent of the buttons and let the system decide where and how to present them depending on the space available and the device. For instance, the structure returned by the `primaryAction` property usually places the buttons on the right, and the one returned by the `secondaryAction` property tells the system that the buttons are not essential for the application and therefore are placed inside a popup menu.

```
struct ContentView: View {
    @Environment(ApplicationData.self) private var appData
```

```
var body: some View {
    NavigationStack {
        List(appData.userData) { book in
            CellBook(book: book)
        }
        .navigationTitle(Text("Books"))
        .navigationBarTitleDisplayMode(.inline)
        .toolbar {
            ToolbarItemGroup(placement: .primaryAction) {
                Button(action: {
                    print("Adding Book...")
                }, label: {
                    Image(systemName: "plus.app")
                })
            }
            ToolbarItemGroup(placement: .secondaryAction) {
                Button(action: {
                    print("Sorting Books...")
                }, label: {
                    Label("Sort Books", systemImage: "arrow.up.arrow.down")
                })
            }
        }
        .toolbarRole(.editor)
    }
}
```

Listing 8-6: *Defining the buttons intent*

In the code in Listing 8-6, The `toolbar()` modifier includes two `ToolbarItemGroup` items with one button each. The purpose of the button in the first group is to add books to the list, which is a primary function and therefore we declare it as a primary action, but the purpose of the button included in the second group is to sort the list and therefore we declare it as secondary. On an iPhone, the system places both buttons on the right, but includes the second button in a popup menu.

Figure 8-7: *Primary and secondary buttons*

The navigation bar is split into three areas: leading, center, and trailing. By default, the title is positioned at the center and the buttons on the sides, but we can change this behavior with the `toolbarRole()` modifier. This is specially useful on iPads and Mac computers, where larger screens and windows allow us to add more elements to the bar. For instance, if we declare the role as `editor` or `browser`, as we did in the example in Listing 8-6, on iPads the title is shown on the leading area and the secondary buttons at the center.

Figure 8-8: Secondary buttons on an iPad

There is a built-in tool that allows the user to add or remove buttons to the navigation bar when they are declared as secondary actions. To activate this feature, we must declare the identifiers for the `toolbar()` modifier and the items, as shown below.

```
struct ContentView: View {
   @Environment(ApplicationData.self) private var appData

   var body: some View {
      NavigationStack {
         List(appData.userData) { book in
            CellBook(book: book)
         }
         .navigationTitle(Text("Books"))
         .toolbar(id: "mybar") {
            ToolbarItem(id: "sort", placement: .secondaryAction) {
               Button(action: {
                  print("Sorting Books...")
               }, label: {
                  Label("Sort Books", systemImage: "arrow.up.arrow.down")
               })
            }
            ToolbarItem(id: "settings", placement: .secondaryAction) {
               Button(action: {
                  print("Settings...")
               }, label: {
                  Label("Settings", systemImage: "gearshape")
               })
            }
         }
         .toolbarRole(.editor)
      }
   }
}
```

Listing 8-7: Customizing the bar

In this example, we declare the bar with the "mybar" identifier and two buttons with the identifiers "sort" and "settings". The system uses these identifiers to store the last configuration and restore it the next time the app is launched. On iPhones the buttons are shown in a popup menu, as any other secondary action, but on iPads and Mac computers the system shows the buttons at the center and an additional button with an option to configure the bar.

Figure 8-9: Button to customize the toolbar

When this option is selected, the system opens a window were the user can drag and drop the buttons to configure the bar.

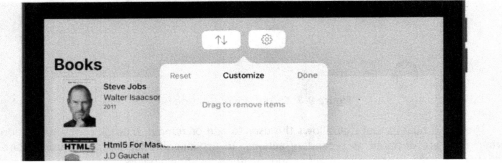

Figure 8-10: Toolbar customization

If we want to manually create a popup menu, instead of a button we need to add a `Menu` view to the toolbar.

▷ **Menu**(String, **content:** Closure)—This initializer creates a menu with the title specified by the first argument. The closure assigned to the **content** argument provides the **Button** views to create the options. The view also includes the `Menu(content: Closure, label: Closure)` initializer to declare the title with a view.

The `Menu` view works with any button, but it is usually implemented with toolbar buttons, as illustrated in the following example.

```
struct ContentView: View {
   @Environment(ApplicationData.self) private var appData

   var body: some View {
      NavigationStack {
         List(appData.userData) { book in
            CellBook(book: book)
         }
         .navigationTitle(Text("Books"))
         .toolbar {
            Menu(content: {
               Button("Option 1") { print("Option 1") }
               Button("Option 2") { print("Option 2") }
               Button("Option 3") { print("Option 3") }
            }, label: {
               Image(systemName: "filemenu.and.selection")
            })
         }
      }
   }
}
```

Listing 8-8: Creating a popup menu

Our `Menu` view includes three buttons. In this case, we print messages in the console, but the buttons can perform any task we want. The view is represented by a button with an SF Symbol. Pressing this button opens the menu, as shown below.

Figure 8-11: Custom popup menu

Search

A `NavigationStack` view can include a search bar to allow the user to search for values in the model. The following is the modifier we need to apply to this view to enable that feature.

▷ **searchable(text:** Binding, **tokens:** Binding, **suggestedTokens:** Binding, **placement:** SearchFieldPlacement, **prompt:** String, **token:** Closure**)**—This modifier adds and configures a search bar. The **text** argument stores the value inserted by the user. The **tokens** argument keeps track of the search tokens shown to the user. The **suggestedTokens** argument provides a list of tokens to suggest values to the user. The **placement** argument specifies the place where the bar will be located. For this purpose, the structure includes the type properties **automatic**, **navigationBar-Drawer**, **sidebar**, and **toolbar**, and the method **navigationBarDrawer-(displayMode: NavigationBarDrawerDisplayMode)** that can take the type properties **always** and **automatic** to always display or automatically hide the bar. The **prompt** argument specifies the bar's placeholder text. And the **token** argument provides the views to display the tokens.

This modifier comes in different versions, which allow us to implement only the arguments we need. For instance, to perform a simple search, all we need is a binding property for the **text** argument to store the user's input. The rest of the arguments are only required if we want to provide additional functionality, as we will see in the examples below.

The **searchable()** modifier displays the search bar, but how the search is performed depends on the characteristics of our model. In a model that stores values in an array, as the one we are using in this chapter, the search can be performed by filtering the values with the **filter()** method. The following are the changes we need to introduce to the **ApplicationData** class in our model to filter books.

```
@Observable class ApplicationData: @unchecked Sendable {
    @ObservationIgnored var userData: [Book] {
        didSet {
            filterValues(search: "")
        }
    }
    var filteredItems: [Book] = []

    func filterValues(search: String) {
        if search.isEmpty {
            filteredItems = userData.sorted(by: { $0.title < $1.title })
        } else {
            let list = userData.filter( { item in
                return item.title.localizedStandardContains(search)
            })
            filteredItems = list.sorted(by: { $0.title < $1.title })
        }
    }
    static let shared: ApplicationData = ApplicationData()
    private init() {
        userData = [
            Book(title: "Steve Jobs", author: "Walter Isaacson", cover:
"book1", year: 2011, selected: false),
            Book(title: "HTML5 for Masterminds", author: "J.D Gauchat",
cover: "book2", year: 2017, selected: false),
            Book(title: "The Road Ahead", author: "Bill Gates", cover:
"book3", year: 1995, selected: false),
            Book(title: "The C Programming Language", author: "Brian W.
Kernighan", cover: "book4", year: 1988, selected: false),
            Book(title: "Being Digital", author: "Nicholas Negroponte",
cover: "book5", year: 1996, selected: false),
```

```
            Book(title: "Only the Paranoid Survive", author: "Andrew S.
Grove", cover: "book6", year: 1999, selected: false),
            Book(title: "Accidental Empires", author: "Robert X. Cringely",
cover: "book7", year: 1996, selected: false),
            Book(title: "Bobby Fischer Teaches Chess", author: "Bobby
Fischer", cover: "book8", year: 1982, selected: false),
            Book(title: "New Guide to Science", author: "Isaac Asimov",
cover: "book9", year: 1993, selected: false),
            Book(title: "Christine", author: "Stephen King", cover:
"book10", year: 1983, selected: false),
            Book(title: "IT", author: "Stephen King", cover: "book11", year:
1987, selected: false),
            Book(title: "Ending Aging", author: "Aubrey de Grey", cover:
"book12", year: 2007, selected: false)
        ]
      filterValues(search: "")
   }
}
```

Listing 8-9: Filtering the data in the model

In this model, we have applied the `@ObservationIgnored` macro to the `userData` property so that changes to this property are not reported to the views. This is because this property is used to store all the available books, but the data for the views is provided by a new property called `filteredItems`, which contains only the books that match the search performed by the user. To keep this property up to date, we define the `filterValues()` method that we call each time a new search is performed or books are added to or removed from the model.

The `filterValues()` method receives a string with the value inserted by the user in the search bar. If the value is empty, we assign all the books in the `userData` property to the `filteredItems` property to show the full list on the screen, but if there is a value to search, we filter the books in the `userData` property with the `filter()` method. This method receives a value and must return `true` or `false` to determine if it is going to be included in the result. In this case, we return `true` only when the book's title contains the value inserted by the user. The resulting array is assigned to the `filteredItems` property to make it available to the views. Note that in both cases, the arrays are sorted with the `sorted()` method, so the values are displayed in alphabetical order.

After we store the testing data in the `userData` property, we call the `filterValues()` method with an empty array to initialize the list. Now we can use the `filteredItems` property to show the books.

```
struct ContentView: View {
   @Environment(ApplicationData.self) private var appData
   @State private var searchTerm: String = ""

   var body: some View {
      NavigationStack {
         List(appData.filteredItems) { book in
            CellBook(book: book)
         }.navigationTitle(Text("Books"))
      }
      .searchable(text: $searchTerm, prompt: Text("Insert title"))
      .onChange(of: searchTerm, initial: false) { old, value in
         let search = value.trimmingCharacters(in: .whitespaces)
         appData.filterValues(search: search)
      }
   }
}
```

Listing 8-10: Displaying a search bar

This view includes a `@State` property to store the value inserted by the user, and two modifiers to manage the search. The `searchable()` modifier asks the system to display a search bar. For this example, we only need to provide two values, the binding property to store the value (`searchTerm`) and a `Text` view with the placeholder to show in the bar. This stores the value inserted by the user, but the search is performed by the `onChange()` modifier added below. This modifier executes a closure every time the value of the `searchTerm` property changes. In this closure, we trim the value to make sure there are no spaces at the beginning or the end, and then call the `filterValues()` method in the model. The method filters the values, assigns the result to the `filteredItems` property, and because we used this property to define the `List` view, only the books that match the search are shown on the screen.

Figure 8-12: *Search bar*

 Do It Yourself: Update the `ApplicationData` class with the code in Listing 8-9 and the `ContentView` view with the code in Listing 8-10. Run the application on the simulator or a device. Tap on the bar and perform a search. The list should only show the books which titles match what you type on the bar.

 IMPORTANT: In this example, we filter the items with a function in the model. This means that every time the filter changes or books are added, modified or removed, we must call the function again to update the views. This is why we declared the `didSet` method for the `userData` property, so every time a book is added or removed from this property, we call the `filterValues()` method to update the views. There are different programming patterns available. An alternative is to create a computed property inside the view to filter the items and use that property to provide the values for the list, as we did in the example of Listing 7-30. All you need to remember is that the views take the values from the observable properties, so you always have to make sure that these properties are up-to-date.

By default, the search bar disappears when the user scrolls the list, but we can keep it permanently on the screen by defining the display mode. This is an additional argument included in the `searchable()` modifier called **placement**. This argument defines the location of the bar, which depends on the system and the organization of the interface, but it can also define the bar's display mode. For this purpose, the structure used to define this value includes the `navigationBarDrawer()` method. If we specify this method with the value **always**, as shown below, the bar is permanently displayed on the screen.

```
.searchable(text: $searchTerm,
placement: .navigationBarDrawer(displayMode: .always), prompt:
Text("Insert title"))
```

Listing 8-11: *Keeping the search bar on the screen*

We can also activate the search field from code by setting the focus state. The `View` protocol defines the following modifier to assign a `FocusState` property to the field.

> ▷ **searchFocused**(FocusState)—This modifier associates a `FocusState` property of type `Bool` to the search field to control its focus state.

In the following example, we define a property to store the state of the field with the `@FocusState` property wrapper (see Listing 6-23), assign this property to the field with the `searchFocused()` modifier, and create a button that allows the user to set the state to `true`.

```
struct ContentView: View {
    @Environment(ApplicationData.self) private var appData
    @State private var searchTerm: String = ""
    @FocusState private var isFocused: Bool

    var body: some View {
        NavigationStack {
            List {
                Button("Search") {
                    isFocused = true
                }.padding()
                ForEach(appData.filteredItems) { book in
                    CellBook(book: book)
                }
            }
            .navigationTitle(Text("Books"))
        }
        .searchable(text: $searchTerm, prompt: Text("Insert title"))
        .searchFocused($isFocused)
        .onChange(of: searchTerm, initial: false) { old, value in
            let search = value.trimmingCharacters(in: .whitespaces)
            appData.filterValues(search: search)
        }
    }
}
```

Listing 8-12: Changing the focus state of the search field

When the Search button is pressed, the focus is set on the search field, the cursor appears to allow the user to type, and the keyboard opens.

Figure 8-13: Focus on the search field

The `searchable()` modifier automatically stores every character typed by the user into the binding property. This means that the search is performed for each character typed or removed from the bar. If we want the user to decide when the search takes place, we can include the `onSubmit()` modifier. We have implemented this modifier before with `TextField` views to process a value when the Return/Done key is pressed on the keyboard, but if we declare it with the `search` value, we can use it to perform a search, as shown below.

```
struct ContentView: View {
    @Environment(ApplicationData.self) private var appData
    @State private var searchTerm: String = ""
```

```
    var body: some View {
        NavigationStack {
            List(appData.filteredItems) { book in
                CellBook(book: book)
            }
            .navigationTitle(Text("Books"))
        }
        .searchable(text: $searchTerm, prompt: Text("Insert title"))
        .onSubmit(of: .search) { performSearch() }
        .onChange(of: searchTerm, initial: false) { old, value in
            if value.isEmpty {
                performSearch()
            }
        }
    }
    func performSearch() {
        let search = searchTerm.trimmingCharacters(in: .whitespaces)
        appData.filterValues(search: search)
    }
}
```

Listing 8-13: Performing the search when the Return/Done key is pressed

Since we need to perform the search from two different modifiers, we move the process to a new method called **performSearch()**. When the Return/Done key is pressed, the closure assigned to the **onSubmit()** modifier is executed and the **performSearch()** method is called to trim the text and filter the books. This method is also called from the **onChange()** modifier, but only when the search is empty. This is because we don't want to update the list every time the user types or removes a character, as we did before, but still need to do it when the user cancels the search. If the user presses the Cancel button, the system assigns an empty string to the **searchTerm** property, so we check this condition and update the list accordingly.

Another important feature is the possibility of showing a list of values to suggest to the user what to type. SwiftUI includes the following modifier to create this list for a search field.

▷ **searchSuggestions(Closure)**—This modifier creates a list of values that are displayed to the user as a suggestion. The argument is a closure that provides the list of **Text** views we need to present the values.

The suggestions are provided with a list of **Text** views defined in a closure. If the views are created with the same model used to create the **List** view, only values that match the search are shown. The user can close the suggestion list by pressing the Return/Done key or by selecting one of the values. To allow selection, the framework includes the following modifier.

▷ **searchCompletion(String)**—This modifier associates a search value with a view. The argument is the value we want the search bar to contain when the view is selected.

The **Text** views with the suggestions may be declared manually to create a static list, or with a **ForEach** loop to create a dynamic list. In our case, we want to show suggestions according to the value inserted by the user, so we create a dynamic list with a **ForEach** loop.

```
struct ContentView: View {
    @Environment(ApplicationData.self) private var appData
    @State private var searchTerm: String = ""

    var body: some View {
        NavigationStack {
            List(appData.filteredItems) { book in
                CellBook(book: book)
            }
```

```
            .navigationTitle(Text("Books"))
    }
    .searchable(text: $searchTerm, prompt: Text("Insert title"))
    .searchSuggestions({
        ForEach(appData.filteredItems) { item in
            Text("\(item.title) - \(item.author)")
                .searchCompletion(item.title)
        }
    })
    .onChange(of: searchTerm, initial: false) { old, value in
        let search = value.trimmingCharacters(in: .whitespaces)
        appData.filterValues(search: search)
    }
    }
  }
}
```

Listing 8-14: Suggesting terms to the user

In this example, we applied the **searchable()** modifier, as before, but also included the **searchSuggestions()** modifier to display a list of suggested values. The closure assigned to this modifier creates a list of **Text** views with the values of the **filteredItems** property, so only the books that match the current search are included. To help the user identify the books, the **Text** view shows the book's title and author, but when the user selects a suggestion, only the title is assigned to the search bar by the **searchCompletion()** modifier.

Figure 8-14: Suggestions

The search bar includes two buttons, one to clear the bar and another to allow the user to cancel the search, but we can also do it programatically. The environment includes the following values to control the process.

▷ **isSearching**—This is a Boolean value that determines if the user is currently performing a search or not.

▷ **dismissSearch**—This property creates an action to cancel the search. It is a **DismissSearchAction** structure. The structure exposes a handler we can call to perform the action.

The **searchable()** modifier sends the information down the view hierarchy through the environment, so the system can determine where and when to show the search bar. This means that the environment values are only available within the views in the hierarchy. Therefore, to be able to read them, we must embed the list of books in a custom view. In the following example, we call this view **SearchableView**.

```
struct ContentView: View {
    @Environment(ApplicationData.self) private var appData
    @State private var searchTerm: String = ""

    var body: some View {
        NavigationStack {
```

Chapter 8 - Navigation

```
            SearchableView()
                .navigationTitle(Text("Books"))
        }
        .searchable(text: $searchTerm, prompt: Text("Insert title"))
        .onChange(of: searchTerm, initial: false) { old, value in
            let search = value.trimmingCharacters(in: .whitespaces)
            appData.filterValues(search: search)
        }
    }
}
struct SearchableView: View {
    @Environment(ApplicationData.self) private var appData
    @Environment(\.isSearching) var isSearching
    @Environment(\.dismissSearch) var dismissSearch

    var body: some View {
        List {
            if isSearching {
                Button("Dismiss") {
                    dismissSearch()
                }
            }
            ForEach(appData.filteredItems) { book in
                CellBook(book: book)
            }
        }
    }
}
```

Listing 8-15: *Cancelling the search programmatically*

The `SearchableView` view implements a `ForEach` view to generate the list of books, so we are able to include an additional row at the top with a button to dismiss the search. But to avoid interfering with the content, the button is only shown when the user is performing a search. For this purpose, we check whether a search is taking place with the `isSearching` value and cancel the search with the `dismissSearch` value when the Dismiss button is pressed. Note that the `dismissSearch` value is a structure that exposes a closure that we can call as we do with any other closure or function. The result is shown below.

Figure 8-15: *Custom cancel button*

Another feature we can add to a search bar are scope buttons. These are buttons placed below the bar that allow the user to specify the scope of the search (e.g., search by title or by author). To incorporate these buttons, SwiftUI includes the following modifier.

▷ **searchScopes(**Binding, **scopes:** Closure**)**—This modifier defines a list of search scopes. The first argument is a binding property to store the currently selected scope, and the **scopes** argument provides the views to create the buttons.

This modifier needs two things: the values to represent the scopes and a binding property to keep track of the scope selected by the user.

```
import SwiftUI

enum Scopes {
   case title, author
}
struct ContentView: View {
   @Environment(ApplicationData.self) private var appData
   @State private var searchTerm: String = ""
   @State private var searchScope: Scopes = .title

   var body: some View {
      NavigationStack {
         List(appData.filteredItems) { book in
            CellBook(book: book)
         }.navigationTitle(Text("Books"))
      }
      .searchable(text: $searchTerm, prompt: Text("Insert title"))
      .searchScopes($searchScope, scopes: {
         Text("Title").tag(Scopes.title)
         Text("Author").tag(Scopes.author)
      })
      .onChange(of: searchTerm, initial: false) { _, _ in
         performSearch()
      }
      .onChange(of: searchScope, initial: false) { _, _ in
         performSearch()
      }
   }
   func performSearch() {
      let search = searchTerm.trimmingCharacters(in: .whitespaces)
      appData.filterValues(search: search, scope: searchScope)
   }
}
```

Listing 8-16: Adding scope buttons

In this example, we define the scopes with an enumeration and two values: `title` and `author`. The `@State` property is initialized with the `title` value, so the searches are first performed by title. The closure assigned to the `searchScopes()` modifier includes two `Text` views to create two scope buttons, one to select the `title` scope and another to select the `author` scope. To perform the search in the current scope, we send the value of the `searchScope` property to the `filterValues()` method in the model. The method must now check the selected scope and search the value accordingly, as shown below.

```
func filterValues(search: String, scope: Scopes = .title) {
   if search.isEmpty {
      filteredItems = userData.sorted(by: { $0.title < $1.title })
   } else {
      let list = userData.filter( { item in
         let value = scope == .title ? item.title : item.author
         return value.localizedStandardContains(search)
      })
      filteredItems = list.sorted(by: { $0.title < $1.title })
   }
}
```

Listing 8-17: Searching by title and author

The search bar now includes two buttons below. If the user presses the Title button, we search by title, and if the user presses the Author button, we search by author.

Figure 8-16: *Search scopes*

Another feature we can incorporate to a search bar are search tokens. These are values that appear inside the bar to help the user perform complex search queries. For instance, if we want to allow the user to search books by author, we can create a token that shows the current selected author so the user knows the current constraint applied to the search and can also remove it.

As with scopes, we need a binding property to store the current tokens and also provide a `Text` view to present the tokens on the screen, but because tokens must be created from values that conform to the `Identifiable` protocol, we need to define a custom data type. (The data type must also conform to the `Equatable` protocol to be able to track changes with the `onChange()` modifier. See Chapter 3 for more information on these protocols).

```
import SwiftUI
struct Tokens: Identifiable, Equatable {
    let id = UUID()
    let name: String
}
struct ContentView: View {
    @Environment(ApplicationData.self) private var appData
    @State private var searchTerm: String = ""
    @State private var searchTokens: [Tokens] = []

    var body: some View {
        NavigationStack {
            List(appData.filteredItems) { book in
                CellBook(book: book)
            }.navigationTitle(Text("Books"))
            .toolbar {
                let list = appData.userData.map { $0.author }
                let authors = Set(list).sorted()
                Menu(content: {
                    ForEach(authors, id: \.self) { author in
                        Button(author) {
                            let token = Tokens(name: author)
                            searchTokens = [token]
                        }
                    }
                }, label: {
                    Image(systemName: "pencil.circle")
                })
            }
        }
        .searchable(text: $searchTerm, tokens: $searchTokens, token:
{ token in
            Text(token.name)
        })
        .onChange(of: searchTerm, initial: false) { _, _ in
            performSearch()
        }
```

```
    .onChange(of: searchTokens, initial: false) { _, _ in
        performSearch()
    }
}
func performSearch() {
    let search = searchTerm.trimmingCharacters(in: .whitespaces)
    appData.filterValues(search: search, author:
searchTokens.first?.name ?? "")
}
}
```

Listing 8-18: Adding tokens

In this example, we define a structure called `Tokens` to create the tokens. The structure includes the required `id` property to identify the value and a `String` property to store the name of the token. The `searchable()` modifier stores the tokens in an array, so we define the `@State` property as an array of `Tokens` structures. To create the tokens, we have added a `toolbar()` modifier with a `Menu` view. The menu's options are defined with the name of the authors available in the model. This creates a button in the navigation bar the user can press to select an author. Note that to get the list of authors, we map the `userData` array, extract the author's name, turn the array into a `Set` to remove duplicates, and sort them in alphabetical order.

Once an author is selected, we create an instance of the `Tokens` structure with the author's name and assign it to the `searchTokens` property. This adds a token to the search bar, which tells the user that the search will be performed on the books written by that author. As always, we need to modify the `filterValues()` method in the model for this search to work.

```
func filterValues(search: String, author: String = "") {
    if search.isEmpty && author.isEmpty {
        filteredItems = userData.sorted(by: { $0.title < $1.title })
    } else {
        let list = userData.filter( { item in
            var valid = true
            if !author.isEmpty && author != item.author {
                valid = false
            }
            if valid && !search.isEmpty && !
item.title.localizedStandardContains(search) {
                valid = false
            }
            return valid
        })
        filteredItems = list.sorted(by: { $0.title < $1.title })
    }
}
```

Listing 8-19: Filtering books by author

In this new method, we must check if the user has selected an author and then filter the array by author and title. The easiest way to do it is to start with a valid condition (`valid = true`) and then invalidate it if something doesn't match. We first check if the user selected an author and compare it with the author of the book. If they don't match, the condition becomes invalid. Next, we do the same for the title, but only if the condition was not already invalidated by the author. As a result, when the user selects an author, a token with the author's name appears in the search bar and the search is only performed on the books written by that author.

Figure 8-17: *Tokens*

Basic **Navigation Link**

The **NavigationStack** view can manage a stack of views, but there is no stack if we only have one view. To allow the user to open additional views, SwiftUI includes the **NavigationLink** view. This is a control view that creates a button the user can press to replace the current view with another. The following are the view's initializers.

▷ **NavigationLink**(String, **destination:** View)—This initializer creates a button for navigation. The first argument is the text we want to assign to the button's label, and the **destination** argument is the view we want to open when the button is pressed. If we want to define a complex label for the button, we can use the initializer **NavigationLink(destination: View, label: Closure)** instead.

▷ **NavigationLink**(String, **value:** Value)—This initializer creates a button for dynamic navigation. The first argument is the text we want to assign to the button's label, and the **value** argument is a value that identifies the link. If we want to define a complex label for the button, we can use the initializer **NavigationLink(value: Value, label: Closure)** instead.

The **NavigationLink** view requires a view to open and a label the user can tap to perform the action. For instance, the following example adds a link to the navigation bar to open a view the user can use to change the app's settings.

```
struct ContentView: View {
   @Environment(ApplicationData.self) private var appData

   var body: some View {
      NavigationStack {
         List(appData.userData) { book in
            CellBook(book: book)
         }.navigationTitle(Text("Books"))
         .toolbar {
            ToolbarItem(placement: .navigationBarTrailing) {
               NavigationLink(destination: SettingsView(), label: {
                  Image(systemName: "gearshape")
               })
            }
         }
      }
   }
}
```

Listing 8-20: *Including a navigation link*

Like the **Button** view, the **NavigationLink** view creates a button but with the purpose of replacing the current view with another one. In this case, we create the button with an SF Symbol image of a gear, and set the destination view to be a custom view we call **SettingsView**.

```
import SwiftUI

struct SettingsView: View {
    @State private var showPictures: Bool = true
    @State private var showYear: Bool = true

    var body: some View {
        Form {
            Toggle("Show Pictures", isOn: $showPictures)
            Toggle("Show Year", isOn: $showYear)
        }.navigationTitle("Settings")
    }
}
#Preview{
    NavigationStack {
        SettingsView()
    }
}
```

Listing 8-21: Defining a second view

Our `SettingsView` view includes two `@State` properties to store the values of the two `Toggle` views we use to create a form. Other than that, the view is the same as any other we have created before, but because it represents the interface for the whole screen, we should put it in a separate SwiftUI file (see Figure 5-106).

The `SettingsView` view is opened from the `ContentView` view and therefore it is part of its hierarchy, so we don't have to embed it in a `NavigationStack` view, but we still need to declare its title with the `navigationTitle()` modifier, as we did for the initial view.

When the user taps the button in the `ContentView` view, an instance of the `SettingsView` view is created and presented on the screen transitioning from right to left.

Figure 8-18: Interface with two views

Do It Yourself: Create a Multiplatform project. Create a Swift file called ApplicationData.swift with the model from Chapter 7, Listing 7-3 and inject an instance of the `ApplicationData` class into the environment and the previews, as we did in Chapter 7, Listing 7-4. Download the book covers from our website and add them to the Asset Catalog. Update the `ContentView` view with the code in Listing 8-20. You also need the `CellBook` view from Listing 8-1. Press Command + N or select the options New/Empty File from the File menu at the top of the screen to create a new SwiftUI file with the name SettingsView.swift (see Figure 5-106). Update this file with the code in Listing 8-21. Run the application. Press the button on the navigation bar. You should see the `SettingsView` view appear on the screen, transitioning from right to left, as shown in Figure 8-18.

IMPORTANT: The views defined by the `SettingsView` structure in Listing 8-21 are not embedded in a `NavigationStack` view because the `SettingsView` view is opened from the `ContentView` view and therefore it is already part of a navigation hierarchy, but the instance of this view created for the preview is not part of that hierarchy and therefore if we want to see on the canvas what this view is going to look like when it is presented to the user, we must embed it in a `NavigationStack` view, as we did in Listing 8-21.

The view opened by a `NavigationLink` view includes a button in the navigation bar that the user can tap to go back to the previous view. This button is automatically generated by SwiftUI and it is part of the basic tools provided for navigation. Usually, it is displayed with the label "Back", but it changes according to the title of the previous view. If the title is short enough, it is assigned to the button's label, and that's why in our example it is called "Books" (see Figure 8-18, right). This helps the user identify the view that is going to appear on the screen if the button is pressed. But that is about all the configuration options we have for this button. If we need something different, we must remove the back button with the `navigationBarBackButton-Hidden()` modifier and create our own.

Custom back buttons must provide a way for the user to remove the view. An alternative is to modify the state of the presentation from the environment. For this purpose, the environment includes the following values.

▷ **dismiss**—This property creates an action to dismiss the view. It is a `DismissAction` structure. The structure exposes a handler we can call to perform the action.

▷ **isPresented**—This is a Boolean value that determines whether the view is being presented or not.

We have worked with values from the environment before (see Listing 5-94). All we have to do is to add an `@Environment` property to the view and then read or modify its values. The `dismiss` value is a structure that provides access to a closure with code to dismiss the view, so all we need to do to remove the `SettingsView` view is to define an `@Environment` property with this value and then execute the closure when a button is pressed, as shown below.

```
struct SettingsView: View {
    @Environment(\.dismiss) var dismiss
    @State private var showPictures: Bool = true
    @State private var showYear: Bool = true

    var body: some View {
        Form {
            Toggle("Show Pictures", isOn: $showPictures)
            Toggle("Show Year", isOn: $showYear)
        }.navigationTitle("Settings")
        .navigationBarBackButtonHidden(true)
        .toolbar {
            ToolbarItem(placement: .navigationBarLeading) {
                Button("Go Back") {
                    dismiss()
                }
            }
        }
    }
}
```

Listing 8-22: Dismissing the view from the environment

As always, it is recommended to use the name of the environment value to define the property. In this example, we call it `dismiss`. To add a custom back button, we first remove the one provided by the system with the `navigationBarBackButtonHidden()` modifier, and then add a new button on the left side of the navigation bar (leading) with the `toolbar()` modifier. When the button is pressed, we execute the closure provided by the `DismissAction` structure in the `dismiss` property, and the view is removed.

Figure 8-19: Custom back button

 Do It Yourself: Update the `SettingsView` view with the code in Listing 8-22. Run the application. Press the button to open the `SettingsView` view and then press the Go Back button to close this view and show the list of books on the screen again.

In the previous example, we used an `Image` view to declare the label for the `NavigationLink` view, but we can use any view we want, including custom views. A common practice is to declare the rows of a list as the labels of a `NavigationLink` view, so when the user taps on a row, another view opens to show additional information.

```
struct ContentView: View {
    @Environment(ApplicationData.self) private var appData

    var body: some View {
        NavigationStack {
            List(appData.userData) { book in
                NavigationLink(destination: {
                    DetailView(book: book)
                }, label: {
                    CellBook(book: book)
                })
            }.navigationTitle(Text("Books"))
        }
    }
}
```

Listing 8-23: Selecting rows with a navigation link

The view that opens when a row is selected is usually referred to as the Detail view, as its purpose is to display the details of the selected item. In our example, we want to show additional information about the book selected by the user. For this purpose, the `NavigationLink` view opens a new view called `DetailView` and sends to it a copy of the `Book` structure that represents the book. The view receives this instance and displays the values on the screen.

```
import SwiftUI

struct DetailView: View {
    let book: Book

    var body: some View {
        VStack {
            Text(book.title)
                .font(.title)
            Text(book.author)
```

```
            Image(book.cover)
                .resizable()
                .scaledToFit()
        }.padding()
        .navigationTitle("Book")
        .navigationBarTitleDisplayMode(.inline)
    }
}
#Preview {
    NavigationStack {
        DetailView(book: ApplicationData.shared.userData[0])
    }
}
```

Listing 8-24: Defining a Detail view

When the user selects a row in the `ContentView` view, an instance of the `DetailView` view is created and presented on the screen transitioning from right to left, and the values of the book are shown to the user.

Figure 8-20: Detail view

 Do It Yourself: Update the `ContentView` view with the code in Listing 8-23. Create a new SwiftUI file called DetailView.swift and update the code generated by the template with the code in Listing 8-24. Tap on a book. You should see the information of the book on the screen, as in Figure 8-20 (right).

Although this is a valid approach, we don't have much control over the navigation process. The system automatically includes back buttons that we can replace with custom buttons and the `dismiss` value, as we did in previous examples (see Listing 8-22), but these buttons only remove the current view. Professional applications allow the user to navigate through many views that comprise long navigation paths. Navigating through the views one by one is tedious and time-consuming. To have more control over the navigation path, we can access the views through the `NavigationStack` view. This view can keep track of all the views opened by the user and store references to those views in a binding property. By changing the values stored in this property, we can navigate through the views programmatically (add or remove as many views as we want).

There are a few steps we need to follow to control the navigation path. First, we must create the navigation links with the `NavigationLink(String, value: Value)` initializer. This initializer identifies the link with the value provided by the **value** argument. Once the link is identified, we must add the following modifier to tell the system what to open.

▷ **navigationDestination(for:** Type, **destination:** Closure)—This modifier specifies the destination view for a `NavigationLink` view. The **for** argument is the data type of the values used by the `NavigationLink` view to identify the link, and the **destination** argument creates an instance of the destination view.

The **NavigationLink** view and the **navigationDestination()** modifier are connected by the data type of the value used by the view to identify the link. When the user taps on a **NavigationLink** view identified with a value, the **navigationDestination()** modifier associated to that data type creates a destination view and presents it on the screen. Once the destination view is presented on the screen, the **NavigationStack** view stores it in a navigation stack and the value assigned to the **NavigationLink** is added to a binding property that we can modify later to control the navigation path. The values in this property are stored in a collection, but because they can be of different data types, SwiftUI provides the following structure to manage them.

▷ **NavigationPath()**—This initializer creates a structure to store values associated with views in a navigation path. This initializer defines an empty path, but there are two more that create instances with predefined paths. We can create it from a collection of values or from a **CodableRepresentation** structure, which allows us to restore previous navigation paths when the app is launched. (We will learn more about the **CodableRepresentation** structure in Chapter 12.)

The **NavigationPath** structure includes the following properties and methods to manage the values.

▷ **isEmpty**—This property returns a Boolean value that indicates if the path is empty.

▷ **count**—This property returns the number of values (views) in the path.

▷ **append(**Value**)**—This method adds a value (a view) to the path.

▷ **removeLast(**Int**)**—This method removes the last value from the path. The argument is the number of values (views) to remove. By default, only the last value is removed.

When we add a value to the **NavigationPath** structure, the view associated to that value is shown on the screen, and when we remove a value, the view is removed from the navigation path (and the screen if it is currently active). For this process to work, we need to define a binding property with a **NavigationPath** structure (this could be a **@State** property inside the view or an observable property in the model), initialize the **NavigationStack** view with a reference to this property, create the **NavigationLink** views with a value, and implement the **navigationDestination()** modifier to tell the system which view to open when a link is followed by the user. The next example shows how to implement these changes to control navigation.

```
struct ContentView: View {
    @Environment(ApplicationData.self) private var appData
    @State private var viewPath = NavigationPath()

    var body: some View {
        NavigationStack(path: $viewPath) {
            List(appData.userData) { book in
                NavigationLink(value: book, label: {
                    CellBook(book: book)
                })
            }
            .navigationTitle(Text("Books"))
            .navigationBarTitleDisplayMode(.inline)
            .toolbar {
                ToolbarItem(placement: .navigationBarTrailing) {
                    NavigationLink(value: "Settings View", label: {
                        Image(systemName: "gear")
                    })
                }
            }
        }
```

```
    .navigationDestination(for: Book.self, destination: { book in
        DetailView(viewPath: $viewPath, book: book)
    })
    .navigationDestination(for: String.self, destination: { viewID in
        if viewID == "Settings View" {
            SettingsView(viewPath: $viewPath)
        }
    })
    }
  }
}
```

Listing 8-25: *Defining custom navigation*

As we already mentioned, the `NavigationLink` view and the `navigationDestination()` modifier are connected by the data type of the value that identifies the link. In the example in Listing 8-25, we define two `NavigationLink` views, one to open a detail view with information about the selected book and another to open a settings view. The navigation link for the detail view is identified with the `Book` structure that represents the book selected by the user, and the one for the settings view is identified with a string. To tell the system which view to open when a link is activated by the user, we implement two `navigationDestination()` modifiers, one associated with the `Book` data type to open the `DetailView` view and another associated with the `String` data type to open the `SettingsView` view. When a link is activated, the system finds the right destination based on the data type and opens the corresponding view.

To control the navigation path from other views in the interface, we must pass a reference of the `viewPath` property and then add or remove values from it, as we do in the `DetailView` view below.

```
struct DetailView: View {
    @Binding var viewPath: NavigationPath
    var book: Book

    var body: some View {
        VStack {
            Text(book.title)
                .font(.title)
            Text(book.author)
            Image(book.cover)
                .resizable()
                .scaledToFit()
                .frame(width: 100)
            Spacer()
        }.padding()
        .navigationTitle(Text("Book"))
        .navigationBarBackButtonHidden(true)
        .toolbar {
            ToolbarItem(placement: .navigationBarLeading) {
                Button("Go Back") {
                    viewPath.removeLast()
                }
            }
        }
    }
}
#Preview {
    @Previewable @State var navigation = NavigationPath()

    NavigationStack {
        DetailView(viewPath: $navigation, book:
ApplicationData.shared.userData[0])
    }
```

}

Listing 8-26: Adding and removing views from the path

The `DetailView` view receives a reference to the `viewPath` property, so we can add or remove values from the `NavigationPath` structure and in consequence add or remove views from the navigation path. In this example, we add a button to the navigation bar that calls the `removeLast()` method. This method removes the last value in the `NavigationPath` structure, which in our case is the `Book` structure that represents the `DetailView` view, so this view is removed from the screen when the button is pressed.

We do something similar in the `SettingsView` view. In this case, the view is opened when a button in the navigation bar is pressed, but the procedure for removing the view is the same.

```
struct SettingsView: View {
    @Binding var viewPath: NavigationPath

    var body: some View {
        VStack {
            Text("My Settings")
            Spacer()
        }.padding()
        .navigationBarBackButtonHidden(true)
        .toolbar {
            ToolbarItem(placement: .navigationBarLeading) {
                Button("Go Back") {
                    viewPath.removeLast()
                }
            }
        }
    }
}
#Preview {
    @Previewable @State var navigation = NavigationPath()

    NavigationStack {
        SettingsView(viewPath: $navigation)
    }
}
```

Listing 8-27: Removing a view from the path

 Do It Yourself: Update the `ContentView` view with the code in Listing 8-25, the `DetailView` view with the code in Listing 8-26, and the `SettingsView` view with the code in Listing 8-27. Run the application. Select a book to open the detail view or tap on the button in the navigation bar to open the Settings view. You should see a Go Back button at the top of the screen to go back to the initial view.

Removing a value from the navigation path with the `removeLast()` method is similar to what we can do with the `dismiss` value (see Listing 8-22), but a navigation path can span multiple views. In these cases, we need to keep two things in mind. First, if we store the navigation path in a `@State` property, as we did in the `ContentView` view of our example, we must pass a reference of this property to each view we want to control. This can be tedious and error-prone, so it is better to store the path in the model instead. Second, the `NavigationStack` view gives precedence to the `navigationDestination()` modifier that is higher in the view hierarchy. For example, if we define two `navigationDestination()` modifiers to process `String` values, the `NavigationStack` view will process only the one that is higher in the view hierarchy, which means that all the navigation links identified with a string will be processed from the same place.

The following example shows an alternative way to control a long navigation path. For this purpose, we create two properties in the model: one to store the navigation path, and another to store a reference to the book selected by the user.

```
@Observable class ApplicationData: @unchecked Sendable {
   var userData: [Book] = []
   var viewPath = NavigationPath()
   var selectedBook: Book? = nil

   static let shared: ApplicationData = ApplicationData()
   private init() {
      userData = [
         Book(title: "Steve Jobs", author: "Walter Isaacson", cover:
"book1", year: 2011, selected: false),
         Book(title: "HTML5 for Masterminds", author: "J.D Gauchat",
cover: "book2", year: 2017, selected: false),
         Book(title: "The Road Ahead", author: "Bill Gates", cover:
"book3", year: 1995, selected: false),
         Book(title: "The C Programming Language", author: "Brian W.
Kernighan", cover: "book4", year: 1988, selected: false),
         Book(title: "Being Digital", author: "Nicholas Negroponte",
cover: "book5", year: 1996, selected: false),
         Book(title: "Only the Paranoid Survive", author: "Andrew S.
Grove", cover: "book6", year: 1999, selected: false),
         Book(title: "Accidental Empires", author: "Robert X. Cringely",
cover: "book7", year: 1996, selected: false),
         Book(title: "Bobby Fischer Teaches Chess", author: "Bobby
Fischer", cover: "book8", year: 1982, selected: false),
         Book(title: "New Guide to Science", author: "Isaac Asimov",
cover: "book9", year: 1993, selected: false),
         Book(title: "Christine", author: "Stephen King", cover:
"book10", year: 1983, selected: false),
         Book(title: "IT", author: "Stephen King", cover: "book11", year:
1987, selected: false),
         Book(title: "Ending Aging", author: "Aubrey de Grey", cover:
"book12", year: 2007, selected: false)
      ]
   }
}
```

Listing 8-28: *Controlling the navigation path from the model*

Now we can store the path in the observable object and manage the whole navigation from the `ContentView` view, as shown below.

```
struct ContentView: View {
   @Environment(ApplicationData.self) private var appData

   var body: some View {
      @Bindable var appData = appData

      NavigationStack(path: $appData.viewPath) {
         List(appData.userData) { book in
            NavigationLink(value: book, label: {
               CellBook(book: book)
            })
         }
         .navigationTitle(Text("Books"))
         .navigationBarTitleDisplayMode(.inline)
         .toolbar {
            ToolbarItem(placement: .navigationBarTrailing) {
               NavigationLink(value: "Settings View", label: {
                  Image(systemName: "gear")
```

```
                })
            }
        }
        .navigationDestination(for: Book.self, destination: { book in
            DetailView(book: book)
        })
        .navigationDestination(for: String.self, destination: { viewID in
            if viewID == "Settings View" {
                SettingsView()
            } else if viewID == "Picture View" {
                PictureView()
            }
        })
        }
    }
}
```

Listing 8-29: Controlling the navigation path from the initial view

The `navigationDestination()` modifier declared to process navigation links identified with a `String` value now opens two views, the `SettingsView` view, as before, and the `PictureView` view that opens when the user taps the book's cover. Below are the changes we need to introduce to the `DetailView` view to create this link.

```
struct DetailView: View {
    @Environment(ApplicationData.self) private var appData
    var book: Book

    var body: some View {
        VStack {
            Text(book.title)
                .font(.title)
            Text(book.author)
            Button(action: {
                appData.selectedBook = book
                appData.viewPath.append("Picture View")
            }, label: {
                Image(book.cover)
                    .resizable()
                    .scaledToFit()
                    .frame(width: 100)
            })
            Spacer()
        }.padding()
        .navigationTitle(Text("Book"))
        .navigationBarBackButtonHidden(true)
        .toolbar {
            ToolbarItem(placement: .navigationBarLeading) {
                Button("Go Back") {
                    appData.viewPath.removeLast()
                }
            }
        }
    }
}
#Preview {
    NavigationStack {
        DetailView(book: ApplicationData.shared.userData[0])
            .environment(ApplicationData.shared)
    }
}
```

Listing 8-30: Adding views to the navigation path programmatically

To create the navigation link, we use a `Button` view instead of the `NavigationLink` view implemented before. This is to be able to assign the book selected by the user to the `selectedBook` property in the model, so that the `PictureView` view knows which cover to display. To open the `PictureView` view, we add the string "Picture View" to the `Navigation-Path` structure using the `append()` method. Below is our implementation of this view.

```
struct PictureView: View {
   @Environment(ApplicationData.self) private var appData

   var body: some View {
      VStack {
         Image(appData.selectedBook?.cover ?? "nopicture")
            .resizable()
            .scaledToFit()
         Spacer()
      }
      .navigationTitle(Text("Cover"))
      .navigationBarBackButtonHidden()
      .toolbar {
         ToolbarItem(placement: .navigationBarLeading) {
            Button("Go Back") {
               appData.viewPath.removeLast()
            }
         }
         ToolbarItem(placement: .navigationBarTrailing) {
            Button("Back to List") {
               appData.viewPath = NavigationPath()
            }
         }
      }
   }
}
#Preview {
   NavigationStack {
      PictureView()
         .environment(ApplicationData.shared)
   }
}
```

Listing 8-31: Returning to different views

When the user taps the cover of the book in the `DetailView` view, the string "Picture View" is added to the `NavigationPath` structure, the `NavigationStack` view looks for the `navigationDestination()` modifier that responds to `String` values, and the modifier opens the `PictureView` view. At this point, the `NavigationPath` structure contains two values: the `Book` structure, which represents the `DetailView` view, and the string "Picture View", which represents the `PictureView` view. This means that we now have two views to return to: the `DetailView` view and the `ContentView` view. To show how to navigate to any of these views, the navigation bar of the `PictureView` view defined in Listing 8-31 includes two buttons. The first button removes the last value in the `NavigationPath` structure using the `removeLast()` method. This is the string "Picture View" and thus the `PictureView` view is removed from the screen. The second button returns the user to the initial view, but the process is a little different. As mentioned earlier, the values stored in the `NavigationPath` structure represent the views opened by the user. In our example, an empty `NavigationPath` structure represents the `ContentView` view (the initial view), the `Book` structure stored first represents the `DetailView` view, and the "Picture View" string stored second represents the `PictureView` view. Therefore, to return to the initial view, we can remove these two values using the `removeLast()` method (`removeLast(2)`) or simply assign a new `NavigationPath` structure with an empty path to the `viewPath` property. The last approach is recommended and is followed in this example. This avoids the error of removing more values than are present in the path. The result is shown below.

Figure 8-21: Custom navigation path

Do It Yourself: Update the `ApplicationData` class with the code in Listing 8-28, the `ContentView` view with the code in Listing 8-29, and the `DetailView` view with the code in Listing 8-30. Create a new SwiftUI file called PictureView.swift for the view in Listing 8-31. Remember to update the `SettingsView` view to work with the `viewPath` property in the model. Select a book and tap on the cover. You should see the `PictureView` view on the screen with an enlarged image of the cover. If you press the Go Back button, you should go back to the `DetailView` view, but if you press the Back to List button, the interface should transition back to the list of books.

(Basic) **Zoom Transition**

By default, a `NavigationStack` view creates a transition from side to side, but we can turn it into a zoom transition. This type of transition zooms in and out of a view from another view. To set the transition we need to indicate which view is going to be presented and from which view the animation is going to start. SwiftUI provides the following modifiers for this purpose.

▷ **navigationTransition(**NavigationTransition**)**—This modifier sets the navigation style for the view. The argument is a protocol with the property **automatic** to set the transition by default and the method `zoom(sourceID: Value, in: Namespace.ID)` to set a zoom transition.

▷ **matchedTransitionSource(id:** Value, **in:** Namespace.ID**)**—This modifier determines which view is the origin for the animation. The **id** argument is a value that associates the source view with the view to be presented, and the **in** argument is the namespace used by the system to coordinate the transition.

The `navigationTransition()` modifier specifies which view is to be opened, and the `matchedTransitionSource()` modifier specifies the view from which the animation is to be performed. To connect these two views, we need to provide an identifier, usually a string, and a namespace. A namespace is a name that objects and structures use to work together. SwiftUI defines the following property wrapper to create a namespace.

▷ **@Namespace**—This property wrapper defines a new namespace.

To open a view with a zoom transition, we need to define a property with the `@Namespace` property wrapper and then apply the modifiers to the views involved. If there are multiple views participating in the process, we need to identify each animation with different values. For example, if we want to open the `DetailView` view for each book in our project with a zoom transition, we can identify each animation with the book's `id` property, as shown below.

```
struct ContentView: View {
   @Environment(ApplicationData.self) private var appData
   @Namespace var zoomBooks
```

```
var body: some View {
    @Bindable var appData = appData

    NavigationStack(path: $appData.viewPath) {
        List(appData.userData) { book in
            NavigationLink(value: book, label: {
                CellBook(book: book)
                    .matchedTransitionSource(id: book.id, in: zoomBooks)
            })
        }
        .navigationTitle(Text("Books"))
        .navigationBarTitleDisplayMode(.inline)
        .toolbar {
            ToolbarItem(placement: .navigationBarTrailing) {
                NavigationLink(value: "Settings View", label: {
                    Image(systemName: "gear")
                })
            }
        }
        .navigationDestination(for: Book.self, destination: { book in
            DetailView(book: book)
                .navigationTransition(.zoom(sourceID: book.id, in:
zoomBooks))
        })
        .navigationDestination(for: String.self, destination: { viewID in
            if viewID == "Settings View" {
                SettingsView()
            } else if viewID == "Picture View" {
                PictureView()
            }
        })
    }
}
```

Listing 8-32: Opening a view with a zoom transition

 Do It Yourself: Update the **ContentView** view with the code in Listing 8-32. Run the application. Select a row. The **DetailView** view with the selected book should open and the animation should start from the view you tapped.

(Basic) **8.2 Modal Views**

In addition to the views opened by navigation links, we can extend the interface with modal views. Modal views are normal views but are presented on top of the rest of the views.

(Basic) **Sheets**

Sheets are general-purpose modal views. On iPhones, they occupy the whole screen, and on iPads and Mac computers they are shown as a rectangular view at the center of the screen. The **View** protocol defines the following modifiers to present a sheet.

▷ **sheet(isPresented:** Binding, **onDismiss:** Closure?, **content:** Closure)—This modifier displays a sheet. The **isPresented** argument is a binding property of type **Bool** that determines whether the sheet has to be presented (**true**) or removed (**false**), the **onDismiss** argument is a closure that is executed when the sheet is removed, and the **content** argument is a closure that defines the view to be shown on the screen.

▷ **sheet(item:** Binding, **onDismiss:** Closure?, **content:** Closure)—This modifier displays a sheet. The **item** argument is an optional binding value that determines whether the sheet has to be presented or removed (**nil**), the **onDismiss** argument is a closure that is executed when the sheet is removed, and the **content** argument is a closure that defines the view to be shown on the screen. The closure receives the value stored in the binding property.

These modifiers create a sheet that partially covers the interface. SwiftUI also includes the following modifiers to create a full-screen sheet.

▷ **fullScreenCover(isPresented:** Binding, **onDismiss:** Closure, **content:** Closure)—This modifier displays a full-screen sheet. The **isPresented** argument is a binding property of type **Bool** that determines whether the sheet has to be presented (**true**) or removed (**false**), the **onDismiss** argument is a closure that is executed when the sheet is removed, and the **content** argument is a closure that defines the view to be shown on the screen.

▷ **fullScreenCover(item:** Binding, **onDismiss:** Closure, **content:** Closure)— This modifier displays a full-screen sheet. The **item** argument is an optional binding value that determines whether the sheet has to be presented or removed (**nil**), the **onDismiss** argument is a closure that is executed when the sheet is removed, and the **content** argument is a closure that defines the view to be shown on the screen. The closure receives the value stored in the binding property.

Sheets are controlled from a binding property. When the property contains a value or the value is **true**, the modifier opens the view on top of the current interface, and we can use this view for anything we want. A common practice is opening sheets to allow the user to add values to the model. For instance, we can open a sheet to allow the user to add a book to the list.

```
struct ContentView: View {
    @Environment(ApplicationData.self) private var appData
    @State private var showSheet: Bool = false

    var body: some View {
        NavigationStack {
            List(appData.userData) { book in
                CellBook(book: book)
            }.navigationTitle(Text("Books"))
            .toolbar {
                ToolbarItem(placement: .navigationBarTrailing) {
                    Button(action: {
                        showSheet = true
                    }, label: { Image(systemName: "plus") })
                }
            }
            .sheet(isPresented: $showSheet) {
                AddBookView()
            }
        }
    }
}
```

Listing 8-33: Displaying a sheet

This view defines a **@State** property to control the state of the sheet and adds a **Button** view to the navigation bar that assigns the value **true** to this property to open the sheet when pressed. The sheet is managed by the **sheet()** modifier applied to the **List** view. The modifier is connected to the **showSheet** property, so when the value of this property is **true** a custom view called **AddBookView** is presented on the screen. This is the view we are using to allow the user to add new books. The view includes `TextField` views to insert the book's title, author and year, and a button to store the values in the model.

```
import SwiftUI

struct AddBookView: View {
    @Environment(ApplicationData.self) private var appData
    @Environment(\.dismiss) var dismiss
    @State private var titleInput: String = ""
    @State private var authorInput: String = ""
    @State private var yearInput: String = ""

    var body: some View {
        VStack(alignment: .trailing, spacing: 10) {
            HStack {
                Spacer()
                Button("Close") {
                    dismiss()
                }.padding([.top, .bottom], 10)
            }
            TextField("Insert Title", text: $titleInput)
                .textFieldStyle(.roundedBorder)
            TextField("Insert Author", text: $authorInput)
                .textFieldStyle(.roundedBorder)
            TextField("Insert Year", text: $yearInput)
                .textFieldStyle(.roundedBorder)
                .keyboardType(.numbersAndPunctuation)
            Button("Save") {
                storeBook()
                dismiss()
            }.buttonStyle(.borderedProminent)
            Spacer()
        }.padding()
    }
    func storeBook() {
        let title = titleInput.trimmingCharacters(in: .whitespaces)
        let author = authorInput.trimmingCharacters(in: .whitespaces)
        if let year = Int(yearInput), !title.isEmpty && !author.isEmpty {
            let newBook = Book(title: title, author: author, cover:
"nocover", year: year, selected: false)
            appData.userData.append(newBook)
        }
    }
}
#Preview {
    NavigationStack {
        AddBookView()
            .environment(ApplicationData.shared)
    }
}
```

Listing 8-34: Defining the view for the sheet

There is nothing new in this view, all we do is to take the input from the user, trim the values to remove additional space, check whether the values are valid, and store a new book in the model. For this purpose, we create a new `Book` structure with the values inserted by the user and add it to the `userData` array in the model. After the process is over, we perform the `dismiss` handler, the view is closed, and the new book appears at the end of the list.

Figure 8-22: Sheet to insert new values

Do It Yourself: Update the `ContentView` view from the previous example with the code in Listing 8-33. Create a new SwiftUI file called AddBookView.swift for the code in Listing 8-34. Press the + button in the navigation bar. You should see a sheet with three input fields. Insert the values and press Save. The book should be added at the end of the list.

IMPORTANT: The views opened in a sheet are not part of the hierarchical structure created by the `NavigationStack` view, and therefore they do not participate in the path created by this view. To remove it, we must implement the `dismiss` property, as we did in Listing 8-34.

In this example, we have included a button to close the view, but there is a built-in feature that allows the user to remove the view by dragging it down with the finger. SwiftUI includes the following modifier to disable this tool.

▷ **interactiveDismissDisabled(**Bool**)**—This modifier enables or disables the possibility of dragging down the view to close it (`true` disabled, `false` enabled).

There are also modifiers to configure the sheet. The following are the most frequently used.

▷ **presentationDetents(**Set, **selection:** Binding**)**—This modifier determines the sheet's height. The first argument is a set of values that determine all the different sizes the sheet can take. The values are defined by a structure of type `PresentationDetent`. The structure includes the type properties `large` and `medium` to set predefined sizes, and the type methods `custom(Type)`, `fraction(CGFloat)`, and `height(CGFloat)` to set custom sizes. And the **selection** argument is a binding property we can use to keep track of the current height.

▷ **presentationDragIndicator(**Visibility**)**—This modifier shows or hides the indicator that is provided by the system to drag the sheet when there are multiple heights available. The argument is an enumeration with the values `automatic`, `visible`, and `hidden`.

▷ **presentationBackground(**ShapeStyle**)**—This modifier defines the sheet's background. The argument specifies a color or a pattern, such as those provided by `Color` views or `Material` structures.

▷ **presentationCornerRadius(**CGFloat?**)**—This modifier defines the sheet's corner radius.

▷ **presentationBackgroundInteraction(**PresentationBackgroundInteraction **)**—This modifier determines if the user can interact with the content behind the sheet.

These modifiers are applied directly to the view presented by the sheet. For instance, the modifiers implemented in the following example give the sheet a translucent background and don't allow the user to drag it down to close it.

```
.sheet(isPresented: $showSheet) {
   AddBookView()
      .interactiveDismissDisabled(true)
      .presentationBackground(.thinMaterial)
}
```

Listing 8-35: Disabling the interactive feature to dismiss the sheet

To determine the sheet's height, we have different options available. By default, the height is set to `large`, which means that the view will take up as much space as possible. The value `medium` sets the height to around half the space available.

```
.sheet(isPresented: $showSheet) {
   AddBookView()
      .presentationDetents([.medium])
}
```

Listing 8-36: Assigning a predefined height

The sheet now takes up less space on the screen, but we can go further and specify a custom height. With the `height()` method we can specify a height in points, and with the `fraction()` method we can specify a height proportional to that of the screen (values from 0.0 to 1.0). In the following example, we reduce it to 250 points.

```
.sheet(isPresented: $showSheet) {
   AddBookView()
      .presentationDetents([.height(250)])
}
```

Listing 8-37: Assigning a custom height

 Do It Yourself: Replace the `sheet()` modifier in the `ContentView` view with the modifier you want to try. Press the + button to open the sheet. Try to assign multiple values to the first argument of the `presentationDetents()` modifier to see how the sheet adapts to different heights.

On iPhones, the sheets are displayed full screen, but on iPads and Mac computers they partially cover the screen. The size and shape of the view is determined by the system, but we can change it with the following modifier.

▷ **presentationSizing(**PresentationSizing**)**—This modifier determines the shape of the sheet and how it is going to adapt to the size of its content. The argument is a structure that conforms to the **PresentationSizing** protocol. The framework includes properties to return predefined structures that conform to this protocol. The currently available are **automatic**, **fitted**, **form** and **page**.

The structure returned by the **page** property is the one used by default. It presents a view over the content with a size determined by the space available on the screen. The one returned by the **form** property presents a narrow view, which is ideal to display forms. And the structure returned by the **fitted** property adapts the view to the size of the content. For example, we can assign a fixed size to the view with the **frame()** modifier and then ask the sheet to adapt to it.

```
.sheet(isPresented: $showSheet) {
   AddBookView()
      .frame(width: 350, height: 250)
```

```
        .presentationSizing(.fitted)
}
```

Listing 8-38: Declaring the size of the sheet

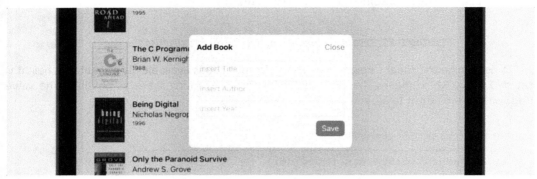

Figure 8-23: *Custom sheet on iPads*

There is a second **sheet()** modifier designed to open a sheet for each of the values in the model. It is usually implemented to open a sheet for each row on a list. The modifier needs an optional binding property of the same data type of the items in our model (the data type must conform to the **Identifiable** protocol). If the property contains a value, a sheet is opened with that value, and when the value **nil** is assigned to the property, the sheet is closed.

In the following example, we implement this modifier to allow the user to edit the values of the books. When a row is selected, we assign a copy of the **Book** structure that represents the book to the **@State** property, so the sheet is opened with this value.

```
struct ContentView: View {
    @Environment(ApplicationData.self) private var appData
    @State private var showSheet: Bool = false
    @State private var editItem: Book?

    var body: some View {
        NavigationStack {
            List(appData.userData) { book in
                CellBook(book: book)
                    .background(.white)
                    .onTapGesture {
                        editItem = book
                    }
            }.navigationTitle(Text("Books"))
            .toolbar {
                ToolbarItem(placement: .navigationBarTrailing) {
                    Button(action: {
                        showSheet = true
                    }, label: { Image(systemName: "plus") })
                }
            }
            .sheet(isPresented: $showSheet) {
                AddBookView()
            }
            .sheet(item: $editItem) { item in
                AddBookView(book: item)
            }
        }
    }
}
```

Listing 8-39: Presenting a sheet for every value on the list

This view defines a **@State** property called **editItem** to store the **Book** value for the sheet. To allow the user to select a row, we add the **onTapGesture()** modifier to the **CellBook** view. We have implemented this modifier before to perform a task when the user taps a row (see Listing 7-37). In this case, we assign the row's **Book** structure to the **editItem** property. When this value changes, the sheet is opened with a second **sheet()** modifier added to the **List** view. The closure assigned to this modifier receives a copy of the **Book** structure that we send to the **AddBookView** view so the user is able to edit the values.

The **AddBookView** view must be updated to be able to receive the book selected by the user and show the current values in the input fields. But we also must contemplate that the view might be opened by the user to insert a new book. The following are the modifications we need to introduce to the view for this purpose.

```
struct AddBookView: View {
   @Environment(ApplicationData.self) private var appData
   @Environment(\.dismiss) var dismiss
   @State private var titleInput: String = ""
   @State private var authorInput: String = ""
   @State private var yearInput: String = ""
   var book: Book?

   var body: some View {
      VStack(alignment: .trailing, spacing: 10) {
         HStack {
            Text(book == nil ? "Add Book" : "Edit Book")
               .font(.body.weight(.bold))
            Spacer()
            Button("Close") {
               dismiss()
            }.padding([.top, .bottom], 10)
         }
         TextField("Insert Title", text: $titleInput)
            .textFieldStyle(.roundedBorder)
         TextField("Insert Author", text: $authorInput)
            .textFieldStyle(.roundedBorder)
         TextField("Insert Year", text: $yearInput)
            .textFieldStyle(.roundedBorder)
            .keyboardType(.numbersAndPunctuation)
         Button("Save") {
            storeBook()
            dismiss()
         }.buttonStyle(.borderedProminent)
         Spacer()
      }.padding()
      .onAppear {
         titleInput = book?.title ?? ""
         authorInput = book?.author ?? ""
         yearInput = book?.displayYear ?? ""
      }
   }
   func storeBook() {
      let title = titleInput.trimmingCharacters(in: .whitespaces)
      let author = authorInput.trimmingCharacters(in: .whitespaces)
      if let year = Int(yearInput), !title.isEmpty && !author.isEmpty {
         if let index = appData.userData.firstIndex(where: { $0.id ==
book?.id }) {
            let newBook = Book(title: title, author: author, cover:
appData.userData[index].cover, year: year, selected: false)
            appData.userData[index] = newBook
         } else {
            let newBook = Book(title: title, author: author, cover:
"nocover", year: year, selected: false)
```

```
            appData.userData.append(newBook)
         }
      }
   }
}
```

Listing 8-40: Editing a book

There are a few differences in this view from the one defined in Listing 8-34. First, we added an optional property called **book** to receive the book. If the user opens the view to add a new book, the value of this property will be **nil**, but if the view is opened by selecting a row, the property will contain the **Book** structure with the information about the selected book. By checking this value, we can perform tasks for each situation. For instance, at the top of the view, we added a **Text** view to display the texts "Add Book" or "Edit Book" depending on the value of this property. At the bottom, the **onAppear()** modifier was included to load the values. If the **book** property contains a book, we assign the values to the input fields so the user can change them.

The **storeBook()** method updates or adds the book to the model. We first get the index of the selected book with the **firstIndex()** method. If an index is returned, we create a new **Book** structure with the values inserted by the user and the current image, otherwise, we create the structure with an image by default and add it to the **userData** array.

Figure 8-24: Sheet to edit values

 Do It Yourself: Update the **ContentView** view with the code in Listing 8-39 and the **AddBookView** view with the code ih Listing 8-40. Select a row. You should see the values of the book on the screen. Edit a value and press Save. You should see the new value on the list.

(Basic) **Inspector**

SwiftUI also provides a modal view, similar to sheets, that opens on the right side of the screen on iPads and Macs and as a sheet on iPhones. This view is called *Inspector* and is used to provide additional information and functionality related to the content selected by the user. Below is the modifier we need to implement to present this view.

▷ **inspector(isPresented:** Binding, **content:** Closure)—This modifier presents a modal view. The **isPresented** argument is a Boolean property that determines whether the view is presented or not, and the **content** argument is the closure that provides the view to be presented.

SwiftUI also provides a modifier to determine the size of the inspector.

▷ **inspectorColumnWidth(min:** CGFloat?, **ideal:** CGFloat, **max:** CGFloat?)— This modifier defines the inspector's width. The **min** argument determines the minimum width possible, the **ideal** argument determines the initial width (it can be changed by the user), and the **max** argument determines the maximum width possible.

The `inspector()` modifier works like the `sheet()` modifier; it takes a binding property to determine whether the inspector should be open or not, and a closure to define its content.

```
struct ContentView: View {
    @Environment(ApplicationData.self) private var appData
    @State private var presentInspector: Bool = false

    var body: some View {
        NavigationStack {
            List(appData.userData) { book in
                CellBook(book: book)
            }
            .navigationTitle(Text("Books"))
            .navigationBarTitleDisplayMode(.inline)
            .inspector(isPresented: $presentInspector) {
                InspectorView()
            }
            .toolbar {
                Spacer()
                Button("Inspector") {
                    presentInspector.toggle()
                }
            }
        }
    }
}
```

Listing 8-41: *Presenting the inspector*

The view in Listing 8-41 includes a Boolean property called `presentInspector` to determine whether the inspector is open or not, and a button in the navigation bar to toggle the value. When the button is pressed, the `inspector()` modifier opens the `InspectorView` view. For this example, we defined the view with a `VStack` and three `Text` views to show some content. On an iPad or Mac, this view is displayed on the right side of the screen, while on iPhones it is presented as a sheet.

Figure 8-25: *Inspector on the iPhone and iPad*

The inspector adopts a size depending on the system, but we can specify the width we want with the `inspectorColumnWidth()` modifier. This modifier is applied to the view and can take a specific width or specify a maximum, minimum, and ideal size, as shown below.

```
.inspector(isPresented: $presentInspector) {
    InspectorView()
        .inspectorColumnWidth(min: 200, ideal: 250, max: 300)
}
```

Listing 8-42: *Defining the size of the inspector*

Another type of views we can add to our interface are popovers. Popovers are presented like sheets on iPhones, but as small views on iPads and Mac computers. The **View** protocol defines the following modifier to present them.

▷ **popover(isPresented:** Binding, **attachmentAnchor:** PopoverAttachment-Anchor, **arrowEdge:** Edge, **content:** Closure)—This modifier displays a popover. The **isPresented** argument is a binding property of type **Bool** that determines whether the popover has to be displayed (**true**) or removed (**false**). The **attachmentAnchor** argument is an enumeration of type **PopoverAttachmentAnchor** that includes the **point()** and **rect()** methods to determine the part of the view to which the popover should be anchored. The **arrowEdge** argument is an enumeration of type **Edge** that determines the side in which the popover's arrow should be placed. The values available are **bottom**, **leading**, **top**, and **trailing**. And the **content** argument is a closure that defines the view to be shown on the screen.

In iPhones, a popover is presented as a sheet, but on iPads they are presented as small views with a size determined by the view that defines the content. The position is determined by the view to which the modifier is applied and the location of the popover's arrow (top, left, right, or bottom). For instance, the following example shows a popover anchored to a **Button** view with a **top** arrow, so it appears below the button.

```
struct ContentView: View {
    @State private var showPopover: Bool = false

    var body: some View {
        VStack {
            Button("Show Popover") {
                showPopover = true
            }
            .popover(isPresented: $showPopover, arrowEdge: .top) {
                HelpView()
            }
            Spacer()
        }.font(.title)
    }
}
```

Listing 8-43: Showing a popover

The **popover()** modifier in Listing 8-43 has two arguments: the **isPresented** argument to control when the popover is shown, and the **arrowEdge** argument to determine the side where the arrow is placed, which in turn determines the position of the view relative to the anchor view. When the value of the **showPopover** property is **true**, the modifier creates an instance of the **HelpView** view and shows it on the screen.

The **HelpView** view is the custom view we use to define the popover's content. From this view, we can also determine the size of the popover with a **frame()** modifier, as shown below.

```
import SwiftUI

struct HelpView: View {
    @Environment(\.dismiss) var dismiss

    var body: some View {
        VStack {
            HStack {
                Spacer()
```

```
            Button("X") {
                dismiss()
            }.padding(.trailing, 16)
        }
        Text("Press this button when you need help")
            .font(.title)
            .padding()
    }.frame(width: 250, height: 250)
    }
}
```

Listing 8-44: Defining the content of the popover

The view can be removed by dragging it down with the finger on iPhones and by clicking outside the view on iPads, but we can also do it programmatically with the `dismiss` value, as we do in this example.

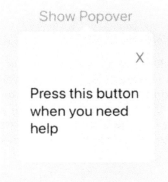

Figure 8-26: Popover on iPad

 Do It Yourself: Create a Multiplatform project. Update the **ContentView** view with the code in Listing 8-43. Create a SwiftUI file called HelpView.swift for the view in Listing 8-44. Run the application on the iPad simulator and press the Show Popover button. You should see the popover illustrated in Figure 8-26.

Basic Alert Views

Alert views are predefined modal views that can display messages and receive input from the user. Their purpose is to deliver to the user important information that requires immediate attention. For example, an alert view may be used to ask confirmation from the user before deleting data from the model. The following is the most frequently used modifier provided by the framework to create these views.

▷ **alert**(String, **isPresented:** Binding, **actions:** Closure, **message:** Closure)—
This modifier presents an alert view. The first argument is the title, the **isPresented** argument is a binding value of type **Bool** that determines whether the alert view has to be presented (**true**) or removed (**false**), the **actions** argument is a closure with **Button** views to create the buttons for the view, and the **message** argument is a closure with the view that provides the message.

The process to open alert views is the same as with sheets. We have to define a **@State** property to manage the state of the view and then apply the **alert()** modifier.

```
struct ContentView: View {
    @State private var name: String = ""
    @State private var openAlert: Bool = false
```

```
var body: some View {
   VStack(spacing: 10) {
      TextField("Insert your Name", text: $name)
         .textFieldStyle(.roundedBorder)
      HStack {
         Spacer()
         Button("Save") {
            openAlert = name.isEmpty
         }
      }
      Spacer()
   }.padding()
   .alert("Error", isPresented: $openAlert, actions: {
      Button("Cancel", role: .cancel, action: {
         openAlert = false
      })
   }, message: { Text("Insert your name") })
   }
}
```

Listing 8-45: Displaying an alert view

The **@State** property for this view is called **openAlert**. The view includes a **TextField** view and a button. When the button is pressed, the code checks whether the user inserted a value. If not, the value **true** is assigned to the **openAlert** property to present the alert view. The view was defined with the title "Error", the message "Insert your name", and a **Button** view that allows the user to dismiss it. Note that the button has been assigned a role that corresponds to the action performed (in this case, **cancel**) so that the system knows its purpose and can style it appropriately.

Figure 8-27: Alert view

 Do It Yourself: Create a Multiplatform project. Update the **ContentView** view with the code in Listing 8-45. Press the Save button. If you didn't insert anything in the text field, you should see the alert view illustrated in Figure 8-27.

In the example in Listing 8-45, we assign the value **false** to the **openAlert** property to remove the alert view when the Cancel button is pressed, but this is not necessary. After the action is performed, the view is automatically closed.

Our current view contains only one button, but we can include more. If there are two buttons, they are shown side by side, but three or more are displayed on a list, with the Cancel button at the end, as shown next.

```
.alert("Error", isPresented: $openAlert, actions: {
   Button("Cancel", role: .cancel, action: {})
   Button("Delete", role: .destructive, action: {
      name = ""
   })
   Button("Save Anyway", role: .none, action: {
      print("Save value")
   })
}, message: { Text("Insert your name") })
```

Listing 8-46: Defining an Alert view with multiple buttons

Chapter 8 - Navigation

This modifier includes three buttons. A button to cancel the action and two more to perform other tasks. The Cancel button was defined first, but because the role is set to `cancel`, the system places it at the end of the list.

Figure 8-28: *Alert view with multiple buttons*

(Basic) Confirmation Dialog

SwiftUI includes another type of alert views called *Confirmation Dialogs* (also known as Action Sheets). These views are usually presented when our application needs the user to make a decision and there is more than one option available. The following is the modifier we need to apply to create this view.

▷ **confirmationDialog(**String, **isPresented:** Binding, **titleVisibility:** Visibility, **actions:** Closure, **message:** Closure**)**—This modifier creates a confirmation dialog. The first argument is the text for the title, the **isPresented** argument is a binding value of type **Bool** that determines whether the view has to be presented (**true**) or removed (**false**), the **titleVisibility** argument is an enumeration with the values **automatic**, **hidden**, and **visible** that determines the visibility of the title, the **actions** argument defines the buttons to include in the view, and the **message** argument provides the text for the message.

There is not much difference between confirmation dialogs and alert views other than the design and location. For instance, in iPhones, a confirmation dialog is presented at the bottom of the screen. The following example creates a confirmation dialog with three buttons. The buttons don't perform any action but illustrate how to implement and work with these kinds of views.

```
struct ContentView: View {
   @State private var openDialog: Bool = false
   var body: some View {
      VStack(spacing: 10) {
         Button("Open Confirmation Dialog") {
            openDialog = true
         }
         Spacer()
      }.padding()
      .confirmationDialog("Email", isPresented: $openDialog, actions: {
         Button("Move to Inbox", role: .none, action: {})
         Button("Delete", role: .destructive, action: {})
         Button("Cancel", role: .cancel, action: {})
      }, message: {
         Text("What do you want to do with the message?")
      })
   }
}
```

Listing 8-47: *Defining an action sheet*

As always, we define a **@State** property to manage the view. When the value **true** is assigned to this property, the **confirmationDialog()** modifier opens a view with three buttons. There is a standard button to perform a normal operation, a **destructive** button to delete data, and a **cancel** button to allow the user to dismiss the view.

Figure 8-29: Confirmation dialog

 Do It Yourself: Create a Multiplatform project. Update the **ContentView** view with the code in Listing 8-47. Run the application and press the Open Confirmation Dialog button to open the view.

Basic   Tip Views

Tip views are small views we can show to help users find features in our app and learn how they work. They can be displayed along with the rest of the views in the interface or as popups.

Figure 8-30: Tip View

Tip views and all the tools required to configure and display tips are defined by a framework called TipKit. To define the tips, the framework provides the **Tip** protocol. This protocol includes the following properties to declare the content of the tip.

▷ **title**—This property returns a **Text** view to display the title of the tip.

▷ **message**—This property returns a **Text** view to display the message of the tip.

▷ **image**—This property returns an **Image** view with the image to display with the tip.

▷ **id**—This property returns a **String** value with the tip's identifier.

▷ **options**—This property returns an array of structures that conform to the **TipOption** protocol and are used to configure the tip. There are two structures available: The **IgnoresDisplayFrequency** structure is initialized with a Boolean value that determines if the tip is going to ignore the display frequency set by the system, and the **MaxDisplayCount** is initialized with an integer value that determines the maximum number of times the tip will be displayed to the user.

▷ **rules**—This property returns an array of **Rule** structures that determine the condition to meet before displaying a tip.

▷ **actions**—This property returns an array of **Action** structures that define the buttons to include with the tip to allow users to perform actions.

To create a tip, we need to import the TipKit framework, create a structure that conforms to the `Tip` protocol, and define the properties. The `title` property is required for the tip to be valid, but the rest are optional. In the following example, we define the `title` and `message` properties to specify the tip's title and message (recommended).

```
import SwiftUI
import TipKit

struct TipButton: Tip {
   var title: Text {
      Text("Press to Save")
   }
   var message: Text? {
      Text("Press this button to save your progress.")
   }
}
```

Listing 8-48: Defining a tip

TipKit defines an enumeration called `Tips` that provides access to configuration options and the following method to configure the tips.

▷ **configure(**[Tips.ConfigurationOption]**)**—This type method configures the tips. The argument is an array of **ConfigurationOption** structures. The framework includes two methods to return these structures: The **datastoreLocation-(DatastoreLocation)** method determines where the state of the tips is going to be stored, and the **displayFrequency()** method determines when the tips are eligible to be displayed.

After the tips are defined and the system is configured, we can show the tips with a `TipView` view. The following is the view's initializer.

▷ **TipView(**Tip, **arrowEdge:** Edge?, **action:** Closure**)**—This initializer creates a view to show a tip. The first argument is the `Tip` structure that defines the tip, the **arrowEdge** argument is an **Edge** enumeration that determines the direction of the view's indicator (**top**, **bottom**, **leading** and **trailing**), and the **action** argument is a closure with the code we want to execute when a tip button is pressed. The closure receives a reference of the **Action** structure that represents the button pressed by the user.

To display a tip, we need to create an instance of the `Tip` structure and use it to initialize a `TipView` view. It is recommended to store the instance in a constant so we can reference the tip later and work with it. In the following example, we store an instance of our `TipButton` structure in a constant called `tipButton` and then present it with a `TipView` view below a button to let the user know what the button is for.

```
import SwiftUI
import TipKit

struct ContentView: View {
   let tipButton = TipButton()

   var body: some View {
      VStack {
         Button("Save") {
            print("Action Performed")
         }
         TipView(tipButton)
      }
```

```
        .padding()
        .task {
          try? Tips.configure([
              .displayFrequency(.immediate),
              .datastoreLocation(.applicationDefault)
          ])
        }
        Spacer()
    }
}
```

Listing 8-49: Presenting a tip

For the tips to appear, we must configure the system. In this example, we use a `task()` modifier. This modifier executes the code in a closure as soon as the view is loaded, like the `onAppear()` modifier, but it runs the code in the background. (We will learn more about concurrency and how to execute background code in Chapter 9) There are two options for configuration. First, we can determine the frequency in which the tip is going to appear with the `displayFrequency()` method. This method takes the values `immediate`, `daily`, `hourly`, `weekly` and `monthly`. In this example we use the value `immediate` to show the tip when the view appears on the screen for the first time. The second configuration option is provided by the `datastoreLocation()` method. With this method we can determine where the states of the tips are going to be stored. Depending on the frequency, a tip can be shown one or multiple times. To know if the tip is eligible to be shown to the user, the system stores the states of the tips in a file. There are three options available: We can store the states in a file inside the application's support directory, in a specific file, or in CloudKit. In this example, we use the `applicationDefault` property to store the states in a file selected by the system (default), but the `DatastoreLocation` structure also includes the methods `url(URL)` to select our own file and `groupContainer(identifier: String)` to select a container in CloudKit to share the state with other devices. (We will learn how to work with files and URLs in Chapter 10 and how to share information between devices in Chapter 10 and Chapter 15)

 Do It Yourself: Create a Multiplatform project. Create a new file called Tips.swift for the code in Listing 8-48. Update the ContentView.swift file with the code in Listing 8-49. You should see the tip on the screen, as shown in Figure 8-30.

The example in Listing 8-49 displays the tip view along with the rest of the views in the interface (see Figure 8-30). If instead of a view, we want to show the tip over the interface in a popup window, we can use the following method provided by SwiftUI.

▷ **popoverTip(**Tip, **arrowEdge:** Edge, **action:** Closure**)**—This method creates a popover to show a tip. The first argument is the `Tip` structure that defines the tip, the **arrowEdge** argument is an `Edge` enumeration that determines the direction of the arrow of the popover (`top`, `bottom`, `leading` and `trailing`), and the **action** argument is a closure with the code we want to execute when a tip button is pressed. The closure receives the `Action` structure that represents the button pressed by the user.

To present the tip as a popover, we need to remove the `TipView` view and assign the `popoverTip()` modifier to the view associated with the tip, as shown below.

```
Button("Save") {
    print("Action Performed")
}
.popoverTip(tipButton)
```

Listing 8-50: Presenting a tip in a popover

Tips only appear when they are eligible according to the frequency set by the system. In our example, we set the frequency to `immediate` and therefore the tip is shown when the view appears on the screen for the first time and never again. This means that if we introduce changes to the tip or the interface, we won't be able to see the tip again on the canvas. To help us work with tips and design the interface, the framework includes the following methods.

▷ **showAllTipsForTesting()**—This method configures the system to show all the tips as soon as the view appears on the screen.

▷ **hideAllTipsForTesting()**—This method configures the system to never show tips.

Like the configuration options, these methods are also accessible from the `Tips` enumeration. In the following example, we show how to call the `showAllTipsForTesting()` method to always show the tips on the screen.

```
.task {
    try? Tips.configure([
        .displayFrequency(.immediate)
    ])
    Tips.showAllTipsForTesting()
}
```

Listing 8-51: Showing the tips for testing

 Do It Yourself: Update the `ContentView` view with the code in Listing 8-51. You should see the tip on the canvas again. Update the `ContentView` view with the code in Listing 8-50. You should now see the tip in a popover.

The `immediate` value configures the tips to appear the first time the view is shown to the user and then never again, but we can get the tip to appear every hour, day, week or month (`daily`, `hourly`, `immediate`, `monthly` and `weekly`). This means that a tip will appear over and over again at the frequency determined by the system. To stop showing a tip, the `Tip` protocol defines the following method.

▷ **invalidate(reason:** InvalidationReason**)**—This method invalidates the tip. The **reason** argument determines the reason why the tip was invalidated. It is an enumeration with the values **actionPerformed**, **displayCountExceeded**, and **tipClosed**.

In the following example, we configure the tips to be shown daily and then invalidate the tip when a button is pressed.

```
struct ContentView: View {
    let tipButton = TipButton()

    var body: some View {
        VStack {
            Button("Save") {
                print("Action Performed")
                tipButton.invalidate(reason: .actionPerformed)
            }
            .popoverTip(tipButton)
        }
        .padding()
        .task {
            try? Tips.configure([
                .displayFrequency(.daily)
            ])
        }
    }
```

```
        Spacer()
    }
}
```

Listing 8-52: Invalidating a tip

We can also control the display frequency from the tip itself. There are two options available: we can configure the tip to ignore the display frequency set by the system with a `IgnoresDisplayFrequency` structure or limit the times the tip is displayed with the `MaxDisplayCount` structure. In the following example, we configure our tip to be shown only one time.

```
struct TipButton: Tip {
    var title: Text {
        Text("Press to Save")
    }
    var message: Text? {
        Text("Press this button to save your progress.")
    }
    var options: [any TipOption] {
        [MaxDisplayCount(1)]
    }
}
```

Listing 8-53: Showing the tip only once

Tips can also include buttons that perform actions. The actions are defined by the `Action` structure and assigned to the `actions` property of the `Tip` structure, as shown below.

```
struct TipButton: Tip {
    var title: Text {
        Text("Press to Save")
    }
    var message: Text? {
        Text("Press this button to save your progress.")
    }
    var actions: [Action] {
        [Action(id: "tipButton", title: "More Into")]
    }
}
```

Listing 8-54: Adding actions to a tip

There are two ways to perform an action. We can assign a closure to the `Action` structure with the code we want to execute when the button is pressed, or assign an identifier to the action and then run the code from the view. In this example, we identified the action with the string "tipButton", so we can perform the action from the view.

```
.popoverTip(tipButton, action: { action in
    if action.id == "tipButton" {
        print("Help")
    }
})
```

Listing 8-55: Performing an action

When the button in the tip view is pressed, the system calls the closure assigned to the tip view. In this closure, we check if the action's identifier is equal to "tipButton" and execute the code.

       Chapter 8 - Navigation

Figure 8-31: Action

 Do It Yourself: Update the `TipButton` structure with the code in Listing 8-54. Update the `popoverTip()` modifier in the `ContentView` view with the code in Listing 8-55. Remember to call the `showAllTipsForTesting()` method to get the tip to show again, as we did in Listing 8-51. You should see a popover like the one in Figure 8-31. Press the button. The string "Help" should be printed on the console.

 IMPORTANT: TipKit also offers the possibility to set rules that determine conditions for the tip to appear, it allows the app to display multiple tips for the same view, and also to define a custom style for the tip views. The topic is beyond the scope of this book. For more information, visit our website and follow the links for this chapter.

(Basic) **8.3 Tab Views**

Another way to organize multiple views (screens), is with a Tab View. This view offers the user several options for opening views. By default, the view creates a bar with buttons that users can tap to open the view they want. On iPhones, the buttons are displayed as tabs at the bottom of the screen, whereas on iPads they are displayed in a bar at the top.

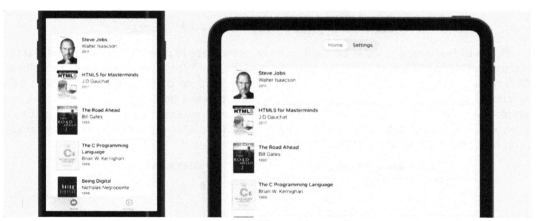

Figure 8-32: Tab View with two views

SwiftUI includes the `TabView` and `Tab` structures to create a Tab View and the tabs. The following are the initializers.

▷ **TabView(selection:** Binding, **content:** Closure)—This initializer creates a `TabView` view. The **selection** argument returns the value that identifies the view currently open, and the **content** argument is a closure with the list of `Tab` views the `TabView` view is going to include.

▷ **Tab(value:** Value, **role:** TabRole?, **content:** Closure)—This initializer creates a **Tab** view. The **value** argument is the value used to identify the tab for selection purposes. The **role** argument is a structure that defines the purpose of the tab. At the moment, the structure only includes the **search** property to declare that the tab is used for searching. The **content** argument is a closure that provides the view to be shown when the tab is selected.

A **TabView** view can have many configurations. The user can select the views using the tabs at the bottom or top of the screen, as shown in Figure 8-32, but also by turning them like the pages of a book or using a sidebar. To select the configuration, the **TabView** structure includes the following modifier.

▷ **tabViewStyle(**TabViewStyle)—This modifier defines the appearance of a **TabView** view. The argument is a structure that conforms to the **TabViewStyle** protocol. The framework includes many predefined structures with properties to configure the view. The most frequently used are **automatic**, **page**, **verticalPage**, **grouped**, **sidebarAdaptable** and **tabBarOnly**.

The following example shows how to create a standard Tab View with two tabs, one for the main content and another for settings.

```
struct ContentView: View {
    var body: some View {
        TabView {
            Tab("Home", systemImage: "book.circle") {
                Text("Main Screen")
            }
            Tab("Settings", systemImage: "gear") {
                Text("Settings")
            }
        }
    }
}
```

Listing 8-56: Defining a TabView *view with two tabs*

The **TabView** view defined in Listing 8-56 includes two tabs to present two views. The first tab is created with an SF Symbol called "book.circle" and the text "Home" and the second tab with an SF Symbol called "gear" and the text "Settings". The purpose of the tabs is to present fully functional views, as we did with the **NavigationStack** view before, but in this case we use simple **Text** views to simplify the example. When a tab is selected on iPhones or a button is pressed on iPads, the Tab View creates a new view with the corresponding **Text** view at the center of the screen, as shown below.

Figure 8-33: Views in a TabView *view*

Do It Yourself: Create a Multiplatform project. Update the `ContentView` view with the code in Listing 8-56. Select the iPhone simulator. You should see the screen illustrated in Figure 8-33. Click on the tabs to switch between the views.

We can include all the `Tab` views we want in a `TabView` view. If there is no space in the toolbar to display all of them, the system shows an additional button so that the user can select the remaining tabs.

Figure 8-34: *More tabs*

A `TabView` view shows one view at a time. This means that the user may not be aware that the content of a view has been updated. To alert the user that new information is available, we can display a badge over the button. The `View` protocol includes the following modifier for this purpose.

▷ **badge(**Value**)**—This modifier creates a badge with the value provided by the argument. The argument can be an integer, a string, or a `Text` view.

The `badge()` modifier is applied to the tab whose view has been updated. For instance, we can apply it to the Settings view to indicate how many issues require the user's attention.

```
struct ContentView: View {
    var body: some View {
        TabView {
            Tab("Home", systemImage: "book.circle") {
                Text("Main Screen")
            }
            Tab("Settings", systemImage: "gear") {
                Text("Settings")
            }
            .badge(12)
        }
    }
}
```

Listing 8-57: *Displaying a badge on a tab*

In this case, the badge is created with the number 12, so it will always show that value, but badges are usually defined with values from properties or counters used to alert the user of important issues that need attention.

Figure 8-35: *Badge*

The user can select the tabs at the bottom of the screen to open a view, but we can also do it from code. The `TabView` view can use a binding property to store a value that determines which view is currently opened. By modifying the value of this property, we can open a view programmatically. For this to work, we must assign the binding property to the **selection** argument of the `TabView` initializer and assign the tab's identifier to the **value** argument of the `Tab` initializer, as shown below.

```
struct ContentView: View {
    @State private var selectedView: Int = 2

    var body: some View {
        TabView(selection: $selectedView) {
            Tab("Home", systemImage: "book.circle", value: 1) {
                Text("Main Screen")
            }
            Tab("Settings", systemImage: "gear", value: 2) {
                Text("Settings")
            }
        }
    }
}
```

Listing 8-58: *Selecting the Settings view*

Every time a new value is assigned to the `@State` property, the tab with that identifier is shown on the screen. This also means that we can determine the view to show by default by initializing the property with that view's identifier. In our example, we assign the value 2 to the property, so the Settings view is shown first.

(Basic) Search

In addition to creating custom tabs, the `Tab` view also offers the option of creating a predefined tab that the user can use to search for information. This tab contains the icon of a magnifying glass, which makes it perfect for the compact design of iPads, as shown below.

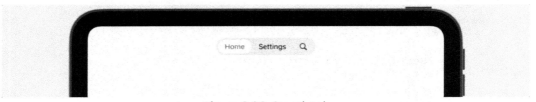

Figure 8-36: *Search tab*

The search tab is created by assigning the value `search` to the **role** argument of the `Tab` view's initializer. In the following example, we add a search tab to our `TabView` view to reproduce the design in Figure 8-36.

```
struct ContentView: View {
    var body: some View {
        TabView {
            Tab("Home", systemImage: "book.circle") {
                Text("Main Screen")
            }
            Tab("Settings", systemImage: "gear") {
                Text("Settings")
            }
            Tab(role: .search) {
                Text("Search")
            }
        }
    }
}
```

Listing 8-59: *Adding a search tab*

IMPORTANT: A search tab works just like any other tab. When you click on the tab, a view opens. In this case, the view should contain all the tools required for the user to perform a search. In the example in Listing 8-59, we open a simple `Text` view, as we have done for the other tabs, to illustrate how a `TabView` view works, but we will develop a more realistic example later in this chapter.

(Basic) Pages

By default, the design of a `TabView` view shows the tabs as a bar at the bottom of the screen on iPhones and as a series of buttons at the top of the screen on iPads, but we can change it with the `tabViewStyle()` modifier. An alternative for iOS devices is to show the views as the pages of an book with the `page` style.

When the content of a `TabView` view is displayed as the pages of a book, the toolbars are hidden. To help the user navigate between views, the `TabView` view shows indicators at the bottom of the screen. The `View` protocol includes the following modifier to change the aspects of these indicators.

▷ **indexViewStyle(**IndexViewStyle**)**—This modifier defines the appearance of the scroll indicators. The argument is a structure that includes the type method `page(backgroundDisplayMode: BackgroundDisplayMode)` to specify the style. The method takes a structure of type `BackgroundDisplayMode`. This structure includes the type properties **always**, **automatic**, **interactive**, and **never**.

The `page` style is usually implemented when we need to provide easy access to visual content, such as images. To illustrate how these types of views work, we are going to use the same `Text` views as before, but expanded to occupy the whole screen.

```
struct ContentView: View {
    var body: some View {
        TabView {
            Tab(content: {
                Text("Screen One")
                    .frame(minWidth: 0, maxWidth: .infinity, minHeight: 0,
maxHeight: .infinity)
                    .background(.orange)
            })
            Tab(content: {
                Text("Screen Two")
                    .frame(minWidth: 0, maxWidth: .infinity, minHeight: 0,
maxHeight: .infinity)
                    .background(.blue)
            })
        }
        .tabViewStyle(.page)
        .indexViewStyle(.page(backgroundDisplayMode: .always))
        .ignoresSafeArea(.all)
    }
}
```

Listing 8-60: Configuring the `TabView` *view to show content in pages*

This view creates a `TabView` view with two `Text` views, but because we declare the `tabViewStyle()` modifier with the value `page`, instead of showing the tabs at the bottom, the `TabView` view allows the user to swipe the views to the left or the right. Note that we've also implemented the `indexViewStyle()` modifier with the value **always** to show a background view below the page indicator.

Figure 8-37: Pages

 Do It Yourself: Update the `ContentView` view with the code in Listing 8-60. You should be able to swipe the views to the left to unveil the next one, as shown in Figure 8-37.

(Basic) **Sidebar**

The `tabViewStyle()` modifier also provides the option on iPads to access the buttons in a sidebar with the `sidebarAdaptable` style. On iPhones, the tabs are added to the tab bar as always, but on iPads the `TabView` view includes an additional button on the left to open the sidebar.

Figure 8-38: Sidebar button

To add this button and allow the user to open the sidebar, all we need to do is to apply the modifier to the `TabView` view, as shown below.

```
struct ContentView: View {
    var body: some View {
        TabView {
            Tab("Home", systemImage: "book.circle") {
                Text("Main Screen")
            }
            Tab("Settings", systemImage: "gear") {
                Text("Settings")
            }
        }
        .tabViewStyle(.sidebarAdaptable)
    }
}
```

Listing 8-61: Expanding the `TabView` view with a sidebar

When the button is pressed, the `TabView` view replaces the toolbar with a sidebar. If there is enough space, the sidebar is placed on the left side of the screen and the content on the right, otherwise, the sidebar is displayed over the content, as shown below.

Chapter 8 - Navigation

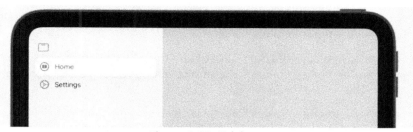

Figure 8-39: Sidebar

In addition to the buttons, the sidebar can include a header, a footer, and a toolbar at the bottom. The `View` protocol includes the following modifiers for this purpose.

▷ **tabViewSidebarHeader(content:** Closure**)**—This modifier inserts a view above the buttons. The **content** argument is the closure that provides the view to be displayed.

▷ **tabViewSidebarFooter(content:** Closure**)**—This modifier inserts a view below the buttons. The **content** argument is the closure that provides the view to be displayed.

▷ **tabViewSidebarBottomBar(content:** Closure**)**—This modifier inserts a view at the bottom of the sidebar. The **content** argument is the closure that provides the view to be displayed.

In the following example, we show how to create a header with a simple **Text** view.

```
struct ContentView: View {
    var body: some View {
        TabView {
            Tab("Home", systemImage: "book.circle") {
                Text("Main Screen")
            }
            Tab("Settings", systemImage: "gear") {
                Text("Settings")
            }
        }
        .tabViewStyle(.sidebarAdaptable)
        .tabViewSidebarHeader {
            Text("My Menu")
                .padding()
        }
    }
}
```

Listing 8-62: Adding a header to the sidebar

Figure 8-40: Sidebar header

The toolbar can only display a short list of buttons at a time, but the sidebar can display more buttons to help users find additional content. For this purpose, SwiftUI includes the **TabSection** structure. With this structure, we can create a section with tabs that can only be selected in the sidebar. The following is the structure's initializer.

▷ **TabSection(Closure, header:** Closure)—This initializer creates a container for sidebar tabs. The first argument is the closure that provides the tabs, and the **header** argument is the closure that provides the view for the section's header.

The `TabSection` structure creates a container for `Tab` views. In the following example, we add a section called More Info below the Settings tab of our previous example. The section includes two `Tab` views and therefore two new buttons are added to the sidebar.

```
struct ContentView: View {
    var body: some View {
        TabView {
            Tab("Home", systemImage: "book.circle") {
                Text("Main Screen")
            }
            Tab("Settings", systemImage: "gear") {
                Text("Settings")
            }
            TabSection("More Info") {
                Tab("Additional One", systemImage: "plus") {
                    Text("Additional Tab One")
                }
                Tab("Additional Two", systemImage: "pencil") {
                    Text("Additional Tab Two")
                }
            }
        }
        .tabViewStyle(.sidebarAdaptable)
    }
}
```

Listing 8-63: *Creating a section for the sidebar*

The contents of the sections are only visible in the sidebar and the Sections are displayed below individual tabs, as shown in Figure 8-41.

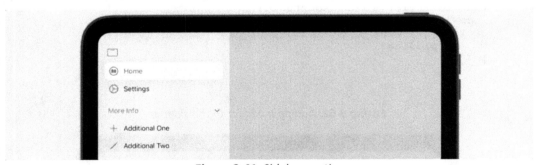

Figure 8-41: *Sidebar section*

Because the sidebar can contain additional buttons, the `TabView` view offers the possibility for the users to select the buttons they want to include in the sidebar and toolbar. To store the current selection, the framework defines the `TabViewCustomization` structure and the following modifiers to enable customization, and also to identify and configure the tabs.

▷ **tabViewCustomization(**TabViewCustomization**)**—This modifier applies the configuration selected by the user to the `TabView` view. The argument is the binding property used to store and read the current configuration.

▷ **customizationID**(String)—This modifier set the identifier for a tab.

▷ **customizationBehavior**(TabCustomizationBehavior, **for:** AdaptableTab-BarPlacement)—This modifier sets the configuration behavior for a tab. The first argument determines what the user is allowed to do with the tab. It is a structure with the properties `automatic`, `disabled`, and `reorderable`. The **for** argument determines where the behavior is going to be applied. It is a structure with the properties `automatic`, `sidebar`, and `tabBar`. (More than one value can be declared separated by comma.)

▷ **defaultVisibility**(Visibility, **for:** AdaptableTabBarPlacement)—This modifier determines whether the tab is going to be included or not. The first argument is an enumeration with the values `automatic`, `visible`, and `hidden`, and the **for** argument determines where the behavior is going to be applied. It is a structure with the properties `automatic`, `sidebar`, and `tabBar`. (More than one value can be declared separated by comma.)

To enable customization, we need a binding property to store the `TabViewCustomization` structure, we have to apply the `tabViewCustomization()` modifier to tell the `TabView` view to use this property to save and read the configuration, and finally apply the `customizationID()` modifier with a unique identifier to each tab we want the user to be able to modify.

```
struct ContentView: View {
    @State private var configuration = TabViewCustomization()

    var body: some View {
        TabView {
            Tab("Home", systemImage: "book.circle") {
                Text("Main Screen")
            }
            Tab("Settings", systemImage: "gear") {
                Text("Settings")
            }
            TabSection("More Info") {
                Tab("Additional One", systemImage: "plus") {
                    Text("Additional Tab One")
                }
                .customizationID("com.formasterminds.additional1")

                Tab("Additional Two", systemImage: "pencil") {
                    Text("Additional Tab Two")
                }
                .customizationID("com.formasterminds.additional2")
            }
            .customizationID("com.formasterminds.more")
        }
        .tabViewStyle(.sidebarAdaptable)
        .tabViewCustomization($configuration)
    }
}
```

Listing 8-64: *Customizing the* TabView *view*

When customization is enabled, the sidebar shows a button at the top to edit the tabs. After activating the editing mode, the user can drag tabs from the sidebar to the toolbar, decide which tabs are going to be shown in the sidebar or remove tabs from the toolbar.

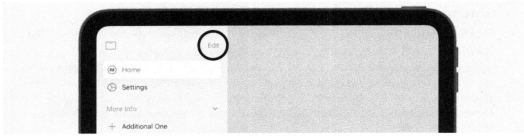

Figure 8-42: Edit button

 IMPORTANT: In this example, we use a `@State` property to save the configuration selected by the user. This means that every time the application is closed, the configuration is lost. To permanently store the changes made by the user, we can create an `@AppStorage` property. This type of property stores its values in a database so that they are preserved even after the application is closed. We will learn more about this property wrapper in Chapter 10.

Basic **Real-Life Application**

A `TabView` view is no different from a `NavigationStack` view except for the way it presents the views to the user, so we can use it with our model and define each screen as before. For instance, we can define a `TabView` view that opens three views: one to show a list of books, another to configure the list, and one more to allow the user to search for a book. The following is the `TabView` view we need for this example.

```
import SwiftUI
struct ContentView: View {
    var body: some View {
        TabView {
            Tab("Home", systemImage: "book.circle") {
                BooksView()
            }
            Tab("Settings", systemImage: "gear") {
                SettingsView()
            }
            Tab(role: .search) {
                SearchView()
            }
        }
        .tabViewStyle(.sidebarAdaptable)
    }
}
#Preview {
    ContentView()
        .environment(ApplicationData.shared)
}
```

Listing 8-65: Designing a `TabView` view for content

To allow the user to change the app's configuration, we need to store the values in the model. The following are the changes we need to introduce to our previous model.

```
@Observable class ApplicationData: @unchecked Sendable {
    var showPictures: Bool = true
    var showYear: Bool = true

    @ObservationIgnored var userData: [Book] {
```

```
        didSet {
           filterValues(search: "")
        }
     }
     var filteredItems: [Book] = []
     func filterValues(search: String) {
        if search.isEmpty {
           filteredItems = []
        } else {
           let list = userData.filter( { item in
              return item.title.localizedStandardContains(search)
           })
           filteredItems = list.sorted(by: { $0.title < $1.title })
        }
     }
     static let shared: ApplicationData = ApplicationData()
     private init() {
        userData = [
           Book(title: "Steve Jobs", author: "Walter Isaacson", cover:
"book1", year: 2011, selected: false),
           Book(title: "HTML5 for Masterminds", author: "J.D Gauchat",
cover: "book2", year: 2017, selected: false),
           Book(title: "The Road Ahead", author: "Bill Gates", cover:
"book3", year: 1995, selected: false),
           Book(title: "The C Programming Language", author: "Brian W.
Kernighan", cover: "book4", year: 1988, selected: false),
           Book(title: "Being Digital", author: "Nicholas Negroponte",
cover: "book5", year: 1996, selected: false),
           Book(title: "Only the Paranoid Survive", author: "Andrew S.
Grove", cover: "book6", year: 1999, selected: false),
           Book(title: "Accidental Empires", author: "Robert X. Cringely",
cover: "book7", year: 1996, selected: false),
           Book(title: "Bobby Fischer Teaches Chess", author: "Bobby
Fischer", cover: "book8", year: 1982, selected: false),
           Book(title: "New Guide to Science", author: "Isaac Asimov",
cover: "book9", year: 1993, selected: false),
           Book(title: "Christine", author: "Stephen King", cover:
"book10", year: 1983, selected: false),
           Book(title: "IT", author: "Stephen King", cover: "book11", year:
1987, selected: false),
           Book(title: "Ending Aging", author: "Aubrey de Grey", cover:
"book12", year: 2007, selected: false)
        ]
        filterValues(search: "")
     }
}
```

Listing 8-66: Updating the model

This model is based on the one introduced in Listing 8-9, but now we include two new properties to store Boolean values that users can change from the Settings tab, and the **filterValues()** method returns an empty string when there is nothing to search, so the user only see results when a value is inserted into the field.

The values stored in the **showPictures** and **showYear** properties from the Settings view determine whether the list of books should show the books' covers and year of publication, so we must use them in the **BooksView** view to configure the rows, as shown below.

```
import SwiftUI

struct BooksView: View {
   @Environment(ApplicationData.self) private var appData

   var body: some View {
```

```
        List(appData.userData) { book in
            CellBook(book: book)
        }
    }
}
struct CellBook: View {
    @Environment(ApplicationData.self) private var appData
    let book: Book

    var body: some View {
        HStack(alignment: .top) {
            if appData.showPictures {
                Image(book.cover)
                    .resizable()
                    .scaledToFit()
                    .frame(width: 80, height: 100)
            }
            VStack(alignment: .leading, spacing: 2) {
                Text(book.title).bold()
                Text(book.author)
                if appData.showYear {
                    Text(book.displayYear).font(.caption)
                }
                Spacer()
            }.padding(.top, 5)
            Spacer()
        }
    }
}
#Preview {
    BooksView()
        .environment(ApplicationData.shared)
}
```

Listing 8-67: Designing the rows according to the app's configuration

The list is created from the values in the **userData** array, as always, but the rows are now designed according to the app's configuration. If the value of the **showPictures** property is **true**, we show the book's cover, and if the value of the **showYear** property is **true**, we show the year of publication.

To allow the user to set these values, we must provide a form in the **SettingsView** view.

```
import SwiftUI

struct SettingsView: View {
    @Environment(ApplicationData.self) private var appData

    var body: some View {
        @Bindable var appData = appData

        Form {
            Section(header: Text("Settings"), footer: Text("Select what you
want to see")) {
                Toggle("Show Pictures", isOn: $appData.showPictures)
                Toggle("Show Year", isOn: $appData.showYear)
            }
        }
    }
}
#Preview {
    SettingsView()
        .environment(ApplicationData.shared)
}
```

Listing 8-68: Configuring the app

This view includes two `Toggle` views to set the values in the model. Now the user can decide what to show on the list. To complete the application, we need a view with a `TextField` view to allow the user to search for a book when the search tab is selected.

```
import SwiftUI

struct SearchView: View {
    @Environment(ApplicationData.self) private var appData
    @State private var searchBook: String = ""

    var body: some View {
        VStack {
            TextField("Insert Title", text: $searchBook)
                .textFieldStyle(.roundedBorder)
                .padding()
            List(appData.filteredItems) { book in
                CellBook(book: book)
            }
        }
        .onChange(of: searchBook, initial: true, {
            appData.filterValues(search: searchBook)
        })
    }
}
#Preview {
    SearchView()
        .environment(ApplicationData.shared)
}
```

Listing 8-69: Searching for books

Every time the user inserts a character in the field, we call the `filterValues()` method in the model. This method finds the books whose titles contain the text inserted by the user and adds them to the `filteredItems` array, so only the books that match the search appear on the list.

The application now includes a view to show the whole list of books, another to select the information we want to see on the list, and another to search for books.

Figure 8-43: `TabView` view *application*

 Do It Yourself: Update the `ContentView` view with the code in Listing 8-65. Create a new Swift file called ApplicationData.swift with the model in Chapter 7, Listing 7-3. Update the `ApplicationData` class with the code in Listing 8-66. Remember to inject the `ApplicationData` object into the environment for the app and the previews (Chapter 7, Listing 7-4). Download the books covers from our website and add them to the Asset Catalog. Create new files called BooksView.swift, SettingsView.swift and SearchView.swift for the codes in

Listings 8-67, 8-68 and 8-69. Run the application. Select the Settings tab and turn off the switches. You should see the books on the list without the cover and year of publication, as illustrated in Figure 8-43, right.

Basic 8.4 Adaptivity

SwiftUI views can adapt to the space available. We can implement flexible views to expand the interface or align the views using alignment values, but in practice this is only useful when the proportions of the window remain the same. For example, the screen of an iPhone 15 in portrait mode is slightly taller than the screen of an older iPhone in the same orientation, but the proportions between width and height are similar. Adapting the interface to these variations only requires simple transformations, such as extending or contracting the views. Things change when we compare devices with very different screens, such as iPhones and iPads, or the same device in different orientations. The interface must be drastically modified to adapt to these disparate conditions. To know when to perform these changes, the system defines values that represent the relative size of the space in which the interface is being presented. The classification is based on the magnitude of the horizontal and vertical dimensions of the space available. The value is called *Regular* if the space is large enough to fit a regular interface, or *Compact* otherwise. These values make up a unit of measurement called *Size Classes*.

Basic Size Classes

Because of the rectangular shape of the screen, the interface is defined by two size classes, one for the horizontal and another for the vertical space. Every device is assigned different size classes, depending on the size of their screens and orientations, as illustrated below.

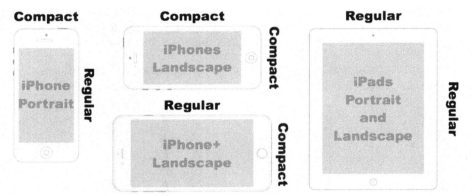

Figure 8-44: *Size classes assigned to mobile devices*

The illustration in Figure 8-44 represents the only four possible combinations of size classes, but they change according to the current layout. For instance, the horizontal size class changes from Regular to Compact if the screen is split in two on an iPad, or when an iPhone is rotated from landscape to portrait mode. But no matter what causes the change, we can detect it and adapt the interface accordingly. For this purpose, the environment includes the following values.

▷ **horizontalSizeClass**—This value is a **UserInterfaceSizeClass** enumeration that represents the current horizontal size class of the space occupied by the view. The values available are **compact** and **regular**.

▷ **verticalSizeClass**—This value is a **UserInterfaceSizeClass** enumeration that represents the current vertical size class of the space occupied by the view. The values available are **compact** and **regular**.

As explained before, we access these environment values with the **@Environment** property wrapper (see Listing 5-93). Once the **@Environment** properties are created, adapting the interface is a matter of organizing the views according to their values (**compact** or **regular**). For instance, in the following example we define the interface with two custom views, **HeaderView** and **BodyView**, and then display them in a vertical or horizontal stack depending on the current horizontal size class.

```
struct ContentView: View {
    @Environment(\.horizontalSizeClass) var horizontalClass

    var body: some View {
        Group {
            if horizontalClass == .compact {
                VStack(spacing: 0) {
                    HeaderView(isCompact: true)
                    BodyView()
                }
            } else {
                HStack(spacing: 0) {
                    HeaderView(isCompact: false)
                    BodyView()
                }
            }
        }.ignoresSafeArea()
    }
}
struct HeaderView: View {
    let isCompact: Bool

    var body: some View {
        Text("Food Menu")
            .frame(minWidth: 0, maxWidth: .infinity, minHeight: 0,
maxHeight: isCompact ? 150 : .infinity)
            .background(Color.yellow)
    }
}
struct BodyView: View {
    var body: some View {
        Text("Content Title")
            .frame(minWidth: 0, maxWidth: .infinity, minHeight: 0,
maxHeight: .infinity)
            .background(Color.gray)
    }
}
```

***Listing 8-70:** Detecting changes in the horizontal size class*

For didactic purposes we have defined all the views in the same file. The **ContentView** view creates two layouts according to the horizontal size class. If the size class is **compact**, which means that the interface is being presented in a small space, we create a **VStack** to show the views on top of each other, otherwise, we create an **HStack** to show them side by side.

Organizing the views on the screen is not enough to adapt the interface to the space available, sometimes we also must adapt their content. In this case, we do it by passing a value to the **HeaderView** to indicate whether the interface is been shown in a compact or a regular space, and then use this value inside the view to select the appropriate height.

The **HeaderView** and **BodyView** views are flexible, so the space available is distributed between the two, but we limit the height of the **HeaderView** view to 150 when it is presented in a vertical layout, so this view will only be 150 points tall in a vertical layout but extend from top to bottom in a horizontal layout.

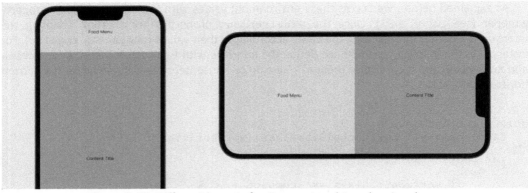

Figure 8-45: Different layouts for Compact and Regular size classes

 Do It Yourself: Create a Multiplatform project. Update the ContentView.swift file with the code in Listing 8-70. Select a large iPhone that presents the interface in two size classes, such as the iPhone 15 Pro Max. Rotate the preview. You should see the interfaces illustrated in Figure 8-45.

 IMPORTANT: Note that `isCompact` is a normal property. We didn't have to use a binding property in this case because every time the value of the `horizontal` property changes, the views are redrawn and the `isCompact` property is updated with the current value.

(Medium) GeometryReader View

Apple recommends to always adapt the interface according to the size classes, but there are times when this information is not enough. For instance, apps running fullscreen on iPads are always Regular and Regular (see Figure 8-44), but the difference between the width and height in portrait and landscape orientation is still significant. In cases like this, we must adapt the interface according to the size of the views, the window, or the screen. SwiftUI includes a view called `GeometryReader` that can help us on this task. The `GeometryReader` view takes the size of its container and sends this information to its children, so they can adapt to those values.

▷ **GeometryReader(content:** Closure)—This initializer creates a `GeometryReader` view. The closure assigned to the **content** argument contains the views we want to measure. This closure receives a `GeometryProxy` value with the view's position and dimensions.

The `GeometryReader` view calculates its position and size and sends this information to the closure that defines the content. The values are stored in an instance of the `GeometryProxy` structure. This structure provides the following properties and method to get the values.

▷ **size**—This property returns a `CGSize` value with the width and height of the `GeometryReader` view.

▷ **safeAreaInsets**—This property returns an `EdgeInsets` value with the insets of the safe area.

▷ **frame(in:** CoordinateSpace)—This method returns a `CGRect` value with the position and size of the `GeometryReader` view. The values are returned according to the coordinate space specified by the **in** argument. The argument is an enumeration with the values `global`, `local`, and `named(String)`.

The `GeometryReader` view works like a flexible view. It stretches to occupy all the space available and sends a `GeometryProxy` value with its position and size to the closure. Using these values, we can adapt the views or change the content, as shown below.

```
struct ContentView: View {
    var body: some View {
        GeometryReader { geometry in
            let isPortrait = geometry.size.height > geometry.size.width
            let message = isPortrait ? "Portrait" : "Landscape"

            HStack {
                Text(message)
            }.frame(minWidth: 0, maxWidth: .infinity, minHeight: 0,
maxHeight: .infinity, alignment: .center)
        }.ignoresSafeArea()
    }
}
```

Listing 8-71: Using a GeometryReader *to detect orientation*

In this example, we embed the whole interface inside a **GeometryReader** view, so the view expands to fill the screen. This means that the values produced by the view reflect the size of the screen, so we use them to determine whether the view is being shown in a portrait or landscape orientation. For this purpose, we get the values sent to the closure and compare the **height** and **width** properties of the **CGSize** structure returned by the **size** property. If the view's height is greater than the width, we are in portrait orientation, otherwise, the orientation is landscape.

Figure 8-46: Orientations

 Do It Yourself: Create a Multiplatform project. Update the **ContentView** view with the code in Listing 8-71. Run the application on the iPhone simulator. Rotate the screen. The text should change according to the orientation.

 IMPORTANT: With a **GeometryReader** view we can determine the orientation of the view, but this not always matches the device's orientation. For instance, the view may be shown inside an overlay on an iPad in landscape orientation, and the values will still indicate a portrait orientation. SwiftUI does not provide a way to determine the orientation of the device, but we can resort to the tools included in the UIKit framework for this purpose, as we will see in Chapter 14.

In the previous example, we select the content of a **Text** view depending on the view's orientation, but we can also adapt any other aspect of the content, including the views and sizes. For instance, we can set the size of an image.

```
struct ContentView: View {
    var body: some View {
        GeometryReader { geometry in
            HStack {
```

```
            Image(.spot1)
                .resizable()
                .scaledToFit()
                .frame(width: geometry.size.width / 2, height:
geometry.size.height / 4)
                .background(Color.gray)
            }.frame(minWidth: 0, maxWidth: .infinity, minHeight: 0,
maxHeight: .infinity)
        }
    }
}
```

Listing 8-72: Adapting an `Image` *view to the size of its container*

This code creates an **Image** view, but the view is embedded in a **GeometryReader** view, so we know the space available for it. In this example, we have decided to give the image a width that is half of the width of the container (**geometry.size.width / 2**) and a height that is a quarter of its height (**geometry.size.height / 4**). This determines the size of the **Image** view, but the aspect ratio of the image was set to **fit**, so the image is reduced even more to fit within the view's frame. (We gave the view a gray background to make the frame visible.)

Figure 8-47: Image of relative size

 Do It Yourself: Update the **ContentView** view with the code in Listing 8-72. Download the spot1.jpg image from our website and add it to the Asset Catalog. Run the application on the iPhone simulator. Rotate the screen. You should see the **Image** view adapting to the space available on the screen.

In addition to the size, we can also get the position of the **GeometryReader** view. This information is returned by the **frame()** method of the **GeometryProxy** structure and the values depend on the selected coordinate space. A SwiftUI interface defines two types of coordinates spaces, one called **global** that represents the coordinates of the screen and another called **local** that represents the coordinates of the view (every view has its own coordinate space). If we read the values considering the **local** coordinate space, the position is 0,0 (0 horizontal points and 0 vertical points), because the coordinate space of the **GeometryReader** view always starts at the position 0,0, but if we select the **global** coordinate space, the values returned by the method represent the position of the view relative to the screen. The following example implements this method to show how to work with these values.

```
struct ContentView: View {
    var body: some View {
        GeometryReader { geometry in
            let globalX = Int(geometry.frame(in: .global).origin.x)
            let globalY = Int(geometry.frame(in: .global).origin.y)
```

```
         Text("Position: \(globalX) / \(globalY)")
            .frame(minWidth: 0, maxWidth: .infinity, minHeight: 0,
maxHeight: .infinity)
      }.frame(width: 200, height: 250)
      .background(.gray)
   }
}
```

Listing 8-73: *Reading the position of the* `GeometryReader` *view*

This view includes a **Text** view embedded in a **GeometryReader** view. We made the **Text** view flexible to fill the container, and gave the **GeometryReader** view a fixed size of 200 by 250. Because of this, the views are positioned at the center of the screen, which means that the position of the **GeometryReader** view on the screen will be different in portrait and landscape orientation. Figure 8-48, below, shows what we see when we run this application on a small iPhone. In portrait, the **GeometryReader** view is 60 points from the left and 169 points from the top, but in landscape, the view is 184 points from the left and 35 points from the top.

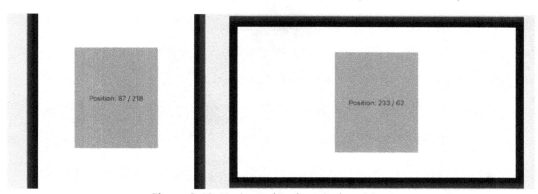

Figure 8-48: *Horizontal and vertical positions*

 Do It Yourself: Update the **ContentView** view with the code in Listing 8-73. Run the application on the iPhone simulator. Rotate the screen. You should see the values of the x and y coordinates change because of the changes in the **GeometryReader** view's position relative to the screen.

The **GeometryReader** view is a flexible view and therefore it takes all the space available in its container. This means that we can use it to calculate the size and position of any view by presenting the **GeometryReader** view as a secondary view. Secondary views are those assigned to other views, like the ones assigned to the view's background. For instance, we can add a background to an image and embed the background view in a **GeometryReader** view to determine the size of the image.

```
struct ContentView: View {
   @State private var size: CGSize = .zero

   var body: some View {
      VStack {
         Image(.spot1)
            .resizable()
            .scaledToFit()
            .background(
               GeometryReader { geometry in
                  Color.clear
                     .onAppear {
                        size = geometry.size
                     }
               })
```

```
        Text("\(Int(size.width)) x \(Int(size.height))")
    }.padding(100)
  }
}
```

Listing 8-74: Reading the position and size of a view

This example includes an **Image** view with a clear background (**Color.clear**). The **GeometryReader** view is used to embed the **Color** view. Views assigned to the background adopt the size of the original view. In this case, the **GeometryReader** view expands to occupy the space of the **Image** view and therefore its values reflect the image's position and size.

175 x 234

Figure 8-49: View measured by a GeometryReader *view*

 Do It Yourself: Update the **ContentView** view with the code in Listing 8-74. Run the application on the iPhone simulator. You should see the size of the **Image** view at the bottom, as shown in Figure 8-49.

 IMPORTANT: Note that the **onAppear()** modifier is only called the first time the view appears on the screen. This means that the values are not updated when the device is rotated. To have access to these values at any time, we need to implement Preferences, as shown next.

(Medium) **Preferences**

The **GeometryReader** view sends the information down the hierarchy. Only the views within the **GeometryReader** view can read and use these values. If we need to send the values up the hierarchy, we must use Preferences.

Despite what the name suggests, Preferences are just named values that we can generate from a view and read from the rest of the views in the hierarchy. For instance, if we have a **Text** view inside a **VStack** view, the preference values generated by the **Text** view are accessible from the **VStack** view.

Preference values are stored in what is called a Preference Key. This is a structure that conforms to the **PreferenceKey** protocol. The protocol has the following requirements.

▷ **Value**—This property is an associated type that defines the data type of the values we are going to work with.

▷ **defaultValue**—This property defines the value the Preference Key is going to have by default.

▷ **reduce(value:** Value, **nextValue:** Closure)—This method adds a new value to the structure. The **value** argument is a reference to the values stored in the structure from previous calls, and the **nextValue** argument is a closure that returns the new value.

We must define a structure that conforms to the **PreferenceKey** protocol and then use it to pass the values from one view to another with the following modifiers.

Chapter 8 - Navigation

- ▷ **preference(key:** Type, **value:** Value)—This modifier sets a value for a specific preference key. The **key** argument is a reference to the key's data type, and the **value** argument is the value we want to assign to that key.

- ▷ **onPreferenceChange(**Type, **perform:** Closure)—This modifier executes a closure when the value of a preference key changes. The first argument is a reference to the key's data type, and the **perform** argument is the closure to be executed when the value changes.

The process to pass a value from one view to another begins by defining a structure that conforms to the **PreferenceKey** protocol. Then, we must apply the **preference()** modifier to a view with the value we want to send. And finally, we must apply the **onPreferenceChange()** modifier to a view in the hierarchy (a parent view or a container of the previous view) to process the value. The following example illustrates how the process works. We implement a **GeometryReader** view to determine the size of an image, as we did in the previous example, but send the values to the rest of the views using a **PreferenceKey** structure.

```
import SwiftUI

struct BoxPreference: PreferenceKey {
   typealias Value = CGSize
   static let defaultValue: CGSize = .zero

   static func reduce(value: inout CGSize, nextValue: () -> CGSize) {
      value = nextValue()
   }
}
struct ContentView: View {
   @State private var size: CGSize = .zero

   var body: some View {
      VStack {
         Image(.spot1)
            .resizable()
            .scaledToFit()
            .background(
               GeometryReader { geometry in
                  Color.clear
                     .preference(key: BoxPreference.self, value:
geometry.size)
               })
         Text("\(Int(size.width)) x \(Int(size.height))")
      }.padding()
      .onPreferenceChange(BoxPreference.self) { value in
         size = value
      }
   }
}
```

Listing 8-75: Setting and reading preferences

The first thing we do in Listing 8-75 is to define the structure to store the values. To conform to the **PreferenceKey** protocol, this structure must meet some requirements. First, we must define a typealias called **Value**. Because we are going to store the **CGSize** value returned by the **size** property of the **GeometryProxy** structure, we define **Value** as a typealias of **CGSize**. Next comes a type property called **defaultValue**. This property defines the value of the structure by default. Since we are working with a **CGSize** structure, we define it as a **CGSize** structure with its values set to 0 (**zero**). Finally, we implement the **reduce()** method. This method receives a reference to the values already stored in the structure and a closure that returns the new value. To store this new value, we must execute the closure and add the value returned to the values already stored in the structure. In this case, we are working only with one value (a **CGSize** structure), so we assign it directly to the property (**value = nextValue()**).

In the view, we embed an **Image** view with a **VStack** view and apply a **GeometryReader** view to the background, as done before, but this time we store the values in an instance of our **BoxPreference** structure with the **preference()** modifier. Now, this value is defined as a Preference and therefore we can read it from the views in the hierarchy with the **onPreferenceChange()** modifier. In this example, the modifier is applied to the **VStack** view. When a new value is received, we assign it to a **@State** property to update the view. As a result, the view always shows the size of the image on the screen, even when the device is rotated.

Figure 8-50: *Interface updated with preferences*

Do It Yourself: Update the ContentView.swift file with the code in Listing 8-75. Run the application on the iPhone simulator. Rotate the screen. You should see the size of the image change according to the orientation.

IMPORTANT: In this example, we store a single **CGSize** value, but the **PreferenceKey** protocol was designed to manage values from multiple views and therefore they are usually stored in arrays. For more information on Preferences, visit our website and follow the links for this chapter.

(Basic) **8.5 Universal Interface**

Working with one view per screen is enough for small devices, like iPhones and the Apple Watch, but iPads and Macs require a more elaborated design. SwiftUI offers a container view called **NavigationSplitView** to present two or three views on the screen at the same time. The advantage of using this container view is not only that we can get multiple views to share the screen, but also that it adapts to small screens or windows, so we can use it to create universal interfaces that work seamlessly on iPhones, iPads and Macs.

▷ **NavigationSplitView(columnVisibility:** Binding, **sidebar:** Closure, **content:** Closure, **detail:** Closure)—This initializer creates a container view to present two or three views on the screen simultaneously. The **columnVisibility** argument is a binding property that determines the visibility of the columns. This value is determined by a **NavigationSplitViewVisibility** structure, which includes the type properties **automatic**, **all**, **doubleColumn**, and **detailOnly**. And the **sidebar**, **content**, and **detail** arguments return the views we want to present in each column. If we only want to present two columns, we must omit the **content** argument.

The columns are called Sidebar, Content, and Detail, and they are interconnected. A **NavigationLink** view in the Sidebar column updates the content of the Content column, and a **NavigationLink** view in the Content column updates the content of the Detail column.

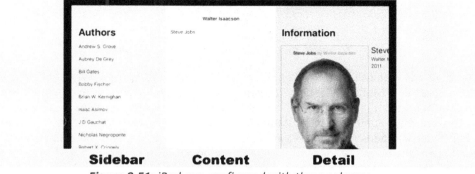

| Sidebar | Content | Detail |

Figure 8-51: *iPad app configured with three columns*

The Sidebar and Content columns are removable, and are presented on the screen depending on the number of columns and the space available. By default, on iPads in landscape mode, only one of the removable columns is shown. In a two-column design, the `NavigationSplitView` view displays the sidebar column, while in a three-column design the content column is shown instead. In iPads on portrait mode and large iPhones in landscape mode, only the Detail column is displayed, and a button is provided in the navigation bar to open the removable columns. iPhones in portrait mode present a different configuration; the columns are displayed as in a `NavigationStack` view; they replace one another and buttons are included to navigate back.

Figure 8-52: `NavigationSplitView` view *on iPhones in portrait mode*

A `NavigationSplitView` view may contain two or three columns. A two columns design is very common. The interface is simple. We define the `NavigationSplitView` view and assign the view we want to show on the left to the **sidebar** argument and the one we want to show on the right to the **detail** argument.

```
struct ContentView: View {
   @State private var selectedBook: Book?
   @State private var visibility: NavigationSplitViewVisibility
= .automatic

   var body: some View {
      NavigationSplitView(columnVisibility: $visibility, sidebar: {
         BooksView(selectedBook: $selectedBook)
      }, detail: {
         if let book = selectedBook {
            DetailView(book: book)
         } else {
            PlaceholderView()
         }
      })
   }
}
#Preview {
   ContentView()
```

```
        .environment(ApplicationData.shared)
}
```

Listing 8-76: Defining a two-column split view

To keep track of the selected items, the `NavigationSplitView` view works with `List` selection (see Edit Mode in Chapter 7). In our example, we include a `@State` property called `selectedBook` to store the book selected by the user, another for the `NavigationSplitView` view to store the columns' visibility state, and the view itself with two columns. The column on the left (Sidebar) opens the `BooksView` view with a list of books, and the column on the right (Detail) opens the `DetailView` view with information about the selected book (or a placeholder view if no book was selected yet).

When a book is selected, the `Book` structure that represents the book is assigned to the `selectedBook` property, the content of the `ContentView` view is recreated, and a new `DetailView` view opens on the right column to present the book on the screen.

To know when a new row has been selected, we pass a reference of the `selectedBook` property to the `BooksView` view. Therefore, every time the user selects a book in the `BooksView` view, the value is stored in the `selectedBook` property, and the interface is updated. For the selection to work, the `BooksView` view must include a `List` view connected to the `selectedBook` property and also create the rows with a `NavigationLink` view identified with a value that matches the value stored in that property, as shown below.

```
import SwiftUI

struct BooksView: View {
    @Environment(ApplicationData.self) private var appData
    @Binding var selectedBook: Book?

    var body: some View {
        List(appData.userData, selection: $selectedBook) { book in
            NavigationLink(value: book, label: {
                Text(book.title)
            })
        }
        .listStyle(.sidebar)
        .navigationTitle("Books")
    }
}
#Preview {
    @Previewable @State var selected: Book? = nil

    BooksView(selectedBook: $selected)
        .environment(ApplicationData.shared)
}
```

Listing 8-77: Defining the view for the left column

When a `NavigationLink` is selected, the value is assigned to the `selectedBook` property and the selection is performed on the interface. Note that we have assigned the `sidebar` style to the list to reproduce the interface in Figure 8-51.

No functionality is required for the `PlaceholderView` view. This view only opens on some devices to have something to show before the user selects a book, so we only need it to display a message.

```
import SwiftUI

struct PlaceholderView: View {
    var body: some View {
```

```
        VStack {
            Text("Select a Book")
            Spacer()
        }.padding(50)
    }
}
```

Listing 8-78: Defining a placeholder view for the right column

The **PlaceholderView** view is displayed on the right column until the user selects a book, in which case it is replaced with a **DetailView** view. The **DetailView** view is similar to the one we have created before for an iPhone application, but now we must consider that it may be shown on devices with very different characteristics, such as an iPhone in portrait orientation or an iPad in landscape. For this types of applications, Apple recommends adapting the interface according to the size classes (see Chapter 6). For instance, if the horizontal size class is compact, we can display the values on a list, as we did before, otherwise, we can take advantage of the larger screen and present the values side by side.

Selecting the right view for the device and the space available is quite simple in SwiftUI. All we need to do is to get the view's horizontal size class from the environment and display one view or the other, as we do in the following example.

```
import SwiftUI

struct DetailView: View {
    @Environment(\.horizontalSizeClass) var horizontal
    let book: Book

    var body: some View {
        Group {
            if horizontal == .regular {
                DetailLarge(book: book)
            } else {
                DetailSmall(book: book)
            }
        }.padding()
        .navigationTitle(Text("Information"))
    }
}
struct DetailLarge: View {
    let book: Book

    var body: some View {
        HStack {
            VStack {
                Image(book.cover)
                    .resizable()
                    .scaledToFit()
                    .frame(maxWidth: 300)
                Spacer()
            }
            VStack(alignment: .leading, spacing: 4) {
                Text(book.title)
                    .font(.title)
                Text(book.author)
                Text(book.displayYear)
                Spacer()
            }.frame(minWidth: 0, maxWidth: .infinity, alignment: .leading)
            Spacer()
        }
    }
}
```

```
struct DetailSmall: View {
   let book: Book

   var body: some View {
      VStack {
         Text(book.title)
            .font(.title)
         Text(book.author)
         Text(book.displayYear)
            .font(.caption)
         Image(book.cover)
            .resizable()
            .scaledToFit()
            .frame(maxWidth: 300)
      }.multilineTextAlignment(.center)
   }
}
#Preview {
   DetailView(book: ApplicationData.shared.userData[1])
}
```

Listing 8-79: Defining a Multiplatform Detail view

The views can be declared in the same file or in separate files, depending on their complexity. In this example, we have declared two additional views in the same file: the `DetailLarge` view to define the interface for a regular size class, and the `DetailSmall` view for the interface of a compact size class. When the `DetailView` is loaded, we check the value of the `horizontalSizeClass` property in the environment and load the corresponding view. As a result, the `DetailView` view shows the book's information next to the cover on iPads and on top of the cover on iPhones.

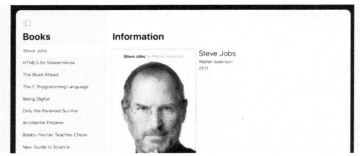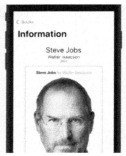

Figure 8-53: Different design for iPhones and iPads

 Do It Yourself: Create a Multiplatform project. Create a Swift file called ApplicationData.swift for the model in Chapter 7, Listing 7-3. Update the ContentView.swift file with the code in Listing 8-76. Create a new SwiftUI file called BooksView.swift for the code in Listing 8-77, another called PlaceholderView.swift for the code in Listing 8-78, and another called DetailView.swift for the code in Listing 8-79. Download the covers from our website and add them to the Asset Catalog. Remember to inject the `ApplicationData` object into the environment for the app and the previews (Chapter 7, Listing 7-4). Run the application on the iPad simulator in landscape mode and select a book. You should see the interface illustrated in Figure 8-53, left. Repeat the process on the iPhone simulator to see how it looks on that device.

When our app is launched on a device with a large screen, the interface is presented in two columns. The column on the left shows the list of books, and the column on the right shows the `PlaceholderView` view with a message to indicate to the user what to do. This view is replaced

Chapter 8 - Navigation

by the `DetailView` view when a book is selected from the list. Depending on the characteristics of our application, sometimes it might be better to show an item by default. For instance, we can show the `DetailView` view instead of the `PlaceholderView` view when there are books available in the model, as shown below.

```
struct ContentView: View {
   @Environment(ApplicationData.self) private var appData
   @State private var selectedBook: Book?
   @State private var visibility: NavigationSplitViewVisibility
= .automatic

   var body: some View {
      NavigationSplitView(columnVisibility: $visibility, sidebar: {
         BooksView(selectedBook: $selectedBook)
      }, detail: {
         if let book = selectedBook {
            DetailView(book: book)
         } else {
            PlaceholderView()
         }
      })
      .onAppear {
         if let book = appData.userData.first {
            selectedBook = book
         }
      }
   }
}
```

Listing 8-80: Showing an item by default

Although we could get a book from the model and show the `DetailView` view with it, it is better to assign that book to the `selectedBook` property instead. This way, the item is also selected in the `List` view. In our example, we use the `onAppear()` modifier for this purpose. On iPhones in portrait, the application works as before, but on iPads in landscape, the first row is selected and the book is shown on the screen.

Do It Yourself: Update the `ContentView` view with the code in Listing 8-80. Run the application on the iPad simulator in landscape mode. You should see on the screen the first book found in the `userData` array.

The view on the right is just one view, but we can allow the user to navigate to other views by embedding the `DetailView` view in a `NavigationStack` view. To control the navigation, we need to add a `NavigationPath` property, as shown below.

```
struct ContentView: View {
   @State private var selectedBook: Book?
   @State private var path = NavigationPath()
   @State private var visibility: NavigationSplitViewVisibility
= .automatic

   var body: some View {
      NavigationSplitView(columnVisibility: $visibility, sidebar: {
         BooksView(selectedBook: $selectedBook)
      }, detail: {
         NavigationStack(path: $path) {
            if let book = selectedBook {
               DetailView(path: $path, book: book)
            } else {
```

```
                    PlaceholderView()
                }
            }
        })
        .onChange(of: selectedBook, initial: false) { _, _ in
            path = NavigationPath()
        }
    }
}
```

Listing 8-81: Enabling navigation in the right column

The procedure is the same used before to control the navigation path. We declare the **NavigationPath** property and then use it to initialize the **NavigationStack** view, but because we are enabling navigation for the right column, we need to pass a reference of the path to the **DetailView** view. Note that to make sure the navigation path always begins with the **DetailView** view, we clear the **NavigationPath** structure when a book is selected (when the value of the **selectedBook** property changes).

When this application is launched, the **DetailView** view becomes the initial view of the navigation stack, so the rest of the navigation is managed from this view. We can, for instance, allow the user to tap on the cover to expand it, as we did in previous examples.

```
import SwiftUI

struct DetailView: View {
    @Environment(\.horizontalSizeClass) var horizontal
    @Binding var path: NavigationPath
    let book: Book

    var body: some View {
        Group {
            if horizontal == .regular {
                DetailLarge(path: $path, book: book)
            } else {
                DetailSmall(path: $path, book: book)
            }
        }.padding()
        .navigationTitle(Text("Information"))
        .navigationDestination(for: String.self, destination: { _ in
            PictureView(book: book)
        })
    }
}
struct DetailLarge: View {
    @Binding var path: NavigationPath
    let book: Book

    var body: some View {
        HStack {
            VStack {
                Button(action: {
                    path.append("Picture View")
                }, label: {
                    Image(book.cover)
                        .resizable()
                        .scaledToFit()
                        .frame(maxWidth: 300)
                })
                Spacer()
            }
            VStack(alignment: .leading, spacing: 4) {
                Text(book.title)
```

```
                .font(.title)
            Text(book.author)
            Text(book.displayYear)
            Spacer()
        }.frame(minWidth: 0, maxWidth: .infinity, alignment: .leading)
        Spacer()
    }
  }
}
struct DetailSmall: View {
    @Binding var path: NavigationPath
    let book: Book

    var body: some View {
        VStack {
            Text(book.title)
                .font(.title)
            Text(book.author)
            Text(book.displayYear)
                .font(.caption)
            Button(action: {
                path.append("Picture View")
            }, label: {
                Image(book.cover)
                    .resizable()
                    .scaledToFit()
                    .frame(maxWidth: 300)
            })
        }.multilineTextAlignment(.center)
    }
}
#Preview {
    @Previewable @State var navigation = NavigationPath()

    DetailView(path: $navigation, book:
ApplicationData.shared.userData[1])
}
```

Listing 8-82: Creating a navigation path for the right column

This **DetailView** view receives a reference to the **path** property to add or remove views from the navigation stack. We pass this reference to the subviews and then embed the book's cover in a **Button** view to append a value to the path. We use a **Button** view instead of a **NavigationLink** view because there is no **List** view in this interface to control selection, but the result is the same. When the user presses the button, the **append()** method adds a string to the **path** property, the **navigationDestination()** modifier detects that a **String** value has been added to the path, and the **NavigationStack** view opens the **PictureView** view to show the expanded cover on the screen.

The **PictureView** view is similar to previous examples, but this time we must adapt the interface to the space available (the size class).

```
import SwiftUI

struct PictureView: View {
    @Environment(\.horizontalSizeClass) var horizontal
    let book: Book

    var body: some View {
        VStack {
            if horizontal == .regular {
                Image(book.cover)
                    .resizable()
```

```
                .scaledToFit()
                .padding([.top, .bottom], 20)
                .padding([.leading, .trailing], 50)
        } else {
            Image(book.cover)
                .resizable()
                .scaledToFit()
        }
        Spacer()
    }.navigationBarTitleDisplayMode(.inline)
  }
}
#Preview {
    NavigationStack {
        PictureView(book: ApplicationData.shared.userData[0])
    }
}
```

Listing 8-83: Expanding the cover in a Multiplatform application

 Do It Yourself: Update the `ContentView` view with the code in Listing 8-81 and the DetailView.swift file with the code in Listing 8-82. Create a SwiftUI file called PictureView.swift for the view in Listing 8-83. Run the application on the iPad simulator in landscape orientation, select a book and tap the cover. You should see the `PictureView` view on the right column transitioning from right to left. Select another book. You should see the `DetailView` view again in the right column. Try removing the `onChange()` modifier in the `ContentView` view and repeat the process. You should see that the cover in the `PictureView` view changes, but the interface does not transition back to the `DetailView` view because the path was not cleared.

We can also add navigation to the left column (Sidebar). The problem is that the `NavigationSplitView` view is configured by default to always open navigation links on the Detail column. In a two-column layout, the `NavigationLink` views in the left column will always open the destination view in the right column, but we can change this behavior with the following modifier.

▷ **isDetailLink(Bool)**—This modifier determines whether the link will open in the Detail column or not (**true** or **false**).

If we apply this modifier with the value **false** to a `NavigationLink` view in the left column, the view will open in the same column. For instance, we can embed the `BooksView` view in a `NavigationStack` view and add a button to the navigation bar to allow the user to configure the list of books.

```
struct ContentView: View {
    @State private var selectedBook: Book?
    @State private var path = NavigationPath()
    @State private var visibility: NavigationSplitViewVisibility
= .automatic

    var body: some View {
        NavigationSplitView(columnVisibility: $visibility, sidebar: {
            NavigationStack {
                BooksView(selectedBook: $selectedBook)
            }
        }, detail: {
            NavigationStack(path: $path) {
```

```
                    if let book = selectedBook {
                       DetailView(path: $path, book: book)
                    } else {
                       PlaceholderView()
                    }
                 }
            })
            .onChange(of: selectedBook, initial: false) { _, _ in
                 path = NavigationPath()
            }
        }
    }
}
```

Listing 8-84: Adding navigation to the left column

To open the view, we must add the button in the **BooksView** view with a **NavigationLink** associated to a value. In this case, we use a string and open a view called **SettingsView** when the button is pressed.

```
struct BooksView: View {
    @Environment(ApplicationData.self) private var appData
    @Binding var selectedBook: Book?

    var body: some View {
        List(appData.userData, selection: $selectedBook) { book in
            NavigationLink(value: book, label: {
                Text(book.title)
            })
        }
        .listStyle(.sidebar)
        .navigationTitle("Books")
        .toolbar {
            ToolbarItem(placement: .navigationBarTrailing) {
                NavigationLink(value: "Settings View", label: {
                    Image(systemName: "gear")
                })
                .isDetailLink(false)
            }
        }
        .navigationDestination(for: String.self, destination: { _ in
            SettingsView()
        })
    }
}
```

Listing 8-85: Opening a view on the left column

The **BooksView** view now includes an item in the navigation bar defined by a **NavigationLink** view and an SF Symbol that opens a view to configure the application, but because we applied the **isDetailLink()** modifier with the value **false**, the **SettingsView** view opens in the same column, as shown below.

Figure 8-54: Link opens the view in the left column

Do It Yourself: Update the `ContentView` view with the code in Listing 8-84 and the `BooksView` view with the code in Listing 8-85. Create a SwiftUI file called SettingsView.swift. Modify the `SettingsView` view with a `Text` view to show the message "Settings View". Run the application on the iPad simulator in landscape orientation. Press the Settings button in the navigation bar. You should see the `SettingsView` view open in the left column.

(Basic) Three-Columns Layout

A `NavigationSplitView` view can present up to three columns. So far, we have been using the two-column layout, but we can add one more by including the **content** argument in the `NavigationSplitView`'s initializer. In a three-column layout, the links in the Sidebar column update the content in the Content column, and the links in the Content column update the content in the Detail column. Therefore, we have two columns on the left to select information and a column on the right to show it.

This process is not automatic, we need to prepare the data in the model to feed the views. For instance, if we want to show a list of authors in the first column, and the books that belong to the selected author in the second column, as we do in the example in Figure 8-51, the model must provide the list of values in that order. How we organize and store this data in our model depends on the characteristics of the application. For our example, we are going to store the list of books in an array and implement a method that extracts the names of the authors from it.

```
@Observable class ApplicationData: @unchecked Sendable {
    @ObservationIgnored var userData: [Book] = [] {
        didSet {
            updateAuthors()
        }
    }
    var listAuthors: [String] = []

    func updateAuthors() {
        var list: [String] = []
        for name in userData.map({ $0.author }) {
            if !list.contains(name) {
                list.append(name)
            }
        }
        listAuthors = list.sorted(by: { $0 < $1 })
    }
    static let shared: ApplicationData = ApplicationData()
    private init() {
        userData = [
            Book(title: "Steve Jobs", author: "Walter Isaacson", cover:
"book1", year: 2011, selected: false),
            Book(title: "HTML5 for Masterminds", author: "J.D Gauchat",
cover: "book2", year: 2017, selected: false),
            Book(title: "The Road Ahead", author: "Bill Gates", cover:
"book3", year: 1995, selected: false),
            Book(title: "The C Programming Language", author: "Brian W.
Kernighan", cover: "book4", year: 1988, selected: false),
            Book(title: "Being Digital", author: "Nicholas Negroponte",
cover: "book5", year: 1996, selected: false),
            Book(title: "Only the Paranoid Survive", author: "Andrew S.
Grove", cover: "book6", year: 1999, selected: false),
            Book(title: "Accidental Empires", author: "Robert X. Cringely",
cover: "book7", year: 1996, selected: false),
            Book(title: "Bobby Fischer Teaches Chess", author: "Bobby
Fischer", cover: "book8", year: 1982, selected: false),
```

```
            Book(title: "New Guide to Science", author: "Isaac Asimov",
     cover: "book9", year: 1993, selected: false),
            Book(title: "Christine", author: "Stephen King", cover:
     "book10", year: 1983, selected: false),
            Book(title: "IT", author: "Stephen King", cover: "book11", year:
     1987, selected: false),
            Book(title: "Ending Aging", author: "Aubrey de Grey", cover:
     "book12", year: 2007, selected: false)
        ]
        updateAuthors()
    }
}
```

Listing 8-86: Providing the list of authors

This new **ApplicationData** class defines the **userData** property as a normal property to store the books, and includes a new observable property called **listAuthors** to store the names of the authors. To get the authors from the data, we have created a method called **updateAuthors()**. The method gets the names of the authors with the **map()** method and assigns it to the **listAuthors** property in alphabetical order. Note that before adding the name, we check if it already exists to avoid duplicates (**!list.contains(name)**).

The **updateAuthors()** method should be called every time the values in the **userData** property change to keep the views up to date. In our example, we call it after the property is initialized with testing values, and also with a property observer applied to the **userData** property, so the authors are updated every time a book is added or removed from the model.

Now that we have the values for the first column, it is time to define the three-column layout in the **ContentView** view.

```
struct ContentView: View {
    @State private var selectedAuthor: String?
    @State private var selectedBook: Book?
    @State private var visibility: NavigationSplitViewVisibility
= .automatic

    var body: some View {
        NavigationSplitView(columnVisibility: $visibility, sidebar: {
            AuthorsView(selectedAuthor: $selectedAuthor)
        }, content: {
            BooksView(selectedBook: $selectedBook, selectedAuthor:
selectedAuthor)
        }, detail: {
            if let book = selectedBook {
                DetailView(book: book)
            } else {
                PlaceholderView()
            }
        })
    }
}
```

Listing 8-87: Defining a three-column layout

Because we now have two columns with list of values the user can choose from, we need two properties to store the selection. We call them **selectedAuthor** and **selectedBook**. The view in the first column, called **AuthorsView**, presents the list of authors available, so we pass a reference to the **selectedAuthor** property to capture the user's selection. On the other hand, the view in the second column, called **BooksView**, presents the list of books that belong to the selected author, so we need to pass a reference to the **selectedBook** property to control selection and also the value of the **selectedAuthor** property to filter the books by author.

The **AuthorsView** view must create a list of authors and allow the user to select one. The code is similar to previous examples.

```
import SwiftUI

struct AuthorsView: View {
    @Environment(ApplicationData.self) private var appData
    @Binding var selectedAuthor: String?

    var body: some View {
        List(appData.listAuthors, id: \.self, selection: $selectedAuthor) {
author in
            NavigationLink(value: author, label: {
                Text(author)
            })
        }
        .listStyle(.sidebar)
        .navigationTitle("Authors")
    }
}
#Preview {
    @Previewable @State var selected: String? = nil

    AuthorsView(selectedAuthor: $selected)
        .environment(ApplicationData.shared)
}
```

Listing 8-88: Showing the authors

The **BooksView** view is also similar to previous examples, but now we must show only the list of books that belong to the author selected by the user. To filter the values, we define a computed property called **listBooks** and use it to feed the **List** view.

```
struct BooksView: View {
    @Environment(ApplicationData.self) private var appData
    @Binding var selectedBook: Book?
    let selectedAuthor: String?

    var listBooks: [Book] {
        let list = appData.userData.filter({ item in
            return item.author == selectedAuthor
        })
        return list.sorted(by: { $0.title < $1.title })
    }
    var body: some View {
        List(listBooks, selection: $selectedBook) { book in
            NavigationLink(value: book, label: {
                Text(book.title)
            })
        }.listStyle(.grouped)
        .navigationBarTitleDisplayMode(.inline)
        .navigationTitle(selectedAuthor ?? "Undefined")
    }
}
#Preview {
    @Previewable @State var selected: Book? = nil

    BooksView(selectedBook: $selected, selectedAuthor: nil)
        .environment(ApplicationData.shared)
}
```

Listing 8-89: Showing the books

The **listBooks** property gets the author's books and returns them in alphabetical order. The rest of the view is the same as before. We create a **List** view with these values and embed the rows in a **NavigationLink** view to update the **selectedBook** property when a book is selected.

 Do It Yourself: Update the **ApplicationData** class in the ApplicationData.swift file with the code in Listing 8-86. Update the **ContentView** view with the code in Listing 8-87. Create a new SwiftUI file called AuthorsView.swift and update the view with the code in Listing 8-88. Update the **BooksView** view with the code in Listing 8-89. The **PlaceholderView** view and the **DetailView** view used in this example are the same defined for previous examples (see Listings 8-78 and 8-79). Run the application on the iPad simulator in landscape orientation. Press the button on the top-left corner. You should see the three columns on the screen, as shown in Figure 8-51. Run the application again on the iPhone simulator to see how the columns are presented on that device.

(Basic) Configuration

The width of the columns, which columns will be visible, and how they are going to be presented on the screen, is determined by the space available, but we can suggest a specific configuration and the system will try to comply when possible. One of the things we can do is to suggest the number of columns we want to be visible by modifying the value of the binding property assigned to the **columnVisibility** argument. We can ask the system to show all the columns (**all**), only the Content and Detail (**doubleColumn**), and only the Detail column (**detailOnly**). For example, we can hide the column on the left when an item is selected.

```
struct ContentView: View {
    @State private var selectedAuthor: String?
    @State private var selectedBook: Book?
    @State private var visibility: NavigationSplitViewVisibility
= .automatic

    var body: some View {
        NavigationSplitView(columnVisibility: $visibility, sidebar: {
            AuthorsView(selectedAuthor: $selectedAuthor)
        }, content: {
            BooksView(selectedBook: $selectedBook, selectedAuthor:
selectedAuthor)
        }, detail: {
            if let book = selectedBook {
                DetailView(book: book)
            } else {
                PlaceholderView()
            }
        })
        .onChange(of: selectedBook, initial: false) { _, _ in
            visibility = .detailOnly
        }
    }
}
```

Listing 8-90: Hiding columns programmatically

This example applies the **onChange()** modifier to change the value of the **visibility** property to **detailOnly** when a book is selected. This closes the columns on the left and expands the column on the right to take up all the space available.

Do It Yourself: Update the `ContentView` view with the code in Listing 8-90. Run the application on the iPad simulator. Press the button to open the columns on the left. Select an author and a book. You should see the selected book on the right and the columns should be removed from the screen.

In a three-column design, the Detail column is blurred and displaced to the right when the columns on the left become visible. The `NavigationSplitView` view implements the following modifiers to configure this behavior and define the width of the columns.

▷ **navigationSplitViewStyle(**NavigationSplitViewStyle**)**—This modifier defines how the Detail column is displayed when other columns are present. The argument is a structure that conforms to the `NavigationSplitViewStyle` protocol. The protocol defines the type properties `automatic` (default), `balanced` (the size of the Detail column is reduced to make room for the rest of the columns), and `prominentDetail` (the size of the Detail column is maintain and the rest of the columns are overlaid on top).

▷ **navigationSplitViewColumnWidth(**CGFloat**)**—This modifier defines a fixed width for the column.

▷ **navigationSplitViewColumnWidth(min:** CGFloat?, **ideal:** CGFloat, **max:** CGFloat?**)**—This modifier defines a flexible column but with constraints.

The style is applied to the `NavigationSplitView` view, but the width is applied to the columns. In the following example, we set the width for the Sidebar and Content columns to 200 points, and apply the `prominentDetail` style to the view, so the columns on the left open over the Detail column but take up only a portion of the screen.

```
struct ContentView: View {
    @State private var selectedAuthor: String?
    @State private var selectedBook: Book?
    @State private var visibility: NavigationSplitViewVisibility
= .automatic

    var body: some View {
        NavigationSplitView(columnVisibility: $visibility, sidebar: {
            AuthorsView(selectedAuthor: $selectedAuthor)
                .navigationSplitViewColumnWidth(200)
        }, content: {
            BooksView(selectedBook: $selectedBook, selectedAuthor:
selectedAuthor)
                .navigationSplitViewColumnWidth(200)
        }, detail: {
            if let book = selectedBook {
                DetailView(book: book)
            } else {
                PlaceholderView()
            }
        })
        .navigationSplitViewStyle(.prominentDetail)
    }
}
```

Listing 8-91: Configuring the columns

(Basic) 9.1 Asynchronous and Concurrent Tasks

Apple systems can take advantage of the large number of cores in modern processors to execute multiple pieces of code simultaneously, increasing the amount of work a program can do at any given time. For example, one code may be downloading a file from the Internet while another is displaying the progress on the screen. In such cases, we can't wait for one code to finish to run the other; we have to perform both tasks at the same time.

To process many codes simultaneously, the system groups code units into tasks. In Swift, tasks can be implemented with asynchronous and concurrent programming. Asynchronous programming is a programming pattern in which the code waits for a process to finish before completing the task. While waiting, the system can use the resources for other tasks. This allows the system to share computing resources among many processes. Concurrent programming, on the other hand, implements code that can take advantage of multiple cores to execute tasks simultaneously.

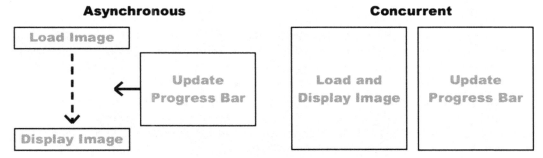

Figure 9-1: Asynchronous and concurrent programming

Since multiple applications can run at the same time, the system doesn't allocate a specific number of cores per application. What it does is to create execution threads, assign the tasks to these threads, and then decide which threads are going to be executed by which core depending on the available resources. In the example in Figure 9-1, left, there is an asynchronous task that loads an image from the web and then displays it on the screen. While waiting for the server to respond, the thread is free to perform other tasks, so the system may use it to execute the code that updates the progress bar. On the right, the tasks were created as concurrent tasks and therefore they are executed simultaneously in different threads.

(Basic) Tasks

Asynchronous and concurrent code is defined by tasks. The Swift Standard Library includes the **Task** structure to create and manage these tasks. The following is the structure's initializer.

▷ **Task(priority:** TaskPriority?, **operation:** Closure)—This initializer creates and runs a new task. The **priority** argument is a structure that helps the system decide when to execute the task. The structure includes type properties to defined standard priorities. The currently available are **background**, **high**, **low**, **medium**, **userInitiated**, and **utility**. The **operation** argument is a closure with the statements to be executed by the task.

The **Task** structure includes the following properties to cancel a task.

▷ **isCancelled**—This property returns a Boolean value that indicates if the task was cancelled.

▷ **cancel()**—This method cancels the task.

There are also a few type properties and methods available to get information from the current task or create tasks that perform specific processes. The following are the most frequently used.

▷ **currentPriority**—This property returns the priority of the current task. It is a **TaskPriority** structure with the properties **background, high, low, medium, userInitiated**, and **utility**.

▷ **isCancelled**—This property returns a Boolean value that indicates whether the current task was cancelled.

▷ **sleep(nanoseconds:** UInt64)—This method suspends the current task the time specified by the **nanoseconds** argument.

Although we can create **Task** structures anywhere in our code to initiate an asynchronous task, SwiftUI includes the following modifiers to do it when the view appears. The task is perform as soon as the view appears and it is automatically canceled when the view disappears.

▷ **task(priority:** TaskPriority, Closure)—This modifier executes the task specified by the second argument when the view appears. The **priority** argument is a structure that helps the system decide when to execute the task. The values available are **background, high, low, medium, userInitiated**, and **utility**.

▷ **task(id:** Value, **priority:** TaskPriority, Closure)—This modifier executes the task specified by the third argument when the view appears. The **id** argument is a value used to identify the task. Every time this value changes, the task is restarted. And the **priority** argument is a structure that helps the system decide when to execute the task. The values available are **background, high, low, medium, userInitiated**, and **utility**.

(Basic) **Async and Await**

Asynchronous and concurrent tasks are defined in Swift with the **async** and **await** keywords. For example, to create an asynchronous task, we mark a method with **async** and then wait for that method to complete with **await**. This means that an asynchronous method can only be called with the **await** keyword from inside another asynchronous method, which creates an indefinite cycle. To start the cycle, we can initiate the asynchronous task when the view appears with the **task()** modifier, as shown below.

```
struct ContentView: View {
    var body: some View {
        VStack {
            Text("Hello, world!")
                .padding()
        }
        .task(priority: .background) {
            let imageName = await loadImage(name: "image1")
            print(imageName)
        }
    }
    func loadImage(name: String) async -> String {
        try? await Task.sleep(nanoseconds: 3 * 1000000000)
```

```
        return "Name: \(name)"
    }
}
```

Listing 9-1: Initiating an asynchronous task

The task in this example is created with a **background** priority, which means that it is not going to have priority over other parallel tasks. In the closure, we call the **loadImage()** method and then print on the console the value returned. This is a method we define to simulate the process of downloading an image form the web. We will learn how to download data and connect to the web later, but for now we use the **sleep()** method to pause the task for 3 seconds and pretend that the image is downloading (the method takes a value in nanoseconds). Once this pause is over, the method returns a string with the file's name. To define the method as asynchronous, we add the **async** keyword after the parameters, and then call it with the **await** keyword to indicate that the task must wait for this process to be over.

The **task()** modifier creates the task and adds it to a thread. When the view is loaded, the closure assigned to the modifier is executed. In the closure, we call the **loadImage()** method and wait for its completion. The method pauses for 3 seconds and then returns a string. After this, the task continues executing the statements and a message is printed on the console.

 Do It Yourself: Create a Multiplatform project. Update the **ContentView** view with the code in Listing 9-1. Run the application on the simulator. You should see a message appear on the console after 3 seconds.

A task can perform multiple asynchronous processes. For instance, in the following example we call the **loadImage()** method three times to download three images.

```
struct ContentView: View {
    var body: some View {
        VStack {
            Text("Hello, world!")
                .padding()
        }.task(priority: .background) {
            let imageName1 = await loadImage(name: "image1")
            let imageName2 = await loadImage(name: "image2")
            let imageName3 = await loadImage(name: "image3")
            print("\(imageName1), \(imageName2), and \(imageName3)")
        }
    }
    func loadImage(name: String) async -> String {
        try? await Task.sleep(nanoseconds: 3 * 1000000000)
        return "Name: \(name)"
    }
}
```

Listing 9-2: Running multiple asynchronous processes

The processes are executed one by one, in sequential order. The task waits for a process to be over before executing the next. In this case, the whole task is going to take 9 seconds to finish (3 seconds per process).

 Do It Yourself: Update the **ContentView** view with the code in Listing 9-2. Run the application on the simulator. You should see a message appear on the console after 9 seconds (3 seconds per process).

The **task()** modifier is useful when all we need is to run an asynchronous task after the views are loaded, but most of the time tasks are not dependent on the views' life cycle and must be created explicitly with the **Task** initializer. For instance, we can reproduce the previous example with the **onAppear()** method and a **Task** structure.

```
struct ContentView: View {
    var body: some View {
        VStack {
            Text("Hello, world!")
                .padding()
        }
        .onAppear {
            Task(priority: .background) {
                let imageName1 = await loadImage(name: "image1")
                let imageName2 = await loadImage(name: "image2")
                let imageName3 = await loadImage(name: "image3")
                print("\(imageName1), \(imageName2), and \(imageName3)")
            }
        }
    }
    func loadImage(name: String) async -> String {
        try? await Task.sleep(nanoseconds: 3 * 1000000000)
        return "Name: \(name)"
    }
}
```

Listing 9-3: *Defining a task explicitly*

This view performs the same three processes as before, but now the task is defined explicitly, which gives us more control over it. For instance, now we can assign the task to a variable and then call the **cancel()** method to cancel it.

The **cancel()** method cancels the task, but the processes are not automatically cancelled; we must detect whether the task has been cancelled with the **isCancelled** property and stop the process ourselves, as shown below.

```
struct ContentView: View {
    var body: some View {
        VStack {
            Text("Hello, world!")
                .padding()
        }
        .onAppear {
            let myTask = Task(priority: .background) {
                let imageName = await loadImage(name: "image1")
                print(imageName)
            }
            Timer.scheduledTimer(withTimeInterval: 2.0, repeats: false)
{ (timer) in
                print("The time is up")
                myTask.cancel()
            }
        }
    }
    func loadImage(name: String) async -> String {
        try? await Task.sleep(nanoseconds: 3 * 1000000000)
        if !Task.isCancelled {
            return "Name: \(name)"
        } else {
            return "Task Cancelled"
        }
    }
}
```

Listing 9-4: *Cancelling a task*

Chapter 9 - Concurrency

This example assigns the previous task to a constant and then creates a timer to call the `cancel()` method on the task 2 seconds later. In the `loadImage()` method, we read the `isCancelled` property and respond accordingly. If the task was cancelled, we return the "Task Cancelled" message, otherwise, the name is returned as before. Note that in this case we are working inside a process executed by the task, so we use the type property instead of the instance property (we read the `isCancelled` property from the data type, not the instance). This property returns `true` or `false` depending on the state of the current task. As a result, the task is cancelled before it is completed.

Tasks can receive and return values. The `Task` structure includes the `value` property to provide access to the value returned by the task. Of course, we also need to wait for the task to complete before reading this value, as shown below.

```
struct ContentView: View {
    var body: some View {
        VStack {
            Text("Hello, world!")
                .padding()
        }
        .onAppear {
            Task(priority: .background) {
                let imageName = await loadImage(name: "image1")
                print(imageName)
            }
        }
    }
    func loadImage(name: String) async -> String {
        let result = Task(priority: .background) { () -> String in
            let imageData = await getMetadata()
            return "Name: \(name) Size: \(imageData)"
        }
        let message = await result.value
        return message
    }
    func getMetadata() async -> Int {
        try? await Task.sleep(nanoseconds: 3 * 1000000000)
        return 50000
    }
}
```

Listing 9-5: Reading a value returned by a task

Because we need to wait for the task to finish before using the value, we have defined a second task. The process starts as always, with a task that calls the `loadImage()` method, but now we create a second task that returns a string. This task executes another asynchronous method that waits for 3 seconds and returns the number 50000. After this process is over, the task creates a string with the name and the number and returns it. We then get the string from the `value` property, and return it to the original task, which prints it on the console.

So far, we have worked with asynchronous methods, but we can also define asynchronous properties. All we need to do is to define the getter with the `async` keyword.

```
struct ContentView: View {
    var thumbnail: String {
        get async {
            try? await Task.sleep(nanoseconds: 3 * 1000000000)
            return "mythumbnail"
        }
    }
    var body: some View {
```

```
        VStack {
            Text("Hello, world!")
                .padding()
        }
        .onAppear {
            Task(priority: .background) {
                let imageName = await thumbnail
                print(imageName)
            }
        }
    }
}
```

Listing 9-6: *Defining asynchronous properties*

This time, instead of calling a method, the task reads a property. The property suspends the tasks for 3 seconds and returns a string. Again, we are suspending the task for didactic purposes, but we can perform any demanding task we want in this property, such as processing or downloading data.

(Basic) **Errors**

Asynchronous tasks are not always successful, so we must be prepared to process the errors returned. If we are creating our own tasks, we can define the errors with an enumeration that conforms to the **Error** protocol, as explain in Chapter 3 (see Listing 3-189). The following example defines a structure with two errors, one to return when no metadata is found on the server (**noData**), and another for when the image is not available (**noImage**).

```
import SwiftUI

enum MyErrors: Error {
    case noData, noImage
}
struct ContentView: View {
    var body: some View {
        VStack {
            Text("Hello, world!")
                .padding()
        }
        .onAppear {
            Task(priority: .background) {
                do {
                    let imageName = try await loadImage(name: "image1")
                    print(imageName)
                } catch MyErrors.noData {
                    print("Error: No Data Available")
                } catch MyErrors.noImage {
                    print("Error: No Image Available")
                }
            }
        }
    }
    func loadImage(name: String) async throws -> String {
        try? await Task.sleep(nanoseconds: 3 * 1000000000)

        let error = true
        if error {
            throw MyErrors.noImage
        }
        return "Name: \(name)"
    }
}
```

}

Listing 9-7: Responding to errors

The **loadImage()** method in this example always throws a **noImage** error to test the code. The task checks for errors with a **do catch** statement and prints a message on the console to report the result. Note that to indicate that the asynchronous function can throw errors, we must declare the **throws** keyword after **async**.

(Basic) **Concurrency**

Asynchronous tasks are useful when we want to free resources so that the system can perform other tasks, such as updating the interface, but when we want to run two tasks simultaneously, we need concurrency. For this purpose, the Swift Standard Library defines the **async let** statement. To turn an asynchronous task into multiple concurrent tasks, all we need to do is to declare the processes with the **async let** statement, as shown next.

```
struct ContentView: View {
    var body: some View {
        VStack {
            Text("Hello, world!")
                .padding()
        }
        .onAppear {
            let currentTime = Date()

            Task(priority: .background) {
                async let imageName1 = loadImage(name: "image1")
                async let imageName2 = loadImage(name: "image2")
                async let imageName3 = loadImage(name: "image3")

                let listNames = await "\(imageName1), \(imageName2), and \
(imageName3)"
                print(listNames)
                print("Total Time: \(Date().timeIntervalSince(currentTime))")
            }
        }
    }
    func loadImage(name: String) async -> String {
        try? await Task.sleep(nanoseconds: 3 * 1000000000)
        return "Name: \(name)"
    }
}
```

Listing 9-8: Defining a concurrent task

Every time a process is declared with the **async let** statement the system creates a new concurrent task that runs in parallel with the rest of the tasks. In the example in Listing 9-8, we create three concurrent tasks (**imageName1**, **imageName2**, and **imageName3**). The process is the same as before, the **loadImage()** method is executed, it pauses the task for 3 seconds and returns a string, but because this time the processes run in parallel, the time they take to complete is around 3 seconds (not 9 seconds, as previous examples).

Do It Yourself: Update the **ContentView** view with the code in Listing 9-8. Run the application on the simulator. After a few seconds, you should see a message on the console with the time that took for the processes to be over.

Data Races

When working with concurrent tasks, we may encounter a problem called data race. A data race occurs when two or more concurrent tasks try to access or modify the same data at the same time. This can lead to errors or serious bugs and is one of the main reasons why applications crash. Up until this point, it was up to the developer to make sure the values were safe, but with Swift 6, everything has changed. When we develop our application with Swift 6, the compiler detects when our code could cause a data race and we have to fix the problem or our application will not work.

Due to the amount of work required to make sure that our code doesn't generate data races, Swift 6 is disabled by default. If we are working with multiple background tasks and want to make sure that our code doesn't produce data races, we can enable it from Settings. The option is available in the Build Settings panel.

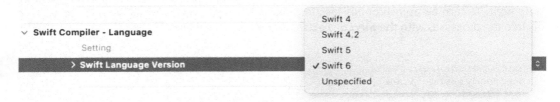

Figure 9-2: Swift 6 option

IMPORTANT: When we develop an application with Swift 6, we need to restructure our code and think about how we want to pass values between threads. If you are not ready yet or find concurrency confusing, you can set your project to work with Swift 5 until you are ready to switch over.

To help us avoid creating data races, Swift introduces the concept of isolation domains. As the name suggests, these are independent units of code that isolate their values from external threads. Swift includes many tools for creating and controlling these isolation domains. The most important is Actors. Actors are data types that isolate parallel tasks from each other. They are reference types and are defined like classes, but instead of the **class** keyword, they are declared with the **actor** keyword. Another important difference with classes is that the properties and methods must be accessed asynchronously (we must wait with the **await** keyword). This ensures that the code waits for the actor to be free (no other task is accessing the actor).

The following example illustrates how actors work. The code declares an actor with a property and a method, creates an instance, and then calls the method from multiple tasks.

```
import SwiftUI

actor ItemData {
   var counter: Int = 0

   func incrementCount() -> String {
      counter += 1
      return "Value: \(counter)"
   }
}
struct ContentView: View {
   var item: ItemData = ItemData()
   var body: some View {
      Button("Start Process") {
         Timer.scheduledTimer(withTimeInterval: 0.1, repeats: true)
{ (timer) in
            Task(priority: .background) {
               async let operation = item.incrementCount()
```

```
                print(await operation)
            }
        }
        Timer.scheduledTimer(withTimeInterval: 0.2, repeats: true)
{ (timer) in
            Task(priority: .high) {
                async let operation = item.incrementCount()
                print(await operation)
            }
        }
    }
}
```

Listing 9-9: Defining an actor

The interface includes a button to start two timers that repeat indefinitely, one every 0.1 seconds and another every 0.2 seconds. The timers perform a task with a concurrent operation that calls the `incrementCount()` method in the actor. This means that different tasks in different threads will be calling the same method, and eventually they will do it at the same time, creating a data race. If we declare `ItemData` as a class, we will have errors, unexpected behavior, or even crashes, but because we declared this data type as an actor, the code works correctly. Every time a task calls the `incrementCount()` method, the actor takes control and makes sure that the tasks only access the method one at a time.

As we mentioned, the actor isolates the properties and methods from the rest of the code and other threads, but in some circumstances this isolation is not required. In these cases, we can revert the condition of isolation with the following keyword.

▷ **nonisolated**—This keyword breaks the isolation of a property or a method.

Non-isolated properties and methods may be necessary to conform to protocols and can also simplify our code when all we need is to access immutable values in the actor. For instance, in the following example we add a constant to the `ItemData` actor called `maximum` and a method that prints its value. Because the value of the constant never changes, we can declare the method non-isolated and call it without waiting for the actor to give us access to it.

```
import SwiftUI

actor ItemData {
   var counter: Int = 0
   let maximum: Int = 50

   func incrementCount() -> String {
      counter += 1
      return "Value: \(counter)"
   }
   nonisolated func maximumValue() -> String {
      return "Maximum Value: \(maximum)"
   }
}
struct ContentView: View {
   var item: ItemData = ItemData()

   var body: some View {
      Button("Start Process") {
         let value = item.maximumValue()
         print(value)
      }
   }
}
```

Listing 9-10: Defining a non-isolated method

In these examples, we have worked with values defined by the actor, but usually values are also sent to the actor for processing. Sending values to a method in the actor is dangerous. Since an actor's job is to make sure that two or more asynchronous tasks don't modify values simultaneously, not every value is safe. Value types, including custom structures and primitive data types like `Int` and `String`, are thread safe because they are copied; when we call a method in the actor with one of these values, the system creates a copy and sends that copy to the method, so the original value is not modified. But objects are reference types and therefore only a reference to the object is sent to the actor, which means that the object may be modified from elsewhere in the code, potentially creating a data race. To ensure that the values we want to sent to an actor are safe, the Swift Standard Library defines the following protocol and attribute.

▷ **Sendable**—This protocol tells the system that the values created from the data type can be safely shared between asynchronous threads.

▷ **@Sendable**—This attribute indicates to the system that a method or a closure can be safely shared between asynchronous threads.

The `Sendable` protocol doesn't do anything other than telling the compiler that the data type is thread safe. When a data type conforms to this protocol, the compiler shows errors if it includes unsafe values. For instance, although structures are safe, we can make them conform to this protocol to make sure we don't add any unsafe properties later. Classes are also safe if they only include immutable values, but subclasses may not be safe, so we have to mark the class with the `final` keyword to make sure that nobody can create a subclass from it, as shown below.

```
import SwiftUI

final class Product: Sendable {
    let name: String

    init(name: String) {
        self.name = name
    }
}
actor ItemData {
    var stock: Int = 100

    func sellProduct(product: Product, quantity: Int) {
        stock = stock - quantity
        print("Stock: \(stock) \(product.name)")
    }
}
struct ContentView: View {
    var item: ItemData = ItemData()

    var body: some View {
        Button("Start Process") {
            Task(priority: .background) {
                let product = Product(name: "Lamp")
                await item.sellProduct(product: product, quantity: 5)
            }
        }
    }
}
```

***Listing 9-11:** Defining a non-isolated method*

This example defines a class called `Product` that is final (no subclasses can be created from it) and includes an immutable property (`let`). Also, the property is of type `String`, a sendable data type. This means that objects created from this class are thread safe and can be sent to an actor.

If we really need to include unsafe values and we know for sure that they are not going to be modified from different threads, we can tell the compiler not to check for errors with the following attribute.

▷ **@unchecked**—This attribute asks the compiler not to check whether the data type conforms to the `Sendable` protocol or not.

We have used this attribute and the `Sendable` protocol before in our models. By conforming our model to the `Sendable` protocol, we tell the compiler that other threads can safely access its values, and by applying the `@unchecked` attribute, we also allow the model to work with not sendable values that we know are safe (Usually required when working with old frameworks). But we can also use the `@unchecked` attribute in other structures and classes that we know are safe. For instance, in the following example, we turn the `Product` class into a structure and use the `name` property to store an `NSString` value. The `NSString` data type is not sendable and therefore the `Product` structure does not meet the requirements of the `Sendable` protocol, but since we know that the value will not be changed anywhere else, we apply the `@unchecked` attribute to ask the compiler not to worry about it.

```
struct Product: @unchecked Sendable {
    let name: NSString
}
```

Listing 9-12: Asking the compiler not to check conformity to the `Sendable` *protocol*

Another way to get the system to ignore an unsafe value is to explicitly declare it unsafe with the `nonisolated` keyword and the parameter `unsafe`. For example, global variables are not safe. Many tasks can access a global variable simultaneously. One way to solve this issue is to turn it into a constant, but if we still need to modify its value, we can use the `nonisolated(unsafe)` keyword to tell the system that we are going to take care of safety ourselves.

```
import SwiftUI

nonisolated(unsafe) var myvalue = NSString(string: "Hello!")
struct ContentView: View {
    var body: some View {
        Button("Start Process") {
            Task(priority: .background) {
                myvalue = NSString(string: "Goodbye!")
            }
        }
    }
}
```

Listing 9-13: Declaring a global variable unsafe

In this example, we have a global variable called `myvalue`. If we declare it as a normal variable, Xcode will return an error, but because we know that only one task is accessing the value at a time, we can declare it unsafe to solve the problem.

Swift also offers the following attribute to suppress warnings and data race errors.

▷ **@preconcurrency**—This attribute tells the compiler that the code was designed before concurrency was available.

This attribute is useful when working with old frameworks that have not yet implemented Swift concurrency. We can declare it when the framework is imported (e.g. `@preconcurrency import OldFramework`) or before the name of an old protocol (e.g. `class MyClass: @preconcurrency OldProtocol`). We will see some practical examples in further chapters.

IMPORTANT: How you isolate data in Swift depends on the characteristics of your application, the organization of your code, and also the type of frameworks you use. In this book, we simply ignore many of the issues because we know that the values are not going to be modified by another thread, but that may not be the case in your project. If you want to learn more about concurrency and how to avoid data races in Swift 6, visit our website and follow the links for this chapter.

(Basic) Main Actor

Tasks are assigned to execution threads and then the system distributes these threads among the multiple cores of a processor to perform the tasks as fast and smoothly as possible. A thread can manage multiple tasks, and multiple threads may be created for our application. Besides the threads initialized by asynchronous and concurrent tasks, the system always creates a thread called *Main Thread* to start the application and run non-asynchronous code, including the code that creates and updates the user interface. This means that if we try to modify the interface from an asynchronous or concurrent task, we may cause a data race or a serious bug. To avoid these conflicts, the Swift Standard Library defines the Main Actor. The Main Actor is an actor created by the system that makes sure that every task that wants to interact with the main thread or modify the elements of the interface waits for other tasks to finish.

Swift provides two easy ways to make sure that our code runs on the Main Actor: the **@MainActor** modifier and the **run()** method. With the **@MainActor** modifier we can mark an entire method to run on the main thread, while the **run()** method executes a closure in the main thread. For instance, in the following example we mark the **loadImage()** method with **@MainActor** to make sure that the code inside the method is executed in the main thread and we are able to modify the value of a **Text** view with no issues.

```
struct ContentView: View {
    @State private var myText: String = "Hello, world!"

    var body: some View {
        VStack {
            Text(myText)
                .padding()
        }
        .onAppear {
            Task(priority: .background) {
                await loadImage(name: "image1")
            }
        }
    }
    @MainActor func loadImage(name: String) async {
        myText = name
    }
}
```

Listing 9-14: Executing a method in the Main Actor

This code creates an asynchronous task as before, but now the method is marked with **@MainActor**, so the code is executed in the main thread and we can safely update the **myText** property and the interface.

Most of the time, only part of our code deals with the interface, but the rest can be executed in the current thread. For cases like this, we can implement the **run()** method. This is a type method defined by the **MainActor** structure (the structure used to create the Main Actor). The method takes a closure with the statements we need to execute in the main thread.

```
struct ContentView: View {
   @State private var myText: String = "Hello, world!"

   var body: some View {
      VStack {
         Text(myText)
            .padding()
      }
      .onAppear {
         Task(priority: .background) {
            await loadImage(name: "image1")
         }
      }
   }
   func loadImage(name: String) async {
      await MainActor.run {
         myText = name
      }
      print(name)
   }
}
```

Listing 9-15: Executing code in the Main Actor

The **loadImage()** method now includes a statement at the end to print the string on the console, but only the statement that assigns the new value to the **myText** property needs to run in the main thread, so we execute it within the **run()** method. Note that this method is marked with **await**. The **await** keyword is necessary because the method may have to wait for the main thread to be free to execute the statements.

The **run()** method can also return a value. This is useful when we need to report the result of a complex operation. All we need to remember is that we must declare the type of value returned by the closure, as shown below.

```
func loadImage(name: String) async {
   let result: String = await MainActor.run {
      myText = name
      return "Name: \(name)"
   }
   print(result)
}
```

Listing 9-16: Returning a value from the Main Actor

We can also use **@MainActor** to initiate tasks in the Main Actor. In the following example, we change the value of the **Text** view directly from a task.

```
struct ContentView: View {
   @State private var myText: String = "Hello, world!"

   var body: some View {
      VStack {
         Text(myText)
            .padding()
      }
      .onAppear {
         Task { @MainActor in
            myText = "Goodbye, world!"
         }
      }
   }
}
```

```
}
```

Listing 9-17: Accessing the Main Actor from a task

The `@MainActor` can also be used to avoid data races. For example, we can declare a global variable in the Main Actor so it can only be accessed from that domain.

```
import SwiftUI

@MainActor
var myvalue = NSString(string: "Hello!")
struct ContentView: View {
    var body: some View {
        Button("Start Process") {
            Task(priority: .background) {
                myvalue = NSString(string: "Goodbye!")
            }
        }
    }
}
```

Listing 9-18: Declaring global variables in the Main Actor

Medium Asynchronous Sequences

Sometimes, information is returned as a sequence of values, but the values may not be available all at once. In cases like this, we can create an asynchronous sequence. This sequence is like an array, but the values are returned asynchronously, so we must wait for each value to be ready.

The Swift Standard Library includes two protocols to create asynchronous sequences: the `AsyncSequence` protocol to define the sequence and the `AsyncIteratorProtocol` protocol to define the code that iterates through the sequence to return the values. The `AsyncSequence` protocol requires the data type to include a typealias with the name `Element` that represents the data type returned by the sequence and also the following method.

> **makeAsyncIterator()**—This method returns the instance of the iterator in charge of producing the values. The value returned is an instance of a data type that conforms to the `AsyncIteratorProtocol` protocol.

On the other hand, the `AsyncIteratorProtocol` protocol only requires the data type to implement the following method.

> **next()**—This method returns the next element on the list. The method is called over and over again until the value returned is `nil`, which indicates the end of the sequence.

To create an asynchronous sequence, we must define two data types, one that conforms to the `AsyncSequence` to describe the data type of the values returned by the sequence and initialize the iterator, and another that conforms to the `AsyncIteratorProtocol` protocol to produce the values. In the following example, we define an asynchronous sequence that processes an array of strings one by one and returns a sequence of `String` values.

```
import SwiftUI

struct ImageIterator : AsyncIteratorProtocol {
    let imageList: [String]
    var current = 0

    mutating func next() async -> String? {
        guard current < imageList.count else {
```

```
          return nil
      }
      try? await Task.sleep(nanoseconds: 3 * 1000000000)

      let image = imageList[current]
      current += 1
      return image
   }
}
struct ImageLoader : AsyncSequence {
   typealias Element = String
   let imageList: [String]

   func makeAsyncIterator() -> ImageIterator {
      return AsyncIterator(imageList: imageList)
   }
}
struct ContentView: View {
   let list = ["image1", "image2", "image3"]

   var body: some View {
      VStack {
         Text("Hello World!")
            .padding()
      }
      .onAppear {
         Task(priority: .background) {
            let loader = ImageLoader(imageList: list)
            for await image in loader {
               print(image)
            }
         }
      }
   }
}
```

Listing 9-19: Defining an asynchronous sequence

The code in Listing 9-19 simulates the process of asynchronously downloading images from the web. The iterator is defined first with the **next()** method. In this method, we read the strings from the **list** array and update a counter to know when we have reached the end (the value of the counter is equal or greater than the number of elements in the array). The asynchronous sequence is defined next by the **ImageLoader** structure. The structure includes a typealias called **Element** to indicate that the sequence returns **String** values, and the **makeAsyncIterator()** method to initialize the iterator.

Everything is ready to read the values in the sequence, so we start a task, create an instance of the **ImageLoader** sequence, and then iterate through the elements with a **for in** loop. Note that the **for in** loop requires the **await** keyword to wait for each element of the sequence. The loop runs until the value returned by the iterator is **nil**.

 Do It Yourself: Update the ContentView.swift file with the code in Listing 9-19. Run the application on the simulator. You should see the values in the **list** array printed on the console every 3 seconds.

Medium **Task Group**

A task group is a container for dynamically generated tasks. Once the group is created, we can add and manage tasks from code as required by the application. The Swift Standard Library defines the following global methods to create a group.

▷ **withTaskGroup(of:** Type, **returning:** Type, **body:** Closure)—This method creates a task group. The **of** argument defines the data type returned by the tasks, the **returning** argument defines the data type returned by the group, and the **body** argument is the closure where the tasks are defined. If no values are returned, the arguments may be ignored.

▷ **withThrowingTaskGroup(of:** Type, **returning:** Type, **body:** Closure)—This method creates a task group that can throw errors. The **of** argument defines the data type returned by the tasks, the **returning** argument defines the data type returned by the group, and the **body** argument is the closure where the tasks are defined. If no values are returned, the arguments may be ignored.

The group is defined by an instance of the `TaskGroup` structure, which includes properties and methods to manage the tasks in the group. The following are the most frequently used.

▷ **isCancelled**—This property returns a Boolean value that indicates whether the group was cancelled.

▷ **isEmpty**—This property returns a Boolean value that indicates whether the group has any remaining tasks.

▷ **addTask(priority:** TaskPriority?, **operation:** Closure)—This method adds a task to the group. The **priority** argument is a structure that helps the system decide when to execute the task. The structure includes type properties to defined standard priorities. The currently available are `background`, `high`, `low`, `medium`, `userInitiated`, and `utility`. And the **operation** argument is a closure with the statements to be executed by the task.

▷ **cancelAll()**—This method cancels all the tasks in the group.

A task group is an asynchronous sequence of tasks. This sequence is generic, which means that the tasks and the group can return any types of values. This is the reason why the methods to create a task group have two arguments, one to specify the data type returned by the tasks and another to specify the data types returned by the group.

The two methods available to create a task group are the same. The one we implement depends on whether we want to throw errors or not. These methods create a `TaskGroup` structure that works with the data types specified by the arguments and send the instance to the closure. Using this value inside the closure, we can add to the group all the tasks we want, as shown below.

```
struct ContentView: View {
    var body: some View {
        VStack {
            Text("Hello World!")
                .padding()
        }
        .onAppear {
            Task(priority: .background) {
                await withTaskGroup(of: String.self) { group in
                    group.addTask(priority: .background) {
                        let imageName = await self.loadImage(name: "image1")
                        return imageName
                    }
                    group.addTask(priority: .background) {
                        let imageName = await self.loadImage(name: "image2")
                        return imageName
                    }
                    group.addTask(priority: .background) {
                        let imageName = await self.loadImage(name: "image3")
```

Chapter 9 - Concurrency

```
                    return imageName
                }
                for await result in group {
                    print(result)
                }
            }
        }
    }
}
func loadImage(name: String) async -> String {
    try? await Task.sleep(nanoseconds: 3 * 1000000000)
    return "Name: \(name)"
}
}
```

Listing 9-20: Defining a task group

In this example, we create a task group that doesn't throw errors. The group doesn't return a value either, but the tasks return a string, so we declare the **of** argument of the **withTaskGroup()** method as a **String** data type (**String.self**). The tasks are added to the group one after another. Each task performs the same process as before. They call the **loadImage()** method asynchronously and get a string in return.

Because a task group is an asynchronous sequence of tasks, we can iterate though the values with a **for in** loop, as we did for the asynchronous sequence created in the previous section of this chapter. Every time a task is completed, the group returns the value produced by the task until no tasks remain, in which case the value **nil** is returned to finish the loop.

 IMPORTANT: Task Groups store the tasks in sequence. You can remove, filter, or even check whether a group contains a specific task. The topic is beyond the scope of this book. For more information, visit our website and follow the links for this chapter.

(Basic) Asynchronous Images

Although the tools introduced in this chapter allow us to perform any type of asynchronous or concurrent task we need, SwiftUI offers the **AsyncImage** view to simplify our work when loading images. This view takes care of downloading an image from a server and displaying the image on the screen when it is ready. The following are the most frequently used initializers.

▷ **AsyncImage(url:** URL, **scale:** CGFloat)—This view downloads an image from a server and displays it on the screen. The **url** argument is a **URL** structure with the image's url, and the **scale** argument is the scale we want to assign to the image (1 by default).

▷ **AsyncImage(url:** URL, **scale:** CGFloat, **content:** Closure, **placeholder:** Closure)—This view downloads an image from a server and displays it on the screen. The **url** argument is a **URL** structure with the image's url, the **scale** argument is the scale we want to assign to the image (1 by default), the **content** argument is a closure to process the image, and the **placeholder** argument is a closure that returns a view to show in place of the image while we wait for the image to download.

The location of the image is determined by a **URL** structure. These structures are used to store the addresses of local and remote documents, files, and resources. The following are the initializers we need to create URLs to access documents and resources on the web.

▷ **URL(string:** String)—This initializer creates a **URL** structure with the URL specified by the **string** argument.

▷ **URL(string:** String, **relativeTo:** URL?**)**—This initializer creates a `URL` structure with the URL specified by the arguments. The URL is created by adding the value of the **string** argument to the value of the **relativeTo** argument.

▷ **URL(dataRepresentation:** Data, **relativeTo:** URL?, **isAbsolute:** Bool**)**—This initializer creates a `URL` structure with the URL specified by the arguments. The URL is created by adding the value of the **dataRepresentation** argument to the value of the **relativeTo** argument. The `isAbsolute` argument is a Boolean value that determines if the URL is absolute or not (it includes all the information required to access the resource).

There are two types of URL: secure and non-secure. Non-secure URLs are identified with the http protocol (Hypertext Transfer Protocol) and secure URLs are identified with the https protocol (Hypertext Transfer Protocol Secure). Secure URLs are allowed by default, but if we need to open non-secure URLs we must configure our app to circumvent a security system called ATS (App Transport Security) implemented by Apple devices.

The option to configure the App Transport Security system is called "App Transport Security Settings", and it is added to the app's configuration from the Info panel. We have introduced this panel before (see Figure 5-13) and use it to add custom fonts (see Figure 5-34). As explained before, new options are added from the + button on the right side of the items.

Key	Type	Value
Bundle name	String	$(PRODUCT_NAME)
Bundle identifier	String	$(PRODUCT_BUNDLE_IDENTIFIER)
InfoDictionary version	String	6.0
> Supported interface orientations (iPho...	Array	(3 items)

Figure 9-3: Button to add configuration options

After we click on the + button (circled in Figure 9-3), a new empty text field is added below the option. If we start typing, a drop down menu shows the options available and we can select it from the list.

Key	Type	Value
Bundle name	String	$(PRODUCT_NAME)
App Transport Security Settings	Dictionary	(0 items)
Bundle identifier	String	$(PRODUCT_BUNDLE_IDENTIFIER)
InfoDictionary version	String	6.0
> Supported interface orientations (iPho...	Array	(3 items)

Figure 9-4: App Transport Security option

The App Transport Security Settings option is just a container. To configure the option, we must add subitems. To add a subitem, we must click on the arrow on the left (circled in Figure 9-4), and then press the + button again. The option to allow the app to open non-secure URLs is called "Allow Arbitrary Loads".

Key	Type	Value
Bundle name	String	$(PRODUCT_NAME)
∨ App Transport Security Settings	Dictionary	(1 item)
Allow Arbitrary Loads	Boolean	YES
Bundle identifier	String	$(PRODUCT_BUNDLE_IDENTIFIER)

Figure 9-5: App Transport Security configured to allow non-secure URLs

The Allow Arbitrary Loads key takes a Boolean value specified with the strings YES and NO (or 1 and 0, respectively). Setting this key to YES (1) allows any URL to be opened. If what we want is to allow only specific domains, we must use the Exception Domains key and add to the key additional items with the domains we want to include. These items in turn require at least three more items with the keys **NSIncludesSubdomains** (Boolean), **NSTemporaryException-AllowsInsecureHTTPLoads** (Boolean), and **NSTemporaryExceptionMinimumTLSVersion** (String). For example, the following configuration allows documents from the formasterminds.com domain to be opened.

Key		Type	Value
Bundle name	⌃	String	$(PRODUCT_NAME)
⌄ App Transport Security Settings	⌃	Dictionary	(1 item)
⌄ Exception Domains	⌃	Dictionary	(1 item)
formasterminds.com	⊙⊖	Dictionary ⌃	(3 items)
NSIncludesSubdomains		Boolean	1
NSTemporaryExceptionAllowsInsec...		Boolean	1
NSTemporaryExceptionMinimumTL...		String	TLSv1.1

Figure 9-6: App Transport Security configured to allow URLs from formasterminds.com

Configuring the App Transport Security system may be necessary or not, depending on the type of URLs we want our users to be able to access. Secure URLs are allowed by default, but if we want to allow our users to access non-secure URLs, we must add the options to the app configuration, as shown above. For instance, the following example loads an image from the non-secure version of our website (http protocol).

```
struct ContentView: View {
    let website = URL(string: "http://www.formasterminds.com/images/
coveruikit4big.png")

    var body: some View {
        VStack {
            AsyncImage(url: website)
        }.padding()
    }
}
```

Listing 9-21: Loading an image asynchronously

All the **AsyncImage** view needs to download and display an image is a URL. In this example, we store a URL in a constant and then implement the view to load the image. Although the image is effectively loaded and displayed, the **AsyncImage** view doesn't allow any configuration, so the image is shown in its original size.

Figure 9-7: Image loaded asynchronously

If we want to configure the image, we must provide a closure for the **content** argument. This closure receives an **Image** view that we can configure with view modifiers, as before.

```
struct ContentView: View {
    let website = URL(string: "https://www.formasterminds.com/images/
coveruikit4big.png")

    var body: some View {
        VStack {
            AsyncImage(url: website, content: { image in
                image
                    .resizable()
                    .scaledToFit()
            }, placeholder: {
                Image(.nopicture)
            })
            Spacer()
        }.padding()
    }
}
```

Listing 9-22: Configuring the image after it is downloaded

When we provide the **content** argument, the `AsyncImage` view delegates the job of displaying the image to the `Image` view received by the closure, so we can configure this view as before. In this example, we resize the image with the `resizable()` modifier and scale it to fit within the view with the `scaledToFit()` modifier. Note that we have also defined the **placeholder** argument to show a temporary image while the final image is downloading.

Figure 9-8: Image configuration

Do It Yourself: Create a Multiplatform project. Download the nopicture.png image from our website and add it to the Asset Catalog. Update the `ContentView` view with the code in Listing 9-22. Click on the item at the top of the Navigator Area to open the app's configuration panels (Chapter 5, Figure 5-4, number 6). Open the info panel and follow the steps explained in Figures 9-2, 9-3, and 9-4 to add the Allow Arbitrary Loads option with the value YES. After a few seconds, you should see the cover of the UIKit for Masterminds book replacing the nopicture.png image.

Chapter 9 - Concurrency

Chapter 10
Storage

(Basic) **10.1 User Defaults**

Up to this point, we stored all data in arrays created in the model, and the values were hard-coded, meaning they were always the same when the user launched the application. Any changes applied to the model were retained only as long as the application was running, and were deleted as soon as the application was closed. To preserve the values and all the changes made by the user, we need to store the data permanently on the device. Apple offers several systems for storing data. They all work with files, but can take different forms, from simple text files to databases (indexed data).

(Basic) **App Storage**

The simplest storage system available on Apple devices is called Users Defaults. This system is designed to store user preferences, which can include values set by the user to determine how the app should operate, or values set by the app to restore previous states. These values are stored in a system-managed database and therefore persist after the app is closed for as long as the user or the app requires. SwiftUI includes the following property wrapper for storing and retrieving User Defaults values.

▷ **@AppStorage(**String**)**—This property wrapper stores or retrieves a value from User Defaults. The argument is a string with the key of the value we want to access.

The User Defaults system can store any type of data, but it is recommended to use it for storing short strings and small values. Its main purpose is to store the app's settings. For example, we can use it to allow the user to store a limit on the number of items managed by the app, and then reset that limit each time the app is launched. To create this application, all we need is to define a property with the **@AppStorage** property wrapper and then use it as we do with a **@State** property.

```
struct ContentView: View {
    @AppStorage("counter") var mycounter: Double = 0

    var body: some View {
        HStack {
            Stepper("", value: $mycounter)
                .labelsHidden()
            Text("\
(mycounter.formatted(.number.precision(.fractionLength(0))))")
                .font(.title)
        }
    }
}
```

Listing 10-1: Storing and reading values from User Defaults

This view defines an **@AppStorage** property with the "counter" key and the name **mycounter**, and includes a **Stepper** and a **Text** view to let the user select a value and show it on the screen.

An **@AppStorage** property is used like a **@State** property, but now the value is stored in the User Defaults system. As a result, the value of the property is preserved after the app is closed. When the app is closed and reopened, the **mycounter** property retrieves the last value stored by the user from User Defaults and displays it on the screen.

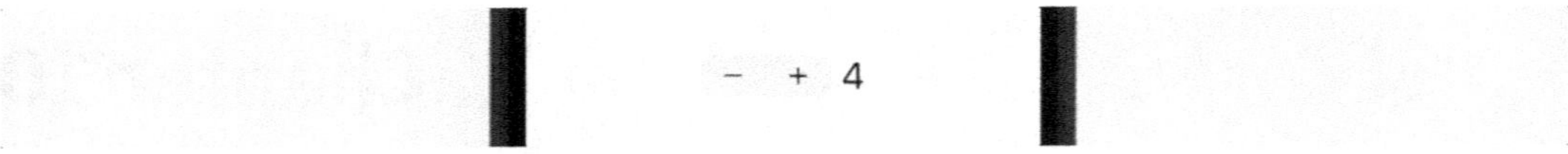

Figure 10-1: *Interface to store settings*

Do It Yourself: Create a Multiplatform project. Update the `ContentView` view with the code in Listing 10-1. Run the application on the iPhone simulator. Press the buttons on the stepper to change the value. Wait a few seconds. Stop the execution of the app from the Stop button in Xcode. Run the application again. The value displayed on the screen should be the last one you selected.

IMPORTANT: The `@AppStorage` property wrapper can only store simple values like strings and numbers, but you can also store other types of values, including custom data types, by converting them into `Data` structures (see Archiving).

As we already mentioned, we can also store values generated by the application. For example, we can add a value to User Defaults to check how long it's been since the last time the app was launched. The process to read and store the value is the same, but this time we need to store a date. The `@AppStorage` property wrapper doesn't take `Date` structures, but we can store a `TimeInterval` value from a reference date, and then create the `Date` structure from this value when necessary.

```
struct ContentView: View {
    @AppStorage("interval") var interval =
Date.timeIntervalSinceReferenceDate
    @State private var message: String = ""

    var body: some View {
        HStack {
            Text("\(message)")
                .lineLimit(nil)
        }.onAppear {
            let calendar = Calendar.current
            let lastDate = Date(timeIntervalSinceReferenceDate: interval)
            let components =
calendar.dateComponents([.year, .month, .day, .hour, .minute, .second],
from: lastDate, to: Date())
            message = "You haven't use this app in \(components.year!)
years, \(components.month!) months, \(components.day!) days, \
(components.hour!) hours, \(components.minute!) minutes, \
(components.second!) seconds"
            interval = Date.timeIntervalSinceReferenceDate
        }
    }
}
```

Listing 10-2: *Storing app settings in User Defaults*

This view creates a property of type `TimeInterval` called `interval` with the number of seconds from a reference date (January 1st, 2001). When the view appears, the `onAppear()` modifier turns this value into a `Date` structure, extracts the components of the date, creates a string with these values, and assigns it to a `@State` property to show it on the screen. At the end, we update the `interval` property with the current interval to be able to calculate the time again when the app is relaunched.

You haven't use this app in 0 years, 0 months, 0 days, 0 hours, 0 minutes, 17 seconds

Figure 10-2: *Displaying app settings*

Chapter 10 - Storage

Do It Yourself: Update the `ContentView` view with the code in Listing 10-2. Run the application on the iPhone simulator. The first time, you should see all the date components set to 0. Stop the app from Xcode and run it again. You should see how long it has been since the last time the app was launched.

The previous examples were intended for didactic purposes. User Defaults is often used to store the app's settings and users are provided with a separate view where they can change these values and configure the app to their liking. In the following example, we will follow this approach to allow the user to configure the rows of a `List` view that presents a list of books. By changing the values in the Settings view, the user can decide whether to show or hide the cover and year of each book.

Figure 10-3: *App settings*

For this example, we use the model defined in Chapter 7, Listing 7-3 and define two `@AppStorage` properties, `showYear` and `showCover`, to store Boolean values that indicate whether the year and the cover should be shown or hidden. By reading the values of these properties, we can configure the list, as shown below.

```
struct ContentView: View {
    @Environment(ApplicationData.self) private var appData
    @AppStorage("showYear") var showYear: Bool = true
    @AppStorage("showCover") var showCover: Bool = true

    var body: some View {
        NavigationStack {
            List(appData.userData) { book in
                VStack {
                    HStack(alignment: .top) {
                        if showCover {
                            Image(book.cover)
                                .resizable()
                                .scaledToFit()
                                .frame(width: 80, height: 100)
                        }
                        VStack(alignment: .leading, spacing: 2) {
                            Text(book.title).bold()
                            Text(book.author)
                            if showYear {
                                Text(book.displayYear).font(.caption)
                            }
                        }.padding(.top, 5)
                        Spacer()
                    }.padding([.leading, .trailing], 10)
                    .padding([.top, .bottom], 5)
                }
            }
            .navigationBarTitle("Books")
            .toolbar {
                ToolbarItem(placement: .navigationBarTrailing) {
                    NavigationLink("Settings", destination: {
```

```
                    SettingsView()
               })
          }
       }
     }
   }
}
```

Listing 10-3: Adapting the interface to the app's settings

Each row on the list is configured according to the values in User Defaults. The **Image** view is only displayed when the value of the **showCover** property is **true** and the year is shown depending on the value of the **showYear** property.

The navigation bar of the **ContentView** view includes a button on the right to open a view called **SettingsView**. This is the view where we allow the user to change the configuration.

```
struct SettingsView: View {
   @AppStorage("showYear") var showYear: Bool = true
   @AppStorage("showCover") var showCover: Bool = true

   var body: some View {
      Form {
         List {
            Toggle("Show Picture", isOn: $showCover)
            Toggle("Show Year", isOn: $showYear)
         }
      }
      .navigationBarTitle("Settings")
   }
}
```

Listing 10-4: Modifying the app's settings

Since the **@AppStorage** properties always access the same values from the User Defaults system, we can recreate them wherever we need them. In this example, we have redefined the two properties to access the showYear and showCover values. The view includes two **Toggle** views to toggle these values. When the user interacts with these controls, the values in User Defaults are updated and the views are redrawn, as shown in Figure 10-3 above.

 Do It Yourself: Download the book covers from our website and add them to the Asset Catalog. Create a Swift file called ApplicationData.swift for the model in Chapter 7, Listing 7-3. Update the **ContentView** view with the code in Listing 10-3. Create a SwiftUI file called SettingsView.swift for the view in Listing 10-4. Remember to inject the **ApplicationData** object into the environment for the app and the preview (Chapter 7, Listing 7-4). Run the application on the iPhone simulator. You should see the interface in Figure 10-3, left. Press the Settings button. In the Settings view, turn the switches off (Figure 10-3, center). Press the Back button to see the changes on the interface (Figure 10-3, right).

(Basic) **10.2 SwiftData**

The User Defaults system is intended to store the configuration and state of the app, and therefore cannot be used to store large amounts of data. For this purpose, Apple provides the SwiftData framework. This framework takes advantage of macros and property wrappers to create the code we need to permanently store the app's model in a database. The framework creates a system that includes a container to manage the database, a context to send and retrieve data from the container, and an API to interact with the context to retrieve and permanently store the data.

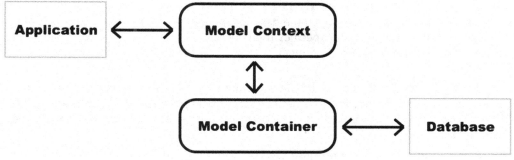

Figure 10-4: *Model structure*

The model container is the object in charge of managing the database and storing the data permanently on file. This object is created from the `ModelContainer` class, which includes the following initializer.

▷ **ModelContainer(for:** PersistentModel.Type..., **migrationPlan:** Schema-MigrationPlan.Type, **configurations:** ModelConfiguration...)—This initializer creates a container for the models specified by the arguments. The **for** argument is a list of references to the data types used to create the models. The **migrationPlan** argument is a reference to the data type that describes how to migrate to a new version of the container. And the **configurations** argument is a list of `ModelConfiguration` structures that specify the container's configuration.

To configure the container, the SwiftData framework includes the `ModelConfiguration` structure. The following are some of the structure's initializers.

▷ **ModelConfiguration(isStoredInMemoryOnly:** Bool)—This initializer creates a structure to configure a model container. The **isStoredInMemoryOnly** argument determines whether the data is stored permanently on disk or temporarily in memory.

▷ **ModelConfiguration(**String, **schema:** Schema?, **url:** URL, **allowsSave:** Bool, **cloudKitDatabase:** CloudKitDatabase)—This initializer creates a structure to configure a container. The first argument is the name we want to give the configuration, the **schema** argument is an object that maps the classes describing the model to the container, the **url** argument determines where the database is stored, the **allowsSave** argument specifies whether the changes in the context are automatically saved to the container (`true` by default), and the **cloudKitDatabase** argument is a structure that specifies the identifier of the CloudKit container used to share data with other devices. The structure defines the properties `automatic` and `none` to determine how the system is going to find the container, and the method `private(String)` to declare a specific container.

The container takes care of managing the data, but our application accesses that data through the context. This is an object created by the `ModelContext` class. Although we can create the context manually, the container provides its own. Below is the property included by the `ModelContainer` class to return a reference to this object.

▷ **mainContext**—This property returns a reference to the `ModelContext` object assigned to the container.

The context is the object that allows our application to access and modify the data managed by the container. For this purpose, the `ModelContext` class defines multiple properties and methods. The following are the most frequently used.

▷ **fetch(FetchDescriptor, batchSize:** Int)—This method retrieves from the container the objects that match the description specified by the arguments. The first argument is a structure that specifies the criteria and sort order used to retrieve the objects, and the **batchSize** argument specifies the maximum number of objects to retrieve.

▷ **fetchCount(**FetchDescriptor)—This method returns an `Int` value with the number of objects found by the container that match the description specified by the argument. The argument is a structure that specifies the criteria and sort order used to find the objects.

▷ **insert(**Object)—This method inserts an object into the context.

▷ **delete(**Object)—This method removes an object from the context.

▷ **save()**—This method saves the changes in the context to the container.

(Basic) Model

The first step in working with a database is to tell the system the types of values we want to store. The procedure in SwiftData is simple. We must define a class with all the properties we need to store the user's data, and then use it to represent our data model. For this purpose, SwiftData provides the following macro.

▷ **@Model**—This macro adds to a class all the code necessary to permanently store any object created from that class in a database, and also to update the views when a value in that object changes.

To create a SwiftData model, all we need is to apply the `@Model` macro to a class. For example, we can convert the `Book` structure from our previous examples into a class and apply the `@Model` macro to turn it into a SwiftData model, as shown below.

```
import SwiftUI
import SwiftData

@Model
class Book: Identifiable {
    var id: UUID = UUID()
    var title: String = ""
    var author: String = ""
    var cover: String = ""
    var year: Int = 0

    init(title: String, author: String, cover: String, year: Int) {
        self.title = title
        self.author = author
        self.cover = cover
        self.year = year
    }
    var displayYear: String {
        get {
            let value = year > 0 ? String(year) : "Undefined"
            return value
        }
    }
}
```

Listing 10-5: Defining a SwiftData model

The **@Model** macro is defined in the SwiftData framework. After importing this framework, we apply the macro to the **Book** class and define the properties as before. We have a property to store a unique identifier for each book, and all the properties necessary to store the information, including title, author, cover, and year. Note that SwiftData requires that the properties have a value by default or be optional.

Store properties are used to define the structure of the data stored in the database, but we can also include any computed properties and methods we need to prepare and process the data. The macro defines the data model with the stored properties and ignores the rest of the members of the class. In this example, we include the **displayYear** property, which formats the value of the **year** property for the views (**Text** views can only display strings).

(Basic) **Container**

The **@Model** macro uses a class to define the structure of the data our app can store. So we can create objects from this class, insert them into the context, and they will be permanently stored in the database. But we still need to create the container that will process the data and manage the database. Although we can do this manually by creating an instance of the **ModelContainer** class, as we will see later, SwiftUI includes the following modifier to create the container and inject it into the environment.

▷ **modelContainer(for: [Type], inMemory: Bool, isAutosaveEnabled: Bool, isUndoEnabled: Bool, onSetup: Closure)**—This modifier creates a container with the configuration specified by the arguments and injects it into the environment. The **for** argument is a set with references to all the classes that make up the data model, the **inMemory** argument specifies whether the data is stored permanently on disk or temporarily in memory (**false** by default), the **isAutosaveEnabled** argument specifies whether the changes in the context are automatically saved to the container (**true** by default), the **isUndoEnabled** argument specifies whether the user should be able to undo and redo changes (**false** by default), and the **onSetup** argument provides a closure that is executed after the container is set up.

Like any data model, the SwiftData model must be injected into the environment from the window or the main view to make it available to all the views in the interface. Below we show how to work with a SwiftData model along with the observable data models introduced in previous chapters.

```
import SwiftUI
import SwiftData

@main
struct TestApp: App {
   @State private var appData = ApplicationData.shared

   var body: some Scene {
      WindowGroup {
         ContentView()
            .environment(appData)
            .modelContainer(for: [Book.self])
      }
   }
}
```

Listing 10-6: Creating the container

Unless we want to provide a specific configuration, the only argument required to create the container is a set with the data types of the classes we want to use to store the data in the database. In our example, this is the **Book** class defined in Listing 10-5.

Context

The `modelContainer()` modifier creates a container, but our application must interact with the context. To access the context assigned to the container, the environment includes the following property.

▷ **modelContext**—This environment property returns a reference to the context assigned to the container.

Once we have access to the context, we can read, save, modify, or delete objects. When a value is modified, the system detects the change and automatically stores it in the container. When reading data, the process is reversed. The container retrieves the objects from the database and then moves them to the context. Once the objects are in the context, we can read their properties, change their values, or delete them. The problem with retrieving data from a database is that thousands or even millions of objects may be available. Getting all this information at once takes time and consumes resources. Therefore, we need to retrieve only the objects that the user needs at any given time. For this purpose, SwiftData defines the `Query` macro.

▷ **@Query(filter:** Predicate?, **sort:** KeyPath, **order:** SortOrder, **transaction:** Transaction?)—This macro performs a query on the container and keeps the objects synchronized. The **filter** argument provides a predicate for filtering the objects, the **sort** argument specifies the property used to sort the objects, the **order** argument is an enumeration with the values `forward` and `reverse` to determine whether the objects are listed in ascending or descending order, and the **transaction** argument specifies the type of animation used to insert or remove objects from the list.

▷ **@Query(**FetchDescriptor, **transaction:** Transaction?)—This macro performs a query on the container and keeps the objects synchronized. The first argument is a structure that defines the criteria to filter and sort the objects, and the **transaction** argument specifies the type of animation used to insert or remove objects from the list.

Implementing SwiftData

Using SwiftData to store user data in a database is simple. We define the model using the `@Model` macro to tell the system how to structure the data (Listing 10-5), create the container and inject it into the environment with the `modelContainer(for:)` modifier (Listing 10-6), and then access the context from the views to read, create, and modify the objects.

To show how to implement all the features provided by SwiftData, we will recreate a previous application for storing and listing books. Although the books are managed and stored by the SwiftData model, we still need to use an observable object to control the app's states. For this first example, we only need a single property to store the navigation path (see Listing 8-28).

```
import SwiftUI
import Observation

@Observable class ApplicationData: @unchecked Sendable {
   var viewPath = NavigationPath()

   static let shared: ApplicationData = ApplicationData()
   private init() { }
}
```

Listing 10-7: Controlling the navigation path from an observable object

From the `ContentView` view, we read the books in the database with a `@Query` property and allow the user to open an additional view to add more.

```
import SwiftUI
import SwiftData

struct ContentView: View {
    @Environment(ApplicationData.self) private var appData
    @Environment(\.modelContext) var dbContext
    @Query var listBooks: [Book]

    var body: some View {
        @Bindable var appData = appData

        NavigationStack(path: $appData.viewPath) {
            List(listBooks) { book in
                CellBook(book: book)
            }.listStyle(.plain)
            .navigationTitle("Books")
            .toolbarTitleDisplayMode(.inline)
            .toolbar {
                ToolbarItem(placement: .navigationBarTrailing) {
                    NavigationLink(value: "Add Book", label: {
                        Image(systemName: "plus")
                    })
                }
            }
            .navigationDestination(for: String.self, destination: { viewID in
                if viewID == "Add Book" {
                    AddBook()
                }
            })
        }
    }
}
struct CellBook: View {
    let book: Book

    var body: some View {
        HStack(alignment: .top) {
            Image(book.cover)
                .resizable()
                .scaledToFit()
                .frame(width: 80, height: 100)
            VStack(alignment: .leading, spacing: 2) {
                Text(book.title).bold()
                Text(book.author)
                Text(book.displayYear).font(.caption)
                Spacer()
            }
            Spacer()
        }.padding([.top], 10)
    }
}
#Preview {
    ContentView()
        .environment(ApplicationData.shared)
        .modelContainer(for: [Book.self], inMemory: true)
}
```

Listing 10-8: Fetching books from the database

As before, we need to import the SwiftData framework to implement its macros and modifiers. In this case, we use the `@Query` macro to fetch the list of books from the database. Because we want to get all the objects in the database, the query does not require any parameters other than the name of the property used to store the values. The `List` view takes the values in this property and shows the list of books on the screen.

The list of values is processed as in previous examples, but there are two things to note in this view. First, we have added a property for accessing the context from the environment. The `@Query` macro can access the context without this property, but we will need it later to get information or delete objects from this view. Second, we applied the `modelContainer()` modifier to the preview, but now with the **inMemory** argument set to `true`. This will store any data we insert for testing in memory and therefore automatically remove it each time the preview is recreated (we will learn how to work with previews later).

The view in Listing 10-8 also includes a `NavigationLink` view and a `navigation-Destination()` modifier to take users to a view called `AddBook()` where they can insert books. In this view, we need to create a new instance of the `Book` class with the information provided by the user and then implement the `insert()` method of the `ModelContext` object to insert it into the context, as shown below.

```
import SwiftUI
import SwiftData

struct AddBook: View {
    @Environment(ApplicationData.self) private var appData
    @Environment(\.modelContext) var dbContext

    @State private var titleInput: String = ""
    @State private var authorInput: String = ""
    @State private var yearInput: String = ""

    var body: some View {
        VStack(alignment: .trailing, spacing: 10) {
            TextField("Insert Title", text: $titleInput)
                .textFieldStyle(.roundedBorder)
            TextField("Insert Author", text: $authorInput)
                .textFieldStyle(.roundedBorder)
            TextField("Insert Year", text: $yearInput)
                .textFieldStyle(.roundedBorder)
                .keyboardType(.numbersAndPunctuation)
            Button("Save") {
                storeBook()
            }.buttonStyle(.borderedProminent)
            Spacer()
        }.padding()
    }
    func storeBook() {
        let title = titleInput.trimmingCharacters(in: .whitespaces)
        let author = authorInput.trimmingCharacters(in: .whitespaces)
        if let year = Int(yearInput), !title.isEmpty && !author.isEmpty {
            let newBook = Book(title: title, author: author, cover:
"nocover", year: year)
            dbContext.insert(newBook)
            try? dbContext.save()
            appData.viewPath.removeLast()
        }
    }
}
#Preview {
    AddBook()
        .environment(ApplicationData.shared)
        .modelContainer(for: [Book.self], inMemory: true)
}
```

Listing 10-9: *Storing a book in the database*

This view contains three `TextField` views to allow the user to enter the title, author, and the year the book was published. Below the text fields there is also a button to store the book. For this purpose, the `Button` view calls a method that we use to trim the values, check that they are valid, and then save them to the database. To save the data in the database, we need to create an instance of the class we are using as a model (in our case, this is the `Book` class), insert it into the context using the `insert()` method, and finally call the `save()` method to save the changes in the context to the database. The `@Query` macro detects the change and updates the views with the new entry. The result is shown below.

Figure 10-5: Interface to save and list books stored in a database

Do It Yourself: Create a Multiplatform project. Update the `App` structure with the code in Listing 10-6. Create a new Swift file called ApplicationData.swift for the model in Listing 10-7 and another called BookModel.swift for the SwiftData model in Listing 10-5. Update the ContentView.swift file with the code in Listing 10-8. Create a new SwiftUI file called AddBook.swift for the view in Listing 10-9. Download the book covers from our website and add them to the Asset Catalog. Run the application. Press the + button to add a book. Insert the information and press Save. You should see something similar to Figure 10-5.

(Basic) Attributes

The properties in the `Book` class tell the database the type of values we want to store, but not how to store them. The database can store the values as they are, but it can also assign special attributes to them. For example, a value may be encrypted for security reasons or stored in a separate file for efficiency. To apply these attributes, SwiftData includes the following macros.

▷ **@Attribute(**Option, **originalName:** String?, **hashModifier:** String?**)**—This macro assigns attributes to the properties of the model. The first argument is a structure with properties that determine the type of attribute we want to assign to the value, the **originalName** argument is used to migrate a value to a different name, and the **hashModifier** argument identifies the new version for migration.

▷ **@Transient**—This macro tells SwiftData that the property shouldn't be stored in the database.

The `@Attribute` macro works with an `Option` structure. This structure determines the type of attribute to assign to the property. For this purpose, the structure includes the properties `allowsCloudEncryption` (it stores the value in an encrypted form), `externalStorage` (it stores the value in an external file), `preserveValueOnDeletion` (it preserves the value in the persistent history after deletion), `spotlight` (it indexes the value so it can appear in Spotlight search results), `ephemeral` (it tells the system not to store the value in the database), and `unique` (it ensures the value is unique). The structure also includes the `transformable(by: ValueTransformer.Type)` method to transform a value of a custom data type into a form that can be stored in the database.

Probably the most useful of these attributes are the `allowsCloudEncryption` attribute, frequently used to store encrypted passwords, the `externalStorage` attribute, used to store images in external files to improve database performance, and the `unique` attribute, used to avoid duplicate values. For example, with the `unique` attribute we can ensure that the identifiers for each book are unique.

```
@Model
class Book: Identifiable {
   @Attribute(.unique) var id: UUID = UUID()
   var title: String = ""
   var author: String = ""
   var cover: String = ""
   var year: Int = 0

   init(title: String, author: String, cover: String, year: Int) {
      self.title = title
      self.author = author
      self.cover = cover
      self.year = year
   }
   var displayYear: String {
      get {
         let value = year > 0 ? String(year) : "Undefined"
         return value
      }
   }
}
```

Listing 10-10: Storing unique values

The `UUID` structure guarantees that each value is unique, but we can make the mistake of using the identifier of one book to store another, for example. By implementing the `@Attribute` macro with the value `unique`, we ensure that this can never happen. The database will refuse to store a book with the same identifier as another book.

 Do It Yourself: Update the `Book` class with the code in Listing 10-10. The application should work as before, but now SwiftData checks for duplicates and does not allow you to store books with the same identifier. We will see more examples on how to apply attributes later.

If the values of many properties are required to determine the uniqueness of the object, we can use the `#Unique` macro. This macro ensures that the objects are unique based on all the required values.

▷ **#Unique([PartialKeyPath])**—This macro determines which properties SwiftData has to check to make sure that the objects are unique. The argument is an array of key paths that specify the properties involved.

For example, books may have the same title, author or year of publication, but we don't want those three values to be the same. If we want to make sure that the user doesn't insert two books with the same title, author and year, we can include a `#Unique` macro, as shown below.

```
@Model
class Book: Identifiable {
   #Unique<Book>([\.title, \.author, \.year])

   @Attribute(.unique) var id: UUID = UUID()
   var title: String = ""
   var author: String = ""
   var cover: String = ""
   var year: Int = 0

   init(title: String, author: String, cover: String, year: Int) {
      self.title = title
      self.author = author
      self.cover = cover
      self.year = year
```

```
   }
   var displayYear: String {
      get {
         let value = year > 0 ? String(year) : "Undefined"
         return value
      }
   }
}
```

Listing 10-11: Using the #Unique macro to avoid duplicates

When we set multiple properties to determine the uniqueness of an object, the system must perform a search to compare the values with every object already in the database. This consumes resources and can take too much time. To improve performance, we can create indexes. Indexes are an additional list of selected values that are used to speed up queries. The framework includes the following macro to create these indexes.

▷ **#Index([PartialKeyPath])**—This macro creates indexes for a SwiftData model. The argument is an array of key paths that specify the properties we want to create the indexes for.

The syntax for the **#Index** macro is the same used for the **#Unique** macro. So if we want to use the title, author and year as unique values, as we did in the previous example, we should create an **#Index** macro with these properties too, as shown below.

```
@Model
class Book: Identifiable {
   #Unique<Book>([\.title, \.author, \.year])
   #Index<Book>([\.title, \.author, \.year])

   @Attribute(.unique) var id: UUID = UUID()
   var title: String = ""
   var author: String = ""
   var cover: String = ""
   var year: Int = 0

   init(title: String, author: String, cover: String, year: Int) {
      self.title = title
      self.author = author
      self.cover = cover
      self.year = year
   }
   var displayYear: String {
      get {
         let value = year > 0 ? String(year) : "Undefined"
         return value
      }
   }
}
```

Listing 10-12: Creating indexes for better performance

(Basic) **Relationships**

The **Book** class includes properties to store all the values we need for a book, including the author's name. This approach has the problem that users have to re-enter the author's name every time they insert a new book. This is error-prone and time-consuming, and if there are multiple books by the same author, there is no way to ensure that they all have exactly the same name (e.g., one book might have the author's middle name, others just the first name). Without the certainty that all books have exactly the same name, we cannot include important features in our app, such as sorting books by author or listing only the books published by one author. It gets even worse when we want to store other information about the author besides the name, such as his or her date of birth or nationality. Proper organization of this information requires separate models, and therefore we need to create new classes to represent them. For our example, we can create a new class called **Author** to store the author's name, so every time we store a book, we can associate that **Book** object with the **Author** object that represents the author.

```swift
import SwiftUI
import SwiftData

@Model
class Author: Identifiable {
    @Attribute(.unique) var id: UUID = UUID()
    var name: String = ""
    var books: [Book]? = []

    init(name: String, books: [Book]) {
        self.name = name
        self.books = books
    }
}
```

Listing 10-13: *Creating a second model to store the authors*

Since an author can have multiple books, we need to tell the system which **Book** objects the author is associated with. For this purpose, the **Author** class includes a property called **books** to store an array of **Book** objects. This establishes a relationship between the **Author** class and the **Book** class, but it is not enough for the system to recognize the connection. We also need a property in the **Book** class to establish the reverse relationship with the **Author** class.

```swift
@Model
class Book: Identifiable {
    @Attribute(.unique) var id: UUID = UUID()
    var title: String = ""
    var author: Author?
    var cover: String = ""
    var year: Int = 0

    init(title: String, author: Author?, cover: String, year: Int) {
        self.title = title
        self.author = author
        self.cover = cover
        self.year = year
    }
    var displayYear: String {
        get {
            let value = year > 0 ? String(year) : "Undefined"
            return value
        }
    }
}
```

Listing 10-14: *Creating a relationship with the* Author *class*

In this example, we have turned the **author** property into an optional property of type **Author** to store an instance of the **Author** class (the properties that are used to create relationships must be optional). This creates a connection between the **Book** object and the **Author** object. From this property and the **books** property in the **Author** class, the system can see what **Author** object is associated with each book, and which **Book** objects are associated with each author. (In this example, we assume that our app only stores books written by one author.)

The connection between the `Book` and `Author` class we just created is called a *Relationship*. Relationships are created automatically by SwiftData when an instance of one class references an instance of another. However, since there can be different types of relationships, SwiftData provides the following macro to define them explicitly.

▷ **@Relationship(**Option, **deleteRule:** DeleteRule, **minimumModelCount:** Int?, **maximumModelCount:** Int?, **originalName:** String?, **inverse:** AnyKeyPath?, **hashModifier:** String?**)**—This macro establishes a relationship between models. The first argument is used to assign an attribute to the property (these are the same attributes applied by the `@Attribute` macro). The **deleteRule** argument is an enumeration with values to specify the rule to follow when an object in a relationship is deleted. The possible values are `cascade`, `deny`, `noAction`, and `nullify`. The **minimumModelCount** and **maximumModelCount** arguments define the minimum and maximum objects allowed in the relationship. The **originalName** argument is used to migrate a value to a different name. The **inverse** argument tells SwiftData which property in the other object is participating in the relationship. And the **hashModifier** argument identifies the version for migration purposes.

The most important values in a relationship are the deletion rule and the inverse property. The deletion rule determines what happens to the destination of a relationship when the object is deleted. For example, if we delete a `Book` object, should the `Author` object assigned to the `author` property also be deleted? There are four deletion rules available: `cascade` (the `Author` object is deleted when the `Book` object is deleted), `deny` (the `Book` object is not deleted when it is linked to an `Author` object), `noAction` (the `Author` object is not affected by what happens to the `Book` object), and `nullify` (when a `Book` object is deleted, the `Author` object linked to that book loses the connection with the book, but is not deleted). On the other hand, the inverse property helps the system determine the bidirectional connection between objects so that the system knows what to do with the other side of the relationship when an object is changed or removed.

By default, the system defines the deletion rule as `nullify`, which means that the value of the property involved in the relationship is set to `nil` but the object is not deleted. For example, if we delete an `Author` object, the `author` property in the `Book` object is set to `nil`, but the `Book` object is not deleted. This is probably the best approach, because it gives us absolute control over what is deleted and what is not.

Although we can use the relationships set by default, it is always recommended to declare them explicitly with the `@Relationship` macro, especially if we are working in a team, so that everyone knows what properties are involved in the relationship and what kind of relationship we are working with. For our example, we should declare the `author` property in the `Book` class as follows.

```
@Relationship(deleteRule: .nullify, inverse: \Author.books) var author:
Author?
```

Listing 10-15: Defining the relationship in the Book *class*

This relationship nullifies the connection in the `Author` class when a book is deleted (it removes the `Book` object from the array), and declares the inverse property as the `books` property in the `Author` class so that the system knows what to do when a book or an author is modified.

The inverse relationship is only declared on one side of the relationship, so all we need to do in the `Author` class is to declare the delete rule for the relationship, as shown below.

```
@Relationship(deleteRule: .nullify) var books: [Book]? = []
```

Listing 10-16: Defining the relationship in the Author *class*

Now our model is ready to store books and authors, we just need to provide the interface for the user to create and associate these objects. For this example, we will create two additional views, one to list the available authors and another to add more.

Figure 10-6: Interface to add and select authors

How we build this interface depends on the type of navigation we use and how our application is organized. In our example, we need to add two properties to the data model, one to store a reference to the book selected by the user, and another for the author.

```
import SwiftUI
import Observation

@Observable class ApplicationData: @unchecked Sendable {
    var viewPath = NavigationPath()
    var selectedBook: Book? = nil
    var selectedAuthor: Author? = nil

    static let shared: ApplicationData = ApplicationData()
    private init() { }
}
```

Listing 10-17: Controlling the values selected by the user from the model

As shown in Figure 10-6, we need two new views to allow the user to associate an author with a book. One view lists the existing authors, and the other allows the user to add more. Because we use strings to identify the links, we need to open these views from the **navigationDestination()** modifier defined in the **ContentView** view, as we did earlier for the **AddBook** view (see Listing 10-9).

```
.navigationDestination(for: String.self, destination: { viewID in
    if viewID == "Add Book" {
        AddBook()
    } else if viewID == "List Authors" {
        ListAuthors()
    } else if viewID == "Add Author" {
        AddAuthor()
    }
})
```

Listing 10-18: Opening additional views for navigation

The option to select an author must be added to the **AddBook** view. For this purpose, we need to replace the text field used before to enter the author's name with a button that opens the **ListAuthors** view, as shown below.

```
struct AddBook: View {
    @Environment(ApplicationData.self) private var appData
    @Environment(\.modelContext) var dbContext
```

```
    @State private var titleInput: String = ""
    @State private var yearInput: String = ""
    var body: some View {
        VStack(alignment: .leading, spacing: 10) {
            TextField("Insert Title", text: $titleInput)
                .textFieldStyle(.roundedBorder)
            TextField("Insert Year", text: $yearInput)
                .textFieldStyle(.roundedBorder)
                .keyboardType(.numbersAndPunctuation)
            VStack(alignment: .leading) {
                Text("Author")
                NavigationLink(value: "List Authors", label: {
                    Text(appData.selectedAuthor?.name ?? "Select")
                })
            }
            HStack {
                Spacer()
                Button("Save") {
                    storeBook()
                }.buttonStyle(.borderedProminent)
            }
            Spacer()
        }.padding()
    }
    func storeBook() {
        let title = titleInput.trimmingCharacters(in: .whitespaces)
        if let year = Int(yearInput), !title.isEmpty {
            let newBook = Book(title: title, author: appData.selectedAuthor,
cover: "nocover", year: year)
            dbContext.insert(newBook)
            try? dbContext.save()
            appData.selectedAuthor = nil
            appData.viewPath.removeLast()
        }
    }
}
```

Listing 10-19: *Assigning an author to a book*

In this application, we will use the **selectedAuthor** property in the model to store the **Author** object representing the author selected by the user, so we can use the value of this property to define the label for the button. If the property contains a value, it means that an author has already been selected, otherwise we display the string "Select" to indicate to the user that the button can be pressed to select one.

Since we no longer store a string with the author's name, we also need to modify the **storeBook()** method. The **Book** object is created as before, but instead of specifying a string for the author, we use the value of the **selectedAuthor** property. After the book is inserted into the context, we assign the value **nil** to that property to remove the user's selection.

When the user taps on the **NavigationLink** view added to the **AddBook** view, the **ListAuthors** view opens to allow the user to select an author. Just like with the books, we need to create a property with the **@Query** macro to retrieve the authors from the database and then display the list with a **List** view, but this time we also need a **@State** property to control the selection so we know which author was selected by the user and can assign it to the **selectedAuthor** property in the model.

```
import SwiftUI
import SwiftData

struct ListAuthors: View {
    @Environment(ApplicationData.self) private var appData
```

```
@Query private var authorsList: [Author]
@State private var selection: Author.ID? = nil

var body: some View {
    List(authorsList, selection: $selection) { author in
        Text(author.name)
    }
    .onChange(of: selection, initial: false) { old, idAuthor in
        appData.selectedAuthor = authorsList.first(where: { $0.id ==
idAuthor })
        appData.viewPath.removeLast()
    }
    .toolbar {
        ToolbarItem(placement: .navigationBarTrailing) {
            NavigationLink(value: "Add Author", label: {
                Image(systemName: "plus")
            })
        }
    }
}
}
#Preview {
    NavigationStack {
        ListAuthors()
            .environment(ApplicationData.shared)
            .modelContainer(for: [Book.self, Author.self], inMemory: true)
    }
}
```

Listing 10-20: Listing the authors

When the user selects an author, we get the reference from the **authorsList** property, assign it to the **selectedAuthor** property in the model, and then close the view so that the user can proceed with inserting the rest of the information for the book.

To add new authors to the list, we added a button to the navigation bar. This **NavigationLink** is identified with the string "Add Author" so that the **AddAuthor** view opens when the button is pressed (see Listing 10-18). The **AddAuthor** view provides a text field to insert the name of the author and creates the **Author** object with this information.

```
import SwiftUI
import SwiftData

struct AddAuthor: View {
    @Environment(ApplicationData.self) private var appData
    @Environment(\.modelContext) var dbContext
    @State private var nameInput: String = ""

    var body: some View {
        VStack(alignment: .leading, spacing: 10) {
            TextField("Insert Name", text: $nameInput)
                .textFieldStyle(.roundedBorder)
            HStack {
                Spacer()
                Button("Save") {
                    storeAuthor()
                }.buttonStyle(.borderedProminent)
            }
            Spacer()
        }.padding()
    }
    func storeAuthor() {
        let name = nameInput.trimmingCharacters(in: .whitespaces)
        if !name.isEmpty {
```

```
            let newAuthor = Author(name: name, books: [])
            dbContext.insert(newAuthor)
            try? dbContext.save()
            appData.selectedAuthor = newAuthor
            appData.viewPath.removeLast(2)
        }
    }
}
#Preview {
    NavigationStack {
        AddAuthor()
            .environment(ApplicationData.shared)
            .modelContainer(for: [Book.self, Author.self], inMemory: true)
    }
}
```

Listing 10-21: Adding new authors

The procedure for adding a new author to the database is the same as for books. We need to create the object, in this case from the **Author** class, insert it into the context using the **insert()** method, and then save the change to the container with the **save()** method. Note that we specify an empty array for the **books** property, since this author has not yet been assigned to a book. After the **Author** object is created and inserted into the context, we assign it to the **selectedAuthor** property to tell the application that the new author is now the one selected by the user, and then remove two views from the navigation path. This takes users directly back to the **AddBook** view, so they do not have to go the extra step of selecting the new author from the list.

Once the rest of the information is inserted and the user saves the new book, the **listBooks** property in the **ContentView** view is updated and the book is added to the list on the screen. In order for this to be possible, we need to make another change to our interface. Since we no longer store a string with the author's name, we need to update the **CellBook** view to display the value of the **name** property in the **Author** book instead.

```
struct CellBook: View {
    let book: Book

    var body: some View {
        HStack(alignment: .top) {
            Image(book.cover)
                .resizable()
                .scaledToFit()
                .frame(width: 80, height: 100)
            VStack(alignment: .leading, spacing: 2) {
                Text(book.title).bold()
                Text(book.author?.name ?? "Undefined")
                Text(book.displayYear).font(.caption)
                Spacer()
            }
            Spacer()
        }.padding([.top], 10)
    }
}
```

Listing 10-22: Displaying the author's name

Because a book may not have an author (the value of the **author** property may be **nil**), we check the value with the nil-coalescing operator and display the string "Undefined" if no author is found.

There is only one more change we need to perform for this example to be ready. When we add a new model to our application, as we did with the **Author** class in this example, SwiftData can recognize it based on the relationships and automatically add it to the container, but it is always recommended to do this explicitly via the `modelContainer()` modifier, as we did for the previews in Listings 10-20 and 10-21. The new modifier for the `App` structure should be declared as follows.

```
WindowGroup {
   ContentView()
      .environment(appData)
      .modelContainer(for: [Book.self, Author.self])
}
```

Listing 10-23: *Including all the models in the container*

 Do It Yourself: Create a new Swift file called AuthorModel.swift for the code in Listing 10-13. Update the `Book` class with the code in Listing 10-14. Update the `author` property in the `Book` class with the code in Listing 10-15 and the `books` property in the `Author` class with the code in Listing 10-16. Update the `ApplicationData` class with the code in Listing 10-17, the `navigation-Destination()` modifier of the `ContentView` view with the code in Listing 10-18, and the `AddBook` view with the code in Listing 10-19. Create two new SwiftUI files called ListAuthors.swift and AddAuthor.swift for the codes in Listings 10-20 and 10-21. Update the `CellBook` view with the code in Listing 10-22 and the `App` structure with the code in Listing 10-23. Run the application. Press the + button to add a book. You should see the interface in Figure 10-6 (left). Press the Select button to select an author for the book. You should see an empty list. Press the + button to add an author. Enter the author's name and press Save. Enter the title for the book and the year of publication, and press Save. You should see the book on the list, including the name of the author.

(Basic) Deleting Objects

Deleting an object from the database is no different than any other value (see Chapter 7, Listing 7-31). We need to implement a `ForEach` view to list the values, apply the `onDelete()` modifier to this view, and then remove the objects from the context with the `delete()` method.

```
List {
   ForEach(listBooks) { book in
      CellBook(book: book)
   }
   .onDelete { indexes in
      for index in indexes {
         dbContext.delete(listBooks[index])
      }
      try? dbContext.save()
   }
}
```

Listing 10-24: *Deleting objects*

The indexes received by the `onDelete()` modifier are the indexes of the objects the user wants to delete from the array in the `listBooks` property. Therefore, to remove the objects selected by the user, we iterate through the indexes with a `for in` loop, get the objects from the `listOfBooks` array in those indexes, and remove them from the context with the `delete()` method. Once the objects are removed from the context, the `listOfBooks` property is automatically updated and the changes are displayed on the screen.

Do It Yourself: Update the `List` view in the `ContentView` view with the code in Listing 10-24. Press the + button to add a new book. From the list of books, drag the book to the left. You should see the Delete button. Press the button to remove the book.

 IMPORTANT: When you apply the `onDelete()` modifier to the `ForEach` view, the system automatically includes a swipe action to allow the user to delete the rows, but you can create custom actions with the `swipeActions()` modifier, as we did in the example in Chapter 7, Listing 7-39.

(Basic) Sorting Objects

Objects returned by a query are usually in the order in which they were created, but this is not guaranteed. To specify a particular order, the `@Query` macro can take two arguments. The **sort** argument is the key path to the property we want to use to sort the objects, and the **order** argument determines whether the objects are listed in ascending or descending order (`forward` or `reverse`). For example, the following query retrieves the books sorted by title in ascending order.

```
@Query(sort: \Book.title, order: .forward) private var listBooks: [Book]
```

Listing 10-25: Sorting objects

To sort the objects, the `@Query` macro takes the values we specify for the arguments and creates a Foundation structure called `SortDescriptor`, but if we want more control over the process, we can create and provide this structure ourselves. The following is the initializer.

▷ **SortDescriptor(**KeyPath, **comparator:** StandardComparator, **order:** SortOrder**)**—This initializer creates a `SortDescriptor` structure that sorts the objects according to the value of the property specified by the first argument. The **comparator** argument determines how to compare the values. It is a structure with the type properties `lexical`, `localized`, and `localizedStandard` (default). And the **order** argument determines if the objects will be sorted in ascending or descending order. It is an enumeration with the values `forward` and `reverse`.

The `@Query` macro can take an array of `SortDescriptor` structures to determine the sort order of the objects. For instance, the following query sorts the objects by title in ascending order, as in the previous example.

```
@Query(sort: [SortDescriptor(\Book.title, order: .forward)]) private var
listBooks: [Book]
```

Listing 10-26: Sorting objects with a `SortDescriptor` structure

The advantage of using `SortDescriptor` structures is that we can specify multiple conditions for sorting the list. The final order is determined based on the position of the `SortDescriptor` structures in the array. For example, the following query sorts the books first by author and then by year.

```
@Query(sort: [SortDescriptor(\Book.author?.name, order: .forward),
SortDescriptor(\Book.year)]) private var listBooks: [Book]
```

Listing 10-27: Sorting books by author and year

The values are sorted according to a comparator. The `String` structure defines the `StandardComparator` structure to create it. The structure includes type properties to create instances for common comparators. The ones currently available are `lexical`, `localizedStandard` (default), and `localized`. The structure returned by the `lexical` property sorts the values alphabetically. For instance, if we have an array with the values 1, 2, and 10, the order will be 1, 10, 2 (the value 10 begins with 1, which comes before 2). This also applies to letters. Uppercase letters come before lowercase letters, so words beginning with a lowercase letter are moved to the end of the list. The structure returned by the `localizedStandard` property sorts the values numerically (1, 2, 10), which is also true for letters (words beginning with uppercase letters are sorted along with lowercase letters). And finally, the structure returned by the `localized` property sorts the values alphabetically like the `lexical` structure, but uppercase and lowercase letters are sorted together, as with the `localizedStandard` structure.

By default, the values are sorted with the `localizedStandard` structure. The following example shows how to apply a `lexical` structure instead.

```
@Query(sort: [SortDescriptor(\Book.title, comparator: .lexical,
order: .forward)]) private var listBooks: [Book]
```

Listing 10-28: Sorting with a lexical comparator

 Do It Yourself: Update the `@Query` macro in the `ContentView` view with the example you want to try. Insert books with different values to see if they are sorted as specified in the query. At the moment of writing, the query implemented in Listing 10-27 returns an error on the canvas, but it works properly on the simulator or a device.

(Basic) **Filtering Objects**

So far we have retrieved all the books in the database, but the `@Query` macro can take an additional argument to filter the objects. The argument is called **filter** and takes a structure called `Predicate` to specify the condition for the filter. SwiftData includes the following macro to create this structure.

▷ **#Predicate(Closure)**—This macro produces the code to create a predicate. The argument is a closure that specifies the condition to filter the objects.

The closure assigned to the `#Predicate` macro receives a value representing the object to be filtered, so we can use that value to set the condition. For instance, in the following example, we use a predicate to filter the books by year.

```
@Query(filter: #Predicate<Book> { $0.year == 1986 }) private var
listBooks: [Book]
```

Listing 10-29: Filtering books by year

The `Predicate` structure is generic, so we need to specify the data type of the values we want to filter. In this case, it is the `Book` class. Inside the closure, we get the instance of the `Book` class and compare the value of the `year` property with the number 1986. If the values match, the condition returns `true` and the book is included in the list, otherwise the book is ignored.

The condition in Listing 10-29 implements the == operator to compare the values, but all other comparison operators are available, including <, <=, >, >=, ==, and !=, and also logical operators such as && (AND), || (OR), and ! (NOT). For example, we can look for books that have been assigned an author and were published after the year 2000.

```
@Query(filter: #Predicate<Book> {
    $0.author != nil && $0.year > 2000
}) private var listBooks: [Book]
```

Listing 10-30: Filtering books by author and year

For collections and sequences of values, we can also implement the methods `allSatisfy()`, `filter()`, `contains()`, `contains(where:)`, and `starts(with:)`. And to perform a case-insensitive search, we can use the `localizedStandardContains()` method. For example, we can use this method to get only the books whose author contains the name "Stephen".

```
@Query(filter: #Predicate<Book> {
    $0.author?.name.localizedStandardContains("Stephen") == true
}) private var listBooks: [Book]
```

Listing 10-31: Filtering books by text

For more complex predicates, we can create expressions. These expressions are useful when we need to perform tasks that produce different results than true or false, such as when we need to count objects. The Foundation framework includes the following macro for this purpose.

▷ **#Expression(Closure)**—This macro produces the code to create an expression for a predicate. The argument is a closure that specifies the condition to filter the objects.

This macro creates a generic structure that we need to evaluate inside the predicate. The structure includes the following method for this purpose.

▷ **evaluate(Value)**—This method evaluates an expression and returns the result. The argument is the value we want to send to the expression to be processed.

The `#Expression` macro is built with a generic structure, so it needs to know the type of values is going to receive and return. To illustrate how the process works, we are going to create a simple expression that returns `true` or `false` depending on whether the book was published after the year 2000 or not.

```
let expression = #Expression<Int, Bool> { year in
    year > 2000
}
```

Listing 10-32: Defining an expression

This expression takes an integer and returns a Boolean value. Now we can use it to create our predicate.

```
@Query(filter: #Predicate<Book> {
    expression.evaluate($0.year)
}) private var listBooks: [Book]
```

Listing 10-33: Evaluating an expression

This predicate evaluates the expression with the value of the `year` property. If the value is greater than 2000, the expression returns `true` and the book is included on the list.

Do It Yourself: To use the expression with the `@Query` macro, we need to define it as a global variable. Insert the code in Listing 10-32 at the beginning or end of the ContentView.swift file and then replace the `@Query` macro in this view with the one in Listing 10-33. Insert some books. You should only see the books that were published after the year 2000.

(Basic) Dynamic Query

In the previous sections we used a predefined criteria to sort and filter the objects, but we can allow users to specify their own. To do this, we need to define the query with the values selected by the user when the view is initialized. For instance, in the following example we move the `List` view in the `ContentView` view into a separate view called `ListBooksView` to be able to initialize the query with the `SortOrder` value selected by the user.

```swift
struct ContentView: View {
    @Environment(ApplicationData.self) private var appData
    @Environment(\.modelContext) var dbContext
    @State private var orderBooks: SortOrder = .forward

    var body: some View {
        @Bindable var appData = appData

        NavigationStack(path: $appData.viewPath) {
            ListBooksView(orderBooks: orderBooks)
                .listStyle(.plain)
                .navigationTitle("Books")
                .toolbarTitleDisplayMode(.inline)
                .toolbar {
                    ToolbarItem(placement: .navigationBarTrailing) {
                        Button(action: {
                            orderBooks = orderBooks
== .forward ? .reverse : .forward
                        }, label: {
                            Image(systemName: "gear")
                        })
                    }
                    ToolbarItem(placement: .navigationBarTrailing) {
                        NavigationLink(value: "Add Book", label: {
                            Image(systemName: "plus")
                        })
                    }
                }
                .navigationDestination(for: String.self, destination:
{ viewID in
                    if viewID == "Add Book" {
                        AddBook()
                    } else if viewID == "List Authors" {
                        ListAuthors()
                    } else if viewID == "Add Author" {
                        AddAuthor()
                    }
                })
        }
    }
}
struct ListBooksView: View {
    @Query var listBooks: [Book]

    init(orderBooks: SortOrder) {
        _listBooks = Query(sort: \Book.title, order: orderBooks)
    }
    var body: some View {
```

```
        List {
            ForEach(listBooks) { book in
                CellBook(book: book)
            }
        }
    }
}
```

Listing 10-34: Defining a dynamic query

This **ContentView** view includes a **@State** property to store the **SortOrder** value selected by the user. This value is passed to the new **ListBooksView** view, where we use it to create a new **Query** structure and assign it to the **@Query** property. Note that to access the **Query** structure created by the **@Query** macro we need to prefix the name of the property with an underscore, as we did for **@State** properties in Chapter 6 (see Listing 6-6).

When the user taps a button in the navigation bar, we toggle the value of this property, the views are updated, the **Query** structure is recreated, and the order of the list changes.

Figure 10-7: Order of objects set by the user

 Do It Yourself: Update the ContentView.swift file with the views in Listing 10-34. Add a few books and press the button in the navigation bar. You should see the list of books alternate between ascending and descending order.

(Basic) Search

With a dynamic query we can also search for values provided by the user. For example, we can allow the user to search books by title.

```
struct ContentView: View {
    @Environment(ApplicationData.self) private var appData
    @Environment(\.modelContext) var dbContext
    @State private var searchValue: String = ""

    var body: some View {
        @Bindable var appData = appData

        NavigationStack(path: $appData.viewPath) {
            ListBooksView(search: searchValue)
                .listStyle(.plain)
                .navigationTitle("Books")
                .toolbarTitleDisplayMode(.inline)
                .toolbar {
                    ToolbarItem(placement: .navigationBarTrailing) {
                        NavigationLink(value: "Add Book", label: {
                            Image(systemName: "plus")
                        })
                    }
                }
                .navigationDestination(for: String.self, destination:
{ viewID in
```

```
                if viewID == "Add Book" {
                    AddBook()
                } else if viewID == "List Authors" {
                    ListAuthors()
                } else if viewID == "Add Author" {
                    AddAuthor()
                }
            })
        }
        .searchable(text: $searchValue, prompt: Text("Search"))
    }
}
struct ListBooksView: View {
    @Query private var listBooks: [Book]

    init(search: String) {
        var predicate = #Predicate<Book> { _ in true }
        if !search.isEmpty {
            let searching = search.lowercased()
            predicate = #Predicate<Book> { book in
                book.title.localizedStandardContains(searching)
            }
        }
        _listBooks = Query<Book, [Book]>(filter: predicate, sort:
\Book.title, order: .forward)
    }
    var body: some View {
        List {
            ForEach(listBooks) { book in
                CellBook(book: book)
            }
        }
    }
}
```

Listing 10-35: *Searching books by title*

To allow the user to search for a value, we implement the **searchable()** modifier (see Chapter 8, Listing 8-10). This modifier displays a search box and stores the value entered by the user in a **@State** property, so we pass the value of this property to the **ListBooksView** view to create a query. When this view is initialized, we create a predicate that searches for books whose title contains the text entered by the user. To ensure that the values match, the term entered by the user is lowercased and then compared to the title of the book using the **localizedStandardContains()** method. The result is shown below.

Figure 10-8: *User search*

 Do It Yourself: Update the ContentView.swift file with the views in Listing 10-35. Run the application in the simulator, add new books, and perform a search. You should only see the books whose titles contain the string entered in the search bar.

So far we have used the tools provided by SwiftData to work with SwiftUI views, but there are situations where we need to access the objects in the database from outside a view. The `ModelContext` class includes the `fetch()` and `fetchCount()` methods to fetch objects, but to specify the predicate and sort descriptors, we need to implement a structure provided by SwiftData called `FetchDescriptor`. The following is the structure's initializer.

> ▷ **FetchDescriptor(predicate:** Predicate?, **sortBy:** [SortDescriptor])—This initializer creates a structure for filtering and sorting objects. The **predicate** argument is a `Predicate` structure to filter the objects, and the **sortBy** argument is an array of `SortDescriptor` structures to sort them.

The `FetchDescriptor` structure includes the following properties to change the values or provide additional configuration.

> ▷ **predicate**—This property sets or returns the `Predicate` structure assigned to the fetch descriptor.
> ▷ **sortBy**—This property sets or returns the array of `SortDescriptor` structures assigned to the fetch descriptor.
> ▷ **fetchLimit**—This property sets or returns an `Int` value that determines the maximum number of objects to fetch.
> ▷ **fetchOffset**—This property sets or returns an `Int` value that determines where the fetching should begin.
> ▷ **includePendingChanges**—This property sets or returns a Boolean value that determines whether the pending changes in the context are included in the result.

We can use a fetch descriptor to prepare the information for the views or to process objects in the background. The following example creates a fetch descriptor to retrieve all the books that haven't yet been assigned an author and prints the titles on the console.

```
.onAppear {
    let predicate = #Predicate<Book> { book in
        book.author?.name == nil
    }
    let sort = SortDescriptor<Book>(\.title, order: .forward)

    let descriptor = FetchDescriptor<Book>(predicate: predicate, sortBy:
[sort])
    if let list = try? dbContext.fetch(descriptor) {
        for book in list {
            print(book.title)
        }
    }
}
```

Listing 10-36: Fetching objects manually

Although we can use this same procedure to count objects in the database, they are loaded into memory and therefore consume too many resources. To avoid this problem, the `ModelContext` class includes the `fetchCount()` method. This method returns an integer with the number of objects we would get if we called the `fetch()` method with the same request.

```
.onAppear {
    let predicate = #Predicate<Book> { book in
        book.author == nil
    }
    let sort = SortDescriptor<Book>(\.title, order: .forward)
    let descriptor = FetchDescriptor<Book>(predicate: predicate, sortBy:
[sort])
    if let count = try? dbContext.fetchCount(descriptor) {
        print(count)
    }
}
```

Listing 10-37: Counting objects

 Do It Yourself: Add the `onAppear()` modifier in Listing 10-36 to the `ListBooksView` view (below the `navigationDestination()` modifier). Run the application on the simulator. Insert a book without an author. You should see the title of the book in the console. Update the modifier with the code in Listing 10-37, now you should see the number of books printed on the console.

Another practical use of fetch descriptors and the `fetchCount()` method is to check for duplicates. Although we can modify a property in the model with the `@Attribute` macro and the value `unique` to ensure that no object with the same value is stored in the database, sometimes we need to be able to warn the user before a duplicate is created or have more control over the situation. In such cases, we can use a fetch descriptor with a predicate that searches for existing objects before creating a new one. In the following example, the `AddAuthor` view checks if the author entered by the user already exists in the database.

```
struct AddAuthor: View {
    @Environment(ApplicationData.self) private var appData
    @Environment(\.modelContext) var dbContext
    @State private var nameInput: String = ""
    @State private var openAlert: Bool = false

    var body: some View {
        VStack(alignment: .leading, spacing: 10) {
            TextField("Insert Name", text: $nameInput)
                .textFieldStyle(.roundedBorder)
            HStack {
                Spacer()
                Button("Save") {
                    storeAuthor()
                }.buttonStyle(.borderedProminent)
            }
            Spacer()
        }.padding()
        .alert("Error", isPresented: $openAlert, actions: {
            Button("OK", role: .cancel, action: {})
        }, message: { Text("The author already exists") })
    }
    func storeAuthor() {
        let name = nameInput.trimmingCharacters(in: .whitespaces)
        if !name.isEmpty {
            let predicate = #Predicate<Author> { $0.name == name }
            let descriptor = FetchDescriptor<Author>(predicate: predicate)
            if let count = try? dbContext.fetchCount(descriptor), count > 0 {
                openAlert = true
            } else {
                let newAuthor = Author(name: name, books: [])
```

```
            dbContext.insert(newAuthor)
            try? dbContext.save()
            appData.selectedAuthor = newAuthor
            appData.viewPath.removeLast(2)
         }
      }
   }
}
```

Listing 10-38: Checking for duplicates

The code in Listing 10-38 creates a fetch descriptor for the **Author** model. The predicate searches for objects with a name that matches the value entered by the user. Using this descriptor, we call the **fetchCount()** method in the context to get the total number of objects that match the condition. If the returned value is 0, we know that there are no authors with that name and we can create a new one.

 Do It Yourself: Update the **AddAuthor** view with the code in Listing 10-38. Run the application. Press the + button to add a book. Press the Select button to select an author. Press the + button to add an author. You should only be able to insert a new author if there is no other with the same name in the database.

(Basic) Previews

So far, we have created the container for the previews in memory with the **modelContainer()** modifier. This is enough to make the preview work on the canvas, but it's not good for testing. Every time we update the view, the preview is recreated and all data is deleted. To always have values to work with, we can create a custom container with some sample data, but recreating the container and the data every time the view is updated can affect performance. To avoid these issues, SwiftUI provides the **PreviewModifier** protocol. With this protocol, we can create a structure that creates and preprocess the content and then provides that content to any preview that needs it. The protocol requires the implementation of the following methods.

▷ **makeSharedContext()**—This type method is used to create the content we want to assign to the previews.

▷ **body(content:** Content, **context:** Context)—This method is called to assign the content to the preview. The **content** argument is a reference to the view the preview is going to show, and the **context** attribute is the context we want to associate with the view.

The first step to preprocess data for previews is to define a structure that conforms to the **PreviewModifier** protocol and implement its methods. In our example, we need to create a custom SwiftData container with the **ModelContainer** class and then apply it to the preview with the **modelContainer()** modifier, as shown below.

```
struct PreviewData: PreviewModifier {
    static func makeSharedContext() throws -> ModelContainer {
        let config = ModelConfiguration(isStoredInMemoryOnly: true)
        let container = try ModelContainer(for: Book.self, Author.self,
configurations: config)

        let author = Author(name: "Stephen King", books: [])
        container.mainContext.insert(author)

        let book1 = Book(title: "Christine", author: author, cover:
"book10", year: 1987)
        let book2 = Book(title: "IT", author: author, cover: "book11",
year: 1986)
```

```
        container.mainContext.insert(book1)
        container.mainContext.insert(book2)

        return container
    }
    func body(content: Content, context: ModelContainer) -> some View {
        content.modelContainer(context)
    }
}
```

Listing 10-39: Providing sample data for the previews

The structure in Listing 10-39 defines the two methods required by the protocol. In the `makeSharedContext()` method, we create a `ModelConfiguration` structure with the **isStoredInMemoryOnly** argument set to **true** to store the data in memory, then use that configuration to create the `ModelContainer` object for the `Book` and `Author` models, create a new `Author` object and two `Book` objects to have something to work with, and finally return the container so we can assign it later to the previews.

Every time a preview needs the information created by the `makeSharedContext()` method, it calls the `body()` method in our structure with a reference to the view (`content`). In this method, we can assign the content to the view as we did before. In our example, we assign the SwiftData container to the view with the `modelContainer()` modifier.

When we work with preprocessed data, the previews are defined as before, but the data is provided as a trait using the `modifier()` method, as shown below.

```
#Preview(traits: .modifier(PreviewData())) {
    ContentView()
        .environment(ApplicationData.shared)
}
```

Listing 10-40: Implementing a custom container in the preview

The preview in Listing 10-40 is for the `ContentView` view of our previous example, but we should apply the modifier to every view in the interface, so they all work with the same container. The preview is now created from the container returned by the `PreviewData` structure and therefore it includes two books and an author.

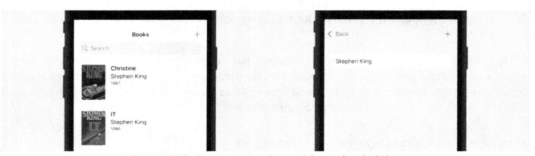

Figure 10-9: Custom container with pre-loaded data

 Do It Yourself: Add the `PreviewData` structure in Listing 10-39 at the bottom of the ApplicationData.swift file. Remember to import the SwiftData framework. Update the preview of the `ContentView` view with the code in Listing 10-40. Remember to update the previews for the other views as well so they all use the same container. You should see the preview on the canvas with two books and an author, as shown in Figure 10-9.

(Basic) Modifying Objects

Usually, users need to modify the values of objects stored in the database. With SwiftData, this is quite simple. All we need to do is get the object from the container, as we have done so far, and then pass it to a view that allows the user to change the values of its properties. Once a property is updated, SwiftData takes care of saving the object back to the database and reporting the change to the system so that the views are updated with the new values.

Although we can provide a new view to modify the values, we can also use our **AddBook** view to serve both purposes: add new books and edit the values of those already stored in the database. For this purpose, we can use the **selectedBook** property added to the model in Listing 10-17. If the property contains a **Book** object, it means that the user has selected a book and wants to edit its values, otherwise it means that the user wants to add a new book. The new interface is shown below.

Figure 10-10: *Editing values*

For this to work, we need to update the + button in the navigation bar of the **ContentView** view so we can make sure that the value of the **selectedBook** property is **nil** every time the user wants to add a new book.

```
struct ContentView: View {
    @Environment(ApplicationData.self) private var appData
    @Environment(\.modelContext) var dbContext
    @Query private var listBooks: [Book]

    var body: some View {
        @Bindable var appData = appData

        NavigationStack(path: $appData.viewPath) {
            List {
                ForEach(listBooks) { book in
                    NavigationLink(value: book, label: {
                        CellBook(book: book)
                    })
                }
            }
            .listStyle(.plain)
            .navigationTitle("Books")
            .toolbarTitleDisplayMode(.inline)
            .toolbar {
                ToolbarItem(placement: .navigationBarTrailing) {
                    Button(action: {
                        appData.selectedBook = nil
                        appData.viewPath.append("Add Book")
                    }, label: {
                        Image(systemName: "plus")
                    })
                }
            }
            .navigationDestination(for: String.self, destination: { viewID in
```

```
                if viewID == "Add Book" {
                    AddBook()
                } else if viewID == "List Authors" {
                    ListAuthors()
                } else if viewID == "Add Author" {
                    AddAuthor()
                }
            })
            .navigationDestination(for: Book.self, destination: { book in
                DetailView(book: book)
            })
        }
    }
}
```

Listing 10-41: Preparing the `selectedBook` *property to add new books*

For this example, we also embedded the `CellBook` view into a `NavigationLink` view and added an additional `navigationDestination()` modifier at the bottom to open a view called `DetailView` when a book is selected. This view displays the book's data, but it also includes a button in the navigation bar to open the `AddBook` view to allow the user to edit the values.

```
import SwiftUI
import SwiftData
struct DetailView: View {
    @Environment(ApplicationData.self) private var appData
    let book: Book

    var body: some View {
        VStack {
            Text(book.title)
                .font(.title)
            Text(book.author?.name ?? "Undefined")
            Image(book.cover)
                .resizable()
                .scaledToFit()
                .frame(width: 100)
            Spacer()
        }.padding()
        .navigationTitle(Text("Book"))
        .toolbar {
            ToolbarItem(placement: .navigationBarTrailing) {
                Button(action: {
                    appData.selectedBook = book
                    appData.selectedAuthor = book.author
                    appData.viewPath.append("Add Book")
                }, label: {
                    Image(systemName: "pencil.circle")
                })
            }
        }
    }
}
#Preview(traits: .modifier(PreviewData())) {
    @Previewable @Query var listBooks: [Book]

    NavigationStack {
        DetailView(book: listBooks[0])
            .environment(ApplicationData.shared)
    }
}
```

Listing 10-42: Opening the view to edit a book

When the button that opens the `AddBook` view is pressed, we assign the `Book` object selected by the user and the `Author` object to the `selectedBook` and `selectedAuthor` properties in the model, so that the `AddBook` view knows that a book has been selected and can show the values to the user.

```swift
struct AddBook: View {
    @Environment(ApplicationData.self) private var appData
    @Environment(\.modelContext) var dbContext
    @State private var titleInput: String = ""
    @State private var yearInput: String = ""

    var body: some View {
        VStack(alignment: .leading, spacing: 10) {
            TextField("Insert Title", text: $titleInput)
                .textFieldStyle(.roundedBorder)
            TextField("Insert Year", text: $yearInput)
                .textFieldStyle(.roundedBorder)
                .keyboardType(.numbersAndPunctuation)
            VStack(alignment: .leading) {
                Text("Author")
                NavigationLink(value: "List Authors", label: {
                    Text(appData.selectedAuthor?.name ?? "Select")
                })
            }
            HStack {
                Spacer()
                Button("Save") {
                    storeBook()
                }.buttonStyle(.borderedProminent)
            }
            Spacer()
        }.padding()
        .onAppear {
            if let selectedBook = appData.selectedBook, titleInput.isEmpty
&& yearInput.isEmpty {
                titleInput = selectedBook.title
                yearInput = selectedBook.displayYear
            }
        }
    }
    func storeBook() {
        let title = titleInput.trimmingCharacters(in: .whitespaces)
        if let year = Int(yearInput), !title.isEmpty {
            if let oldBook = appData.selectedBook {
                oldBook.title = title
                oldBook.year = year
                oldBook.author = appData.selectedAuthor
                try? dbContext.save()
            } else {
                let newBook = Book(title: title, author:
appData.selectedAuthor, cover: "nocover", year: year)
                dbContext.insert(newBook)
                try? dbContext.save()
            }
            appData.selectedAuthor = nil
            appData.selectedBook = nil
            appData.viewPath.removeLast()
        }
    }
}
```

Listing 10-43: Editing a book

To determine if the user wants to edit a book or create a new one, we check the value of the `selectedBook` property (see the `onAppear()` modifier). If the property contains a value and the text fields are empty, we assign the title and year of the book to these fields to show them to the user. We do the same thing when the Save button is pressed. In this case, if the `selectedBook` property contains a `Book` object, we modify the properties with the values entered by the user, otherwise we create a new book. Note that at the end we clear the values of both properties, `selectedBook` and `selectedAuthor`, to reset the system.

 Do It Yourself: Update the ContentView.swift file with the code in Listing 10-41. Create a SwiftUI file for the `DetailView` view in Listing 10-42. Update the `AddBook` view with the code in Listing 10-43. Run the application on the canvas. Select a book. Tap on the button in the navigation bar to edit the book. Modify the values and press Save. The changes should be visible in the `DetailView` view and in the list.

(Basic) Images

In the previous examples, we loaded an image from the Asset Catalog to represent the cover of the book (nocover). However, the images supplied by users are stored as data and come from a variety of sources, such as the camera, the network, or a storage device. Therefore, to store an image in a database, we need to convert it into data, and to load it and display it on the screen, we must perform the reverse process and convert the data back into an image. For this purpose, the Foundation framework provides the `Data` structure and the UIKit framework provides the `UIImage` class (`NSImage` for Mac applications). The `Data` structure stores the data, while the `UIImage` class provides all the tools to perform the conversions and prepare the images for the views. The following are some of the initializers provided by this class.

▷ **UIImage(named: String)**—This initializer creates an object that contains the image from the file specified by the **named** argument. The argument is a string with the name of the file or the image set in the Asset Catalog.

▷ **UIImage(data: Data, scale: CGFloat)**—This initializer creates an object that contains an image generated from the data provided by the **data** argument and with an associated scale specified by the **scale** argument. If the last argument is ignored, the image is assigned a scale of 1.

▷ **UIImage(contentsOfFile: String)**—This initializer creates an object that contains the image stored in the file indicated by the **contentsOfFile** argument. The argument is a string with a path that determines the location of the file.

▷ **UIImage(cgImage: CGImage, scale: CGFloat, orientation: Orientation)**—This initializer creates an object that contains an image generated from a `CGImage` object and with a scale and orientation defined by the arguments. The `CGImage` class is defined by the Core Graphics framework to store a low-level representation of an image, and the **orientation** argument is an enumeration with the values **up**, **down**, **left**, **right**, **upMirrored**, **downMirrored**, **leftMirrored**, and **rightMirrored**.

The `UIImage` class includes properties and methods to get information about the image and process it. The following are the most frequently used.

▷ **size**—This property returns a `CGSize` value with the size of the image.

▷ **scale**—This property returns a `CGFloat` value with the scale of the image.

▷ **imageOrientation**—This property returns a value that identifies the image's orientation. It is an enumeration called **Orientation**. The values available are **up**, **down**, **left**, **right**, **upMirrored**, **downMirrored**, **leftMirrored**, and **right-Mirrored**.

▷ **cgImage**—This property returns the image in the Core Graphic format. It is of type `CGImage`, a Core Graphic data type.

The size of photographs taken by the camera or images loaded from the Photo Library are often too large for processing and storage. Storing these images in files and databases can consume too much storage space and memory. The `UIImage` class includes the following methods to optimize an image and reduce its size.

▷ **preparingThumbnail(of:** CGSize)—This method returns a new image created from the original and with a size determined by the **of** argument.

▷ **byPreparingThumbnail(ofSize: CGSize)**—This asynchronous method creates a new image from the original. The **ofSize** argument determines the size of the image.

▷ **preparingForDisplay()**—This method decompresses the original image and returns a new one ready to be shown on the screen.

▷ **byPreparingForDisplay()**—This asynchronous method decompresses the original image.

And to convert an image into data, the `UIImage` class includes the following methods.

▷ **pngData()**—This method converts the image into raw data in the PNG format and returns a **Data** structure with it.

▷ **jpegData(compressionQuality:** CGFloat)—This method converts the image into raw data in the JPEG format and returns a **Data** structure with it. The **compression-Quality** argument is a value between 0.0 and 1.0 to determine the level of compression.

Images are represented by large amounts of data. Storing this data in a database can affect the performance of the system and slow down essential processes such as searching for values or migrating the model. An alternative is to store the images in separate files and keep a link to the file in the database. However storing and synchronizing this information can be tedious and error-prone when hundreds or even thousands of images are available. Fortunately, SwiftData can take care of this process for us. All we have to do is define a property that can store a **Data** structure, and then modify it with the **externalStorage** attribute, as shown below.

```
@Model
class Book: Identifiable {
    @Attribute(.unique) var id: UUID = UUID()
    var title: String = ""
    @Relationship(deleteRule: .nullify, inverse: \Author.books) var
author: Author?
    @Attribute(.externalStorage) var cover: Data?
    var year: Int = 0

    init(title: String, author: Author?, cover: Data?, year: Int) {
        self.title = title
        self.author = author
        self.cover = cover
        self.year = year
    }
    var displayYear: String {
        get {
            let value = year > 0 ? String(year) : "Undefined"
            return value
        }
    }
    var displayCover: UIImage {
        if let data = cover, let image = UIImage(data: data) {
```

```
            return image
        } else {
            return UIImage(named: "nocover")!
        }
    }
}
```

Listing 10-44: Storing images externally

The image for the cover is now stored as a **Data** structure in an external file. This means that every time we want to process or show this image to the user, we have to convert the **Data** structure into a **UIImage** object. For this purpose, we added an additional computer property to the model called **displayCover**. This property checks if there is data stored in the **cover** property and converts it to a **UIImage** object using the **UIImage(data:)** initializer. If no data is found, we create a **UIImage** object with the nocover image from the Asset Catalog, and return that instead.

Once we have the **UIImage** object with the image we want to show, we can turn it into an **Image** view using the **Image(uiImage:)** initializer introduced earlier. The following is the change we need to make to the **CellBook** view to display the covers in the list.

```
struct CellBook: View {
    let book: Book

    var body: some View {
        HStack(alignment: .top) {
            Image(uiImage: book.displayCover)
                .resizable()
                .scaledToFit()
                .frame(width: 80, height: 100)
            VStack(alignment: .leading, spacing: 2) {
                Text(book.title).bold()
                Text(book.author?.name ?? "Undefined")
                Text(book.displayYear).font(.caption)
                Spacer()
            }
            Spacer()
        }.padding([.top], 10)
    }
}
```

Listing 10-45: Displaying an image from a UIImage object

The same change is required in the **DetailView** view. Instead of providing a string to load the image from the Asset Catalog, we now get it from the **UIImage** object returned by the **displayCover** property.

```
Image(uiImage: book.displayCover)
    .resizable()
    .scaledToFit()
    .frame(width: 100)
```

Listing 10-46: Displaying the image in the DetailView view

The images that users load into the app usually come from the camera or a storage device, but the process to convert them to and from **UIImage** objects is always the same. As the **displayCover** property shows, to convert a **Data** structure into a **UIImage** object, we implement the **UIImage(data:)** initializer. And to perform the reverse process, the **UIImage** class offers the **pngData()** and **jpegData(compressionQuality:)** methods. The implementation of these methods is very simple. For example, when the user creates a new book in our application, we can load the nocover image from the Asset Catalog into a `UIImage` object, convert it to data using the `pngData()` method, and then use the `Data` structure returned by this method to create the `Book` object. The following are the changes we need to make to the `storeBook()` method in the `AddBook` view for this purpose.

```
func storeBook() {
    let title = titleInput.trimmingCharacters(in: .whitespaces)
    if let year = Int(yearInput), !title.isEmpty {
        if let oldBook = appData.selectedBook {
            oldBook.title = title
            oldBook.year = year
            oldBook.author = appData.selectedAuthor
            try? dbContext.save()
        } else {
            let cover = UIImage(named: "nocover")?.pngData()
            let newBook = Book(title: title, author: appData.selectedAuthor,
cover: cover, year: year)
            dbContext.insert(newBook)
            try? dbContext.save()
        }
        appData.selectedAuthor = nil
        appData.selectedBook = nil
        appData.viewPath.removeLast()
    }
}
```

Listing 10-47: Converting a `UIImage` *object into data*

Since the cover of the book is now stored as a `Data` structure instead of a string, we also need to modify the objects inserted into the database in the `PreviewData` structure. The following are the changes we need to make to the `makeSharedContext()` method.

```
struct PreviewData: PreviewModifier {
    static func makeSharedContext() throws -> ModelContainer {
        let config = ModelConfiguration(isStoredInMemoryOnly: true)
        let container = try ModelContainer(for: Book.self, Author.self,
configurations: config)

        let author = Author(name: "Stephen King", books: [])
        container.mainContext.insert(author)

        let book10 = UIImage(named: "book10")?.pngData()
        let book11 = UIImage(named: "book11")?.pngData()
        let book1 = Book(title: "Christine", author: author, cover: book10,
year: 1987)
        let book2 = Book(title: "IT", author: author, cover: book11, year:
1986)
        container.mainContext.insert(book1)
        container.mainContext.insert(book2)

        return container
    }
    func body(content: Content, context: ModelContainer) -> some View {
        content.modelContainer(context)
    }
}
```

Listing 10-48: Creating `Book` *objects with images from the Asset Catalog*

Do It Yourself: Update the `Book` model with the code in Listing 10-44. Update the `CellBook` view in the ContentView.swift file with the code in Listing 10-45. Update the `Image` view in the `DetailView` view with the code in Listing 10-46. Update the `storeBook()` method in the `AddBook` view with the code in Listing 10-47. Update the `makeSharedContext()` method in the `PreviewData` structure with the code in Listing 10-48. Run the application. Add a new book. You should see that the book is created with the image nocover.png, as before, but this time it is stored in the database as a `Data` structure. We will learn how to work with the camera and load images from the Photo library in Chapter 18.

(Basic) **Sections**

The information in the database can be presented in sections. At the time of writing, SwiftData does not include tools for creating sections, but we can structure our models to present the data in this way. For example, we can list books in sections, with each section representing an author. We just need to create a query that gets the authors, and then read the books published by each author from the **books** property of the **Author** class. There is only one change we need to make to this class. This is because the order of the books in the **books** array is not guaranteed. To ensure that we get the books in the order we want, we need to reorganize the **books** array before the values are used by the view. For our example, we decided to create a computed property that returns the list of books sorted by title.

```
@Model
class Author: Identifiable {
    @Attribute(.unique) var id: UUID = UUID()
    var name: String = ""
    @Relationship(deleteRule: .nullify) var books: [Book]? = []

    init(name: String, books: [Book]) {
        self.name = name
        self.books = books
    }
    var listBooks: [Book] {
        get {
            let sortList: [Book] = books?.sorted(by: { $0.title <
$1.title }) ?? []
            return sortList
        }
    }
}
```

Listing 10-49: Sorting the books

The idea for this app is to create a section per author, but only for those authors who are associated with at least one book. For this purpose, we must create the **Section** view only if the array returned by the **listBooks** property contains a value, as shown below.

```
struct ContentView: View {
    @Environment(ApplicationData.self) private var appData
    @Environment(\.modelContext) var dbContext
    @Query(sort: \Author.name, order: .forward) private var listAuthors:
[Author]

    var body: some View {
        @Bindable var appData = appData

        NavigationStack(path: $appData.viewPath) {
            List {
```

```
ForEach(listAuthors) { author in
    if !author.listBooks.isEmpty {
        Section(author.name) {
            ForEach(author.listBooks) { book in
                NavigationLink(value: book, label: {
                    CellBook(book: book)
                })
            }
        }.headerProminence(.increased)
    }
}
.id(UUID())
}
.listStyle(.insetGrouped)
.navigationTitle("Books")
.toolbarTitleDisplayMode(.inline)
.toolbar {
    ToolbarItem(placement: .navigationBarTrailing) {
        Button(action: {
            appData.selectedBook = nil
            appData.viewPath.append("Add Book")
        }, label: {
            Image(systemName: "plus")
        })
    }
}
.navigationDestination(for: String.self, destination: { viewID in
    if viewID == "Add Book" {
        AddBook()
    } else if viewID == "List Authors" {
        ListAuthors()
    } else if viewID == "Add Author" {
        AddAuthor()
    }
})
.navigationDestination(for: Book.self, destination: { book in
    DetailView(book: book)
})
}
}
}
```

Listing 10-50: *Displaying the books in sections*

Figure 10-11: *Sections by author*

 IMPORTANT: Note that in the example in Listing 10-50 we have applied the `id()` modifier to the `ForEach` view. At the moment of writing, SwiftData does not always update the views within a `ForEach` view when a new value is assigned to a relationship. By assigning a new `UUID` value to this view, we force the system to update the view's content when a new value is available. To learn more about the `id()` modifier, see Chapter 6, Listing 6-54.

If we want to use a different value to create the sections, we need to organize the database accordingly. For example, if we want to display the list of books in alphabetical order with one section per letter, we need to create an additional model to store the letters. In our example, this means that we need a model with two properties, one property to store a letter and another to store the list of books whose title starts with that letter, as shown below.

```
import SwiftUI
import SwiftData

@Model
class SortLetters: Identifiable {
   @Attribute(.unique) var id: UUID = UUID()
   var letter: String = ""
   @Relationship(deleteRule: .nullify) var books: [Book]? = []

   init(letter: String, books: [Book]) {
      self.letter = letter
      self.books = books
   }
   var listBooks: [Book] {
      get {
         let sortList: [Book] = books?.sorted(by: { $0.title <
$1.title }) ?? []
         return sortList
      }
   }
}
```

Listing 10-51: Storing the letters for the sections

Once we have the model to store the letters, we need to create the inverse relationship in the **Book** model.

```
@Model
class Book: Identifiable {
   @Attribute(.unique) var id: UUID = UUID()
   var title: String = ""
   @Relationship(deleteRule: .nullify, inverse: \Author.books) var
author: Author?
   @Attribute(.externalStorage) var cover: Data?
   var year: Int = 0
   @Relationship(deleteRule: .nullify, inverse: \SortLetters.books) var
sortLetter: SortLetters?

   init(title: String, author: Author?, cover: Data?, year: Int,
sortLetter: SortLetters?) {
      self.title = title
      self.author = author
      self.cover = cover
      self.year = year
      self.sortLetter = sortLetter
   }
   var displayYear: String {
      get {
         let value = year > 0 ? String(year) : "Undefined"
         return value
      }
   }
   var displayCover: UIImage {
      if let data = cover, let image = UIImage(data: data) {
         return image
      } else {
```

```
            return UIImage(named: "nocover")!
        }
    }
}
```

Listing 10-52: Adding the relationship to sort the books by letter

For this to work, each time a new book is created or the title is modified by the user, we need to get the first letter of the new title, create a **SortLetters** object with this value, and then assign it to the **sortLetter** property. This process can be done from the model or from the views. In our example, we decided to do it from within the **AddBook** view. Below are the changes we need to make to the **storeBook()** method in this view and also the new method we need to add to the view to get the first letter of the book title and store it in the database.

```
func storeBook() {
    let title = titleInput.trimmingCharacters(in: .whitespaces)
    if let year = Int(yearInput), !title.isEmpty {
        if let oldBook = appData.selectedBook {
            oldBook.title = title
            oldBook.year = year
            oldBook.author = appData.selectedAuthor
            oldBook.sortLetter = getFirstLetter(newTitle: title)
            try? dbContext.save()
        } else {
            let letter = getFirstLetter(newTitle: title)
            let cover = UIImage(named: "nocover")?.pngData()

            let newBook = Book(title: title, author: appData.selectedAuthor,
cover: cover, year: year, sortLetter: letter)
            dbContext.insert(newBook)
            try? dbContext.save()
        }
        appData.selectedAuthor = nil
        appData.selectedBook = nil
        appData.viewPath.removeLast()
    }
}
func getFirstLetter(newTitle: String) -> SortLetters {
    var firstLetter = String(newTitle[newTitle.startIndex]).uppercased()
    if let _ = Int(firstLetter), firstLetter.isEmpty {
        firstLetter = "#"
    }
    let predicate = #Predicate<SortLetters> {
        $0.letter == firstLetter
    }
    let descriptor = FetchDescriptor<SortLetters>(predicate: predicate)
    if let request = try? dbContext.fetch(descriptor), request.count > 0 {
        let oldLetter = request[0]
        return oldLetter
    } else {
        let newLetter = SortLetters(letter: firstLetter, books: [])
        dbContext.insert(newLetter)
        try? dbContext.save()
        return newLetter
    }
}
```

Listing 10-53: Getting the SortLetters *object that correspond to the book*

Every time a book is modified or a new book is created, we call the **getFirstLetter()** method to get the **SortLetters** object that represents the first letter of the book's title. In this method, we use the **startIndex** property to get the first letter in the string and make sure it is capitalized. If the letter is a number, we convert it to the numeral character and then check whether or not there is already a `SortLetters` object with that value. If an object is found, we return it, otherwise we create a new one. Back in the `storeBook()` method, the `SortLetters` object is assigned to the book so now we can sort the books in alphabetical sections.

The process for creating the sections is the same as before, but instead of creating the query with the `Author` model, we do it with the `SortLetters` model.

```
struct ContentView: View {
    @Environment(ApplicationData.self) private var appData
    @Environment(\.modelContext) var dbContext
    @Query(sort: \SortLetters.letter, order: .forward) private var
listLetters: [SortLetters]

    var body: some View {
        @Bindable var appData = appData

        NavigationStack(path: $appData.viewPath) {
            List {
                ForEach(listLetters) { letter in
                    if !letter.listBooks.isEmpty {
                        Section(letter.letter) {
                            ForEach(letter.listBooks) { book in
                                NavigationLink(value: book, label: {
                                    CellBook(book: book)
                                })
                            }
                        }.headerProminence(.increased)
                    }
                }
                .id(UUID())
            }
            .listStyle(.insetGrouped)
            .navigationTitle("Books")
            .toolbarTitleDisplayMode(.inline)
            .toolbar {
                ToolbarItem(placement: .navigationBarTrailing) {
                    Button(action: {
                        appData.selectedBook = nil
                        appData.viewPath.append("Add Book")
                    }, label: {
                        Image(systemName: "plus")
                    })
                }
            }
            .navigationDestination(for: String.self, destination: { viewID in
                if viewID == "Add Book" {
                    AddBook()
                } else if viewID == "List Authors" {
                    ListAuthors()
                } else if viewID == "Add Author" {
                    AddAuthor()
                }
            })
            .navigationDestination(for: Book.self, destination: { book in
                DetailView(book: book)
            })
        }
    }
}
```

Listing 10-54: Listing books in alphabetical sections

As before, we also need to modify the **container** property in the **PreviewContainer** class to work with the new models. In this case, we need to create the **SortLetters** objects manually and assign them to the books.

```
struct PreviewData: PreviewModifier {
    static func makeSharedContext() throws -> ModelContainer {
        let config = ModelConfiguration(isStoredInMemoryOnly: true)
        let container = try ModelContainer(for: Book.self, Author.self,
configurations: config)

        let author = Author(name: "Stephen King", books: [])
        container.mainContext.insert(author)

        let letter1 = SortLetters(letter: "C", books: [])
        let letter2 = SortLetters(letter: "I", books: [])
        container.mainContext.insert(letter1)
        container.mainContext.insert(letter2)

        let book10 = UIImage(named: "book10")?.pngData()
        let book11 = UIImage(named: "book11")?.pngData()
        let book1 = Book(title: "Christine", author: author, cover: book10,
year: 1987, sortLetter: letter1)
        let book2 = Book(title: "IT", author: author, cover: book11, year:
1986, sortLetter: letter2)
        container.mainContext.insert(book1)
        container.mainContext.insert(book2)

        return container
    }
    func body(content: Content, context: ModelContainer) -> some View {
        content.modelContainer(context)
    }
}
```

Listing 10-55: Listing books in alphabetical sections

Figure 10-12: Alphabetical sections

 Do It Yourself: Create a new Swift file called SortLettersModel.swift for the model in Listing 10-51. Update the **Book** model with the code in Listing 10-52. Update the **AddBook** view with the methods in Listing 10-53, the **ContentView** view with the code in Listing 10-54, and the **makeShared-Context()** method in the **PreviewData** structure with the code in Listing 10-55. Run the application on the canvas. You should see the books organized in alphabetical sections, as in Figure 10-12.

(Medium) Archiving

Although we can add as many properties to a model as we want and define as many models as we need, professional applications usually rely on more sophisticated models that include collection of values and custom data types. To give us more flexibility, Foundation provides the

`NSCoder` class. This class can encode and decode values into `Data` structures for storage in a process called *Archiving*.

Archiving works with Property List values. These are values that can be converted to raw data and reconstructed later, such as `NSNumber`, `NSString`, `NSDate`, `NSArray`, `NSDictionary`, `NSData`, and the equivalents in Swift. If our values are of one of these data types, they can be archived and stored without any problem, but if we want to archive our own data types, we first need to convert them to Property List values. Foundation provides two classes for this purpose, `PropertyListEncoder` and `PropertyListDecoder`, which include the following methods for encoding and decoding the values.

▷ **encode(**Value**)**—This method of the `PropertyListEncoder` class encodes a value into a Property List value.

▷ **decode(**Type, **from:** Data**)**—This method of the `PropertyListDecoder` class decodes a Property List value into a value of the type specified by the first argument. The **from** argument is a `Data` structure with the data to be decoded.

Another requirement for custom structures is that they must implement the initializers and methods defined in a protocol called `NSCoding`. These initializers and methods tell the system how to encode and decode data for storage or distribution. Fortunately, the Swift Standard Library defines a protocol called `Codable` that simplifies our work by turning a structure into an encodable and decodable data type. All we have to do is to get our structure to conform to this protocol, and the compiler takes care of adding all the methods needed to encode and decode the values.

In the following example, we store the author's date and place of birth, but archive the data and assign it to a single property. For this purpose, we need to create a `Codable` structure and encode/decode the values as needed. We call this structure `AuthorInfo`.

```
import SwiftUI

struct AuthorInfo: Codable {
   var birthday: Date?
   var placeOfBirth: String = ""
}
```

Listing 10-56: Defining a `Codable` *structure*

To store an instance of this structure, we need to add a property to the `Author` model, as shown below.

```
@Model
class Author: Identifiable {
   @Attribute(.unique) var id: UUID = UUID()
   var name: String = ""
   @Relationship(deleteRule: .nullify) var books: [Book]? = []
   var info: Data?

   init(name: String, books: [Book], info: Data?) {
      self.name = name
      self.books = books
      self.info = info
   }
   var listBooks: [Book] {
      get {
         let sortList = books?.sorted(by: { $0.title < $1.title }) ?? []
         return sortList
      }
   }
   var showBirthday: String? {
```

```
        let decoder = PropertyListDecoder()
        if let info, let authorInfo = try? decoder.decode(AuthorInfo.self,
from: info) {
            if let date = authorInfo.birthday, date < Date() {
                return authorInfo.birthday?.formatted(date: .abbreviated,
time: .omitted)
            }
        }
        return nil
    }
    var showPlaceOfBirth: String? {
        let decoder = PropertyListDecoder()
        if let info, let authorInfo = try? decoder.decode(AuthorInfo.self,
from: info) {
            if !authorInfo.placeOfBirth.isEmpty {
                return authorInfo.placeOfBirth
            }
        }
        return nil
    }
}
```

Listing 10-57: Storing and decoding data

This model includes a new property called `info` that stores a `Data` structure, and two computed properties to prepare the values for the views. To decode the `Data` structure into an `AuthorInfo` structure, we create an instance of the `PropertyListDecoder` class and call the `decode()` method. This method takes the `Data` structure in the `info` property and creates an instance of the `AuthorInfo` class with that data. Once we have this structure, we format the values and return them so that the view can show them on the screen.

The next step is to provide the controls for the user to enter the author's date and place of birth, and then to encode these values before creating the new `Author` object. The following are the changes we need to make to the `AddAuthor` view.

```
struct AddAuthor: View {
    @Environment(ApplicationData.self) private var appData
    @Environment(\.modelContext) var dbContext
    @State private var nameInput: String = ""
    @State private var openAlert: Bool = false
    @State private var birthday: Date = Date()
    @State private var placeOfBirth: String = ""

    var body: some View {
        VStack(alignment: .leading, spacing: 10) {
            TextField("Insert Name", text: $nameInput)
                .textFieldStyle(.roundedBorder)
            DatePicker("Birthday", selection: $birthday,
displayedComponents: .date)
            TextField("Insert Address", text: $placeOfBirth)
                .textFieldStyle(.roundedBorder)
            HStack {
                Spacer()
                Button("Save") {
                    storeAuthor()
                }.buttonStyle(.borderedProminent)
            }
            Spacer()
        }.padding()
            .alert("Error", isPresented: $openAlert, actions: {
                Button("OK", role: .cancel, action: {})
            }, message: { Text("The author already exists") })
    }
```

```
func storeAuthor() {
    let name = nameInput.trimmingCharacters(in: .whitespaces)
    if !name.isEmpty {
        let predicate = #Predicate<Author> { $0.name == name }
        let descriptor = FetchDescriptor<Author>(predicate: predicate)
        if let count = try? dbContext.fetchCount(descriptor), count > 0 {
            openAlert = true
        } else {
            let newAuthor = Author(name: name, books: [], info:
archiveInfo())
            dbContext.insert(newAuthor)
            try? dbContext.save()
            appData.selectedAuthor = newAuthor
            appData.viewPath.removeLast(2)
        }
    }
}
func archiveInfo() -> Data? {
    var newBirthday = Date.distantFuture
    if birthday < Date(timeIntervalSinceNow: -86400) {
        newBirthday = birthday
    }
    let authorInfo = AuthorInfo(birthday: newBirthday, placeOfBirth:
placeOfBirth)
    let encoder = PropertyListEncoder()
    let infoData = try? encoder.encode(authorInfo)
    return infoData
}
}
```

Listing 10-58: Encoding data

This view includes two new **@State** properties called **birthday** and **placeOfBirth** to store the values entered by the user. As always, when the user presses the Save button, we create the **Author** object and insert it into the context, but this time we call an additional method to encode the data for the **info** property. In this method, we check if the date is older than the current date (minus one day) to confirm that the user has selected a date of birth. If no date is selected, we store a **distantFuture** date to later determine if a date is available or not, and then create the **AuthorInfo** structure with that value. To encode the structure, we create an instance of the **PropertyListEncoder** class and call the **encode()** method.

The values are now encoded and stored in the database, so we can read them from the stored properties defined in the model and show them on the screen. The following are the changes we need to make to the **DetailView** view.

```
struct DetailView: View {
    @Environment(ApplicationData.self) private var appData
    let book: Book

    var body: some View {
        VStack {
            Text(book.title)
                .font(.title)
            Image(uiImage: book.displayCover)
                .resizable()
                .scaledToFit()
                .frame(width: 100)
            Text(book.author?.name ?? "Undefined")
            Text(book.author?.showBirthday ?? "Undefined")
            Text(book.author?.showPlaceOfBirth ?? "Undefined")
            Spacer()
        }.padding()
        .navigationTitle(Text("Book"))
```

```
    .toolbar {
        ToolbarItem(placement: .navigationBarTrailing) {
            Button(action: {
                appData.selectedBook = book
                appData.selectedAuthor = book.author
                appData.viewPath.append("Add Book")
            }, label: {
                Image(systemName: "pencil.circle")
            })
        }
    }
  }
 }
}
```

Listing 10-59: *Displaying encoded data*

Figure 10-13: *Encoded data*

 Do It Yourself: Create a Swift file called AuthorInfo.swift for the code in Listing 10-56. Update the **Author** model with the code in Listing 10-57, the **AddAuthor** view with the code in Listing 10-58, and the **DetailView** view with the code in Listing 10-59. You also need to add the **info** argument to the **Author** initializer in the **PreviewData** structure for the previews to work (**let author = Author(name: "Stephen King", books: [], info: nil)**). Run the application. Press the + button to add a new book. Press the Select button to select the author. Press the + button to add a new author. You should see the form in Figure 10-13 (left). Enter the information and press Save. Select the book from the list. You should see the values on the screen, as in Figure 10-13 (right).

Another way to encode and decode custom data types is with JSON (JavaScript Object Notation). This format was developed for transmitting information on the Internet, but the fact that it is easy to read and write made it suitable to store data for applications. Apple systems adopted JSON a long time ago to store and retrieve information. Foundation includes the **JSONDecoder** class to decode JSON data into Swift structures and the **JSONEncoder** class to encode Swift structures into JSON data. The classes define their respective methods for decoding and encoding the values.

▷ **decode(**Type, **from:** Data**)**—This method returns a value of the type specified by the first argument with the information provided by the **from** argument. The **from** argument is a **Data** structure that contains the JSON data we want to decode.

▷ **encode(**Value**)**—This method returns a **Data** structure with the JSON representation of the value provided by the argument.

A JSON file is just a text file that stores the data in a specific syntax. The syntax includes the values of an object or structure as key/value pairs separated by a colon, like dictionaries. The property name becomes the key for the value, and each object or structure is enclosed in curly braces. The following example shows how a JSON file looks like when we store an instance of our **AuthorInfo** structure.

```
{
    "placeOfBirth": "Toronto",
    "birthday": 271479840
}
```

Listing 10-60: JSON file

As always, the objects or structures we want to encode must conform to the **Codable** protocol, and the data must be encoded and decoded before it can be stored or read. Therefore, adapting our application to work with JSON is simple. We just have to replace the Property List encoders and decoders with those defined for the JSON format. Below are the computed properties that were previously defined for the **Author** model, but now the values are decoded by the **JSONDecoder** class.

```
var showBirthday: String? {
    let decoder = JSONDecoder()
    if let info, let authorInfo = try? decoder.decode(AuthorInfo.self,
from: info) {
        if let date = authorInfo.birthday, date < Date() {
            return authorInfo.birthday?.formatted(date: .abbreviated,
time: .omitted)
        }
    }
    return nil
}
var showPlaceOfBirth: String? {
    let decoder = JSONDecoder()
    if let info, let authorInfo = try? decoder.decode(AuthorInfo.self,
from: info) {
        if !authorInfo.placeOfBirth.isEmpty {
            return authorInfo.placeOfBirth
        }
    }
    return nil
}
```

Listing 10-61: Decoding with JSON

The changes in the **AddAuthor** view are also simple. We just need to update the **archiveInfo()** method to encode the data with the **JSONEncoder** class.

```
func archiveInfo() -> Data? {
    var newBirthday = Date.distantFuture
    if birthday < Date(timeIntervalSinceNow: -86400) {
        newBirthday = birthday
    }
    let encoder = JSONEncoder()
    let authorInfo = AuthorInfo(birthday: newBirthday, placeOfBirth:
placeOfBirth)
    let infoData = try? encoder.encode(authorInfo)
    return infoData
}
```

Listing 10-62: Encoding with JSON

 Do It Yourself: Update the computed properties in the **Author** model with the code in Listing 10-61, and the **archiveInfo()** method in the **AddAuthor** view with the code in Listing 10-62. The app should work as before.

Basic 10.3 CloudKit

CloudKit is a database system in iCloud. With this system, we can store structured data online with different levels of accessibility so that our users can access it from any device they own. The system offers three types of databases to determine who has access to the information: private, public and shared. The private database is used for sharing data between devices (only the user can access the information stored in this database), while the public and shared databases are used for sharing information between users. (The information stored in the public database is accessible to all users running our app and the information stored in the shared database is accessible to the users with whom the user wants to share the data.)

Basic Enabling CloudKit

SwiftData can automatically create a private database in CloudKit to share data between the user's devices, but we need to enable the service. The first step is to enable iCloud. This is done from the Signing & Capabilities panel located in Settings (Figure 5-4, number 6). In the panel's upper left corner is the +Capability button that allows us to add a new capability to the app (Figure 10-14, number 1). The button opens a view with all the capabilities available. We just have to look for the iCloud option and double-click it or select it and press Return to add it to our app.

Figure 10-14: *Enabling iCloud for our app*

 IMPORTANT: iCloud services are only available to developers that are members of the Apple Developer Program. At the time of writing, the membership costs $99 US Dollars per year. You also must register your account with Xcode, as explained in Chapter 5 (see Figure 5-3).

After iCloud is added to the app, it will appear on the panel under the Signing section. From here, we can select the iCloud services we want to enable. For CloudKit, we must check the CloudKit option, as shown below.

Figure 10-15: *CloudKit service*

CloudKit requires a container on Apple servers to store and manage the database. To create a new container, we must press the + button (Figure 10-15, number 1). This will open a window where we can enter the name of the container. The name must be unique, and the best way to ensure this is to use the app's bundle identifier. In our example, we used the bundle identifier to create the container for an app called TestCloudKit. Once the container is created, we should press the Refresh button to ensure that the information is immediately uploaded to Apple servers (Figure 10-15, number 2). The container will then be added and selected as the active container for the application.

Because CloudKit uses Remote Notifications to report changes in the database, when we activate CloudKit, Xcode automatically includes an additional service called *Push Notifications*.

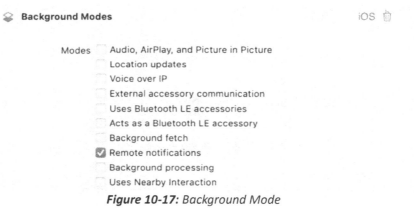

Figure 10-16: *Push Notifications*

Push Notifications (also known as Remote Notifications) are messages sent from a server to inform our app that something has changed or needs attention. Remote Notifications posted by CloudKit are sent from Apple servers when something changes in the database. Since this can happen not only when the user is working with the app, but also when the app is running in the background, we need to add the Background Mode capability and enable a service called *Remote Notifications* to receive these notifications at any time.

Figure 10-17: *Background Mode*

In theory, this is all we need for the system to start uploading and downloading data from CloudKit, but in practice CloudKit has some additional requirements. First, all properties of the model must have a value by default or be optional. This includes the properties used to create relationships, which must be optional for the connections to work in the CloudKit database. And second, CloudKit cannot work with the `unique` attribute, so we must remove this attribute from all our models.

Since we have already assigned values to the properties by default or declared them as optionals, all that is left to do for our models to work is to remove the `@Attribute` macro for the `id` property, as shown in the `Book` model below.

```
@Model
class Book: Identifiable {
    var id: UUID = UUID()
    var title: String = ""
    @Relationship(deleteRule: .nullify, inverse: \Author.books) var
author: Author?
    @Attribute(.externalStorage) var cover: Data?
    var year: Int = 0
```

```
    @Relationship(deleteRule: .nullify, inverse: \SortLetters.books) var
sortLetter: SortLetters?
    init(title: String, author: Author?, cover: Data?, year: Int,
sortLetter: SortLetters?) {
        self.title = title
        self.author = author
        self.cover = cover
        self.year = year
        self.sortLetter = sortLetter
    }
    var displayYear: String {
        get {
            let value = year > 0 ? String(year) : "Undefined"
            return value
        }
    }
    var displayCover: UIImage {
        if let data = cover, let image = UIImage(data: data) {
            return image
        } else {
            return UIImage(named: "nocover")!
        }
    }
}
```

Listing 10-63: *Preparing the models for CloudKit*

 Do It Yourself: Open the project created for previous examples, click on the app's settings option at the top of the Navigator Area (Figure 5-4, number 6), and open the Signing & Capabilities panel. Click on the +Capability button at the top-left corner of the panel to add a capability. Select the iCloud option, press return, and check the option CloudKit. Press the + button to add a container (Figure 10-15, number 1). Insert the app's bundle identifier for the container's name (you can find your app's bundle identifier at the top of panel). If the app doesn't recognize the container, press the Refresh button to upload the information to Apple servers (Figure 10-15, number 2). Click on the + Capability button again to add another capability. Select the Background Modes capability and check the option Remote Notifications (Figure 10-17). Remove the `@Attribute` macro from the `id` property in the `Book`, `Author` and `SortLetter` models, as shown in Listing 10-63. Run the application on two devices connected to the same iCloud account. Insert a book with an author on one device. After a few seconds, the book and the author should appear on the second device.

(Basic) **CloudKit Dashboard**

Objects created from SwiftData models are stored on CloudKit servers as records. In order to know what type of records the database may contain, CloudKit creates a model on its servers every time a new object is added to the local database. For example, if we create an object of type **Book**, CloudKit adds a record type called "CD_Book" to the model and creates fields representing each of the object's properties. In this way, the system sets up the structure of the database based on the data we store during development, saving us the trouble of configuring the database beforehand. The process is automatic, but if we want to check or change this structure, we can access it through the CloudKit dashboard. This is an online control panel that allows us to manage CloudKit databases, add, update or remove records and configure the model (also called schema).

The panel is available at **icloud.developer.apple.com/dashboard/** or by clicking the CloudKit Dashboard button at the bottom of the iCloud section in the Signing & Capabilities panel. The Dashboard home page contains several buttons for accessing tools and documentation. We can configure the database, check its performance, control user activity, and manage our account.

Figure 10-18: CloudKit Dashboard

If we click on the CloudKit Database button, a panel is loaded to edit the database. The panel includes an option at the top to select the container (Figure 10-19, number 1), a panel on the left to edit the data and the schema, and another on the right to show and edit the values.

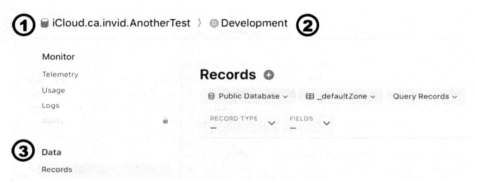

Figure 10-19: CloudKit Database

Once we have selected the container, we can see the database structure and records. Next to the container, there is an option to choose between two configurations: Development and Production (Figure 10-19, number 2). The Development option shows the configuration of the database that will be used during development. This is the database that will be created for us as to test the application. The Production option shows the configuration of the database that we will ship with our application (the one that will be available to our users). Below these buttons is the Data section (Figure 10-19, number 3), where we can edit the data stored by our application, including records, zones, and subscriptions.

CloudKit automatically creates records, zones and subscriptions for us. Records are the data structures that represent the objects created by SwiftData, zones are containers in the database where those records are stored, and subscriptions are messages that CloudKit sends to notify each device of changes in the database, so the devices stay in sync. When we enable CloudKit for our application and start adding objects to the database, the system creates a zone in the private database called com.apple.coredata.cloudkit.zone to store the records and a subscription called com.apple.coredata.cloudkit.private.subscription to send notifications when changes are introduced to the database.

To represent the SwiftData models, CloudKit creates record types. These record types are like classes that describe how the data is structured. CloudKit defines a record type for each SwiftData model in our application and creates fields to represent their properties. Record types are managed from the Schema section in the left panel. When we select the Record Types option, we get a list of record types created by our application on the right. Note that the names of the record types and the fields are defined by prefixing the SwiftData model name with the string "CD_". In our example, we get the record types CD_Author, CD_Book, and CD_SortLetters.

Figure 10-20: Database schema

The SwiftData objects added to the database by our app during testing are uploaded to CloudKit servers and stored as records. If we add a **Book** object, CloudKit creates a CD_Book record with those values. From CloudKit's dashboard, we can list these records and create more. The panel is available when we click on the Records option in the Data section, as shown in Figure 10-19 (number 3). As mentioned earlier, the records for SwiftData are stored in the private database and a zone called com.apple.coredata.cloudkit.zone, so we must select these values to be able to list the records created by our app.

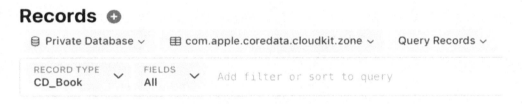

Figure 10-21: List of records

To list the records, we must select the Record Type, as shown in Figure 10-21, and then click the Query Records button. However, when we do this with the default configuration, we get the error message "Field 'recordName' is not marked queryable." This is because the CloudKit dashboard is trying to sort the objects by the recordName field. This is a field that CloudKit adds to a record type to identify the records. The problem is that there is no index associated with the recordName field. Indexes are values that are added to the database to improve performance. To search for a value, the fields must be associated with a Queryable index. All the fields created to represent the properties of SwiftData objects are associated with a Queryable index, but not the recordName field. To add a Queryable index to the recordName field, we must select the Indexes option in the Schema section. This option lists the available record types in the right panel and shows a button on the top-right corner to add more (Figure 10-22, number 1).

Figure 10-22: Indexes

When we press the + button, a new window asks for the Record Type we want to modify and the type of Index we want to create.

Add Index

Record types have fields that allow you to store to different types on the record, such as a string, a list, reference, asset, etc.

Record Type

Name

Type

Figure 10-23: Add Index

Once we select the Record Type and the type Queryable, a new option appears to select the Field, including the recordName field that we need to query records.

Type

QUERYABLE

Field

recordName

Cancel   Add

Figure 10-24: Queryable index for the recordName field

After the Queryable index for the recordName field is added to the list, we can query records.

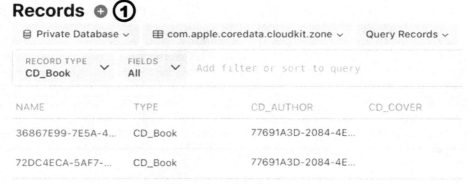

Figure 10-25: List of CD_Book records

The records in this list are those added to the database during testing. From this panel, we can check that the records were uploaded correctly to the CloudKit server and also add new records. This is useful when we only have one device. We can add a record from the CloudKit dashboard and see if it appears on the device. The option to add a new record is at the top of the list (Figure 10-25, number 1). When we press this button, a third panel opens on the right with text fields to provide all the information for the record. (Note that to associate an author to the book, we must provide the author's record name.)

Deploy to Production

In CloudKit's dashboard, at the bottom of the left panel, there is a list of options for working with the database schema. We can export the schema, import a schema from our computer, reset the schema to start from scratch, and deploy the schema to production. This last option is the one we have to choose if we want to prepare our app for distribution (to sell it in the App Store).

The option called Deploy Schema Changes opens a window that displays the features that are to be transferred to the Production environment. These include record types and indexes, but not the records added during testing. If we agree, we need to click the Deploy button to complete the process, and our database in CloudKit is ready for distribution.

 IMPORTANT: The Production environment is used by apps that are submitted to Apple for distribution. This step is required for, your application to be published in the App Store. If you don't deploy the changes to production, the database is not going to be available to your users. To learn how to submit your app to the App Store, read Chapter 21.

Basic **10.4 Files**

Although the User Defaults system and SwiftData are perfect storage solutions, we can also work directly with files stored on the device. For this purpose, the Foundation framework defines a class called `FileManager`. An instance of this class is assigned to the application and from this object we can create, delete, copy and move files and directories in the storage space reserved for our application. The class provides the following type property to get a reference to this object.

▷ **default**—This type property returns a reference to the app's `FileManager` object.

The `FileManager` class provides several properties and methods for managing files and directories. The following are the most frequently used.

▷ **urls(for:** SearchPathDirectory, **in:** SearchPathDomainMask)—This method returns an array with the locations of a directory. The **for** argument is an enumeration with values that represent common system directories. The most frequently used are `documentDirectory` to represent the Documents directory, and `application-SupportDirectory` to reference the Application Support directory. And the **in** argument is an enumeration with values that determine the domain in which the files are located. The most frequently used is `userDomainMask` to represent the user's home directory.

▷ **createFile(atPath:** String, **contents:** Data?, **attributes:** Dictionary?)—This method creates a file. The **atPath** argument specifies the location of the file, including its name and extension, the **contents** argument represents the content of the file, and the **attributes** argument is a dictionary with values that determine the file's arguments (e.g., ownership). The value `nil` sets the arguments by default, which are usually enough.

▷ **createDirectory(at:** URL, **withIntermediateDirectories:** Bool, **attributes:** Dictionary?)—This method creates a new directory. The **at** argument specifies the location of the directory, including its name, the **withIntermediateDirectories** argument indicates whether intermediate directories will also be created or not, and the **attributes** argument is a dictionary with values that determine the directory's arguments (e.g., ownership). The value `nil` sets the arguments by default.

▷ **contents(atPath:** String)—This method returns the contents of the file at the path specified by the **atPath** argument. The value returned is an optional of type `Data`.

- **contentsOfDirectory(atPath: String)**—This method returns an array with the paths of the files and directories inside the directory indicated by the **atPath** argument.
- **copyItem(atPath: String, toPath: String)**—This method copies the file or directory at the path specified by the **at** argument to the path specified by the **to** argument.
- **moveItem(atPath: String, toPath: String)**—This method moves the file or directory at the path specified by the **at** argument to the path specified by the **to** argument.
- **removeItem(atPath: String)**—This method removes the file or directory at the path indicated by the **atPath** argument.
- **fileExists(atPath: String)**—This method returns a Boolean value that determines if the file or the directory at the path specified by the **atPath** argument exists.
- **attributesOfItem(atPath: String)**—This method returns a dictionary with the arguments of the file or directory at the location indicated by the **atPath** argument. The `FileManager` class includes constants to define the arguments, including `creationDate`, `modificationDate`, `size`, and `type`, among others.

Basic URLs and Paths

As in any other operating system, files are organized in directories (folders). There is a directory called root, which can contain other files and directories in a tree-like structure. To specify the location of a file, Apple systems use a conventional syntax that separates each component with a slash (/) and begins with a single slash to indicate the root directory (e.g., /Pictures/Travels/ Hawaii.png). This is called a path and can be used to access any file on the system. Paths are an easy way to access files, but they are not enough to determine the location of a file in the storage system. This is because in practice, files are usually not stored in a single storage location, but in multiple units or even on remote servers. Tracing a long path to find a file also takes time and consumes resources. For these reasons, storage locations are always identified with URLs (Uniform Resource Locator). We introduced URLs in Chapter 9 and use them to asynchronously download images from a server. They are created from the **URL** structure provided by the Foundation framework and can be used for multiple purposes, including referencing remote and local resources. Below are some of the initializers, properties, and methods included in this structure to work with local files and directories.

- **URL(fileURLWithPath: String)**—This initializer returns a **URL** object referencing a local file or directory. The **fileURLWithPath** argument is a string with the file's path.
- **URL(fileURLWithPath: String, relativeTo: URL)**—This initializer returns a **URL** object referencing a local file or directory. The **fileURLWithPath** argument is a string with the file's path, and the **relativeTo** argument is a **URL** object referencing the base URL.
- **path**—This property returns the path of a URL. It is a conditional of type **String**.
- **pathComponents**—This property returns an array of **String** values that represent the components of a path extracted from a URL (the strings between forward slashes).
- **lastPathComponent**—This property returns a string with the last component of a path extracted from a URL. It is usually used to get the file's name and extension.
- **pathExtension**—This property returns a string with the extension of the path extracted from a URL. It is used to get the file's extension.
- **appendingPathComponent(String)**—This method returns a new **URL** structure with the URL of the original object plus the component specified by the argument.

IMPORTANT: The `FileManager` class includes methods that work with both paths and URLs. For example, there are two versions of the `create-Directory()` method, one for creating the directory from a path and another to do it from a URL. The methods that work with paths take care of converting the path to a URL and are usually easier to implement. For a complete list, visit our website and follow the links for this chapter.

(Basic) Files and Directories

Apple's operating systems allow users to create and access any files and directories they want, but mobile applications are restricted to their own storage space to ensure that they do not interfere with each other. This means that we can only access the files and directories that belong to our application.

When the application is installed on the device, the system creates a group of standard directories that we can use to store our files. The most useful are the Documents directory, where we can store the user's files, and the Application Support directory, for files that our application needs to create at runtime but are not directly generated by the user. The location of these directories is not guaranteed, so we must always ask the system for the current URL that points to the directory or file we want to access. To determine the location of common directories such as Documents, the `FileManager` class includes the `urls()` method. This method takes two arguments, one that represents the directory we want to access and another that specifies the domain in which the directory is located (the domain of the user's home directory is represented by the value `userDomainMask`). In consequence, to get the URL of one of the directories provided by the system to our application and create files to store the user's data, we need to get a reference to the `FileManager` object and then call the `urls()` method with the values that represent the location we want to access.

Although we can read and create files from anywhere in the code, it is recommended that we manage all of our files from the model. The following is a simple model that illustrates how to access the directories available to the application and how to create files.

```
import SwiftUI
import Observation

@Observable class ApplicationData: @unchecked Sendable {
    @ObservationIgnored let manager: FileManager
    @ObservationIgnored let directories: [URL]?

    static let shared: ApplicationData = ApplicationData()
    private init() {
        manager = FileManager.default
        directories = manager.urls(for: .documentDirectory,
in: .userDomainMask)
    }
    func saveFile(name: String) {
        if let docURL = directories?.first {
            let newFileURL = docURL.appendingPathComponent(name)
            let path = newFileURL.path

            if let contentData = UIImage(named: "husky")?.pngData() {
                manager.createFile(atPath: path, contents: contentData,
attributes: nil)
            }
        }
    }
}
```

Listing 10-64: Saving files

This model includes two non-observable properties, one to store a reference to the **FileManager** object assigned to the application and another to store the directories returned by the **urls()** method. After initializing these properties, we define a method called **saveFile()** that the views are going to call to create a file. This method receives a string and creates a file with that name. First, we get the URL of the Documents directory from the **directories** property (the Documents directory is always the first item in the array), and then use the **appendingPathComponent()** method to add the name of the file to the URL. Once we have this URL, we get the path from the **path** property and finally create the file.

For this example, we define the contents of the file as an image that we get from the Assets Catalog. (We will learn how to get images from the Photo Library and the camera in Chapter 18) Files can only store data, so we convert the image to a **Data** structure with the **pngData()** method and then use that value to call the **createFile()** method to create the file. (If the file already exists, the method updates its contents.)

Since in this example we are storing the same image in every file, the interface only needs a view to list the files and another with a text field to allow the user to create more.

Figure 10-26: *Interface to create files*

The following is the code for the initial view.

```
struct ContentView: View {
    @Environment(ApplicationData.self) private var appData
    @State private var openSheet: Bool = false

    var body: some View {
        NavigationStack {
            VStack {
                Text("No Files")
                Spacer()
            }.padding()
            .navigationBarTitle("Files")
            .toolbar {
                ToolbarItem(placement: .navigationBarTrailing) {
                    Button("Add File") {
                        openSheet = true
                    }
                }
            }
            .sheet(isPresented: $openSheet) {
                AddFileView()
            }
        }
    }
}
```

Listing 10-65: *Opening a sheet to add files to the model*

At the moment, this view only displays a message on the screen, but it provides a button in the navigation bar to open a sheet with a view called **AddFileView**, which allows the user to create new files.

```
struct AddFileView: View {
    @Environment(ApplicationData.self) private var appData
    @Environment(\.dismiss) var dismiss
    @State private var nameInput: String = ""

    var body: some View {
        VStack {
            HStack {
                Text("Name:")
                TextField("Insert File Name", text: $nameInput)
                    .textFieldStyle(.roundedBorder)
                    .autocapitalization(.none)
                    .disableAutocorrection(true)
            }.padding(.top, 25)
            HStack {
                Spacer()
                Button("Create") {
                    var fileName =
nameInput.trimmingCharacters(in: .whitespaces)
                    if !fileName.isEmpty {
                        fileName += ".dat"
                        appData.saveFile(name: fileName)
                        dismiss()
                    }
                }
            }
            Spacer()
        }.padding()
    }
}
```

Listing 10-66: Creating new files

This view includes a `TextField` view where the user can enter the name of the file, and a `Button` view to create it. When the button is pressed, the string is truncated to remove spaces at the beginning and the end, the string ".dat" is appended to the name (adding an extension is not necessary), and then the `saveFile()` method is called in the model to create the file. After that, the Documents directory will contain a file with the name entered by the user, the extension .dat, and the image of a husky.

 Do It Yourself: Create a Multiplatform project. Create a Swift file called ApplicationData.swift for the model in Listing 10-64. Update the **ContentView** view with the code in Listing 10-65. Create a SwiftUI View file called AddFileView.swift for the view in Listing 10-66. Remember to inject the **ApplicationData** object into the environment for the app and the previews (Chapter 7, Listing 7-4). Download the image husky.png from our website and add it to the Asset Catalog. Run the application on the iPhone simulator and press the Add File button. Insert the name of the file and press the Create button. The file is created, and the sheet is closed.

At the moment, the initial view only shows the message "No Files", but the purpose of this application is to allow the user to create multiple files and show them on the screen. For this purpose, the **FileManager** class includes methods to list the contents of a directory. For example, we can use the **contentsOfDirectory()** method to get an array of strings with the names of the files and directories in a given path, store them in an array, and then display them on the screen with a **List** view. For this purpose, we need to modify our model to store the names of the files along with an identifier, as we did for books before, and include a property to provide the list for the views. The following is the new model for this project.

```
struct File: Identifiable, Hashable {
    let id: UUID = UUID()
    var name: String
}
@Observable class ApplicationData: @unchecked Sendable {
    var listOfFiles: [File] = []
    @ObservationIgnored let manager: FileManager
    @ObservationIgnored let directories: [URL]?

    static let shared: ApplicationData = ApplicationData()
    private init() {
        manager = FileManager.default
        directories = manager.urls(for: .documentDirectory,
in: .userDomainMask)
        if let docURL = directories?.first {
            if let list = try? manager.contentsOfDirectory(atPath:
docURL.path) {
                for name in list {
                    let newFile = File(name: name)
                    listOfFiles.append(newFile)
                }
            }
        }
    }
    func saveFile(name: String) {
        if let docURL = directories?.first {
            let newFileURL = docURL.appendingPathComponent(name)
            let path = newFileURL.path

            if let contentData = UIImage(named: "husky")?.pngData() {
                if manager.createFile(atPath: path, contents: contentData,
attributes: nil) {
                    let newFile = File(name: name)
                    listOfFiles.append(newFile)
                }
            }
        }
    }
}
```

Listing 10-67: Getting the list of files

The first structure, called `File`, is the model we use to store the name of each file. The structure conforms to the `Identifiable` protocol so that it can be easily managed by the views, and also the `Hashable` protocol so that we can later use these values to identify the links with the `NavigationLink` view.

When the observable object is initialized, we initialize the properties as before and then retrieve the list of files in the directory with the `contentsOfDirectory()` method. This method returns an array of strings with the names of the files, so we create a loop, initialize an instance of the `File` structure with each name, and add it to an observable property called `listOfFiles` to make it available to the views.

The `saveFile()` method is the same as before, but after the `createFile()` method is called, we now check if the file has been created and add the `File` structure to the `listOfFiles` property only if there is no other file with that name.

After the `ApplicationData` structure is initialized, the `listOfFiles` property contains the names of all the files in the directory, so we can show them to the user.

```
struct ContentView: View {
    @Environment(ApplicationData.self) private var appData
    @State private var openSheet: Bool = false
```

```
var body: some View {
    NavigationStack {
        List {
            ForEach(appData.listOfFiles) { file in
                Text(file.name)
            }
        }
        .navigationBarTitle("Files")
        .toolbar {
            ToolbarItem(placement: .navigationBarTrailing) {
                Button("Add File") {
                    openSheet = true
                }
            }
        }
        .sheet(isPresented: $openSheet) {
            AddFileView()
        }
    }
}
```

Listing 10-68: *Listing the files created by the user*

The **List** view includes a **ForEach** view that lists the values of the **listOfFiles** property. Each row includes the name of a file, as shown below.

Figure 10-27: *List of files*

 Do It Yourself: Update the ApplicationData.swift file with the code in Listing 10-67 and the **ContentView** view with the code in Listing 10-68. Run the application on the iPhone simulator. Press the Add File button to add a file. Insert the name of the file and press the Create button. You should see on the screen the list of all the files you have created so far, as shown in Figure 10-27.

Creating and listing files is only the first step, we must also allow the user to read their contents. To read files, we need to check if the file exists and then read its contents with the **contents()** method. The following is the function we need to include in our model for this purpose.

```
func loadFile(name: String) -> UIImage? {
    if let docURL = directories?.first {
        let fileURL = docURL.appendingPathComponent(name)
        let filePath = fileURL.path

        if manager.fileExists(atPath: filePath) {
            if let content = manager.contents(atPath: filePath) {
                return UIImage(data: content)
            }
        }
    }
}
```

```
        return nil
   }
```

Listing 10-69: Reading the content of a file

To read the contents of a file, we get the URL as before, then use the `fileExists()` method to check if the file exists, and read the contents with the `contents()` method. Since in this case we know that the file contains an image, we create the `UIImage` object and return it.

In the views, we need a way to allow users to open the files. For this example, we will add a `NavigationLink` to the items in the list to open an additional view that displays the contents of the file. The following are the changes we need to make to the `ContentView` view.

```
struct ContentView: View {
    @Environment(ApplicationData.self) private var appData
    @State private var openSheet: Bool = false

    var body: some View {
        NavigationStack {
            List {
                ForEach(appData.listOfFiles) { file in
                    NavigationLink(value: file, label: {
                        Text(file.name)
                    })
                }
            }
            .navigationBarTitle("Files")
            .toolbar {
                ToolbarItem(placement: .navigationBarTrailing) {
                    Button("Add File") {
                        openSheet = true
                    }
                }
            }
            .navigationDestination(for: File.self, destination: { file in
                ShowFile(file: file)
            })
            .sheet(isPresented: $openSheet) {
                AddFileView()
            }
        }
    }
}
```

Listing 10-70: Allowing the user to open a file

When the user selects a file from the list, the `navigationDestination()` modifier receives a `File` structure and opens the `ShowFile` view with that value. In this view, we need to call the `loadFile()` method in the model and show the user the image returned by it.

```
import SwiftUI

struct ShowFile: View {
    @Environment(ApplicationData.self) private var appData
    @State private var imageContent: UIImage?
    let file: File

    var body: some View {
        VStack {
            Text(file.name)
            Image(uiImage: imageContent ?? UIImage(named: "nopicture")!)
                .resizable()
                .scaledToFit()
```

```
            Spacer()
         }.padding(.horizontal)
          .toolbarTitleDisplayMode(.inline)
          .task {
             imageContent = appData.loadFile(name: file.name)
          }
       }
    }
}
#Preview {
    ShowFile(file: File(name: "Test File"))
       .environment(ApplicationData.shared)
}
```

Listing 10-71: Displaying the contents of a file

This view includes a @State property to store a UIImage object. When the view appears, the task() modifier calls the loadFile() method with the name of the file selected by the user, the method reads the file, converts the contents to a UIImage object, returns it, and the object is assigned to the property to display the image on the screen.

Figure 10-28: File content

 Do It Yourself: Add the method in Listing 10-69 to the ApplicationData class. Update the ContentView view with the code in Listing 10-70. Create a new file called ShowFile.swift for the view in Listing 10-71. Download the file nopicture.png from our website and add it to the Asset Catalog. Run the application on the simulator and select a file. You should see the picture of the husky, as shown in Figure 10-28.

Of course, we can also delete files. The process is the same we used earlier to remove items from the model. We need to implement the onDelete() method and then remove the file from the Documents directory and the File structure from the listOfFiles array. The following is the method we need to add to our model for this purpose.

```
func deleteFile(index: Int) {
    let file = listOfFiles[index]
    let name = file.name

    if let docURL = directories?.first {
        let fileURL = docURL.appendingPathComponent(name)
        do {
            try manager.removeItem(atPath: fileURL.path)
            listOfFiles.remove(at: index)
        } catch {
            print("File was not removed")
        }
    }
}
```

```
}
```

Listing 10-72: Deleting a file

This method receives the index of the file the user wants to delete, gets the `File` structure, builds the file's URL, and then removes the file from the Documents directory with the `removeItem()` method and the `File` structure from the `listOfFiles` array.

In the view, we just need to add the `onDelete()` modifier to the `ForEach` view and then call the `deleteFile()` method in the model every time the user decides to delete a file.

```
List {
    ForEach(appData.listOfFiles) { file in
        NavigationLink(value: file, label: {
            Text(file.name)
        })
    }
    .onDelete { indexSet in
        for index in indexSet {
            appData.deleteFile(index: index)
        }
    }
}
```

Listing 10-73: Allowing the user to delete files

Figure 10-29: File deleted

Files can store anything we want as long as we convert the information into raw data. For custom data types, we can use the archiving process presented earlier, but if we just want to store a string, the `String` structure includes a method that converts a string to data, and also an initializer that can get back a string from a `Data` structure.

▷ **String(data:** Data, **encoding:** Encoding)—This initializer creates a `String` value with the text in the `Data` structure provided by the **data** argument. The **encoding** argument is a structure that determines the type of encoding used to generate the string. The encoding usually depends on the language the text was written in. The most frequently used are the structures returned by the properties `utf8` and `ascii`.

▷ **data(using:** Encoding, **allowLossyConversion:** Bool)—This method returns a `Data` structure containing the string from a `String` value. The **using** argument is a structure that determines the type of encoding used to generate the string. The encoding usually depends on the language the text was written in. The most frequently used are the structures returned by the properties `utf8` and `ascii`. The **allowLossyConversion** argument determines the precision of the conversion.

The `String` structure also includes a convenient method to turn a string into data and store it in a file, all at once.

- ▷ **write(to:** URL, **atomically:** Bool, **encoding:** Encoding)—This method converts a string into a **Data** structure and stores it in the file located at the URL specified by the **to** argument. The **atomically** argument determines if we want the data to be stored in an auxiliary file first to ensure that the original file is not corrupted (recommended). And the **encoding** argument is a structure that determines the type of encoding used to generate the string. The encoding usually depends on the language the text was written in. The most frequently used are the structures returned by the properties **utf8** and **ascii**.

There is also a similar method provided by the **Data** structure to save the data directly into a file.

- ▷ **write(to:** URL, **options:** WritingOptions)—This method stores the **Data** structure in the file located at the URL specified by the **to** argument. The **options** argument is a structure that determines how the file should be saved. The structure includes the type properties **atomic, withoutOverwriting, noFileProtection, completeFileProtection, completeFileProtectionUnlessOpen, complete-FileProtectionUntilFirstUserAuthentication**, and **fileProtectionMask**.

As an example, we can create an application that allows the user to write a text and save it to a file. The model must read the file and load the text each time the application is launched, and it must also provide a property that saves the text to a file when changes are introduced by the user.

```
import SwiftUI
import Observation

@Observable class ApplicationData: @unchecked Sendable {
    var textInFile: String = "" {
        didSet {
            if let docURL = directories?.first {
                let fileURL = docURL.appendingPathComponent("textdata.dat")
                let filePath = fileURL.path
                if let textData = textInFile.data(using: .utf8,
allowLossyConversion: true) {
                    manager.createFile(atPath: filePath, contents: textData,
attributes: nil)
                }
            }
        }
    }
    @ObservationIgnored var manager: FileManager
    @ObservationIgnored var directories: [URL]?

    static let shared: ApplicationData = ApplicationData()
    private init() {
        manager = FileManager.default
        directories = manager.urls(for: .documentDirectory,
in: .userDomainMask)
        if let docURL = directories?.first {
            let fileURL = docURL.appendingPathComponent("textdata.dat")
            let filePath = fileURL.path
            if manager.fileExists(atPath: filePath) {
                if let content = manager.contents(atPath: filePath) {
                    if let text = String(data: content, encoding: .utf8) {
                        textInFile = text
                    }
                }
            }
        }
    }
}
```

```
}
```

Listing 10-74: Storing text in a file

To automatically save the text to a file, we use property observers. As we saw in Chapter 3, property observers are methods that are executed when a value is assigned to the property (see Chapter 3, Listing 3-44). In this example, we implemented the `didSet()` method for the `textInFile` property to store the property's value in a file whenever a new value is assigned to it. In the method, we convert the string into a `Data` structure using the `data()` method and then store the data in the file with the `createFile()` method of the `FileManager` object, as we did earlier for images.

In the initializer, we look for a file named textdata.dat. If the file exists, we get its contents with the `contents()` method, convert the data to a string with the `String(data:)` initializer, and assign the result to the `textInFile` property to update the view.

The view for this example must include a `TextEditor` view to show the text currently stored in the file and allow the user to change it.

```
struct ContentView: View {
    @Environment(ApplicationData.self) private var appData

    var body: some View {
        @Bindable var appData = appData

        GroupBox("Editor") {
            TextEditor(text: $appData.textInFile)
        }.padding()
    }
}
```

Listing 10-75: Editing the content of a file

Figure 10-30: Interface to insert and store a text

Do It Yourself: Create a Multiplatform project. Create a Swift file called ApplicationData.swift for the model in Listing 10-74. Update the **ContentView** view with the code in Listing 10-75. Remember to inject the **Application-Data** object into the environment for the app and the previews (Chapter 7, Listing 7-4). Run the application on the iPhone simulator. Type a text. Stop the application from Xcode and run it again. You should see the same text on the screen.

(Basic) Bundle

In the previous examples, we worked with files created by the user. However, if we want to load files that were added to the project during development, we need to read them from the bundle. Bundles are directories assigned to each application by the system. They create a hierarchical structure to organize all the files and resources for the application. To create and manage bundles, Foundation includes the `Bundle` class. The class provides properties and methods to work with bundles and determine their location, including the following type property to return a reference to the bundle created by default for our application.

▷ **main**—This type property returns a reference to the app's bundle.

The problem with accessing the files in the bundle is that the bundle is created by the system after the app is installed on the device. Therefore, we don't know what URLs are assigned to the files. To get these URLs, we need to retrieve them from the `Bundle` object. For this purpose, the class provides the following methods.

▷ **url(forResource: String?, withExtension: String?)**—This method returns a `URL` structure with the URL of a file or directory inside the bundle. The first argument specifies the name of the file or directory we are looking for, and the **withExtension** argument specifies the extension.

▷ **path(forResource: String?, ofType: String?)**—This method returns the path of a file or directory inside the bundle. The first argument specifies the name of the file or directory we are looking for, and the **ofType** argument specifies the extension.

The files in the bundle are usually required to load initial data or restore the application's initial state. The following example illustrates how this process works by loading a single file with some content. The application loads a text file called quote.txt from the bundle when the application is launched. The file must be added to the project during development by dragging it from Finder to the Navigator Area (see Chapter 5, Figure 5-32).

```
import SwiftUI
import Observation

@Observable class ApplicationData: @unchecked Sendable {
   var textInFile: String = ""

   static let shared: ApplicationData = ApplicationData()
   private init() {
      let manager = FileManager.default
      let bundle = Bundle.main
      if let path = bundle.path(forResource: "quote", ofType: "txt") {
         if let data = manager.contents(atPath: path) {
            if let message = String(data: data, encoding: .utf8) {
               textInFile = message
            }
         }
      } else {
         textInFile = "File Not Found"
      }
   }
}
```

***Listing 10-76:** Loading a file from the bundle*

The model's initializer gets a reference to the app's bundle and then calls the `path()` method to find the path for a file called quote.txt. Once we get the path, we can read the file as before. The value is stored in an observable property to update the view. The view for this example just needs to read this property and display the text on the screen.

```
struct ContentView: View {
   @Environment(ApplicationData.self) private var appData

   var body: some View {
      VStack {
```

```
        Text(appData.textInFile)
            .lineLimit(nil)
            .padding(15)
            .frame(minWidth: 0, maxWidth: .infinity)
            .background(Color(white: 0.8))
        Spacer()
    }.padding()
  }
}
```

Listing 10-77: Displaying the content of a file stored in the bundle

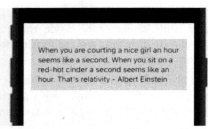

When you are courting a nice girl an hour seems like a second. When you sit on a red-hot cinder a second seems like an hour. That's relativity - Albert Einstein

Figure 10-31: Content of a text file stored in the bundle

Do It Yourself: Create a Multiplatform project. Create a Swift file called ApplicationData.swift for the model in Listing 10-76. Update the `ContentView` view with the code in Listing 10-77. Download the file quote.txt from our website or create your own and add it to the project. Remember to inject the `ApplicationData` object into the environment for the app and the previews (Chapter 7, Listing 7-4). Run the application. You should see the text loaded from the file on the screen, as shown in Figure 10-31.

(Medium) **Documents**

The `FileManager` class provides the tools we need to create and store files in the storage space designated by the system for our application, but sometimes users need to share that information with other applications. For this purpose, Apple systems allow users to create and share documents. Documents are containers that can process and store a specific type of information in a file. They can be stored on the device and shared with other apps, sent to servers, or stored in iCloud to make them available to other devices.

Creating, editing and sharing documents has become so important nowadays that SwiftUI includes two Scenes for creating applications with the specific purpose of handling documents.

▷ **DocumentGroup(newDocument:** Closure, **editor:** Closure)—This initializer creates a `DocumentGroup` structure that defines a Scene with all the tools required to open, create, edit, and save documents. The **newDocument** argument is a closure that returns a document model to create the documents, and the **editor** argument is a closure that provides the view used to edit the document's content.

▷ **DocumentGroupLaunchScene(**String, Closure, **background:** Closure, **backgroundAccessoryView:** Closure, **overlayAccessoryView:** Closure)— This initializer creates a `DocumentGroupLaunchScene` structure to use along with a `DocumentGroup` structure to define the launch screen for a `DocumentGroup` scene. The first argument is the window's title, the second argument is a closure that provides the actions we want the user to initiate from this screen, the **background** argument is a closure with the views we want to show in the background, the **backgroundAccessory-View** argument is a closure with the accessory views we want to show in the background (usually images), and the **overlayAccessoryView** argument is the closure with the accessory views we want to show in the overlay.

The **DocumentGroup** structure replaces the **WindowGroup** structure we have been using so far to create the Scene (the window). Once we have implemented the **DocumentGroup** structure, the system presents an interface for creating and loading documents, as shown below.

Figure 10-32: Document app

The documents are created from a document model. This is a structure or class that defines the type of data managed by the document and how the information is converted into a format that the application can process. The model is defined using a structure that conforms to the **FileDocument** protocol or a class that conforms to the **ReferenceFileDocument** protocol. Which protocol to use depends on the requirements of our application, but both define similar properties and methods for configuration. For example, below are the requirements of the **FileDocument** protocol.

▷ **readableContentTypes**—This property returns an array of **UTType** structures to indicate the type of values managed by the document.

▷ **init(configuration: ReadConfiguration)**—This initializer is used by the Document app to get the data when the user wants to read it. The **configuration** argument is a structure with information about the document. The structure includes the **file** property to return a **FileWrapper** structure, which in turn includes properties to return information about the document. The most frequently used are **filename** and **preferredFilename** to return the file's name and extension, **fileAttributes** to return the file's attributes, and **regularFileContents** to return the file's content.

▷ **fileWrapper(configuration: WriteConfiguration)**—This method is called by the Document app to get the content we want to include in the document. The **configuration** argument is a structure with information about the current document. The structure includes the **existingFile** property to return a **File-Wrapper** structure with this information or the value **nil** if the document was not saved yet. The method must return a **FileWrapper** structure with the content we want to save.

The content of the document is managed by an instance of the **FileWrapper** structure. The following is the structure's initializer.

▷ **FileWrapper(regularFileWithContents:** Data**)**—This initializer creates a file wrapper for a document with the data provided by the argument.

To allow the user to work with documents, we need to define the document model using the tools presented above. This can be a structure or a class, depending on what we need for our application. The following example shows how to define a document model with a structure that conforms to the **FileDocument** protocol.

```
import SwiftUI
import UniformTypeIdentifiers

struct TextDocument: FileDocument {
   static let readableContentTypes: [UTType] = [.plainText]

   var documentText: String
   init() {
      documentText = ""
   }
   init(configuration: ReadConfiguration) throws {
      if let data = configuration.file.regularFileContents {
         if let text = String(data: data, encoding: .utf8) {
            documentText = text
         } else {
            throw CocoaError(.fileReadCorruptFile)
         }
      } else {
         throw CocoaError(.fileReadCorruptFile)
      }
   }
   func fileWrapper(configuration: WriteConfiguration) throws ->
FileWrapper {
      let data = documentText.data(using: .utf8)
      let wrapper = FileWrapper(regularFileWithContents: data!)
      return wrapper
   }
}
```

Listing 10-78: Defining a document model

Among other things, the document model defines the type of data that the document can process. This is determined by a **UTType** structure. This structure provides a universal identifier that any application can recognize. Although we can define our own, as we will see in Chapter 12, the structure provides type properties to represent the most common types, including **png**, **gif**, **jpeg**, **pdf**, **mp3**, **avi**, **json**, **image**, **text**, and **plainText**. In this example, we assign the **plainText** type to the **readableContentTypes** property to configure the document to store plain text. (Note that to use the **UTType** data type we had to import the UniformTypeIdentifiers framework where the structure is defined.)

To store the contents of the document, we define a **String** property called **documentText** and use the structure's initializer to initialize it with an empty string. Any document created from this model will be empty by default.

The document model requires an initializer to read the content of the document and a method to write it. The initializer is used to recreate the model when the user selects the document. The system reads the file and provides the data with a **FileWrapper** object, which we can read from the **regularFileContents** property. So we read this property, convert the data to a string using the **String** initializer, and assign it to the **documentText** property. To write the content of this property back to the document, we implement the **fileWrapper()** method. In this case, we just need to convert the value of the **documentText** property into a **Data** structure, create a **FileWrapper** object with it, and return it.

 IMPORTANT: Note that we must return an error if the process of reading the document fails. The Foundation framework defines a class called **CocoaError** that returns common error codes. The class includes an initializer to create an object from a **Code** structure and several type properties to return **Code** values. The most commonly used for reading files are **fileReadCorruptFile**, **fileReadNoSuchFile**, and **fileReadUnknown**.

Now that the document model is ready, we can create the Scene with the `DocumentGroup` structure. The structure's initializer requires an instance of our document model and a closure with the view we want to use to edit the documents. This closure receives a `FileDocument-Configuration` structure with a reference to the document and its properties. The structure includes the following properties to return these values.

▷ **document**—This is a binding property with a reference to the document.

▷ **fileURL**—This property returns a `URL` structure with the file's URL.

▷ **isEditable**—This property returns a Boolean value that indicates whether the user is allowed to edit the document or not.

The `DocumentGroup` structure creates a Scene for processing documents and therefore it can replace the `WindowGroup` structure implemented in previous examples, as shown below.

```
import SwiftUI

@main
struct TestApp: App {
  var body: some Scene {
    DocumentGroup(newDocument: TextDocument(), editor: { config in
      ContentView(document: config.$document)
    })
  }
}
```

Listing 10-79: *Creating a Document app*

This `App` structure creates an app for managing documents. We initialize the `DocumentGroup` structure with an instance of our `TextDocument` structure to tell the app how to create the documents, and a closure that returns a `ContentView` view to provide a view for editing the documents. Note that we take the property from the `FileDocument-Configuration` structure received by the closure and pass it to the view so that the view can access the document and edit its content. For the view to receive this value, it must contain a binding property, as shown below.

```
struct ContentView: View {
   @Binding var document: TextDocument

   var body: some View {
      GroupBox("Editor") {
         TextEditor(text: $document.documentText)
      }.padding()
       .navigationBarTitleDisplayMode(.inline)
   }
}
#Preview {
   @Previewable @State var document = TextDocument()
   ContentView(document: $document)
}
```

Listing 10-80: *Editing the document*

With a document app, users can save and share documents on the device, in iCloud, or on a server. The user interface consists of a home screen with a button at the top to create a new document and a sheet at the bottom with tabs to select recent documents and create new ones. When we press a button to create or open a document, the app opens the `ContentView` view to edit the content.

Figure 10-33: Custom Document app

 Do It Yourself: Create a Multiplatform project. Create a Swift file called TextDocument.swift for the structure in Listing 10-78. Update the **App** structure with the code in Listing 10-79 and the **ContentView** view with the code in Listing 10-80. Run the application on the iPhone simulator. Select the Browse tab on the sheet and tap the Create Document button (Figure 10-33, left). You should see the document editor (Figure 10-33, right).

The **DocumentGroup** structure provides an interface with all the tools the user needs to create, modify, and remove documents, but sometimes all we need is to allow the user to export or import documents from our own custom interface. For this purpose, SwiftUI includes the following modifiers.

▷ **fileExporter(isPresented:** Binding, **document:** FileDocument, **content-Type:** UTType, **defaultFilename:** String, **onCompletion:** Closure)—This modifier presents an interface to allow the user to save a document on the device, iCloud, or a remote location. The **isPresented** argument is a binding property of type **Bool** that indicates whether the interface is shown or hidden. The **document** argument is the document model we want to use to create the document. The **contentType** argument determines the type of content the document is going to handle. The **defaultFilename** argument is the name we want to assign to the document. And finally, the **onCompletion** argument is the closure to execute when the process is over. The closure receives a **Result** value with the document's URL and an **Error** value to report errors.

▷ **fileImporter(isPresented:** Binding, **allowedContentTypes:** [UTType], **onCompletion:** Closure)—This modifier presents an interface to allow the user to open a document. The **isPresented** argument is a binding property of type **Bool** that indicates whether the interface is shown or hidden. The **allowedContentTypes** argument determines the type of document we want to allow the user to open. And the **onCompletion** argument is the closure to execute when the process is over. The closure receives a **Result** value with the document's URL and an **Error** value to report errors.

▷ **fileMover(isPresented:** Binding, **file:** URL, **onCompletion:** Closure)—This modifier presents an interface to allow the user to move a document. The **isPresented** argument is a binding property of type **Bool** that indicates whether the interface is shown or hidden. The **file** argument is the URL of the document we want to move. And the **onCompletion** argument is the closure to execute when the process is over. The closure receives a **Result** value with the document's URL and an **Error** value to report errors.

These modifiers open their own interface, so we no longer need to create the window using the **DocumentGroup** structure. For example, the **fileExporter()** modifier opens an interface that allows the user to export and share a file. This modifier creates a document from a document model, as before, but from our own application, as shown below.

```
struct ContentView: View {
    @State private var document = TextDocument()
    @State private var openExport: Bool = false

    var body: some View {
        NavigationStack {
            GroupBox("Editor") {
                TextEditor(text: $document.documentText)
            }.padding()
            .navigationTitle("Document")
            .navigationBarTitleDisplayMode(.inline)
            .toolbar {
                ToolbarItem(placement: .navigationBarTrailing) {
                    Button(action: {
                        openExport = true
                    }, label: {
                        Image(systemName: "square.and.arrow.up")
                    })
                }
            }
        }
        .fileExporter(isPresented: $openExport, document: document,
contentType: .plainText, defaultFilename: "My Document", onCompletion:
{ result in
            print("Document exported") })
    }
}
```

Listing 10-81: *Exporting a document*

To create the document, we need an instance of the document model. In this example, we create a **@State** property called **document** and initialize it with an instance of the same **TextDocument** structure used in the previous example. The view includes a **TextEditor** view so that the user can edit the contents of the document. And for exporting, we provide a button in the navigation bar. When the button is pressed, we assign the value **true** to a **@State** property and the **fileExporter()** modifier opens the interface. Now we can insert a text and export it as a document from our application without having to create the Scene with the **DocumentGroup** structure.

Figure 10-34: *Export a document*

 Do It Yourself: Create a Multiplatform project. Create a Swift file called TextDocument.swift for the document model in Listing 10-79. Update the **ContentView** view with the code in Listing 10-81. Run the application on the simulator. Type some text. Press the Export button to export the text as a document, as shown in Figure 10-34.

In the same way that we can create and export a document with the text inserted by the user, we can import a document, read it, and display the text to the user by implementing the `fileImporter()` modifier. The only difference is that we do not work with a document but with the file associated with the document. The `fileImporter()` modifier returns a `URL` structure with the location of the file. To read the file at this URL and extract the data, the `Data` structure includes the following initializer.

▷ **Data(contentsOf:** URL)—This initializer creates a `Data` structure with the content of the file at the location specified by the **contentsOf** argument.

Since the files we access with the `fileImporter()` modifier are not stored in our app's storage space but in the file system, they are protected and inaccessible by default. To allow our app to access these files, the `URL` structure includes the following methods.

▷ **startAccessingSecurityScopedResource()**—This method grants access to the resource referenced by the `URL` structure. The method returns a Boolean value to report whether access was granted or not.

▷ **stopAccessingSecurityScopedResource()**—This method revokes the access granted to the application to the resource referenced by the `URL` structure.

The implementation of the `fileImporter()` modifier is very similar to the `fileExporter()` modifier. We must apply it to a view and define a Boolean state to indicate when we want to open the interface. In the following example, we add an additional button to the navigation bar. When the button is pressed, we assign the value **true** to the `@State` property to open the interface, then read the document selected by the user and assign the text to the `TextEditor` view to show it on the screen.

```
struct ContentView: View {
    @State private var document = TextDocument()
    @State private var openExport: Bool = false
    @State private var openImport: Bool = false

    var body: some View {
        NavigationStack {
            GroupBox("Editor") {
                TextEditor(text: $document.documentText)
            }.padding()
            .navigationTitle("Document")
            .navigationBarTitleDisplayMode(.inline)
            .toolbar {
                ToolbarItem(placement: .navigationBarLeading) {
                    Button(action: {
                        openImport = true
                    }, label: {
                        Image(systemName: "square.and.arrow.down")
                    })
                }
                ToolbarItem(placement: .navigationBarTrailing) {
                    Button(action: {
                        openExport = true
                    }, label: {
                        Image(systemName: "square.and.arrow.up")
                    })
                }
            }
        }
    }
```

```
        .fileExporter(isPresented: $openExport, document: document,
contentType: .plainText, defaultFilename: "My Document", onCompletion:
{ result in
        print("Document exported")
    })
        .fileImporter(isPresented: $openImport, allowedContentTypes:
[.plainText], onCompletion: { result in
        if let fileURL = try? result.get() {
            if fileURL.startAccessingSecurityScopedResource() {
                if let data = try? Data(contentsOf: fileURL) {
                    if let text = String(data: data, encoding: .utf8) {
                        document.documentText = text
                    }
                }
                fileURL.stopAccessingSecurityScopedResource()
            }
        }
    })
    }
}
```

Listing 10-82: Importing a document

The `fileImporter()` modifier imports the document and calls the closure assigned to the **onCompletion** argument to report the result. This closure receives a `Result` value that we can read to get the file's URL (see Chapter 3, Listing 3-195). In this example, we use the `get()` method to get the URL and then read the file with the `Data(contentsOf:)` initializer. The data is converted to a string and assigned to the document so that the text is shown on the screen.

Figure 10-35: Interface to import a document

 Do It Yourself: Update the `ContentView` view with the code in Listing 10-82. Run the application again on your device. Press the Import button and select the document created before. You should see the content of the document on the screen.

Basic **11.1 Shapes**

All the views we have used so far are containers or are designed to display predefined content on the screen, but SwiftUI also includes graphical views to create custom controls or to use them for decoration. These views work like the ones introduced before and can use most of the modifiers presented so far, but are specifically designed to draw custom graphics on the screen.

Basic **Common Shapes**

SwiftUI allows us to create predefined or custom shapes. The following are the views available for creating standard shapes.

▷ **Rectangle()**—This initializer creates a `Rectangle` view. The size of the rectangle is determined by the view's frame.

▷ **RoundedRectangle(cornerRadius:** CGFloat, **style:** RoundedCornerStyle)— This initializer creates a `RoundedRectangle` view. The **cornerRadius** argument determines the radius of the curvature of the corners, and the **style** argument is an enumeration of type `RoundedCornerStyle` that determines the type of curvature to use. The values available are `circular` and `continuous`. The view also includes the following initializer to define the radius with a `CGSize` value: `RoundedRectangle-(cornerSize: CGSize, style: RoundedCornerStyle)`.

▷ **Circle()**—This initializer creates a `Circle` view. The diameter of the circle is determined by the view's frame.

▷ **Ellipse()**—This initializer creates an `Ellipse` view. The size of the ellipse is determined by the width and height of the view's frame.

▷ **Capsule(style:** RoundedCornerStyle)—This initializer creates a `Capsule` view. The **style** argument is an enumeration that determines the type of curvature to apply to the corners. The values available are `circular` and `continuous`.

As with many other views, graphical views adopt the size of their container if no size is specified, but we can declare a particular size with the **frame()** modifier. The following example shows all the standard shapes available. We have put the views in a horizontal **ScrollView** view so that the list can be scrolled.

```
struct ContentView: View {
    var body: some View {
        VStack {
            ScrollView(.horizontal, showsIndicators: true) {
                HStack {
                    Rectangle()
                        .frame(width: 100, height: 100)
                    RoundedRectangle(cornerRadius: 25, style: .continuous)
                        .frame(width: 100, height: 100)
                    Circle()
                        .frame(width: 100, height: 100)
                    Ellipse()
                        .frame(width: 100, height: 50)
                    Capsule()
                        .frame(width: 100, height: 50)
```

```
            }.padding()
        }
        Spacer()
      }
    }
}
```

Listing 11-1: Drawing standard shapes

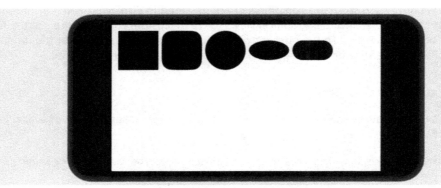

Figure 11-1: Standard shapes

 Do It Yourself: Create a Multiplatform project. Update the **ContentView** view with the code in Listing 11-1. If you don't see all the shapes on the screen, scroll the views to the left. Use this project to test the rest of the examples in this chapter.

By default, views are rendered with a color that depends on the appearance mode (black for light and white for dark), but we can change what we use to fill and outline shapes with the following modifiers.

▷ **fill(**View**)**—This modifier fills the shape with the view specified by the argument. The argument is a view that represents a color, a gradient or an image.

▷ **stroke(**View, **lineWidth:** CGFloat**)**—This modifier defines the border of the shape. The first argument is a view that represents a color, a gradient, or an image, and the **lineWidth** argument defines the border's width.

▷ **stroke(**View, **style:** StrokeStyle**)**—This modifier defines the border of the shape. The first argument is a view that represents a color, a gradient or an image, and the **style** argument is a structure of type **StrokeStyle** that defines the border's width, cap, join, miter limit, dash, and dash phase.

▷ **strokeBorder(**View, **lineWidth:** CGFloat**)**—This modifier defines the inner border of the shape. The first argument is a view that represents a color, a gradient, or an image, and the **lineWidth** argument defines the border's width.

▷ **strokeBorder(**View, **style:** StrokeStyle**)**—This modifier defines the inner border of the shape. The first argument is a view that represents a color, a gradient or an image, and the **style** argument is a structure of type **StrokeStyle** that defines the border's width, cap, join, miter limit, dash, and dash phase.

There are two aspects of a shape that we can change with these modifiers: the view we use to fill the shape and the border. The view used to fill the shape can be any other view, such as the **Color** view, and it is applied with the **fill()** modifier, as shown below.

```
struct ContentView: View {
    var body: some View {
```

```
        RoundedRectangle(cornerRadius: 25)
            .fill(Color.red)
            .frame(width: 100, height: 100)
    }
}
```

Listing 11-2: Filling a shape with a color

Note that the `fill()` modifier is implemented by the `RoundedRectangle` view, but the `frame()` modifier returns a different view. Therefore, any modifier defined for shapes, such as `fill()`, must be applied before other modifiers such as `frame()`. In this example, we use these modifiers to create a red rectangle with rounded corners.

Figure 11-2: Rectangle

Adding a border requires a similar process, but there are two types of modifiers that give a slightly different result. The `stroke()` modifier expands the border outward and inward, while the `strokeBorder()` modifier creates an inner border.

```
struct ContentView: View {
    var body: some View {
        HStack {
            RoundedRectangle(cornerRadius: 25)
                .stroke(Color.red, lineWidth: 20)
                .frame(width: 100, height: 100)
                .padding()
            RoundedRectangle(cornerRadius: 25)
                .strokeBorder(Color.red, lineWidth: 20)
                .frame(width: 100, height: 100)
                .padding()
        }
    }
}
```

Listing 11-3: Defining a border

This view includes two `RoundedRectangle` views with a border of 20 points, but because we are using different modifiers, the borders are different. Half of the border for the first rectangle is drawn outside the shape, while the other half is drawn inside the view's frame, but the border for the second rectangle is all inside the frame, as shown below.

Figure 11-3: Rectangles with different strokes

These two modifiers can also take a `StrokeStyle` structure to fine-tune the border. The structure provides the following initializer.

▷ **StrokeStyle(lineWidth:** CGFloat, **lineCap:** CGLineCap, **lineJoin:** CGLine-Join, **miterLimit:** CGFloat, **dash:** [CGFloat], **dashPhase:** CGFloat)—This initializer creates a **StrokeStyle** structure to configure a stroke. The **lineWidth** argument determines the width. The **lineCap** argument determines the style of the end of the lines. It is an enumeration with the values **butt** (squared end), **round** (rounded end), and **square** (squared end). The **lineJoin** argument sets the style of the joint of two connected lines. It is an enumeration with the values **miter** (sharp end), **round** (rounded end), and **bevel** (squared end). The **miterLimit** argument determines how long the lines extend when the **lineJoin** argument is set to **miter**. The **dash** argument determines the length of the segments for a dashed stroke. And the **dashPhase** argument determines where the dashed line begins.

The following example creates a **RoundedRectangle** view where the outline is configured as a dashed line with a width of 15 points and rounded tips.

```
struct ContentView: View {
    let lineStyle = StrokeStyle(lineWidth: 15, lineCap: .round,
lineJoin: .round, miterLimit: 0, dash: [20], dashPhase: 0)

    var body: some View {
        RoundedRectangle(cornerRadius: 25)
            .stroke(Color.red, style: lineStyle)
            .frame(width: 100, height: 100)
    }
}
```

Listing 11-4: Defining a custom border

Figure 11-4: Rectangle with a custom stroke

Shapes are views and therefore can be combined with other SwiftUI views and controls. For instance, the following example assigns a **Capsule** shape as the background of a button.

```
struct ContentView: View {
    @State private var setActive: Bool = true

    var body: some View {
        VStack {
            Button(action: {
                setActive.toggle()
            }, label: {
                Text(setActive ? "Active" : "Inactive")
                    .font(.title)
                    .foregroundColor(Color.white)
                    .padding(.horizontal, 30)
                    .padding(.vertical, 10)
            })
            .background(
                Capsule()
                    .fill(setActive ? Color.green : Color.red)
            )
```

```
        Spacer()
    }.padding()
    }
}
```

Listing 11-5: Combining shapes with other views

There is also a version of the **background()** modifier specifically designed for shapes.

▷ **background**(Color, **in:** Shape)—This modifier assigns a shape to the background of a view. The first argument specifies the color, and the **in** argument the shape.

Using this modifier, we can declare the background of the button in the previous example with a single line of code.

```
.background(setActive ? Color.green : Color.red, in: Capsule())
```

Listing 11-6: Assigning a shape as the background of a button

The button toggles the value of a **@State** property. If the value is **true**, we show the label "Active" and assign a green capsule to the button's background, otherwise we display the label "Inactive" and turn the capsule red.

Figure 11-5: Graphic button

(Basic) Gradients

We can also use color gradients to fill the shapes and the borders. SwiftUI includes four structures for creating gradients: **LinearGradient**, **RadialGradient**, **AngularGradient**, and **EllipticalGradient**. These structures conform to the **ShapeStyle** protocol, which defines the following methods to create customized instances.

▷ **linearGradient**(Gradient, **startPoint:** UnitPoint, **endPoint:** UnitPoint)— This method returns a linear gradient. The **gradient** argument is the gradient of colors to be used, and the **startPoint** and **endPoint** arguments determine the points inside the shape where the gradient starts and ends.

▷ **radialGradient**(Gradient, **center:** UnitPoint, **startRadius:** CGFloat, **endRadius:** CGFloat)—This method returns a circular gradient. The **gradient** argument is the gradient of colors to be used. The **center** argument determines the position of the center of the circle, and the **startRadius** and **endRadius** arguments determine where the gradient starts and ends.

▷ **ellipticalGradient**(Gradient, **center:** UnitPoint, **startRadiusFraction:** CGFloat, **endRadiusFraction:** CGFloat)—This method returns a radial gradient with the shape of an ellipse. The **gradient** argument is the gradient of colors to be used. The **center** argument determines the center of the ellipse, and the **startRadiusFraction** and **endRadiusFraction** argument determine the radius of the ellipse.

▷ **angularGradient**(Gradient, **center:** UnitPoint, **startAngle:** Angle, **endAngle:** Angle)—This method returns an angular gradient. The **gradient** argument is the gradient of colors to be used. The **center** argument determines the center of the shape, the **startAngle** argument determines the angle at the beginning of the gradient and the **endAngle** determines the angle at the end.

▷ **conicGradient(**Gradient, **center:** UnitPoint, **angle:** Angle)—This method returns a conic gradient. The **gradient** argument is the gradient of colors to be used. The **center** argument determines the position of the tip of the cone, and the **angle** argument determines the angle where the gradient begins.

These methods return an instance of one of the gradient structures introduced before, but the gradient of colors is defined by the `Gradient` structure.

▷ **Gradient(colors:** [Color])—This initializer creates a gradient with the colors specified by the argument. The **colors** argument is an array of **Color** views.

▷ **Gradient(stops:** [Gradient.Stop])—This initializer creates a gradient with the colors specified by the argument. The **stops** argument is an array of **Stop** structures that determine the colors and when they stop.

Another value required to present a gradient is the `UnitPoint` structure. This is like the `CGPoint` structure but specifically designed to work with graphical structures.

▷ **UnitPoint(x:** CGFloat, **y:** CGFloat)—This initializer creates a `UnitPoint` structure. The **x** and **y** arguments determine the x and y coordinates of the point. For gradients, these arguments are defined with values from 0.0 to 1.0.

The `UnitPoint` structure also includes the type properties **bottom**, **bottomLeading**, **bottomTrailing**, **center**, **leading**, **top**, **topLeading**, **topTrailing**, **trailing**, and **zero** to define common points. For example, we can apply a linear gradient with the values **bottom** and **top** to draw the gradient from the bottom to the top of the shape.

```
struct ContentView: View {
    let gradient = Gradient(colors: [Color.red, Color.green])

    var body: some View {
        RoundedRectangle(cornerRadius: 25)
            .fill(.linearGradient(gradient, startPoint: .bottom,
endPoint: .top))
            .frame(width: 100, height: 100)
    }
}
```

Listing 11-7: *Defining a linear gradient*

The code in Listing 11-7 defines a gradient with two colors, red and green, and then applies the gradient to a **RoundedRectangle** view with the structure returned by the `linear-Gradient()` method. Because we declare the value **bottom** as the starting point and the value **top** as the ending point, the colors are displayed from bottom to top in the order declared by the `Gradient` structure.

Figure 11-6: *Linear gradient*

When a gradient is created without specifying color stops, the colors are distributed evenly over the entire area occupied by the gradient. If we want to adjust the distribution, we must define the colors for the gradient with **Stop** structures.

- ▷ **Stop(color:** Color, **location:** CGFloat)—This initializer creates a color with a stop value. The **color** argument determines the color, and the **location** argument determines the position in the gradient where the color begins (it's a value from 0.0 to 1.0).

The following example reproduces the previous gradient, but this time the green color begins at the position 0.4 (40% of the area occupied by the gradient).

```
struct ContentView: View {
   let gradient = Gradient(stops: [
      Gradient.Stop(color: Color.red, location: 0.0),
      Gradient.Stop(color: Color.green, location: 0.4)
   ])
   var body: some View {
      RoundedRectangle(cornerRadius: 25)
         .fill(.linearGradient(gradient, startPoint: .bottom,
endPoint: .top))
         .frame(width: 100, height: 100)
   }
}
```

***Listing 11-8:** Defining a linear gradient with custom stops*

***Figure 11-7:** Linear gradient with custom stops*

In addition to the linear gradient, we can also create gradients with different shapes. For example, radial and elliptical gradients are created with circular layers drawn outward from the center of a circle, as shown below.

```
struct ContentView: View {
   let gradient = Gradient(colors: [Color.red, Color.white])

   var body: some View {
      RoundedRectangle(cornerRadius: 25)
         .fill(.radialGradient(gradient, center: .center, startRadius: 0,
endRadius: 120))
         .frame(width: 100, height: 100)
   }
}
```

***Listing 11-9:** Defining a circular gradient*

This example illustrates how to create a radial gradient. The values required are the `Gradient` structure, the center of the circle, and the position within the shape where the gradient begins and ends. These values determine where the gradient begins and ends, but only the part of the gradient that is inside the shape is drawn. In our example, the **endRadius** argument was specified as 120, but because the size of the shape is 100 x 100, only part of the gradient is visible.

Figure 11-8: Circular gradient

Another type of gradient we can use for our shapes are angular or conical gradients. In these gradients, the colors are drawn around a circle so that it looks like a cone when viewed from above. The values required depend on the type of cone we want to define. For a simple cone, we only need the `Gradient` structure, the center of the circle, and the angle at which the gradient begins.

```
struct ContentView: View {
    let gradient = Gradient(colors: [Color.red, Color.white])

    var body: some View {
        RoundedRectangle(cornerRadius: 25)
            .fill(.conicGradient(gradient, center: .center,
angle: .degrees(180)))
            .frame(width: 100, height: 100)
    }
}
```

Listing 11-10: Defining a conic gradient

The angles for the gradient are declared using an instance of the `Angle` structure. This structure includes two type methods to define the value in degrees or radians: `degrees(Double)` and `radians(Double)`. In the example in Listing 11-10, the start of the gradient is specified with an angle of 180 degrees, which is the opposite side of the default start point.

Figure 11-9: Conic gradient

SwiftUI also includes the `MeshGradient` view for creating two-dimensional color gradients. The gradient is created from a grid of points. Each point is associated with a color, so the system can mix the colors between each point and change the gradient as the points are moved.

▷ **MeshGradient(width:** Int, **height:** Int, **points:** [Float], **colors:** [Color], **background:** Color, **smoothsColors:** Bool, **colorSpace:** Gradient.-ColorSpace)—This initializer creates a view for displaying a two-dimensional gradient. The **width** and **height** arguments determine the number of horizontal and vertical points in the grid. The **points** argument is an array of vectors with `Float` values representing the coordinates of the points on the grid. The **colors** argument is an array of `Color` views that represent the colors for each point. The **background** argument determines the background color of the grid (`clear` by default). The **smoothsColors** argument determines whether the transition between the colors is smooth or not (**true** by default). And the **colorSpace** argument determines the color space used to display the colors (the one assigned to the device is used by default).

The **width** and **height** arguments define the side of the grid. For example, a grid of 3 by 3 points includes a total of 9 points. The position of the points is defined with values from 0.0 to 1.0 (left to right and top to bottom) and the colors for each point are declared with **Color** views.

```
struct ContentView: View {
    var body: some View {
        MeshGradient(width: 3, height: 3, points: [
            [0.0, 0.0], [0.5, 0.0], [1.0, 0.0],
            [0.0, 0.5], [0.8, 0.8], [1.0, 0.6],
            [0.0, 1.0], [0.5, 1.0], [1.0, 1.0]
        ], colors: [
            .red, .purple, .indigo,
            .orange, .white, .blue,
            .yellow, .green, .mint
        ])
    }
}
```

Listing 11-11: Defining a mesh gradient

Figure 11-10: Mesh gradient

Basic Effects

The **ShapeStyle** protocol, which defines the type methods implemented in the previous section for creating gradient structures, also specifies several properties and methods for applying other effects to a view. The following are the most frequently used.

▷ **shadow(**ShadowStyle**)**—This method applies a shadow to the view. The argument is a structure with two type methods to create drop and inner shadows: **drop(color: Color, radius: CGFloat, x: CGFloat, y: CGFloat)** and **inner(color: Color, radius: CGFloat, x: CGFloat, y: CGFloat)**.

▷ **opacity(**Double**)**—This method assigns to the view the level of opacity specified by the argument. The argument takes values from 0.0 (fully transparent) to 1.0 (fully opaque).

▷ **blendMode(**BlendMode**)**—This method determines how the view is going to blend with the background and other views. The argument is an enumeration with the values **normal, darken, multiply, colorBurn, plusDarker, lighten, screen, colorDodge, plusLighter, overlay, softLight, hardLight, difference,** exclusion, hue, **saturation**, **color**, luminosity, **sourceAtop**, **destination-Over**, and **destinationOut**.

Many modifiers can take a structure that conforms to the **ShapeStyle** protocol to assign a style to a view. When working with shapes, these styles work better with the **foreground-Style()** modifier. For instance, if we want to apply a shadow to our rectangular shape, we can use this modifier for the shadow and define the fill color with the **foregroundColor()** modifier, as in the following example.

```
struct ContentView: View {
    var body: some View {
        RoundedRectangle(cornerRadius: 25)
            .foregroundStyle(.shadow(.drop(color: .black, radius: 3, x: 4,
y: 4)))
            .foregroundColor(.red)
            .frame(width: 100, height: 100)
    }
}
```

Listing 11-12: Adding a shadow to a view

Figure 11-11: Shadow

(Basic) **Patterns**

In addition to colors and gradients, we can also use images to fill a shape. SwiftUI includes the **ImagePaint** structure for this purpose. The structure includes the following type method to create a custom instance.

▷ **image**(Image, **sourceRect:** CGRect, **scale:** CGFloat)—This method returns an **ImagePaint** structure with the image and configuration specified by the arguments. The first argument provides the **Image** view with the image we want to use, the **sourceRect** argument determines the part of the image to be drawn (by default, the entire image), and the **scale** argument defines the scale of the image (by default, the original scale).

By default, the **ImagePaint** structure uses the entire image at its original scale, so in most cases, specifying the image is enough for the system to create the pattern, as in the following example.

```
struct ContentView: View {
    var body: some View {
        Rectangle()
            .fill(.image(Image(.pattern)))
            .frame(width: 100, height: 100)
    }
}
```

Listing 11-13: Filling a shape with an image

The image repeats indefinitely to fill the entire shape. In this example, we define a square of 100 by 100 points and paint over it with an image of 25 by 25 points. Since the image is smaller than the shape, it is drawn several times to cover the area.

Chapter 11 - Graphics and Animations

Figure 11-12: Pattern

11.2 Paths

The shapes we have implemented so far are defined by paths. A path is a set of instructions that define the outline of a 2D shape. In addition to the paths defined by the standard shapes presented earlier, we can create our own. For this purpose, SwiftUI includes the `Path` view.

Basic **Path View**

The `Path` view is designed to create a view that contains a custom path. The following are some of the initializers.

▷ **Path()**—This initializer creates an empty `Path` view. The path is created by applying modifiers to this instance.

▷ **Path(Closure)**—This initializer creates an empty `Path` view. The argument is a closure to define the path. The closure receives a reference to the `Path` structure that we can use to create the path.

The path is created with a combination of lines and curves. The strokes move from one point to another in the view's coordinates, as if following the movement of a pencil. The `Path` structure defines a set of modifiers to determine the position of the pencil and generate the path. The following are the most frequently used.

▷ **move(to:** CGPoint)—This modifier moves the pencil to the coordinates determined by the **to** argument.

▷ **addLine(to:** CGPoint)—This modifier adds a straight line to the path, from the pencil's current position to the coordinates indicated by the **to** argument.

▷ **addLines(**[CGPoint])—This modifier adds multiple straight lines to the path. The lines are added in sequence according to the order of the points in the array.

▷ **addArc(center:** CGPoint, **radius:** CGFloat, **startAngle:** Angle, **endAngle:** Angle, **clockwise:** Bool)—This modifier adds an arc to the path. The **center** argument specifies the coordinates of the center of the circle formed by the arc, the **radius** argument is the radius of the circle, the **startAngle** and **endAngle** arguments are the angles in which the arc starts and ends, and the **clockwise** argument determines the orientation in which the arc is calculated (**true** clockwise and **false** counterclockwise).

▷ **addArc(tangent1End:** CGPoint, **tangent2End:** CGPoint, **radius:** CGFloat)— This modifier adds an arc to the path using tangent points. The **tangent1End** argument defines the coordinates of the end of the first tangent line, the **tangent2End** argument defines the coordinates of the end of the second tangent line, and the **radius** argument determines the radius of the circle.

▷ **addCurve(to:** CGPoint, **control1:** CGPoint, **control2:** CGPoint)—This modifier adds a cubic Bezier curve to the path with two control points. The **to** argument defines the coordinates of the ending point, and the **control1** and **control2** arguments define the coordinates of the first and second control points, respectively.

- **addQuadCurve(to:** CGPoint, **control:** CGPoint)—This modifier adds a quadratic Bezier curve to the path with a control point. The **to** argument defines the coordinates of the ending point, and the **control** argument defines the coordinates of the control point.

- **addEllipse(in:** CGRect)—This modifier adds an ellipse to the path. The **in** argument determines the area of the ellipse. If the rectangle is a square, the ellipse becomes a circle.

- **addRect(**CGRect**)**—This modifier adds the rectangle defined by the argument to the path. There is a version of this modifier that takes an array of `CGRect` values to add multiple rectangles at a time (`addRects([CGRect])`).

- **addRoundedRect(in:** CGRect, **cornerSize:** CGSize, **style:** RoundedCorner-Style)—This modifier adds a rounded rectangle to the path. The **in** argument determines the dimensions of the rectangle, the **cornerRadius** argument determines the radius of the curvature of the corners, and the **style** argument is an enumeration with the values `circular` and `continuous`.

A custom path works the same way as a predefined path. If we don't specify the fill or stroke, the path is drawn with a color that depends on the appearance mode (black for light and white for dark), but we can change that with the `fill()` and `stroke()` modifiers, as we did before for standard shapes. If we draw the path with the `fill()` modifier, the path is automatically closed, but if we do it with the `stroke()` modifier, it stays open. To close the path and ensure that the lines are connected, the `Path` structure includes the following modifier.

- **closeSubpath()**—This modifier closes the current path. If the path is not a closed path, the modifier adds a line between the end and the beginning of the path to close it.

To create a path, we must apply the modifiers in order, following the line of an imaginary pencil. In the following example, a path is created in the shape of a triangle.

```
struct ContentView: View {
    var body: some View {
        Path { path in
            path.move(to: CGPoint(x: 100, y: 150))
            path.addLine(to: CGPoint(x: 200, y: 150))
            path.addLine(to: CGPoint(x: 100, y: 250))
            path.closeSubpath()
        }.stroke(Color.blue, lineWidth: 5)
    }
}
```

Listing 11-14: Defining a custom path

By default, the initial position of the pencil is at coordinates 0, 0 (upper-left corner of the view). If we want to start drawing from a different position, we must first apply the `move()` modifier. In Listing 11-14, we move the pencil to the coordinates 100, 150 before adding the first line. Subsequent lines are created from the current position of the pencil to the coordinates specified by the modifier. For example, after we set the starting point in our example, we create a line from that point to the point 200, 150, so the next line starts at that point and ends at 100, 250. Notice that we only created two lines. The line that goes from point 100, 250 to point 100, 150 is automatically created by the `closeSubpath()` modifier to close the path. If we want to create an open path, we can ignore this modifier.

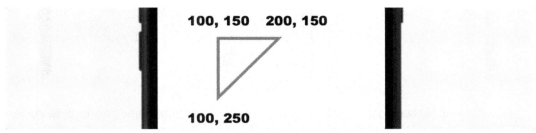

Figure 11-13: Custom path

By combining different modifiers, we can create complex paths. The following path is defined with two lines and an arc.

```
struct ContentView: View {
   var body: some View {
      Path { path in
         path.move(to: CGPoint(x: 100, y: 150))
         path.addLine(to: CGPoint(x: 200, y: 150))
         path.addArc(center: CGPoint(x: 200, y: 170), radius: 20,
startAngle: .degrees(270), endAngle: .degrees(90), clockwise: false)
         path.addLine(to: CGPoint(x: 100, y: 190))
      }.stroke(Color.blue, lineWidth: 5)
   }
}
```

Listing 11-15: Combining lines and arcs

Since arcs are calculated from the coordinates of the center of the circle and the radius, we must consider these two values to connect the arc to the previous line. If the initial coordinates of the arc do not match the current position of the pencil, a line is created between these two points to connect the path. Figure 11-14 below shows the path we get with the example in Listing 11-15, and what we see when we move the center of the arc up 10 points (y: 160).

Figure 11-14: Lines and arcs

The **addRect()** and **addEllipse()** modifiers allow us to add rectangles and circles to the path. The modifiers add the shapes to the current path, but they move the pencil to the position indicated by the **CGRect** value, so they are considered independent shapes.

```
struct ContentView: View {
   var body: some View {
      Path { path in
         path.move(to: CGPoint(x: 100, y: 150))
         path.addLine(to: CGPoint(x: 200, y: 150))
         path.addEllipse(in: CGRect(x: 200, y: 140, width: 20, height: 20))
      }.stroke(Color.blue, lineWidth: 5)
   }
}
```

Listing 11-16: Combining lines and ellipses

In this case, no line is created between the current position of the pencil and the ellipse unless they are connected. Figure 11-15 below shows the path we get with the example in Listing 11-16, and what we see when we move the area of the circle 10 points to the right (x: 210).

Figure 11-15: Lines and ellipses

In addition to **addArc()** and **addEllipse()**, we have two other modifiers to draw curves: The **addQuadCurve()** modifier generates a quadratic Bezier curve, and the **addCurve()** modifier generates a cubic Bezier curve. The difference between these modifiers is that the first one has only one control point and the second has two, creating different types of curves.

```
struct ContentView: View {
    var body: some View {
        Path { path in
            path.move(to: CGPoint(x: 50, y: 50))
            path.addQuadCurve(to: CGPoint(x: 50, y: 200), control:
CGPoint(x: 100, y: 125))
            path.move(to: CGPoint(x: 250, y: 50))
            path.addCurve(to: CGPoint(x: 250, y: 200), control1: CGPoint(x:
200, y: 125), control2: CGPoint(x: 300, y: 125))
        }.stroke(Color.blue, lineWidth: 5)
    }
}
```

Listing 11-17: *Creating complex curves*

To create a quadratic curve, we move the pencil to the point 50, 50, finish the curve at the point 50, 200, and place the control point at the position 100, 125. The cubic curve, created with the **addCurve()** modifier is more complicated. For this curve there are two control points, the first one at the position 200, 125, and the second one at the position 300, 125. These points shape the curve as shown below.

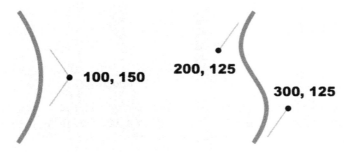

Figure 11-16: *Complex curves*

The paths we have created so far use fixed values. This means that the shape will always be the same size, regardless of the size of the view. To adjust the path to the size of the view, we need to calculate how much space is available with the **GeometryReader** view (see Chapter 8).

```
struct ContentView: View {
    var body: some View {
        GeometryReader { geometry in
            Path { path in
                let width = geometry.size.width / 2
                let height = width
                let posX = (geometry.size.width - width) / 2
                let posY = (geometry.size.height - height) / 2
```

Chapter 11 - Graphics and Animations

```
            path.move(to: CGPoint(x: posX, y: posY))
            path.addLine(to: CGPoint(x: posX + width, y: posY))
            path.addLine(to: CGPoint(x: posX, y: posY + height))
            path.closeSubpath()
        }.stroke(Color.blue, lineWidth: 5)
      }
    }
}
```

Listing 11-18: Adapting the size of the path to the size of the container

The code in Listing 11-18 draws a triangle that is always half the width of its container. To do this, we first calculate the width of the triangle by dividing the width of the geometry by 2. Then we assign this value to the **height** constant to set the height equal to the width. After the dimensions are calculated, we determine the position of the starting point. Since we want to center the triangle in the container, to get the starting point we get the remaining space by subtracting the width of the triangle from the width of the geometry and then dividing the result by 2. We do the same for the vertical position and store the values in the **posX** and **posY** constants. With these values, we can finally draw the path. The **move()** modifier moves the pencil to the starting position defined by **posX** and **posY**. Then the **addLine()** modifier draws a line from this point to the point at the right end of the triangle (**posX + width**). The next **addLine()** modifier draws a line from this point to the point at the bottom left of the triangle (**posY + height**). And finally the **closeSubpath()** modifier draws the vertical line to close the path.

Because we calculate all the coordinates of the path from the values of the geometry, the triangle adjusts to the size of its container and is always half the size and centered in the view, regardless of the device or the size of the screen.

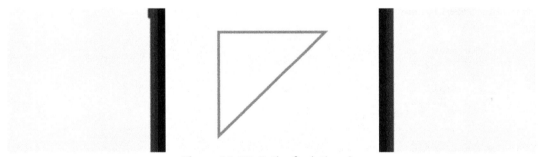

Figure 11-17: Path of relative size

⬭ Medium Custom Shapes

The common shapes introduced at the beginning of this chapter are structures that conform to the **Shape** protocol. A structure that conforms to this protocol defines its own path, which is created in the same way as the path for a **Path** view, but the advantage of working with **Shape** structures instead of **Path** views is that a **Shape** structure is given a **CGRect** value with the dimensions of the view in which the shape is to be drawn, so the shape always adjusts to the size of the container (we do not have to calculate its size using a **GeometryReader** view).

The protocol requires the structure to implement the following method to define the path of the shape.

> ▷ **path(in:** CGRect)—This method receives a **CGRect** value with the dimensions of the view and must return a **Path** view with the path we want to assign to the shape.

Creating a custom shape is easy. We must define a structure that conforms to the **Shape** protocol, implement the **path()** method, and create and return a **Path** view. The following example defines a shape structure called **Triangle** that draws a triangle.

```
import SwiftUI

struct Triangle: Shape {
    func path(in rect: CGRect) -> Path {
        var path = Path()
        let width = rect.width
        let height = rect.height
        let posX = rect.origin.x
        let posY = rect.origin.y

        path.move(to: CGPoint(x: posX, y: posY))
        path.addLine(to: CGPoint(x: posX + width, y: posY))
        path.addLine(to: CGPoint(x: posX, y: posY + height))
        path.closeSubpath()

        return path
    }
}
```

Listing 11-19: Creating a custom shape view

The path is the same as in the previous examples, but now we take the values from the **CGRect** structure received by the method to calculate the size of the shape. In this case, we expand the triangle from left to right and top to bottom to cover the entire view. (The size of the triangle corresponds to the width and height of the view, which is the recommended approach for custom shapes.)

Once the **Shape** view is defined, we can implement it in our interface like any other view. To illustrate how this works, we can instantiate multiple **Triangle** views of different sizes within a horizontal **ScrollView** view.

```
struct ContentView: View {
    var body: some View {
        VStack {
            ScrollView(.horizontal, showsIndicators: true) {
                HStack {
                    Triangle()
                        .fill(Color.blue)
                        .frame(width: 120, height: 50)
                    Triangle()
                        .fill(Color.green)
                        .frame(width: 120, height: 100)
                    Triangle()
                        .fill(Color.yellow)
                        .frame(width: 120, height: 80)
                    Triangle()
                        .fill(Color.red)
                        .frame(width: 50, height: 50)
                }
            }.padding()
            Spacer()
        }
    }
}
```

Listing 11-20: Implementing custom shape views

When a **Triangle** view is created, the **path()** method is called with the dimensions of the view and the triangle is drawn according to those values. Therefore, if we define **Triangle** views of different sizes, we will get triangles of different shapes on the screen.

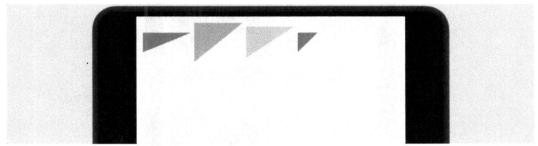

Figure 11-18: Custom shape views

 Do It Yourself: Create a Swift file called Triangle.swift for the code in Listing 11-19. Update the **ContentView** view with the code in Listing 11-20. If you don't see all the triangles, scroll the view or rotate the device (Figure 11-18).

(Medium) 11.3 Transformations

SwiftUI provides a variety of tools to change physical aspects of a view or a **Shape** view, such as the orientation, perspective, or position of the content. The following are some of the modifiers available for this purpose.

> ▷ **offset**(CGSize)—This modifier displaces the content of the view to the horizontal and vertical distance defined by the argument.

> ▷ **rotationEffect**(Angle)—This modifier rotates the content of the view to the angle determined by the argument.

> ▷ **rotation3DEffect**(Angle, Tuple)—This modifier rotates the content of the view in 3D. The first argument declares the angle in degrees or radians, and the second argument is a tuple with three values to represent the axes, as in **(x: Double, y: Double, z: Double)**. Values different than 0 rotate the image in that axis.

> ▷ **clipShape**(Shape)—This modifier clips the view with the shape specified by the argument.

These modifiers affect the content of the view. For example, if we apply an offset to an **Image** view, the image within the view is moved by the distance determined by the modifier, but the frame of the view is not affected.

```
struct ContentView: View {
    var body: some View {
        Image(.spot1)
            .resizable()
            .scaledToFit()
            .frame(width: 150, height: 200)
            .offset(CGSize(width: 75, height: 0))
    }
}
```

Listing 11-21: Displacing an image

The code in Listing 11-21 moves the image 75 points to the right (half the width of the **Image** view).

Figure 11-19: *Image displaced to the right*

The rotation modifiers work in a similar way. They rotate the content of the view in 2D or 3D. The most interesting is the **rotation3DEffect()** which can rotate the content around any axis.

```
struct ContentView: View {
    var body: some View {
        Image(.spot1)
            .resizable()
            .scaledToFit()
            .frame(width: 150, height: 200)
            .scaleEffect(CGSize(width: 0.9, height: 0.9))
            .rotation3DEffect(.degrees(30), axis: (x: 0, y: 1, z: 0))
    }
}
```

Listing 11-22: *Rotating the image*

The **rotation3DEffect()** modifier requires a tuple with values that determine the axes about which the content should be rotated. A value of 0 means that there is no rotation, and a value other than 0 indicates the direction of rotation, negative to one side and positive to the other.

Figure 11-20: *Image rotated in the y axis*

Another transformation we can perform is clipping the view with the **clipShape()** modifier. This modifier overlays the view with a shape and preserves only the parts of the view that are covered by the shape. This is especially useful for images. For example, we can clip our image with a **Circle** shape to create a nice thumbnail.

```
struct ContentView: View {
    var body: some View {
        Image(.spot1)
            .resizable()
            .scaledToFit()
            .frame(width: 150, height: 200)
```

```
        .clipShape(Circle())
    }
}
```

Listing 11-23: Clipping the image

Figure 11-21: Image clipped with a `Circle` *shape*

When a view is clipped, its shape changes. This means that if we want to apply a border, it won't match the shape of the view. To apply a border to a view with an irregular shape, we need to create an overlay using the **overlay()** modifier and draw a view that matches the shape of the original view. For example, we can create a border for the previous image with a **Circle** view and the **stroke()** modifier.

```
struct ContentView: View {
    var body: some View {
        Image(.spot1)
            .resizable()
            .scaledToFit()
            .frame(width: 150, height: 200)
            .clipShape(Circle())
            .overlay {
                Circle().stroke(Color.blue, lineWidth: 10)
            }
    }
}
```

Listing 11-24: Adding a border to an irregular shape

Figure 11-22: Irregular view with a border

SwiftUI also includes modifiers specifically designed for transforming **Shape** views. The following are the most frequently used.

▷ **rotation(Angle, anchor: UnitPoint)**—This modifier rotates the shape to the angle specified by the first argument. The **anchor** argument determines the point around which the shape will rotate. The point is specified with values between 0.0 and 1.0.

▷ **scale(CGFloat, anchor: UnitPoint)**—This modifier changes the scale of the shape. The first argument determines the new scale (1.0 by default), and the **anchor** argument determines the point from which the shape is scaled. There is an additional modifier to change the scale independently for the x and y axes: **scale(x: CGFloat, y: CGFloat, anchor: UnitPoint)**.

▷ **trim(from:** CGFloat, **to:** CGFloat)—This modifier trims the shape from the point determined by the **from** argument to the point determined by the **to** argument.

These modifiers are implemented by `Shape` views and therefore must be applied before other modifiers, as in the following example.

```
struct ContentView: View {
    var body: some View {
        RoundedRectangle(cornerRadius: 20)
            .rotation(.degrees(45))
            .fill(Color.red)
            .frame(width: 100, height: 100)
    }
}
```

Listing 11-25: Rotating a shape

Again, the transformation modifiers affect the content of the view, in this case the shape, but the view itself remains unchanged. In the example in Listing 11-25, we create a `RoundedRectangle` view and rotate it 45 degrees.

Figure 11-23: Rotation

The `scale()` modifier is used not only to change the size of the shape, but also to create cool effects. For example, we can contract or expand shapes by specifying different values for horizontal and vertical scale, or use a negative value to create a mirror image. The following example applies this last trick to invert the coordinate system and draw an inverted shape.

```
struct ContentView: View {
    var body: some View {
        HStack {
            Triangle()
                .fill(Color.blue)
                .frame(width: 100, height: 100)
            Triangle()
                .scale(x: -1, y: 1)
                .fill(Color.blue)
                .frame(width: 100, height: 100)
        }
    }
}
```

Listing 11-26: Inverting a shape with the `scale()` *modifier*

This example implements the **Triangle** view defined in Listing 11-19. The first instance is displayed with a normal scale, but the second instance is transformed with the **scale()** modifier and a horizontal scale of -1, inverting the coordinate system and creating a mirror image.

Figure 11-24: Mirror shapes

Do It Yourself: Update the `ContentView` view with the code in Listing 11-26. To test this example, you also need the Triangle.swift file we created before with the `Triangle` view defined in Listing 11-19. You should see the shapes in Figure 11-24 on the canvas.

As mentioned earlier, paths are drawn from one point to another as if following the movement of a pencil. We can remove part of the process with the `trim()` modifier. This modifier determines which part of the path is drawn with values from 0.0 to 1.0, where 0.0 is the beginning of the path and 1.0 is the end.

```
struct ContentView: View {
    var body: some View {
        HStack {
            Triangle()
                .trim(from: 0, to: 0.70)
                .stroke(Color.blue, lineWidth: 10)
                .frame(width: 100, height: 100)
        }
    }
}
```

Listing 11-27: Trimming a path

This example creates a `Triangle` view, but the path is truncated at the point 0.70, which represents the 70% of the drawing. This allows the system to draw the first and second lines completely, but the process is interrupted so that the triangle is never completed.

Figure 11-25: Incomplete shape

Basic **11.4 Canvas**

With standard and custom shapes, we can add as many graphics as needed to the interface, but performance drops when too many views are required. To overcome these limitations, SwiftUI includes the `Canvas` view. This view is designed specifically for dynamic 2D drawing.

▷ **Canvas(opaque:** Bool, **colorMode:** ColorRenderingMode, **rendersAsynchronously:** Bool, **renderer:** Closure)—This initializer creates a `Canvas` view. The **opaque** argument determines whether the canvas is opaque (`true`) or transparent (`false`). The **colorMode** argument defines the color space used to draw the graphics. It is an enumeration with the values `extendedLinear`, `linear`, and `nonLinear`. The **rendersAsynchronously** argument determines whether the drawing is going to be made synchronously or asynchronously. And the **renderer** argument provides the graphics to be drawn. The closure receives two values, a `GraphicsContext` structure that represents the graphic context where all the drawing is performed, and a `CGSize` value with the canvas' width and height.

The closure assigned to the **Canvas** view provides an instance of the `GraphicsContext` structure that represents the drawing context. All the drawing is performed in this context from methods provided by the structure. The following are some of the methods available for drawing images.

▷ **draw(**Image, **at:** CGPoint, **anchor:** UnitPoint)—This method draws the image specified by the first argument. The **at** argument determines the position of the image in the context, and the **anchor** argument determines the origin of the image.

▷ **draw(**Image, **in:** CGRect, **style:** FillStyle)—This method draws the image specified by the first argument in the area specified by the **in** argument. The **style** argument determines the style of the image. It is a structure with the initializer `FillStyle(eoFill: Bool, antialiased: Bool)`.

The following are some of the methods available for drawing text.

▷ **draw(**Text, **at:** CGPoint, **anchor:** UnitPoint)—This method draws the text specified by the first argument. The **at** argument determines the position in the context, and the **anchor** argument determines the origin of the text.

▷ **draw(**Text, **in:** CGRect)—This method draws the text specified by the first argument within the area specified by the **in** argument. If there is not enough space in the area, the text is truncated.

And the following are the methods available for drawing paths.

▷ **stroke(**Path, **with:** Shading, **lineWidth:** CGFloat)—This method draws the path specified by the first argument. The **with** argument specifies the color or pattern used to stroke the path, and the **lineWidth** argument determines the width.

▷ **stroke(**Path, **with:** Shading, **style:** StrokeStyle)—This method draws the path specified by the first argument. The **with** argument specifies the color or pattern used to stroke the path, and the **style** argument determines the style (see Listing 11-4).

▷ **fill(**Path, **with:** Shading, **style:** FillStyle)—This method draws the path specified by the first arguments and fills the shape. The **with** argument specifies the color or pattern used to fill the shape, and the **style** argument determines the style. It is a structure with the initializer `FillStyle(eoFill: Bool, antialiased: Bool)`.

Paths are drawn with the colors and patterns specified by a `Shading` structure. The structure includes the following type methods to produced custom styles.

▷ **color(**Color)—This method returns a color. The argument is the `Color` view with the color we want to assign to the path.

▷ **color(red:** Double, **green:** Double, **blue:** Double, **opacity:** Double)—This method returns a color. The **red**, **green**, and **blue** arguments determine the levels of red, green, and blue with values from 0.0 (no color) to 1.0 (full color).

▷ **color(white:** Double, **opacity:** Double)—This method returns a color. The **white** argument determines the level of white with a value from 0.0 to 1.0 (black to white), and the **opacity** argument determines the level of opacity with a value from 0.0 (transparent) to 1.0 (opaque). The opacity may be ignored.

- **linearGradient(**Gradient, **startPoint:** CGPoint, **endPoint:** CGPoint)—This method returns a linear gradient. The first argument is the gradient of colors to be used, and the **startPoint** and **endPoint** arguments determine the points inside the shape where the gradient starts and ends.

- **radialGradient(**Gradient, **center:** CGPoint, **startRadius:** CGFloat, **endRadius:** CGFloat)—This method returns a circular gradient. The first argument is the gradient of colors to be used. The **center** argument determines the position of the center of the circle, and the **startRadius** and **endRadius** arguments determine where the gradient starts and ends.

- **conicGradient(**Gradient, **center:** CGPoint, **angle:** Angle)—This method returns a conic gradient. The first argument is the gradient of colors to be used. The **center** argument determines the position of the tip of the cone, and the **angle** argument determines the angle where the gradient begins.

- **tiledImage(**Image, **origin:** CGPoint, **sourceRect:** CGRect, **scale:** CGFloat)— This method draws the image specified by the first argument over and over again to cover the shape. The **origin** argument determines the point in the shape where the initial image is placed. The **sourceRect** argument determines the region of the original image we want to draw. And the **scale** argument defines the scale of the image.

By default, the canvas is non-opaque (the **opaque** argument is assigned the value **false**), the color mode is set to **nonLinear**, and the rendering is performed synchronously. If this configuration is enough for our app, we only need to declare the closure to render the graphics.

```
struct ContentView: View {
    var body: some View {
        Canvas { context, size in
            let imageFrame = CGRect(origin: .zero, size: size)
            context.draw(Image(.spot1), in: imageFrame)
        }.ignoresSafeArea()
    }
}
```

Listing 11-28: Drawing an image on the canvas

This example creates a **Canvas** view the size of the screen. (Notice the **ignoresSafeArea()** modifier at the end.) The **draw()** method takes a **CGRect** value and draws the image in that area. In this case, we decided to use the entire canvas, so we define a **CGRect** value with origin 0,0 and the size of the canvas, but we can also declare a specific size. For example, the image we are using in this example is 644 pixels wide and 864 pixels high. Using these values, we can define the **CGRect** value required to display the image at a smaller size.

```
struct ContentView: View {
    var body: some View {
        Canvas { context, size in
            let imageSize = CGSize(width: 161, height: 216)
            let posX = (size.width - imageSize.width) / 2
            let posY = posX

            let imageFrame = CGRect(x: posX, y: posY, width:
imageSize.width, height: imageSize.height)
            context.draw(Image(.spot1), in: imageFrame)
        }.ignoresSafeArea()
    }
}
```

Listing 11-29: Drawing an image on the canvas

In this example, we specify an area a quarter the size of the original image, and divide the remaining horizontal space by 2 to determine its position. The result is that the image is centered on the canvas.

Figure 11-26: *Image of a custom size*

Of course, we can also draw shapes, including standard and custom shapes and paths. For example, we can combine our image with graphics and text.

```
struct ContentView: View {
    var body: some View {
        Canvas { context, size in
            let imageFrame = CGRect(x: 60, y: 75, width: 215, height: 288)
            context.draw(Image(.spot1), in: imageFrame)

            let circleFrame = CGRect(x: 20, y: 50, width: 60, height: 60)
            context.fill(Circle().path(in: circleFrame),
with: .color(.yellow))

            let rectFrame = CGRect(x: 50, y: 60, width: 250, height: 40)
            context.fill(RoundedRectangle(cornerRadius: 25).path(in:
rectFrame), with: .color(.yellow))

            let textPos = CGPoint(x: 80, y: 80)
            context.draw(Text("My Picture").font(.title.bold()), at:
textPos, anchor: .leading)
        }.ignoresSafeArea()
    }
}
```

Listing 11-30: *Drawing shapes and text*

In this example we create a banner over the image with a circle, a rounded rectangle and a text. The result is shown below.

Figure 11-27: *Shapes and text on the canvas*

The **GraphicsContext** structure also includes methods to perform transformations on the canvas. The following are the most frequently used.

▷ **scaleBy(x:** CGFloat, **y:** CGFloat)—This method determines the horizontal and vertical scale of the canvas. By default, the scale is 1.0.

▷ **rotate(by:** Angle)—This method rotates the canvas the angle specified by the **by** argument.

▷ **translateBy(x:** CGFloat, **y:** CGFloat)—This method moves the point of origin of the canvas to the position determined by the **x** and **y** arguments.

These methods work like those previously implemented for shapes, but they only affect the matrix that the context uses to calculate the position and size of the graphics. For example, if we call the **rotate()** method on the context, the graphics already on the canvas will remain unchanged, only the graphics drawn afterwards will be rotated. As an example, we can draw two copies of the same image on the canvas. The first one is drawn on the default canvas and the second one is drawn after the canvas is rotated by 20 degrees.

```
struct ContentView: View {
    var body: some View {
        Canvas { context, size in
            let imageFrame = CGRect(x: 60, y: 75, width: 161, height: 216)
            context.draw(Image(.spot1), in: imageFrame)

            context.rotate(by: .degrees(20))
            context.draw(Image(.spot1), in: imageFrame)
        }.ignoresSafeArea()
    }
}
```

Listing 11-31: Rotating the canvas

As Figure 11-28 below shows, only the image drawn after applying the **rotate()** method is affected by the rotation; the previous image remains unchanged. This is because the transformation methods do not affect the canvas, but the matrix that the context uses to calculate how to draw the graphics.

Figure 11-28: Rotation

The rotation is about the origin of the canvas, which by default is at coordinates 0, 0 (upper left corner). If instead we want to rotate a graphic around its center, we must first move the origin to that position using the **translateBy()** method, as shown below.

```
struct ContentView: View {
    var body: some View {
        Canvas { context, size in
```

```
        context.translateBy(x: size.width/2, y: size.height/2)
        context.rotate(by: .degrees(45))
        let width = 161
        let height = 216
        let imageFrame = CGRect(x: -width/2, y: -height/2, width: width,
height: height)
        context.draw(Image(.spot1), in: imageFrame)
    }.ignoresSafeArea()
  }
}
```

Listing 11-32: Rotating an image

The code in Listing 11-32 moves the origin to the center of the canvas, rotates the canvas 45 degrees, and then calculates the position and size of the image. In this example, the image is displayed as before at one-quarter its original size, but the position is estimated with respect to the new origin. Since the origin of the image is at the position 0, 0 (upper-left corner) and we want to rotate the image around its center, we need to specify values that place the center of the image at the origin of the canvas, and this means using negative values. The horizontal position is minus half the width of the image (-85) and the vertical position is minus half the height (-108), so that the center of the image coincides with the origin of the canvas.

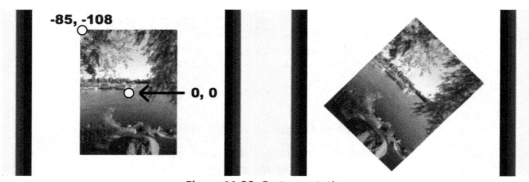

Figure 11-29: Custom rotation

Transformations are cumulative. This means that the transformations performed on the canvas are superimposed on the previous transformations. For example, if we rotate the canvas 45 degrees and then another 45 degrees, the final rotation is 90 degrees.

```
struct ContentView: View {
  var body: some View {
    Canvas { context, size in
      let imageFrame = CGRect(x: 0, y: 0, width: 100, height: 100)
      context.translateBy(x: size.width/2, y: size.height/2)
      for _ in 0..<10 {
        context.rotate(by: .degrees(36))
        context.draw(Image(.spot1), in: imageFrame)
      }
    }.ignoresSafeArea()
  }
}
```

Listing 11-33: Performing multiple transformations

In this example, we create a loop with 10 cycles (from 0 to 9). With each cycle, the context is rotated 36 degrees and then an image is drawn. Because the rotations are cumulative, the rotation of each image adds to the previous rotation to form a complete circle.

Figure 11-30: *Multiple rotations*

Drawing the same image multiple times affects performance. The system must prepare the image each time it is about to be drawn. To improve performance, we can prepare the image beforehand using the following method.

▷ **resolve(**Image**)**—This method returns an image that is configured according to the current context.

This method can also be used to prepare `Text` views and `Shading` values, but it is especially useful with images. The following example is the same as the previous one, but the image is resolved before drawing.

```
struct ContentView: View {
    var body: some View {
        Canvas { context, size in
            let imageReady = context.resolve(Image(.spot1))
            let imageFrame = CGRect(x: 0, y: 0, width: 100, height: 100)
            context.translateBy(x: size.width/2, y: size.height/2)
            for _ in 0..<10 {
                context.rotate(by: .degrees(36))
                context.draw(imageReady, in: imageFrame)
            }
        }.ignoresSafeArea()
    }
}
```

Listing 11-34: *Preparing images*

The **GraphicsContext** structure also includes the following method for creating a clipping mask that specifies which part of the canvas is available for drawing.

▷ **clip(to:** Path**)**—This method creates a clipping mask. Only the parts of the graphics inside the mask are drawn.

The following code applies a circular clipping mask to the canvas of the previous example, so that only the parts of the images that lie within the circle are drawn.

```
struct ContentView: View {
    var body: some View {
        Canvas { context, size in
            let imageFrame = CGRect(x: 0, y: 0, width: 100, height: 100)
            context.translateBy(x: size.width/2, y: size.height/2)

            let clipFrame = CGRect(x: -100, y: -100, width: 200, height: 200)
            context.clip(to: Circle().path(in: clipFrame))

            for _ in 0..<10 {
```

```
            context.rotate(by: .degrees(36))
            context.draw(Image(.spot1), in: imageFrame)
        }
    }.ignoresSafeArea()
    }
}
```

Listing 11-35: Clipping the canvas

Figure 11-31: Clipping mask

   In the previous examples, we applied the changes to the context one on top of the other. If we want to work with multiple configurations, we can create copies of the context. In the following example, an image is rotated in a copy of the context, but then additional graphics are drawn in the original context with default settings.

```
struct ContentView: View {
    var body: some View {
        Canvas { context, size in
            var copyContext = context
            copyContext.translateBy(x: size.width/2, y: size.height/2)
            copyContext.rotate(by: .degrees(45))
            let imageFrame = CGRect(x: -85, y: -108, width: 161, height: 216)
            copyContext.draw(Image(.spot1), in: imageFrame)

            let center = size.width/2
            let rectFrame = CGRect(x: center - 125, y: 160, width: 250,
height: 40)
            context.fill(RoundedRectangle(cornerRadius: 25).path(in:
rectFrame), with: .color(.yellow))

            let textPos = CGPoint(x: center, y: 180)
            context.draw(Text("My Picture").font(.title.bold()), at:
textPos, anchor: .center)
        }.ignoresSafeArea()
    }
}
```

Listing 11-36: Working with different configurations

Figure 11-32: Multiple configurations

Chapter 11 - Graphics and Animations

The **GraphicsContext** structure also allows us to filter the graphics. With filters, we can add effects and configure different aspects of the graphics, such as brightness, contrast, blur, and more. The structure includes the following method for applying a filter.

▷ **addFilter(**Filter**)**—This method applies a filter to the context. The argument defines the type of filter and its configuration. The structure includes multiple type methods to define standard filters. The most frequently used are **brightness(Double)**, **contrast(Double)**, **saturation(Double)**, **colorInvert(Double)**, **color-Multiply(Color)**, **hueRotation(Angle)**, **grayscale(Double)**, **blur(radius: CGFloat)**, and **shadow(color: Color, radius: CGFloat, x: CGFloat, y: CGFloat, blendMode: BlendMode, options: ShadowOptions)**.

Applying a filter is simple. We call the **addFilter()** method in the context for each effect we want to apply, and all the graphics drawn afterwards will be affected. The following example colors an image and blurs it.

```
struct ContentView: View {
    var body: some View {
        Canvas { context, size in
            context.addFilter(.colorMultiply(Color.red))
            context.addFilter(.blur(radius: 5))

            let margin = (size.width - 161) / 2
            let imageFrame = CGRect(x: margin, y: margin, width: 161,
height: 216)
            context.draw(Image(.spot1), in: imageFrame)
        }.ignoresSafeArea()
    }
}
```

***Listing 11-37:** Applying filters to the graphics*

***Figure 11-33:** Filters*

(Basic) **11.5 Charts**

In addition to the tools SwiftUI provides to create and display graphics on the screen, there is also a framework called Swift Charts that we can use to create a graphical representation of the user's data. Below is the structure that the framework provides for creating a chart.

▷ **Chart(**Data, **content:** Closure**)**—This initializer creates a view to display a chart. The first argument is the data we want to represent with the chart, and the **content** argument is the closure that returns the views required to create the chart.

Basic Mark Views

There are several predefined charts available. We can create a bar chart, a line chart, a point chart, and more. The graphics used to create these charts are called *Marks*. The following are the views that are included in the framework to create these marks and some of their initializers.

▷ **BarMark(x:** PlottableValue, **y:** PlottableValue)—This initializer creates a mark that represents the data with a bar. The **x** and **y** arguments represent the position and size of the bar in the chart's coordinates.

▷ **LineMark(x:** PlottableValue, **y:** PlottableValue)—This initializer creates a mark that represents the data with lines between points. The **x** and **y** arguments represent the position of the point that is going to be used to connect the lines.

▷ **PointMark(x:** PlottableValue, **y:** PlottableValue)—This initializer creates a mark that represents the data with points. The **x** and **y** arguments represent the position of the point in the chart's coordinates.

▷ **RectangleMark(x:** PlottableValue, **y:** PlottableValue, **width:** MarkDimension, **height:** MarkDimension)—This initializer creates a mark that represents the data with a rectangle. The **x** and **y** arguments represent the position of the rectangle, and the **width** and **height** arguments determine the size.

▷ **AreaMark(x:** PlottableValue, **y:** PlottableValue)—This initializer creates a mark that represents the data by filling the area below or between the points. The **x** and **y** arguments represent the position of the points used to calculate the area.

▷ **SectorMark(angle:** PlottableValue, **innerRadius:** MarkDimension, **outerRadius:** MarkDimension, **angularInset:** CGFloat?)—This initializer creates a mark that represents the data with a pie chart. The **angle** argument is a value that determines the proportional size of the sector or a range of values that specifies the start and end angles, the **innerRadius** argument specifies the inner radius of the pie chart, the **outerRadius** argument specifies the outer radius of the pie chart, and the **angularInset** argument determines the corner radius for each section.

▷ **RuleMark(x:** PlottableValue, **yStart:** PlottableValue, **yEnd:** PlottableValue)—This initializer creates a view that represents data with a single line. The **x** argument determines the position of the line in the **x** axis, and the **yStart** and **yEnd** arguments determine the position where the line begins and ends in the **y** axis.

The positions in the chart's coordinate system are determined by an instance of the `PlottableValue` structure. The structure includes the following type methods to return these values.

▷ **value(String, Value)**—This type method creates a value for a mark that represents quantitative data. The first argument is a custom string to describe the value, and the second argument is the value itself.

▷ **value(String, Date, unit:** Component, **calendar:** Calendar?)—This type method creates a value for a mark that represents dates. The first argument is a custom string to describe the value. The second argument specifies the date we are representing. The **unit** argument determines the component of the date we want to use to represent the data. And **calendar** is an optional argument we can use to specify the calendar that should be used to determine the date.

A chart can take quantitative values, such as integers, nominal values, such as strings, and temporal values, such as dates. Therefore, we can usually create charts directly from the user's data. For instance, we can use a model that includes food items and their calorie content.

```
import SwiftUI
import Observation

struct Consumables: Identifiable {
    let id = UUID()
    var name: String
    var category: String
    var calories: Int
}
@Observable class ApplicationData: @unchecked Sendable {
    var listOfItems: [Consumables]

    static let shared: ApplicationData = ApplicationData()
    private init() {
        listOfItems = [
            Consumables(name: "Bagels", category: "Baked", calories: 250),
            Consumables(name: "Brownies", category: "Baked", calories: 466),
            Consumables(name: "Butter", category: "Dairy", calories: 717),
            Consumables(name: "Cheese", category: "Dairy", calories: 402),
            Consumables(name: "Cookies", category: "Baked", calories: 502),
            Consumables(name: "Donuts", category: "Baked", calories: 452),
            Consumables(name: "Granola", category: "Baked", calories: 471)
        ]
    }
}
```

Listing 11-38: Providing the data for a chart

The syntax of the **Chart** view is similar to that of the **List** view. We can provide the data in the view initializer or use a **ForEach** loop and then build the views with the value received by the closure, as shown below.

```
import SwiftUI
import Charts

struct ContentView: View {
    @Environment(ApplicationData.self) private var appData

    var body: some View {
        VStack {
            Chart(appData.listOfItems) { item in
                BarMark(x: .value("Name", item.name), y: .value("Calories",
item.calories))
            }.frame(height: 300)
            .padding()
            Spacer()
        }
    }
}
#Preview {
    ContentView()
        .environment(ApplicationData.shared)
}
```

Listing 11-39: Visualizing data with a bar chart

Charts is a separate framework, so we need to import it with an **import** statement. Once we have access to the framework's views, we can create a chart. The **Chart** view generates a loop with the data in the model. In each cycle, the closure assigned to the **content** argument receives a value and creates the view that represents that value. In this example, we use a **BarMark** view to represent the values with bars. The value of the **name** property is assigned to the **x** axis and the number of calories is assigned to the **y** axis. This creates vertical bars, with the names of the foods under the bars and the calories on the side. However, we can easily reverse the axes by swapping the values. (The calories are assigned to the **x** axis and the name to the **y** axis). The result of both configurations is shown below.

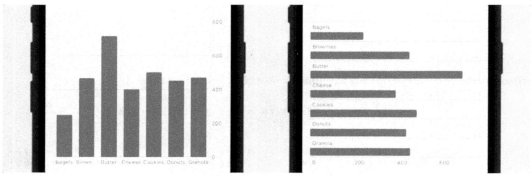

Figure 11-34: Bar Charts

If we want to create a different type of chart, we just need to replace the **BarMark** view with the desired view. For example, we can plot the same data with lines.

```
struct ContentView: View {
    @Environment(ApplicationData.self) private var appData

    var body: some View {
        VStack {
            Chart(appData.listOfItems) { item in
                LineMark(x: .value("Name", item.name), y: .value("Calories",
item.calories))
            }.frame(height: 300)
            .padding()
            Spacer()
        }
    }
}
```

Listing 11-40: Visualizing data with a line chart

This chart creates a line between the points in the plot area determined by the positions assigned to the names on the **x** axis and the calories on the **y** axis. If we want to display only the point, we can implement the **PointMark** view. The **RectangleMark** view represents the values with rectangles, and the **AreaMark** view fills the area under or between the points.

Figure 11-35: Line, Point, Rectangle, and Area charts

 Do It Yourself: Create a Multiplatform project. Create a Swift file called ApplicationData.swift for the model in Listing 11-38. Remember to inject the **ApplicationData** object into the environment for the app and the previews (Chapter 7, Listing 7-4). Update the ContentView.swift file with the code in Listing 11-39 and run the application. You should see a bar chart, as in Figure 11-34, left. Assign the value of the **calories** property to the **x** axis and the value of the **name** property to the **y** axis. Run the application again. You should see a chart with horizontal bars, as in Figure 11-34, right. Update the **ContentView** view with the code in Listing 11-40. Run the application again. You should see a line chart, as in Figure 11-35, left. Replace the **LineMark** view with the **PointMark**, **RectangleMark**, and **AreaMark** views. You should see on the screen the rest of the charts illustrated in Figure 11-35.

Basic — Chart Modifiers

The **View** protocol includes modifiers to customize the chart. The following are those defined to add graphics and views on top or behind the chart.

▷ **chartOverlay(alignment:** Alignment, **content:** Closure)—This modifier adds a view over the chart. The **alignment** argument specifies the alignment of the content. It is a structure with the type properties **bottom**, **bottomLeading**, **bottomTrailing**, **center**, **leading**, **top**, **topLeading**, **topTrailing**, and **trailing**. And the **content** argument defines the views to create the overlay.

▷ **chartBackground(alignment:** Alignment, **content:** Closure)—This modifier adds a view behind the chart. The **alignment** argument specifies the alignment of the content. It is a structure with the type properties **bottom**, **bottomLeading**, **bottom-Trailing**, **center**, **leading**, **top**, **topLeading**, **topTrailing**, and **trailing**. And the **content** argument defines the views to create the background.

The closure assigned to these modifiers receives a structure called **ChartProxy**. This structure contains properties and methods to return information about the chart. The most useful are those that return the position and size of the plot area. The **plotContainerFrame** property returns an **Anchor** structure with a **CGRect** value that specifies the position and size of the visible part of the plot area (not including the axes). The **plotFrame** property returns an **Anchor** structure with a **CGRect** value indicating the position and size of the currently visible part of the plot area (for scrollable charts), and the **plotSize** property returns a **CGSize** value indicating the area's width and height.

The values returned by some of the properties defined by the **ChartProxy** structure are **Anchor** structures that we need to process with a **GeometryProxy** structure to convert them to the coordinate space of the view. The following example shows how these values can be used to add an overlay at the center of the chart.

```
struct ContentView: View {
    @Environment(ApplicationData.self) private var appData

    var body: some View {
        VStack {
            Chart(appData.listOfItems) { item in
                BarMark(x: .value("Name", item.name), y: .value("Calories",
item.calories))
            }.frame(height: 300)
            .padding()
            .chartOverlay(content: { proxy in
                GeometryReader { geometry in
                    if let plotFrame = proxy.plotContainerFrame {
                        let frame = geometry[plotFrame]
                        VStack {
                            Text("My Chart")
                                .padding(30)
                        }
                        .background(.ultraThinMaterial, in: Capsule())
                        .position(x: frame.midX, y: frame.midY)
                    }
                }
            })
        } })
```

```
        Spacer()
      }
   }
}
```

Listing 11-41: Displaying an overlay

To obtain a **GeometryProxy**, we apply the **GeometryReader** to the view. First, we check if the **plotContainerFrame** property contains a value (the property returns **nil** if no chart is found), and then we get the frame in the view's coordinate space from the **GeometryProxy** structure. Using this value, we create a **VStack** with a **Text** view and display it at the center of the chart. The result is shown below.

Figure 11-36: Overlay

The **View** protocol also defines modifiers to configure the scale of the chart. The following are the most frequently used.

▷ **chartXScale(domain:** Domain, **range:** Range, **type:** ScaleType?**)**—This modifier defines the scale for the **x** axis. The **domain** argument specifies the possible values with a range for quantitative values and an array for nominal values. The **range** argument defines the positions corresponding to the scale values in the plot area. And the **type** value is a structure that determines the type of scale to use. The structure includes the type properties **category**, **date**, **linear**, and **log**. The protocol also defines the **chartYScale()** to modify the scale for the **y** axis.

▷ **chartForegroundStyleScale(**Dictionary**)**—This modifier assigns specific foreground styles to a scale of values. The argument is a dictionary with items that map the values to the styles.

The scale used to plot the values is automatically calculated by the **Chart** view based on the data. In the previous examples, the system set a scale between 0 and 800 because the calorie count in our model is estimated in the hundreds and is above 700. If we remove the "Butter" element, for example, the scale is now set from 0 to 600 because there are no more values greater than 600. If we don't want the scale to adapt to the data, we can implement the **chartXScale()** or **chartYScale()** modifiers to configure the axis. For example, if we know that all foods stored in our model have a maximum of 1000 calories, we can set a permanent scale between 0 and 1000.

```
struct ContentView: View {
   @Environment(ApplicationData.self) private var appData

   var body: some View {
      VStack {
         Chart(appData.listOfItems) { item in
            BarMark(x: .value("Name", item.name), y: .value("Calories",
item.calories))
```

```
        }
        .chartYScale(domain: 0...1000)
        .frame(height: 300)
        .padding()
        Spacer()
     }
   }
}
```

Listing 11-42: Defining a custom scale for the y axis

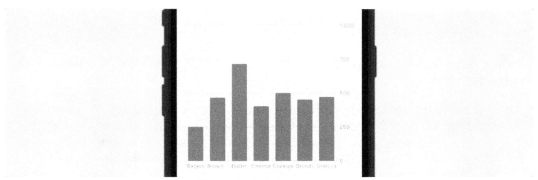

Figure 11-37: Custom scale

The views used to create the chart conform to the `ChartContent` protocol. This protocol defines many modifiers for configuring and styling the views. The following are the most frequently used.

- ▷ **foregroundStyle(**Style**)**—This modifier sets the color or style of the mark.
- ▷ **foregroundStyle(by:** PlottableValue**)**—This modifier assigns different foreground styles to the marks based on a value. The **by** argument specifies the value to consider when assigning the styles.
- ▷ **opacity(**Double**)**—This modifier sets the mark's opacity.
- ▷ **cornerRadius(**CGFloat, **style:** RoundedCornerStyle**)**—This modifier sets the corner radius of each mark. The first argument determines the radius, and the **style** argument specifies the style. It is an enumeration with the values **circular** and **continuous**.

The `ChartContent` protocol also defines modifiers to style the elements in a chart, such as the lines and symbols. The following are the most frequently used.

- ▷ **symbol(by:** PlottableValue**)**—This modifier assigns different symbols to the points in a chart based on a value. The **by** argument specifies the value to consider when assigning the symbols.
- ▷ **symbolSize(**CGFloat**)**—This modifier sets the size of the symbols that represent the points in the chart. The argument specifies the size of the area occupied by the symbol.
- ▷ **lineStyle(**StrokeStyle**)**—This modifier defines the style of the line.
- ▷ **interpolationMethod(**InterpolationMethod**)**—This modifier determines the style used to join the points when the chart contains lines or area marks. The argument is a structure with the type properties **cardinal**, **catmullRom**, **linear**, **monotone**, **stepCenter**, **stepEnd**, and **stepStart**.
- ▷ **chartLegend(**Visibility**)**—This modifier displays or hides the labels below the chart. The argument is an enumeration with the values **automatic**, **visible** and **hidden**.

There are also modifiers to set the position of the content. The following are the most frequently used.

▷ **position(by:** PlottableValue, **axis:** Axis?, **span:** MarkDimension)—This modifier assigns a position for the marks. The **by** argument determines the value used to identify the marks. The **axis** argument specifies the axis used to position the marks. It is an enumeration with the values `horizontal` and `vertical`. And the **span** argument determines the space available for the marks. It is a structure with the type methods `fixed(CGFloat)`, `inset(CGFloat)`, and `ratio(CGFloat)`.

▷ **offset(x:** CGFloat, **y:** CGFloat)—This modifier moves the marks by the offset specified by the arguments.

The protocol also includes modifiers to add labels and views to the chart. The following is the most frequently used.

▷ **annotation(position:** AnnotationPosition, **alignment:** Alignment, **spacing:** CGFloat?, **content:** Closure)—This modifier adds an annotation to the line. The **position** argument specifies the position of the annotation in the plot area. It is a structure with the type properties `automatic`, `bottom`, `bottomLeading`, `bottomTrailing`, `leading`, `overlay`, `top`, `topLeading`, `topTrailing`, and `trailing`. The alignment argument aligns the annotation in relation to the line. It is a structure with the type properties `leading`, `center`, and `trailing`. The **spacing** argument defines the space between the line and the annotation. And the **content** argument provides the views to create the annotation.

Some of these modifiers apply to any view but others are more specific. For example, the `foregroundStyle(by:)` modifier is particularly useful with the `SectorMark` structure. This structure creates a pie chart, and therefore the sectors are only distinguishable if they are drawn in different colors. In the following example, we use this modifier and the names of the foods to determine the colors of the sectors.

```
struct ContentView: View {
    @Environment(ApplicationData.self) private var appData

    var body: some View {
        VStack {
            Chart(appData.listOfItems) { item in
                SectorMark(angle: .value("Value", item.calories))
                    .foregroundStyle(by: .value("Product category",
item.name))
            }.frame(height: 300)
            .padding()
            Spacer()
        }
    }
}
```

Listing 11-43: Assigning different styles based on a value

The **Chart** view checks the values and assigns a different color to each one of them (the colors are automatically assigned by the system). Note that the chart also creates labels at the bottom to inform the user what the colors represent.

Chapter 11 - Graphics and Animations

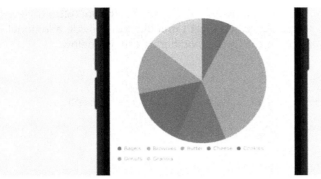

Figure 11-38: *Different styles per value*

Some of the modifiers provided by the **ChartContent** protocol are useful when multiple types of marks are used to represent the values. For example, if lines and points are to be used, the graphics representing the points can be enlarged to make them more visible.

```
struct ContentView: View {
    @Environment(ApplicationData.self) private var appData

    var body: some View {
        VStack {
            Chart(appData.listOfItems) { item in
                LineMark(x: .value("Name", item.name), y: .value("Calories",
item.calories))
                    .interpolationMethod(.catmullRom)
                PointMark(x: .value("Name", item.name), y: .value("Calories",
item.calories))
                    .foregroundStyle(by: .value("Category", item.category))
                    .symbol(by: .value("Category", item.category))
                    .symbolSize(200)
            }.frame(height: 300)
            .padding()
            Spacer()
        }
    }
}
```

Listing 11-44: *Representing the values with different types of marks*

In this example, we apply an interpolation of type **catmullRom** to the **LineMark** view to smooth the lines. For the points, we apply a different color for each category using the **foregroundStyle(by:)** modifier, just as we did for the pie chart in the previous example. We also assign a different symbol to each category with the **symbol()** modifier, and finally enlarge the symbols with the **symbolSize()** modifier. The result can be seen below.

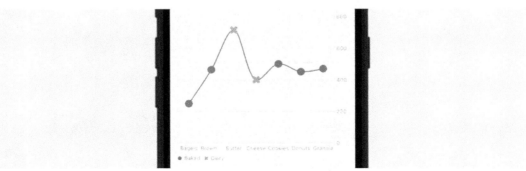

Figure 11-39: *Multiple mark styles*

Other modifiers are useful for certain views. For example, the `RuleMark` view draws a line above or behind the chart and needs to work with modifiers to provide additional information, such as the `lineStyle()` and `annotation()` modifiers, as shown below.

```
struct ContentView: View {
    @Environment(ApplicationData.self) private var appData

    var body: some View {
        VStack {
            Chart {
                ForEach(appData.listOfItems) { item in
                    BarMark(x: .value("Name", item.name),
y: .value("Calories", item.calories))
                        .foregroundStyle(.cyan)
                        .opacity(0.5)
                        .cornerRadius(20)
                }
                RuleMark(y: .value("Average", averageCalories()))
                    .foregroundStyle(.black)
                    .lineStyle(StrokeStyle(lineWidth: 5))
                    .annotation(position: .top, alignment: .leading) {
                        Text("Average Calories")
                    }
            }.frame(height: 300)
            .padding()
            Spacer()
        }
    }
    func averageCalories() -> Int {
        let total = appData.listOfItems.reduce(0, { $0 + $1.calories })
        return total / appData.listOfItems.count
    }
}
```

Listing 11-45: *Drawing a line in the plot area*

In this example, the `Chart` view creates the chart, but the marks are generated by a `ForEach` loop. After this loop, we define a `RuleMark` view to draw a horizontal line across the chart. (To draw the line behind the chart, we need to declare the `RuleMark` view before the `ForEach` view.) To calculate the line's vertical position, we define a method called `averageCalories()` that returns the average number of calories of all the items in the model.

For the design, we set a line width of 5 points and add an annotation at the top with the string "Average Calories". Note that we also implemented some modifiers to design the marks, including a color for the bars, opacity, and round corners. The result can be seen below.

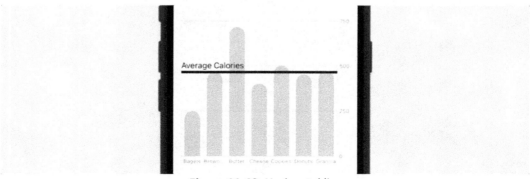

Figure 11-40: *Horizontal line*

(Basic) Selection

A `Chart` view can also allow the user to select a value. The selection is made by pressing and holding or dragging the finger over the plot area or, on Mac computers, by moving the mouse over the chart. The view determines where the finger or mouse is currently located and stores the value in a binding property that we can later use to perform a task or display additional information to the user. The `View` protocol includes the following modifiers to enable this feature.

- ▷ **chartXSelection(value:** Binding**)**—This modifier allows the selection of values on the **x** axis. The **value** argument is the binding property to be used to store the selected value. The protocol also defines the `chartYSelection(value:)` modifier to enable selection for the **y** axis.

- ▷ **chartXSelection(range:** Binding**)**—This modifier allows the selection of a range of values on the **x** axis. The **range** argument is the binding property to be used to store the range of selected values. The protocol also defines the `chartYSelection(range:)` modifier to enable selection for the **y** axis.

- ▷ **chartAngleSelection(value:** Binding**)**—This modifier allows selection of values on pie charts. The **value** argument is the binding property to be used to store the selected value.

The implementation is simple. We need a `@State` property to store the value selected by the user, apply the modifier with this property to enable selection, and then do something with the value. In the following example, we use the property's value to change the color of the selected bar.

```
struct ContentView: View {
    @Environment(ApplicationData.self) private var appData
    @State private var selectedFood: String? = nil

    var body: some View {
        VStack {
            Chart(appData.listOfItems) { item in
                BarMark(x: .value("Name", item.name), y: .value("Calories",
item.calories))
                    .foregroundStyle(item.name ==
selectedFood ? .yellow : .blue)
            }
            .frame(height: 300)
            .padding()
            .chartXSelection(value: $selectedFood)
            Spacer()
        }
    }
}
```

Listing 11-46: Selecting a value

In our model, the values for the **x** axis are names of food, so we declare a `@State` property of type `String` to store this value, and then compare the value used to create each bar with the value selected by the user. If they match, the bar is colored yellow, otherwise the bar is blue.

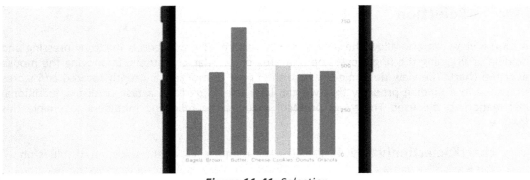

Figure 11-41: *Selection*

(Medium) **Plot Views**

Mark views are well suited for small data sets. To display large amounts of data, SwiftUI includes the following views to create vectorized plots.

▷ **BarPlot(**Collection, **x:** PlottableProjection, **y:** PlottableProjection, **width:** MarkDimensions, **height:** MarkDimensions, **stacking:** MarkStacking-Method**)**—This initializer creates a plot view to represent a large dataset with bars. The first argument is the dataset with the values we want to display, the **x** and **y** arguments represent the position of the point in the chart's coordinates, the **width** and **height** arguments determine the thickness of the bars in horizontal and vertical orientation, and the **stacking** argument is a structure with the properties `center`, `normalized`, `standard` and `unstacked` to determine how the graphics are stacked.

▷ **LinePlot(**Collection, **x:** PlottableProjection, **y:** PlottableProjection, **series:** PlottableProjection**)**—This initializer creates a plot view to represent a large dataset with lines. The first argument is the dataset with the values we want to display, the **x** and **y** arguments represent the position of the point in the chart's coordinates, and the **series** argument is the value used to create regions in the chart.

▷ **PointPlot(**Collection, **x:** PlottableProjection, **y:** PlottableProjection**)**—This initializer creates a plot view to represent a large dataset with points. The first argument is the dataset with the values we want to display, and the **x** and **y** arguments represent the position of the point in the chart's coordinates.

▷ **RectanglePlot(**Collection, **x:** PlottableProjection, **y:** PlottableProjection, **width:** MarkDimensions, **height:** MarkDimensions**)**—This initializer creates a plot view to represent a large dataset with rectangles. The first argument is the dataset with the values we want to display, the **x** and **y** arguments represent the position of the point in the chart's coordinates, and the **width** and **height** arguments determine the size of the rectangles.

▷ **AreaPlot(**Collection, **x:** PlottableProjection, **y:** PlottableProjection, **series:** PlottableProjection, **stacking:** MarkStackingMethod**)**—This initializer creates a plot view to represent a large dataset by filling the area below or between the points. The first argument is the dataset with the values we want to display, the **x** and **y** arguments represent the position of the point in the chart's coordinates, the **series** argument is the value used to create regions in the chart, and the **stacking** argument is a structure with the properties `center, normalized, standard`, and `unstacked` to determine how the regions are going to be stacked.

▷ **SectorPlot(**Collection, **angle:** PlottableProjection, **innerRadius:** Mark-Dimensions, **outerRadius:** MarkDimensions, **angularInset:** CGFloat?**)**—

This initializer creates a plot view that represents a large dataset with a pie chart. The first argument is the dataset with the values we want to display, the **angle** argument determines the proportional size of the sector, the **innerRadius** argument specifies the inner radius of the pie chart, the **outerRadius** argument specifies the outer radius of the pie chart, and the **angularInset** argument determines the corner radius for each section.

▷ **RulePlot(**Collection, **xStart:** PlottableProjection, **xEnd:** Plottable-Projection, **y:** PlottableProjection**)**—This initializer creates a plot view that represents a large dataset with a single line. The first argument is the dataset with the values we want to display, the **xStart** and **xEnd** arguments determine the position where the line begins and ends in the **x** axis, and the **y** argument determines the vertical position of the line.

These views are applied in the same way as the mark views we have seen before, but they take care of reading and processing the values, as shown in the following example.

```
struct ContentView: View {
    @Environment(ApplicationData.self) private var appData

    var body: some View {
        VStack {
            Chart {
                PointPlot(appData.listOfItems, x: .value("Food", \.name),
y: .value("Calories", \.calories))
            }.frame(height: 300)
            .padding()
            Spacer()
        }
    }
}
```

Listing 11-47: Visualizing large datasets with a point plot

The **LinePlot** and **AreaPlot** views can not only display large datasets, but also plot mathematical functions. The following are the initializers.

▷ **LinePlot(x:** String, **y:** String, **domain:** Range, Closure**)**—This initializer creates a plot view to visualize a single mathematical function. The **x** and **y** arguments provide the labels for the **x** and **y** axes, the **domain** argument limits the domain of the function, and the last argument is a closure that provides the function to be plotted.

▷ **AreaPlot(x:** String, **yStart:** String, **yEnd:** String, **domain:** Range, Closure**)** —This initializer creates a plot view to visualize the area covered by a mathematical function. The **x**, **yStart**, and **yEnd** arguments provide the labels for the chart, the **domain** argument limits the domain of the function, and the last argument is a closure that provides the function to be plotted.

The following example plots a mathematical function that returns the sine of every given value.

```
struct ContentView: View {
    @Environment(ApplicationData.self) private var appData

    var body: some View {
        VStack {
            Chart {
                LinePlot(x: "x", y: "y") { x in
                    sin(x)
                }
```

```
        }
        .chartXScale(domain: -5...5)
        .chartYScale(domain: -5...5)
        .frame(width: 300, height: 300)
        Spacer()
      }
    }
  }
}
```

Listing 11-48: *Plotting a mathematical function*

To display the part of the function we want, we need to apply the **chartXScale()** and **chartYScale()** modifiers with the **domain** argument. In this case, we limit the function in both axes to the values -5 and 5.

Figure 11-42: *Chart representing a mathematical function*

(Basic) **Multiple Marks**

A **Chart** view can present multiple series of values. The process is similar than before, but we need to organize the data in the model depending on what we want to achieve. The following example shows a possible implementation. In this model, there is a structure to store the date and number of items sold (**Sales**), and another to store the sales per item (**Products**). To test the application, we initialize it with two products, Bagels and Brownies, and one week of sales each.

```
import SwiftUI
import Observation
struct Sales: Identifiable {
   let id = UUID()
   var date: Date
   var amount: Int
}
struct Products: Identifiable {
   let id = UUID()
   var name: String
   var sales: [Sales]
}
@Observable class ApplicationData: @unchecked Sendable {
   var sales: [Products]

   static let shared: ApplicationData = ApplicationData()
   private init() {
      let salesBagels = [
         Sales(date: Date(timeInterval: -86400 * 7, since: Date()),
amount: 10),
         Sales(date: Date(timeInterval: -86400 * 6, since: Date()),
amount: 12),
         Sales(date: Date(timeInterval: -86400 * 5, since: Date()),
amount: 8),
```

```
        Sales(date: Date(timeInterval: -86400 * 4, since: Date()),
amount: 13),
        Sales(date: Date(timeInterval: -86400 * 3, since: Date()),
amount: 9),
        Sales(date: Date(timeInterval: -86400 * 2, since: Date()),
amount: 7),
        Sales(date: Date(timeInterval: -86400 * 1, since: Date()),
amount: 8) ]
    let salesBrownies = [
        Sales(date: Date(timeInterval: -86400 * 7, since: Date()),
amount: 3),
        Sales(date: Date(timeInterval: -86400 * 6, since: Date()),
amount: 5),
        Sales(date: Date(timeInterval: -86400 * 5, since: Date()),
amount: 2),
        Sales(date: Date(timeInterval: -86400 * 4, since: Date()),
amount: 8),
        Sales(date: Date(timeInterval: -86400 * 3, since: Date()),
amount: 6),
        Sales(date: Date(timeInterval: -86400 * 2, since: Date()),
amount: 5),
        Sales(date: Date(timeInterval: -86400 * 1, since: Date()),
amount: 9) ]
    sales = [
        Products(name: "Bagels", sales: salesBagels),
        Products(name: "Brownies", sales: salesBrownies) ]
    }
}
```

Listing 11-49: Representing the values with different types of marks

To create the chart, we must iterate through the items and then through the sales for each item, so we need two **ForEach** loops.

```
struct ContentView: View {
    @Environment(ApplicationData.self) private var appData

    var body: some View {
        VStack {
            Chart {
                ForEach(appData.sales) { product in
                    ForEach(product.sales) { sale in
                        LineMark(x: .value("Date", sale.date, unit: .day),
y: .value("Sales", sale.amount))
                        }.foregroundStyle(by: .value("Products", product.name))
                    }
                }.frame(height: 300)
                .padding()
                Spacer()
            }
        }
    }
}
```

Listing 11-50: Visualizing two series of values

This example creates a line chart. The first **ForEach** loop gets the products from the **sales** property in the model and then reads the **sales** property of each product to visualize the sales. Because we use dates to define the **x** axis, we implement the **value()** method to specify the date and the unit we want to use to represent the value (**day**). As a result, we get two line charts, one for Bagels and another for Brownies.

Figure 11-43: Multiple series of values

In a line chart, the series of values are independent, but bar and area charts add the marks on top of each other to display the total per value, as shown in the following example.

```
struct ContentView: View {
    @Environment(ApplicationData.self) private var appData

    var body: some View {
        VStack {
            Chart {
                ForEach(appData.sales) { product in
                    ForEach(product.sales) { sale in
                        BarMark(x: .value("Date", sale.date, unit: .day),
y: .value("Sales", sale.amount))
                        }.foregroundStyle(by: .value("Products", product.name))
                }
            }.chartForegroundStyleScale([
                "Bagels": .red,
                "Brownies": .orange
            ])
            .frame(height: 300)
            .padding()
            Spacer()
        }
    }
}
```

Listing 11-51: Visualizing two series of values with a bar chart

In this chart, we replace the **LineMark** view with a **BarMark** view, but we also implement the **chartForegroundStyleScale()** modifier to assign custom colors to the bars. The modifier takes a dictionary. The keys are the values used by the **foregroundStyle(by:)** modifier to identify each series of values, and the values are the styles we want to assign to the bars. (In this case, the color red for Bagels and orange for Brownies).

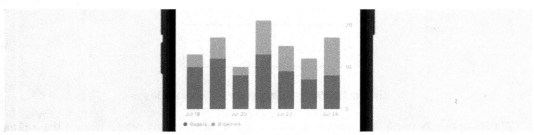

Figure 11-44: Bar chart with two series of values

By default, the bars are added to show the total, but we can use the **position()** modifier to adjust the position. In the following example, we specify a different position for each product and separate the bars with a space.

```
struct ContentView: View {
   @Environment(ApplicationData.self) private var appData

   var body: some View {
      VStack {
         Chart {
            ForEach(appData.sales) { product in
               ForEach(product.sales) { sale in
                  BarMark(x: .value("Date", sale.date, unit: .day),
y: .value("Sales", sale.amount))
               }.foregroundStyle(by: .value("Products", product.name))
               .position(by: .value("Product", product.name))
            }
         }.frame(height: 300)
         .padding()
         Spacer()
      }
   }
}
```

Listing 11-52: Defining the positions of the bars

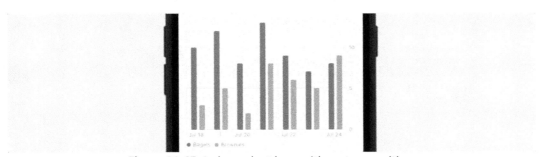

Figure 11-45: Independent bars with custom positions

 IMPORTANT: The Charts framework includes additional tools to customize the charts and achieve any layout we need. There are also initializers for the marks that we can use to provide maximum and minimum values to limit the graphics. The topic is beyond the scope of this book. For more information, visit our website and follow the links for this chapter.

(Basic) Scrolling

Models often store long lists of values. It would be unreasonable to try to create a chart that displays all of these values on the screen at once. For a better presentation, we can enable scrolling. The **view** protocol defines the following modifiers for this purpose.

▷ **chartScrollableAxes(Axis)**—This modifier enables scrolling for the axis specified by the argument. The argument is an enumeration with the values **horizontal** and **vertical**. It can take a set to enable scrolling for both axes.

▷ **chartXVisibleDomain(length: Value)**—This modifier determines the number of values to present per screen on the **x** axis. The **length** argument determines the length of the range of values to be displayed. The protocol defines the **chartYVisible-Domain(length:)** modifier for the **y** axis.

▷ **chartScrollPosition(x: Binding)**—This modifier determines the scrolling position in the **x** axis and stores it in a binding property. The protocol includes the **chartScroll-Position(y:)** modifier for the **y** axis.

▷ **chartScrollTargetBehavior(**ChartScrollTargetBehavior**)**—This modifier determines the scrolling behavior. The argument is a structure that conforms to the **ChartScrollTargetBehavior** protocol. The protocol includes several type methods called **valueAligned()** with different parameters to determine the behavior according to the values represented by the chart.

The last example in the previous section displays the bars side by side, and so the width of the bars is reduced to fit the available space, but we can make them look better by displaying a few at a time and allowing the user to scroll the chart, as shown below.

```
struct ContentView: View {
    @Environment(ApplicationData.self) private var appData

    var body: some View {
        VStack {
            Chart {
                ForEach(appData.sales) { product in
                    ForEach(product.sales) { sale in
                        BarMark(x: .value("Date", sale.date, unit: .day),
y: .value("Sales", sale.amount))
                    }.foregroundStyle(by: .value("Products", product.name))
                    .position(by: .value("Product", product.name))
                }
            }.frame(height: 300)
            .chartLegend(.hidden)
            .chartScrollableAxes(.horizontal)
            .chartXVisibleDomain(length: 3600 * 24 * 4)
            .padding()
            Spacer()
        }
    }
}
```

Listing 11-53: *Scrolling the chart*

In this example, we implement the **chartScrollableAxes()** modifier to make the chart scrollable on the **x** axis, and then use the **chartXVisibleDomain()** modifier to tell the **Chart** view how many bars to display at a time. Since the **x** axis in our model is determined by **Date** values, we calculate the number of seconds in four days to display four days at a time (3600 * 24 * 4).

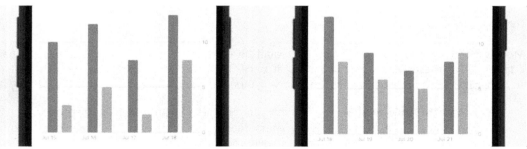

Figure 11-46: *Scrollable chart*

Basic 11.6 Image Renderer

All the graphics and charts we defined in the previous examples are created on the spot. If we want to recreate a graphic or a complex view, we have to redraw every line and circle. But sometimes we need to reuse a graphic or save it to a file or a database. In such cases, we can convert the view into an image. SwiftUI includes the **ImageRenderer** class for this purpose.

Chapter 11 - Graphics and Animations

▷ **ImageRenderer(content:** View)—This initializer creates an image from the view specified by the **content** argument.

The image is created by the `ImageRenderer` object and then returned by its properties. Three properties are available: `uiImage` returns a `UIImage` object (UIKit), `cgImage` returns a `CGImage` object (Core Graphics), and `nsImage` returns an `NSImage` object (Appkit).

To convert a view into an image, we need to store the view in a property so we can use that property to reference the view from the `ImageRenderer`'s initializer. For instance, the following example defines a separate view called `NewPictureView` with an `Image` view that presents a circular image. The view is stored in a property called `newPicture` which we use to display it on the screen and then convert it to a `UIImage` object.

```
struct ContentView: View {
    @State private var pattern: UIImage?
    let newPicture = NewPictureView()

    var body: some View {
        VStack {
            newPicture
            Button("Export Image") {
                let renderer = ImageRenderer(content: newPicture)
                if let img = renderer.uiImage {
                    pattern = img.preparingThumbnail(of: CGSize(width: 25,
height: 25))
                }
            }
            if let pattern {
                Image(uiImage: pattern)
                    .resizable(resizingMode: .tile)
                    .frame(width: 200, height: 200)
            }
            Spacer()
        }
    }
}
struct NewPictureView: View {
    var body: some View {
        Image(.spot1)
            .resizable()
            .scaledToFit()
            .frame(width: 150, height: 200)
            .clipShape(Circle())
    }
}
```

Listing 11-54: Creating an image from a view

The interface includes a button. When the button is pressed, we create the `ImageRenderer` object from the view in the `newPicture` property and read the `uiImage` property to get the `UIImage` object with the new image. Once we have this object, we can process it like any other. In this example, we shrink it to 25 by 25 points using the `preparingThumbnail()` method and create a pattern with an `Image` view in the `tile` resizing mode. The result is shown below.

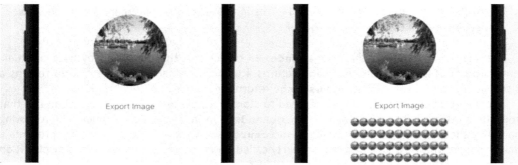

Figure 11-47: *Custom image*

 Do It Yourself: Create a Multiplatform project. Update the ContentView.swift file with the code in Listing 11-54. Download the spot1.jpg image from our website and add it to the Asset Catalog. Press the Export Image button. You should see the rectangle filled with a pattern created with the new image (Figure 11-47).

Basic 11.7 Animations

SwiftUI automatically animates views when they change or transition to a new view, but not always. To create our own animations, the framework includes the following functions.

▷ **withAnimation(**Animation?, Closure**)**—This function performs an animation and returns the result. The first argument defines the type of animation to use (if ignored, the animation is defined as **default**). The second argument specifies the closure that performs the changes we want to animate.

▷ **withAnimation(**Animation?, **completionCriteria:** AnimationCompletion-Criteria, Closure, **completion:** Closure**)**—This function performs an animation and executes a closure when finished. The first argument defines the type of animation to use (if ignored, the animation is defined as **default**). The **completionCriteria** argument determines when the animation is considered to be completed. It is a structure with the properties **logicallyComplete** (the animation is complete when the logical process is over) and **removed** (the animation is complete when the entire process is over). The third argument is the closure that performs the changes we want to animate, and the **completion** argument is the closure we want to execute after completion.

These functions apply the animation to the states, but the animation is determined by an instance of the **Animation** structure. The structure provides properties and methods to create and configure the animation, including the following type properties to define standard animations.

▷ **default**—This type property returns the animation defined by the system by default.

▷ **easeIn**—This type property returns an animation that is slow at the beginning and faster at the end.

▷ **easeInOut**—This type property returns an animation that is slow at the beginning and the end.

▷ **easeOut**—This type property returns an animation that is fast at the beginning and slow at the end.

▷ **linear**—This type property returns an animation that is always performed at the same speed.

The animation returned by the value **default** is a spring animation with a specific configuration (a response of 0.55, a damping fraction of 1.0, and a blend duration of 0.0). The **Animation** structure includes the following properties to specify spring animations with different configurations.

- ▷ **bouncy**—This type property returns a spring animation with a predefined duration and a high bounce effect.
- ▷ **smooth**—This type property returns a spring animation with a predefined duration and no bounce effect.
- ▷ **snappy**—This type property returns a spring animation with a predefined duration and a small bounce effect that feels more snappy.

The **withAnimation()** function asks the system to perform an animation if a state changes. For example, if a state modifies the opacity of the view, SwiftUI calculates the values between the initial opacity and the new, and then recreates the view for each of those values to produce every frame of the animation. The process is easy to implement. We set the new state, declare the type of animation we want, and SwiftUI takes care of producing the animation. For example, we can change the scale of a **Rectangle** view from 1 to 2 when a button is pressed, but if we do it in the closure of the **withAnimation()** function, the change is animated.

```
struct ContentView: View {
    @State private var boxScale: CGFloat = 1

    var body: some View {
        VStack {
            HStack {
                Rectangle()
                    .fill(Color.blue)
                    .frame(width: 50, height: 50)
                    .scaleEffect(boxScale)
            }.frame(width: 250, height: 120)
            Button("Animate") {
                withAnimation(.default) {
                    boxScale = 2
                }
            }
        }.padding()
    }
}
```

Listing 11-55: Animating a view

This view defines a **@State** property of type **CGFloat** with the value 1, uses this value to define the scale of a **Rectangle** view with the **scaleEffect()** modifier, and provides a button to change it. When the button is pressed, we assign the value 2 to the property, expanding the view, but because the assignment is done within an animation closure, the change is animated.

Figure 11-48: Animation by default

The animation in this example is of type **default**, which on most systems is set as an **easeInOut** animation, but we can specify a different type if we think it will look better on our interface. The following example applies a **linear** animation instead.

```
Button("Animate") {
   withAnimation(.linear) {
      boxScale = 2
   }
}
```

Listing 11-56: Applying a linear animation

 Do It Yourself: Create a Multiplatform project. Update the **ContentView** view with the code in Listing 11-55. Press the Animate button. You should see the blue square grow, as shown in Figure 11-48. Specify another type of animation as we did in Listing 11-56 to see the difference between one type and another.

The duration of a standard animation is set by default, but the **Animation** structure includes the following methods to specify our own.

▷ **easeIn(duration: Double)**—This type method creates an **easeIn** animation with the duration determined by the argument.

▷ **easeInOut(duration: Double)**—This type method creates an **easeInOut** animation with the duration determined by the argument.

▷ **easeOut(duration: Double)**—This type method creates an **easeOut** animation with the duration determined by the argument.

▷ **linear(duration: Double)**—This type method creates a **linear** animation with the duration determined by the argument.

There are also methods available to customize spring animations.

▷ **bouncy(duration: TimeInterval, extraBounce: Double)**—This type method creates a **bouncy** animation with the duration specified by the **duration** argument and an additional bounce effect specified by the **extraBounce** argument.

▷ **smooth(duration: TimeInterval, extraBounce: Double)**—This type method creates a **smooth** animation with the duration specified by the **duration** argument and an additional bounce effect specified by the **extraBounce** argument.

▷ **snappy(duration: TimeInterval, extraBounce: Double)**—This type method creates a **snappy** animation with the duration specified by the **duration** argument and an additional bounce effect specified by the **extraBounce** argument.

For example, we can run the previous animation for 5 seconds.

```
Button("Animate") {
   withAnimation(.linear(duration: 5)) {
      boxScale = 2
   }
}
```

Listing 11-57: Declaring a specific duration

The **Animation** structure also includes the following methods to set the animation's behavior.

▷ **delay(Double)**—This method sets the seconds the animator waits before starting the animation.

▷ **repeatCount(**Int, **autoreverses:** Bool**)**—This method sets the number of times the animator performs an animation. The first argument determines the number of animations to be performed, and the **autoreverses** argument determines if the process of going back to the initial state is going to be animated as well (**true** by default).

▷ **repeatForever(autoreverses:** Bool**)**—This method determines if the animator is going to perform the animation indefinitely. The **autoreverses** argument determines if the process of going back to the initial state is going to be animated as well (**true** by default).

▷ **speed(**Double**)**—This method sets the speed of the animation (1 by default).

These methods are applied to the **Animation** structure, similar to how modifiers are applied to views. We create the **Animation** structure, call the methods to configure the animation, and then apply it to the state with the **withAnimation()** method, as in the following example.

```
Button("Animate") {
    let animation = Animation.bouncy
        .delay(1)
        .speed(2)
        .repeatCount(3)
    withAnimation(animation) {
        boxScale = 2
    }
}
```

Listing 11-58: Configuring the animation

This animation is delayed by 1 second, reproduced at twice the normal speed, and repeated 3 times. Note that by default, the **repeatCount()** method defines the auto-reverse option to **true**. This means that the view is going to animate back to its initial state. But because we specified 3 cycles, the animation is going forward and backward a total of 3 times (forward, backward, and forward again).

 Do It Yourself: Update the **Button** view in the **ContentView** view with the code in Listing 11-58. Press the Animate button. You should see that the square is animated twice forwards and once backwards.

Standard animations are enough for most applications, but the **Animation** structure also includes the possibility to set any parameter we need. The following are some of the methods available to create custom animations.

▷ **spring(duration:** TimeInterval, **bounce:** Double, **blendDuration:** Double**)** —This type method creates a spring animation. The **duration** argument specifies the duration of the animation, the **bounce** argument specifies the bounce effect, and the **blendDuration** argument determines the time it takes for the animation to stop and the next animation to begin.

▷ **spring(response:** Double, **dampingFraction:** Double, **blendDuration:** Double**)**—This type method creates a spring animation. The **response** argument determines the duration of one animation period, the **dampingFraction** argument determines the amount of oscillation, and the **blendDuration** argument determines the time it takes for the animation to stop and the next animation to begin.

▷ **interpolatingSpring(duration:** TimeInterval, **bounce:** Double, **initialVelocity:** Double**)**—This type method creates a spring animation that combines the values with previous animations. The **duration** argument determines the duration of the animation, the **bounce** argument specifies the bounce effect, and the **initialVelocity** argument determines the initial velocity of the animation.

- **interpolatingSpring(mass: Double, stiffness: Double, damping: Double, initialVelocity: Double)**—This type method creates a spring animation that combines the values with previous animations. The **mass** argument determines the mass we want to assign to the view, the **stiffness** argument determines the stiffness of the spring, the **damping** argument determines the amount of oscillation, and the **initialVelocity** determines the initial velocity of the animation.

- **interactiveSpring(response: Double, dampingFraction: Double, blendDuration: Double)**—This type method creates a spring animation that can interact with the user. The **response** argument determines the duration of one animation period, the **dampingFraction** argument determines the amount of oscillation, and the **blendDuration** argument determines the time it takes for the animation to stop and the next animation to begin.

- **timingCurve(UnitCurve, duration: TimeInterval)**—This type method creates an animation with a custom timing curve. The first argument specifies the characteristics of the curve. It is a structure with the type properties `linear`, `easeIn`, `easeOut`, `easeInOut`, `circularEaseIn`, `circularEaseOut`, and `circularEase-InOut`, and the type method `bezier(startControlPoint: UnitPoint, endControlPoint: UnitPoint)`. The **duration** argument determines the duration of the animation.

- **timingCurve(Double, Double, Double, Double, duration: Double)**—This type method creates an animation with a custom timing curve. The four initial arguments determine the coordinates of the control points of a cubic Bezier curve, and the **duration** argument determines the duration of the animation.

These custom animations are created in the same way as the standard animations, and they can even use the same methods for configuration. For example, we can create a custom spring animation with a specific speed and repetition cycle.

```
Button("Animate") {
    let animation = Animation.interpolatingSpring(mass: 0.15, stiffness:
0.8, damping: 0.5, initialVelocity: 5)
        .speed(5)
        .repeatForever()
    withAnimation(animation) {
        boxScale = 2
    }
}
```

Listing 11-59: Defining a custom animation

 Do It Yourself: Update the **Button** view in the **ContentView** view with the code in Listing 11-59. Press the Animate button. You should see the square bouncing indefinitely. Try different values for the **interpolatingSpring()** animation and implement other types of animations to see how they work.

The **withAnimation()** function can animate multiple states at a time. The system takes care of combining the animations, as shown in the following example.

```
struct ContentView: View {
    @State private var boxScale: CGFloat = 1
    @State private var roundCorners: Bool = false

    var body: some View {
        VStack {
            HStack {
                Rectangle()
```

Chapter 11 - Graphics and Animations

```
                     .fill(Color.blue)
                     .frame(width: 50, height: 50)
                     .clipShape(RoundedRectangle(cornerRadius: roundCorners ?
15 : 0))
                     .scaleEffect(boxScale)
            }.frame(width: 250, height: 120)
            Button("Animate") {
                withAnimation(.easeInOut(duration: 2)) {
                    boxScale = 2
                    roundCorners = true
                }
            }
        }.padding()
    }
}
```

Listing 11-60: Animating multiple states at a time

This example defines two **@State** properties, one to control the scale of the box and another to change the radius of the corners. When the button is pressed, we change the values of these two properties, and both changes are animated.

 Do It Yourself: Update the **ContentView** view with the code in Listing 11-60. Press the Animate button. You should see the square grow and the corners become round, all happening at the same time.

In the last example, we applied the same animation to both values (**easeInOut**), but SwiftUI allows us to perform as many animations as we need. All we have to do is to implement the **withAnimation()** function for each value we want to animate with the type of animation we want to use. For instance, the **Button** view in the following example performs two types of animations. We animate the **roundCorners** state with an **easeOut** animation, and the **boxScale** state with a **linear** animation. The effect is similar than before, but now each state is controlled by a different type of animation.

```
Button("Animate") {
    withAnimation(.easeOut) {
        roundCorners = true
    }
    withAnimation(.linear) {
        boxScale = 2
    }
}
```

Listing 11-61: Applying a different animation to each state

Medium Animating Custom Shapes

The system knows how to animate the views because they conform to a protocol included in SwiftUI called **Animatable**. The protocol defines a computed property called **animatableData** that provides the data required to create the frames for the animation. Every time we animate a view, the system gets the value from this property, increases or decreases it by a small amount, redraws the view, and repeats the process until the value matches the new one. For instance, the view returned by the **opacity()** modifier includes an **animatableData** property that provides the view's opacity value, so the system can gradually increase or decrease this value and redraw the view each time with a different opacity to make it look like it's being animated.

Most SwiftUI views include the **animatableData** property and therefore the system knows how to animate them, but if we want to animate a path in a custom **Shape** view, we must do it ourself. For this purpose, we need to make the structure conform to the **Animatable** protocol and implement the **animatableData** property to tell the system what is the value that it has to modify to get all the frames for the animation.

The **Shape** protocol already inherits from the **Animatable** protocol, so all we need to do is to implement the **animatableData** property to provide the value to animate. This value has to be something we can use to draw the path. For instance, if we want to animate a circle, we can provide its radius. If the animation goes from a radius of 0 to a radius of 10, the view will be able to draw the intermediate values required to create the animation (1, 2, 3, etc.). If the value we use to create the path is not animatable, we must turn it into something that can be animated. For instance, in the following example, we use a Boolean **@State** property to determine whether the mouth in the illustration of a face should be smiling or not, but we turn this value into the number 0 or 1, so the system can generate values in between to animate the path.

```
struct ContentView: View {
    @State private var smiling: Bool = true

    var body: some View {
        VStack {
            Face(smile: smiling ? 1 : 0)
                .stroke(Color.blue, lineWidth: 5)
                .frame(width: 100, height: 120)
            Button("Change") {
                withAnimation(.default) {
                    smiling.toggle()
                }
            }
        }
    }
}
```

Listing 11-62: *Instantiating a view with a value that can be animated*

If the **smiling** property is **true**, we send the value 1 to the view, otherwise, we send the value 0. This means that the system can create an animation by instantiating this view with values from 0 to 1. The view takes this value and draws a mouth with the curve defined by the **addCurve()** method.

```
import SwiftUI

struct Face: Shape {
    var smile: CGFloat
    var animatableData: CGFloat {
        get {
            return smile
        }
        set {
            self.smile = newValue
        }
    }
    func path(in rect: CGRect) -> Path {
        let width = rect.width
        let smileClamp = min(max(smile, 0), 1)
        let section = rect.height / 5
        let smilePos = section + (section * 3 * smileClamp)

        var path = Path()
        path.addEllipse(in: CGRect(x: width/10*2 - 10, y: rect.minY + 10,
width: 20, height: 20))
        path.addEllipse(in: CGRect(x: width/10*8 - 10, y: rect.minY + 10,
width: 20, height: 20))

        path.move(to: CGPoint(x: width/10*2, y: rect.midY))
```

```
      path.addCurve(to: CGPoint(x: width/10*8, y: rect.midY), control1:
CGPoint(x: width / 4, y: smilePos), control2: CGPoint(x: width / 4 * 3,
y: smilePos))
      return path
   }
}
```

Listing 11-63: Defining an animatable path

The only difference with previous **Shape** structures is that now we have an **animatableData** property that provides the system with the value to animate. The system accesses this property, gets the value of the **smile** property from it, increases or decreases this value by a small amount, sends the result back to the **animatableData** property, and the path is redrawn with this new value.

Because the values received by the **Face** view are between 0 and 1 (0.1, 0.2, 0.3, etc.), we must convert them to a range we can use to draw the mouth. First, we make sure that the value is between 0 and 1 with the **min()** and **max()** functions. After that, we calculate the position of the bottom of the mouth according to this value. If the value is close to 0, the bottom of the mouth will be near the top of the view, and if the value is close to 1, it will be near the bottom, so we get a happy or a sad face.

Figure 11-49: Animated path

 Do It Yourself: Update the **ContentView** view with the code in Listing 11-62. Create a new Swift file called Face.swift for the structure of Listing 11-63. Press the Change button. You should see the curves illustrated in Figure 11-49.

(Medium) Canvas Animations

The content of a **Canvas** view can also be animated. The process requires to redraw the canvas over and over again. For this purpose, SwiftUI includes the following view.

▷ **TimelineView(**Schedule, **content:** Closure**)**—This initializer creates a view that redraws its content according to a schedule. The first argument specifies the schedule the view must follow, and the **content** argument is a closure with the views we want to redraw at each point in time. The closure receives a **Context** structure, which includes the **date** property with the schedule date that triggered the update, and the **cadence** property with the rate at which the views are updated.

The **TimelineView** view needs a schedule to know when to perform the task again. This schedule is defined by a structure that conforms to the **TimelineSchedule** protocol. SwiftUI defines several structures to create built-in schedules. These structures include the following type properties and methods.

▷ **explicit(**Dates**)**—This type method creates a schedule from the **Date** values specified by the argument. The argument is an array of **Date** values with the dates and times to schedule the task.

▷ **periodic(from:** Date, **by:** TimeInterval**)**—This type method creates a schedule from the dates specified by the arguments. The **from** argument determines when the process begins, and the **by** argument determines the intervals at which the task is performed.

▷ **everyMinute**—This type property creates a schedule that performs the task every minute.

▷ **animation**—This type property creates a schedule that performs the task over and over again to produce an animation.

▷ **animation(minimumInterval: Double?, paused: Bool)**—This type method creates a schedule to produce an animation that can be paused. The **minimumInterval** argument specifies the interval at which the animation should be performed (the value **nil** sets the interval by default), and the **paused** argument determines if the animation should be running or paused.

The **TimelineView** view can be used for any task that requires updating the interface after a period of time. This may involve anything from single strings to complex graphics. When the interface needs simple updates, we can use a periodic or explicit schedule, as shown below.

```
struct ContentView: View {
    var body: some View {
        TimelineView(.periodic(from: Date(), by: 2)) { time in
            let calendar = Calendar.current
            let components = calendar.dateComponents([.second], from:
time.date)
            HStack {
                Text("Time: \(components.second ?? 0)")
                    .font(.largeTitle.bold())
            }
        }
    }
}
```

Listing 11-64: Updating the interface

In this example, the **TimelineView** view begins drawing the views from the current date and does it again every two seconds. In the closure, we use the value produced by the view to get the date when the drawing is performed, extract the seconds, and show the number on the screen.

The **TimelineView** view works with any content, but it is particularly useful with the **Canvas** view. SwiftUI even defines a specific schedule structure to create animations with a canvas that can be obtained from the **animation** property or the **animation()** method. There is a caveat, though. The system doesn't know what we want to animate on the canvas, so we must take care of everything, including the frequency of the animation, the positions of the graphics, and more. The following example illustrates how to create a simple animation that repositions a circle on the screen after a few fractions of a second.

```
class ContentViewData {
    var posX: CGFloat = 0
    var posY: CGFloat = 0
    var lastTime: Double = 0
    var maxTime: Double = 0.2
}
struct ContentView: View {
    let contentData = ContentViewData()

    var body: some View {
        TimelineView(.animation) { time in
            let interval = time.date.timeIntervalSinceReferenceDate
            let delta = interval - contentData.lastTime
```

```
     Canvas { context, size in
         if delta > contentData.maxTime {
             contentData.posX = CGFloat.random(in: 0..<size.width - 20)
             contentData.posY = CGFloat.random(in: 0..<size.height - 20)
             contentData.lastTime = interval
         }
         let circleFrame = CGRect(x: contentData.posX, y:
contentData.posY, width: 20, height: 20)
             context.fill(Circle().path(in: circleFrame),
with: .color(.red))
         }.ignoresSafeArea()
     }
   }
}
```

Listing 11-65: Animating the canvas

For this example, we have defined a simple class called **ContentViewData** to be able to store and update the position of the circle and all the values required to control the frequency of the animation.

The timing is controlled from the date produced by the **TimelineView** view. From this value, we get the current date, extract the seconds with the **timeIntervalSinceReferenceDate** property, check how many seconds have passed since the last iteration, and update the position of the circle if the difference is greater than the maximum time set by the **maxTime** property. Note that after the position of the circle is determined, we assign the current date in seconds to the **lastTime** property to know when the last iteration happened, so the graphics are only updated every 0.2 seconds.

 Do It Yourself: Update the ContentView.swift file with the code in Listing 11-65. You should see a red circle appearing in different locations on the screen every 0.2 seconds.

The previous example shows how the graphics are updated on the canvas, but no animation is created. To animate a graphic on the canvas, we need to manually draw each frame. This means that the position of each graphic must be calculated for each step of the animation. To show how this works, we will animate a circle in the center of the screen. The animation is created by changing the radius of the circle.

```
import SwiftUI

class ContentViewData {
   var radius: CGFloat = 0
   var step: CGFloat = 5
   var lastTime: Double = 0
   var maxTime: Double = 0.02
}
struct ContentView: View {
   let contentData = ContentViewData()

   var body: some View {
      TimelineView(.animation) { time in
          let interval = time.date.timeIntervalSinceReferenceDate
          let delta = interval - contentData.lastTime

          Canvas { context, size in
             if delta > contentData.maxTime {
                 calculateRadius()
                 contentData.lastTime = interval
             }
             let rad = contentData.radius
```

```
            let circleFrame = CGRect(x: size.width/2 - rad, y:
size.height/2 - rad, width: rad * 2, height: rad * 2)
            context.fill(Circle().path(in: circleFrame),
with: .color(.red))
         }.ignoresSafeArea()
      }
   }
   func calculateRadius() {
      contentData.radius = contentData.radius + contentData.step
      if contentData.step < 0 && contentData.radius < 0 {
         contentData.radius = 0
         contentData.step = 5
      }
      if contentData.step > 0 && contentData.radius > 150 {
         contentData.radius = 150
         contentData.step = -5
      }
   }
}
```

Listing 11-66: *Creating a real animation*

The process of controlling the frequency of the animation is the same as before, but we have defined a function to calculate the radius. If the radius is small, we add 5 points to expand the circle, otherwise we start the opposite animation by reducing the radius by -5 points. To know whether the circle is expanding or contracting, we store the difference in an additional property called **step**. When the value of this property is negative, it means that the circle is contracting, otherwise it is expanding.

(Medium) Transitions

As we have already seen, we can add or remove views to the interface depending on a state (see Chapter 6, Listing 6-14). The process by which the view appears or disappears on the screen is called *transition*. By default, the system doesn't use a transition, it simply displays or removes the views, but we can assign a specific transition to a view using the following modifiers.

▷ **transition(**AnyTransition**)**—This modifier assigns the transition specified by the argument to the view.

▷ **contentTransition(**ContentTransition**)**—This modifier assigns the transition specified by the argument to the content of the view.

SwiftUI defines standard transitions. The following are the type properties provided by the **AnyTransition** structure to create them.

▷ **opacity**—This type property returns a transition that inserts or removes a view by modifying its opacity.

▷ **scale**—This type property returns a transition that inserts or removes a view by modifying its scale.

▷ **slide**—This type property returns a transition that inserts or removes a view by sliding it from or to the sides.

▷ **identity**—This type property returns a transition that inserts or removes a view without any effect. This is the transition by default.

The **AnyTransition** structure determines the type of transition, but in order for the transition to be applied, we must specify how it should be animated. For this purpose, the **AnyTransition** structure provides the following method.

▶ **animation**(Animation)—This method applies an animation to the transition.

The **animation()** method is called on the instance of the **AnyTransition** structure, so we have to define the transition and then call this method to determine the animation we are going to apply to it. In the following example, we show and hide a **Text** view with a transition of type **scale** and an animation of type **default**.

```
struct ContentView: View {
   @State private var showInfo = false

   var body: some View {
      VStack {
         Button("Show Information") {
            showInfo.toggle()
         }.padding()
         if showInfo {
            Text("This is the information")
               .transition(.scale.animation(.default))
         }
         Spacer()
      }
   }
}
```

Listing 11-67: Adding and removing a view with a transition

The button in this view toggles the value of the **showInfo** property. When the value is **true**, a **Text** view is added to the interface, otherwise, the view is removed. But because of the **scale** transition, the view expands until it reaches its natural size when the value of the property is **true**, and contracts until it disappears from the screen when it is **false**.

 Do It Yourself: Create a Multiplatform project. Update the **ContentView** view with the code in Listing 11-67. Run the application on the iPhone simulator. Press the Show Information button. You should see the **Text** view appear or disappear from the screen every time the button is pressed. Replace the **scale** transition by the **opacity** and **slide** types to see how they work.

In the previous example, we use a standard animation (**default**). In this case, the code is easy to read, but it can become cumbersome when we apply our own animations or combine custom transitions with custom animations. To improve readability and organize the code, it is better to define the transition externally. There are different ways to do it, but what is considered best practice is to declare an extension of the **AnyTransition** structure and define our custom transition as if it belonged to the structure itself. In the following example, we extend the **AnyTransition** structure to define a custom transition called **mytransition**.

```
struct ContentView: View {
   @State private var showInfo = false

   var body: some View {
      VStack {
         Button("Show Information") {
            showInfo.toggle()
         }.padding()
         if showInfo {
            Text("This is the information")
               .transition(.mytransition)
         }
         Spacer()
      }
   }
```

```
}
extension AnyTransition {
    static var mytransition: AnyTransition {
        let animation = Animation.easeInOut(duration: 2)
        let transition = AnyTransition.scale
            .animation(animation)
        return transition
    }
}
```

Listing 11-68: Extending the `AnyTransition` *structure*

The code in Listing 11-68 defines an extension of the **AnyTransition** structure with a type property called **mytransition**. This is a computed property that creates and returns a custom transition. Of course, we can define any transition with any animation we want, the only requirement is that the property returns a structure of type **AnyTransition**, so we can use it to specify the transition for a view. In this example, we create a custom **easeInOut** animation with a duration of 2 seconds and apply it to a standard transition of type **scale**.

Because we declare our custom transition as an extension of the **AnyTransition** structure, we can assign it to the view as we do with any standard transition already defined by the structure.

 Do It Yourself: Update the ContentView.swift file with the code in Listing 11-68. Run the application on the iPhone simulator. Press the Show Information button. You should see the **Text** view appear with a **scale** transition, but the animation should last 2 seconds.

The transitions we have implemented so far are symmetric; they are the same when the view is added to the interface and when the view is removed. To create an asymmetric transition, the **AnyTransition** structure includes the following type method.

▷ **asymmetric(insertion:** AnyTransition, **removal:** AnyTransition)—This type method defines an asymmetric transition. The **insertion** argument specifies the transition to use when the view is inserted, and the **removal** argument specifies the transition to use when the view is removed.

For example, we can fade-in the view by modifying the opacity when it is added to the interface, and then remove it by reducing the scale.

```
extension AnyTransition {
    static var mytransition: AnyTransition {
        let animation = Animation.easeInOut(duration: 2)
        let transition = AnyTransition.asymmetric(insertion: .opacity,
removal: .scale)
            .animation(animation)
        return transition
    }
}
```

Listing 11-69: Defining an asymmetric transition

 Do It Yourself: Update the **AnyTransition** extension from the previous example with the code in Listing 11-69. Run the application on the iPhone simulator. Press the Show Information button. You should see the text fade-in and then shrink when the button is pressed again.

In addition to defining one transition for the insertion and another for the removal, we can combine two transitions with the following method.

▷ **combined(with:** AnyTransition**)**—This method combines the transition with the transition specified by the **with** argument.

The following example combines a type **scale** transition with a type **opacity** transition. The text fades in and out and also scales as it appears and disappears on the screen.

```
extension AnyTransition {
    static var mytransition: AnyTransition {
        let animation = Animation.easeInOut(duration: 2)
        let transition = AnyTransition.scale.combined(with: .opacity)
            .animation(animation)
        return transition
    }
}
```

Listing 11-70: Combining transitions

 Do It Yourself: Update the **AnyTransition** extension from the previous example with the code in Listing 11-70. Run the application on the iPhone simulator. Press the Show Information button. You should see the text fade in as it expands until it reaches the final size and position.

The **AnyTransition** structure also includes the following type methods to create custom transitions.

▷ **move(edge:** Edge**)**—This type method defines a transition that moves the view in and out of the interface from the side defined by the argument. The **edge** argument is an enumeration of type **Edge** with the values **bottom**, **leading**, **top**, and **trailing**.

▷ **offset(x:** CGFloat, **y:** CGFloat**)**—This type method defines a transition that moves the view in and out of the interface by the space determined by the arguments. The **x** and **y** arguments specify the offset of the view from the center of the frame.

▷ **scale(scale:** CGFloat, **anchor:** UnitPoint**)**—This type method defines a transition that scales the view. The **scale** argument determines the initial scale for the transition, and the **anchor** argument determines the point from which the view is going to be scaled.

Custom transitions require an explicit animation. This means that instead of animating the transition itself, we must animate the change of the state with the **withAnimation()** function.

```
struct ContentView: View {
    @State private var showInfo = false

    var body: some View {
        VStack {
            Button("Show Information") {
                withAnimation {
                    showInfo.toggle()
                }
            }.padding()
            if showInfo {
                Text("This is the information")
                    .transition(.offset(x: 400, y: 0))
            }
            Spacer()
        }
    }
}
```

```
}
```

Listing 11-71: Customizing the transition

This example creates a transition that moves the view in and out of the interface from the left side of the screen. Note that this transition reproduces the `slide` transition, but in this case the view always uses the same side of the screen.

Do It Yourself: Update the `ContentView` view with the code in Listing 11-71. Run the application on the iPhone simulator. Press the Show Information button. You should see the text slide from the left side of the screen and then slide back to the same side when the button is pressed again.

Of course, multiple views can transition at the same time, and because the interface is updated all at once, the animations are coordinated. For instance, we can use the same `showInfo` property to show and hide two `Text` views.

```
struct ContentView: View {
    @State private var showInfo = false

    var body: some View {
        VStack {
            Button("Show Information") {
                showInfo.toggle()
            }.padding()
            HStack {
                if !showInfo {
                    Text("Left")
                        .transition(.scale.animation(.default))
                }
                Spacer()
                if showInfo {
                    Text("Right")
                        .transition(.scale.animation(.default))
                }
            }.padding()
            Spacer()
        }
    }
}
```

Listing 11-72: Coordinating transitions

As always, the `showInfo` property is initialized with the value `false`. This means that the `Text` view with the string "Left" is shown on the left hand side of the screen. But when the button is pressed, the value of the `showInfo` property is toggled and the `Text` view with the string "Right" is shown instead. Both transitions are animated with a `scale` effect, so they shrink or expand to appear or disappear from the screen.

The transitions in this example look coordinated, but the strings are displayed by two different `Text` views and therefore each animation is independent. If we want to transition from one view to another with a single animation, we must declare both views to be the same. SwiftUI includes the following modifier for this purpose.

▷ **matchedGeometryEffect(id:** Value, **in:** Namespace.ID, **properties:** MatchedGeometryProperties, **anchor:** UnitPoint, **isSource:** Bool)—This modifier includes a view in an animation group for synchronization. The `id` argument is a hashable value that identifies the associated views. The **in** argument is the namespace that groups the animations together. The **properties** argument is a structure that indicates the types of properties we want to synchronize. The type properties available to create these structures are **frame** (default), **position**, and **size**. The **anchor** argument determines the position shared by the views (**center** by default). And the **isSource** argument determines if the view should be used as the source of geometry for the rest of the views (**true** by default).

This modifier can be used to group and associate multiple views. To associate the views, we need to provide a common identifier, usually a string, but to create an animation group, we need to define a namespace (see Chapter 8, Listing 8-32). In the following example, we create a **@Namespace** property and then apply the **matchedGeometryEffect()** modifier to each view with this value.

```
struct ContentView: View {
    @Namespace private var myAnimations
    @State private var showInfo = false

    var body: some View {
        VStack {
            Button("Show Information") {
                withAnimation(.easeInOut) {
                    showInfo.toggle()
                }
            }.padding()
            HStack {
                if !showInfo {
                    Text("Left")
                        .matchedGeometryEffect(id: "TextAnimation", in:
myAnimations)
                }
                Spacer()
                if showInfo {
                    Text("Right")
                        .matchedGeometryEffect(id: "TextAnimation", in:
myAnimations)
                }
            }.padding()
            Spacer()
        }
    }
}
```

Listing 11-73: Coordinating views

This example includes the same views as before. There is a **Text** view that appears on the left and another on the right, but because we apply the **matchedGeometryEffect()** modifier to the views with the same identifier and assign them to the same namespace, they are animated as one view. In this case, when the value of the **showInfo** property changes, the views move from left to right and right to left, and also the text gradually changes from "Left" to "Right", and vice versa. Note that for the transition to be animated, we had to animate the state change with the **withAnimation()** function.

 Do It Yourself: Update the **ContentView** view with the code in Listing 11-73. Run the application on the iPhone simulator. Press the Show Information button. You should see the text sliding from the left side of the screen to the right, and the text gradually changing from "Left" to "Right".

(Medium) **Animating SF Symbols**

SF Symbols are graphical symbols provided by Apple to create buttons and indicators. We introduced static SF Symbols in Chapter 5, but they can also be animated. The **View** protocol defines the following modifiers to apply a transition to changes in the content of a single view.

- ▷ **symbolEffect(**SymbolEffect, **options:** SymbolEffectOptions, **isActive: Bool)**—This modifier creates a content transition to animate a symbol. The first argument defines the effect to apply to the transition, the **options** argument defines the configuration of the effect, and the **isActive** argument is a Boolean binding property that determines whether the symbol is animated or not.

- ▷ **symbolEffect(**SymbolEffect, **options:** SymbolEffectOptions, **value: Binding)**—This modifier creates a content transition to animate a symbol. The first argument defines the effect to apply to the transition, the **options** argument defines the configuration of the effect, and the **value** argument is a binding property used to run the animation each time its value changes.

The effect applied by these modifiers is defined by a structure that conforms to the **SymbolEffect** protocol. Apple provides a framework called Symbols that defines a set of structures with predefined effects, as well as type properties to return instances of these structures. The properties currently available are **appear**, **automatic**, **bounce**, **breathe**, **disappear**, **pulse**, **replace**, **rotate**, **scale**, **variableColor**, and **wiggle**. The structures returned by these properties in turn contain their own properties for configuration. Some share the same properties, such as **up** and **down**, which can be used to specify whether the animation should be upwards or downwards, but others are more specific, as we will see later.

By default, the animation is not repeated and runs at a speed of 1.0, but we can change these values by specifying a **SymbolEffectOptions** structure. The structure includes the following properties and methods for configuration.

- ▷ **repeating**—This property returns a set of options that repeat the effect indefinitely.

- ▷ **nonRepeating**—This property returns a set of options that specify that the effect is not repeated.

- ▷ **repeat(**Int?**)**—This method creates a set of options that repeat the effect as many times as specified by the argument.

- ▷ **speed(**Double**)**—This method creates a set of options that determine the speed of the effect according to the value specified by the argument.

Animating an SF Symbol that was designed for animation is easy. All we have to do is display the symbol with an **Image** view and apply the **symbolEffect()** modifier with the desired effect and configuration.

```
struct ContentView: View {
   @State private var isActive = false

   var body: some View {
      VStack(spacing: 10) {
         Image(systemName: "wifi")
            .font(.largeTitle)
            .symbolEffect(.variableColor.iterative,
options: .nonRepeating, isActive: isActive)
         Button("Animate") {
            isActive.toggle()
         }
      }
   }
}
```

Listing 11-74: *Animating an SF Symbol*

In this example, we use the **variableColor** effect. This property returns a **Variable-ColorSymbolEffect** structure that contains properties for configuring the effect. The most useful are **cumulative** and **iterative** to determine how the layers should be animated, and **dimInactiveLayers** and **hideInactiveLayers** to dim or hide the inactive layers. To simulate the propagation of radio waves, we use the **iterative** version of the effect.

To start or stop the animation, we assign a Boolean **@State** property to the **isActive** argument. If the property is **true**, the symbol will be animated, otherwise it will be displayed as a static symbol.

The **isActive** argument takes a Boolean value, but we can also use the **value** argument to control the animation with any value. For example, the following modifier starts or stops the animation when the value changes. In this case, we use the same **isActive** property as before, but the argument can take any type of value. The animation is activated when the value changes, regardless of the value itself.

```
.symbolEffect(.bounce, value: isActive)
```

Listing 11-75: Animating an SF Symbol when a value changes

In this example, we use the **bounce** effect. This effect animates each layer of the symbol individually, so that the symbol looks like it is bouncing off the screen. The effect plays only once, but can be configured to repeat. In the following example, we use the **repeat()** method to repeat the effect twice.

```
.symbolEffect(.bounce, options: .repeat(2), value: isActive)
```

Listing 11-76: Animating an SF Symbol multiple times

The structure returned by the **bounce** property includes the properties **up** and **down** to determine the direction of the effect (e.g, **.bounce.down**), but each effect includes its own configuration properties. For example, the structure returned by the **wiggle** property includes properties to determine the angle of the effect. The properties available are **backward**, **byLayer**, **clockwise**, **counterClockwise**, **down**, **forward**, **left**, **right**, **up**, and **wholeSymbol**. The structure also includes the **custom(angle: Double)** method to specify a custom angle between 0 and 360 degrees, as shown below.

```
.symbolEffect(.wiggle.custom(angle: 45), value: isActive)
```

Listing 11-77: Configuring animations

The previous effects execute the animation and then show the symbol again in its initial state. However, some effects execute the animation and remain in that state until the animation is deactivated. For example, if we enlarge the symbol with the **scale** effect, it will remain in that state until we scale it down.

```
.symbolEffect(.scale.up, isActive: isActive)
```

Listing 11-78: Scaling a symbol

The same happens with other effects like **disappear**. In this case, the symbol appears or disappears from the screen and remains in that state until the animation is activated again.

```
.symbolEffect(.disappear, isActive: isActive)
```

Listing 11-79: Removing a symbol from the screen

This effect removes the symbol from the screen, but the layout remains unchanged. If we want the layout to adapt to the new space, we must apply the effect within a transition, as in the following example.

```
struct ContentView: View {
   @State private var isActive = true

   var body: some View {
      VStack(spacing: 10) {
         if isActive {
            Image(systemName: "wifi")
               .font(.largeTitle)
               .transition(.symbolEffect(.disappear))
         }
         Button("Animate") {
            isActive.toggle()
         }
      }
   }
}
```

Listing 11-80: Adapting the layout to the effect

In this example, the **Image** view is displayed only if the value of the **isActive** property is **true**, but because we apply the **transition()** modifier, the symbol is added to or removed from the interface with an animation. And in this case, the animation is the one provided by the **disappear** property.

In addition to removing a symbol, we can also replace it with the **replace** effect. This effect is called *Magic Replace* because, if the symbols are related, it can animate the transition. The only condition is that it must be applied with the **contentTransition()** modifier so that the effect is applied to the content of the view and not to the view itself. In the following example, we replace the wifi symbol with the same symbol with a slash.

```
struct ContentView: View {
   @State private var isActive = false

   var body: some View {
      VStack(spacing: 10) {
         Image(systemName: isActive ? "wifi" : "wifi.slash")
            .font(.largeTitle)
            .contentTransition(.symbolEffect(.replace))
         Button("Animate") {
            isActive.toggle()
         }
      }
   }
}
```

Listing 11-81: Replacing a symbol

 IMPORTANT: Graphics and animations can be combined in infinite ways to create the most astonishing interfaces. The topic is beyond the scope of this book. For more information, visit our website and follow the links for this chapter.

Basic # 12.1 Gesture Recognizers

Gestures are actions that the user performs on the screen, such as tapping, swiping, or pinching. These gestures are difficult to recognize because the only thing the screen returns is the position of the fingers. For this reason, Apple offers gesture recognizers. A gesture recognizer does all the calculations needed to recognize a gesture, so instead of processing multiple events and values, we simply wait for the notifications the system sends when complex gestures are detected and react accordingly.

Basic ## Gesture Modifiers

The most common gesture used in a mobile device is a tap gesture, which is recognized when the user touches the screen with a finger. Since this gesture is used very frequently, SwiftUI defines two handy modifiers to handle it.

▷ **onTapGesture(count:** Int, **perform:** Closure)—This modifier recognizes a single or multiple taps. The **count** argument determines how many taps are required for the gesture to be recognized (1 by default), and the **perform** argument is the closure to be executed when the gesture is detected. The closure receives a `CGPoint` value with the location of the tap in the view's coordinates.

▷ **onLongPressGesture(minimumDuration:** Double, **maximumDistance:** CGFloat, **perform:** Closure, **onPressingChanged:** Closure)—This modifier recognizes a long press gesture (the user keeps pressing the screen with a finger). The **minimumDuration** argument is the time in seconds the user must press the screen with the finger until the gesture is recognized. The **maximumDistance** argument is the distance in points the user can move the finger from the original position before the gesture is no longer recognized. The **perform** argument is the closure to be executed when the gesture is confirmed. And finally, the **onPressingChanged** argument is the closure to be executed when the user begins and ends pressing the view. The closure receives a Boolean value to indicate whether the user is pressing or not.

We have often worked with the `onTapGesture()` modifier to detect a tap and perform an action (see Chapter 7, Listing 7-37). What we haven't done in the previous examples is to determine the position of the finger where the tap occurred. This is done using the `CGPoint` value received by the closure, which contains the x and y coordinates of the finger within the view. In the following example, we open a sheet when an image is tapped and show how to access this value.

```
struct ContentView: View {
   @State private var expand: Bool = false

   var body: some View {
      Image(.spot1)
         .resizable()
         .scaledToFit()
         .frame(width: 160, height: 200)
         .onTapGesture { location in
            expand = true
            print("Location: \(location)")
         }
```

```
            .sheet(isPresented: $expand) {
                ShowImage()
            }
        }
    }
}
```

Listing 12-1: Detecting a tap gesture on an image

The code in Listing 12-1 defines an **Image** view of a size of 160 by 200 points. The **onTapGesture()** and **sheet()** modifiers are applied to the view to detect the tap and present a sheet. The following is the **ShowImage** view opened by the sheet.

```
import SwiftUI

struct ShowImage: View {
    var body: some View {
        Image(.spot1)
            .resizable()
            .scaledToFill()
            .edgesIgnoringSafeArea(.all)
    }
}
```

Listing 12-2: Showing the image

This view creates an **Image** view and expands it to fill the sheet, including the safe area. As a result, the interface presents a small image on the screen, and when the user taps on it, a sheet is opened to show it in full size.

Figure 12-1: Image responds to the tap gesture

 Do It Yourself: Create a Multiplatform project. Download the spot1.jpg image from our website and add it to the Asset Catalog. Update the **ContentView** view with the code in Listing 12-1. Create a SwiftUI file called ShowImage.swift and update the view with the code in Listing 12-2. You should see the interface illustrated in Figure 12-1 (left). Tap the image to open the sheet and print the location on the console.

The long press gesture is similar to the tap gesture, but the system waits a moment before acknowledging the gesture and performing the task. With the **onLongPressGesture()** modifier, we can set the waiting time and also execute a task while the user presses and waits for the gesture to complete, as in the following example.

```
struct ContentView: View {
    @State private var expand: Bool = false
    @State private var pressing: Bool = false

    var body: some View {
        Image(.spot1)
            .resizable()
            .scaledToFit()
            .frame(width: 160, height: 200)
            .opacity(pressing ? 0 : 1)

            .onLongPressGesture(minimumDuration: 1, maximumDistance: 10,
                perform: {
                    expand = true
                }, onPressingChanged: { value in
                    withAnimation(.easeInOut(duration: 1.5)) {
                        pressing = value
                    }
                })
            .sheet(isPresented: $expand) {
                ShowImage()
            }
    }
}
```

Listing 12-3: *Detecting a long press gesture*

This is the same example as before, but now we apply a long press gesture to the **Image** view so that the user must hold down their finger for a moment to open the sheet. In this case, we set the wait time to 1 second and the maximum distance to 10 points, so that the user cannot move the finger more than 10 points away from the initial position, otherwise the gesture is cancelled.

The closure assigned to the **onPressingChanged** argument is executed when the user starts touching the image, and again when the finger is lifted. In this closure, we change the value of a **@State** property called **pressing**, which we use to set the opacity of the view. When the gesture begins, the value received by the closure is **true**, so the opacity is set to 0. But when the user moves the finger away, lifts the finger, or ends the gesture, the closure receives the value **false**, so the opacity is set to 1. The change in opacity is animated with an **easeInOut** animation that lasts 1.5 seconds, so the sheet is opened before the image completely disappears, giving the user the necessary feedback to know they must wait until the process is complete.

 Do It Yourself: Update the **ContentView** view with the code in Listing 12-3. Press and hold the finger on the image (long click). You should see the image fading-out and the sheet opening after 1 second.

Basic Hit Testing

Because views sometimes overlap, the system must decide whether a view should process a gesture or pass it on to the views in the back. The process of finding the view that the user wants to interact with and deciding whether or not to respond to the gesture is called *hit testing*. The **View** protocol defines the following modifiers to control this process.

▷ **allowsHitTesting(**Bool**)**—This modifier determines whether the detection of hits is enabled on the view or not.

▷ **contentShape(**Shape, eoFill: Bool**)**—This modifier defines the shape of the hitting area. The first argument is a shape view that determines the area the user can interact with, and the **eoFill** argument determines the algorithm to use to detect the hit.

The **allowsHitTesting()** modifier can be used to disable a gesture. For instance, we can enable or disable the tap gesture on the **Image** view of the previous example.

```
struct ContentView: View {
    @State private var expand: Bool = false
    @State private var allowExpansion: Bool = false

    var body: some View {
        VStack(spacing: 20) {
            Image(.spot1)
                .resizable()
                .scaledToFit()
                .frame(width: 160, height: 200)
                .onTapGesture {
                    expand = true
                }
                .allowsHitTesting(allowExpansion)
                .sheet(isPresented: $expand) {
                    ShowImage()
                }
            Toggle("", isOn: $allowExpansion)
                .labelsHidden()
        }
    }
}
```

Listing 12-4: Disabling the tap gesture

The view in Listing 12-4 adds a **Toggle** view below the image to control the value of a **@State** property. This property determines whether hit testing is allowed for the **Image** view. The initial value of the property is set to **false** so that the user cannot tap the image to open the sheet, but when the switch is turned on, the value **true** is assigned to the property, and the gesture is therefore recognized by the **Image** view.

 Do It Yourself: Update the **ContentView** view with the code in Listing 12-4. Tap on the image. Nothing should happen. Turn on the switch below the image. Now, the image should open the sheet when you tap on it.

The **contentShape()** modifier also plays an important role in gesture recognition. When we apply a gesture recognizer to an **Image** view or a **Text** view, the gesture is recognized when the user touches any part of the area occupied by the view. However, this is not always the case. Container views, such as **VStack** and **HStack**, recognize the gesture only when it is performed on the area occupied by their content. To ensure that every part of the view can recognize a gesture, we need to force the content to occupy the entire area. We have encountered this problem before (see Chapter 7, Listing 7-37). In those examples, we had to define a background with a **Color** view to create an area for the tap gesture to be recognized. This is enough to get the container to recognize the gesture, but it creates content that is not required by the interface. A better solution is to apply the **contentShape()** modifier. This modifier allows us to define the hitting area for the gesture without adding any real content to the view.

In the following example, we recreate the views used in previous projects to create the rows of a list, but this time we do not use a **Color** view to respond to the tap gesture, instead we define the content of the row with a **Rectangle** view and the **contentShape()** modifier. This allows the user to tap anywhere on the row to select it.

```
struct ContentView: View {
    @State private var selected: Bool = false

    var body: some View {
        VStack {
```

```
        HStack(alignment: .top) {
            Image(.spot1)
                .resizable()
                .scaledToFit()
                .frame(width: 80, height: 100)
                .border(selected ? Color.yellow : Color.clear, width: 5)
            VStack(alignment: .leading, spacing: 2) {
                Text("Balmy Beach").bold()
                Text("Toronto")
                Text("2020").font(.caption)
                Spacer()
            }
            Spacer()
        }.frame(height: 100)
        .padding(5)
        .border(.gray, width: 1)
        .contentShape(Rectangle())
        .onTapGesture {
            selected.toggle()
        }
        Spacer()
    }
  }
}
```

Listing 12-5: Defining the shape of the content

The view in Listing 12-5 displays a row with information about a location. If the user taps anywhere on the row, the gesture recognizer toggles the value of a **@State** property called **selected**, which we use to define the color for the border of the image. The value **true** makes the border yellow (selected) and the value **false** makes it transparent (deselected).

Figure 12-2: Responsive row

Basic # 12.2 Gesture Structures

The gestures processed by the **onTapGesture()** and **onLongPressGesture()** modifiers are defined by structures that conform to the **Gesture** protocol. The following are the most frequently used.

▷ **TapGesture(count: Int)**—This initializer creates a gesture recognizer to detect a tap gesture. The **count** argument determines the number of taps required for the gesture to be recognized.

▷ **LongPressGesture(minimumDuration: Double, maximumDistance: CGFloat)**—This initializer creates a gesture recognizer to detect a long-press gesture. The **minimumDuration** argument is the time in seconds the user must press the screen with the finger until the gesture is recognized. The **maximumDistance** argument is the distance in points the user can move the finger from the original position before the gesture is no longer recognized.

▷ **MagnificationGesture(minimumScaleDelta: CGFloat)**—This initializer creates a gesture recognizer to detect a magnification gesture. The **minimumScaleDelta** argument is the minimum increment or decrement on the scale required for the gesture to be recognized.

▷ **RotationGesture(minimumAngleDelta:** Angle)—This initializer creates a gesture recognizer to detect a rotation gesture. The **minimumAngleDelta** argument is the minimum increment or decrement on the angle of the view required for the gesture to be recognized.

These initializers configure the gestures recognizers, but to respond to the different states of the gesture, the structures implement the following methods.

▷ **onChanged(**Closure)—This method executes a closure when the state of the gesture changes. The closure receives a value with information about the state of the gesture.

▷ **onEnded(**Closure)—This method executes a closure when the gesture ends. The closure receives a value with information about the state of the gesture.

▷ **updating(**GestureState, **body:** Closure)—This method executes a closure when the state of the gesture is updated, either because its value changed or the gesture was cancelled. The first argument is a binding property that stores the gesture's state values, and the **body** argument is the closure to be executed every time the state is updated. The closure receives a value with information about the state of the gesture, a reference to the binding property, and a value of type **Transaction** that contains information about the animation.

Because of the frequency with which the **updating()** method is called, we cannot use a normal **@state** property to track the state of the gesture. Any attempt to change a state within the updating closure will result in an error. Therefore, SwiftUI defines the following property wrapper to work with this method.

▷ **@GestureState**—This property wrapper stores the state of a gesture and resets its value to its initial value when the gesture ends.

Once we have an instance of the gesture recognizer properly configured, we must apply it to the view. The **View** protocol defines the following modifiers for this purpose.

▷ **gesture(**Gesture)—This modifier assigns a gesture recognizer to the view with a lower priority than the gesture recognizers already applied to the view.

▷ **highPriorityGesture(**Gesture)—This modifier assigns a gesture recognizer to the view with a higher priority than the gesture recognizers already applied to the view.

▷ **simultaneousGesture(**Gesture)—This modifier assigns a gesture recognizer to the view that is processed along with the gesture recognizers already applied to the view.

The process is simple. We need to instantiate a **Gesture** structure to define the gesture recognizer, apply the **onChanged()**, **onEnded()**, or **updating()** methods to the structure depending on what we want to do during the process, and assign that instance to the view with a modifier like **gesture()**. Which methods are applied depends on the gesture and what we want to accomplish, and the values received by these methods also depend on the type of gesture recognizer we are using. So there are several options available, as we will see in next.

(Basic) **Tap Gesture**

Because of the simplicity of the tap gesture, there is not much difference between applying the **onTapGesture()** modifier and implementing the **TapGesture** structure. As well as the modifier, the structure can also define the number of taps required to detect the gesture, and since there are no changes to report over time, only the `onEnded()` method is useful. The following example reproduces the previous project, but this time we define the gesture recognizer with a `TapGesture` structure.

```
struct ContentView: View {
   @State private var expand: Bool = false

   var body: some View {
      Image(.spot1)
         .resizable()
         .scaledToFit()
         .frame(width: 160, height: 200)
         .gesture(
            TapGesture(count: 1)
               .onEnded {
                  expand = true
               }
         )
         .sheet(isPresented: $expand) {
            ShowImage()
         }
   }
}
```

Listing 12-6: *Defining a* `TapGesture` *recognizer*

The `TapGesture` structure defines the gesture recognizer, but to associate it with a view we must apply the `gesture()` modifier. The result is the same as before. When the image is tapped, the closure assigned to the `onEnded()` method is executed, and the value `true` is assigned to the `expand` property to open the sheet. Note that the `onEnded()` method belongs to the `TapGesture` structure and therefore it is called on the instance of that structure, not the view.

 Do It Yourself: For this example, you need the **ShowImage** view defined in Listing 12-2. Update the **ContentView** view with the code in Listing 12-6. You should see a small image on the screen. Tap the image to open the sheet.

Basic) Long Press Gesture

Like the `TapGesture` structure, the `LongPressGesture` structure creates a simple gesture recognizer, but in this case there is some activity while the gesture is being performed, so in addition to the `onEnded()` method, we can also implement the `updating()` method if we want to perform a task while the view is being pressed.

When implementing the `updating()` method, we need to keep a few things in mind. First, as mentioned earlier, this method requires a `@GestureState` property instead of a `@State` property. A `@GestureState` property stores the current state, but also resets itself to the initial value when the gesture ends, so we should make sure that the initial value is what the property should have by default. Second, we need to update the state ourselves from the closure assigned to the method, but not directly, we must do it from the reference received by the method (usually called `state`). And third, because we are processing the changes inside the `updating()` method, the system cannot animate the process. For this purpose, we need to assign an `Animation` structure to the `animation` property of the `Transaction` structure created by the gesture, as shown below.

```
struct ContentView: View {
   @GestureState private var pressing: Bool = false
   @State private var expand: Bool = false
```

```
    var body: some View {
        Image(.spot1)
            .resizable()
            .scaledToFit()
            .frame(width: 160, height: 200)
            .opacity(pressing ? 0 : 1)

            .gesture(LongPressGesture(minimumDuration: 1)
                .updating($pressing) { value, state, transaction in
                    state = value
                    transaction.animation = Animation.easeInOut(duration: 1.5)
                }
                .onEnded { value in
                    expand = true
                }
            )
            .sheet(isPresented: $expand) {
                ShowImage()
            }
    }
}
```

Listing 12-7: Defining a LongPressGesture *recognizer*

This is the same application created with the **onLongPressGesture()** modifier (see Listing 12-3). When the user touches the image for a second, the opacity changes, and when the time is up, the sheet opens. The values are processed in the same way as before, but instead of working directly with the **@State** property, we assign the new value received by the closure to a reference of the **pressing** property. In this case, we identify the value and the reference with the names **value** and **state**, but these names are arbitrary. Once the new value is assigned to **state**, the value of the **pressing** property changes and the opacity is adjusted accordingly. After one second, the **onEnded()** method is executed, and the value **true** is assigned to the **expand** property to open the sheet.

Although we can work directly with the values generated by the **updating()** method, as we did in Listing 12-7, this method is designed to process the state through an enumeration. Instead of assigning the value received by the method directly to the **@GestureState** property, we assign an enumeration value to that property and then get the state from the enumeration.

```
import SwiftUI

enum PressingState {
    case active
    case inactive

    var isActive: Bool {
        switch self {
        case .active:
            return true
        case .inactive:
            return false
        }
    }
}
struct ContentView: View {
    @GestureState private var pressingState = PressingState.inactive
    @State private var expand: Bool = false

    var body: some View {
        Image(.spot1)
            .resizable()
            .scaledToFit()
            .frame(width: 160, height: 200)
            .opacity(pressingState.isActive ? 0 : 1)
```

Chapter 12 -Gestures

```
    .gesture(LongPressGesture(minimumDuration: 1)
        .updating($pressingState) { value, state, transaction in
            state = value ? .active : .inactive
            transaction.animation = Animation.easeInOut(duration: 1.5)
        }
        .onEnded { value in
            expand = true
        }
    )
    .sheet(isPresented: $expand) {
        ShowImage()
    }
    }
   }
}
```

Listing 12-8: Controlling the states of a gesture with an enumeration

This example works as before, but now we use an enumeration to capture the state of the gesture. The enumeration is called **PressingState** and contains two cases, **active** and **inactive**, as well as a computed property that returns a Boolean value corresponding to the current value of the instance (**true** for active and **false** for inactive). Now, instead of defining a **@GestureState** property of type **Bool** to store the value received by the **updating()** method, we can define a property of type **PressingState** and store an enumeration value. We call this property **pressingState** and assign it to the **updating()** method. When the method is called, we assign this property the value **active** or **inactive**, depending on the value the method receives. When it is time to read the state in the **opacity()** modifier, we get the Boolean value from the **isActive** property instead of the **@GestureState** property. If the current value of the **pressingState** property is active, the **isActive** property returns **true** and the opacity is set to 0. Otherwise, the returned value is **false** and the opacity is set to 1.

The result is the same as before, but the use of enumeration values becomes necessary when working with more complex gestures or when several gestures are combined.

(Basic) Magnification Gesture

The magnification gesture is often called the pinch gesture because it is recognized when the user spreads or pinches two fingers together. This gesture is usually implemented to allow the user to zoom in or out on an image.

The value sent to the **updating()**, **onChanged()** and **onEnded()** methods is a **CGFloat** that represents a multiple of the scale that we must multiply by the current scale to get the final scale of the image, as in the following example.

```
struct ContentView: View {
    @GestureState private var magnification: CGFloat = 1
    @State private var zoom: CGFloat = 1

    var body: some View {
        Image(.spot1)
            .resizable()
            .scaledToFit()
            .frame(width: 160, height: 200)
            .scaleEffect(zoom * magnification)

            .gesture(MagnificationGesture()
                .updating($magnification) { value, state, transaction in
                    state = value
                }
                .onEnded { value in
                    zoom = zoom * value
                }
            )
```

```
        }
    }
```

Listing 12-9: Defining a `MagnificationGesture` *recognizer*

The code in Listing 12-9 defines two states, one to track the magnification and another to store the final value. The idea is to allow the user to zoom in and out multiple times. While the gesture is being performed, the magnification value is stored in the `magnification` property, but the value of the `zoom` property is not changed until the gesture is over, so the next time the user tries to zoom in or out, the new scale is calculated based on the last one.

To set the scale of the image to the one chosen by the user, we apply the `scaleEffect()` modifier to the `Image` view and calculate the new scale by multiplying the value of the `zoom` property (the last scale set by the user) by the value of the `magnification` property (the multiple produced by the gesture). The result is that the image is zoomed in and out according to the movement of the fingers.

 Do It Yourself: Update the ContentView.swift file with the code in Listing 12-9. Pinch the view with two fingers to zoom in or out. When you run the application in the simulator or the canvas, press the Option key on your keyboard to activate the gesture.

The example in Listing 12-9 allows users to zoom an image in and out as much as they want, but in most cases we need to limit the scale of the view to values that make sense for the interface and the purpose of our application. To set these limits, we need to control the scale in two places: when it is applied to the view with the `scaleEffect()` modifier, and when the gesture ends and the final scale is assigned to the `zoom` property.

```
struct ContentView: View {
    @GestureState private var magnification: CGFloat = 1
    @State private var zoom: CGFloat = 1

    var body: some View {
        Image(.spot1)
            .resizable()
            .scaledToFit()
            .frame(width: 160, height: 200)
            .scaleEffect(getCurrentZoom(magnification: magnification))
            .gesture(MagnificationGesture()
                .updating($magnification) { value, state, transaction in
                    state = value
                }
                .onEnded { value in
                    zoom = getCurrentZoom(magnification: value)
                }
            )
    }
    func getCurrentZoom(magnification: CGFloat) -> CGFloat {
        let minZoom: CGFloat = 1
        let maxZoom: CGFloat = 2

        var current = zoom * magnification
        current = max(min(current, maxZoom), minZoom)
        return current
    }
}
```

Listing 12-10: Determining a minimum and a maximum scale

In this example, the view scaling is limited to a minimum of 1 and a maximum of 2. Since we need to perform some operations to limit the scaling to these values, we move the process to a method called `getCurrentZoom()` and call it every time it is needed. The method defines two constants with the minimum and maximum values for the scale, then calculates the current scale by multiplying the values of the `zoom` property and the magnification, and finally limits the result to a minimum of 1 and a maximum of 2 using the `min()` and `max()` functions. The `min()` function compares the scale with the maximum scale allowed and returns the smallest value (if the value is greater than 2, it returns 2), and then the `max()` function compares the result with the minimum scale allowed and returns the largest value (if the value is less than 1, it returns 1). The `getCurrentZoom()` method is called by the `scaleEffect()` modifier to set the scale for the view, and by the `onEnded()` method to set the final scale. Consequently, the user can zoom the image in and out, but up to a maximum of 2 and a minimum of 1.

 Do It Yourself: Update the `ContentView` structure with the code in Listing 12-10 and run the application. You should be able to scale the view to the limits set by the `minZoom` and `maxZoom` constants.

(Basic) **Rotation Gesture**

The rotation gesture is recognized when the user touches the screen with two fingers and makes a circular motion. It is often used to rotate an image. As with the previous gestures, if we want the user to perform the gesture multiple times, we need to store two states, one for the current rotation and another for the last rotation. The value generated by the gesture is a structure of type `Angle`. We have worked with this structure before. It contains two type methods, one to create an instance with a value in degrees (`degrees(Double)`) and another for a value in radians (`radians(Double)`), but in our example we are going to rotate an image to follow the fingers, and for that we only need to add the current angle to the delta angle produced by the gesture.

```
struct ContentView: View {
    @GestureState private var rotationAngle: Angle = Angle.zero
    @State private var rotation: Angle = Angle.zero

    var body: some View {
        Image(.spot1)
            .resizable()
            .scaledToFit()
            .frame(width: 160, height: 200)
            .rotationEffect(rotation + rotationAngle)

            .gesture(RotationGesture()
                .updating($rotationAngle) { value, state, transaction in
                    state = value
                }
                .onEnded { value in
                    rotation = rotation + value
                }
            )
    }
}
```

Listing 12-11: Defining a `RotationGesture` *recognizer*

This example applies the **`rotationEffect()`** modifier to rotate the view. The angle is calculated by adding the values of the two state properties. We also add the current rotation to the previous one when the gesture ends to preserve the current state in case the user wants to rotate the image again from that angle.

Figure 12-3: Image rotated by the user

 Do It Yourself: Update the `ContentView` view with the code in Listing 12-11. You should be able to rotate the view with your fingers, as shown in Figure 12-3. When you run the application in the simulator or the canvas, press the Option key on your keyboard to activate the gesture.

(Basic) ## Drag and Drop Gesture

Drag and drop is an operation that allows us to move an item from one app to another or between sections of the same app. This tool is useful on devices that can share the screen with two or more windows, such as iPads and Mac computers. On Mac computers, the process is quite simple. We open two or more windows at the same time and drag an item from one window to the other with the mouse. On iPads, we need to split the screen in half. For this purpose, iPads have a three-dot icon at the top that we can tap to share the screen with other applications.

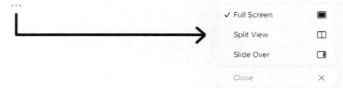

Figure 12-4: Tool to split the screen on iPads

When we tap the three dots, the system displays a menu with three options. The Full Screen option assigns the entire screen to the app, the Split View option splits the screen in half to show the current app on the left and another app on the right, and the Slide Over option moves the app to an overlay window that appears above other apps. If we choose the second or third option, the screen will be shared by two apps so that we can drag and drop items between them.

To allow the user to drag and drop items, we need to tell the system which views can be dragged and dropped. SwiftUI includes the following modifiers for this purpose.

▷ **draggable(**Transferable, **preview:** Closure**)**—This modifier designates the view as the source of a drag and drop operation. The first argument is a value that conforms to the `Transferable` protocol and represents the data that will be transferred in the process. The **preview** argument provides the view to show to the user while the drag gesture is performed.

▷ **dropDestination(for:** Type, **action:** Closure**)**—This modifier designates the view as the destination of a drag and drop operation. The **for** argument is a reference to the data type of the values we want the view to be able to receive, and the **action** argument provides a closure to process the data transferred by the gesture.

Drag-and-drop gestures are performed in the views, but the data to be transferred is determined by the code. This doesn't mean that we cannot send any value we want, but the data must be presented in such a way that applications can recognize it. For this purpose, the framework defines the `Transferable` protocol. This protocol prepares the data to be sent and processes the data received in an operation. Although our custom data types can conform to this protocol, some Swift data types and SwiftUI views do so by default. For example, if we want to let the user drag an image from our app to another app, we can use the `Image` view.

```
struct ContentView: View {
   var body: some View {
      VStack {
         Image(.husky)
            .resizable()
            .scaledToFit()
            .frame(width: 300, height: 400)
            .draggable(Image(.husky))
         Spacer()
      }
   }
}
```

Listing 12-12: *Allowing the user to drag an image*

This is a simple application with an `Image` view to show the image of a husky, but since we applied the `draggable()` modifier, the user can drag the image to another application. To tell the system what data to share between applications, we provide the modifier another `Image` view with the same picture. The `Image` view conforms to the `Transferable` protocol, so the system knows how to pass the data, and the external applications know how to process it. Figure 12-5 below shows the app running on an iPad and sharing the screen with the Photo Library. When we drag the husky into an album on the right, the image is added to that album.

Figure 12-5: *Drag and drop operation between apps*

 Do It Yourself: Create a Multiplatform project. Download the husky.png image from our website and add it to the Asset Catalog. Update the `ContentView` view with the code in Listing 12-12. Run the application on the iPad simulator. Tap the three dots at the top of the screen and select the Split View option (Figure 12-4). Open the Photo Library. You should see something like Figure 12-5. Open an album in the Photo Library and drag and drop the husky inside. The husky image should be added to the album.

The system creates an image from the view being dragged and uses it to show a preview to the user, but we can assign an additional view to the `draggable()` modifier to create a custom preview. For instance, the following example shows an SF Symbol instead.

```
struct ContentView: View {
   var body: some View {
      VStack {
         Image(.husky)
            .resizable()
            .scaledToFit()
            .frame(width: 300, height: 400)
            .draggable(Image(.husky), preview: {
```

```
                Image(systemName: "scope")
                    .font(.system(size: 50))
            })
        Spacer()
    }
  }
}
```

Listing 12-13: Providing a custom preview for the gesture

Figure 12-6: Custom preview

On the other hand, if what we want is to allow the user to drop items into our app, we need to provide a view that can receive that data. To turn a view into a possible destination for a drag-and-drop operation, we must apply the `dropDestination()` modifier. This modifier takes a data type that determines the type of data the view can receive and a closure to process it. As before, the type must conform to the `Transferable` protocol. For example, we can use an `Image` view.

```
struct ContentView: View {
    @State private var picture: Image = Image(.nopicture)

    var body: some View {
        VStack {
            picture
                .resizable()
                .scaledToFit()
                .frame(minWidth: 0, maxWidth: .infinity)
                .frame(height: 400)
                .dropDestination(for: Image.self, action: { elements,
location in
                    if let image = elements.first {
                        picture = image
                        return true
                    }
                    return false
                })
            Spacer()
        }
    }
}
```

Listing 12-14: Dropping images into an `Image` *view*

The closure assigned to the **action** argument receives two values: an array containing a list of the items dropped by the user, and a `CGPoint` structure with the position in the view where the items were dropped. Since we are processing the data as `Image` structures, the user can only drop images and the values are automatically converted to `Image` views, so we can assign them directly to a `@State` property and show them on the screen. Note that the closure must return a Boolean value to indicate the result of the operation. If we are able to get and process the values, we must return `true`, otherwise `false`.

Figure 12-7: *Dropping an image into our app*

Do It Yourself: Update the `ContentView` view with the code in Listing 12-14. Download the nopicture.png image from our website and add it to the Asset Catalog. Run the application on the iPad simulator and split the screen to share it with the Photo Library. Drag the image of the husky back to the app. The nopicture.png image should be replaced by the husky.

The `dropDestination()` modifier can use a binding property to tell the application when the item dragged by the user enters or leaves the area occupied by the view. For example, we can add a `@State` property to our previous example to change the color of the view when the item enters or leaves the area.

```
struct ContentView: View {
    @State private var picture: Image = Image(.nopicture)
    @State private var didEnter: Bool = false

    var body: some View {
        VStack {
            picture
                .resizable()
                .scaledToFit()
                .frame(minWidth: 0, maxWidth: .infinity)
                .frame(height: 400)
                .overlay(didEnter ? Color.green.opacity(0.2) : Color.clear)
                .dropDestination(for: Image.self, action: { elements,
location in
                    if let image = elements.first {
                        picture = image
                        return true
                    }
                    return false
                }, isTargeted: { value in
                    didEnter = value
                })
            Spacer()
        }
    }
}
```

Listing 12-15: *Providing feedback to the user*

The `didEnter` property stores a Boolean value. If the item is inside the area of the view, the `dropDestination()` modifier assigns the value `true` to this property, so we can use it to provide feedback to the user. In this case, we have created an overlay for the `Image` view. If the value of the `didEnter` property is `true`, we show a green overlay, otherwise the color is clear.

Figure 12-8: Feedback for the drag and drop operation

Do It Yourself: Update the `ContentView` view with the code in Listing 12-15. Run the application on the iPad simulator and split the screen as before. The drop area should turn green when you drag the image over it.

So far we have used an `Image` view to transfer the data. This data type conforms to the `Transferable` protocol, so it can be used to transfer data via drag and drop without any additional effort. However, custom data types, including structures and classes, can also be used. All we need to do is make them conform to the `Transferable` protocol. The protocol's only requirement is the implementation of the following type property.

▷ **transferRepresentation**—This type property returns a structure that represents the data to be transferred.

The property must return a structure that conforms to a protocol called `Transfer-Representation`. The framework defines several structures for creating these representations. The most frequently used are `CodableRepresentation` for sending and receiving encodable and decodable data, `DataRepresentation` for raw data, `FileRepresentation` for files, and `ProxyRepresentation` for using predefined representations. The following are some of the initializers available to create these structures.

▷ **CodableRepresentation(for:** Type, **contentType:** UTType)—This initializer creates a structure that represents data that can be encoded and decoded. The **for** argument is a reference to the data type itself, and the **contentType** argument determines the type of values the user is allowed to drag and drop.

▷ **DataRepresentation(contentType:** UTType, **exporting:** Closure, **importing:** Closure)—This initializer creates a structure that represents raw data. The **contentType** argument determines the type of values the user is allowed to drag and drop, the **exporting** argument provides the data to send when the view is dragged, and the **importing** argument creates an instance of the data type with the data dropped by the user. The structure also includes two more initializers to only import or export data: `DataRepresentation(importedContentType: UTType, importing: Closure)` and `DataRepresentation(exportedContentType: UTType, exporting: Closure)`.

▷ **FileRepresentation(contentType:** UTType, **shouldAttemptToOpenIn-Place:** Bool, **exporting:** Closure, **importing:** Closure)—This initializer creates a structure that represents files. The **contentType** argument determines the types of files the user is allowed to drag and drop, the **shouldAttemptToOpenInPlace** argument indicates if the receiver can access the original file, the **exporting** argument provides the file to be sent in a drag operation, and the **importing** argument creates the file from the information received from a drop operation. The structure also includes two more initializers to only import or export files: `FileRepresentation(importedContent-Type: UTType, shouldAttemptToOpenInPlace: Bool, importing:`

```
Closure) and FileRepresentation(exportedContentType:    UTType,
shouldAllowToOpenInPlace: Bool, exporting: Closure).
```

▷ **ProxyRepresentation(exporting:** Closure, **importing:** Closure)—This
  initializer creates a structure that uses an existent transfer representation that is
  suitable for the type. The **exporting** argument provides a reference to the transfer
  representation used when an element is dragged, and the **importing** argument provides
  a reference to the transfer representation used when an element is dropped. The
  structure also includes two more initializers to only import or export data:
  `ProxyRepresentation(importing:    Closure)` and `ProxyRepresentation-`
  `(exporting: Closure)`.

The purpose of these structures is to prepare the data to be sent and to process the data
received in a drag-and-drop operation. But no matter what structure we use, the values are
transferred as `Data` structures. In order for the applications to know how to process this data, we
need to declare the content type with a `UTType` structure. We have already introduced this
structure in Chapter 10. As we will see later, we can define our own types, but we can also use
the standard types provided by the framework. In the following example, we use the type `png` to
send a PNG image when the view is dragged to other applications.

```
import SwiftUI
struct ImageRepresentation: Transferable {
   let name: String
   let image: UIImage

   static var transferRepresentation: some TransferRepresentation {
      DataRepresentation(exportedContentType: .png, exporting: { value in
         return value.image.pngData()!
      })
   }
}
struct ContentView: View {
   @State private var picture: UIImage = UIImage(named: "nopicture")!

   var body: some View {
      VStack {
         Image(uiImage: picture)
            .resizable()
            .scaledToFit()
            .draggable(ImageRepresentation(name: "My Picture", image:
picture))
            .dropDestination(for: Data.self, action: { elements, location in
               if let data = elements.first, let image = UIImage(data:
data) {
                  picture = image
                  return true
               }
               return false
            })
         Spacer()
      }
   }
}
```

Listing 12-16: Dragging custom values

For this application, we want to transfer only the image, so we define a structure called
`ImageRepresentation`, get the structure to conform to the `Transferable` protocol,
implement the `transferRepresentation` property, and define a `DataRepresentation`
structure to get the data from the image and return it.

Although we are transferring data that represents an image, we are using our own custom data type to process it. When the user drags the view, the `draggable()` modifier creates an instance of the `ImageRepresentation` structure and the structure is sent to the closure assigned to the `DataRepresentation` structure so we can get the `UIImage` object in the `image` property, convert it to data using the `pngData()` method, and return it. The external application receives this data, recognizes it as a PNG image thanks to the `UTType` structure and processes it as such.

Note that to know which image the user is dragging, we have changed the data type of the `picture` property to a `UIImage` object, and therefore we need to display the image on the screen using the `Image(uiImage:)` initializer. And because we are processing the image with a `UIImage` object instead of an `Image` view, we have also updated the `dropDestination()` modifier to work with this value. The process is simple. We tell the `dropDestination()` modifier that the value received is a `Data` structure, and then convert that value to an image using the `UIImage(data:)` initializer (see Images in Chapter 10). Now the user can drag and drop images between this view and an external application, and everything is automatically converted from data to image and vice versa.

 Do It Yourself: Update the ContentView.swift file with the code in Listing 12-16. Run the application on the iPad simulator. Split the screen. Open the Photo Library. You should be able to drag and drop images back and forward between the apps.

In the last example, we use a `DataRepresentation` structure to prepare the data to be sent in a drag operation (exporting), but use a `Data` type to receive an image dropped by the user. This is because we have no control over the data that other applications send to us. However, we can send and receive custom data types as long as the application knows how to process them. For example, when we allow the user to drag and drop items within our application, we have control over the entire process and can therefore transfer any custom data type we want. The only requirement is that the data be encoded. When data is sent, it must be encoded, and when data is received, it must be decoded. This is easily accomplished with the `Codable` protocol and the `CodableRepresentation` structure, but since we are using custom data types, we also need to define a custom `UTType`. The following is the structure's initializer.

▷ **UTType(exportedAs:** String, **conformingTo:** UTType?)—This initializer creates a custom `UTType` identified by the string assigned to the **exportedAs** argument. The **conformingTo** argument is a predefined `UTType` that the custom type uses as reference.

The `UTType` structure requires an identifier, which we must create from settings. We need to go to the project's settings (Figure 5-4, number 6), open the Info panel, expand the Exported Type Identifiers section, press the + button, and insert the values.

⌄ **Exported Type Identifiers (1)**

Pictures

Description	Pictures	Extensions
Identifier	com.formasterminds.pictures	Mime Types
Conforms To	public.data	
Reference URL	None	

Figure 12-9: Custom content type

The values we need are the Description, the Identifier, and the Conforms To. The Description is just text describing the type, the Identifier must be unique, so it is recommended to declare it with an inverted domain, as we did in our example, and the Conforms to option is a predefined **UTType** that closely matches what our type will represent. In this case, we use the public.data type, so that the system knows we are transferring raw data.

Once we have the custom content type, we need to extend the **UTType** structure to include a type property that represents it. In the following example, we create a custom structure to manage the data (an image and an identifier), and extend the **UTType** structure with a property called **product** to store our custom type.

```
import SwiftUI
import Observation
import UniformTypeIdentifiers

struct PictureRepresentation: Identifiable, Codable, Transferable {
   var id = UUID()
   var image: Data

   static var transferRepresentation: some TransferRepresentation {
      CodableRepresentation(for: PictureRepresentation.self, contentType:
.product)
   }
}
extension UTType {
   static let product = UTType(exportedAs: "com.formasterminds.pictures")
}

@Observable class ApplicationData: @unchecked Sendable {
   var listPictures: [PictureRepresentation]

   static let shared: ApplicationData = ApplicationData()
   private init() {
      listPictures = [
         PictureRepresentation(image: UIImage(named:
"spot1")!.pngData()!),
         PictureRepresentation(image: UIImage(named:
"spot2")!.pngData()!),
         PictureRepresentation(image: UIImage(named:
"spot3")!.pngData()!)
      ]
   }
}
```

Listing 12-17: Using a custom content type

After defining the **PictureRepresentation** structure to contain the data and extending the **UTType** to include our content type, we initialize the model with three instances containing the images spot1, spot2, and spot3. The purpose of this application is to allow the user to drag these images from the top of the screen to a view at the bottom. Note that after dropping an image, we want that image to be deleted from the list, so we include a **UUID** value to identify it.

For the interface, we need a **ForEach** loop to list all the images available at the top and another **Image** view at the bottom where the user can drop them.

```
struct ContentView: View {
   @Environment(ApplicationData.self) private var appData
   @State private var currentPicture: UIImage = UIImage(named:
"nopicture")!

   var body: some View {
      VStack {
         HStack(spacing: 10) {
            ForEach(appData.listPictures) { picture in
               Image(uiImage: UIImage(data: picture.image) ??
UIImage(named: "nopicture")!)
```

```
                 .resizable()
                 .frame(width: 80, height: 100)
                 .draggable(picture)
         }
     }.frame(height: 120)
     Image(uiImage: currentPicture)
         .resizable()
         .scaledToFit()
         .padding(10)
         .dropDestination(for: PictureRepresentation.self, action:
{ elements, location in
             if let picture = elements.first {
                 currentPicture = UIImage(data: picture.image) ??
UIImage(named: "nopicture")!
                 appData.listPictures.removeAll(where: { $0.id ==
picture.id })
                 return true
             }
             return false
         })
     }
   }
}
#Preview {
   ContentView()
      .environment(ApplicationData.shared)
}
```

Listing 12-18: Dragging and dropping custom values

The `draggable()` and `dropDestination()` modifiers work with the `Picture-Representation` structure to transfer the data. When the user drags an image, the structure encodes the data, including the identifier and the image, and when the user drops the image into the target view, the data is decoded, an instance of the `PictureRepresentation` structure is created, and we can process the values. In this case, we assign the image to the `Image` view and then remove the original picture from the list. The result is shown below.

Figure 12-10: Drag and drop custom data

 Do It Yourself: Create a Swift file called ApplicationData.swift for the model in Listing 12-17. Update the `ContentView` view with the code in Listing 12-18. Download the spot1.jpg, spot2.jpg and spot3.jpg images from our website and add them to the Asset Catalog. Go to the project's settings (Figure 5-4, number 6), open the Info panel, expand the Exported Type Identifiers section, press the + button, and insert the values, as shown in Figure 12-9. Run the application on the iPhone simulator. Drag an image and drop it over the nopicture.png image. The original image should be removed, as shown in Figure 12-10 (right).

Chapter 13
MapKit Framework

(Basic) **13.1 Map View**

Often, users need to visualize their location or the places they want to go on a map to position themselves in the world. For these types of applications, Apple offers the MapKit framework. The framework includes all the tools necessary to create and configure maps, including the `Map` view to add a map to the user interface. The following are some of the view's initializers.

▷ **Map(initialPosition:** MapCameraPosition, **bounds:** MapCameraBounds?, **interactionModes:** MapInteractionModes, **selection:** Binding, **scope:** Namespace.ID?, **content:** Closure)—This initializer creates a map with the configuration defined by the arguments. The **initialPosition** argument specifies the initial position of the camera. The **bounds** argument is a structure that defines the area of the map that the user is allowed to use. The **interactionModes** argument defines the user interaction allowed. It is a structure with the properties `all`, `pan`, `zoom`, `pitch`, and `rotate`. The **selection** argument is a binding property used to store the map item that was selected by the user. The **scope** argument is a value that can be used to identify the map and associate it with external controls. And the **content** argument specifies the additional content for the view.

▷ **Map(position:** Binding, **bounds:** MapCameraBounds?, **interaction-Modes:** MapInteractionModes, **selection:** Binding, **scope:** Namespace.ID?, **content:** Closure)—This initializer creates a map with the configuration defined by the arguments. The **position** argument is a binding of type `MapCameraPosition` that sets and keeps track of the position of the camera. The **bounds** argument is a structure that defines the area of the map that the user is allowed to use. The **interactionModes** argument defines the user interaction allowed. It is a structure with the properties `all`, `pan`, `zoom`, `pitch`, and `rotate`. The **selection** argument is a binding property used to store the map item selected by the user. The **scope** argument is a value that can be used to identify the map and associate it with external controls. And the **content** argument specifies the additional content for the view.

If all we want is to display a map, we just need to insert the `Map` view without any parameters, as shown below.

```
import SwiftUI
import MapKit

struct ContentView: View {
   var body: some View {
      Map()
         .ignoresSafeArea()
   }
}
```

Listing 13-1: Displaying a map

The `Map` view takes up all available space, but considers the safe area before placing labels and tools, such as the Apple logo. If we want the view to ignore the safe area, we can apply the `ignoresSafeArea()` modifier, as we did in this example.

If we don't specify the position of the camera, the `Map` view shows the whole world, but the user can zoom in to find a location.

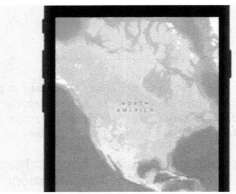

Figure 13-1: *Standard map*

By default, the view shows a representation of the map that includes the names of roads and locations, as well as icons to indicate points of interest, but it can also show a satellite image or a combination of both. To set the style, the framework includes the following modifier.

▷ **mapStyle(**MapStyle**)**—This modifier sets the style of the map. The argument is a structure with properties and methods to define and configure the style.

The `MapStyle` structure includes the properties `hybrid`, `imagery`, and `standard` to represent the three possible styles, but also provides the following methods for configuration.

▷ **hybrid(elevation:** Elevation, **pointsOfInterest:** PointOfInterestCategories, **showsTraffic:** Bool**)**—This method returns the style for rendering a hybrid map with the configuration specified by the arguments. The **elevation** argument specifies whether the map displays elevations. It is a structure with the properties `automatic` (standard 2D map), `flat` (2D map), and `realistic` (3D map). The **pointsOfInterest** argument is a structure with properties and methods for specifying the points of interest that the map should contain. And the **showsTraffic** argument determines whether the map should contain roads.

▷ **imagery(elevation:** Elevation**)**—This method returns the style for rendering a satellite map with the configuration specified by the argument. The **elevation** argument specifies whether the map displays elevations. It is a structure with the properties `automatic` (standard 2D map), `flat` (2D map), and `realistic` (3D map).

▷ **standard(elevation:** Elevation, **emphasis:** StandardEmphasis, **pointsOf-Interest:** PointOfInterestCategories, **showsTraffic:** Bool**)**—This method returns the style for rendering a standard map with the configuration specified by the arguments. The **elevation** argument specifies whether the map displays elevations. It is a structure with the properties `automatic` (standard 2D map), `flat` (2D map), and `realistic` (3D map). The **emphasis** argument determines whether map features are highlighted. It is a structure with the properties `automatic` and `muted`. The **pointsOf-Interest** argument is a structure with properties and methods for specifying the points of interest that the map should contain. And the **showsTraffic** argument determines whether the map should contain roads.

If it is just a matter of displaying a particular map, we can apply the `mapStyle()` modifier with the property that represents the map we want to use.

```
struct ContentView: View {
   var body: some View {
      Map()
         .mapStyle(.hybrid)
         .ignoresSafeArea()
   }
}
```

Listing 13-2: *Displaying a hybrid map*

In this example, we use the `hybrid` property to get a map that shows satellite imagery along with roads, locations, and icons to represent points of interest.

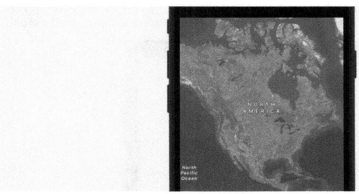

Figure 13-2: *Hybrid map*

By default, the map displays all points of interest in the area, but we can select the ones we want by specifying an instance of the `PointOfInterestCategories` structure. The structure includes the following initializer.

▷ **PointOfInterestCategories(arrayLiteral:** MKPointOfInterestCategory...**)**— This initializer creates a structure to represent points of interest. The **arrayLiteral** argument is a list of structures representing the points of interest to be included. The values are separated by commas.

The `PointOfInterestCategories` structure also defines the following type methods to include or exclude specific points of interest.

▷ **excluding(**[MKPointOfInterestCategory]**)**—This method returns a `PointOf-InterestCategories` structure that excludes the points of interest specified by the argument.

▷ **including(**[MKPointOfInterestCategory]**)**—This method returns a `PointOf-InterestCategories` structure that includes only the points of interest specified by the argument.

The points of interest are represented by an instance of the `MKPointOfInterestCategory` structure. The structure includes a long list of type properties to return structures that represent every category available. These properties are `airport`, `amusementPark`, `aquarium`, `atm`, `bakery`, `bank`, `beach`, `brewery`, `cafe`, `campground`, `carRental`, `evCharger`, `fireStation`, `fitnessCenter`, `foodMarket`, `gasStation`, `hospital`, `hotel`, `laundry`, `library`, `marina`, `movieTheater`, `museum`, `nationalPark`, `nightlife`, `parkparking`, `pharmacy`, `police`, `postOffice`, `publicTransport`, `restaurant`, `restroom`, `school`, `stadium`, `store`, `theater`, `university`, `winery`, and `zoo`.

With these properties, we can specify exactly what should be displayed on the map. For example, we can show only coffee shops.

```
struct ContentView: View {
    var body: some View {
        Map()
            .mapStyle(.standard(pointsOfInterest: .including([.cafe])))
            .ignoresSafeArea()
    }
}
```

Listing 13-3: *Selecting points of interest*

If we zoom in on the map enough to see a neighborhood, the `Map` view will automatically load and display icons representing the points of interest we have selected. In this case, coffee shops.

Figure 13-3: *Points of interest*

 Do It Yourself: Create a Multiplatform project. Update the **ContentView** view with the code in Listing 13-3. You should see the world map. Zoom in until you see a neighborhood. You should see icons representing the coffee shops in the area, as shown in Figure 13-3. If you are testing the application on the canvas, hold down the Option key to zoom in or out on the map.

(Basic) Camera

The area of the map that the user sees is determined by a camera. The MapKit framework includes the following structure to create it.

▷ **MapCamera(centerCoordinate:** CLLocationCoordinate2D, **distance:** Double, **heading:** Double, **pitch:** Double)—This initializer creates a camera with the configuration defined by the arguments. The **centerCoordinate** argument specifies the coordinates at the center of the visible map, the **distance** argument specifies the distance in meters from the center of the visible map to the camera, the **heading** argument specifies the orientation of the camera in degrees relative to the true north, and the **pitch** argument specifies the viewing angle in degrees.

The `Map` view automatically creates a camera for us, so we don't have to provide our own, but it sets the camera's viewpoint to show the entire planet. To move the camera, the framework includes the `MapCameraPosition` structure. The structure defines the following methods to set the position of the camera.

▷ **camera(**MapCamera**)**—This method configures the camera based on the configuration of the camera specified by the argument.

▷ **region(**MKCoordinateRegion**)**—This method directs the camera to the region of the map specified by the argument.

▷ **rect(**MKMapRect**)**—This method directs the camera to the rectangle on the map defined by the argument. The argument is a structure that represents a rectangular area on a two-dimensional map.

▷ **item(**MKMapItem, **allowsAutomaticPitch:** Bool**)**—This method directs the camera to the point of interest indicated by the first argument. The first argument is a structure representing a point of interest or the user's location, and the **allowsAutomaticPitch** argument determines whether the camera automatically selects a pitch.

▷ **userLocation(followsHeading:** Bool, **fallback:** MapCameraPosition**)**—This method directs the camera to the user's location. The **followsHeading** argument determines whether the camera should follow the user, and the **fallback** argument specifies a position the camera should point to when the user's location cannot be determined.

The most frequently used method for setting the camera position is `region()`. This method requires the region to be specified with an `MKCoordinateRegion` structure. The structure includes the following initializer.

▷ **MKCoordinateRegion(center:** CLLocationCoordinate2D, **latitudinal-Meters:** CLLocationDistance, **longitudinalMeters:** CLLocationDistance**)**— This initializer creates an `MKCoordinateRegion` structure with the values specified by the arguments. The **center** argument specifies the region's coordinates, and the **latitudinalMeters** and **longitudinalMeters** arguments determine the vertical and horizontal size of the region in meters (`CLLocationDistance` is a typealias of `Double`).

The latitude and longitude of a location are determined by a `CLLocationCoordinate2D` structure. The structure includes the following initializer.

▷ **CLLocationCoordinate2D(latitude:** CLLocationDegrees, **longitude:** CLLocationDegrees**)**—This initializer creates an `CLLocationCoordinate2D` structure with the values specified by the arguments. The **latitude** argument is a typealias of `Double` that determines the location's latitude, and the **longitude** argument is a typealias of `Double` that determines the location's longitude.

With these values, we can move the camera and zoom in and out the map to show the area we want, but because they may change or more may be required later, it is better to manage the location from the model, as we do in the following example.

```
import SwiftUI
import Observation
import MapKit

@Observable class ApplicationData: @unchecked Sendable {
    var cameraPos: MapCameraPosition

    static let shared: ApplicationData = ApplicationData()
    private init() {
        let coordinates = CLLocationCoordinate2D(latitude:
40.7637825011971, longitude: -73.9731328627541)
        let region = MKCoordinateRegion(center: coordinates,
latitudinalMeters: 1000, longitudinalMeters: 1000)
        cameraPos = MapCameraPosition.region(region)
    }
```

```
}
```

Listing 13-4: Configuring the map from the model

In this model, we include a property to store the `MapCameraPosition` structure, and then initialize it with the coordinates of the Apple Store in New York City and a region of 1000 meters around that location. Now we can set the map to this location.

```
struct ContentView: View {
    @Environment(ApplicationData.self) private var appData

    var body: some View {
        @Bindable var appData = appData

        Map(position: $appData.cameraPos)
    }
}
```

Listing 13-5: Zooming on a region on the map

When we specify a location, the map is automatically zoomed to that region. In this case, the area around the Apple Store in New York City.

Figure 13-4: Map showing a specific region of New York City

Do It Yourself: Create a Swift file called ApplicationData.swift for the model in Listing 13-4. Remember to inject the `ApplicationData` object into the environment for the app and the previews (Chapter 7, Listing 7-4). Update the `ContentView` view with the code in Listing 13-5. You should see the map of New York City with the Apple Store in the center.

In the previous example, we specified the map's initial location, but when the user scrolls the map, the values are not updated. To respond to these changes, the framework includes the following modifier.

▷ **onMapCameraChange(frequency:** MapCameraUpdateFrequency, **Closure)**—This modifier executes a closure when the location of the camera changes. The **frequency** argument determines how often the system should check for updates. It is a structure with the properties **continuous** (while the interaction is taking place) and **onEnd** (when the interaction is over).

The closure assigned to the `onMapCameraChange()` modifier receives a `MapCamera-UpdateContext` structure with information about the camera. The structure includes the following properties.

- **camera**—This property returns a reference to the `MapCamera` structure that represents the camera assigned to the map.

- **rect**—This property returns an `MKMapRect` structure with a rectangle representing the visible area on the map.

- **region**—This property returns an `MKCoordinateRegion` structure with values representing the visible region on the map.

When the user scrolls the map, it is our job to update the values in the `MapCameraPosition` structure. For example, we can get the region returned by the `MapCameraUpdateContext` structure and assign it to the camera every time the closure of the `onMapCameraChange` modifier is executed.

```
struct ContentView: View {
    @Environment(ApplicationData.self) private var appData

    var body: some View {
        @Bindable var appData = appData

        Map(position: $appData.cameraPos)
            .safeAreaInset(edge: .bottom) {
                HStack {
                    if let region = appData.cameraPos.region {
                        Text(String(region.center.latitude))
                        Text(String(region.center.longitude))
                    }
                }.padding([.top, .bottom])
                .frame(minWidth: 0, maxWidth: .infinity)
                .background(.white)
            }
            .onMapCameraChange { context in
                appData.cameraPos = .region(context.region)
            }
    }
}
```

Listing 13-6: Showing the current latitude and longitude

Once the `MapCameraPosition` structure is updated, we can use this value to present information to the user. In this example, we display the current latitude and longitude at the bottom of the map. Note that we use the `safeAreaInset()` modifier so that the safe area is expanded and the view does not obscure the labels on the map.

Figure 13-5: Current latitude and longitude

By default, the `Map` view allows the user to zoom and pan the map, but the view's initializer can include the **interactionModes** argument to restrict interaction. For example, we can enable only zooming to not allow the user to change the region.

```
struct ContentView: View {
   @Environment(ApplicationData.self) private var appData

   var body: some View {
      @Bindable var appData = appData

      Map(position: $appData.cameraPos, interactionModes: .zoom)
   }
}
```

Listing 13-7: Disabling panning

Another option is to limit the area through which the user can navigate. The framework includes the following structure to determine the area available to the user.

▷ **MapCameraBounds(centerCoordinateBounds:** MKCoordinateRegion, **minimumDistance:** Double?, **maximumDistance:** Double?)—This initializer creates a `MapCameraBounds` structure to limit user interaction. The **centerCoordinate-Bounds** argument determines the center of the visible area, and the **minimumDistance** and **maximumDistance** arguments specify how large this area may be.

If we specify the **centerCoordinateBounds** argument, the structure limits how far the user can scroll the map, and if this argument is ignored, the structure limits how far the user can zoom in or out. For example, in the following application, the user cannot move further than 1000 meters from the center. As always, we define the values in the model, but they could also be provided by the view or a method.

```
@Observable class ApplicationData: @unchecked Sendable {
   var cameraPos: MapCameraPosition
   var cameraBounds: MapCameraBounds

   static let shared: ApplicationData = ApplicationData()
   private init() {
      let coordinates = CLLocationCoordinate2D(latitude:
40.7637825011971, longitude: -73.9731328627541)
      let region = MKCoordinateRegion(center: coordinates,
latitudinalMeters: 1000, longitudinalMeters: 1000)
      cameraPos = MapCameraPosition.region(region)
      cameraBounds = MapCameraBounds(centerCoordinateBounds: region,
minimumDistance: 200, maximumDistance: 1000)
   }
}
```

Listing 13-8: Defining the boundaries for the camera

Applying this bounds to the camera is easy. All we need to do is to provide the `MapCameraBounds` structure to the `Map` view initializer.

```
struct ContentView: View {
   @Environment(ApplicationData.self) private var appData

   var body: some View {
      @Bindable var appData = appData

      Map(position: $appData.cameraPos, bounds: appData.cameraBounds)
   }
}
```

Listing 13-9: Applying the boundaries to the map

Do It Yourself: Update the **ApplicationData** class with the code in Listing 13-8 and the **ContentView** view with the code in Listing 13-9. You shouldn't be able to scroll the map more than 1000 meters.

Basic **Map Content**

The previous examples set the visible area around the Apple Store. Since this is a relevant location, the **Map** view displays an icon with the name of the store, but this is not always the case. For most locations, no indication is shown at all, and the user has to guess where the location actually is. To mark locations, the framework includes the **Marker** structure. The structure defines many initializers. The following are the most frequently used.

▷ **Marker(String, coordinate: CLLocationCoordinate2D)**—This initializer creates a standard pin for a **Map** view with the title and at the location specified by the arguments. The first argument specifies the text that appears under the pin, and the **coordinate** argument specifies the location.

▷ **Marker(item: MKMapItem)**—This initializer creates a standard pin for a **Map** view that represents the map item specified by the argument. The **item** argument is a structure used to represent a location.

The **Marker** structure adds a standard pin to the map. If we need more customization, we can create an annotation instead. For this purpose, the framework provides the **Annotation** structure.

▷ **Annotation(String, coordinate: CLLocationCoordinate2D, anchor: UnitPoint, content: Closure)**—This initializer creates an annotation for a **Map** view. The first argument specifies the text that appears under the annotation, the **coordinate** argument specifies the location, the **anchor** argument determines where to position the annotation around that location, and the **content** argument defines the views that represent the annotation.

The **Marker** and **Annotation** structures display a title below the pin. The framework includes the following modifier to specify the visibility of this title.

▷ **annotationTitles(Visibility)**—This modifier determines the visibility of the pin's title. The argument is an enumeration with the values **automatic**, **visible**, and **hidden**.

The framework also includes the following structures for using graphics to represent areas on the map.

▷ **MapCircle(center: CLLocationCoordinate2D, radius: CLLocationDistance)** —This initializer creates a circular overlay to represent an area on the map. The **center** argument specifies the location, and the **radius** argument specifies the radius of the circle.

▷ **MapPolygon(coordinates: [CLLocationCoordinate2D])**—This initializer creates a polygonal overlay to represent an area on the map. The **coordinates** argument is an array with the locations of each corner of the polygon.

▷ **MapPolyline(coordinates: [CLLocationCoordinate2D], contourStyle: ContourStyle)**—This initializer creates an overlay with a single line. The **coordinates** argument is an array of locations for the line to follow, and the **contourStyle** argument specifies the style of the line. This is a structure with the properties **geodesic** (the line follows the contours of the earth) and **straight** (a straight line between points).

The overlays are displayed along with the rest of the content, including labels and icons. To determine which content should be displayed on top, the framework provides the following modifier.

▷ **mapOverlayLevel(level:** MKOverlayLevel**)**—This modifier specifies the position of the overlay. The **level** argument is an enumeration with the values **aboveRoads** and **aboveLabels**.

The framework also includes a list of modifiers for styling overlays, pins and annotations.

▷ **tint(**ShapeStyle**)**—This modifier applies a color or pattern to the view. The argument is a value that conforms to the **ShapeStyle** protocol, such as **Color**.

▷ **stroke(**ShapeStyle, **lineWidth:** CGFloat**)**—This modifier applies a stroke with the style specified by the arguments. The first argument is a value that conforms to the **ShapeStyle** protocol, such as **Color**, and the **lineWidth** argument specifies the width of the stroke.

▷ **stroke(**ShapeStyle, **style:** StrokeStyle**)**—This modifier applies a stroke with the style specified by the arguments. The first argument is a value that conforms to the **ShapeStyle** protocol, such as **Color**, and the **style** argument specifies a style (see **StrokeStyle** in Chapter 11).

▷ **foregroundStyle(**ShapeStyle**)**—This modifier fills the view with the color or pattern specified by the argument. The argument is a value that conforms to the **ShapeStyle** protocol, such as **Color**.

The markers, annotations and graphics are added to the map from the closure assigned to the **Map** view's initializer. For example, we can add a marker at the location of the Apple Store in New York City.

```
struct ContentView: View {
    @Environment(ApplicationData.self) private var appData
    let coordinatesApple = CLLocationCoordinate2D(latitude:
40.7637825011971, longitude: -73.9731328627541)

    var body: some View {
        @Bindable var appData = appData

        Map(position: $appData.cameraPos) {
            Marker("Apple Store", coordinate: coordinatesApple)
                .tint(.blue)
        }
    }
}
```

Listing 13-10: Adding markers to the map

In this example, we store the location of the Apple Store in a property and use that value to add a marker to the map. The marker is represented by a red pin, but we change its color to blue with the **tint()** modifier. The result is shown below.

Figure 13-6: Marker

The **Marker** view creates a pin in the shape of a balloon. We can change the color, the title, and the symbol inside the balloon, but if we want more customization, we need to create an annotation. Annotations work like markers, but can be represented by any view we want. In the following example, we use an **Image** view with the picture of the Apple Store.

```
Map(position: $appData.cameraPos) {
    Annotation("Apple Store", coordinate: coordinatesApple, content: {
        Image(.appstore)
    })
}
```

Listing 13-11: Displaying annotations

Figure 13-7: Annotation

 Do It Yourself: Update the **ContentView** view with the code in Listing 13-10. You should see a blue pin at the Apple Store location in New York City (Figure 13-6). Update the **Map** view with the code in Listing 13-11. Download the appstore.png image from our website and add it to the Asset Catalog. You should see a custom marker with the picture of the Apple Store (Figure 13-7).

If what we need is to highlight an area of the map, we can show graphics instead. In the following example, we display a circle at the Apple Store location.

```
Map(position: $appData.cameraPos) {
    MapCircle(center: coordinatesApple, radius: 100)
        .foregroundStyle(.blue)
        .mapOverlayLevel(level: .aboveLabels)
}
```

Listing 13-12: Drawing a circle over the labels

In this example, we apply the **mapOverlayLevel()** modifier to the **MapCircle** view to draw the circle over the labels. Figure 13-8 below shows the difference when the modifier is applied or not.

Figure 13-8: Graphics over or under the labels

In addition to circles, we can also draw rectangles and lines to represent areas on the map. In the following example, we show how to draw a line from the Apple Store to Trump Tower in New York City.

```
struct ContentView: View {
   @Environment(ApplicationData.self) private var appData
   let coordinatesApple = CLLocationCoordinate2D(latitude:
40.7637825011971, longitude: -73.9731328627541)
   let coordinatesTower = CLLocationCoordinate2D(latitude:
40.76260429912616, longitude: -73.97378658614556)

   var body: some View {
      @Bindable var appData = appData

      Map(position: $appData.cameraPos) {
         MapPolyline(coordinates: [coordinatesApple, coordinatesTower])
            .stroke(.red, lineWidth: 5)
      }
   }
}
```

Listing 13-13: Drawing a line

The `MapPolyline` view draws a straight line between two or more points on the map, but it can also be used to trace routes, as we will see later. In this example, we use it to show the direct connection between two locations. Note that we use the `stroke()` modifier to draw the line in red and with a width of 5 points.

Figure 13-9: Straight lines

(Basic) **Search**

The MapKit framework includes a service for translating addresses into locations and finding places of interest. The service is called Local Search. The system can take a free-form query string and return an array with the results. The query is created by the `Request` class, which is defined in the `MKLocalSearch` class. Below are some of the properties defined by the `Request` class to configure the query.

▷ **naturalLanguageQuery**—This property sets or returns a string with the term or address we want to search.

▷ **region**—This property sets or returns an `MKCoordinateRegion` structure that specifies the region in which the search is performed.

To perform a search, the `MKLocalSearch` class includes the following initializer and method.

▷ **MKLocalSearch(request:** MKLocalSearchRequest)—This initializer creates an `MKLocalSearch` object to perform a search request.

▷ **start()**—This asynchronous method performs a search and returns an `MKLocalSearchResponse` object with the results.

The search returns an `MKLocalSearchResponse` object that contains the following properties.

▷ **mapItems**—This property returns an array of `MKMapItem` objects that represent the results produced by the search.

Chapter 13 -Maps

▷ **boundingRegion**—This property returns an `MKCoordinateRegion` structure that determines the region occupied by the results produced by the search.

The Local Search service is designed to find all the locations that match the query. The framework defines the `MKMapItem` class to represent a location. Below are some of the properties included in the class to return the data.

▷ **name**—This property sets or returns a string with the name of the location.

▷ **phoneNumber**—This property sets or returns a string with the location's phone number.

▷ **url**—This property sets or returns a `URL` value with the URL of the location's website.

▷ **placemark**—This property sets or returns an `MKPlacemark` object with additional information about the place. The `MKPlacemark` class inherits from the `CLPlacemark` class, which includes many properties to return information about the location. The most frequently used are `thoroughfare` and `subThoroughfare` (address), `locality` (city), `postalCode`, `administrativeArea` (state), `country` and `location` (a `CLLocation` structure that includes the `coordinate` property we can use to retrieve the `CLLocationCoordinate2D` structure with the location's latitude and longitude).

There are several ways an app can perform a search and display the results. As an example, we can search for places related to the word "Pizza" every time the position of the camera changes. First, we need a property in the model to store the locations found by the system and a method to perform the search.

```
import SwiftUI
import Observation
import MapKit

@Observable class ApplicationData: @unchecked Sendable {
    var cameraPos: MapCameraPosition
    var listLocations: [MKMapItem] = []

    static let shared: ApplicationData = ApplicationData()
    private init() {
        let coordinates = CLLocationCoordinate2D(latitude:
40.7637825011971, longitude: -73.9731328627541)
        let region = MKCoordinateRegion(center: coordinates,
latitudinalMeters: 1000, longitudinalMeters: 1000)
        cameraPos = MapCameraPosition.region(region)
    }
    func findPlaces() async {
        if let region = cameraPos.region {
            let request = MKLocalSearch.Request()
            request.naturalLanguageQuery = "Pizza"
            request.region = region

            let search = MKLocalSearch(request: request)
            if let results = try? await search.start() {
                let items = results.mapItems
                await MainActor.run {
                    listLocations = []
                    for place in items {
                        listLocations.append(place)
                    }
                }
            }
        }
    }
}
```

```
}
```

Listing 13-14: Finding places with Local Search

Now we can perform a search, store the results in the model, and display the locations on the map.

```
struct ContentView: View {
    @Environment(ApplicationData.self) private var appData

    var body: some View {
        @Bindable var appData = appData
        Map(position: $appData.cameraPos) {
            ForEach(appData.listLocations, id: \.self) { place in
                Marker(item: place)
            }
        }
        .onMapCameraChange(frequency: .onEnd) { context in
            appData.cameraPos = .region(context.region)
            Task(priority: .background) {
                await appData.findPlaces()
            }
        }
    }
}
```

Listing 13-15: Searching for places

The code in Listing 13-15 defines the `findPlaces()` method to search for places associated with the term "Pizza" and adds each location found to the `listLocations` property. When the view is loaded, the `onMapCameraChange()` modifier calls this method asynchronously to start the process. The method creates a request with the query "Pizza" and the region the camera is pointed at. This query is used to create the `MKLocalSearch` object, and then the search is initiated by calling the `start()` method. This method is asynchronous, so we have to wait for the results. Once the results come back from the Apple servers, we remove the current locations in the `listLocations` property and save the new ones found by the search. The `Map` view is updated and the `Marker` views are created with a `ForEach` loop to display the current locations.

Figure 13-10: Places found by the Local Search system

 Do It Yourself: Update the ApplicationData.swift file with the code in Listing 13-14 and the `ContentView` view with the code in Listing 13-15. You should see the pizzerias around the Apple Store in New York City. Scroll through the map. The app should search for and display the pizzerias around the new location.

The `Map` view allows users to select locations on the map. To enable this feature, we just need to provide a property to store the value that identifies the selected item and initialize the `Map` view with that property. The framework includes the `MapSelection` structure to store the selected value.

▷ **MapSelection**(SelectionValue)—This initializer creates a structure to store the identifier of the item selected by the user. The argument is the value we use to identify the item.

The `MapSelection` structure includes the following properties to return the information about the selected item.

▷ **value**—This property returns the value used to identify the item selected by the user.

▷ **feature**—This property returns a `MapFeature` structure with information about the feature selected by the user.

The `MapSelection` structure is generic, so we can use any value we want to identify the markers. In the following example, we create a property to store the selected value and then use the `MKMapItem` value to identify the markers. When a marker is selected by the user, the `MapSelection` structure associated with that marker is assigned to the property so we know which one was selected.

```
struct ContentView: View {
    @Environment(ApplicationData.self) private var appData
    @State private var selectedItem: MapSelection<MKMapItem>?

    var body: some View {
        @Bindable var appData = appData

        Map(position: $appData.cameraPos, selection: $selectedItem) {
            ForEach(appData.listLocations, id: \.self) { place in
                Marker(item: place)
                    .tag(MapSelection(place))
            }
        }
        .onMapCameraChange(frequency: .onEnd) { context in
            if selectedItem == nil {
                appData.cameraPos = .region(context.region)
                Task(priority: .background) {
                    await appData.findPlaces()
                }
            }
        }
        .onChange(of: selectedItem, { old, value in
            if let item = value?.value {
                print(item.name ?? "Undefined")
                print(item.phoneNumber ?? "Undefined")
                print(item.placemark.locality ?? "Undefined")
            }
        })
    }
}
```

Listing 13-16: Selecting markers

When a marker is selected by the user, the `Map` view assigns the marker's identifier to the `selectedItem` property. It is now up to us to process the selected value and do something with it. In this example, we just print some of the values to the console, but we could also have saved them in the model or displayed them to the user. Displaying information to the user is actually quite common in this type of application. For this reason, the framework includes some modifiers to simplify our work.

▷ **mapItemDetailSelectionAccessory(**MapItemDetailSelectionAccessorySty le**)**—This modifier specifies the type of accessory to be shown when an item on the map is selected. The argument is a structure with the properties `automatic`, `callout`, `caption` and `sheet`, and also the `callout(CalloutStyle)` method to select a specific callout style (`automatic`, `compact` or `full`).

▷ **mapFeatureSelectionAccessory(**MapItemDetailSelectionAccessoryStyle**)** —This modifier specifies the type of accessory to be shown when a feature on the map is selected. The argument is a structure with the properties `automatic`, `callout`, `caption` and `sheet`, and also the `callout(CalloutStyle)` method to select a specific callout style (`automatic`, `compact` or `full`).

The `mapItemDetailSelectionAccessory()` modifier is applied to the markers. For example, we can use it to show a small callout window with additional information for the location selected by the user.

```
Map(position: $appData.cameraPos, selection: $selectedItem) {
    ForEach(appData.listLocations, id: \.self) { place in
        Marker(item: place)
            .tag(MapSelection(place))
    }
    .mapItemDetailSelectionAccessory(.callout)
}
```

Listing 13-17: Showing a callout with additional information

Figure 13-11: Map callouts

There are different styles for the callout. We can show only a link to Apple Maps, a small callout (Figure 13-11), or open a popover or a sheet. Showing the information in a popover or a sheet is useful because it allows us to include more valuable data about a location. Since we may need to open this sheets outside the `Map` view, the framework includes the following modifiers.

▷ **mapItemDetailSheet(isPresented:** Binding, **item:** MKMapItem, **displaysMap:** Bool**)**—This modifier opens a view in a sheet with information about a location. The **isPresented** argument is a Boolean binding property that determines if the sheet is open or not, the **item** argument specifies the location we want to show, and the **displaysMap** argument determines whether the sheet is going to include a small map showing the location.

▷ **mapItemDetailPopover(isPresented:** Binding, **item:** MKMapItem, **displaysMap:** Bool, **attachmentAnchor:** PopoverAttachmentAnchor, **arrowEdge:** Edge)—This modifier opens a view in a popover with information about a location. The **isPresented** argument is a Boolean binding property that determines if the popover is open or not, the **item** argument specifies the location we want to show, the **displaysMap** argument determines whether the sheet is going to include a small map showing the location, the **attachmentAnchor** argument is an enumeration with two cases, `point()` and `rect()`, to specify a point or a rectangle inside the view where the popover is going to be anchored, and the **arrowEdge** argument is an enumeration that determines the direction of the arrow (`top`, `bottom`, `leading` and `trailing`).

These modifiers can be applied to any view. All we need is a `@State` property that stores a Boolean value to control the sheet or popover, and an action to change the value of this property when we want the view to be opened. In this case, we use the `onChange()` modifier again. Every time a new marker is selected by the user, a sheet opens to display additional information.

```
struct ContentView: View {
    @Environment(ApplicationData.self) private var appData
    @State private var selectedItem: MapSelection<MKMapItem>?
    @State private var showCallout = false

    var body: some View {
        @Bindable var appData = appData

        Map(position: $appData.cameraPos, selection: $selectedItem) {
            ForEach(appData.listLocations, id: \.self) { place in
                Marker(item: place)
                    .tag(MapSelection(place))
            }
        }
        .onMapCameraChange(frequency: .onEnd) { context in
            appData.cameraPos = .region(context.region)
            Task(priority: .background) {
                await appData.findPlaces()
            }
        }
        .onChange(of: selectedItem, { old, value in
            if value != nil {
                showCallout = true
            }
        })
        .mapItemDetailSheet(isPresented: $showCallout, item:
selectedItem?.value, displaysMap: true)
    }
}
```

Listing 13-18: Opening a sheet with additional information

In this example, we use the same map and locations as before to show how to open a sheet, but sheet and popovers can be opened from anywhere in the app as long as we have the `MKMapItem` structure that represents the location we want to show.

Figure 13-12: Map sheets

(Basic) **Controls**

A map can display controls on the screen to change the map orientation, check the zoom level, find the user's location, and more. The framework includes the following modifiers to add these controls to the map.

▷ **mapControls(**Closure**)**—This modifier adds controls to the map. The argument is a closure that provides the views to create the controls to be included.

▷ **mapControlVisibility(**Visibility**)**—This modifier determines the visibility of the controls. The argument is an enumeration with the values **automatic**, **visible** and **hidden**.

▷ **mapScope(**Namespace.ID**)**—This modifier creates a space to connect external controls to the map.

Each control is represented by a view and added to the map from the closure assigned to the **mapControls()** modifier. The following are the views available to create controls for iOS applications (the framework also defines views to present controls that are exclusive to Mac computers).

▷ **MapCompass(scope:** Namespace.ID?**)**—This initializer creates a view that displays the current orientation of the map. The **scope** argument specifies the space used to connect the control with a map.

▷ **MapPitchToggle(scope:** Namespace.ID?**)**—This initializer creates a view that displays a button to toggle the map between 2D and 3D views. The **scope** argument specifies the space used to connect the control with a map.

▷ **MapScaleView(anchorEdge:** HorizontalEdge, **scope:** Namespace.ID?**)**— This initializer creates a view that displays the zoom level of the map. The **anchorEdge** argument determines the side from which the scale grows. It is an enumeration with the values **leading** and **trailing**. And the **scope** argument specifies the space used to connect the control with a map.

▷ **MapUserLocationButton(scope:** Namespace.ID?**)**—This initializer creates a view that displays a button to show the user's location. The **scope** argument specifies the space used to connect the control with a map.

Adding controls is simple. We need to apply the **mapControls()** modifier to the **Map** view and provide all the views we want to include. In the following example, we add a compass, a scale view, and a pitch toggle.

```
struct ContentView: View {
   @Environment(ApplicationData.self) private var appData

   var body: some View {
      @Bindable var appData = appData

      Map(position: $appData.cameraPos)
         .mapControls {
            MapCompass()
            MapScaleView()
            MapPitchToggle()
         }
         .mapControlVisibility(.visible)
   }
}
```

Listing 13-19: Displaying map controls

In this example, we also included the `mapControlVisibility()` modifier to keep the controls visible, but some controls are still hidden until the user performs an action. For example, the compass is only shown on the screen when the map is rotated.

Figure 13-13: Map controls

The position of the controls on the screen is automatically determined by the `Map` view. If we want to customize the interface, we need to define the controls as independent views and associate them to the map using a namespace. We have implemented this tool before (see Chapter 11, Listing 11-73). A namespace is declared with the `@Namespace` property wrapper and is used to provide a name that objects and structures can use to identify themselves. To connect the `Map` view to the control views, we need to declare a property with the namespace we want to use and then assign it to all the views involved, including the `Map` view and the control views. In addition, we must implement the `mapScope()` modifier to create a scope that the views can use to connect to each other, as shown below.

```
struct ContentView: View {
   @Environment(ApplicationData.self) private var appData
   @Namespace var mapSpace

   var body: some View {
      @Bindable var appData = appData

      Map(position: $appData.cameraPos, scope: mapSpace)
         .mapControlVisibility(.hidden)
         .safeAreaInset(edge: .top) {
            HStack {
               MapCompass(scope: mapSpace)
```

```
                .padding(5)
                .background {
                    Circle()
                        .fill(.thinMaterial)
                        .stroke(.red, lineWidth: 3)
                }
            Spacer()
            MapPitchToggle(scope: mapSpace)
                .padding(5)
                .background {
                    Circle()
                        .fill(.thinMaterial)
                        .stroke(.red, lineWidth: 3)
                }
        }.padding()
        .frame(minWidth: 0, maxWidth: .infinity)
    }
    .mapScope(mapSpace)
    }
}
```

Listing 13-20: Creating custom controls

For this example, we create a namespace called `mapSpace` and then define a scope for the map with the `mapScope()` modifier. Once we have this scope, we assign it to each view, so the `Map` view and the control views are connected. For the user interface, we add a compass and a pitch toggle at the top of the screen. The controls are still managed by the `Map` view, so they are shown or hidden depending on user interaction. To make them easier for the user to see, a red circle is displayed in the background. The result is shown below.

Figure 13-14: Custom controls

(Basic) Look Around

The `Map` view includes a feature called *Look Around*, which provides interactive street-level panoramas, similar to the Street View service provided by Google Map. To enable this feature, we need to perform a request to Apple servers with the location we want to show to the user. The MapKit framework includes the `MKLookAroundSceneRequest` class for this purpose. The following are the initializers.

▷ **MKLookAroundSceneRequest(coordinate:** CLLocationCoordinate2D)—
This initializer creates a Look Around request for the location specified by the argument.

▷ **MKLookAroundSceneRequest(mapItem:** MKMapItem)—This initializer creates a Look Around request for the location of the item specified by the argument.

The scenes returned by Apple servers are represented by an `MKLookAroundScene` object. This is a utility class that encapsulates all the information needed to render the scene for the user. To get this object, the `MKLookAroundSceneRequest` structure includes the following property.

▷ **scene**—This property returns the `MKLookAroundScene` object produced by the request or `nil` in case of failure.

There are two ways to present this scene to the user. We can create a preview that the user can tap to open the scene, or present the scene directly with a modifier. To create the preview, the framework defines the `LookAroundPreview` structure. The following is the most frequently used initializer.

▷ **LookAroundPreview(initialScene:** MKLookAroundScene?, **allows-Navigation:** Bool, **showsRoadLabels:** Bool, **pointsOfInterest:** PointOfInterestCategories, **badgePosition:** MKLookAroundBadgePosition)—This initializer creates a preview of a scene with the configuration specified by the arguments. The **initialScene** argument is a reference to the scene returned by the request. The **allowsNavigation** argument determines whether the user is allowed to navigate through the scene. The **showsRoadLabels** argument specifies whether the scene should display road labels. The **pointsOfInterest** argument specifies the items we want to include in the scene. And the **badgePosition** argument specifies the position of the labels that will appear above the scene. It is an enumeration with the values `bottomTrailing`, `topLeading` and `topTrailing`.

The framework also includes modifiers to open a sheet with the scene and all the tools for the user to navigate. The following is the most frequently used.

▷ **lookAroundViewer(isPresented:** Binding, **initialScene:** MKLookAround-Scene?, **allowsNavigation:** Bool, **showsRoadLabels:** Bool, **pointsOfInterest:** PointOfInterestCategories, **onDismiss:** Closure)—This initializer opens a sheet with a scene configured with the values specified in the arguments. The **isPresented** argument is a Boolean binding property that determines whether the sheet is open or not. The **initialScene** argument is a reference to the scene returned by the request. The **allowsNavigation** argument determines whether the user is allowed to navigate through the scene. The **showsRoadLabels** argument specifies whether the scene should display road labels. The **pointsOfInterest** argument specifies the items we want to include in the scene. And the **onDismiss** argument is the closure that should be executed when the sheet is closed.

The following example shows how to perform a request for a scene and how to present a preview to the user. As we did in previous examples, we are going to manage the process from the model.

```
@Observable class ApplicationData: @unchecked Sendable {
    var cameraPos: MapCameraPosition
    var openView: Bool = false
    var lookScene: MKLookAroundScene?

    static let shared: ApplicationData = ApplicationData()
    private init() {
        let coordinates = CLLocationCoordinate2D(latitude:
40.7637825011971, longitude: -73.9731328627541)
        let region = MKCoordinateRegion(center: coordinates,
latitudinalMeters: 1000, longitudinalMeters: 1000)
        cameraPos = MapCameraPosition.region(region)
    }
```

```
func lookAround() {
    if let region = cameraPos.region {
        Task {
            let request = MKLookAroundSceneRequest(coordinate:
region.center)
            if let scene = try? await request.scene {
                lookScene = scene
                openView = true
            }
        }
    }
}
```

Listing 13-21: Creating a Look Around preview

This model includes two properties, one to control the view and another to store the **MKLookAroundScene** object, as well as a method to create it. After the object is created, we request the scene of the camera's location from Apple servers and assign the information to the properties when the values are received.

In the view, we need to present the preview with the **LookAroundPreview** structure and provide the buttons for the user to start and finish the process.

```
struct ContentView: View {
    @Environment(ApplicationData.self) private var appData

    var body: some View {
        @Bindable var appData = appData

        Map(position: $appData.cameraPos)
            .safeAreaInset(edge: .bottom) {
                if appData.openView {
                    VStack {
                        LookAroundPreview(initialScene: appData.lookScene)
                            .frame(height: 200)
                            .padding()
                        Button("Hide Street") {
                            appData.openView = false
                        }.buttonStyle(.borderedProminent)
                    }
                } else {
                    Button("Show Street") {
                        appData.lookAround()
                    }.buttonStyle(.borderedProminent)
                }
            }
    }
}
```

Listing 13-22: Presenting a Look Around preview

In this example, we use the **safeAreaInset()** modifier to present views at the bottom of the screen without obscuring the map's labels. The modifier displays different views depending on the value of the **openView** property. If the property is **false**, we show a button to perform a request, and when the values are received, the modifier displays the preview with the **LookAroundPreview** structure and a button to close it.

The view created by the **LookAroundPreview** structure adapts to the space available. In our example, we set the height of the view to 200 and give it a standard padding.

Figure 13-15: Look Around preview

When the Show Street button is pressed, the application shows a Look Around preview, and when the user taps on this preview, a sheet opens showing the scene (Figure 13-15, right). However, we can also open this sheet directly with the `lookAroundViewer()` modifier, as shown below.

```
struct ContentView: View {
   @Environment(ApplicationData.self) private var appData

   var body: some View {
      @Bindable var appData = appData

      Map(position: $appData.cameraPos)
         .safeAreaInset(edge: .bottom) {
            Button("Show Street") {
               appData.lookAround()
            }.buttonStyle(.borderedProminent)
         }
         .lookAroundViewer(isPresented: $appData.openView, initialScene:
appData.lookScene)
   }
}
```

Listing 13-23: Presenting the Look Around sheet

The request is created as before, but instead of showing a preview, we use the `openView` property to display the scene with the `lookAroundViewer()` modifier. When the `openView` property is assigned the value `true`, the modifier opens a sheet to display the scene.

Basic | Directions

Maps are not only used to find places, but also to find routes that indicate how to get from one place to another. The MapKit framework includes a number of classes to calculate a route and draw it on the map. The first class we need to implement is called `Request` and is defined inside the `MKDirections` class. The `Request` class generates a request for a route between two locations. The following are the properties available in this class to configure the request.

▷ **source**—This property sets or returns the route's starting point. It is of type `MKMapItem`.

▷ **destination**—This property sets or returns the route's destination. It is of type `MKMapItem`.

▷ **requestsAlternateRoutes**—This property sets or returns a Boolean value that determines whether multiple routes will be returned when available.

▷ **transportType**—This property sets or returns a value that determines the type of transportation used to travel the route. It is an **MKDirectionsTransportType** structure with the properties **automobile**, **walking**, **transit**, and **any**.

▷ **departureDate**—This property sets or returns a **Date** structure that determines the date of departure to help the system estimate the better route.

▷ **arrivalDate**—This property sets or returns a **Date** structure that determines the date of arrival to help the system estimate the better route.

The request is sent to Apple servers for processing. The framework defines the **MKDirections** class to perform the request and process the results. The class includes the following initializer and method.

▷ **MKDirections(request:** Request)—This initializer creates an **MKDirections** object with the request specified by the **request** argument.

▷ **calculate()**—This asynchronous method performs the request and returns an **MKDirectionsResponse** object with the routes found.

The routes are returned as objects of the **MKRoute** class. The class includes the following properties to get the route's information.

▷ **polyline**—This property sets or returns the route's geometry that we can use to draw the route on the map. It is an object of the **MKPolyline** class.

▷ **steps**—This property sets or returns an array of **MKRouteStep** objects that describe every step the user needs to take to reach the destination.

▷ **advisoryNotices**—This property sets or returns an array of strings with additional information that the user may need to travel the route, such as traffic jams or interruptions.

▷ **distance**—This property sets or returns a **CLLocationDistance** value (a typealias of **Double**) with the route distance in meters.

▷ **expectedTravelTime**—This property sets or returns a **TimeInterval** value with the expected travel time in seconds.

After the server has returned the **MKRoute** object with the description of the route, we need to present it to the user. The **MapPolyline** structure introduced earlier defines the following initializer for this purpose.

▷ **MapPolyline(**MKRoute)—This initializer draws a route on the map.

The values assigned to the **origin** and **destination** properties of the request define the origin and destination of the route. These are objects of a class we have introduced before called **MKMapItem**. Objects of this class are usually returned by methods, but we can also create our own with the following initializer.

▷ **MKMapItem(placemark:** MKPlacemark)—This initializer creates an **MKMapItem** object that represents the map item at the location specified by an **MKPlacemark** object. The **MKPlacemark** class provides a convenient way to represent a location on the map. The class includes the initializer **MKPlacemark(coordinate: CLLocationCoordinate2D)**.

The following example shows how to display a route between two places. All we need is a property to store the route and a method to perform the request.

```
@Observable class ApplicationData: @unchecked Sendable {
    var cameraPos: MapCameraPosition
    var route: MKRoute?

    static let shared: ApplicationData = ApplicationData()
    private init() {
        let coordinates = CLLocationCoordinate2D(latitude:
40.7637825011971, longitude: -73.9731328627541)
        let region = MKCoordinateRegion(center: coordinates,
latitudinalMeters: 1000, longitudinalMeters: 1000)
        cameraPos = MapCameraPosition.region(region)
    }
    func calculateRoute() {
        let coordOrigin = CLLocationCoordinate2D(latitude:
40.7637825011971, longitude: -73.9731328627541)
        let placeOrigin = MKPlacemark(coordinate: coordOrigin)
        let origin = MKMapItem(placemark: placeOrigin)

        let coordDestination = CLLocationCoordinate2D(latitude:
40.7523809365088, longitude: -73.9778321046893)
        let placeDestination = MKPlacemark(coordinate: coordDestination)
        let destination = MKMapItem(placemark: placeDestination)

        let request = MKDirections.Request()
        request.source = origin
        request.destination = destination
        request.requestsAlternateRoutes = false

        Task {
            let directions = MKDirections(request: request)
            let results = try await directions.calculate()
            let routes = results.routes
            route = routes.first!
        }
    }
}
```

Listing 13-24: Calculating a route

The `calculateRoute()` method creates a request, assigns the locations to the `origin` and `destination` constants, and then runs an asynchronous task to perform the request. The task creates the `MKDirections` object to process the request and then calls the `calculate()` method to determine the route. This method returns the results in an `MKDirectionsResponse` object, which contains the `routes` property. This property returns an array of `MKRoute` objects representing all the routes found by the system. However, since we have set the `requestsAlternateRoutes` property to `false`, the array contains only one object. Once we get this object, we assign it to the `route` property, and show the route on the map.

```
struct ContentView: View {
    @Environment(ApplicationData.self) private var appData

    var body: some View {
        @Bindable var appData = appData

        Map(position: $appData.cameraPos) {
            if let route = appData.route {
                MapPolyline(route)
                    .stroke(.red, lineWidth: 5)
            }
```

```
    }.onAppear {
        appData.calculateRoute()
    }
  }
}
```

Listing 13-25: Displaying a route

The `MapPolyline` structure creates the path, but we need to specify how it should be drawn. In this example, we use the `stroke()` modifier to display a red line with a width of 5 points.

Figure 13-16: Route

(Basic) User Location

A `Map` view can show the user's location. The MapKit framework includes the `MapUserLocationButton` structure to add a button to the map that, when pressed, moves the camera to the user's location, and also the `UserAnnotation` structure to show an icon at that location. The following is the initializer for this structure.

▷ **UserAnnotation(anchor:** UnitPoint, **content:** Closure**)**—This initializer creates an annotation that is displayed at the user's location. The **anchor** argument determines the position of the icon around the user's location, and the **content** argument is the closure that provides the views to be displayed on the map.

Before we display the user's location, we must ask for permission. The Core Location framework defines the `CLServiceSession` structure for this purpose. An instance of this structure is automatically created for our app, so all we need to do is to check for updates. To manage updates, the framework includes the `CLLocationUpdate` structure which in turn defines the following type method.

▷ **liveUpdates(**LiveConfiguration**)**—This type method returns an instance of the `CLLocationUpdate` structure with information about the current location. The argument is an enumeration that determines the types of updates the framework is going to deliver. The possible values are `default`, `airborne`, `automotive-Navigation`, `fitness` and `otherNavigation`.

For this method to work, we need to add an option in the app configuration that explains to users why we need to access their location. The option is called "Privacy - Location When In Use Usage Description" and is added from the Info panel, just as we did for other options in Chapter 5 (see Figure 5-34).

Key	Type	Value
Bundle name	⇕ String	$(PRODUCT_NAME)
Privacy - Location When In Use Usage Description	⇕ String	We need to access your location to show it on the map
Bundle identifier	⇕ String	$(PRODUCT_BUNDLE_IDENTIFIER)
InfoDictionary version	⇕ String	6.0
Bundle version	⇕ String	$(CURRENT_PROJECT_VERSION)

Figure 13-17: *Privacy - Location When In Use Usage Description option*

The `liveUpdates()` method returns `CLLocationUpdate` structures representing the current location. The `CLLocationUpdate` structure includes properties to report for errors (`accuracyLimited`, `authorizationDenied`, `authorizationDeniedGlobally`, `authorizationRequestInProgress`, `authorizationRestricted`, `insufficientlyIn-Use`, `locationUnavailable`, `serviceSessionRequired` and `stationary`), and also the `location` property to report the user's current location, which returns a `CLLocation` object with properties that contain information about the location, including the `coordinate` property, which returns a `CLLocationCoordinate2D` structure with the latitude and longitude.

The `liveUpdates()` method returns an asynchronous sequence and throw errors, so we need to check the values with a `for in` loop and the `try await` keywords, but the rest of the implementation depends on what we want for our app. The following is a basic implementation that checks for updates in the user's location and respond to errors.

```
@Observable class ApplicationData: @unchecked Sendable {
   var cameraPos: MapCameraPosition
   var lastLocation = CLLocation()
   var isAuthorized: Bool = false

   static let shared: ApplicationData = ApplicationData()
   private init() {
      let coordinates = CLLocationCoordinate2D(latitude:
40.7637825011971, longitude: -73.9731328627541)
      let region = MKCoordinateRegion(center: coordinates,
latitudinalMeters: 1000, longitudinalMeters: 1000)
      cameraPos = MapCameraPosition.region(region)
   }
   func requestAuthorization() {
      Task {
         do {
            let updates = CLLocationUpdate.liveUpdates()
            for try await update in updates {
               if let loc = update.location {
                  lastLocation = loc

                  if !isAuthorized {
                     let coordinates = CLLocationCoordinate2D(latitude:
loc.coordinate.latitude, longitude: loc.coordinate.longitude)
                     let region = MKCoordinateRegion(center: coordinates,
latitudinalMeters: 1000, longitudinalMeters: 1000)
                     cameraPos = MapCameraPosition.region(region)
                     isAuthorized = true
                  }
               } else {
                  checkErrors(update: update)
               }
            }
         } catch {
            print("Error: \(error)")
         }
      }
   }
```

```
func checkErrors(update: CLLocationUpdate) {
   if update.authorizationDeniedGlobally {
      print("Error: Authorization denied globally")
      isAuthorized = false
   } else if update.authorizationDenied {
      print("Error: Authorization denied")
      isAuthorized = false
   } else if update.authorizationRestricted {
      print("Error: Authorization restricted")
      isAuthorized = false
   } else if update.accuracyLimited {
      print("Error: Accuracy limited")
      isAuthorized = false
   } else if update.insufficientlyInUse {
      print("Error: Insufficientrly in use")
      isAuthorized = false
   }
  }
}
```

Listing 13-26: Asking permission and responding to errors

This model includes a method called `requestAuthorization()` that we are going to call from the view to start the process. The method starts an asynchronous task to call the `liveUpdates()` method on the `CLLocationUpdate` structure. Every time this method returns a value, we read the `location` property. If this property contains a value, it means that the user authorized the device to access his or her location and a location was found so we use the value to change the position of the camera, otherwise we call a method to check for errors.

In the view, we need to call the `requestAuthorization()` method to start the process when the view appears on the screen, and then add the `UserAnnotation` view to the map to show the location.

```
struct ContentView: View {
   @Environment(ApplicationData.self) private var appData

   var body: some View {
      @Bindable var appData = appData

      Map(position: $appData.cameraPos) {
         if appData.isAuthorized {
            UserAnnotation()
         }
      }
      .mapControls {
         if appData.isAuthorized {
            MapUserLocationButton()
         }
      }
      .onAppear {
         appData.requestAuthorization()
      }
   }
}
```

Listing 13-27: Requesting authorization and showing the user's location

This example also includes the `MapUserLocationButton` control, so the user can tap the button to see his or her location on the map. The result is shown below.

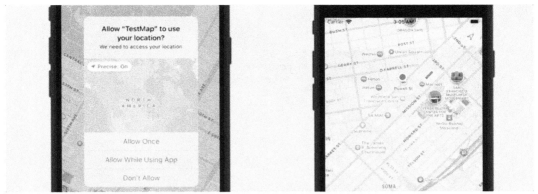

Figure 13-18: User's location on the map

 Do It Yourself: Update the ApplicationData.swift file with the code in Listing 13-26 and the **ContentView** view with the code in Listing 13-27. Add the "Privacy - Location When In Use Usage Description" option to the app configuration, as explained in Chapter 5 (see Figure 5-34). Run the application on the iPhone simulator. If you want to see your current location, you must run it on a real device. Allow the application to access your location. You should see a blue circle over your location on the map.

Sometimes all we need is to have quick access to the user's location. For this purpose, SwiftUI includes the **LocationButton** view.

▷ **LocationButton**(Title, **action:** Closure)—This view creates a button to prompt the user for a one-time access to his or her location. The first argument is a predefined title determined by a **Title** structure. To define these values, the structure includes the type properties **currentLocation** ("Current Location"), **sendCurrentLocation** ("Send Current Location"), **sendMyCurrentLocation** ("Send My Current Location"), **shareCurrentLocation** ("Share Current Location"), and **shareMyCurrent-Location** ("Share My Current Location"). And the **action** argument is a closure that is executed after the user grants or denies access.

When we implement the **LocationButton** view, we no longer need to ask permission from the model, but the process works the same way. The button opens a view that requests one-time access to the user's location, and when access is granted, it shows the location on the map.

```
import SwiftUI
import MapKit
import CoreLocationUI

struct ContentView: View {
    @Environment(ApplicationData.self) private var appData

    var body: some View {
        @Bindable var appData = appData

        Map(position: $appData.cameraPos) {
            if appData.isAuthorized {
                UserAnnotation()
            }
        }
        .mapControls {
            if appData.isAuthorized {
```

```
            MapUserLocationButton()
        }
    }
    .safeAreaInset(edge: .bottom) {
        LocationButton(.currentLocation) {
            appData.cameraPos = .userLocation(fallback: .automatic)
        }.padding()
    }
}
}
```

Listing 13-28: *Implementing the user location button*

Note that the `LocationButton` structure is defined in the CoreLocationUI framework, so we need to import that framework for the view to become available. When the button is pressed, the system displays a simplified Alert View with two buttons to grant or deny access. If the user grants access, the `LocationButton` view changes the position of the camera and the user's location is displayed on the screen.

Figure 13-19: *User location button*

Do It Yourself: Update the ContentView.swift file with the code in Listing 13-28. Run the application on the iPhone simulator. If you want to see your current location, you must run it on a real device. Press the Location button. You should see a window asking for authorization. Authorize the app. You should see a circle over your location on the map.

IMPORTANT: Apple Maps are available for the web and Apple offers a service to configure maps, find locations, create unique identifiers to share locations, and more. The topic is beyond the scope of this book. For more information visit **https://developer.apple.com/maps/resources/**.

Chapter 14
Notifications

(Basic) **14.1 Notification Center**

In addition to the techniques we have seen so far to pass data between different parts of an application, such as sending values from one view to another or providing a common model from which each view can get the information it needs, we can also send notifications across the application to report changes. Foundation includes the `NotificationCenter` class to create an object that serves as a notification center for the entire application. We send notifications (messages) to this object and then listen to these notifications from anywhere in the code. The class includes the following type property to get a reference to this object.

▷ **default**—This type property returns the `NotificationCenter` object assigned to the application by default.

The Notification Center is like a bulletin board; we can post a notification and then read it from anywhere in the code. The `NotificationCenter` class defines the following methods to post and read notifications.

▷ **post(name:** Name, **object:** Any?, **userInfo:** Dictionary)—This method posts a notification to the Notification Center. The **name** argument determines the name of the notification, the **object** argument is a reference to the object that sent the notification, and the **userInfo** argument is a dictionary with the information we want to send with the notification.

▷ **notifications(named:** Name, **object:** AnyObject?)—This method returns a `Notifications` object with an asynchronous sequence that contains all the notifications posted to the Notification Center. The **named** argument is the name of the notification we want to read, and the **object** argument is a reference to the object that sent the notification (set to `nil` if we want to read notifications posted by any object).

Notifications are created by the `Notification` class. The `post()` method automatically creates a `Notification` object to represent the notification to be sent, but we can also create these objects ourselves using the `Notification` class initializer.

▷ **Notification(name:** Name, **object:** Any?, **userInfo:** Dictionary)—This initializer creates a `Notification` object with the information provided by the arguments. The **name** argument determines the name of the notification, the **object** argument is a reference to the object that is sending the notification, and the **userInfo** argument is a dictionary with the information we want to send with the notification.

The class includes the following properties to read the values of the notification.

▷ **name**—This property returns the name of the notification.

▷ **object**—This property returns a reference to the object that posted the notification.

▷ **userInfo**—This property returns the dictionary attached to the notification.

The name of the notification is created from a structure included in the `Notification` class called `Name`. The structure provides the following initializer to define custom names.

▷ **Name(String)**—This initializer creates a structure that represents the notification's name. The argument is a string with the name we want to assign to the notification.

Notifications are used for multiple purposes. We can send a notification after a long process is complete to tell the system that it is time to update the interface, we can communicate views with each other, or we can keep a view up to date by sending notifications from the model with the information we receive from the Internet, to name a few. In the following example, a notification is sent every time a new value is entered by the user. For didactic purposes, we use a simple interface with two views, one that allows the user to enter the title of a book and another that shows the number of books already stored in the model.

Figure 14-1: *Interface to test notifications*

The model must store the values inserted by the user, as always, but also read the notifications to update the main view.

```
import SwiftUI
import Observation
@Observable class ApplicationData: @unchecked Sendable {
   var total: Int = 0
   @ObservationIgnored var titles: [String] = []

   static let shared: ApplicationData = ApplicationData()
   private init() {
      Task(priority: .background) {
         await readNotifications()
      }
   }
   func readNotifications() async {
      let center = NotificationCenter.default
      let name = Notification.Name("Update Data")

      for await _ in center.notifications(named: name, object: nil) {
         await MainActor.run {
            total = titles.count
         }
      }
   }
}
```

Listing 14-1: *Listening to notifications from the model*

This model defines a property of type `Int` to update the view with the total number of titles inserted by the user, and a non-observable property called `titles` to store the values.

The Notification Center creates an asynchronous sequence with all the notifications (see Asynchronous Sequences in Chapter 9). The sequence is managed by a `Notifications` object, which we get from the `notifications()` method. To read this sequence, we create an asynchronous `for in` loop with this object. Each time a notification arrives, the loop performs one cycle, we get the total number of titles stored in the `titles` array and assign it to the label. Note that we call the `run()` method on the Main Actor to ensure that the statement interacting with the label is executed in the main thread.

The initial view needs to show the value of the `total` property on the screen and include a button in the navigation bar to open a second view where the user can insert new values.

```
import SwiftUI

struct ContentView: View {
   @Environment(ApplicationData.self) private var appData

   var body: some View {
      NavigationStack {
         VStack {
            HStack {
               Text("Total Books:")
               Text("\(appData.total)")
                  .font(.largeTitle)
            }
            Spacer()
         }.padding()
          .navigationTitle("Books")
          .toolbar {
             ToolbarItem(placement: .navigationBarTrailing) {
                NavigationLink("Add Book", destination: {
                   AddBook()
                })
             }
          }
      }
   }
}
```

Listing 14-2: Listening to notifications

The values in the model for this example are added from the **AddBook** view, which is opened by the button in the navigation bar. This view must contain a **TextField** view where the user can enter a new value and a button to save it. When the button is pressed, we save the value in the model and send a notification.

```
import SwiftUI

struct AddBook: View {
   @Environment(ApplicationData.self) private var appData
   @Environment(\.dismiss) var dismiss
   @State private var titleInput: String = ""

   var body: some View {
      VStack {
         HStack {
            Text("Title")
            TextField("Insert title", text: $titleInput)
               .textFieldStyle(.roundedBorder)
         }
         HStack {
            Spacer()
            Button("Save") {
               let title =
titleInput.trimmingCharacters(in: .whitespaces)
               if !title.isEmpty {
                  addValue(title: title)
                  dismiss()
               }
            }
         }
         Spacer()
      }.padding()
       .navigationBarTitle("Add Book")
   }
```

```
    func addValue(title: String) {
        appData.titles.append(title)

        let center = NotificationCenter.default
        let name = Notification.Name("Update Data")
        center.post(name: name, object: nil, userInfo: nil)
    }
}
```

Listing 14-3: Adding new values to the model

When a name is inserted into the `TextField` view and the Save button is pressed, we call a method to store the value and post the notification. To post the notification, we get a reference to the `NotificationCenter` object assigned to the app, define a custom name for the notification ("Update Data"), and post it using the `post()` method.

In the model, the asynchronous `for in` loop defined in the `readNotifications()` method detects that there is a new notification, performs a new cycle, the number of titles stored in the `titles` property is assigned to the `total` property, and the initial view is updated with the new value.

 Do It Yourself: Create a Multiplatform project. Create a Swift file called ApplicationData.swift for the model in Listing 14-1. Update the `ContentView` view with the code in Listing 14-2. Create a SwiftUI file called AddBook.swift for the code in Listing 14-3. Remember to inject the `ApplicationData` object into the environment for the app and the previews (Chapter 7, Listing 7-4). Run the application on the iPhone simulator. Press the Add Book button to go to the second scene. Insert a title and press the Save button. The view should be closed and the interface should show the total number of titles inserted so far.

The `Notification` object includes the `userInfo` property, which allows us to attach additional information to the notification. The values that can be included in the dictionary assigned to this property are Property List values (`NSNumber`, `NSString`, `NSDate`, `NSArray`, `NSDictionary`, `NSData`, and the equivalents in Swift), but beyond that there are no other restrictions on what we can assign to this property. For example, we could modify our code to pass the string inserted by the user and perform an additional task if the value matches a specific title. The following are the changes we need to make to the `addValue()` method in the `AddBook` view to attach the title to the notification.

```
func addValue(title: String) {
    appData.titles.append(title)

    let center = NotificationCenter.default
    let name = Notification.Name("Update Data")
    let info = ["type": title]
    center.post(name: name, object: nil, userInfo: info)
}
```

Listing 14-4: Adding information to the notification

The code in Listing 14-4 declares a dictionary with the key "type" and the value entered by the user, and assigns it to the **userInfo** argument of the `post()` method. Now we can check this value in our model every time a notification is received.

```
func readNotifications() async {
    let center = NotificationCenter.default
    let name = Notification.Name("Update Data")

    for await notification in center.notifications(named: name, object:
nil) {
```

```
if let info = notification.userInfo {
    let type = info["type"] as? String
    if type == "Miracle" {
        print("Miracle was inserted")
    }
}
await MainActor.run {
    total = titles.count
}
    }
}
```

Listing 14-5: Reading the value in the notification

The values from the dictionary are returned as values of type `Any`, so we need to cast them to the correct type. In the `for in` loop in Listing 14-5, we read the value of the "type" key, cast it as a `String`, and then compare it to the string "Miracle". If the values match, a message is printed on the console.

 Do It Yourself: Update the `addValue()` method in the **AddBook** view with the code in Listing 14-4, and the `readNotifications()` method in the **ApplicationData** class with the code in Listing 14-5. Run the application on the iPhone simulator. A message should be printed on the console every time you insert the title "Miracle".

If we do not want to post any more notifications, we can stop the process in the **AddBook** view, but if we want to stop processing the notifications from a receiver, we must cancel the task by calling the `cancel()` method, as we did in Chapter 9 (see Listing 9-4). In the following example, we create a timer in the initializer of the **ApplicationData** class to cancel the task after 20 seconds, so that the initial view is no longer updated with the values entered by the user after the time expires.

```
private init() {
    let myTask = Task(priority: .background) {
        await readNotifications()
    }
    Timer.scheduledTimer(withTimeInterval: 20, repeats: false) { timer in
        myTask.cancel()
    }
}
```

Listing 14-6: Cancelling the task

 Do It Yourself: Update the `init()` method in the **ApplicationData** class with the code in Listing 14-6. Run the application on the iPhone simulator. Press the Add Book button to insert a title. The initial view should stop counting new values after 20 seconds.

Medium System Notifications

In addition to the notifications sent by our app, the system also sends notifications to the Notification Center to report changes to the interface or the device. There are dozens of notifications available. They work just like the custom notifications introduced before but are predefined as type properties of UIKit classes. We will probably never need most of them, but some are very useful. For example, the UIKit framework defines a class called **UIWindow**, which is used to create the app's windows and send notifications about the state of the keyboard. The following are the most frequently used.

- **keyboardDidShowNotification**—This notification is posted after the keyboard was shown.

- **keyboardDidHideNotification**—This notification is posted after the keyboard was hidden.

SwiftUI provides automatic behavior to adapt the interface to the keyboard, so we usually don't need to listen to these notifications. For example, the following interface presents an image and a text field where the user can insert a caption. When the user taps on the text field, the keyboard opens and the image is resized to fit the screen.

```
struct ContentView: View {
    @FocusState var focusTitle: Bool
    @State private var inputTitle: String = ""

    var body: some View {
        VStack {
            Image(.spot1)
                .resizable()
                .scaledToFit()
            HStack {
                TextField("Insert Title", text: $inputTitle)
                    .textFieldStyle(.roundedBorder)
                    .focused($focusTitle)
                Button("Save") {
                    focusTitle = false
                }
            }
            Spacer()
        }.padding()
    }
}
```

Listing 14-7: Interface to test the keyboard

The view includes a `@FocusState` property to be able to remove focus from the `TextField` view and close the keyboard (see Chapter 6). When the keyboard opens, the `Image` view adapts to the space available, and when it closes, the `Image` view expands back to its initial state.

Figure 14-2: Interface adapting to the keyboard

If we don't want the interface to adapt to the space available, we can embed it in a `ScrollView` view.

```
struct ContentView: View {
    @FocusState var focusTitle: Bool
    @State private var inputTitle: String = ""
```

```
    var body: some View {
        ScrollView {
            VStack {
                Image(.spot1)
                    .resizable()
                    .scaledToFit()
                HStack {
                    TextField("Insert Title", text: $inputTitle)
                        .textFieldStyle(.roundedBorder)
                        .focused($focusTitle)
                    Button("Save") {
                        focusTitle = false
                    }
                }
                Spacer()
            }.padding()
        }
    }
}
```

Listing 14-8: Scrolling the interface to make room for the keyboard

The only difference from the previous example is that we now have the views embedded in a **ScrollView** view. So instead of adapting the interface, the system scrolls the views to keep the **TextField** view visible when the keyboard is opened.

Figure 14-3: The interface scrolls to adapt to the keyboard

This is the automatic behavior provided by SwiftUI, but we can customize the process by listening to keyboard notifications. For example, if the interface is embedded in a **ScrollView** view, the **TextField** view scrolls up enough to be visible, but there is no space between that view and the keyboard (see Figure 14-3, right). If we want to improve the design, we can apply some modifiers to the views and change the styles when the state of the keyboard changes.

Although we can make these changes in the views, it is better to do so in the model. For example, the following model listens to keyboard notifications and changes the value of a property to apply a -20 point offset to the **ScrollView** view when the keyboard is opened.

```
import SwiftUI
import Observation

@Observable class ApplicationData: @unchecked Sendable {
    @ObservationIgnored let center = NotificationCenter.default
    var scrollOffset: CGFloat = 0

    static let shared: ApplicationData = ApplicationData()
    private init() {
        Task(priority: .background) {
            await receiveNotificationOpen()
```

```
    }
    Task(priority: .background) {
        await receiveNotificationClose()
    }
}
func receiveNotificationOpen() async {
    let name = UIWindow.keyboardDidShowNotification
    for await _ in center.notifications(named: name, object: nil) {
        await MainActor.run {
            scrollOffset = -20
        }
    }
}
func receiveNotificationClose() async {
    let name = UIWindow.keyboardDidHideNotification
    for await _ in center.notifications(named: name, object: nil) {
        await MainActor.run {
            scrollOffset = 0
        }
    }
}
}
```

Listing 14-9: *Listening to keyboard notifications*

The asynchronous `for in` loop waits for new values to arrive. This means that we cannot declare one loop after the other, since the second loop will never be executed. For this reason, we created two tasks, one that waits for a `keyboardDidShowNotification` notification and another that waits for a `keyboardDidHideNotification` notification. When a `keyboardDidShowNotification` notification is received, we assign the value -20 to the `scrollOffset` property, and when a `keyboardDidHideNotification` notification is received, we assign the value 0.

In the view, we can use the value of the `scrollOffset` property to set the offset of the `ScrollView`.

```
struct ContentView: View {
    @Environment(ApplicationData.self) private var appData
    @FocusState var focusTitle: Bool
    @State private var inputTitle: String = ""

    var body: some View {
        ScrollView {
            VStack {
                Image(.spot1)
                    .resizable()
                    .scaledToFit()
                HStack {
                    TextField("Insert Title", text: $inputTitle)
                        .textFieldStyle(.roundedBorder)
                        .focused($focusTitle)
                    Button("Save") {
                        focusTitle = false
                    }
                }
                Spacer()
            }.padding()
        }
        .offset(CGSize(width: 0, height: appData.scrollOffset))
    }
}
```

Listing 14-10: *Modifying the interface when the keyboard state changes*

The `ScrollView` view now moves up 20 points when the keyboard is opened, and returns to its original position when it is closed, creating padding between the views and the keyboard.

 Do It Yourself: Create a Multiplatform project. Create a Swift file called ApplicationData.swift for the model in Listing 14-9. Update the `ContentView` view with the code in Listing 14-10. Download the spot1.jpg image from our website and add it to the Asset Catalog. Remember to inject the `ApplicationData` object into the environment for the app and the previews (Chapter 7, Listing 7-4). Run the application on the iPhone simulator. Tap on the text field to activate the keyboard. You should see the interface scrolling up, creating a padding between the views and the keyboard.

In Chapter 8, we determined the rotation of the device by detecting the Size Classes (see Listing 8-70) or by reading the values generated by the `GeometryReader` view (see Listing 8-71). While these tools are useful, they are not applicable in all situations. To really know the current orientation and detect changes, we need direct access to the device. For this purpose, the UIKit framework defines the `UIDevice` class. This class creates an object that controls the device and provides information about it, including the orientation. The class includes the following notification to report changes.

▷ **orientationDidChangeNotification**—This notification is posted by the `UIDevice` object when the orientation of the device changes.

For accurate detection, the device needs to activate the accelerometer. For this purpose, the `UIDevice` class defines the following methods.

▷ **beginGeneratingDeviceOrientationNotifications()**—This method enables the accelerometer and begins delivering notifications to communicate changes in the orientation.

▷ **endGeneratingDeviceOrientationNotifications()**—This method tells the system that the accelerometer is no longer required and stops the delivery of notifications.

And the following are the properties defined by the `UIDevice` class to access the device and return the current orientation.

▷ **current**—This type property returns the instance of the `UIDevice` class that represents the device in which the app is currently running.

▷ **orientation**—This property returns a value that determines the current orientation of the device. It is an enumeration of type `UIDeviceOrientation` with the values `unknown`, `portrait`, `portraitUpsideDown`, `landscapeLeft`, `landscapeRight`, `faceUp`, and `faceDown`. The enumeration also includes properties that return a Boolean value to report the main orientation: `isPortrait`, `isLandscape`, and `isFlat`.

As always, we can listen to the notification from the model and make the necessary changes. In this case, we decided to include an observable property to update the views when the orientation of the device changes from portrait to landscape and vice versa.

```
import SwiftUI
import Observation

@Observable class ApplicationData: @unchecked Sendable {
    var isLandscape: Bool = false

    static let shared: ApplicationData = ApplicationData()
```

```
    private init() {
        Task(priority: .background) {
            await receiveNotification()
        }
    }
    func receiveNotification() async {
        let center = NotificationCenter.default
        let name = UIDevice.orientationDidChangeNotification
        for await _ in center.notifications(named: name, object: nil) {
            await MainActor.run {
                let device = UIDevice.current
                let orientation = device.orientation
                isLandscape = orientation.isLandscape
            }
        }
    }
}
```

Listing 14-11: Detecting changes in the orientation

When the **orientationDidChangeNotification** notification is received, we read the **current** property to get a reference to the **UIDevice** object that represents the device on which the application is running, access the object's **orientation** property, and assign the value of the **isLandscape** property to our property with the same name. If the device is in landscape orientation, the value assigned to this property is **true**, otherwise it is **false**.

In the view, we need to read the **isLandscape** property to organize the views according to the current orientation, but also call **UIDevice** methods to get the system to start posting notifications when the device is rotated and stop when it is no longer necessary. For this purpose, we can apply the **onAppear()** and **onDisappear()** modifiers, as shown below.

```
struct ContentView: View {
    @Environment(ApplicationData.self) private var appData

    var body: some View {
        Group {
            if !appData.isLandscape {
                VStack(spacing: 0) {
                    HeaderView(isCompact: true)
                    BodyView()
                }
            } else {
                HStack(spacing: 0) {
                    HeaderView(isCompact: false)
                    BodyView()
                }
            }
        }.ignoresSafeArea()
        .onAppear {
            let device = UIDevice.current
            device.beginGeneratingDeviceOrientationNotifications()
        }
        .onDisappear {
            let device = UIDevice.current
            device.endGeneratingDeviceOrientationNotifications()
        }
    }
}
struct HeaderView: View {
    let isCompact: Bool

    var body: some View {
        Text("Food Menu")
```

```
        .frame(minWidth: 0, maxWidth: .infinity, minHeight: 0,
maxHeight: isCompact ? 150 : .infinity)
        .background(Color.yellow)
    }
}
struct BodyView: View {
    var body: some View {
        Text("Content Title")
            .frame(minWidth: 0, maxWidth: .infinity, minHeight: 0,
maxHeight: .infinity)
            .background(Color.gray)
    }
}
```

Listing 14-12: Adapting the interface to changes in the orientation

This app is the same as the one created in Chapter 8 (see Listing 8-70), but instead of organizing the views according to the horizontal Size Class, we do it according to the value of the **isLandscape** property from the model. Now the position of the views always depends on the orientation of the device.

Figure 14-4: Different interface for portrait and landscape orientations

 Do It Yourself: Update the ApplicationData.swift file with the code in Listing 14-11 and the ContentView.swift file with the code in Listing 14-12. Run the application on the iPhone simulator. Rotate the device. You should see different interfaces, as illustrated in Figure 14-4.

(Basic) 14.2 User Notifications

Another type of notifications are User Notifications. These are notifications that the system displays to the user when the app has an event to report, such as the completion of a task or real-life events that the user wants to be reminded of. There are three different types of User Notifications: Alert, Badge, and Sound. A Badge notification displays a badge with a number over the app's icon, a Sound notification plays a sound, and an Alert notification can be displayed as a banner, as an Alert View, or as a message on the lock screen, depending on the current state of the device and the configuration set by the user. They can be scheduled all at once or independently. For example, one notification can be scheduled to display an alert and play a sound, another to display an alert and show a badge, or another to only play a sound.

 IMPORTANT: User Notifications are divided into Local Notifications and Remote Notifications (also known as Push Notifications). Local Notifications are notifications generated by the application running on the device, while Remote Notifications are generated by remote servers and received by the system through the network. In this chapter, we are going to study Local Notifications. For more information on Remote Notifications, visit our website and follow the links for this chapter.

(Basic) User Notifications Framework

User Notifications are created and managed by classes of the User Notifications framework. The framework includes the `UNUserNotificationCenter` class to create a Notification Center that we can use to schedule and manage user notifications. This is like the Notification Center we have worked with earlier, but specifically designed for User Notifications. The class includes the following type method to get the `UNUserNotificationCenter` object assigned to the app.

▷ **current()**—This type method returns a reference to the `UNUserNotification-Center` object assigned to the app.

The notifications are managed from the `UNUserNotificationCenter` object. The first step is to request authorization from the user. For this purpose, the class includes the following methods.

▷ **requestAuthorization(options:** UNAuthorizationOptions)—This asynchronous method requests authorization from the user to show notifications and returns a Boolean value to report the result. The **options** argument is a set of properties that determine the type of notifications we want to show. The properties available are `badge, sound, alert, carPlay, criticalAlert, provisional,` and `announcement`.

▷ **notificationSettings()**—This asynchronous method returns a `UNNotification-Settings` object with the current settings. The most useful property is `authorizationStatus`, which returns an enumeration value with the authorization status. (The user may change the status of the authorization anytime from the Settings app.) The possible values are **notDetermined, denied, authorized, provisional,** and **ephemeral**.

For the notifications to be sent, they must be added to the User Notification Center. The `UNUserNotificationCenter` class includes the following methods to add and remove them.

▷ **add(**UNNotificationRequest)—This asynchronous method schedules a new notification in the User Notification Center. The argument is the request for the notification.

▷ **removePendingNotificationRequests(withIdentifiers:** [String])—This method removes the pending notifications with the identifiers specified by the argument.

The framework includes the `UNMutableNotificationContent` class to store the content of a notification. The following are the properties included in this class to set the values.

▷ **title**—This property sets or returns the notification's title.
▷ **subtitle**—This property sets or returns the notification's subtitle.
▷ **body**—This property sets or returns the notification's message.
▷ **badge**—This property sets or returns a number to show over the app's icon.
▷ **sound**—This property sets or returns the sound we want to play when the notification is delivered to the user. It is an object of type `UNNotificationSound`.
▷ **userInfo**—This property sets or returns a dictionary with the information we want to send with the notification.

Some of these properties store strings, except for the **badge** property, which takes an **NSNumber** object, and the **sound** property, which takes an object of the **UNNotification-Sound** class. This class includes the following initializer and property to get the object.

▷ **UNNotificationSound(named:** UNNotificationSoundName)—This initializer creates a **UNNotificationSound** object with the sound specified by the **named** argument.

▷ **default**—This type property returns a **UNNotificationSound** object with the sound defined by the system.

The names of the sounds are defined by a structure of type **UNNotificationSoundName**. The structure includes the following initializer.

▷ **UNNotificationSoundName(rawValue:** String)—This initializer creates a **UNNotificationSoundName** object with the name of the file that contains the sound we want to play with the notification.

The **UNMutableNotificationContent** class also allows us to specify the level of interruption. By default, notifications are active, which means they turn on the screen and play a sound, but they can also be set to passive (they do not turn on the screen), time sensitive (they are displayed immediately but take user settings into account), and critical (they bypass user settings). The class includes the following property to define the interruption level.

▷ **interruptionLevel**—This property sets or returns a value that determines the importance and delivery timing of the notification. It is a **UNNotification-InterruptionLevel** enumeration with the values **active** (default), **critical**, **passive**, and **timeSensitive**.

User Notifications are posted to the User Notification Center and then displayed by the system when a certain condition is met. These conditions are set by objects called *triggers*. There are three types of triggers for local notifications: Time Interval (the notification is delivered after a specified period of time), Calendar (the notification is delivered on a specified date), and Location (the notification is delivered at a specified location). The framework defines three classes to create these triggers: **UNTimeIntervalNotificationTrigger**, **UNCalendar-NotificationTrigger** and **UNLocationNotificationTrigger**.

▷ **UNTimeIntervalNotificationTrigger(timeInterval:** TimeInterval, **repeats:** Bool)—This initializer creates a Time Interval trigger that will deliver the notification after the period of time determined by the **timeInterval** argument (in seconds). The **repeats** argument determines if the notification will be delivered once or infinite times.

▷ **UNCalendarNotificationTrigger(dateMatching:** DateComponents, **repeats:** Bool)—This initializer creates a Calendar trigger that delivers the notification at the date determined by the. **dateMatching** argument. The **repeats** argument determines if the notification will be delivered once or infinite times.

▷ **UNLocationNotificationTrigger(region:** CLCircularRegion, **repeats:** Bool) —This initializer creates a Location trigger that delivers the notification when the device is inside a region in the real world determined by the **region** argument. The **repeats** argument determines if the notification will be delivered once or infinite times.

To deliver a notification, we must create a request that contains the notification, an identifier, and a trigger. For this purpose, the framework defines the **UNNotificationRequest** class.

▷ **UNNotificationRequest(identifier:** String, **content:** UNNotification-Content, **trigger:** UNNotificationTrigger?)—This initializer creates a request to deliver the notification specified by the **content** argument and at the time or place specified by the **trigger** argument. The **identifier** argument is a string that we can use later to identify and manage the request.

As we mentioned earlier, before sending user notifications, we need to ask the user for permission. Apple recommends that we do this only when it is really necessary. For example, if our application includes a view with a switch that allows the user to enable notifications, or a button to send notifications, we should ask the user for permission in that view and not right after the application is launched. The following example shows how the process works.

```
import SwiftUI
import Observation
import UserNotifications

@Observable class ApplicationData: @unchecked Sendable {
    @ObservationIgnored let center = UNUserNotificationCenter.current()

    static let shared: ApplicationData = ApplicationData()
    private init() { }

    func askAuthorization() async -> Bool {
        do {
            let authorized = try await center.requestAuthorization(options:
[.alert, .sound])
            return authorized
        } catch {
            print("Error: \(error)")
            return false
        }
    }
    func postNotification(message: String) async {
        let authorization = await center.notificationSettings()
        if authorization.authorizationStatus == .authorized {
            let content = UNMutableNotificationContent()
            content.title = "Reminder"
            content.body = message

            let trigger = UNTimeIntervalNotificationTrigger(timeInterval:
10, repeats: false)
            let id = "reminder-\(UUID())"
            let request = UNNotificationRequest(identifier: id, content:
content, trigger: trigger)

            do {
                try await center.add(request)
            } catch {
                print("Error: \(error)")
            }
        }
    }
}
```

Listing 14-13: Sending notifications

This model gets a reference to the `UNUserNotificationCenter` object assigned to our app and then defines two asynchronous methods: The `askAuthorization()` method to ask the user permission to post notifications and the `postNotification()` method to create a notification and send it to the Notification Center.

The `askAuthorization()` method calls the `requestAuthorization()` method to ask the user for authorization to post notifications of type `alert` and `sound`, and then returns a

Boolean value to report the decision to the view. The **postNotification()** method, on the other hand, takes care of posting the notification. When the user presses the button to post a notification, we check if the app is still allowed to send notifications with the **notificationSettings()** method (This is a recommended practice), and if the value of the **authorizationStatus** property is equal to **authorized**, we schedule the notification. The procedure is simple, we need to create an instance of the **UNMutableNotificationContent** class with the values we want to include in the notification, create a trigger (in this case, we use a time interval trigger), create an instance of the **UNNotificationRequest** class with those values to request the delivery of the notification, and finally add the request to the User Notification Center with the **add()** method. Note that the identifier of the request must be unique. In our example, we define it with the word "reminder" followed by a random value generated with the **UUID()** function.

Since everything is processed by the model, all we need to do in the view is to allow the user to send the notification and call the methods. For this example, we are going to include a **TextField** view where users can insert the message they want to send with the notification, and a button to post it.

```
import SwiftUI

struct ContentView: View {
    @Environment(ApplicationData.self) private var appData
    @State private var inputMessage: String = ""
    @State private var isButtonDisabled: Bool = false

    var body: some View {
        @Bindable var appData = appData

        VStack(spacing: 12) {
            HStack {
                Text("Message:")
                TextField("Insert Message", text: $inputMessage)
                    .textFieldStyle(.roundedBorder)
            }
            HStack {
                Spacer()
                Button("Post Notification") {
                    Task(priority: .background) {
                        let message =
inputMessage.trimmingCharacters(in: .whitespaces)
                        if !message.isEmpty {
                            inputMessage = ""
                            await appData.postNotification(message: message)
                        }
                    }
                }.disabled(isButtonDisabled)
            }
            Spacer()
        }.padding()
        .task(priority: .background) {
            let authorization = await appData.askAuthorization()
            isButtonDisabled = !authorization
        }
    }
}
```

Listing 14-14: *Scheduling a notification*

To ask for authorization, we initiate a task as soon as the view is loaded with the **task()** modifier. Once the user inserts a text and presses the button, the notification is scheduled and we can see it appear later in the home screen.

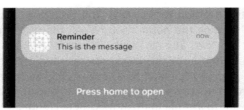

Figure 14-5: Notification

Do It Yourself: Create a Multiplatform project. Create a file called ApplicationData.swift for the model in Listing 14-13. Update the ContentView.swift file with the code in Listing 14-14. Remember to inject the **ApplicationData** object into the environment for the app and the previews (Chapter 7, Listing 7-4). Run the application on the iPhone simulator. The first time you run the application the system will ask you to allow the app to deliver notifications. Press the Allow button. Type a message and press the Post Notification button to post the notification. Press the Home button to close the app. You should see the notification popping up on the screen after 10 seconds.

Notifications can also play a sound. All we need to do is to add the sound file to the project, create the **UNNotificationSound** object with it, and assign it to the **sound** property.

```
func postNotification(message: String) async {
    let authorization = await center.notificationSettings()
    if authorization.authorizationStatus == .authorized {
        let content = UNMutableNotificationContent()
        content.title = "Reminder"
        content.body = message
        content.sound = UNNotificationSound(named:
UNNotificationSoundName(rawValue: "alarm.mp3"))

        let trigger = UNTimeIntervalNotificationTrigger(timeInterval: 10,
repeats: false)
        let id = "reminder-\(UUID())"
        let request = UNNotificationRequest(identifier: id, content:
content, trigger: trigger)

        do {
            try await center.add(request)
        } catch {
            print("Error: \(error)")
        }
    }
}
```

Listing 14-15: Playing a sound

Do It Yourself: Update the **postNotification()** method with the code in Listing 14-15. Download the file alarm.mp3 from our website and drag it to your project. Run the application on the iPhone simulator. Insert a message and press the button to post the notification. Go to the Home screen. After 10 seconds, you should see the notification and hear the alert sound.

(Basic) **Media Attachments**

In addition to sound, notifications can also contain other media types such as images and videos. The **UNMutableNotificationContent** class includes the following property to attach media files to the notification.

▷ **attachments**—This property sets or returns an array of **UNNotification-Attachment** objects with the media files we want to show in the notification.

The attachments are loaded by an object of the **UNNotificationAttachment** class. The class includes the following initializer.

▷ **UNNotificationAttachment(identifier:** String, **url:** URL, **options:** Dictionary?)—This initializer creates an attachment with the media loaded from the URL specified by the **url** argument. The **identifier** argument is the attachment's unique identifier. And the **options** argument is a dictionary with predefined values to configure the media. The most useful are **UNNotificationAttachmentOptionsThumbnail-ClippingRectKey** to use only a portion of an image, and **UNNotification-AttachmentOptionsThumbnailTimeKey** to select a frame from a video.

To attach an image or a video to the notification, we must create the **UNNotification-Attachment** object and assign it to the content's **attachments** property. This object takes a unique identifier, that we can create as we always do, and the URL of the file that contains the media we want to add to the notification. This means that we need the media to be in a file or to create the file ourselves. The following example illustrates how to take an image from the Asset Catalog, store it in a file, and assign it to the notification.

```
func postNotification(message: String) async {
    let content = UNMutableNotificationContent()
    content.title = "Reminder"
    content.body = message

    let idImage = "attach-\(UUID())"
    if let urlImage = await getThumbnail(id: idImage) {
        if let attachment = try? UNNotificationAttachment(identifier:
idImage, url: urlImage, options: nil) {
            content.attachments = [attachment]
        }
    }
    let trigger = UNTimeIntervalNotificationTrigger(timeInterval: 10,
repeats: false)

    let id = "reminder-\(UUID())"
    let request = UNNotificationRequest(identifier: id, content: content,
trigger: trigger)
    do {
        let center = UNUserNotificationCenter.current()
        try await center.add(request)
    } catch {
        print("Error: \(error)")
    }
}
func getThumbnail(id: String) async -> URL? {
    let manager = FileManager.default
    if let docURL = manager.urls(for: .documentDirectory,
in: .userDomainMask).first {
        let fileURL = docURL.appendingPathComponent("\(id).png")
        if let image = UIImage(named: "husky") {
            if let thumbnail = await image.byPreparingThumbnail(ofSize:
CGSize(width: 100, height: 100)) {
                if let imageData = thumbnail.pngData() {
                    if let _ = try? imageData.write(to: fileURL) {
                        return fileURL
                    }
                }
            }
        }
    }
```

```
        }
    }
    return nil
}
```

Listing 14-16: Attaching an image to a notification

Because we need to load the image, process it, and save it to a file, we moved the code to a new method called `getThumbnail()`. In this method, we get the URL of the Documents directory, append the name of the file, then load the image from the Asset Catalog, convert it to data, resize it using the `byPreparingThumbnail()` method, and store it. The URL of the file is returned by the method and used by the code to attach the image to the notification. The result can be seen below. The image is displayed inside the banner and expands when the user taps and holds over the notification (or drags the notification down, depending on the state of the application).

Figure 14-6: Media Attachment

 Do It Yourself: Update the `postNotification()` method with the code in Listing 14-16 and add the `getThumbnail()` method below. Download the husky.png image from our website and add it to the Asset Catalog. Run the application on the iPhone simulator. Insert a message and press the button to post the notification. Go to the Home screen. You should see a notification with the picture of the husky, as in Figure 14-6.

(Basic) Notifications Delegate

If the user is working with the app at the time a notification is delivered, the notification will not be displayed on the screen. To change this behavior, we can assign a delegate to the User Notification Center. For this purpose, the framework defines the `UNUserNotification-CenterDelegate` protocol, which allows us to do two things: We can decide whether to display the notification when the app is running, and we can also respond to the actions performed by the user. For this purpose, the protocol defines the following methods.

▷ **userNotificationCenter**(UNUserNotificationCenter, **willPresent:** UNNotification)—This asynchronous method is called by the User Notification Center on the delegate when the application is active and a notification has to be delivered. The method must return a structure of type **UNNotification-PresentationOptions** to indicate how we want to alert the user. The structure includes the type properties **badge**, **banner**, **list**, and **sound**.

▷ **userNotificationCenter**(UNUserNotificationCenter, **didReceive:** UNNotificationResponse)—This method is called by the User Notification Center when the user interacts with the notification (performs an action). The **didReceive** argument is an object with information about the notification and the action performed.

When a notification is triggered and the application is running, the User Notification Center calls the `userNotificationCenter(UNUserNotificationCenter, willPresent:)` method on its delegate to ask the application what to do. In this method, we can perform any task we want and then return a `UNNotificationPresentationOptions` value to specify the type of notification to display.

As always, we can declare any object as the delegate. For this example, we decided to create a separate class called `CenterDelegate`.

```
import SwiftUI
import UserNotifications

class CenterDelegate: NSObject, UNUserNotificationCenterDelegate {
   func userNotificationCenter(_ center: UNUserNotificationCenter,
willPresent notification: UNNotification) async ->
UNNotificationPresentationOptions {
      return [.banner]
   }
}
```

Listing 14-17: Defining a delegate for the User Notification Center

This class conforms to the `UNUserNotificationCenterDelegate` protocol and implements the `userNotificationCenter(UNUserNotificationCenter, willPresent:)` method to show the notification in a banner while the app is running. Note that the `UNUserNotificationCenterDelegate` protocol was defined in Objective-C and therefore it needs the class to inherit the functionality provided by the `NSObject` class to work properly.

Once the delegate class is defined, we need to create an instance from the model and assign it as the delegate, as shown below.

```
@Observable class ApplicationData: @unchecked Sendable {
   @ObservationIgnored let center = UNUserNotificationCenter.current()
   @ObservationIgnored let centerDelegate: CenterDelegate =
CenterDelegate()

   static let shared: ApplicationData = ApplicationData()
   private init() {
      center.delegate = centerDelegate
   }
   func askAuthorization() async -> Bool {
      do {
         let authorized = try await center.requestAuthorization(options:
[.alert, .sound])
         return authorized
      } catch {
         print("Error: \(error)")
         return false
      }
   }
   func postNotification(message: String) async {
      let content = UNMutableNotificationContent()
      content.title = "Reminder"
      content.body = message

      let trigger = UNTimeIntervalNotificationTrigger(timeInterval: 10,
repeats: false)
      let id = "reminder-\(UUID())"
      let request = UNNotificationRequest(identifier: id, content:
content, trigger: trigger)
```

```
    do {
        let center = UNUserNotificationCenter.current()
        try await center.add(request)
    } catch {
        print("Error: \(error)")
    }
  }
}
```

Listing 14-18: Showing notifications while the app is running

When a notification is received, the system calls the delegate method and the notification is shown on the screen.

Figure 14-7: Notifications in an active application

 Do It Yourself: Create a new file called CenterDelegate.swift for the code in Listing 14-17 and update the **ApplicationData** class with the code in Listing 14-18. Run the application on the iPhone simulator and post a notification. After a few seconds, the notification should appear over the app at the top of the screen, as shown in Figure 14-7.

(Basic) Groups

The system automatically groups notifications by app. For example, if our application sends multiple notifications to the Notification Center, they will all be grouped, with the last one at the top. This is the automatic behavior, but we can separate them in custom groups using identifiers. The **UNMutableNotificationContent** class includes the following property for this purpose.

▷ **threadIdentifier**—This property sets or returns a string used to identify each group of notifications.

Notifications with the same identifier are grouped together. As an example, we will post multiple notifications and separate them into two groups called "Group One" and "Group Two".

```
func postNotification(message: String) async {
    let listGroups = ["Group One", "Group Two"]

    for group in listGroups {
        for index in 1...3 {
            let content = UNMutableNotificationContent()
            content.title = "Reminder \(group)"
            content.body = "\(index) - \(message)"
            content.threadIdentifier = group

            let trigger = UNTimeIntervalNotificationTrigger(timeInterval:
10, repeats: false)
            let id = "reminder-\(UUID())"
            let request = UNNotificationRequest(identifier: id, content:
content, trigger: trigger)
```

```
        do {
            let center = UNUserNotificationCenter.current()
            try await center.add(request)
        } catch {
            print("Error: \(error)")
        }
      }
    }
}
```

Listing 14-19: Organizing notifications into groups

For didactic purposes, we defined an array with the names of the groups ("Group One" and "Group Two") and a **for in** loop to post three notifications per group (`1...3`). To identify the notifications and the groups, we assign these values to the **title** and **body** properties of the **UNMutableNotificationContent** object, and to tell the system which group each notification belongs to, we assign the name of the group to the **threadIdentifier** property. A total of six notifications are posted, three per group, as shown below.

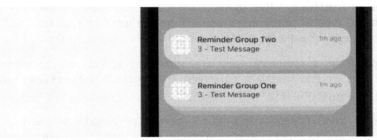

Figure 14-8: Notifications in two groups

 Do It Yourself: Update the **postNotification()** method with the code in Listing 14-19. Run the application on the iPhone simulator or a device and post a notification. Go to the lock screen. After 10 seconds, you should see all the notifications organized in two groups, as shown in Figure 14-8.

(Basic) Summary

Users can create notification summaries to receive a single alert at a specific time of day with all the notifications in a single group. A summary can contain notifications from one or more applications. The tool that allows users to create a summary is available under the Notifications option in the Settings app.

Figure 14-9: Summary option in Settings app

To configure the summary from our application, we must create a category and add this category to the User Notification Center. Categories are objects that define actions and behaviors related to a notification or a group of notifications. The framework provides the **UNNotificationCategory** class to create these objects. The following is the initializer for configuring a summary.

▷ **UNNotificationCategory(identifier:** String, **actions:** [UNNotification-Action], **intentIdentifiers:** [String], **hiddenPreviewsBodyPlaceholder:** String?, **categorySummaryFormat:** String?, **options:** UNNotificationCategoryOptions)—This initializer creates a category to configure a summary. The **identifier** argument is a string that identifies the category, the **actions** argument defines the actions available for the summary, the **intentIdentifiers** argument is an array of strings used to guide Siri to produce a better response, the **hiddenPreviewsBodyPlaceholder** argument is the string to show instead of the notifications when the previews are disabled, the **categorySummaryFormat** argument is the string that describes the summary, and the **options** argument is an array of properties that determine how the notifications associated to the category are going to be handled. The properties available are `customDismissAction` (processes the dismiss action) and `allowInCarPlay` (allows car play to show notifications).

The `UNUserNotificationCenter` class includes the following method to register a category in the User Notification Center.

▷ **setNotificationCategories(**Set)—This method configures the User Notification Center to work with the type of notifications and actions we want to support. The argument is the set of categories we want to associate to the notifications center.

When notifications appear in a summary, they are sorted by relevance. The system determines the relevance, but we can specify it ourselves. The `UNMutableNotificationContent` class contains the following property for this purpose.

▷ **relevanceScore**—This property sets or returns a value of type `Double` between 0 and 1 to tell the system how to sort the app's notifications. The notification with the highest relevance gets featured in the notification summary.

The following are the modifications we need to introduce to the `sendNotification()` method to include the notifications in a summary.

```
func postNotification(message: String) async {
    let center = UNUserNotificationCenter.current()
    let groupID = "Group One"
    let totalMessages = 3

    let summaryFormat = "\(totalMessages) messages"
    let category = UNNotificationCategory(identifier: groupID, actions:
[], intentIdentifiers: [], hiddenPreviewsBodyPlaceholder: nil,
categorySummaryFormat: summaryFormat, options: [])
    center.setNotificationCategories([category])

    for index in 1...totalMessages {
        let content = UNMutableNotificationContent()
        content.title = "Reminder"
        content.body = "\(index) - \(message)"
        content.threadIdentifier = groupID

        let trigger = UNTimeIntervalNotificationTrigger(timeInterval: 10,
repeats: false)
        let id = "reminder-\(UUID())"
        let request = UNNotificationRequest(identifier: id, content:
content, trigger: trigger)
        do {
            try await center.add(request)
        } catch {
            print("Error: \(error)")
        }
    }
```

```
        }
    }
}
```

Listing 14-20: Configuring a summary of notifications

In this example, we create a group of three notifications. To include the notifications in the summary, we create a category with a summary message that contains the number of notifications included in the summary. The rest of the process is the same as before.

If we just run the app, the notifications will appear as before, but we can go to the Settings app and set a summary for this application, as shown in Figure 14-9. Below is what the summary created by our app looks like when it is displayed to the user.

Figure 14-10: Notifications summary in the Lock screen

 Do It Yourself: Update the `postNotification()` method with the code in Listing 14-20. Run the application on a device. Press the Home button, open the Settings app, and set a summary for the application, as shown in Figure 14-9. (Remember to go to the list at the bottom and select the app to include it in the summary.) Run the application and post a notification. You should see a summary in the Lock screen with all the notifications at the time specified in Settings (Figure 14-10).

Basic Actions

Notifications can show custom actions in the form of buttons and input fields that the user can interact with to provide feedback without having to open our app. Actions are defined by two classes: **UNNotificationAction** and **UNTextInputNotificationAction**.

▷ **UNNotificationAction(identifier:** String, **title:** String, **options:** UNNotificationActionOptions)—This initializer creates an action represented by a custom button. The **identifier** argument is a string that we can use to identify the action, the **title** argument is the text shown on the button, and the **options** argument is a set of properties that determine how the action should be performed. The properties available are **authenticationRequired** (the user is required to unlock the device), **destructive** (the button is highlighted), and **foreground** (the app is opened to perform the action).

▷ **UNTextInputNotificationAction(identifier:** String, **title:** String, **options:** UNNotificationActionOptions, **textInputButtonTitle:** String, **textInput-Placeholder:** String)—This initializer creates an action represented by a custom button that when pressed prompts the system to display an input field. In addition to the arguments included by a normal action, these types of actions also include the **textInputButtonTitle** and **textInputPlaceholder** arguments to define the button and the placeholder for the input field.

After the actions are defined, we must create a category to group them together. The **UNNotificationCategory** class includes the following initializer to add actions to a notification.

▷ **UNNotificationCategory(identifier:** String, **actions:** [UNNotification-Action], **intentIdentifiers:** [String], **options:** UNNotificationCategory-Options)—This initializer creates a category with the actions specified by the **actions** argument. The **identifier** argument is a string that identifies the category, the **intentIdentifiers** argument is an array of strings used to guide Siri to produce a better response, and the **options** argument is an array of properties that determine how the notifications associated to the category are going to be handled. The properties available are **customDismissAction** (processes the dismiss action) and **allowInCarPlay** (allows car play to show notifications).

When an action is performed, the User Notification Center calls the **userNotification-Center(UNUserNotificationCenter, didReceive:)** method on its delegate. The method receives a **UNNotificationResponse** object with information about the action and the notification. The class includes the following properties to read the values.

▷ **actionIdentifier**—This property sets or returns the string that identifies the action.

▷ **notification**—This property sets or returns a **UNNotification** object representing the notification. The object includes the **date** property to get the date the notification was delivered and the **request** property with a reference to the **UNNotificationRequest** object used to schedule the notification, which in turn offers the **content** property to access the values of the notification.

As an example, we are going to add an action that shows a Delete button when the notification is opened. The following are the modifications we need to introduce to our model.

```
func postNotification(message: String) async {
    let center = UNUserNotificationCenter.current()
    let groupID = "listActions"
    let actionDelete = UNNotificationAction(identifier: "deleteButton",
title: "Delete", options: .destructive)
    let category = UNNotificationCategory(identifier: groupID, actions:
[actionDelete], intentIdentifiers: [], options: [])
    center.setNotificationCategories([category])

    let content = UNMutableNotificationContent()
    content.title = "Reminder"
    content.body = message
    content.categoryIdentifier = groupID

    let trigger = UNTimeIntervalNotificationTrigger(timeInterval: 10,
repeats: false)
    let id = "reminder-\(UUID())"
    let request = UNNotificationRequest(identifier: id, content: content,
trigger: trigger)
    do {
        try await center.add(request)
    } catch {
        print("Error: \(error)")
    }
}
```

Listing 14-21: *Adding an action to a notification*

This method creates a **UNNotificationAction** object to represent the Delete button, and then defines a category with that action and the "listActions" identifier. Categories must be added to the User Notification Center using the **setNotificationCategories()** method and then assigned to the notification's **categoryIdentifier** property, as we did earlier.

To respond to the user, we must implement the protocol method on the delegate, as we did in Listing 14-17.

```
import SwiftUI
import UserNotifications

class CenterDelegate: NSObject, @preconcurrency
UNUserNotificationCenterDelegate {
    func userNotificationCenter(_ center: UNUserNotificationCenter,
willPresent notification: UNNotification) async ->
UNNotificationPresentationOptions {
        return [.banner]
    }
    @MainActor
    func userNotificationCenter(_ center: UNUserNotificationCenter,
didReceive response: UNNotificationResponse) async {
        let identifier = response.actionIdentifier
        if identifier == "deleteButton" {
            print("Delete Message")
        }
    }
}
```

Listing 14-22: *Processing actions for notifications*

Actions are displayed when the user taps and holds his finger over the notification (or drags it down, depending on the current state of the application). In this case, the notification displays a Delete button. When the user presses this button, the User Notification Center calls the delegate method to give our application the chance to perform a task. In our example, we read the `actionIdentifier` property, compare it to the string "deleteButton" to confirm that the user pressed the Delete button, and then print a message on the console.

Figure 14-11: *Actions in a notification*

 Do It Yourself: Update the `postNotification()` method with the code in Listing 14-21 and the `CenterDelegate` class with the code in Listing 14-22. Run the application on the iPhone simulator and post a notification. Tap and hold the finger on the notification to reveal the Delete button (Figure 14-11). Press the button. You should see a message printed on the console.

 IMPORTANT: After the statements in the `userNotificationCenter-(UNUserNotificationCenter, didReceive:)` method are processed, the system executes a closure in the background to finish the operation. Because the method is asynchronous and the closure must be executed in the main thread (the Main Actor), we must mark the method with the `@MainActor` attribute, as we did in Listing 14-22. Also, this method is asynchronous and its values are not sendable, so they can't be used by another threat. Because we know that the values are not going to be modified, we silence the warning by telling the compiler that the protocol was not designed to work with concurrency (`@preconcurrency UNUserNotificationCenterDelegate`).

In the last example, we implemented a simple action that shows a button when the notification is expanded, but we can also include an action that displays an input field so that the user can provide feedback directly from the notification. The following are the changes we need to make to the `postNotification()` method to add an action of this type.

```
func postNotification(message: String) async {
    let center = UNUserNotificationCenter.current()
    let groupID = "listActions"
    let actionDelete = UNNotificationAction(identifier: "deleteButton",
title: "Delete", options: .destructive)
    let actionInput = UNTextInputNotificationAction(identifier:
"inputField", title: "Message", options: [])

    let category = UNNotificationCategory(identifier: groupID, actions:
[actionDelete, actionInput], intentIdentifiers: [], options: [])
    center.setNotificationCategories([category])

    let content = UNMutableNotificationContent()
    content.title = "Reminder"
    content.body = message
    content.categoryIdentifier = groupID

    let trigger = UNTimeIntervalNotificationTrigger(timeInterval: 10,
repeats: false)
    let id = "reminder-\(UUID())"
    let request = UNNotificationRequest(identifier: id, content: content,
trigger: trigger)
    do {
        try await center.add(request)
    } catch {
        print("Error: \(error)")
    }
}
```

Listing 14-23: *Adding an input action to a notification*

And the following are the modifications we need to introduce to the delegate method to process this new action.

```
@MainActor
func userNotificationCenter(_ center: UNUserNotificationCenter,
didReceive response: UNNotificationResponse) async {
    let identifier = response.actionIdentifier
    if identifier == "deleteButton" {
        print("Delete Message")
    } else if identifier == "inputField" {
        print("Send: \((response as!
UNTextInputNotificationResponse).userText)")
    }
}
```

Listing 14-24: *Processing the user's feedback*

The text entered by the user in the text field is sent to the delegate method. The framework offers a special class to represent the response called **UNTextInputNotificationResponse**. To access the value entered by the user, we must cast the response object to this class and then read its **userText** property, as we did in Listing 14-24. The result is shown below.

Figure 14-12: Notification with a button to open a text field

Do It Yourself: Update the `postNotification()` method with the code in Listing 14-23 and the `CenterDelegate` class with the code in Listing 14-24. Run the application on the iPhone simulator and post a notification. Expand the notification to see the actions. Click the Message button, insert a value, and press the Send button. You should see the same text printed on the console.

(Medium) 14.3 Key/Value Observing

KVO (Key/Value Observing) is a system we can use to perform a task when the value of a property is modified. This is similar to what the `didSet()` method does for the properties of our own structures and classes (see Property Observers in Chapter 3), except that we can use it with properties contained in classes defined by frameworks provided by Apple. To perform a task when the property's value changes, we need to add an observer to the object to which the property belongs. Swift includes the following method for this purpose.

▷ **observe(**KeyPath, **options:** NSKeyValueObservingOptions, **change-Handler:** Closure)—This method adds an observer to the object. The first argument is the key path to the property we want to observe, the **options** argument is a Set with enumeration values that determine the values returned by the observer (possible values are `new`, `old`, `initial`, and `prior`), and the **changeHandler** argument is the closure we want to execute when the value of the property changes. The closure receives two values, one with a reference to the object and another that represents the value required by the options.

As we will see later, KVO is typically used to observe properties of classes defined in frameworks provided by Apple, but we can also observe properties in our own objects. The only requirement is that the properties must be defined as Objective-C properties. This is because KVO is a system designed for the Objective-C programming language. To define properties in Swift that behave like Objective-C properties, we need to use the `@objc` and `dynamic` keywords. The `@objc` keyword makes the property available to Objective-C systems, while the `dynamic` keyword is required for the property to work with a system called Dynamic Dispatch, which is designed to perform operations in the background (in this case, reporting when the property has been updated). The following example illustrates how to define these properties.

```
import SwiftUI

class MyObject: NSObject {
   @objc dynamic var testValue: Int = 0
}
```

Listing 14-25: Defining an observable property for KVO

Our class contains only one property called `testValue`, but since it has been modified with the `@objc` and `dynamic` keywords, we can add an observer to keep track of its value. Note that all the classes defined in Objective-C require the basic functionality of the `NSObject` class, so our class inherits from that class to be able to include observable properties.

Once there is a property that we can observe, we must add the observer to the object. In the following model, we define a property to provide a value for the view, but also two other properties to control the process. The `myObject` property contains an instance of our Objective-C class, and the `myObserver` property stores a reference to the observer so we can disable it later from the view.

```
import SwiftUI
import Observation

@Observable class ApplicationData: @unchecked Sendable {
   var showValue: String = ""
   @ObservationIgnored var myObject = MyObject()
   @ObservationIgnored var myObserver: NSKeyValueObservation?

   static let shared: ApplicationData = ApplicationData()
   private init() {
      myObserver = myObject.observe(\.testValue, options: [.new],
changeHandler: { obj, value in
         if let newValue = value.newValue {
            self.showValue = "Value: \(newValue)"
         }
      })
   }
}
```

Listing 14-26: Observing a property

The observer is defined in the initializer by calling the `observe()` method on the `MyObject` object. The arguments specify that we want to observe the `testValue` property, that we only want to check the new value assigned to the property, and what to do with it. In this case, we use the value of the property to create a string and assign it to the `showValue` property, so it can be displayed by the view.

The property's new value is received by the closure in a generic structure called `NSKeyValueObservedChange`. The structure includes the properties `oldValue` and `newValue`, so we read the value from the `newValue` property and create the string.

Now we have to show the string from the view, allow the user to update the value of the observable property, and disable the observer when the view disappears, as shown below.

```
struct ContentView: View {
   @Environment(ApplicationData.self) private var appData

   var body: some View {
      VStack {
         Text(appData.showValue)
         Button("Add Value") {
            appData.myObject.testValue += 100
         }
         Spacer()
      }.padding()
      .onDisappear {
         appData.myObserver = nil
      }
   }
}
```

Listing 14-27: Working with a KVO property

This view includes a `Text` view to show the string created by the observer and a `Button` view to add 100 to the current value of the `testValue` property. When the user presses the button, the value of this property is modified, the observer recognizes the change, and the closure creates the new string that is displayed on the screen.

The `observer()` method returns an object that conforms to the `NSKeyValueObservation` protocol. When the observer is created, we assign it to the `myObserver` property so that we can disable the observer by assigning `nil` to this property, as we do in the `onDisappear()` modifier. This destroys the `NSKeyValueObservation` object and therefore the observer no longer responds to changes in the property.

> **Do It Yourself:** Create a Multiplatform project. Create a Swift file called MyObject.swift for the class in Listing 14-25. Create a Swift file called ApplicationData.swift for the model in Listing 14-26. Update the `ContentView` view with the code in Listing 14-27. Remember to inject the `Application-Data` object into the environment and the preview (Chapter 7, Listing 7-4). Run the application. You should see the value increase by 100 every time the button is pressed.

(Medium) 14.4 App States

An application can be in three different states: active, inactive, or in the background. The app is active when it is visible and the user can interact with it, inactive when it is visible but not in focus, and in the background when it is still open but no longer visible. The states are reported by an environment property called `scenePhase`. This property returns an enumeration value of type `ScenePhase`. The available values are `active`, `inactive`, and `background`. To detect changes in the state of the app, we can track this property with the `onChange()` modifier, as shown below.

```
import SwiftUI

@main
struct TestApp: App {
    @Environment(\.scenePhase) var scenePhase

    var body: some Scene {
        WindowGroup {
            ContentView()
                .onChange(of: scenePhase, initial: false) { old, phase in
                    if phase == .active {
                        print("The app is active")
                    } else if phase == .background {
                        print("The app is in the background")
                    }
                }
        }
    }
}
```

Listing 14-28: Detecting changes in the app's state

It is recommended to respond to changes in the state of the app from the `App` structure. In this example, we compare the value returned by the `scenePhase` property with the values `active` and `background`, so we can print a message to the console when the state changes between these two. If the app becomes active, the message "The app is active" is printed on the console, and when the app moves to the background, the message "The app is in the background" is printed instead.

Do It Yourself: Create a Multiplatform project. Update the **App** structure with the code in Listing 14-28. Run the application on the iPhone simulator. You should see the message "The app is active" when the **ContentView** view appears on the screen. Press the Home button to close the app. This time, you should see on the console the message "The app is in the background".

(Medium) **App Delegates**

Checking the state of the app from the values returned by the **scenePhase** property is more than sufficient for most situations, but some legacy frameworks still rely on delegate objects to read this value. These objects are assigned as delegates of an object created from the **UIApplication** class. This class defines the tools to create the loop that keeps the application running, check for events, and report changes in the state of the app. An object of this class is automatically created when the application is launched. The class includes the following type property for accessing this object.

▷ **shared**—This type property returns the instance of the **UIApplication** class assigned to our app.

From this object, we can check the state of the app. The class includes the following property for this purpose.

▷ **applicationState**—This property returns the app's current state. It is an enumeration of type **State** with the values **active**, **inactive**, and **background**.

We can read this property to get the current state of the app, as we did with the **scenePhase** property, but some frameworks need more information. For this purpose, the **UIApplication** object can also report changes by calling methods in a delegate object. The UIKit framework includes the **UIApplicationDelegate** protocol to define this delegate. The following are some of the methods included in the protocol.

▷ **application(**UIApplication, **didFinishLaunchingWithOptions:** Dictionary**)** —This is the first method called by the **UIApplication** object. It is called to let us know that all the necessary objects have been instantiated, and the app is ready to work.

▷ **application(**UIApplication, **configurationForConnecting:** UISceneSession, **options:** UIScene.ConnectionOptions**)**—This method is called when a new Scene (window) is requested by the system or the user. The method must return a **UISceneConfiguration** object with the Scene's configuration.

▷ **application(**UIApplication, **didDiscardSceneSessions:** Set**)**—This method is called when the user discards a Scene (closes a window). The **didDiscardSceneSessions** argument is a set with references to the **UISceneSession** objects representing the Scenes' sessions.

The most useful method defined by the **UIApplicationDelegate** protocol is **application(UIApplication, didFinishLaunchingWithOptions:)**. This method is called when the application is launched and therefore it is usually implemented to initialize values in the model or prepare resources the app needs to work. The following example shows how to implement it and how to associate the app delegate with our SwiftUI app. The first step is to create a custom class that conforms to the **UIApplicationDelegate** protocol.

```
import UIKit

class CustomAppDelegate: NSObject, UIApplicationDelegate {
    func application(_ application: UIApplication,
didFinishLaunchingWithOptions launchOptions:
[UIApplication.LaunchOptionsKey : Any]? = nil) -> Bool {
        print("App has launched")
        return true
    }
}
```

Listing 14-29: Defining a custom app delegate

Now that we have the delegate class and have implemented a protocol method, we need to connect our SwiftUI app to it so that the method can be called. For this purpose, the SwiftUI framework includes the `@UIApplicationDelegateAdaptor` property wrapper. This property wrapper is created from the `UIApplicationDelegateAdaptor` structure, which includes the following initializer.

▷ **UIApplicationDelegateAdaptor(**DelegateType.Type**)**—This initializer creates an instance of the `UIApplicationDelegateAdaptor` structure associated with the class specified by the argument.

The `@UIApplicationDelegateAdaptor` property wrapper creates an instance of the class specified by the argument and assigns it as the app's delegate, so when the app state changes, the methods in this object are called.

```
import SwiftUI

@main
struct TestApp: App {
    @UIApplicationDelegateAdaptor(CustomAppDelegate.self) var appDelegate

    var body: some Scene {
        WindowGroup {
            ContentView()
        }
    }
}
```

Listing 14-30: Assigning the app delegate from a SwiftUI application

 Do It Yourself: Create a Multiplatform project. Create a Swift file called CustomAppDelegate.swift file for the class in Listing 14-29 and update the **App** structure with the code in Listing 14-30. Run the application on the iPhone simulator. You should see the message "App has launched" on the console.

Some devices can run multiple instances of the same application simultaneously. For example, two instances of the Text Editor may be open at the same time but editing two different documents, or two instances of a browser may be loading two different websites. To control these instances, the UIKit framework defines Scenes.

iPhones can only work with one Scene (one window) at a time, but iPads and Mac computers can work with multiple Scenes (multiple windows). These Scenes are managed by the **UIApplication** object. The class includes the following properties to access them.

▷ **connectedScenes**—This property returns a set with references to the Scenes that are currently connected to the application.

▷ **supportsMultipleScenes**—This property returns a Boolean value to indicate if the application supports multiple Scenes (multiple instances of the app).

To report the state of a Scene, the `UIApplication` object calls methods on the Scene's delegate, which are defined by the `UIWindowSceneDelegate` protocol. The following are the methods available.

▷ **scene**(UIScene, **willConnectTo:** UISceneSession, **options:** UIScene.-ConnectionOptions)—This method is called when a new Scene is created.

▷ **sceneDidDisconnect**(UIScene)—This method is called when a Scene was removed.

▷ **sceneDidBecomeActive**(UIScene)—This method is called when a Scene becomes active and therefore it is responding to user events.

▷ **sceneWillResignActive**(UIScene)—This method is called when a Scene is about to be moved to the background and stop responding to user events.

▷ **sceneWillEnterForeground**(UIScene)—This method is called when a Scene is about to become visible and respond to user events.

▷ **sceneDidEnterBackground**(UIScene)—This method is called when a Scene is no longer visible and does not respond to user events anymore.

The Scenes are configured from the app delegate. For this purpose, the `UIApplication-Delegate` protocol includes the `application(UIApplication, configurationFor-Connecting:, options:)` method. To define the configuration, the UIKit framework includes the `UISceneConfiguration` class.

▷ **UISceneConfiguration(name:** String?, **sessionRole:** Role)—This initializer creates the object required to configure a Scene. The **name** argument is the identifier we want to assign to the Scene, and the **sessionRole** argument specifies the role of the Scene. It is a structure with the type properties `windowApplication`, `window-ExternalDisplay`, and `carTemplateApplication`.

This initializer provides the name and the role of the Scene, but we must also declare the name of the class that is going to be used to create the Scene's delegate. For this purpose, the `UISceneConfiguration` class includes the following property.

▷ **delegateClass**—This property sets or returns the class that is going to be used to create the Scene's delegate.

The first step to define a Scene delegate is to create a custom class that conforms to the `UIWindowSceneDelegate` protocol and implements the protocol methods.

```
import UIKit

class CustomSceneDelegate: NSObject, UIWindowSceneDelegate {
    func scene(_ scene: UIScene, willConnectTo session: UISceneSession,
options connectionOptions: UIScene.ConnectionOptions) {
        print("Scene was created")
    }
}
```

Listing 14-31: Defining a custom Scene delegate

In this example, we have implemented a method that is called when the Scene is initialized. To assign this object as the Scene delegate for our app, we must define the Scene configuration from the app delegate, as shown below.

```
import UIKit

class CustomAppDelegate: NSObject, UIApplicationDelegate {
    func application(_ application: UIApplication,
didFinishLaunchingWithOptions launchOptions:
[UIApplication.LaunchOptionsKey : Any]? = nil) -> Bool {
        print("App has launched")
        return true
    }
    func application(_ application: UIApplication,
configurationForConnecting connectingSceneSession: UISceneSession,
options: UIScene.ConnectionOptions) -> UISceneConfiguration {
        let config = UISceneConfiguration(name: "Custom Delegate",
sessionRole: connectingSceneSession.role)
        if connectingSceneSession.role == .windowApplication {
            config.delegateClass = CustomSceneDelegate.self
        }
        return config
    }
}
```

Listing 14-32: Configuring a Scene

In this example, we define the `UISceneConfiguration` object with the name "Custom Delegate" and the role received by the method. If our app is running on a mobile device or a Mac computer, the role received by the method is `windowApplication`. If this is the case, we assign our custom class to the `delegateClass` property and return the configuration. When the app is launched, the configuration is defined, the Scene is created, and an instance of our `CustomSceneDelegate` class is assigned as the Scene's delegate, so we see the message "Scene was created" printed on the console.

 Do It Yourself: Create a Swift file called CustomSceneDelegate.swift for the class in Listing 14-31 and update the `CustomAppDelegate` class with the code in Listing 14-32. Run the application on the iPhone simulator. You should see the message "Scene was created" on the console.

These delegate methods are usually implemented to set up the application or to communicate the state of the application to the user. This means that most of the time, we will have to access the model. In our example, this is easy to do. All we need is to get a reference to the model from the `shared` property and work with its values as before.

```
import UIKit

class CustomAppDelegate: NSObject, UIApplicationDelegate {
    func application(_ application: UIApplication,
didFinishLaunchingWithOptions launchOptions:
[UIApplication.LaunchOptionsKey : Any]? = nil) -> Bool {
        let appData = ApplicationData.shared
        appData.maintext = "Text From Delegate"
        return true
    }
}
```

Listing 14-33: Modifying the model from the app delegate

Do It Yourself: Update the `CustomAppDelegate` class with the code in Listing 14-33. This example assumes that you have an `ApplicationData` class with a property of type `String` called `maintext`. Add a `Text` view to the `ContentView` view to show the value of the `maintext` property on the screen. Remember to inject the `ApplicationData` object into the environment and the preview (Chapter 7, Listing 7-4). Run the application on the iPhone simulator. You should see the message "Text From Delegate" appear on the screen as soon as the app is launched.

Medium 14.5 Combine Framework

All the features introduced in our model by the `@Observable` macro are defined in a framework called *Combine*. The Combine framework includes protocols and data types we can use to process values over time. If a change is introduced to the data from one part of the code, we can automatically notify to the other parts that a new value is available. There are two main responsibilities the elements of this system can take: they can be publishers or subscribers. A publisher determines how the values and errors are produced and sends those values to subscribers when they change, and a subscriber receives the values produced by a publisher over time.

Figure 14-13: Combine

Because of its declarative syntax, SwiftUI makes extensive use of publishers and subscribers. For instance, the properties defined in classes that are prefixed with the `@Observable` macro are turned into publishers and those defined in the views with property wrappers like `@State` and `@Environment` become the subscribers. When a new value is assigned to an observable property, the `@State` and `@Environment` properties receive these values and the system updates the views. We don't have to do anything; all the code to create the publishers and the subscribers is produced by the Combine and SwiftUI frameworks in the background, but we can also create our own.

Medium Publishers

Combine defines the `Publisher` protocol to create publishers, but we don't have to create the publishers ourselves, the framework includes predefined data types that conform to this protocol and provide all the functionality we need to emit values. The two most frequently used are `Just` and `Future`.

Just(Value)—This initializer creates a `Just` publisher that sends the value specified by the argument just once and then finishes.

Future(Closure)—This initializer creates a `Future` publisher that can be used to send a value downstream when an asynchronous operation is over. The argument is a closure that receives another closure that must be called with a value of type `Result` to indicate whether the operation was successful or not.

Publishers receive the values from a source and then send them downstream to the subscribers. To turn our view into a subscriber and receive values from external publishers, the `View` protocol defines the following modifier.

onReceive(Publisher, perform: Closure)—This modifier adds a subscriber to a view. The first argument is a reference to the publisher to which the view is going to subscribe, and the **perform** argument is the closure to be executed when a value is received.

Publishers are generic, so they can emit different types of values, and they can also include a value of type **Error** to report the error occurred in the transmission. The **Just** publisher never produces an error, so its data type is defined as **Just<Type>**, where **Type** is the data type of the value to be sent. For instance, in the following model we create a publisher of type **Just<String>** to send a string to the views.

```
import SwiftUI
import Observation
import Combine

@Observable class ApplicationData: @unchecked Sendable {
   let myPublisher: Just<String>!

   static let shared: ApplicationData = ApplicationData()
   private init() {
      myPublisher = Just("Hello, World!")
   }
}
```

Listing 14-34: Creating a Just *publisher*

The **Just** publisher defined in Listing 6-60 sends the string "Hello, World!" downstream. To receive this value, all we need is to apply the **onReceive()** modifier on the view, as shown below.

```
struct ContentView: View {
   @Environment(ApplicationData.self) private var appData

   var body: some View {
      VStack {
         Text("Hello, world!")
      }
      .onReceive(appData.myPublisher) { value in
         print(value)
      }
   }
}
```

Listing 14-35: Assigning a subscriber to the view

The **onReceive()** modifier creates a view that acts as a subscriber. When the view receives a value, the modifier executes a closure in response. In this example, we only output a message to the console, but we can perform any task we want.

 Do It Yourself: Create a Multiplatform project. Create a Swift file called ApplicationData.swift for the model in Listing 14-34. Update the **ContentView** view with the code in Listing 14-35. Remember to inject the **ApplicationData** object into the environment and the preview (Chapter 7, Listing 7-4). Run the application. You should see the message "Hello World!" printed on the console.

Subjects

In addition to the publishers created from the **Publisher** protocol, there is another type of publishers called *Subjects*. Subjects are defined by the **Subject** protocol and they differ from other publishers in that they provide a method that we can call to emit a value. The framework includes the following two classes to create a publisher of this type.

PassthroughSubject()—This subject publishes the value it receives from the method or another publisher.

CurrentValueSubject(Value**)**—This subject stores and publishes the last value received from the method or another publisher, so new subscribers always have a value to work with. The argument is the initial value we want the publisher to emit.

The **Subject** protocol defines the following methods to publish values.

send(Value**)**—This method tells the publisher to send the value specified by the argument.

send(completion: Completion**)**—This method tells the publisher to send a completion signal.

Subjects are also generic, so we must specify the data type of the value and the error in the initialization. If we don't need to report errors, we can use the data type **Never**. In the following example, we create a **PassthroughSubject** instance that works with values of type **String** and doesn't produce any errors (**<String, Never>**).

```
import SwiftUI
import Observation
import Combine

@Observable class ApplicationData: @unchecked Sendable {
   let myPublisher = PassthroughSubject<String, Never>()

   static let shared: ApplicationData = ApplicationData()
   private init() {
      Timer.scheduledTimer(withTimeInterval: 10, repeats: false, block: {
timer in
         self.myPublisher.send("Hello World!")
      })
   }
}
```

Listing 14-36: Creating a PassthroughSubject

The process is the same as before, the publisher emits a value and the view receives that value with the **onReceive()** modifier and process it, but now we can send a value any time we want. In the model in Listing 14-36, we set a timer to 10 seconds and then call the **send()** method to send the string "Hello World!".

 Do It Yourself: Update the **ApplicationData** class with the code in Listing 14-36 and run the application again. After 10 seconds, the view should receive the value and print it on the console.

Integrated Publishers

In addition to SwiftUI, other frameworks are also integrated with Combine and provide their own tools for creating publishers. For instance, the **Timer** class, defined in the Foundation framework, includes the following type method to generate a publisher.

publish(every: TimeInterval, **on:** RunLoop, **in:** Mode)—This type method creates a publisher that emits the current date. The **every** argument determines the time the publisher has to wait before sending the next value. The **on** argument determines the queue in which the process is going to be executed. Among other properties and methods, the **RunLoop** structure includes the type properties **current** to represent the current thread and **main** to represent the main thread. And the **in** argument determines the mode of the **RunLoop**. This is a structure of type **Mode** with the properties **default**, **common**, **eventTracking**, **modalPanel**, and **tracking**.

The publisher returned by this method is of type **TimerPublisher**; a class that conforms to the **ConnectablePublisher** protocol. These types of publishers don't emit any value until they are connected to the subscribers. The **ConnectablePublisher** protocol defines the following method, also called operator, to perform the connection.

connect()—This operator connects the publisher with the subscribers.

This operator returns a structure that conforms to the **Cancellable** protocol. This protocol defines the following method to prevent the publisher from emitting further values.

cancel()—This method cancels the process.

In the following example, we create a **TimerPublisher** publisher that emits the current date every two seconds. The model also includes a method that calls the **cancel()** method on the publisher so that we can call it from the view to terminate the process.

```
@Observable class ApplicationData: @unchecked Sendable {
   let timerPublisher: Timer.TimerPublisher!
   let publisher: Cancellable!

   static let shared: ApplicationData = ApplicationData()
   private init() {
      timerPublisher = Timer.publish(every: 2, on: RunLoop.main,
in: .common)
      publisher = timerPublisher.connect()
   }
   func cancelPublisher() {
      publisher.cancel()
   }
}
```

Listing 14-37: Generating a publisher from a Timer

From the view, we need to apply the **onReceive()** modifier to subscribe to this publisher as before and also include a button to cancel the process.

```
struct ContentView: View {
   @Environment(ApplicationData.self) private var appData

   var body: some View {
      VStack {
         Text("Hello, world!")
```

```
      Button("Cancel") {
         appData.cancelPublisher()
      }.padding()
   }
   .onReceive(appData.timerPublisher) { value in
      print(value)
   }
  }
 }
}
```

Listing 14-38: *Cancelling the publisher*

Do It Yourself: Update the `ApplicationData` class with the code in Listing 14-37 and the `ContentView` view with the code in Listing 14-38. Run the application on the iPhone simulator. You should see the current date printed on the console every two seconds. Press the Cancel button. The publisher should stop sending dates to the view.

IMPORTANT: The Combine framework introduces many types of publishers and those publishers provide many operators to not only connect them with subscribers but also process the values. The topic is beyond the scope of this book. For more information, visit our website and follow the links for this chapter.

Chapter 15
iCloud

Basic **15.1 Data in the Cloud**

iCloud is the service provided by Apple to share files and data among users and devices. We used this service in Chapter 10 with SwiftData to share data stored in a database, but iCloud also provides two other important services to share single values and documents.

Basic **15.2 Key-Value Storage**

The Key-Value storage system is the User Defaults system for iCloud. It works the same way, but all the data is stored on iCloud servers instead of the device. We can use it to store the app's preferences, states, or any other value that we need to automatically set on each device owned by the user. To enable the service, we must follow the same steps as for enabling CloudKit (see Chapter 10). Once the iCloud service is added to our app, we can enable the Key-Value Storage service from the Signing & Capabilities panel.

▼ ☁ **iCloud**

Services ☑ Key-value storage
☐ iCloud Documents
☐ CloudKit

***Figure 15-1:** Enabling the Key-Value Storage service*

Foundation defines the `NSUbiquitousKeyValueStore` class to provide access to this service. The class includes the following methods to store and retrieve values.

▷ **set(Value, forKey: String)**—This method stores the value specified by the first argument with the key specified by the **forKey** argument. The class provides versions of this method for every data type we are allowed to store in the system, such as `String`, `Bool`, `Data`, `Double`, `Int64`, dictionaries, arrays, and also Property List values (`NSNumber`, `NSString`, `NSDate`, `NSArray`, `NSDictionary`, `NSData`, and their equivalents in Swift).

▷ **bool(forKey: String)**—This method retrieves a value of type `Bool`.

▷ **double(forKey: String)**—This method retrieves a value of type `Double`.

▷ **longLong(forKey: String)**—This method retrieves a value of type `Int64`.

▷ **string(forKey: String)**—This method retrieves a value of type `String`.

▷ **array(forKey: String)**—This method retrieves an array.

▷ **dictionary(forKey: String)**—This method retrieves a dictionary.

▷ **data(forKey: String)**—This method retrieves a value of type `Data`.

▷ **object(forKey: String)**—This method retrieves an object.

To store or access a value, we must initialize an `NSUbiquitousKeyValueStore` object and then call one of the methods above. The object takes care of connecting to iCloud and downloading or uploading the values, but it doesn't keep the values up to date. When a value is changed on one device, that change needs to be reflected in real time on the other devices. For this purpose, the `NSUbiquitousKeyValueStore` class defines the following notification.

▷ **didChangeExternallyNotification**—This notification is posted by the system when a change in the values on the Key-Value storage is detected.

As mentioned earlier, the system stores discrete values that represent the user's preferences or the app's current status. For example, we may have a stepper that allows the user to set a limit on the number of items the app can manage.

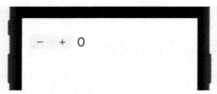

Figure 15-2: Interface to test Key-Value storage

The application must initialize the interface with the current value stored in iCloud, but it also needs to send the value back when the user sets a new one and update it when it is modified from another device. The best way to manage this information is from the model. We need an observable property to store the local value, and a couple of methods to send and receive the value from iCloud.

```
import SwiftUI
import Observation
@Observable class ApplicationData: @unchecked Sendable {
    var control: Double = 0
    @ObservationIgnored let storage: NSUbiquitousKeyValueStore

    static let shared: ApplicationData = ApplicationData()
    private init() {
        storage = NSUbiquitousKeyValueStore()
        control = storage.double(forKey: "control")
    }
    func valueChanged(value: Double) {
        if control != storage.double(forKey: "control") {
            storage.set(value, forKey: "control")
            storage.synchronize()
        }
    }
    func valueReceived() async {
        let center = NotificationCenter.default
        let name =
NSUbiquitousKeyValueStore.didChangeExternallyNotification
        for await notification in center.notifications(named: name, object:
nil) {
            if notification.name == name {
                await MainActor.run {
                    control = storage.double(forKey: "control")
                }
            }
        }
    }
}
```

Listing 15-1: Storing a value in iCloud

This model defines an observable property called `control` that we use to keep track of the value set by the stepper, and a non-observable property to store the `NSUbiquitousKeyValue-`

`Store` object, which we need to access the values in iCloud. When the observable object is initialized, we create the `NSUbiquitousKeyValueStore` object and load a value stored with the key "control". (If the value is not available, the value 0 is returned.)

Next, we define two methods. The `valueChanged()` method is executed each time the value of the `control` property is modified. This method sends the new value to iCloud using the `set()` method and then calls the `synchronize()` method to ensure that the system sends it immediately. Note that we only want to send the value when it is modified by the user, so we only do it when the new value is different from the current value. The second method is called `valueReceived()`. This method initializes an asynchronous `for in` loop that waits for the `didChangeExternallyNotification` notification. When the value is modified from another device, the notification is posted by the system so that we can read the new value from iCloud and update the `control` property.

All the work is done by the model, so the view only needs to include a `Stepper` and a `Text` view to mimic the interface shown in Figure 15-2, and implement the `onChange()` and `task()` modifiers to call the methods in the model when necessary.

```
struct ContentView: View {
    @Environment(ApplicationData.self) private var appData

    var body: some View {
        @Bindable var appData = appData

        VStack {
            HStack {
                Stepper("", value: $appData.control)
                    .labelsHidden()
                Text("\
(appData.control.formatted(.number.precision(.fractionLength(0))))")
                    .font(.title)
                Spacer()
            }
            Spacer()
        }.padding()
        .onChange(of: appData.control, initial: false) { old, value in
            appData.valueChanged(value: value)
        }
        .task {
            await appData.valueReceived()
        }
    }
}
```

Listing 15-2: Defining the interface to store and read values from iCloud

 Do It Yourself: Create a Multiplatform project. Click on the app's settings option at the top of the Navigator Area (see Chapter 5, Figure 5-4, number 6) and open the Signing & Capabilities panel. Click on the + Capability button at the top-left corner of the panel to add a capability (see Chapter 10, Figure 10-14, number 1). Select the iCloud option, press return, and check the option Key-value storage (Figure 15-1). Create a Swift file called ApplicationData.swift for the model in Listing 15-1. Update the `ContentView` view with the code in Listing 15-2. Remember to inject the `ApplicationData` object into the environment for the app and the previews (Chapter 7, Listing 7-4). Run the application on two different devices. Press the stepper's buttons to change the value to 5 on one device. You should see the value changing on the other device (the process may take several seconds). Stop the application from Xcode and run it again. You should see the value 5 on the screen. (Remember to activate the same iCloud account in any of the simulators or devices you use.)

IMPORTANT: The simulator does not update the information automatically. Most of the time, you must force the update. If you modify the value on your device and do not see it changing on the simulator, open the Features menu at the top of the screen and select the option Trigger iCloud Sync. This will synchronize the application with iCloud and update the values right away.

Just as we can store one value, we can store several. The Key/Value storage service can manage multiple values using different keys, but if we want to simplify our work, we can use a structure to store all the values, encode that structure into data using JSON, and then store only one value with that data in iCloud (see JSON in Chapter 10). Our next example follows this approach. We define a structure to store the user's name, address, and city, and then encode and decode an instance of that structure to store the values in iCloud.

```swift
import SwiftUI
import Observation
struct PersonalInfo: Codable {
    var name: String
    var address: String
    var city: String
}
@Observable class ApplicationData: @unchecked Sendable {
    var userInfo: PersonalInfo
    @ObservationIgnored let storage: NSUbiquitousKeyValueStore

    static let shared: ApplicationData = ApplicationData()
    private init() {
        storage = NSUbiquitousKeyValueStore()

        userInfo = PersonalInfo(name: "", address: "", city: "")
        if let dataInfo = storage.data(forKey: "info") {
            let decoder = JSONDecoder()
            if let info = try? decoder.decode(PersonalInfo.self, from:
dataInfo) {
                userInfo = info
            }
        }
    }
    func setInfo() {
        let encoder = JSONEncoder()
        if let data = try? encoder.encode(userInfo) {
            storage.set(data, forKey: "info")
        }
    }
    func valueReceived() async {
        let center = NotificationCenter.default
        let name =
NSUbiquitousKeyValueStore.didChangeExternallyNotification
        for await notification in center.notifications(named: name, object:
nil) {
            if notification.name == name {
                await MainActor.run {
                    if let dataInfo = storage.data(forKey: "info") {
                        let decoder = JSONDecoder()
                        if let info = try? decoder.decode(PersonalInfo.self,
from: dataInfo) {
                            userInfo = info
                        }
                    }
                }
            }
        }
    }
}
```

}

Listing 15-3: Storing multiple values in iCloud

The process is the same as before. We read the value from iCloud when the observable object is initialized, and then implement two methods, one to send the `PersonalInfo` structure to iCloud when the user inserts new values, and another to listen for the `didChangeExternally-Notification` notification and update the structure when new values are inserted from another device. The only difference is how the value is processed. This time we are dealing with a structure that is encoded as a JSON value. Therefore, we need to use a `JSONDecoder` object when a value is received and a `JSONEncoder` object to send the value to iCloud.

For this example, we need two views: one that shows the current values, and another where the user can insert new ones. The initial view is simple. All it needs to do is get the values from the model, display them on the screen, and initialize a task to update them each time they are modified from another device.

```
struct ContentView: View {
    @Environment(ApplicationData.self) private var appData
    @State private var openSheet: Bool = false

    var body: some View {
        NavigationStack {
            VStack {
                HStack {
                    Text("Name:")
                    Text(appData.userInfo.name)
                    Spacer()
                }
                HStack {
                    Text("Address:")
                    Text(appData.userInfo.address)
                    Spacer()
                }
                HStack {
                    Text("City:")
                    Text(appData.userInfo.city)
                    Spacer()
                }
                Spacer()
            }.padding()
            .navigationBarTitle("Personal Info")
            .toolbar {
                ToolbarItem(placement: .navigationBarTrailing) {
                    Button("Change") {
                        openSheet = true
                    }
                }
            }
            .sheet(isPresented: $openSheet) {
                InsertInfoView(openSheet: $openSheet)
            }
            .task {
                await appData.valueReceived()
            }
        }
    }
}
```

Listing 15-4: Reading multiple values from iCloud

This view includes a button in the navigation bar to open a view called **InsertInfoView** in a sheet. The following is our implementation of this view.

```
import SwiftUI

struct InsertInfoView: View {
   @Environment(ApplicationData.self) private var appData
   @Binding var openSheet: Bool

   @State private var inputName: String = ""
   @State private var inputAddress: String = ""
   @State private var inputCity: String = ""

   var body: some View {
      VStack(spacing: 10) {
         TextField("Insert Name", text: $inputName)
            .textFieldStyle(.roundedBorder)
         TextField("Insert Address", text: $inputAddress)
            .textFieldStyle(.roundedBorder)
         TextField("Insert City", text: $inputCity)
            .textFieldStyle(.roundedBorder)
         HStack {
            Spacer()
            Button("Save") {
               appData.userInfo = PersonalInfo(name: inputName, address:
inputAddress, city: inputCity)
               appData.setInfo()
               openSheet = false
            }
         }
         Spacer()
      }.padding()
      .onAppear {
         inputName = appData.userInfo.name
         inputAddress = appData.userInfo.address
         inputCity = appData.userInfo.city
      }
   }
}
#Preview {
   @Previewable @State var open = false
   InsertInfoView(openSheet: $open)
      .environment(ApplicationData.shared)
}
```

Listing 15-5: *Saving multiple values in iCloud*

This is a normal view with three `TextField` views that allow the user to insert and modify the values. Since values may already be stored in iCloud, we assign them to the `@State` properties so that they are displayed to the user when the view appears. When the user presses the button to save the values, we create a new `PersonalInfo` structure and call the `setInfo()` method in the model to encode it and send it to iCloud.

The application is ready. When the user enters new values, they are sent to iCloud, and when the app is launched or a notification is received, the values are downloaded from iCloud and displayed on the screen.

Figure 15-3: *Multiple values stored in the Key/Value storage*

Do It Yourself: Update the ApplicationData.swift file with the code in Listing 15-3. Update the `ContentView` view with the code in Listing 15-4. Create a SwiftUI file called InsertInfoView.swift for the code in Listing 15-5. Run the application on two devices. Press the Change button. Insert new values and press Save. Wait a few seconds for the values to appear on the second device.

Basic 15.3 iCloud Documents

The Key-Value storage system is designed to store small values. The purpose of that system is to allow users to set preferences or configuration parameters across devices. Although useful, it has some limitations, especially in the amount of data we can store (maximum of 1 megabyte). An alternative is to enable the iCloud Documents option in the Capabilities panel and upload files.

Services ◯ Key-value storage
☑ iCloud Documents
◯ CloudKit

Containers ◯ 48S7G5U7J3.ca.invid.MicroTasks
◯ iCloud.ca.invid.AnotherTest
◯ iCloud.ca.invid.Figure-23-6

① + ↻ **②**

Figure 15-4: iCloud Documents service

The operating system uses a container to store iCloud files. This container is a folder in the app's storage space where iCloud files are created. Whenever a file is added, modified, or removed from this container, the system automatically reports the changes to iCloud so that copies of the app running on other devices can modify their own container to stay in sync. As we did to enable CloudKit in Chapter 10, we must create the container by pressing the + button (Figure 15-4, number 1). The name of the container must be unique, and the best way to ensure this is to use the app's bundle identifier, as recommended before.

 Do It Yourself: Create a Multiplatform project. Click on the app's settings option at the top of the Navigator Area (Figure 5-4, number 6) and open the Signing & Capabilities panel. Click on the + Capability button at the upper-left corner of the panel to add a capability (see Chapter 10, Figure 10-14, number 1). Select the iCloud option, press return, and check the option iCloud Documents. Press the + button to add a container (Figure 15-4, number 1). Insert the app's bundle identifier as the name of the container (you can find your app's bundle identifier at the top of panel). If the app doesn't recognize the container, press the Refresh button to upload the information to Apple servers (Figure 15-4, number 2).

An iCloud container is called *Ubiquitous Container* because its content is shared with other devices and therefore available everywhere. The `FileManager` class includes properties and methods to work with an ubiquitous container. The following are the most frequently used.

▷ **url(forUbiquityContainerIdentifier:** String?)—This method returns the URL pointing to the app's iCloud container. The **forUbiquityContainerIdentifier** argument is the name of the container we want to access. The value `nil` returns the container assigned by default.

▷ **evictUbiquitousItem(at:** URL)—This method removes the local copy of the document at the URL specified by the **at** argument.

Although the files are stored in a container on the device and are automatically synchronized by the system, working with iCloud presents some challenges that the `FileManager` class cannot handle. The most important of these is coordination. Due to the unreliability of network connections, iCloud can find different versions of the same file at any given time. Changes made to the file by one device may not have reached iCloud yet and may therefore later conflict with updates made by another device. In this situation, the application must decide which version of the file to keep or which data is more valuable. These problems are not easy to solve and can make the development of these applications a nightmare. Considering all these issues, Apple has introduced a class called `UIDocument`, which is specifically designed to manage files for iCloud. The class can coordinate and synchronize files of any size and provides tools that simplify editing documents on mobile devices, such as progression reports, automatic thumbnail generation, undo manager, and others.

The `UIDocument` class is not meant to be implemented directly in our code; it is like an interface between the app's data and the files we use to store it. To take advantage of this class, we must create a subclass and override some of its methods. Once we have defined the subclass, we can create the object with the following initializer.

▷ **UIDocument(fileURL:** URL**)**—This initializer creates a new `UIDocument` object. The **fileURL** argument is a `URL` structure with the location of the file in the container.

The following are the methods we must override in the subclass of `UIDocument` to provide the data for the file and to retrieve it later.

▷ **contents(forType:** String**)**—This method is called when the `UIDocument` object needs to store the content of the document on file. The method must return an object with the document's data (usually a `Data` structure). The **forType** argument identifies the type of the file (by default, it is determined from the file's extension).

▷ **load(fromContents:** Any, **ofType:** String?**)**—This method is called when the `UIDocument` object loads the content of the document from the file. The **fromContents** argument is an object with the file's content (usually a `Data` structure), and the **ofType** argument is a string that identifies the file's type (by default, it is determined from the file's extension).

Once an object is created from our `UIDocument` subclass, we can manage the file from the asynchronous methods provided by the class. The following are the most frequently used.

▷ **open()**—This asynchronous method asks the `UIDocument` object to open the file and load its content. The method returns a Boolean value to indicate if the operation was successful.

▷ **save(to:** URL, **for:** SaveOperation**)**—This asynchronous method asks the `UIDocument` object to save the content of the document on file. The **for** argument is an enumeration value that indicates the type of operation to perform. The values available are **forCreating** (to save the file for the first time) and **forOverwriting** (to overwrite the file's current version). The method returns a Boolean value to indicate if the operation was successful.

▷ **close()**—This asynchronous method saves any pending changes and closes the document. The method returns a Boolean value to indicate if the operation was successful.

The first thing we have to do to work with documents in iCloud is to define a subclass of `UIDocument`. The following is the one we are going to use for the examples in this chapter.

```
import SwiftUI

class MyDocument: UIDocument {
   var fileContent: Data?

   override func contents(forType typeName: String) throws -> Any {
      return fileContent ?? Data()
   }
   override func load(fromContents contents: Any, ofType typeName:
String?) throws {
      if let data = contents as? Data, !data.isEmpty {
         fileContent = data
      }
   }
}
```

Listing 15-6: Creating the document

The **UIDocument** subclass requires at least three elements: a property to store the contents of the file (**fileContent**), the **contents()** method to provide the data to be stored in the file, and the **load()** method to retrieve the data from the file. When the **UIDocument** object is asked to save or load the data in the file, it calls these methods and uses the **fileContent** property as a proxy to move the data. Therefore, every time we want to access the contents of the file, we need to open the document and read this property.

(Basic) **Metadata Query**

Accessing the files in iCloud is also complicated. We cannot simply retrieve the list of files, as some of them may not have been downloaded to the device yet. Instead, we can retrieve the information associated with the files, known as metadata. The metadata of a file refers to everything related to the file, including its name, extension, creation date and more. In order to retrieve the file's metadata, Foundation defines the **NSMetadataQuery** class. This class provides the necessary properties and methods to retrieve these information and check for updates.

▷ **predicate**—This property sets or returns the predicate for the query. It is an optional of type **NSPredicate**.

▷ **sortDescriptors**—This property sets or returns the sort descriptors for the query. It is an array of **NSSortDescriptor** objects.

▷ **searchScopes**—This property sets or returns a value that indicates the scope of the query. It is an array with constants that represent a predefined scope. The constants available for mobile devices are **NSMetadataQueryUbiquitousDocumentsScope** (searches for all the files in the Documents directory of the iCloud's container) and **NSMetadataQueryUbiquitousDataScope** (searches for all the files that are not in the Documents directory of the iCloud's container).

▷ **results**—This property returns an array with the query's results. By default, the array contains **NSMetadataItem** objects with the metadata of every file found.

▷ **resultCount**—This property returns an **Int** with the number of results produced by the query.

▷ **result(at: Int)**—This method returns the **NSMetadataItem** object from the query's results array at the index specified by the **at** argument.

▷ **start()**—This method initiates the query.

▷ **stop()**—This method stops the query.

▷ **enableUpdates()**—This method enables query updates.

▷ **disableUpdates()**—This method disables query updates.

The **NSMetadataQuery** class also includes some notifications to report when new data is available. The following are the most frequently used.

▷ **NSMetadataQueryDidUpdate**—This notification is posted when the results of the query change.

▷ **NSMetadataQueryDidFinishGathering**—This notification is posted when the query finishes getting all the information.

The predicate used to filter files in a query is similar to the one we used earlier with SwiftData, but it is created from a Foundation class called **NSPredicate**. This class takes in a string with a format that specifies the conditions and comparisons we want to use to filter the values.

▷ **NSPredicate(format:** String, **argumentArray:** [Any]?**)**—This initializer creates an **NSPredicate** object with the conditions set by the **format** argument. The **argumentArray** argument is an optional array of values that replace placeholders in the string assigned to the **format** argument. The **argumentArray** argument may be ignored or replaced by a list of values separated by commas.

The results of a query are returned by the **results** property in the form of an array of **NSMetadataItem** objects. This is a simple class defined to contain the attributes of a file. The class provides the following method to retrieve the values.

▷ **value(forAttribute:** String**)**—This method returns the value of the file's attribute determined by the **forAtttribute** argument. The **NSMetadataItem** class defines a list of constants to represent the attributes. The constants available are **NSMetadataItemFSNameKey** (file's name), **NSMetadataItemDisplayNameKey** (document's name), **NSMetadataItemURLKey** (file's URL), **NSMetadataItemPathKey** (file's path), **NSMetadataItemFSSizeKey** (file's size), **NSMetadataItemFS-CreationDateKey** (date of creation), and **NSMetadataItemFSContentChange-DateKey** (date the file was last modified).

Basic Single Document

The interface of an application that can process documents must allow the user to select the document and provide the tools to process its contents. In the following example, we work with only one document to show how the process works. The initial view includes a button that opens a sheet with a **TextEditor** view where the user can edit the content of the document.

Figure 15-5: Interface to edit a document

The codes listed below make up the model of our application. The first part, next, initializes the **NSMetadataQuery** object and starts listening to the **NSMetadataQueryDidFinish-Gathering** notification to update the document when new information is received.

```
import SwiftUI
import Observation

@Observable class ApplicationData: @unchecked Sendable {
   @ObservationIgnored var document: MyDocument!
   @ObservationIgnored var metaData: NSMetadataQuery!

   static let shared: ApplicationData = ApplicationData()
   private init() {
      metaData = NSMetadataQuery()
      metaData.predicate = NSPredicate(format: "%K == %@",
NSMetadataItemFSNameKey, "myfile.dat")
      metaData.searchScopes = [NSMetadataQueryUbiquitousDocumentsScope]

      Task(priority: .high) {
         let center = NotificationCenter.default
         let name = NSNotification.Name.NSMetadataQueryDidFinishGathering
         for await notification in center.notifications(named: name,
object: nil) {
            if notification.name == name {
               await createFile()
            }
         }
      }
      metaData.start()
   }
}
```

Listing 15-7: *Initializing the model required to store a document in iCloud*

Because of the logic of our application, we only need one property to store the reference to the **MyDocument** object that we will use to access the file, and another property to reference the **NSMetadataQuery** object that we will use to search for the files available in the ubiquitous container. In this example, we call these properties **document** and **metaData**.

Once the model is initialized, we create the **NSMetadataQuery** object, configure the query to search for documents inside the iCloud container (**NSMetadataQueryUbiquitousDocuments-Scope**), listen for the **NSMetadataQueryDidFinishGathering** notification, and initiate the process with the **start()** method. Since we are working with only one document, we make sure that the query returns the correct file with a predicate. The format of the predicate for a query requires comparing the value of a file attribute to the string we are looking for. The attribute is represented by the constants defined in the **NSMetadataItem** class. In this case, we use the **NSMetadataItemFSNameKey** constant to filter the files by name. (Note that the value of the constant is inserted in the string with the placeholder **%K**. This placeholder is called *Dynamic Key* and is used to insert the value without quotes.)

The query gets the document and then posts a **NSMetadataQueryDidFinishGathering** notification. When the notification is received, we can get the list of documents in the container and use them. In this example, we execute a method called **createFile()** to perform that task.

```
@MainActor
func createFile() async {
   if metaData.resultCount > 0 {
      let file = metaData.result(at: 0) as! NSMetadataItem
      let fileURL = file.value(forAttribute: NSMetadataItemURLKey) as! URL
      document = MyDocument(fileURL: fileURL)
   } else {
      let manager = FileManager.default
      if let fileURL = manager.url(forUbiquityContainerIdentifier: nil) {
         let documentURL = fileURL.appendingPathComponent("Documents/
myfile.dat")
```

```
            document = MyDocument(fileURL: documentURL)
            document.fileContent = Data()
            if manager.fileExists(atPath: documentURL.path) {
                let _ = await document.save(to: documentURL,
for: .forOverwriting)
            } else {
                let _ = await document.save(to: documentURL,
for: .forCreating)
            }
        }
    }
}
```

Listing 15-8: *Processing query results*

Since in this application we are working with only one document, the `createFile()` method has only two tasks to perform. If a file is found, we must create an instance of `MyDocument` and assign it to the `document` property to make it available for the views, however if no file is available, we must create one. To know if the query found a document, we check the value of the `resultCount` property of the `NSMetadataQuery` object. This property returns the number of available documents (files). If the number is greater than 0, we get the metadata of the first document in the list using the `result(at:)` method, get its URL with the `value(forAttribute:)` method, and use it to create a `MyDocument` instance.

On the other hand, if no document has been created yet, the `createFile()` method must generate the URL and create a new document. To create the URL of our document, we get the URL of the app's iCloud container with the `url(forUbiquityContainerIdentifier:)` method provided by the `FileManager` object. The URL returned by this method is the root directory of the container, to which we need to append the Documents directory and the name of the file (Documents/myfile.dat). With the URL ready, we create a `MyDocument` object, assign an empty `Data` structure to the `fileContent` property to define the document's initial content, and call the `save()` method to save it. If a document already exists in that URL, we call this method with the `forOverwriting` argument to modify it, otherwise we call it with the `forCreating` argument to create a new one. Internally, the `MyDocument` instance calls the `contents()` method to get the contents of the document and creates the file inside the container.

 IMPORTANT: In this example, we don't need to check the Boolean value returned by the `save()` and `close()` methods, so we ignore the values with an underscore (_), as we did when working with tuples and `switch` statements in Chapter 2 (see Listing 2-38).

From the views, we must open the document, save the changes, and close it. The following are the methods we need to include in the model for this purpose.

```
@MainActor
func openDocument() async -> String {
    let manager = FileManager.default
    if let fileURL = manager.url(forUbiquityContainerIdentifier: nil) {
        let documentURL = fileURL.appendingPathComponent("Documents/
myfile.dat")
        document = MyDocument(fileURL: documentURL)
        let success = await document.open()
        if success {
            if let data = document.fileContent {
                return String(data: data, encoding: .utf8) ?? ""
            }
        }
    }
}
```

```
        return ""
}
@MainActor
func saveDocument(text: String) async {
    let manager = FileManager.default
    if let fileURL = manager.url(forUbiquityContainerIdentifier: nil) {
        let documentURL = fileURL.appendingPathComponent("Documents/
myfile.dat")

        if let data = text.data(using: .utf8) {
            document.fileContent = data
            let _ = await document.save(to: documentURL,
for: .forOverwriting)
        }
    }
}
@MainActor
func closeDocument() async {
    let _ = await document.close()
}
```

Listing 15-9: Updating the document

The `openDocument()` method is called every time the user opens the view to edit the document. In this method, we build the URL, create an instance of **MyDocument** again, open the document with the **open()** method, read the contents, and return a string so that the view can display it on the screen. The **saveDocument()** method performs the opposite process; it takes the text inserted by the user, converts it to a **Data** structure with the **data()** method, assigns it to the document, and saves the document in the container.

At the end, we also add a method called **closeDocument()**. The purpose of this method is to close the document after the user has finished entering the changes.

With these methods, the model is ready. The next step is to provide the views. As always, they are very simple. The initial view only needs a button to open the editor.

```
struct ContentView: View {
    @State private var editDocument: Bool = false

    var body: some View {
        VStack {
            Text("My Document")
                .padding()
            Button("Open Document") {
                editDocument = true
            }.buttonStyle(.borderedProminent)
                .padding()
        }
        .sheet(isPresented: $editDocument) {
            EditDocumentView()
        }
    }
}
```

Listing 15-10: Defining the main interface

The button opens a sheet with a view to edit the document. We call it **EditDocumentView**.

```
struct EditDocumentView: View {
    @Environment(ApplicationData.self) private var appData
    @Environment(\.dismiss) var dismiss
    @State private var inputText: String = ""
```

```
var body: some View {
    VStack {
        HStack {
            Button("Close") {
                dismiss()
            }.padding()
            Spacer()
            Button("Save") {
                Task(priority: .high) {
                    await appData.saveDocument(text: inputText)
                    dismiss()
                }
            }.padding()
        }
        GroupBox {
            TextEditor(text: $inputText)
        }
    }
    .task {
        inputText = await appData.openDocument()
    }
    .onDisappear {
        Task(priority: .background) {
            await appData.closeDocument()
        }
    }
}
}
```

Listing 15-11: Editing the document

This view includes a **TextEditor** view to edit the contents of the document and a button to save it. The editor content is managed by a **@State** property called **inputText**. When the view is loaded, we initiate a task that calls the **openDocument()** method in the model and assigns the value returned by the method to this property, so that the **TextEditor** view is initialized with the document's content.

When the user taps the Save button to save the changes, we call the **saveDocument()** method in the model to store the new value and dismiss the view. Note that we also implemented the **onDisappear()** modifier to ensure that the document is always closed, regardless of how or when the view is dismissed.

 Do It Yourself: In the project you have created before to work with iCloud documents, create a Swift file called MyDocument.swift for the **UIDocument** subclass defined in Listing 15-6 and another called ApplicationData.swift for the model in Listing 15-7. Add the methods in Listings 15-8 and 15-9 to the **ApplicationData** class. Update the **ContentView** view with the code in Listing 15-10. Create a SwiftUI file called EditDocumentView.swift for the view in Listing 15-11. Remember to inject the **ApplicationData** object into the environment for the app and the previews (Chapter 7, Listing 7-4). Run the application on two devices. On the first device, press the Open Document button, insert some text and press the Save button. Wait a few seconds and press the Open Document button on the second device. You should see on the screen the same text you inserted on the first device.

Basic **Multiple Documents**

In the previous example, we worked with only one document, but most applications allow users to create and manage all the documents they need. The requirements for working with a single document or many are the same. We must define a query and listen to the notifications to update the data in our model and the interface. But this time we also need to store information about each document in the model, so the views can show the list of available documents and users can select the one they want to work with. The following model includes a structure called `FileInfo` for this purpose.

```
import SwiftUI
import Observation

struct NotificationWrapper: @unchecked Sendable {
    let value: Notification
}
struct FileInfo: Identifiable {
    let id: UUID = UUID()
    var name: String
    var url: URL
}
@Observable class ApplicationData: @unchecked Sendable {
    var listOfFiles: [FileInfo] = []
    @ObservationIgnored var document: MyDocument!
    @ObservationIgnored var metaData: NSMetadataQuery!

    static let shared: ApplicationData = ApplicationData()
    private init() {
        metaData = NSMetadataQuery()
        metaData.searchScopes = [NSMetadataQueryUbiquitousDocumentsScope]

        Task(priority: .high) {
            let center = NotificationCenter.default
            let name = NSNotification.Name.NSMetadataQueryDidFinishGathering
            for await notification in center.notifications(named: name,
object: nil) {
                if notification.name == name {
                    await getFiles()
                }
            }
        }
        Task(priority: .high) {
            let center = NotificationCenter.default
            let name = NSNotification.Name.NSMetadataQueryDidUpdate
            for await notification in center.notifications(named: name,
object: nil) {
                if notification.name == name {
                    let wrapper = NotificationWrapper(value: notification)
                    await updateFiles(notification: wrapper)
                }
            }
        }
        metaData.start()
    }
}
```

Listing 15-12: Working with multiple documents

The model in Listing 15-12 includes a new structure called `FileInfo` and an observable property called `listOfFiles` to store the instances that represent the documents in the container. In addition to the `NSMetadataQueryDidFinishGathering` notification, we now listen to the `NSMetadataQueryDidUpdate` notification to keep the files up to date. When this notification is received, we execute a method called `updateFiles()`. This method receives the `Notification` object created by the `notifications()` method to learn what changes need to be made in the model. Note that the method is executed in the Main Actor, but the `Notification` object comes from an asynchronous thread. This means that the object is not safe (a data race may occur). To be able to pass this value to the method without receiving warnings and errors from the compiler, we wrap it in a structure called `NotificationWrapper` (for more information on data races and the `Sendable` protocol, see Chapter 9).

The rest of the code in the observable object is the same as before, only the methods change. For example, when the `NSMetadataQueryDidFinishGathering` notification is posted by the `NSMetadataQuery` object, we execute a method called `getFiles()` to process the list of files available in the container.

```
@MainActor
func getFiles() {
   if metaData.resultCount > 0 {
      let files = metaData.results as! [NSMetadataItem]
      for item in files {
         let fileName = item.value(forAttribute: NSMetadataItemFSNameKey)
as! String
         if !listOfFiles.contains(where: { $0.name == fileName }) {
            let documentURL = item.value(forAttribute:
NSMetadataItemURLKey) as! URL
            listOfFiles.append(FileInfo(name: fileName, url:
documentURL))
         }
      }
      listOfFiles.sort(by: { $0.name < $1.name })
   }
}
```

Listing 15-13: Processing the list of files in the container

The `getFiles()` method includes a `for in` loop to go through the list of documents retrieved by the query, get the name of each file, check whether the `listOfFiles` array already contains a file with that name, and add it to the list if necessary.

As mentioned earlier, another method we need to add to the model is the one that is called when an `NSMetadataQueryDidUpdate` notification is received. This notification is sent every time the `NSMetadataQuery` object detects an update in the container (local or remote). In this case, we need to respond when a document is added or removed. To detect the type of change, the `NSMetadataQuery` class defines the following constants.

▷ **NSMetadataQueryUpdateAddedItemsKey**—This constant retrieves an array of `NSMetadataItem` objects that represent the documents added to the container.

▷ **NSMetadataQueryUpdateChangedItemsKey**—This constant retrieves an array of `NSMetadataItem` objects that represent the documents that were modified.

▷ **NSMetadataQueryUpdateRemovedItemsKey**—This constant retrieves an array of `NSMetadataItem` objects that represent the documents that were removed from the container.

This information is returned by the `userInfo` property of the `Notification` object produced by the `NSMetadataQueryDidUpdate` notification and passed to the `updateFiles()` method, so we can process the changes accordingly, as shown below.

```
@MainActor
func updateFiles(notification: NotificationWrapper) {
   metaData.disableUpdates()

   let manager = FileManager.default
   if let modifications = notification.value.userInfo {
```

```
      if let removed =
modifications[NSMetadataQueryUpdateRemovedItemsKey] as? [NSMetadataItem]
{
         for item in removed {
            let name = item.value(forAttribute: NSMetadataItemFSNameKey)
as! String
            if let index = listOfFiles.firstIndex(where: { $0.name ==
name }) {
               listOfFiles.remove(at: index)
            }
         }
      }
      if let added = modifications[NSMetadataQueryUpdateAddedItemsKey]
as? [NSMetadataItem] {
         for item in added {
            let name = item.value(forAttribute: NSMetadataItemFSNameKey)
as! String
            if !listOfFiles.contains(where: { $0.name == name }) {
               if let fileURL =
manager.url(forUbiquityContainerIdentifier: nil) {
                  let documentURL =
fileURL.appendingPathComponent("Documents/\(name)")
                  listOfFiles.append(FileInfo(name: name, url:
documentURL))
               }
            }
         }
         listOfFiles.sort(by: { $0.name < $1.name })
      }
   }
   metaData.enableUpdates()
}
```

Listing 15-14: Updating the container

The **updateFiles()** method in Listing 15-14 receives the wrapper with the **Notification** object, so we can read the notification's **userInfo** property and determine the type of updates performed by the user. If the value is of type **NSMetadataQueryUpdateRemovedItemsKey**, we remove the deleted documents from the **listOfFiles** array, but if the value is of type **NSMetadataQueryUpdateAddedItemsKey**, we create a **FileInfo** structure to represent the file and add it to the **listOfFiles** array as before.

Note that to avoid concurrent updates, we temporarily disable the **NSMetadataQuery** object with the **disableUpdates()** method and re-enable it with the **enableUpdates()** method when the updates are complete.

The remaining methods are those required by the views to process the documents. For example, we need the following two methods to create and remove files from the container.

```
@MainActor
func createFile(name: String) async {
   let manager = FileManager.default
   if let fileURL = manager.url(forUbiquityContainerIdentifier: nil) {
      let documentURL = fileURL.appendingPathComponent("Documents/\
(name)")
      let document = MyDocument(fileURL: documentURL)
      document.fileContent = Data()
      let _ = await document.save(to: documentURL, for: .forCreating)
   }
}
func removeFiles(indexes: IndexSet) async {
   let manager = FileManager.default
   for index in indexes {
```

```
        let fileURL = listOfFiles[index].url
        do {
            try manager.removeItem(atPath: fileURL.path)
            await MainActor.run {
                let _ = listOfFiles.remove(at: index)
            }
        } catch {
            print("Error deleting file: \(error)")
        }
    }
}
```

Listing 15-15: Adding and removing documents from the container

The `createFile()` method defines a URL with the name of the file, creates an empty document, and stores it in the container. The `removeFiles()` method, on the other hand, removes the user-selected files from the container and the corresponding `FileInfo` structures from the array. This last method receives an `IndexSet` value with the indexes of the documents to be removed. This is the value generated by the `onDelete()` modifier. We iterate through these values with a `for in` loop, get the URL of the file from the `url` property, and remove it from the container with the `removeItem()` method and from the `listOfFiles` array with the `remove()` method. Note that the method is asynchronous. This is required by the system. Every time we remove a file from the ubiquitous container, we have to do it in a background thread. This is the reason why we modify the `listOfFiles` property from the Main Actor. (Changes to the interface must always be done from the main thread.)

As before, the model also needs a few more methods to open, save, and close the documents.

```
@MainActor
func openDocument(url: URL) async -> String {
    document = MyDocument(fileURL: url)
    let success = await document.open()
    if success {
        if let data = document.fileContent {
            return String(data: data, encoding: .utf8) ?? ""
        }
    }
    return ""
}
@MainActor
func saveDocument(url: URL, content: String) async {
    if let data = content.data(using: .utf8) {
        document.fileContent = data
        let _ = await document.save(to: url, for: .forOverwriting)
    }
}
@MainActor
func closeDocument() async {
    let _ = await document.close()
}
```

Listing 15-16: Opening, saving, and closing a document

The model is ready, now we must prepare the views. For this example, we need three views: one to list the available documents, one to allow the user to add new documents, and another to edit them. The following are the changes we need to make to the `ContentView` view.

```
struct ContentView: View {
    @Environment(ApplicationData.self) private var appData
    @State private var openSheet: Bool = false

    var body: some View {
        NavigationStack {
            List {
                ForEach(appData.listOfFiles) { file in
                    NavigationLink(destination: EditDocumentView(selectedFile:
file)) {
                        Text(file.name)
                    }
                }
                .onDelete { indexes in
                    Task(priority: .background) {
                        await appData.removeFiles(indexes: indexes)
                    }
                }
            }
            .navigationBarTitle("List of Files")
            .navigationBarTitleDisplayMode(.inline)
            .toolbar {
                ToolbarItem(placement: .navigationBarTrailing) {
                    Button("Create File") {
                        openSheet = true
                    }
                }
            }
            .sheet(isPresented: $openSheet) {
                CreateFileView()
            }
        }
    }
}
```

Listing 15-17: Listing the documents available in the container

This view creates a list with the values in the **listOfFiles** property, applies the **onDelete()** modifier to the **ForEach** view to allow the user to delete a document, and includes a button in the navigation bar to open a sheet to add new documents. The view opened by the **sheet()** modifier is called **CreateFileView**.

```
struct CreateFileView: View {
    @Environment(ApplicationData.self) private var appData
    @Environment(\.dismiss) var dismiss
    @State private var inputFileName: String = ""
    @State private var buttonDisabled: Bool = false

    var body: some View {
        VStack {
            HStack {
                Button("Close") {
                    dismiss()
                }
                Spacer()
                Button("Create") {
                    let fileName =
inputFileName.trimmingCharacters(in: .whitespaces)
                    if !fileName.isEmpty && !
appData.listOfFiles.contains(where: { $0.name == fileName }) {
                        buttonDisabled = true
```

```
                Task(priority: .high) {
                    await appData.createFile(name: fileName)
                    dismiss()
                }
            }
        }.disabled(buttonDisabled)
    }.padding()
    TextField("Insert name and extension", text: $inputFileName)
        .textFieldStyle(.roundedBorder)
        .autocapitalization(.none)
        .autocorrectionDisabled(true)
        .padding()
    Spacer()
    }
  }
}
```

Listing 15-18: Creating new documents

This view includes a `TextField` view where the user can type the name of the document and a button to save it. When the user presses the Save button, the code checks to see if a file with that name already exists in the `listOfFiles` array, disables the button to show the user that the action is being processed, and calls the `createFile()` method to add it to the container.

The `ForEach` loop in the `ContentView` view includes a `NavigationLink` view for the rows. This navigation link opens the `EditDocumentView` view so the user can edit the selected document. The following are the changes we need to make to this view.

```
struct EditDocumentView: View {
    @Environment(ApplicationData.self) private var appData
    @Environment(\.dismiss) var dismiss
    @State private var inputText: String = ""
    let selectedFile: FileInfo

    var body: some View {
        GroupBox {
            TextEditor(text: $inputText)
        }
        .navigationBarTitle(selectedFile.name)
        .navigationBarTitleDisplayMode(.inline)
        .toolbar {
            ToolbarItem(placement: .navigationBarTrailing) {
                Button("Save") {
                    Task(priority: .high) {
                        await appData.saveDocument(url: selectedFile.url,
content: inputText)
                        dismiss()
                    }
                }
            }
        }
        .task {
            inputText = await appData.openDocument(url: selectedFile.url)
        }
        .onDisappear {
            Task(priority: .background) {
                await appData.closeDocument()
            }
        }
    }
}
```

```
#Preview {
   NavigationStack {
      EditDocumentView(selectedFile: FileInfo(name: "", url:
URL(fileURLWithPath: "")))
        .environment(ApplicationData.shared)
   }
}
```

Listing 15-19: Displaying the document's content

This view receives a value of type **FileInfo** with the information about the file selected by the user. Once the view is loaded, we start an asynchronous task to open the document for that file and assign the contents to the **TextEditor** view so the user can see and modify it.

Figure 15-6: Interface to read and save multiple documents

 Do It Yourself: Update the ApplicationData.swift file with the code in Listing 15-12 and the methods in Listings 15-13, 15-14, 15-15, and 15-16. Update the **ContentView** view with the code in Listing 15-17. Create a SwiftUI file called CreateFileView.swift for the view in Listing 15-18, and update the **EditDocumentView** view with the code in Listing 15-19. Run the application simultaneously on two devices. Press the Create File button to add a document. The document should appear on both devices. Move the row to the left and press the Delete button. The document should be removed on both devices.

Basic) **16.1 Integration with UIKit**

SwiftUI was only recently introduced by Apple and therefore not everything we need to build a professional application is available through this framework. This means that sometimes we have to resort to the tools offered by old frameworks such as UIKit (mobile devices) or AppKit (Mac computers).

We have already introduced UIKit. This is the framework SwiftUI implements in the background to create most of the views and controls for mobile applications. Some UIKit classes are used to run the application (`UIApplication`), load images (`UIImage`), manage the device (`UIDevice`) and the windows (`UIWindow`), some are required to define the delegates used to set up the application and the scenes (`UIApplicationDelegate` and `UIWindowSceneDelegate`), and others provide the tools we need to create the interface, including two basic classes to create and manage the views called `UIView` and `UIViewController`.

These last two classes, `UIView` and `UIViewController`, are the ones we need to implement if we want to add UIKit features to our SwiftUI interface. Subclasses of the `UIView` class are used to display information on the screen, such as labels and images, and to create controls, such as buttons, sliders, and switches. The subclasses of the `UIViewController` class, on the other hand, are used to present the views and include the necessary functionality to process their values and interact with the user. To integrate these tools into the SwiftUI interface, the SwiftUI framework defines two protocols: `UIViewRepresentable` and `UIView-ControllerRepresentable`.

Basic) **Representable View**

The `UIViewRepresentable` protocol defines a structure that serves as a wrapper for objects created from the `UIView` class or its subclasses. A structure that conforms to this protocol can present a UIKit view within a SwiftUI interface. To create and manage the UIKit view, the structure must implement the following methods.

▷ **makeUIView(context:** Context)—This method creates the UIKit view and returns it. The **context** argument is a reference to a structure of type `UIViewRepresentable-Context` that provides information about the state of the view.

▷ **updateUIView(**UIViewType, **context:** Context)—This method updates the UIKit view with information provided by the SwiftUI interface through a binding property. The first argument is a reference to the UIKit view, and the **context** argument is a reference to a structure of type `UIViewRepresentableContext` that provides information about the state of the view.

▷ **dismantleUIView(**UIViewType, **coordinator:** Coordinator)—This type method prepares the view to be dismissed. The first argument is a reference to the UIKit view, and the **coordinator** argument is the object that sends values back to the SwiftUI interface.

▷ **makeCoordinator()**—This method creates the object that communicates information from the UIKit view back to the SwiftUI interface.

To include a `UIView` object in a SwiftUI interface (or an object created from one of its subclasses), we need to define a structure that conforms to the `UIViewRepresentable` protocol and implement the methods listed above. The `makeUIView()` and `updateUIView()`

methods are mandatory. In the `makeUIView()` method we must create and return the instance of the UIKit view, and the `updateUIView()` method is used to update the view with values coming from the SwiftUI interface.

The following example creates a UIKit view with a blue background and includes it in a SwiftUI interface. In this case, we only need the `makeUIView()` method to create the UIKit view, but we also have to implement the `updateUIView()` method because it is required by the protocol.

```
import SwiftUI
struct MyCustomView: UIViewRepresentable {
    func makeUIView(context: Context) -> some UIView {
        let view = UIView()
        view.backgroundColor = UIColor(.blue)
        return view
    }
    func updateUIView(_ uiView: UIViewType, context: Context) { }
}
```

Listing 16-1: Preparing a UIKit view to work with SwiftUI

The `makeUIView()` method is called every time a new instance of the `MyCustomView` structure is created. In this method, we create the `UIView` view, give it a blue background, and return it. Therefore, every time we create an instance of the `MyCustomView` structure, a `UIView` is created and included in our SwiftUI interface, as in the following example.

```
struct ContentView: View {
    var body: some View {
        VStack {
            MyCustomView()
                .frame(width: 200, height: 150)
                .padding()
            Spacer()
        }
    }
}
```

Listing 16-2: Showing a UIKit view within a SwiftUI view

A representable view has a flexible size by default, but we can use SwiftUI modifiers to change it. In this example, we use the `frame()` modifier to assign a fixed width and height.

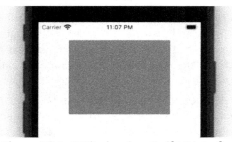

Figure 16-1: UIKit view in a SwiftUI interface

A `UIView` object creates an empty view, but we can also implement views that take input from the user, such as text fields, switches, and more. To pass values from the SwiftUI view to the UIKit view, we use the `updateUIView()` method. However, if we want to send values from the UIKit view to the SwiftUI interface, we need to implement the `makeCoordinator()` method. From this method, we must create an instance of a coordinator object and return it. A coordinator is an object that can send information back from the UIKit view to the SwiftUI interface, usually by modifying binding properties. How to process these values depends on the type of UIKit view we are working with. For example, a `UITextView` view creates an input field where the user can enter multiple lines of text, like the `TextEditor` view in SwiftUI. This view reports changes by calling delegate methods. Therefore, to get the text inserted by the user in a `UITextView` view and process it in SwiftUI, we need to create a coordinator class that conforms to the `UITextViewDelegate` protocol and implements its methods. The following example illustrates how to create a `UIViewRepresentable` structure to work with this class.

```
import SwiftUI
struct TextView: UIViewRepresentable {
   @Binding var input: String

   func makeUIView(context: Context) -> UITextView {
      let view = UITextView()
      view.backgroundColor = UIColor.yellow
      view.font = UIFont.systemFont(ofSize: 17)
      view.delegate = context.coordinator
      return view
   }
   func updateUIView(_ uiView: UITextView, context: Context) {
      uiView.text = input
   }
   func makeCoordinator() -> CoordinatorTextView {
      return CoordinatorTextView(input: $input)
   }
}
class CoordinatorTextView: NSObject, UITextViewDelegate {
   @Binding var inputCoordinator: String

   init(input: Binding<String>) {
      self._inputCoordinator = input
   }
   func textViewDidChange(_ textView: UITextView) {
      inputCoordinator = textView.text
   }
}
```

Listing 16-3: Sending and receiving values from the SwiftUI view

This example creates a `UIViewRepresentable` structure called `TextView`. The structure includes a `@Binding` property called `input` to receive the values and pass them to the SwiftUI view. Below the definition of the `TextView` structure, we define a class called `CoordinatorTextView`. This is our view coordinator whose job is to send values back to the SwiftUI view. For this purpose, we initialize it with a `@Binding` property that is linked to the `input` property defined by the `TextView` structure, and then implement a delegate method that is executed when a character is inserted or removed by the user. The method gets the current text in the input field, so we assign it to the `@Binding` property to send it back to the SwiftUI view.

The `CoordinatorTextView` object is created from the `makeCoordinator()` method when the `UIViewRepresentable` structure is initialized, so the structure is ready from the beginning to receive and send values.

The view is added to the SwiftUI interface as before, but now we need a `@State` property to store and pass the value to the `input` property.

```
struct ContentView: View {
   @State private var inputText: String = "Initial text"

   var body: some View {
      VStack {
```

```
            HStack {
                Text(inputText)
                Spacer()
                Button("Clear") {
                    inputText = ""
                }
            }
            TextView(input: $inputText)
        }.padding()
    }
}
```

Listing 16-4: Receiving and sending values to a UIKit view

This view defines a `@State` property called `inputText`, a `Text` view to display its value, a button to replace the current value with an empty string, and an instance of our `TextInput` view. This view gets a reference to the `inputText` property so that the property is connected to the `input` property in the representable view and we can pass values back and forth.

When the user enters or removes a character in the editor, the representable view calls the `textViewDidChange()` method in the coordinator and the method assigns the current value in the text view to the `inputCoordinator` property (and thus to the `input` property). This means that the value is now available in the `@State` property and the `Text` view can show it on the screen.

On the other hand, when the user presses the Clear button, we assign an empty string to the `@State` property, the system executes the `updateUIView()` method in the representable view, and the value of the `@Binding` property connected to the `@State` property is assigned to the view, so the text view is cleared.

Figure 16-2: `UITextView` view in a SwiftUI interface

 Do It Yourself: Create a Multiplatform project. Create a Swift file called TextView.swift for the code in Listing 16-3. Update the `ContentView` view with the code in Listing 16-4. Insert a text. You should see the text changing at the top. Press the Clear button. You should see the text removed from the text view and also from the view at the top.

 IMPORTANT: A `UIViewRepresentable` structure can represent any UIKit view we want. The implementation always depends on the view we want to use. We will see more examples in following chapters. To learn more about UIKit and UIKit views, read our book **UIKit for Masterminds** (www.formasterminds.com).

(Basic) **Representable View Controller**

The `UIViewControllerRepresentable` protocol defines a structure that serves as a wrapper for objects created from the `UIViewController` class or its subclasses. This class presents a view that can include other views to define the interface for a window or the entire screen, like the views defined by SwiftUI files. A structure that conforms to the `UIViewController-Representable` protocol can present these view controllers within a SwiftUI interface. To create and manage the view controller, the structure must implement the following methods.

- **makeUIViewController(context:** Context)—This method creates the UIKit view controller and returns it. The **context** argument is a reference to a structure of type **UIViewControllerRepresentableContext** that provides information about the state of the view controller.

- **updateUIViewController(**UIViewControllerType, **context:** Context)—This method updates the UIKit view controller with information provided by the SwiftUI interface. The first argument is a reference to the UIKit view controller, and the **context** argument is a reference to a structure of type **UIViewControllerRepresentable-Context** that provides information about the state of the view controller.

- **dismantleUIViewController(**UIViewControllerType, **coordinator:** Coordinator)—This type method prepares the view controller to be dismissed. The first argument is a reference to the UIKit view controller, and the **coordinator** argument is the object that sends values back to the SwiftUI interface.

- **makeCoordinator()**—This method creates the object that communicates information from the UIKit view controller back to the SwiftUI interface.

A UIKit view controller is created from a subclass of the **UIViewController** class. The file is created from the File menu, but the option we need to select to get a subclass of a UIKit class is called Cocoa Touch Class. Once this option is selected, Xcode will display a window where we can enter the name of the file and the class from which we want to create our subclass. For our example, we created a class called **DetailViewController** that inherits from the **UIViewController** class.

```
import UIKit
class DetailViewController: UIViewController {
    override func viewDidLoad() {
        super.viewDidLoad()
        let label = UILabel()
        label.frame = CGRect(x: 20, y: 16, width: 250, height: 30)
        label.font = UIFont.systemFont(ofSize: 30)
        label.text = "Hello World!"
        view.addSubview(label)
    }
}
```

Listing 16-5: *Creating a UIKit view controller*

When the view controller class is instantiated, it creates a view to represent the interface, assigns it to the **view** property, and calls the **viewDidLoad()** method to tell our code that the view is ready. In this method, we can perform all the necessary tasks to initialize the view. In our example, we create a **UILabel** object to display a text on the screen. This object works like the SwiftUI **Text** view, but requires some configuration. In our example, we give it a position and a size by assigning a **CGRect** value to the **frame** property, define a font with a size of 30 pixels, give it the text to display, and then add it to the view controller's view with the **addSubview()** method.

Now that we have the view controller, we need to create a representable view to turn it into a SwiftUI view, as in the following example.

```
import SwiftUI
struct MyViewController: UIViewControllerRepresentable {
    func makeUIViewController(context: Context) -> DetailViewController {
        let controller = DetailViewController()
        return controller
    }
```

```
    func updateUIViewController(_ uiViewController: UIViewControllerType,
context: Context) {
    }
}
```

Listing 16-6: Creating the representable view for a UIKit view controller

The **UIViewControllerRepresentable** protocol works like the **UIViewRepresentable** protocol. We must define a structure that conforms to this protocol, and then add the methods we need to create and update the view. In our example, we only define the **makeUIViewController()** method because we only need to create an instance of our view controller to present it on the screen. The following SwiftUI view loads this view controller inside a **NavigationStack** view when the user presses a button.

```
struct ContentView: View {
    var body: some View {
        NavigationStack {
            VStack {
                NavigationLink("Open UIKit View", destination: {
                    MyViewController()
                }).buttonStyle(.borderedProminent)
                Spacer()
            }.padding()
        }
    }
}
```

Listing 16-7: Loading a UIKit view controller from a SwiftUI view

This view includes a **NavigationLink** view that loads an instance of the **MyViewController** structure, so we can navigate from the initial view to the view controller created by this structure, as we do with normal SwiftUI views.

Figure 16-3: UIKit view controller in a SwiftUI interface

 Do It Yourself: Select the File from Template option from the File menu at the top of the screen to create a new file. Click on the Cocoa Touch Class icon in the iOS section to create a UIKit file. Select the **UIViewController** class from the Subclass option. Insert the name DetailViewController and press Next to save it. Update the **DetailViewController** class with the code in Listing 16-5. Create a Swift file called MyViewController.swift for the code in Listing 16-6. Update the **ContentView** view with the code in Listing 16-7. Run the application. Press the button to open the UIKit view controller.

Chapter 17
Web

Basic **17.1 Web**

Apps can provide users with access to the web, but there are different ways to do it. We can display links that allow the user to open a document in the browser, embed a predefined browser in the app's interface, or download and process data in the background.

Basic **Links**

A link is a text or image associated with a URL that indicates the location of a document. When the user clicks or taps on the link, the document opens. Links were designed for the web, but we can also insert them into our applications and let the system decide where to open the document (in a browser or another application). SwiftUI includes the `Link` view to create them.

▷ **Link(String, destination: URL)**—This initializer creates a button to open a link. The first argument specifies the button's title, and the **destination** argument is a `URL` structure with the location of the document we want to open. If we want to use views to represent the label, we can implement the initializer `Link(destination:, label:)`.

The following example opens the www.formasterminds.com website when the button is pressed. The code defines a `@State` property to store the URL and initializes it with the one we want to open. We use the value of this property to create the `URL` structure and assign it to the `Link` view. When the button is pressed, the system reads the URL, recognizes that it is a web address, and opens the browser to load the website.

```
struct ContentView: View {
    @State private var searchURL = "https://www.formasterminds.com"

    var body: some View {
        VStack {
            Link("Open Web", destination: URL(string: searchURL)!)
                .buttonStyle(.borderedProminent)
            Spacer()
        }.padding()
    }
}
```

Listing 17-1: Opening a website

Figure 17-1: Link

Do It Yourself: Create a Multiplatform project. Update the **ContentView** view with the code in Listing 17-1. Run the application on the iPhone simulator and press the button. The system should open an external browser and load the website.

In this example, we have defined the URL in the code, but sometimes the URL is provided by the user or taken from another document. In such cases, the URL may contain characters that are not allowed and may result in the location not being identified. To ensure that the URL is valid, we need to convert unsafe characters to percent-encoding characters. These are characters represented by the % sign followed by a hexadecimal number. The **String** structure includes the following method for this purpose.

▷ **addingPercentEncoding(withAllowedCharacters:** CharacterSet**)**—This method returns a string with all the characters in the set specified by the argument replaced by percent-encoded characters. The **withAllowedCharacters** argument is a structure with type properties to create instances that represent common sets. The ones available for URLs are **urlFragmentAllowed**, **urlHostAllowed**, **urlPasswordAllowed**, **urlPathAllowed**, **urlQueryAllowed**, and **urlUser-Allowed**.

This method is implemented by the **NSString** class, but we can use it from any instance of the **String** structure. This means that we can apply the method directly to the URL we want to check and assign it to the **Link** view. The only problem is that this view requires a URL that is ready for processing, so we must first check the value using a computed property or a method. To simplify this process, the environment includes a property called **openURL** that returns a method we can use to open a URL. The following example implements a **Button** view that replaces invalid characters in the URL with percentage-encoded characters and then executes the **openURL()** method to open it.

```
struct ContentView: View {
    @Environment(\.openURL) var openURL
    @State private var searchURL = "https://www.formasterminds.com"

    var body: some View {
        VStack {
            Button("Open Web") {
                if let url =
searchURL.addingPercentEncoding(withAllowedCharacters: .urlQueryAllowed)
{
                    openURL(URL(string: url)!)
                }
            }.buttonStyle(.borderedProminent)
            Spacer()
        }.padding()
    }
}
```

Listing 17-2: Encoding URLs

In this example, we are processing a URL that we know works, but that is not always the case. Usually, URLs come from external sources or are provided by the user. In such cases, we not only need to encode the values with the **addingPercentEncoding()** method, but also verify that all the components of the URL are present. For example, if the user only provides the domain (www.formasterminds.com) without the protocol (https), we need to create the full URL before attempting to open it. To read, create, or modify URL components, the Foundation framework defines the **URLComponents** structure. The structure includes the following initializer.

- **URLComponents(string: String)**—This initializer creates a `URLComponents` structure with the components from the URL specified by the **string** argument.

The `URLComponents` structure includes several properties to read and modify the components. The following are the most frequently used.

- **scheme**—This property sets or returns the URL's protocol (e.g., "http").
- **host**—This property sets or returns the URL's domain (e.g., "www.google.com").
- **path**—This property sets or returns the URL's components after the domain (e.g., "/index.php").
- **query**—This property sets or returns the URL's parameters (e.g., "id=22").
- **queryItems**—This property sets or returns an array of `URLQueryItem` structures containing each of the parameters included in the URL.

The `URLComponents` structure also includes the following property to return a string with the URL created from the components.

- **string**—This property returns a string with the URL built from the values of the components.

In the following example, we allow the user to insert a URL, but we make sure that the https protocol is always included.

```
struct ContentView: View {
    @Environment(\.openURL) var openURL
    @State private var searchURL = ""

    var body: some View {
        VStack {
            TextField("Insert URL", text: $searchURL)
                .textFieldStyle(.roundedBorder)
                .autocapitalization(.none)
                .autocorrectionDisabled(true)
            Button("Open Web") {
                if !searchURL.isEmpty {
                    var components = URLComponents(string: searchURL)
                    components?.scheme = "https"
                    if let newURL = components?.string {
                        if let url =
newURL.addingPercentEncoding(withAllowedCharacters: .urlQueryAllowed) {
                            openURL(URL(string: url)!)
                        }
                    }
                }
            }.buttonStyle(.borderedProminent)
            Spacer()
        }.padding()
    }
}
```

Listing 17-3: Encoding custom URLs

The `URLComponents` structure takes a string with the URL, extracts the components, and assigns them to the properties of the structure so that we can read or modify them. In this example, we assign the string "https" to the `scheme` property to ensure that the URL is valid and can be processed by the system. Once the components are ready, we get the full URL from the `string` property, replace invalid characters with percentage-encoded characters, and open it.

Figure 17-2: Custom URLs

Basic Safari View Controller

Links provide access to the web from within our application, but they open the document in an external application. Considering how important it is to capture the user's attention, Apple includes a framework called SafariServices. With this framework, we can open the Safari browser within our application to provide a better experience for our users. The framework includes the **SFSafariViewController** class to create a view controller that includes a view to display web pages and tools for navigation.

▷ **SFSafariViewController(url:** URL, **configuration:** Configuration)—This initializer creates a new Safari view controller that automatically loads the website indicated by the **url** argument. The **configuration** argument is a property of an object of the **Configuration** class included in the **SFSafariViewController** class. The properties available are **entersReaderIfAvailable** and **barCollapsingEnabled**.

The **SFSafariViewController** class creates a UIKit view controller. Therefore, we must define a representable view controller with the **UIViewControllerRepresentable** protocol to add it to our SwiftUI interface, as in the following example. (For more information about representable view controllers, read Chapter 16.)

```
import SwiftUI
import SafariServices
struct SafariBrowser: UIViewControllerRepresentable {
   @Binding var searchURL: URL

   func makeUIViewController(context: Context) -> SFSafariViewController {
      let safari = SFSafariViewController(url: searchURL)
      return safari
   }
   func updateUIViewController(_ uiViewController:
SFSafariViewController, context: Context) {}
}
```

Listing 17-4: Creating a Safari Browser

This structure creates a view controller that contains a functional Safari browser. In the following example, we open this view in a sheet.

```
struct ContentView: View {
   @State private var searchURL: URL = URL(string: "https://
www.formasterminds.com")!
   @State private var openSheet: Bool = false

   var body: some View {
      VStack {
         Button("Open Browser") {
            openSheet = true
         }.buttonStyle(.borderedProminent)
         Spacer()
```

```
      }.padding()
      .sheet(isPresented: $openSheet) {
         SafariBrowser(searchURL: $searchURL)
      }
   }
}
```

Listing 17-5: Opening a Safari Browser

This view defines a **@State** property of type **URL** that is initialized with the URL https:// www.formasterminds.com. When the button is pressed, a **SafariBrowser** view is initialized with this value, the browser is opened in a sheet, and the website is loaded.

Figure 17-3: Safari browser

 Do It Yourself: Create a Multiplatform project. Create a Swift file called SafariBrowser.swift for the code in Listing 17-4. Update the **ContentView** view with the code in Listing 17-5. Run the application on the iPhone simulator and press the button. You should see the Safari browser in a sheet with the www.formasterminds.com website.

The **SFSafariViewController** class also offers the following properties for configuration.

▷ **dismissButtonStyle**—This property sets or returns a value that determines the type of button the view controller is going to show to dismiss the view. It is an enumeration of type **DismissButtonStyle** with the values **done** (default), **close**, and **cancel**.

▷ **preferredBarTintColor**—This property sets or returns a **UIColor** value that determines the color of the bars.

▷ **preferredControlTintColor**—This property sets or returns a **UIColor** value that determines the color of the controls.

The following example takes advantage of these properties to match the colors of the browser with the colors of the www.formasterminds.com website.

```
import SwiftUI
import SafariServices

struct SafariBrowser: UIViewControllerRepresentable {
   @Binding var searchURL: URL

   func makeUIViewController(context: Context) -> SFSafariViewController {
      let safari = SFSafariViewController(url: searchURL)
      safari.dismissButtonStyle = .close
      safari.preferredBarTintColor = UIColor(red: 81/255, green: 91/255,
blue: 119/255, alpha: 1.0)
      safari.preferredControlTintColor = UIColor.white
      return safari
   }
```

```
    func updateUIViewController(_ uiViewController:
SFSafariViewController, context: Context) {}
}
```

Listing 17-6: Configuring the view controller

The code in Listing 17-6 also modifies the **dismissButtonStyle** property to change the type of button displayed by the browser. Instead of Done, the button now says Close.

Figure 17-4: Custom Safari view controller

 IMPORTANT: The **UIColor** class is a class defined in the UIKit framework. The class includes many initializers. The most frequently used is **UIColor(red: CGFloat, green: CGFloat, blue: CGFloat, alpha: CGFloat)**. The class also includes type properties to create predefined colors. The currently available are **systemBlue, systemBrown, systemCyan, systemGreen, systemIndigo, systemMint, systemOrange, systemPink, system-Purple, systemRed, systemTeal, systemYellow, systemGray, systemGray2, systemGray3, systemGray4, systemGray5, systemGray6, clear, black, blue, brown, cyan, darkGray, gray, green, lightGray, magenta, orange, purple, red, white,** and **yellow**. For more information, read our book **UIKit for Masterminds** (www.formasterminds.com).

When the user scrolls the page, the controller collapses the bars to make room for the content. This makes it difficult for the user to exit the view or access the tools. If we think it makes more sense for our application to always leave the bars at their original size, we can initialize the controller with a **Configuration** object. This class is defined inside the **SFSafariViewController** class and includes the following property to configure the bars.

▷ **barCollapsingEnabled**—This property sets or returns a Boolean value that determines whether the navigation bars are collapsed or not.

Once the **Configuration** object is created, we can configure the property and assign it to the Safari View Controller from the controller's initializer.

```
import SwiftUI
import SafariServices

struct SafariBrowser: UIViewControllerRepresentable {
    @Binding var searchURL: URL

    func makeUIViewController(context: Context) -> SFSafariViewController {
        let config = SFSafariViewController.Configuration()
        config.barCollapsingEnabled = false
        let safari = SFSafariViewController(url: searchURL, configuration:
config)
        return safari
    }
```

```
    func updateUIViewController(_ uiViewController:
SFSafariViewController, context: Context) {}
}
```

Listing 17-7: Preserving the bars at their original size

 Do It Yourself: Update the **SafariBrowser** structure with the code in Listing 17-7. Run the application and scroll the page. The bars should remain the same size and the buttons should always be visible.

The framework also defines the **SFSafariViewControllerDelegate** protocol, so we can assign a delegate to the Safari View Controller to control the process. The following are some of the methods defined by this protocol.

▷ **safariViewController(**SFSafariViewController, **didCompleteInitialLoad: Bool)**—This method is called by the controller when the initial website finishes loading.

▷ **safariViewControllerDidFinish(**SFSafariViewController**)**—This method is called by the controller when the view is dismissed (the user pressed the Done button).

The Safari View Controller includes the **delegate** property to assign a delegate. The following example creates a coordinator, assigns it as the view's delegate, and implements the **safariViewControllerDidFinish()** method to disable the button on the interface when the user dismisses the view. (The user can open the view only once.)

```
import SwiftUI
import SafariServices

struct SafariBrowser: UIViewControllerRepresentable {
    @Binding var disable: Bool
    @Binding var searchURL: URL

    func makeUIViewController(context: Context) -> SFSafariViewController {
        let config = SFSafariViewController.Configuration()
        config.barCollapsingEnabled = false
        let safari = SFSafariViewController(url: searchURL, configuration:
config)
        safari.delegate = context.coordinator
        return safari
    }
    func updateUIViewController(_ uiViewController:
SFSafariViewController, context: Context) {}
    func makeCoordinator() -> SafariCoordinator {
        SafariCoordinator(disableCoordinator: $disable)
    }
}
class SafariCoordinator: NSObject, SFSafariViewControllerDelegate {
    @Binding var disableCoordinator: Bool

    init(disableCoordinator: Binding<Bool>) {
        self._disableCoordinator = disableCoordinator
    }
    func safariViewControllerDidFinish(_ controller:
SFSafariViewController) {
        disableCoordinator = true
    }
}
```

Listing 17-8: Assigning a delegate to the Safari View Controller

In the view, we need to define a `@State` property to store a Boolean value and implement the `disable()` modifier in the `Button` view to enable or disable the button depending on this value.

```
struct ContentView: View {
    @State private var searchURL: URL = URL(string: "https://
www.formasterminds.com")!
    @State private var openSheet: Bool = false
    @State private var disableButton: Bool = false

    var body: some View {
        VStack {
            Button("Open Browser") {
                openSheet = true
            }.buttonStyle(.borderedProminent)
            .disabled(disableButton)
            Spacer()
        }.padding()
        .sheet(isPresented: $openSheet) {
            SafariBrowser(disable: $disableButton, searchURL: $searchURL)
        }
    }
}
```

Listing 17-9: Disabling the button from the Safari View Controller delegate

In this example, we include a `@State` property of type `Bool` called `disableButton` and pass it to the representable view controller, so we can modify its value from the coordinator. When the Safari View Controller is dismissed, the `safariViewControllerDidFinish()` method is executed, the value `true` is assigned to the `disableButton` property, and therefore the user can no longer press the button.

 Do It Yourself: Update the SafariBrowser.swift file with the code in Listing 17-8 and the `ContentView` view with the code in Listing 17-9. Run the application on the iPhone simulator and press the button. Press the Done button to close the Safari View Controller. The button should be disabled.

(Basic) WebKit Framework

For some applications, the customization options included in the Safari View Controller are not enough. To provide more alternatives, Apple offers the WebKit framework. With this framework, we can display web content within a view. The view is defined by a subclass of the `UIView` class called `WKWebView`. The class provides the following properties and methods to manage the content.

▷ **title**—This property returns a string with the document's title.

▷ **url**—This property returns a `URL` structure with the document's URL.

▷ **isLoading**—This property returns a Boolean value that determines if the view is in the process of loading a URL or not.

▷ **canGoBack**—This property returns a Boolean value that determines if the view can navigate to the previous page.

▷ **canGoForward**—This property returns a Boolean value that determines if the view can navigate to the next page.

▷ **estimatedProgress**—This property returns a value of type `Double` between 0.0 and 1.0 that determines the fraction of the content that has been already loaded.

▷ **load(**URLRequest**)**—This method loads the content of a URL. The argument is an object with the request for the URL we want to open.

▷ **goBack()**—This method navigates to the previous page on the navigation history.

▷ **goForward()**—This method navigates to the next page on the navigation history.

▷ **go(to:** WKBackForwardListItem**)**—This method navigates to the web page indicated by the argument. The **to** argument is an object that represents a web page in a navigation list.

▷ **reload()**—This method reloads the current page (it refreshes the web page).

▷ **stopLoading()**—This method asks the view to stop loading the content.

To load a website, we must create a request. The UIKit framework offers the `URLRequest` structure for this purpose. The structure includes the following initializer.

▷ **URLRequest(url:** URL, **cachePolicy:** CachePolicy, **timeoutInterval:** TimeInterval**)**—This initializer creates a request to load the URL specified by the **url** argument. The **cachePolicy** argument is an enumeration that determines how the request will work with the cache. The possible values are: `useProtocolCachePolicy` (default), `reloadIgnoringLocalCacheData`, `reloadIgnoringLocalAndRemote-CacheData`, `returnCacheDataElseLoad`, `returnCacheDataDontLoad`, and `reloadRevalidatingCacheData`. The **timeoutInterval** argument is the maximum time allowed for the system to process the request (60.0 by default). Only the first argument is required, the rest of the arguments are defined with values by default.

A WebKit view can report the state of the content through a delegate. For this purpose, the framework defines the `WKNavigationDelegate` protocol. The following are some of the methods included in this protocol.

▷ **webView(**WKWebView, **decidePolicyFor:** WKNavigationAction, **decisionHandler:** Closure**)**—This method is called on the delegate to determine if the view should process a request. The **decidePolicyFor** argument is an object with information about the request, and the **decisionHandler** argument is a closure that we must execute to report our decision. The closure takes a value of type `WKNavigation-ActionPolicy`, an enumeration with the properties `cancel` and `allow`.

▷ **webView(**WKWebView, **didStartProvisionalNavigation:** WKNavigation!**)** —This method is called on the delegate when the view begins loading new content.

▷ **webView(**WKWebView, **didFinish:** WKNavigation!**)**—This method is called on the delegate when the view finishes loading the content.

▷ **webView(**WKWebView, **didFailProvisionalNavigation:** WKNavigation!, **withError:** Error**)**—This method is called on the delegate when an error occurs loading the content.

▷ **webView(**WKWebView, **didReceiveServerRedirectForProvisional-Navigation:** WKNavigation!**)**—This method is called on the delegate when the server redirects the navigator to a different destination.

The WebKit view is a UIKit view and therefore we must use the `UIViewRepresentable` protocol to create it. Once the representable view is defined, the process to load a website in a WebKit view is simple; we provide the URL, create a request, and ask the view to load it.

```
import SwiftUI
import WebKit

struct WebView: UIViewRepresentable {
    let searchURL: URL

    func makeUIView(context: Context) -> WKWebView {
        let view = WKWebView()
        let request = URLRequest(url: searchURL)
        view.load(request)
        return view
    }
    func updateUIView(_ uiView: WKWebView, context: Context) {}
}
```

Listing 17-10: Loading a website with a WebKit View

In this example, we prepare the request with the URL received from the SwiftUI interface and then load the website with the **load()** method. Because we always load the same website, the view only needs to define the URL and pass it to the instance of the **WebView** structure.

```
struct ContentView: View {
    var body: some View {
        WebView(searchURL: URL(string: "https://www.google.com")!)
    }
}
```

Listing 17-11: Showing the WebKit view

Do It Yourself: Create a Multiplatform project. Create a Swift file called WebView.swift for the code in Listing 17-10. Update the **ContentView** view with the code in Listing 17-11. Run the application on the iPhone simulator. You should see Google's website on the screen.

IMPORTANT: In the example in Listing 17-11, we open a secure URL (a URL that begins with the prefix https://) because these are the URLs allowed by default. As we have seen in Chapter 9, Apple implements a system called App Transport Security (ATS) to block insecure URLs. If you want to allow users to load insecure URLs with a **WKWebView** view, you must configure the ATS system with the Allow Arbitrary Loads option (see Figure 9-4).

With a **WKWebView** view, we can load any website, including those specified by the user. We just need to provide a way for the user to enter a URL, as we did in the previous examples, and then execute the **load()** method to load it. To this end, the following view includes a **TextField** view and a button. When the button is pressed, we call a method in the **WebView** structure to update the view with the URL entered by the user.

```
struct ContentView: View {
    @State private var webView: WebView!
    @State private var inputURL: String = ""

    var body: some View {
        VStack {
            HStack {
                TextField("Insert URL", text: $inputURL)
                    .autocapitalization(.none)
                    .autocorrectionDisabled(true)
                Button("Load") {
```

```
            let text = inputURL.trimmingCharacters(in: .whitespaces)
            if !text.isEmpty {
                webView.loadWeb(web: text)
            }
        }
    }.padding(5)
    webView
}.onAppear {
    webView = WebView(inputURL: $inputURL)
}
    }
}
```

Listing 17-12: Allowing the user the insert a URL

In this example, we add a property called `webView` to store a `WebView` structure. The property is initialized when the view appears, and then it is used to call the methods and display the view on the screen.

The URL inserted by the user is stored in a property called **inputURL**, which is passed to the **WebView** structure. This is to be able to update the value of the text field every time the user navigates to a new page.

The **WebView** structure for this example has to create the **WKWebView** view and implement the methods to load new URLs and keep the views updated.

```
import SwiftUI
import WebKit

struct WebView : UIViewRepresentable {
    @Binding var inputURL: String
    let view: WKWebView = WKWebView()

    func makeUIView(context: Context) -> WKWebView  {
        view.navigationDelegate = context.coordinator
        let request = URLRequest(url: URL(string: "https://
www.google.com")!)
        view.load(request)
        return view
    }
    func updateUIView(_ uiView: WKWebView, context: Context) {}

    func loadWeb(web: String) {
        var components = URLComponents(string: web)
        components?.scheme = "https"
        if let newURL = components?.string {
            if let url = newURL.addingPercentEncoding(withAllowedCharacters:
.urlQueryAllowed) {
                if let loadURL = URL(string: url) {
                    let request = URLRequest(url: loadURL)
                    view.load(request)
                }
            }
        }
    }
    func makeCoordinator() -> CoordinatorWebView {
        return CoordinatorWebView(input: $inputURL)
    }
}
class CoordinatorWebView: NSObject, WKNavigationDelegate {
    @Binding var inputURL: String

    init(input: Binding<String>) {
        self._inputURL = input
    }
```

```
    func webView(_ webView: WKWebView, didCommit navigation:
WKNavigation!) {
        if let webURL = webView.url {
            inputURL = webURL.absoluteString
        }
    }
}
```

Listing 17-13: Updating the WKWebView *with the URLs inserted by the user*

We have made several changes to this WebView structure to be able to load multiple URLs. First, we instantiate the WKWebView view outside of the makeUIView() method so that it can be accessed from our custom methods. In the makeUIView() method, we declare the coordinator as the view's delegate by assigning a reference of the coordinator to the view's navigationDelegate property, and then the request is created and loaded. The view is now initialized and will call methods of the coordinator to report changes. However, before we implement the coordinator, we define the loadWeb() method to load the URL entered by the user. This method is executed when the user taps the Load button next to the text field. The method receives a string, prepares the URL, and loads it with the load() method.

The URLs entered by the user are loaded and their content is displayed on the screen. Now we must do the opposite, we need to update the URL in the text field when the content of the view changes. This happens when the user taps on the links on a page to navigate to another one. For this purpose, we make the coordinator conform to the WKNavigationDelegate protocol and implement the webView(WKWebView, didCommit:) method. This method is called by the WKWebView view when new content is loaded. Here, the current URL is retrieved from the url property of the view and assigned to the inputURL property, which changes the value in the TextField view so that the URL in that field matches the website displayed on the screen.

 Do It Yourself: Update the ContentView.swift file with the code in Listing 17-12 and the WebView.swift file with the code in Listing 17-13. Run the application on the iPhone simulator. Insert a URL and press the Load button. The view should load the URL and show the website. Click on a link to navigate to another page. The URL in the text field should match the address of the page on the screen.

In the app we have built so far, the user can visit any URL and navigate by clicking on the links, but our interface does not provide a way to go back or forward in the navigation history. The WKWebView class provides several methods to control the content. For example, there is the goBack() method to go back to the previous page, the goForward() method to go to the page we came back from, and the reload() method to refresh the page. To execute these methods, the example below includes three new buttons.

```
import SwiftUI

struct ContentView: View {
    @State private var inputURL: String = ""
    @State private var backDisabled: Bool = true
    @State private var forwardDisabled: Bool = true
    @State private var webView: WebView!

    var body: some View {
        VStack {
            HStack {
                TextField("Insert URL", text: $inputURL)
                Button("Load") {
                    let text = inputURL.trimmingCharacters(in: .whitespaces)
                    if !text.isEmpty {
```

```
                webView.loadWeb(web: text)
            }
        }
    }.padding(5)

    HStack {
        Button(action: {
            webView.goBack()
        }, label: {
            Image(systemName: "arrow.left.circle")
                .font(.title)
        }).disabled(backDisabled)
        Button(action: {
            webView.goForward()
        }, label: {
            Image(systemName: "arrow.right.circle")
                .font(.title)
        }).disabled(forwardDisabled)
        Spacer()
        Button(action: {
            webView.refresh()
        }, label: {
            Image(systemName: "arrow.clockwise.circle")
                .font(.title)
        })
    }.padding(5)
    webView
    }
    .onAppear {
        webView = WebView(inputURL: $inputURL, backDisabled:
$backDisabled, forwardDisabled: $forwardDisabled)
    }
    }
}
```

Listing 17-14: Providing buttons for navigation

This view defines two more @State properties to determine whether or not the back and forward buttons should be enabled. When the view is first displayed, the buttons should be disabled because only one document has been loaded into the view, but after a new document is loaded, we need to enable the buttons to allow the user to go back and forward in the navigation history. For this purpose we must pass the properties to the WebView structure and modify their values from the coordinator every time a document is loaded.

```
import SwiftUI
import WebKit

struct WebView: UIViewRepresentable {
    @Binding var inputURL: String
    @Binding var backDisabled: Bool
    @Binding var forwardDisabled: Bool

    let view: WKWebView = WKWebView()

    func makeUIView(context: Context) -> WKWebView  {
        view.navigationDelegate = context.coordinator
        let request = URLRequest(url: URL(string: "https://
www.google.com")!)
        self.view.load(request)
        return view
    }
```

```
func updateUIView(_ uiView: WKWebView, context: Context) {}

func loadWeb(web: String) {
    var components = URLComponents(string: web)
    components?.scheme = "https"
    if let newURL = components?.string {
        if let url = newURL.addingPercentEncoding(withAllowedCharacters:
.urlQueryAllowed) {
            if let loadURL = URL(string: url) {
                let request = URLRequest(url: loadURL)
                view.load(request)
            }
        }
    }
}
func goBack(){
    view.goBack()
}
func goForward(){
    view.goForward()
}
func refresh(){
    view.reload()
}
func makeCoordinator() -> CoordinatorWebView {
    return CoordinatorWebView(input: $inputURL, back: $backDisabled,
forward: $forwardDisabled)
}
}
class CoordinatorWebView: NSObject, WKNavigationDelegate {
    @Binding var inputURL: String
    @Binding var backDisabled: Bool
    @Binding var forwardDisabled: Bool

    init(input: Binding<String>, back: Binding<Bool>, forward:
Binding<Bool>) {
        self._inputURL = input
        self._backDisabled = back
        self._forwardDisabled = forward
    }
    func webView(_ webView: WKWebView, didCommit navigation:
WKNavigation!) {
        if let webURL = webView.url {
            inputURL = webURL.absoluteString
            backDisabled = !webView.canGoBack
            forwardDisabled = !webView.canGoForward
        }
    }
}
}
```

Listing 17-15: Navigating back and forth in the navigation history

This code adds three methods to the `WebView` structure to perform the actions selected by the user (move backward, forward, or refresh the page). In the `webView(WKWebView, didFinish:)` method, we update the URL in the text field, as before, but also modify the state of the buttons with the values of the `canGoBack` and `canGoForward` properties so that they are only enabled when there is a page to open.

Figure 17-5: Buttons for navigation

Do It Yourself: Update the ContentView.swift file with the code in Listing 17-14 and the WebView.swift file with the code in Listing 17-15. Run the application on the iPhone simulator. Search a term in Google. Click on a link and press the back button. The view should go back to the previous page.

IMPORTANT: The WebKit framework also offers tools to process cookies and JavaScript code, which allow you to interact with the content of the document. The topic is beyond the scope of this book. For more information, visit our website and follow the links for this chapter.

(Basic) Web Content

The Safari View Controller and the `WKWebView` view are designed to show content to the user, but the integration between the content and our application is limited. Sometimes we need to extract only part of the information from a document or process the data instead of displaying the entire content on the screen. In such cases, we can load and parse the document in the background to extract only what we need.

Foundation includes a group of classes to get the content referenced by a URL. The most important class is called `URLSession`. This class creates a session that manages an HTTP connection for retrieving data and downloading or uploading files. The following are some of the properties and initializers provided by the class to create the session.

▷ **shared**—This type property returns a standard session with a configuration by default that is suitable to perform basic requests.

▷ **URLSession(configuration:** URLSessionConfiguration)—This initializer creates a new session with the configuration set by the argument. The **configuration** argument is an object that specifies the session's behavior.

▷ **URLSession(configuration:** URLSessionConfiguration, **delegate:** URLSessionDelegate?, **delegateQueue:** OperationQueue?)—This initializer creates a new session with the configuration set by the arguments. The **configuration** argument is an object that specifies the session's behavior, the **delegate** argument is a reference to the delegate object we want to assign to the session, and the **delegateQueue** argument is the queue in which the delegate methods are going to be executed.

The session sets up the connection, but it does not perform any tasks. To download or upload data we must implement the following methods defined in the `URLSession` class.

▷ **data(from:** URL, **delegate:** URLSessionTaskDelegate?)—This asynchronous method adds a task to the session to download the data at the URL indicated by the **from** argument. The **delegate** argument is the delegate object used by the task to report updates during the process. The method returns a tuple with two values: a **Data** structure with the data returned by the server and a **URLResponse** object with the status of the request.

▷ **download(from: URL, delegate: URLSessionTaskDelegate?)**—This asynchronous method adds a task to the session to download the file at the URL indicated by the **from** argument. The **delegate** argument is the delegate object used by the task to report updates during the process. The method returns a tuple with two values: a **URL** structure that indicates the location of the downloaded file and a **URLResponse** object with the status of the request.

The following are the methods defined by the class to upload data and files.

▷ **upload(for: URLRequest, from: Data, delegate: URLSessionTask-Delegate?)**—This asynchronous method adds a task to the session to upload the data indicated by the **from** argument. The **delegate** argument is the delegate object used by the task to report updates during the process. The method returns a tuple with two values: a **Data** structure with the data returned by the server and a **URLResponse** object with the status of the request.

▷ **upload(for: URLRequest, fromFile: URL, delegate: URLSessionTask-Delegate?)**—This asynchronous method adds a task to the session to upload the file in the URL indicated by the **fromFile** argument. The **delegate** argument is the delegate object used by the task to report updates during the process. The method returns a tuple with two values: a **Data** structure with the data returned by the server and a **URLResponse** object with the status of the request.

These methods are asynchronous, meaning they return the result after the data has been downloaded or uploaded. The types of values returned depends on the method. For example, the **data()** method returns a value with the data and an object of type **URLResponse** with the status of the request. When we access a URL over the HTTP protocol, the response is represented by an object of type **HTTPURLResponse** (a subclass of **URLResponse**). This class includes the **statusCode** property to return a code that determines the status of the request. Several codes are available, such as the value 200, which reports the success of the request, or the value 301, which reports that the website has moved to a different address. If we just want to make sure that the data was downloaded correctly, we can check if the value of the **statusCode** property is equal to 200 before processing anything. The following example shows how to perform a simple request.

```
import SwiftUI
import Observation

@Observable class ApplicationData: @unchecked Sendable {
   var webContent: String = ""
   var buttonDisabled: Bool = false

   static let shared: ApplicationData = ApplicationData()
   private init() { }

   func loadWeb() async {
      buttonDisabled = true

      let session = URLSession.shared
      let webURL = URL(string: "https://www.yahoo.com")
      do {
         let (data, response) = try await session.data(from: webURL!)
         if let resp = response as? HTTPURLResponse {
            let status = resp.statusCode
```

```
                if status == 200 {
                    if let content = String(data: data, encoding:
String.Encoding.utf8) {
                        await MainActor.run {
                            webContent = content
                            buttonDisabled = false
                        }
                        print(content)
                    }
                } else {
                    print("Error: \(status)")
                }
            }
        } catch {
            print("Error: \(error)")
        }
    }
}
```

Listing 17-16: Loading a remote document

This model loads the content of the website at www.yahoo.com and assigns it to the **webContent** property. The operation is performed by the **loadWeb()** method. The method defines the request with the URL https://www.yahoo.com and then calls the session's **data()** method to download the page. The method downloads the content at that address, checks if the operation was successful (200), takes a string from the data, and updates the **webContent** property with that value to make it available for the view. The following is a simple view for processing this data.

```
struct ContentView: View {
    @Environment(ApplicationData.self) private var appData

    var body: some View {
        VStack {
            Button("Load Web") {
                Task(priority: .high) {
                    await appData.loadWeb()
                }
            }.disabled(appData.buttonDisabled)
            Text("Total Characters: \(appData.webContent.count)")
                .padding()
            Spacer()
        }.padding()
    }
}
```

Listing 17-17: Displaying the document's content

The content returned by www.yahoo.com is extensive. For didactic purposes, we print the entire content on the console and show the number of characters on the screen, but a professional application usually processes the value to extract information.

 Do It Yourself: Create a Multiplatform project. Create a Swift file called ApplicationData.swift for the code in Listing 17-16. Update the **ContentView** view with the code in Listing 17-17. Remember to inject the **Application-Data** object into the environment for the app and the previews (Chapter 7, Listing 7-4). Run the application on the iPhone simulator. Press the Load Web button. After a few seconds, you should see the document downloaded from www.yahoo.com printed on the console and the number of characters on the screen.

A standard session like the one we used in this example comes with a configuration by default that is suitable for most situations, but a custom session requires its own configuration. To configure a session, Foundation provides a class called `URLSessionConfiguration`. The following is the type property we can use to get a configuration object with default values.

▷ **default**—This property returns a `URLSessionConfiguration` object with default settings.

Once we get an object with a standard configuration, we can customize it to meet the needs of our application. The following are some of the properties that the `URLSession-Configuration` class provides to configure the session.

▷ **allowsCellularAccess**—This property sets or returns a Boolean value that determines if the connection should be made when the device is connected to a cellular network.

▷ **timeoutIntervalForRequest**—This property sets or returns a `TimeInterval` value (a typealias of `Double`) that determines the number of seconds the session should wait for a request to be answered. The value by default is 60.

▷ **waitsForConnectivity**—This property sets or returns a Boolean value that determines if the session should wait to perform the request until the device gets connected to the network. The value by default is `false`.

Working with custom sessions only requires us to change how the session is initialized, but the rest of the code remains the same.

```
import SwiftUI
import Observation
@Observable class ApplicationData: @unchecked Sendable {
   var webContent: String = ""
   var buttonDisabled: Bool = false

   static let shared: ApplicationData = ApplicationData()
   private init() { }

   func loadWeb() async {
      buttonDisabled = true

      let config = URLSessionConfiguration.default
      config.waitsForConnectivity = true
      let session = URLSession(configuration: config)

      let webURL = URL(string: "https://www.yahoo.com")
      do {
         let (data, response) = try await session.data(from: webURL!)
         if let resp = response as? HTTPURLResponse {
            let status = resp.statusCode
            if status == 200 {
               if let content = String(data: data, encoding:
String.Encoding.utf8) {
                  await MainActor.run {
                     webContent = content
                     buttonDisabled = false
                  }
                  print(content)
               }
            } else {
               print("Error: \(status)")
            }
         }
      } catch {
```

```
            print("Error: \(error)")
        }
    }
}
```

Listing 17-18: Initializing a custom session

In this example, we haven't implemented the **delegate** argument of the **data()** method. This argument is optional, but we can declare it if we need to respond to and process updates. The framework defines the **URLSessionTaskDelegate** protocol to create this delegate. The following are some of the methods included in the protocol.

▷ **urlSession(**URLSession, **task:** URLSessionTask, **didReceive:** URLAuthenticationChallenge, **completionHandler:** Closure)—This method is called on the delegate when authentication is requested by the server. Our implementation must call the completion handler received by the method with two arguments that define the settings and credentials.

▷ **urlSession(**URLSession, **task:** URLSessionTask, **willPerform-HTTPRedirection:** HTTPURLResponse, **newRequest:** URLRequest, **completionHandler:** Block)—This method is called on the delegate when the server redirected the connection to another URL. Our implementation must call the completion handler received by the method with an argument that defines the new request (the value of the **newRequest** argument) or the value **nil** if we do not want to follow the redirection.

Some websites, such as www.yahoo.com, automatically redirect the user to another address that contains a version of the website tailored to the user's location and preferences. This means that the URL we provide is not the final destination. The server does not return any data, but redirects the user to another document. In such cases, we can define a custom session with a delegate and then implement the **URLSessionTaskDelegate** protocol method to specify what we want to do when the server redirects our application.

```
import SwiftUI
import Observation

@Observable class ApplicationData: NSObject, URLSessionTaskDelegate,
@unchecked Sendable {
    var webContent: String = ""
    var buttonDisabled: Bool = false

    static let shared: ApplicationData = ApplicationData()
    private init() { }

    func loadWeb() async {
        buttonDisabled = true

        let session = URLSession.shared
        let webURL = URL(string: "https://www.yahoo.com")
        do {
            let (data, response) = try await session.data(from: webURL!,
delegate: self)
            if let resp = response as? HTTPURLResponse {
                let status = resp.statusCode
                if status == 200 {
                    if let content = String(data: data, encoding:
String.Encoding.ascii) {
                        await MainActor.run {
                            webContent = content
                            buttonDisabled = false
                        }
```

```
            }
        } else {
            print("Error: \(status)")
        }
    }
    } catch {
        print("Error: \(error)")
    }
}
func urlSession(_ session: URLSession, task: URLSessionTask,
willPerformHTTPRedirection response: HTTPURLResponse, newRequest request:
URLRequest) async -> URLRequest? {
    print(request.url ?? "No URL")
    return request
}
}
```

Listing 17-19: Redirecting the user

 Do It Yourself: Update the `ApplicationData` class with the code in Listing 17-19. Run the application on the iPhone simulator. Press the Load Web button. You should see the URL to which the user was redirected printed on the console.

Web documents, like the one returned by www.yahoo.com, are written in HTML. This is a simple programming language used by any website to organize information. Extracting data from these documents can be tedious and error-prone. For this reason, websites typically provide additional services for sharing data in JSON format. These JSON documents are dynamically generated and contain only the information requested by the application. For example, the website www.openweathermap.org offers a service that generates JSON documents containing information about the weather (https://openweathermap.org/api).

To illustrate how to access and process documents generated by these services, we will read posts from a website called JSONPlaceholder (jsonplaceholder.typicode.com) that generates fake documents. The process doesn't require anything new. We must load the document with a `URLSession` and then decode it with a `JSONDecoder` object.

```
import SwiftUI
import Observation
struct Post: Codable, Identifiable {
    var id: Int
    var userId: Int
    var title: String
    var body: String
}
@Observable class ApplicationData: @unchecked Sendable {
    var listOfPosts: [Post] = []

    static let shared: ApplicationData = ApplicationData()
    private init() {
        Task(priority: .high) {
            await loadJSON()
        }
    }
    func loadJSON() async {
        let session = URLSession.shared
        let webURL = URL(string: "https://jsonplaceholder.typicode.com/
posts")

        do {
            let (data, response) = try await session.data(from: webURL!)
```

```
            if let resp = response as? HTTPURLResponse {
                let status = resp.statusCode
                if status == 200 {
                    let decoder = JSONDecoder()
                    if let posts = try? decoder.decode([Post].self, from:
data) {

                        await MainActor.run {
                            listOfPosts = posts
                        }
                    }
                } else {
                    print("Error: \(status)")
                }
            }
        } catch {
            print("Error: \(error)")
        }
    }
}
```

Listing 17-20: Loading a JSON document

As we learned in Chapter 10, to decode a JSON document, we need to define a structure that matches the JSON values. The URL https://jsonplaceholder.typicode.com/posts returns a list of posts, each with four values: an integer containing the user's identifier, another integer containing the post's identifier, a string containing the title, and a string containing the message. To store these values, the model in Listing 17-20 defines the **Post** structure. This structure conforms to the **Codable** protocol to be able to decode the values, and the **Identifiable** protocol to be able to list the instances with a **List** view.

The process to download the document is the same as before. We get the session, call the **data()** method, decode the data into an array of **Post** structures using a **JSONDecoder** object, and store the values in the **listOfPosts** property to update the view. Since the document is downloaded when the model is initialized, all we need to do in the view is to list the values.

```
struct ContentView: View {
    @Environment(ApplicationData.self) private var appData

    var body: some View {
        VStack {
            List {
                ForEach(appData.listOfPosts) { post in
                    VStack(alignment: .leading) {
                        Text(post.title).bold()
                        Text(post.body)
                    }.padding(5)
                }
            }.listStyle(.plain)
        }.padding()
    }
}
```

Listing 17-21: Listing the values from the document

Do It Yourself: Update the ApplicationData.swift file from the previous project with the code in Listing 17-20 and the **ContentView** view with the code in Listing 17-21. Run the application. You should see 100 messages on the screen. To see the structure of the JSON file returned from the URL https://jsonplaceholder.typicode.com/posts, insert the URL in your browser.

18.1 Pictures

Nowadays, personal devices are mainly used to process images, videos and sound, and Apple devices are no exception. SwiftUI can display an image with an `Image` view, but it needs the support of other frameworks to process the image, present a video on the screen, or play sounds. In this chapter, we present some of the tools Apple provides for this purpose.

Basic **Photos Picker**

SwiftUI includes the `PhotosPicker` structure to generate a view that allows the user to select one or multiple pictures from the Photo Library. The following is the view's initializer.

▷ **PhotosPicker(selection:** Binding, **maxSelectionCount:** Int?, **selection-Behavior:** PhotosPickerSelectionBehavior, **matching:** PHPickerFilter?, **preferredItemEncoding:** EncodingDisambiguationPolicy, **photoLibrary:** PHPhotoLibrary, **label:** Closure)—This initializer creates a `PhotosPicker` view with the configuration specified by the arguments. The **selection** argument is the binding property that stores the references to the selected items. The **maxSelectionCount** argument is the maximum number of items we want to user to be able to select. The **selectionBehavior** argument specifies how the selection is performed. It is a structure with the type properties `default` (checkmark selection), `ordered` (number selection), `continuous` (live selection) and `continuousAnd-Ordered` (live number selection). The **matching** argument determines the type of items the view should include. It is a structure with the type properties `bursts`, `cinematicVideos`, `depthEffectPhotos`, `images`, `livePhotos`, `panoramas`, `screenRecordings`, `screenshots`, `slomoVideos`, `timelapseVideos`, and `videos`. The **preferredItemEncoding** argument determines the encoding to use to process the items. It is a structure with the type properties `automatic` (default), `current`, and `compatible`. The **photoLibrary** argument provides access to the library. It is a structure with the type method `shared()`. And the **label** argument is a closure that provides the label for the button generated by the view.

Since retrieving the items can take time, the picker does not return the images or videos directly, but a reference to the items that we can use to retrieve them later. The framework defines the `PhotosPickerItem` structure for this purpose. The structure includes the following property and method for accessing the media.

▷ **itemIdentifier**—This property returns a string with the item's identifier.

▷ **loadTransferable(type:** Type)—This asynchronous method loads the item and assigns it to an instance of the data type specified by the **type** argument. The data type assigned to this argument must conform to the `Transferable` protocol.

To get access to the `PhotosPicker` structure, we must import the PhotosUI framework. In addition, the view needs a `@State` property to store the selected items. To enable multiple selection, the property must store an array of `PhotosPickerItem` structures, but for single selection, the property only needs to store an optional `PhotosPickerItem` value, as shown below.

```
import SwiftUI
import PhotosUI

struct ContentView: View {
    @State private var selected: PhotosPickerItem?
    @State private var picture: UIImage?

    var body: some View {
        NavigationStack {
            VStack {
                Image(uiImage: picture ?? UIImage(named: "nopicture")!)
                    .resizable()
                    .scaledToFit()
                Spacer()
                PhotosPicker(selection: $selected, matching: .images,
photoLibrary: .shared()) { Text("Select a photo") }
                    .padding()
                    .buttonStyle(.borderedProminent)
            }
            .onChange(of: selected, initial: false) { old, item in
                Task(priority: .background) {
                    if let data = try? await item?.loadTransferable(type:
Data.self) {
                        picture = UIImage(data: data)
                    }
                }
            }
        }
    }
}
```

Listing 18-1: *Creating a Photo picker*

Most of the arguments in the **PhotosPicker** initializer are optional. In this example, we only need to tell the picker where to store the references of the selected items, what kind of items we want to show the user (images), and where to get them from (the shared library).

The **PhotosPicker** structure creates a button that opens a view to select the items when pressed. When an item is selected in this view, a reference is stored in the **@State** property. This means that we can monitor this property for changes with the **onChange()** modifier. When a new image is selected, we start an asynchronous task to call the **loadTransferable()** method for the selected item. This method loads the image, converts it to a **Data** structure, and returns it. If the process is successful, we use the data to initialize a **UIImage** object and assign it to the **picture** property to show it on the screen.

Figure 18-1: *Photo Library's interface (center)*

Do It Yourself: Create a Multiplatform project. Update the `ContentView` view with the code in Listing 18-1. Download the image nopicture.png from our website and add it to the Asset Catalog. Press the Select a photo button. Tap on a picture to select it. The image should be assigned to the `Image` view and displayed on the screen, as shown in Figure 18-1 (right).

 IMPORTANT: In this example, we have used the `Data` structure to transfer the value with the `loadTransferable()` method. We could have used an `Image` view instead, but this data type can only receive PNG images. For more information on the `Transferable` protocol, read the Drag and Drop Gesture section in Chapter 12.

By default, the `PhotosPicker` view creates a button that opens a view on top of our app, but we can also embed the view in our interface with the following modifier.

▷ **photosPickerStyle(**PhotosPickerStyle**)**—This modifier specifies the presentation style for the view. The argument is a structure with the properties `compact`, `inline` and `presentation` (default).

The `presentation` style presents the view in a sheet, as was the case in the previous example. If we want to embed the view in our interface, we can use the `compact` or `inline` styles. These styles are very similar, but the `inline` style provides more options and easy access to the content, as shown by the following example.

```
PhotosPicker(selection: $selected, matching: .images,
photoLibrary: .shared()) { Text("Select a photo") }
    .buttonStyle(.borderedProminent)
    .photosPickerStyle(.inline)
    .frame(height: 300)
```

Listing 18-2: *Embedding the Photos Picker in our interface*

The size of the view presented by a `compact` or `inline` Photos Picker is determined by the available space. This means that the Photos Picker will adjust to the new space when the size of our interface changes. However, we can use the `frame()` modifier to set a fixed size, as we do in our example. The result is shown below.

Figure 18-2: *Inline Photos Picker*

In addition to the `frame()` modifier, we can also use the following modifiers provided by the framework to configure the view.

▷ **photosPickerDisabledCapabilities(**PHPickerCapabilities**)**—This modifier specifies which capabilities are to be excluded from the view. The argument is a structure (or a set of structures) designed to represent a capability. The structure includes the properties `collectionNavigation`, `selectionActions`, `search`, `sensitivityAnalysisIntervention`, and `stagingArea`. We can remove this modifier or specify an empty set if we want all capabilities to be included.

▷ **photosPickerAccessoryVisibility(**Visibility, **edges:** Edge**)**—This modifier specifies whether the controls should be visible or not. The first argument specifies the visibility. It is an enumeration with the values `automatic`, `visible` and `hidden`. And the **edges** argument is a set of `Edge` values that specify the side of the Photos Picker from which the controls should be removed. The `Edge` enumeration includes the values `top`, `bottom`, `leading` and `trailing`.

These modifiers allow us to select the controls we want to include or hide. In the following example, we remove the navigation buttons at the top.

```
PhotosPicker(selection: $selected, matching: .images,
photoLibrary: .shared()) { Text("Select a photo") }
   .buttonStyle(.borderedProminent)
   .photosPickerStyle(.inline)
   .frame(height: 300)
   .photosPickerDisabledCapabilities([.collectionNavigation])
```

Listing 18-3: Hiding controls

Figure 18-3: Photos Picker with custom controls

In the previous example, the user has only been able to select one item at a time. By assigning an array of **PhotosPickerItem** structures to the **@State** property, we can allow the user to select multiple items. Although this is all we need to enable multiple selection, we must consider how the items will be removed from the list when they are deselected by the user. We could clear the array and reload each element, but some of the items may take a while to load. Another option is to store the items in a separate array and compare the values, so we can remove only the deselected elements, but keep the rest. This is the approach we take in the following example. For this purpose, we need a model with a structure to store the images and their identifiers.

```
import SwiftUI
import Observation
import PhotosUI

struct ItemsData: Identifiable {
   var id: String
   var image: UIImage
}
@Observable class ApplicationData: @unchecked Sendable {
   var listPictures: [ItemsData] = []
   var selected: [PhotosPickerItem] = []
```

```
      static let shared: ApplicationData = ApplicationData()
      private init() { }

      func removeDeselectedItems() {
         listPictures = listPictures.filter { value in
            if selected.contains(where: { $0.itemIdentifier == value.id }) {
               return true
            } else {
               return false
            }
         }
      }
      func addSelectedItems() {
         for item in selected {
            Task(priority: .background) {
               if let data = try? await item.loadTransferable(type:
Data.self) {
                  if let id = item.itemIdentifier, let image = UIImage(data:
data) {
                     if !listPictures.contains(where: { $0.id == id }) {
                        let newPicture = ItemsData(id: id, image: image)
                        await MainActor.run {
                           listPictures.append(newPicture)
                        }
                     }
                  }
               }
            }
         }
      }
   }
```

Listing 18-4: *Defining the model for multiple selection*

This model includes two properties, one to store an array of **ItemsData** structures to deliver the currently selected images to the views, and another with an array of **PhotosPickerItem** structures for the **PhotosPicker** view to store the references of the items selected by the user.

There are also two methods in the model: **removeDeselectedItems()** and **addSelectedItems()**. Both are executed by the view every time the user modifies the selection (every time the value of the **selected** property changes). The **removeDeselectedItems()** method iterates through the items in the **listPictures** array to check which ones are still selected by the user, so any item that has been deselected is no longer on the list. On the other hand, the **addSelectedItems()** method adds to the **listPictures** array the items that the user added to the selection. The view can now use the **listPictures** array to display the selected images on the screen and call these methods each time the selection is modified.

```
struct ContentView: View {
   @Environment(ApplicationData.self) private var appData

   let guides = [
      GridItem(.flexible()),
      GridItem(.flexible()),
      GridItem(.flexible())
   ]
   var body: some View {
      @Bindable var appData = appData

      VStack {
         ScrollView {
            LazyVGrid(columns: guides) {
```

```
            ForEach(appData.listPictures) { item in
                Image(uiImage: item.image)
                    .resizable()
                    .scaledToFit()
            }
        }
    }.padding()
    Spacer()
    PhotosPicker(selection: $appData.selected, maxSelectionCount: 4,
selectionBehavior: .continuous, matching: .images,
photoLibrary: .shared()) { Text("Select Photos") }
        .photosPickerStyle(.inline)
        .photosPickerDisabledCapabilities(.selectionActions)
    }
    .onChange(of: appData.selected, initial: false) { old, items in
        appData.removeDeselectedItems()
        appData.addSelectedItems()
    }
  }
 }
}
```

Listing 18-5: *Allowing the user to perform multiple selections*

In this example, we have configured the picker to select a maximum of 4 items, but this is not necessary. If no limit is specified, the user can select all the items he or she wants. Note that because the Photos Picker is embedded in our interface, the selection buttons are not required, and the selection behavior is set to **continuous**, so the selection is updated live (the user doesn't need to press the Add button).

Figure 18-4: *Multiple selection*

Do It Yourself: Create a Swift file called ApplicationData.swift for the model in Listing 18-4. Update the **ContentView** view with the code in Listing 18-5. Remember to inject the **ApplicationData** object into the environment for the app and the previews (Chapter 7, Listing 7-4). Select multiple pictures. You should see the selected pictures on the list, as shown in Figure 18-4 (right).

Basic Camera

One of the most common uses of mobile devices is to take and store photos, and therefore no device is sold without a camera anymore. Since it is quite normal for an application to access the camera and manage images, UIKit offers a controller with built-in functionality that provides the user with all the necessary tools to take photos and videos. The class used to create this controller is called **UIImagePickerController**. The following are the properties that are included in this class for configuration.

- **sourceType**—This property sets or returns a value that determines the type of source we want to use to get the pictures. It is an enumeration called `SourceType` included in the `UIImagePickerController` class. At this moment, only the value `camera` is available.

- **mediaTypes**—This property sets or returns a value that determines the type of media we want to work with. It takes an array of strings with values that represent every media we want to use. The most common are public.image for pictures and public.movie for videos. (These values can be represented by the constants `kUTTypeImage` and `kUTTypeMovie`.)

- **cameraCaptureMode**—This property sets or returns a value that determines the capture mode used by the camera. It is an enumeration called `CameraCaptureMode` included in the `UIImagePickerController` class. The values available are `photo` and `video`.

- **cameraFlashMode**—This property sets or returns a value that determines the flash mode used by the camera. It is an enumeration called `CameraFlashMode` included in the `UIImagePickerController` class. The values available are `on`, `off`, and `auto`.

- **allowsEditing**—This property sets or returns a Boolean value that determines if the user is allowed to edit the image.

- **videoQuality**—This property sets or returns a value that determines the quality of the recorded video. It is an enumeration called `QualityType` included in the `UIImagePickerController` class. The values available are `typeHigh`, `typeMedium`, `typeLow`, `type640x480`, `typeIFrame960x540`, and `typeIFrame1280x720`.

The `UIImagePickerController` class also offers the following type methods to detect the source available and the type of media it can manage.

- **isSourceTypeAvailable(**SourceType**)**—This type method returns a Boolean value that indicates if the source specified by the argument is supported by the device. The argument is an enumeration called `SourceType` included in the `UIImage-PickerController` class. At this moment, only the value `camera` is available.

- **availableMediaTypes(for:** SourceType**)**—This type method returns an array with strings that represent the media types available for the source specified by the argument. The argument is an enumeration called `SourceType` included in the `UIImagePickerController` class. At this moment, only the value `camera` is available.

- **isCameraDeviceAvailable(**CameraDevice**)**—This type method returns a Boolean value that indicates if the camera specified by the argument is available on the device. The argument is an enumeration called `CameraDevice` included in the `UIImagePickerController` class. The values available are `rear` and `front`.

The `UIImagePickerController` class creates a new view where the user can take pictures or record videos. After the image or the video is created, the view must be dismissed, and the media processed. The way our code gets access to the media and knows when to dismiss the view is through a delegate that conforms to the `UIImagePickerControllerDelegate` protocol. The protocol includes the following methods.

- **imagePickerController(**UIImagePickerController, **didFinishPickingMedia-WithInfo:** Dictionary**)**—This method is called on the delegate when the user finishes taking the image or recording the video. The second argument contains a dictionary with the information about the media. The values in the dictionary are identified with properties of the `InfoKey` structure included in the `UIImagePicker-`

Controller class. The properties available are **cropRect**, **editedImage**, **imageURL**, **livePhoto**, **mediaMetadata**, **mediaType**, **mediaURL**, and **originalImage**.

▷ **imagePickerControllerDidCancel**(UIImagePickerController)—This method is called on the delegate when the user cancels the process.

An image picker can be presented with a sheet or a popover, but if we want the view to take up the entire screen, we can embed it in a **NavigationStack** view and open it with a **NavigationLink**. This is the approach we take in the following example. The interface includes a button to open the image picker and an **Image** view to display the photo taken by the user.

Figure 18-5: Interface to work with the camera

 IMPORTANT: To access the camera, you must ask authorization to the user. The process is automatic, but you have to add the "Privacy - Camera Usage Description" option to the Info panel in the app's settings with the message you want to show to the user (see Chapter 5, Figure 5-34).

The image picker controller is a UIKit view controller and is therefore included in the SwiftUI interface with a representable view controller. In order to process the image captured by the camera, we need to include a coordinator and implement the delegate methods. This coordinator must conform to two protocols: **UINavigationControllerDelegate** and **UIImagePickerControllerDelegate**, as shown in the following example.

```
import SwiftUI

struct ImagePicker: UIViewControllerRepresentable {
    @Binding var path: NavigationPath
    @Binding var picture: UIImage?

    func makeUIViewController(context: Context) -> UIImagePickerController {
        let mediaPicker = UIImagePickerController()
        mediaPicker.delegate = context.coordinator
        if UIImagePickerController.isSourceTypeAvailable(.camera) {
            mediaPicker.sourceType = .camera
            mediaPicker.mediaTypes = ["public.image"]
            mediaPicker.allowsEditing = false
            mediaPicker.cameraCaptureMode = .photo
        } else {
            print("The media is not available")
        }
        return mediaPicker
    }
}
```

```
    func updateUIViewController(_ uiViewController:
UIImagePickerController, context: Context) {}

    func makeCoordinator() -> ImagePickerCoordinator {
       ImagePickerCoordinator(path: $path, picture: $picture)
    }
}
class ImagePickerCoordinator: NSObject, UINavigationControllerDelegate,
UIImagePickerControllerDelegate {
    @Binding var path: NavigationPath
    @Binding var picture: UIImage?

    init(path: Binding<NavigationPath>, picture: Binding<UIImage?>) {
       self._path = path
       self._picture = picture
    }
    func imagePickerController(_ picker: UIImagePickerController,
didFinishPickingMediaWithInfo info: [UIImagePickerController.InfoKey :
Any]) {
       if let newpicture = info[.originalImage] as? UIImage {
          picture = newpicture
       }
       path = NavigationPath()
    }
    func imagePickerControllerDidCancel(_ picker: UIImagePickerController) {
       path = NavigationPath()
    }
}
```

Listing 18-6: *Creating the Image Picker Controller to take pictures*

This representable view controller creates an instance of the `UIImagePickerController` class and assigns the `ImagePickerCoordinator` object as its delegate. Next, it checks if the camera is available and configures the controller if successful or displays a message on the console otherwise. The value `camera` is assigned to the `sourceType` property to tell the controller to retrieve the image from the camera, an array with the value public.image is assigned to the `mediaTypes` property to specify images as the media to retrieve, the `allowEditing` property is set to `false` to prevent the user from editing the image, and the value `photo` is assigned to the `cameraCaptureMode` property to allow the user to capture images only.

The camera's interface includes buttons for controlling the camera and capturing the image. After the user takes a picture, a new set of buttons appears, allowing the user to select the image or capture another one. If the user decides to use the current image, the controller calls the `imagePickerController(didFinishPickingMediaWithInfo:)` method on its delegate to report the action. This method receives a parameter called **info**, which we can read to get the media returned by the controller and process it (save it to a file, a database, or display it on the screen). In our example, we read the value of the `originalImage` key to get a `UIImage` object with the picture taken by the user, and assign this object to a `@State` property to make it available for the view. Note that we also implemented the `imagePickerControllerDid-Cancel()` method in the coordinator to dismiss the controller when the user presses the Cancel button.

The view must include a button to open the Image Picker Controller and an **Image** view to show the picture taken by the user.

```
struct ContentView: View {
    @State private var path = NavigationPath()
    @State private var picture: UIImage?

    var body: some View {
       NavigationStack(path: $path) {
          VStack {
```

```
            HStack {
                Spacer()
                NavigationLink("Get Picture", value: "Open Picker")
            }.navigationDestination(for: String.self, destination: { _ in
                ImagePicker(path: $path, picture: $picture)
            })
            Image(uiImage: picture ?? UIImage(named: "nopicture")!)
                .resizable()
                .scaledToFill()
                .frame(minWidth: 0, maxWidth: .infinity, minHeight: 0,
maxHeight: .infinity)
                .clipped()
            Spacer()
        }.padding()
    }.statusBarHidden()
}
}
```

Listing 18-7: Defining the interface to take pictures

This view creates an instance of the **ImagePicker** structure and declares it as the destination of a **NavigationLink** button. When the button is pressed, the view opens. If the user takes a picture and decides to use it, the image is assigned to the **picture** property by the delegate method and the **Image** view is updated to display it on the screen.

Do It Yourself: Create a Multiplatform project. Create a Swift file called ImagePicker.swift for the code in Listing 18-6. Update the ContentView.swift file with the code in Listing 18-7. Download the image nopicture.png from our website and add it to the Asset Catalog. Add the "Privacy - Camera Usage Description" option to the Info panel in the app's settings with the text you want to show to the user. Run the application on a device, press the button and take a picture. You should see the photo on the screen.

(Basic) Storing Pictures

In the previous example, we show the image on the screen, but we can also store it in a file or a database. An alternative, which is sometimes useful when working with the camera, is to store the image in the device's Photo Library so that other applications can access it. The UIKit framework offers the following two functions for saving images and videos.

▷ **UIImageWriteToSavedPhotosAlbum(**UIImage, Any?, Selector?, Unsafe-MutableRawPointer?**)**—This function adds the image specified by the first argument to the camera roll. The second argument is a reference to the object that contains the method we want to execute when the process is over, the third argument is a selector that represents that method, and the last argument is an object with data to pass to the method.

▷ **UISaveVideoAtPathToSavedPhotosAlbum(**String, Any?, Selector?, UnsafeMutableRawPointer?**)**—This function adds the video to the camera roll at the path indicated by the first argument. The second argument is a reference to the object that contains the method we want to execute when the process is over, the third argument is a selector that represents that method, and the last argument is an object with additional data for the method.

IMPORTANT: To store pictures or videos in the device, we must ask permission to the user. As always, this is done from the Info panel in the app's settings. In this case, we must add the "Privacy - Photo Library Additions Usage Description" option with the message we want to show to the user when authorization is requested.

The functions to save a picture are defined in Objective-C, so they require some parameters that are not common in SwiftUI applications, but if all we want is to save the image, we can specify the first argument and define the rest as `nil`, as shown in the following example.

```
struct ContentView: View {
    @State private var path = NavigationPath()
    @State private var picture: UIImage?
    @State private var showAlert: Bool = false

    var body: some View {
        NavigationStack(path: $path) {
            VStack {
                HStack {
                    Button("Share Picture") {
                        showAlert = true
                    }.disabled(picture == nil ? true : false)
                    Spacer()
                    NavigationLink("Get Picture", value: "Open Picker")
                }.navigationDestination(for: String.self, destination: { _ in
                    ImagePicker(path: $path, picture: $picture)
                })
                .alert("Save Picture", isPresented: $showAlert, actions: {
                    Button("Cancel", role: .cancel, action: {
                        showAlert = false
                    })
                    Button("YES", role: .none, action: {
                        if let picture {
                            UIImageWriteToSavedPhotosAlbum(picture, nil, nil, nil)
                        }
                    })
                }, message: { Text("Do you want to store the picture in the
Photo Library?") })
                Image(uiImage: picture ?? UIImage(named: "nopicture")!)
                    .resizable()
                    .scaledToFill()
                    .frame(minWidth: 0, maxWidth: .infinity, minHeight: 0,
maxHeight: .infinity)
                    .clipped()
                Spacer()
            }.padding()
        }.statusBarHidden()
    }
}
```

Listing 18-8: Saving the picture in the Photo Library

The process is the same as before. The image picker controller opens a view for the user to take a picture and then calls the delegate method to process it. The image is assigned to the `picture` property to display it on the screen, but now we have an additional button to present an alert view that allows the user to save the image to the Photo Library.

 Do It Yourself: Update the ContentView.swift file with the code in Listing 18-8. Add the "Privacy - Photo Library Additions Usage Description" option to the Info panel in the app's settings to get access to the Photo Library. (Remember that you also need the "Privacy - Camera Usage Description" option to access the camera, as before.) Run the application on a device and take a picture. You should see the image on the screen. Press the Share Picture button. You should see an alert view asking for permission to save the picture. Press YES. The picture should be available in your Photo Library.

Share Link

Another way to share information with other applications is a share sheet. This is a sheet provided by the system with icons to open the applications with which we can share content, including options to copy and print the information. SwiftUI provides the following view to open the sheet.

▶ **ShareLink(**String, **item:** Item, **subject:** Text?, **message:** Text?, **preview:** SharePreview**)**—This initializer creates a button that presents a sheet to select the application with which we want to share the data. The first argument is the button's label. The **item** argument is the value we want to share (it must conform to the `Transferable` protocol). The **subject** argument is the item's title. The **message** argument is the item's description. And the **preview** argument is a structure that provides a representation of the item.

If we want to share an image, we must provide a preview. SwiftUI includes the `SharePreview` structure for this purpose.

▶ **SharePreview(**String, **image:** Image**)**—This initializer creates a representation of the item to share. The first argument is the description of the item, and the **image** argument is an `Image` view that visually represents the item.

Share links are frequently used to share text, but they can share any type of values we want as long as they conform to the `Transferable` protocol. For instance, we can share the picture taken by the camera.

```
struct ContentView: View {
    @State private var path = NavigationPath()
    @State private var picture: UIImage?

    var body: some View {
        NavigationStack(path: $path) {
            VStack {
                HStack {
                    if let picture = picture {
                        let photo = Image(uiImage: picture)
                        ShareLink("Share Picture", item: photo, preview:
SharePreview("Photo", image: photo))
                    }
                    Spacer()
                    NavigationLink("Get Picture", value: "Open Picker")
                }.navigationDestination(for: String.self, destination: { _ in
                    ImagePicker(path: $path, picture: $picture)
                })
                Image(uiImage: picture ?? UIImage(named: "nopicture")!)
                    .resizable()
                    .scaledToFill()
                    .frame(minWidth: 0, maxWidth: .infinity, minHeight: 0,
maxHeight: .infinity)
                    .clipped()
                Spacer()
            }.padding()
        }.statusBarHidden()
    }
}
```

Listing 18-9: Sharing the image with other applications

The **ShareLink** view creates a button with a predefined label that includes an SF Symbol on the left. In this example, we place it in the upper left corner, but only display it if there is an image to share (if the user has already taken a picture with the camera). When the button is pressed, the system opens a small sheet with icons representing the apps with which we can share information, and when we scroll up the sheet, options are revealed to perform additional actions such as copying and printing the data. For example, if we have the Facebook app installed, we can post a message with our picture, as shown below.

Figure 18-6: Share sheet

 Do It Yourself: Update the **ContentView** view from the previous example with the code in Listing 18-9. Run the application on a device. Press the Get Picture button and take a picture. Press the Share Picture button. You should see the share sheet at the bottom of the screen. Select an app to share the image.

(Medium) **Custom Camera**

The **UIImagePickerController** controller is built from classes defined in the AV Foundation framework. This framework provides the code necessary to process media and control input devices, like the camera and the microphone. So we can use the classes in this framework directly to build our own controller and customize the process and the interface.

Creating a custom controller that accesses the camera and retrieves information from input devices requires the coordination of multiple systems; we need to configure the inputs from the camera and the microphone, process the data received from those inputs, preview it to the user, and produce the output in the form of an image, live photo, video, or audio. Figure 18-7 illustrates all the elements involved.

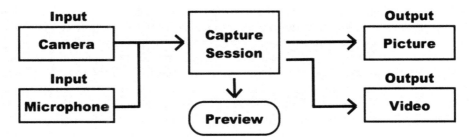

Figure 18-7: System to capture media

The first thing we need to do to build this structure is to determine the input devices. The AV Foundation framework defines the **AVCaptureDevice** class for this purpose. An instance of this class can represent any type of input device, including cameras and microphones. The following are some of the methods included in the class to access and manage a device.

▷ **default(for:** AVMediaType)—This type method returns an `AVCaptureDevice` object that represents the default capture device for the media specified by the argument. The **for** argument is a structure of type `AVMediaType` with properties to define the type of media. The properties available to work with the cameras and microphones are `video` and `audio`.

▷ **requestAccess(for:** AVMediaType)—This asynchronous type method asks the user for permission to access the device. The **for** argument is a structure of type `AVMediaType` with properties to define the type of media. The properties available to work with the cameras and microphones are `video` and `audio`.

▷ **authorizationStatus(for:** AVMediaType)—This type method returns a value that determines the status of the authorization to use the device. The **for** argument is a structure of type `AVMediaType` with properties to define the type of media. The properties available to work with the cameras and microphones are `video` and `audio`. The method returns an enumeration of type `AVAuthorizationStatus` with the values `notDetermined`, `restricted`, `denied`, and `authorized`.

An instance of the `AVCaptureDevice` class represents a capture device, such as the camera or the microphone. The class includes properties and methods for configuring and managing a device. The following are the most commonly used and the ones we will need for our example.

▷ **isSubjectAreaChangeMonitoringEnabled**—This property sets or returns a Boolean value that determines whether the device monitors the area for changes, such as lighting and orientation.

▷ **formats**—This property returns an array of `Format` objects that represent the formats the device supports.

▷ **activeFormat**—This property returns a Format object representing the format in use by the device.

▷ **lockForConfiguration()**—This method requests exclusive access to configure the device.

▷ **unlockForConfiguration()**—This method releases the device for configuration.

To define the capture device as an input device, we must create an object that controls the ports and connections. The framework defines the `AVCaptureDeviceInput` class for this purpose. The class includes the following initializer to create the input object for the device.

▷ **AVCaptureDeviceInput(device:** AVCaptureDevice)—This initializer creates an input for the device specified by the **device** argument.

In addition to inputs, we also need outputs to capture and process the data received from the device. The framework defines subclasses of a base class called `AVCaptureOutput` to describe the outputs. Several subclasses are available, such as `AVCaptureVideoDataOutput` to process the frames of a video and `AVCaptureAudioDataOutput` to get the audio data, but the most useful is the `AVCapturePhotoOutput` class, used to capture a single video frame (take a picture). This class includes many properties and methods to configure the output. Below you can find the property to set the maximum dimensions of the image and the method to capture a photo.

▷ **maxPhotoDimensions**—This property sets or returns the dimensions of the image to be captured. It is a structure of type `CMVideoDimensions` with the properties `width` and `height`.

▷ **capturePhoto(with:** AVCapturePhotoSettings, **delegate:** AVCapture-PhotoCaptureDelegate)—This method initiates a photo capture with the settings specified by the **with** argument. The **delegate** argument is a reference to the object that implements the methods of the `AVCapturePhotoCaptureDelegate` protocol to receive the data generated by the output.

The `AVCapturePhotoOutput` class works with a delegate that conforms to the `AVCapturePhotoCaptureDelegate` protocol, which among other methods defines the following to return a still image.

▷ **photoOutput(**AVCapturePhotoOutput, **didFinishProcessingPhoto:** AVCapturePhoto, **error:** Error?**)**—This method is called on the delegate after the image is captured. The **didFinishProcessingPhoto** argument is a container with information about the image, and the **error** argument is used to report errors.

To control the flow of data from input to output, the framework defines the `AVCaptureSession` class. From an instance of this class, we can control the inputs and outputs and determine when the process begins and ends by calling the following methods.

▷ **addInput(**AVCaptureInput**)**—This method adds an input to the capture session. The argument represents the input device we want to add.

▷ **addOutput(**AVCaptureOutput**)**—This method adds an output to the capture session. The argument represents the output we want to generate from the capture session.

▷ **startRunning()**—This method starts the capture session.

▷ **stopRunning()**—This method stops the capture session.

The framework also defines the `AVCaptureVideoPreviewLayer` class to show a preview to the user. This class creates a layer to display the video captured by the input device. The class includes the following initializer and properties to create and manage the preview layer.

▷ **AVCaptureVideoPreviewLayer(session:** AVCaptureSession**)**—This initializer creates an `AVCaptureVideoPreviewLayer` object with a preview layer connected to the capture session defined by the **session** argument.

▷ **connection**—This property returns an object of type `AVCaptureConnection` that defines the connection between the capture session and the preview layer.

▷ **session**—This property sets or returns an `AVCaptureSession` object representing the session assigned to the preview layer.

The input, output, and preview layer are connected to the capture session by objects of the `AVCaptureConnection` class. The class manages the information for the connection, including ports, data, and orientation. The following are the property and method used to set the orientation of the preview layer.

▷ **videoRotationAngle**—This property sets or returns a `CGFloat` value that represents the rotation angle the connection applies to the preview (the angles are 0.0, 90.0, 180.0 and 270.0).

▷ **isVideoRotationAngleSupported(**CGFloat**)**—This method returns a Boolean value to indicate whether the rotation to the angle specified by the argument is supported.

Rotation angles are determined by a rotation coordinator. To create it, the framework includes a class defined in the `AVCaptureDevice` class called `RotationCoordinator`. The class includes the following initializer.

> **AVCaptureDevice.RotationCoordinator(device:** AVCaptureDevice, **previewLayer:** CALayer?)—This initializer creates a rotation coordinator for the device and the preview layer specified by the arguments.

The `RotationCoordinator` class includes the following two properties that we can read to get the current angle of rotation.

> **videoRotationAngleForHorizonLevelPreview**—This property returns the angle of rotation we need to apply to the preview layer to match the device's orientation.

> **videoRotationAngleForHorizonLevelCapture**—This property returns the angle of rotation we need to apply to the image captured by the camera to match the device's orientation.

The interface for this example needs a button to open the view that allows the user to take a picture with the camera, and an `Image` view to show it on the screen.

Figure 18-8: *Interface for a custom camera*

The process for activating the camera and retrieving the picture taken by the user is independent of the interface, but if we want the user to see the image coming from the camera, we need to create a preview layer. Layers are the way views display graphics on the screen. Views define the area and provide functionality, but the graphics are presented by a layer created from a class called `CALayer`. Each view created from the `UIView` class contains a layer that can be used to display a video, but the layer must be casted as an `AVCaptureVideoPreviewLayer`. To do this, we need to create a subclass of `UIView`, override a type property called `layerClass` to turn the view's layer into a preview layer, and then create a `UIViewRepresentable` structure to be able to display the view in our SwiftUI interface.

```
import SwiftUI
import AVFoundation

class CustomPreviewView: UIView {
    override class var layerClass: AnyClass {
        return AVCaptureVideoPreviewLayer.self
    }
}
struct CustomPreview: UIViewRepresentable {
    let view = CustomPreviewView()

    func makeUIView(context: Context) -> UIView {
        return view
    }
}
```

```
   func updateUIView(_ uiView: UIView, context: Context) { }
}
```

Listing 18-10: Defining a `UIView` subclass to show the camera's preview video

The **layerClass** property is a type property that the system reads to determine the data type of the layer. In this example, we override this property to return a reference to the **AVCaptureVideoPreviewLayer** class so that the system knows that we will use the view layer to display video. The rest of the code for the representable view is created as before.

For this example, we are going to manage all the logic for the camera in the model. The following are the basic elements we need to set up the system.

```
import SwiftUI
import Observation
@preconcurrency import AVFoundation

class ViewData {
    var captureDevice: AVCaptureDevice?
    var captureSession: AVCaptureSession?
    var stillImage: AVCapturePhotoOutput?
    var rotationCoordinator: AVCaptureDevice.RotationCoordinator?
    var previewObservation: NSKeyValueObservation?
}
@Observable class ApplicationData: NSObject,
AVCapturePhotoCaptureDelegate, @unchecked Sendable {
    var path = NavigationPath()
    var picture: UIImage?
    @ObservationIgnored var cameraView: CustomPreview!
    @ObservationIgnored var viewData: ViewData!

    static let shared: ApplicationData = ApplicationData()
    private override init() {
        cameraView = CustomPreview()
        viewData = ViewData()
    }
}
```

Listing 18-11: Defining the properties we need to manage the camera

This code is only the first part of our model, we still need to add some methods to activate and control the camera, but it provides the properties required to store references to every element of the system. Since these properties are required by several methods, we declare them in a separate class called **ViewData**. When the model is initialized, we create an instance of this class and the representable view (**CustomPreview**) and store them in non-observable properties to make them accessible to the rest of the code.

The next step is to define a method to get permission from the user to access the camera. This is done automatically if we use a **UIImagePickerController** controller, but we need to do it ourselves in a custom controller using the type methods provided by the **AVCaptureDevice** class. The following is the method we must add to our model for this purpose.

```
func getAuthorization() async {
    let granted = await AVCaptureDevice.requestAccess(for: .video)
    await MainActor.run {
        if granted {
            self.prepareCamera()
        } else {
            print("Not Authorized")
        }
    }
}
```

}

Listing 18-12: Asking for permission to use the camera

The `requestAccess()` method is asynchronous; it waits for the user to respond and returns a value of type `Bool` to report the result. If the user grants access, we execute a method called `prepareCamera()`. Here we begin to build the network of objects introduced in Figure 18-7. The `prepareCamera()` method must get a reference to the current capture device for video and create the inputs and outputs we need to capture a still image (to take a picture).

```
func prepareCamera() {
    viewData.captureSession = AVCaptureSession()
    viewData.captureDevice = AVCaptureDevice.default(for:
AVMediaType.video)
    if let _ = try? viewData.captureDevice?.lockForConfiguration() {
        viewData.captureDevice?.isSubjectAreaChangeMonitoringEnabled = true
        viewData.captureDevice?.unlockForConfiguration()
    }
    if let device = viewData.captureDevice {
        if let input = try? AVCaptureDeviceInput(device: device) {
            viewData.captureSession?.addInput(input)

            viewData.stillImage = AVCapturePhotoOutput()
            if viewData.stillImage != nil {
                viewData.captureSession?.addOutput(viewData.stillImage!)
                if let max =
viewData.captureDevice?.activeFormat.supportedMaxPhotoDimensions.last {
                    viewData.stillImage?.maxPhotoDimensions = max
                }
            }
            showCamera()
        } else {
            print("Not Authorized")
        }
    } else {
        print("Not Authorized")
    }
}
```

Listing 18-13: Initializing the camera

The method starts by creating a new session and requesting access to the camera. If the `default()` method returns a value, we assign `true` to the `isSubjectAreaChange-MonitoringEnabled` property to start monitoring changes in the orientation of the device.

Once we have a session and access to the device, we can define the inputs and outputs we need. There is no particular order we need to follow in doing this, but since the `AVCaptureDeviceInput()` initializer throws an error, we use it first. This initializer creates an object that manages the input for the capture device. If the initializer succeeds, we add it to the capture session using the `addInput()` method and then create the output.

In this example, we want to use the session to capture a still image. Therefore, we use the `AVCapturePhotoOutput` class to create the output, add it to the session, and then configure it to return images of the maximum size allowed. Note that the maximum size is determined by the `maxPhotoDimensions` property, but we cannot assign an arbitrary value. We need to retrieve the list of possible dimensions that the camera can produce and use the highest one. To do this, we read the `activeFormat` property to get the `Format` object that represents the format currently used by the camera, and read its `supportedMaxPhotoDimensions` property. This property returns an array of `CMVideoDimensions` structures with the dimensions supported by the device, so we get the last one and assign it to the output to get an image of the maximum possible size.

After adding the inputs and outputs to the capture session, the `prepareCamera()` method executes an additional method called `showCamera()` to define the preview layer and display the video coming from the camera on the screen.

```
func showCamera() {
    Task {
        await MainActor.run {
            let previewLayer = cameraView.view.layer as?
AVCaptureVideoPreviewLayer
            previewLayer?.session = viewData.captureSession

            if let device = viewData.captureDevice, let preview =
previewLayer {
                viewData.rotationCoordinator =
AVCaptureDevice.RotationCoordinator(device: device, previewLayer:
preview)
                preview.connection?.videoRotationAngle =
viewData.rotationCoordinator!.videoRotationAngleForHorizonLevelPreview

                viewData.previewObservation =
viewData.rotationCoordinator!.observe(\.videoRotationAngleForHorizonLevel
Preview, changeHandler: { old, value in
                    preview.connection?.videoRotationAngle =
self.viewData.rotationCoordinator!.videoRotationAngleForHorizonLevelPrevi
ew
                })
            }
        }
        viewData.captureSession?.startRunning()
    }
}
```

Listing 18-14: Showing the video from the camera on the screen

As mentioned earlier, the layer included with the view created by the `UIView` class is defined by an object of type `CALayer`. This is a basic class that can display graphics and perform animations. However, to display the video from the camera, we need to cast it as an `AVCaptureVideoPreviewLayer` object. After converting the layer to a preview layer, we can create the rotation coordinator to set the orientation of the video. The coordinator checks the device and the preview layer and stores the current rotation angle in the `videoRotationAngleForHorizonLevelPreview` property, so we assign the value of this property to the `videoRotationAngle` property of the `AVCaptureConnection` object to set the current orientation. To keep this value up to date, we add an observer for the `videoRotationAngleForHorizonLevelPreview` property and set the orientation of the video each time the value of this property changes (see Key/Value Observing in Chapter 14).

Once the preview layer and the rotation coordinator are ready, the capture session is initiated with the `startRunning()` method. (The system requires this method to be executed in a background thread.)

At this point, the video is playing on the screen and the system is ready to capture an image. The process of capturing the image is initiated with the `capturePhoto()` method provided by the `AVCapturePhotoOutput` object, and the type of photo captured by the output is determined by an `AVCapturePhotoSettings` object. This class includes multiple initializers. The following is the most frequently used.

▷ **AVCapturePhotoSettings()**—This initializer creates an `AVCapturePhoto-Settings` object with the format by default.

The following are some of the properties available in this class to configure the image and the preview.

- **maxPhotoDimensions**—This property sets or returns the dimensions of the captured image. It is a structure of type **CMVideoDimensions** with the properties **width** and **height**.

- **previewPhotoFormat**—This property sets or returns a dictionary with keys and values that determine the characteristics of the preview image. The keys available are **kCVPixelBufferPixelFormatTypeKey** (uncompressed format), **kCVPixelBufferWidthKey** (width) and **kCVPixelBufferHeightKey** (height).

- **flashMode**—This property sets or returns the flash mode used when the image is captured. It is an enumeration of type **FlashMode** with the values **on**, **off**, and **auto**.

To capture an image, we have to define the settings with an **AVCapturePhotoSettings** object, call the **capturePhoto()** method of the **AVCapturePhotoOutput** object, and define the delegate method that is going to receive the image. The following is the method we need to add to the model to take the picture.

```
func takePicture() {
    let settings = AVCapturePhotoSettings()
    if let max =
viewData.captureDevice?.activeFormat.supportedMaxPhotoDimensions.last {
        settings.maxPhotoDimensions = max
    }
    viewData.stillImage?.capturePhoto(with: settings, delegate: self)
}
```

Listing 18-15: Taking a picture

When the user presses the button to take a picture, the **takePicture()** method is executed and the **capturePhoto()** method is called to ask the output object to capture an image. After the image is captured, this object sends the result to a delegate method. Note that we have declared the **ApplicationData** class as the delegate object (see Listing 18-11), so we can implement the delegate method in the model. You can see our implementation of this method below.

```
func photoOutput(_ output: AVCapturePhotoOutput, didFinishProcessingPhoto
photo: AVCapturePhoto, error: Error?) {
    Task { @MainActor in
        let scene = UIApplication.shared.connectedScenes.first as?
UIWindowScene
        let scale = scene?.screen.scale ?? 1
        let orientationAngle =
viewData.rotationCoordinator!.videoRotationAngleForHorizonLevelCapture
        var imageOrientation: UIImage.Orientation!
        switch orientationAngle {
        case 90.0:
            imageOrientation = .right
        case 270.0:
            imageOrientation = .left
        case 0.0:
            imageOrientation = .up
        case 180.0:
            imageOrientation = .down
        default:
            imageOrientation = .right
        }
        if let imageData = photo.cgImageRepresentation() {
            picture = UIImage(cgImage: imageData, scale: scale, orientation:
imageOrientation)
            path = NavigationPath()
```

```
            }
        }
    }
```

Listing 18-16: Processing the image

The **photoOutput(AVCapturePhotoOutput, didFinishProcessingPhoto:)** method receives the picture produced by the camera. The value received by this method is an object of type **AVCapturePhoto**, which is a container with information about the image. The class includes two convenient methods to get the data representing the image.

▷ **fileDataRepresentation()**—This method returns a data representation of the image that we can use to create a **UIImage** object.

▷ **cgImageRepresentation()**—This method returns the image as a **CGImage** object (Core Graphics).

In our example, we implemented the **cgImageRepresentation()** method because the **UIImage** class defines a convenient initializer to create an image from a **CGImage** object that includes the scale and orientation. We get the orientation from the **videoRotationAngleFor-HorizonLevelCapture** property of the rotation coordinator. This property returns a **CGFloat** value with the rotation angle, which we can convert to **Orientation** values to set the orientation of the image (see **UIImage** in Chapter 10). To set the scale, we need to access the screen. The screen is managed by an object of the **UIScreen** class, which is automatically created for the device and assigned to a property of the Scene. Therefore, to access the screen and get the scale, we need to read the **UIWindowScene** object that controls the current Scene from the **connectedScenes** property of the **UIApplication** object. We introduced this object in Chapter 14. It is created by the system to control the application. The object is returned by a type property provided by the class called **shared**. To access the Scenes opened by the application, we read the **connectedScenes** property. In this example, we are developing an application for mobile devices, so we only need to access the first available Scene. The **UIWindowScene** object includes the **screen** property to return a reference to the **UIScreen** object that represents the screen, and the **UIScreen** object contains, among other things, the **scale** property to return the current scale and the **bounds** property to return the size of the screen. With these values, we create the **UIImage** object and assign it to the **picture** property to update the view and display the image, as shown below.

```
struct ContentView: View {
    @Environment(ApplicationData.self) private var appData

    var body: some View {
        @Bindable var appData = appData

        NavigationStack(path: $appData.path) {
            VStack {
                HStack {
                    Spacer()
                    NavigationLink("Take Picture", value: "Open Camera")
                }
                .navigationDestination(for: String.self, destination: { _ in
                    CustomCameraView()
                })
                Image(uiImage: appData.picture ?? UIImage(named:
"nopicture")!)
                    .resizable()
                    .scaledToFit()
                    .frame(minWidth: 0, maxWidth: .infinity, minHeight: 0,
maxHeight: .infinity)
```

```
            .clipped()
         Spacer()
      }.padding()
       .navigationBarHidden(true)
   }.statusBar(hidden: true)
   }
}
```

Listing 18-17: Showing the image

There is nothing new in the view in Listing 18-17, with the exception that now instead of opening a **UIImagePickerController** with a standard interface, we open a view that has to provide the buttons and custom controls required for the user to take a picture. The following is our implementation of that view.

```
import SwiftUI

struct CustomCameraView: View {
   @Environment(ApplicationData.self) private var appData

   var body: some View {
      ZStack {
         appData.cameraView
         VStack {
            Spacer()
            HStack {
               Button("Cancel") {
                  appData.path = NavigationPath()
               }
               Spacer()
               Button("Take Picture") {
                  appData.takePicture()
               }
            }.padding()
             .frame(height: 80)
             .background(Color(red: 0.9, green: 0.9, blue: 0.9, opacity:
0.8))
         }
      }
      .edgesIgnoringSafeArea(.all)
      .frame(minWidth: 0, maxWidth: .infinity, minHeight: 0,
maxHeight: .infinity)
      .navigationBarHidden(true)
      .task {
         await appData.getAuthorization()
      }
      .onDisappear {
         appData.viewData.previewObservation = nil
      }
   }
}
```

Listing 18-18: Taking a picture

As shown in Figure 18-8 (right), this view contains our **UIView**, which displays the video coming from the camera, and another view at the top, which provides two buttons, one to cancel the process and dismiss the view, and another to take a picture. When the view appears on the screen, we call the **getAuthorization()** method to start the process. If the user presses the Take Picture button, we call the **takePicture()** method to capture the image. Once the image is processed, the delegate method dismisses the view and displays the image on the screen. Note that we apply the **onDisappear()** modifier to remove the observer. This is necessary to ensure that no observers are active after they are no longer needed.

Do It Yourself: Create a Multiplatform project. Download the nopicture.png image from our website and add it to the Asset Catalog. Create a Swift file called CustomPreviewLayer.swift for the code in Listing 18-10, and another called ApplicationData.swift for the model in Listing 18-11. Add to the model the methods in Listings 18-12, 18-13, 18-14, 18-15, and 18-16. Update the `ContentView` view with the code in Listing 18-17. Create a SwiftUI file called CustomCameraView.swift for the view in Listing 18-18. Remember to add the option "Privacy - Camera Usage Description" to the Info panel in the app's settings and to inject the `ApplicationData` object into the environment for the app and the previews (Chapter 7, Listing 7-4). Run the application on a device and take a picture.

Basic 18.2 Video

Recording and playing videos is probably as important to users as taking and displaying pictures. As with images, Apple frameworks include tools for playing videos and creating a custom video player.

Basic Video Player

SwiftUI defines the `VideoPlayer` view to play videos. This view provides all the controls required to play, stop, and move the video back and forth. The view includes the following initializer.

▷ **VideoPlayer(player:** AVPlayer?, **videoOverlay:** Closure)—This initializer creates a video player to play the video provided by the argument. The **player** argument is the object in charge of playing the media, and the **videoOverlay** argument provides the views we want to show on top of the video.

The `VideoPlayer` view presents the interface for the user to control the video, but the video is played by an object of the `AVPlayer` class. The class includes the following initializer.

▷ **AVPlayer(url:** URL)—This initializer creates an `AVPlayer` object to play the media in the URL indicated by the **url** argument.

The `AVPlayer` class also includes properties and methods to control the video programatically.

▷ **volume**—This property sets or returns a value that determines the player's volume. It is a value of type `Float` between 0.0 and 1.0.

▷ **isMuted**—This property is a Boolean value that determines whether the player's audio is muted or not.

▷ **rate**—This property sets or returns a `Float` value that determines the rate at which the media is being played. A value of 0.0 pauses the video and 1.0 sets the normal rate.

▷ **play()**—This method begins playback.

▷ **pause()**—This method pauses playback.

▷ **addPeriodicTimeObserver(forInterval:** CMTime, **queue:** Dispatch-Queue?, **using:** Closure)—This method adds an observer that executes a closure every certain period of time. The **forInterval** argument determines the time between executions, the **queue** argument is the queue in which the closure should be executed (the main thread is recommended), and the **using** argument is the closure we want to execute. The closure receives a value of type `CMTime` with the time at which the closure was called.

The `VideoPlayer` view requires an `AVPlayer` object to play the video, and that object loads the video from a URL. If we want to play a video available online, we only need the URL, but if the video is provided by the app, we need to get it from the bundle (see Bundle in Chapter 10). In the following model, we add a video called videotrees.mp4 to the project, get the URL that points to the file from the `Bundle` object, and create an `AVPlayer` object with that value.

```
import SwiftUI
import Observation
import AVKit

@Observable class ApplicationData: @unchecked Sendable {
    var player: AVPlayer!

    static let shared: ApplicationData = ApplicationData()
    private init() {
        let bundle = Bundle.main
        if let videoURL = bundle.url(forResource: "videotrees",
withExtension: "mp4") {
            player = AVPlayer(url: videoURL)
        }
    }
}
```

Listing 18-19: Preparing the video to be played

The `VideoPlayer` view and the `AVPlayer` class are defined in the AVKit framework. After importing this framework, we get the URL for the video videotrees.mp4, create the `AVPlayer` object and store it in an observable property to make it available to the view. In the view, we need to check this property and display the `VideoPlayer` view when a video is ready to play.

```
import SwiftUI
import AVKit

struct ContentView: View {
    @Environment(ApplicationData.self) private var appData

    var body: some View {
        if appData.player != nil {
            VideoPlayer(player: appData.player)
                .ignoresSafeArea()
        } else {
            Text("Video not available")
        }
    }
}
```

Listing 18-20: Playing a video

Figure 18-9: Standard video player

Do It Yourself: Create a Multiplatform project. Download the file videotrees.mp4 from our website and add it to your project (make sure that the target is selected). Create a Swift file called ApplicationData.swift for the model in Listing 18-19. Update the `ContentView` view with the code in Listing 18-20. Remember to inject the `ApplicationData` object into the environment for the app and the previews (Chapter 7, Listing 7-4). Run the application. Press play to play the video.

In the previous example, the video doesn't play until the user presses the play button. But we can implement **AVPlayer** properties and methods to control the video programatically. For instance, the following example starts the video as soon as the view is loaded.

```
struct ContentView: View {
   @Environment(ApplicationData.self) private var appData

   var body: some View {
      if appData.player != nil {
         VideoPlayer(player: appData.player)
            .onAppear {
               appData.player.play()
            }
            .ignoresSafeArea()
      } else {
         Text("Video not available")
      }
   }
}
```

Listing 18-21: Automatically playing a video

The **VideoPlayer** view initializer can also include an argument that takes a closure to add a layer of views over the video. In the following example, this initializer is implemented to add a caption with the title of the video at the top.

```
struct ContentView: View {
   @Environment(ApplicationData.self) private var appData

   var body: some View {
      if appData.player != nil {
         VideoPlayer(player: appData.player, videoOverlay: {
            VStack {
               Text("Title: Trees at the park")
                  .font(.title)
                  .padding([.top, .bottom], 8)
                  .padding([.leading, .trailing], 16)
                  .foregroundColor(.black)
                  .background(.ultraThinMaterial)
                  .clipShape(RoundedRectangle(cornerRadius: 10))
                  .padding(.top, 8)
               Spacer()
            }
         })
         .ignoresSafeArea()
      } else {
         Text("Video not available")
      }
   }
}
```

Listing 18-22: Presenting views over the video

The views returned from the closure are above the video but below the controls, so they cannot take input from the user, but we can use them to provide additional information, as in this case. The result is shown below.

Figure 18-10: Overlay views

Medium **Custom Video Player**

In addition to all the code required for the **VideoPlayer** view to function, the AVFoundation framework also provides classes for creating the individual components of the structure required to play media. There is a class responsible for the asset (video or audio), a class responsible for delivering the media to the player, a class responsible for playing the media, and a class responsible for displaying the media on the screen. Figure 18-11 illustrates this structure.

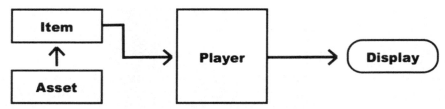

Figure 18-11: System to play media

The media to be played is provided as an asset. An asset consists of one or more tracks of media, including video, audio, subtitles, etc. The AVFoundation framework defines a class called **AVAsset** to load an asset. The class includes the following initializer.

▷ **AVURLAsset(url:** URL)—This initializer creates an **AVURLAsset** object with the media in the location indicated by the **url** argument. The argument is a **URL** structure with the location of a local or remote resource.

An asset contains static information and cannot manage its state when it is played. To control the asset, the framework defines the **AVPlayerItem** class. With this class we can reference an asset and manage its timeline. The class includes several initializers. The following is the most frequently used.

▷ **AVPlayerItem(asset:** AVAsset)—This initializer creates an **AVPlayerItem** object to represent the asset defined by the **asset** argument.

The **AVPlayerItem** class also includes properties and methods to control the status of the asset. The following are the most frequently used.

▷ **status**—This property returns a value that indicates the status of the player item. It is an enumeration called **Status** included in the **AVPlayerItem** class. The values available are **unknown, readyToPlay**, and **failed**.

- **duration**—This property returns a value that indicates the duration of the player item. It is a structure of type `CMTime`.

- **currentTime()**—This method returns a `CMTime` value with the current time of the player item.

- **seek(to:** CMTime**)**—This asynchronous method moves the playback cursor to the time specified by the **to** argument and returns a Boolean value that determines whether the seek operation is finished or not.

The `AVPlayerItem` object manages the information needed for playback, but does not play the media; this is handled by an instance of the `AVPlayer` class. This is the same class we used earlier to load a video for the `VideoPlayer` view. The class includes the following initializer to create a player from an `AVPlayerItem` object.

- **AVPlayer(playerItem:** AVPlayerItem?**)**—This initializer creates an `AVPlayer` object to play the media represented by the **playerItem** argument.

The last object required by the system is the one responsible for displaying the media. It is a subclass of the `CALayer` class called `AVPlayerLayer`, which provides the code necessary to draw the frames on the screen. The class includes the following initializer and property to create and configure the layer.

- **AVPlayerLayer(player:** AVPlayer**)**—This initializer creates an `AVPlayerLayer` object associated with the player specified by the **player** argument.

- **videoGravity**—This property defines how the video adjusts its size to the size of the preview layer. It is a `AVLayerVideoGravity` structure with the type properties `resize`, `resizeAspect`, and `resizeAspectFill`.

All these classes define the system we need to play media, but we also need a way to control time. Since the precision of floating-point values is not suitable for media playback, the framework implements, among other things, the `CMTime` structure from an old framework called Core Media. The structure contains several values to represent time as a fraction. The most important are the value and timescale, which represent the numerator and denominator, respectively. For example, if we want to create a `CMTime` structure to represent 0.5 seconds, we can specify 1 as the numerator and 2 as the denominator (1 divided by 2 equals 0.5). The class includes initializers and type properties to create these values. The following are the most frequently used.

- **CMTime(value:** CMTimeValue, **timescale:** CMTimeScale**)**—This initializer creates a `CMTime` structure with the values specified by the **value** and **timescale** arguments. The arguments are integers of type `Int64` and `Int32`, respectively.

- **CMTime(seconds:** Double, **preferredTimescale:** CMTimeScale**)**—This initializer creates a `CMTime` structure from a floating-point value that represents the time in seconds. The **seconds** argument determines the seconds we want to assign to the structure, and the **preferredTimescale** argument determines the scale we want to use. A value of 1 preserves the value in seconds assigned to the first argument.

- **zero**—This type property returns a `CMTime` structure with the value 0.

The `CMTime` structure also includes several properties for setting and retrieving values. The following are the most frequently used.

- **seconds**—This property returns the time of a `CMTime` structure in seconds. It is of type `Double`.

- ▷ **value**—This property returns the value of a `CMTime` structure.
- ▷ **timescale**—This property returns the time scale of a `CMTime` structure.

To create a custom video player, we must load the asset (`AVURLAsset`), create the item to manage the asset (`AVPlayerItem`), add the item to the player (`AVPlayer`), and associate the player to a layer to display the media on the screen (`AVPlayerLayer`).

As with the preview layer previously used to display the video coming from the camera, we need to convert the layer provided by the `UIView` object into a preview layer (in this case, the `CALayer` object needs to be casted as an `AVPlayerLayer` object). Below is the implementation of the representable view we need for this example.

```
import SwiftUI
import AVFoundation

class CustomPlayerView: UIView {
    override class var layerClass: AnyClass {
        return AVPlayerLayer.self
    }
}
struct PlayerView: UIViewRepresentable {
    var view = CustomPlayerView()

    func makeUIView(context: Context) -> UIView {
        return view
    }
    func updateUIView(_ uiView: UIView, context: Context) { }
}
```

Listing 18-23: *Building a custom video player*

Now that we have the representable view, the next step is to build the video player and then call the `play()` method to start playing the video as soon as it is ready.

```
import SwiftUI
import Observation
import AVFoundation

class ViewData: NSObject, @unchecked Sendable {
    var playerItem: AVPlayerItem?
    var player: AVPlayer?
    var playerLayer: AVPlayerLayer?
    var playerObservation: NSKeyValueObservation?

    func setObserver() {
        playerObservation = playerItem?.observe(\.status, options: .new,
changeHandler: { item, value in
            if item.status == .readyToPlay {
                self.player?.play()
            }
        })
    }
}
@Observable class ApplicationData: @unchecked Sendable {
    @ObservationIgnored var customVideoView: PlayerView!
    @ObservationIgnored var viewData: ViewData

    static let shared: ApplicationData = ApplicationData()
    private init() {
        customVideoView = PlayerView()
        viewData = ViewData()
```

```
        let bundle = Bundle.main
        let videoURL = bundle.url(forResource: "videotrees", withExtension:
"mp4")
        let asset = AVURLAsset(url: videoURL!)
        viewData.playerItem = AVPlayerItem(asset: asset)
        viewData.player = AVPlayer(playerItem: viewData.playerItem)

        Task { @MainActor in
            viewData.playerLayer = customVideoView.view.layer as?
AVPlayerLayer
            viewData.playerLayer?.player = viewData.player
            viewData.setObserver()
        }
    }
}
```

Listing 18-24: Building a custom video player

The media is not immediately available, it has to be loaded and prepared for playback, so we cannot play it right away, we have to wait until it is ready. The status of the media is reported by the **status** property of the **AVPlayerItem** object. This means that we must observe the value of this property to start playing the media only when its value is equal to **readyToPlay**. This requires the use of an observer. Therefore, after defining the three properties we need to store the player item, the player, and the layer, we define a property to store the observer and call the **observer()** method on the **AVPlayerItem** object to keep track of the **status** property. When the current status is **readyToPlay**, we play the video.

To set up the video player, we load the video from the bundle, create the player structure, cast the **UIView** layer as an **AVPlayerLayer** layer, and assign it to the player. Since everything is prepared in the model, all the interface needs to do is to display the representable view. The video fills the screen, adapts to the screen orientation, and plays as soon as the view is loaded.

```
struct ContentView: View {
    @Environment(ApplicationData.self) private var appData

    var body: some View {
        appData.customVideoView
            .ignoresSafeArea()
    }
}
```

Listing 18-25: Showing a video

Do It Yourself: Create a Multiplatform project. Download the file videotrees.mp4 from our website and add it to your project. (Remember to select the target.) Create a Swift file called CustomPlayerView.swift for the code in Listing 18-23 and another called ApplicationData.swift for the model in Listing 18-24. Update the **ContentView** view with the code in Listing 18-25. Run the application. The video should start playing as soon as the application is launched.

The previous example plays the video, but does not provide the user with any tools to control it. The **AVPlayer** class includes methods for playing, pausing, and checking the status of the media, but we are responsible for creating the interface. For the following example, we will create an interface that provides a button and a progress bar so that the user can play, pause, and see the progress.

Figure 18-12: Controls for a custom video player

How we control the process and respond to the interface depends on the requirements of our application. For this example, we decided to define two states, one that indicates whether the video is playing or not, and another that determines the size of the progress bar. Below are the changes we need to make to our model to allow the user to play and pause the video and update the progress bar.

```
import SwiftUI
import Observation
import AVFoundation

class ViewData: NSObject, @unchecked Sendable {
    var playerItem: AVPlayerItem?
    var player: AVPlayer?
    var playerLayer: AVPlayerLayer?
}
@Observable class ApplicationData: @unchecked Sendable {
    var playing: Bool = false
    var progress: CGFloat = 0
    @ObservationIgnored var customVideoView: PlayerView!
    @ObservationIgnored var viewData: ViewData

    static let shared: ApplicationData = ApplicationData()
    private init() {
        customVideoView = PlayerView()
        viewData = ViewData()

        let bundle = Bundle.main
        let videoURL = bundle.url(forResource: "videotrees", withExtension:
"mp4")
        let asset = AVURLAsset(url: videoURL!)
        viewData.playerItem = AVPlayerItem(asset: asset)
        viewData.player = AVPlayer(playerItem: viewData.playerItem)

        Task {
            await MainActor.run {
                viewData.playerLayer = customVideoView.view.layer as?
AVPlayerLayer
                viewData.playerLayer?.player = viewData.player
            }
            let interval = CMTime(value: 1, timescale: 2)
            viewData.player?.addPeriodicTimeObserver(forInterval: interval,
queue: DispatchQueue.main, using: { time in
                if let duration = self.viewData.playerItem?.duration {
                    let position = time.seconds / duration.seconds
                    self.progress = CGFloat(position)
                }
            })
        }
    }
```

```
func playVideo() {
    if viewData.playerItem?.status == .readyToPlay {
        if playing {
            viewData.player?.pause()
            playing = false
        } else {
            viewData.player?.play()
            playing = true
        }
    }
}
}
```

Listing 18-26: Preparing the video player

In this example, we include a method called `playVideo()` that is executed when the user presses the Play button. The method checks whether the media can be played or not, and then performs an action according to the value of the `playing` property. If the video is playing, it is paused, and if it is paused, we play it. In either case, the value of the `playing` property is updated to reflect the new state.

To calculate the size of the progress bar, we must implement an observer. However, this is not a KVO observer like the one implemented before. Normal observers are not fast enough, so the AVFoundation framework includes the `addPeriodicTimeObserver()` method to create an observer that provides a more accurate response. The method requires a `CMTime` value to specify the frequency with which the task should be performed, a reference to the main queue, and a closure with the code to be executed each time the observer is triggered. In this example, we create a `CMTime` value representing a time of 0.5 seconds, and then use it in the call to the `addPeriodicTimeObserver()` method to register the observer. After that, the closure passed to the observer is executed every 0.5 seconds during playback. In this closure, we get the current time and duration of the video in seconds and calculate the progression by converting the seconds to a value between 0.0 and 1.0, which we can later convert to points to display the progress bar on the screen.

 IMPORTANT: The `addPeriodicTimeObserver()` method doesn't work with Swift concurrency. Instead, it requires the thread to be defined by a `DispatchQueue` object. This is an old class defined by the Dispatch framework to create asynchronous tasks. The class includes a type property called `main` to define a task for the main queue (the Main Actor), and this is how we make sure that the closure assigned to this method runs in the main thread.

The player is ready. It is time to define the interface. In this occasion, we need to present the representable view inside a `ZStack` so we can display a toolbar on top (see Figure 18-12).

```
struct ContentView: View {
    @Environment(ApplicationData.self) private var appData

    var body: some View {
        ZStack {
            appData.customVideoView
                .ignoresSafeArea()
            VStack {
                Spacer()
                HStack {
                    Button(appData.playing ? "Pause" : "Play") {
                        appData.playVideo()
                    }.frame(width: 70)
                        .foregroundColor(.black)
                    GeometryReader { geometry in
```

```
                    HStack {
                        Rectangle()
                            .fill(Color(red: 0, green: 0.4, blue: 0.8,
opacity: 0.8))
                            .frame(width: geometry.size.width *
appData.progress, height: 20)
                        Spacer()
                    }
                }.padding(.top, 15)
            }
            .padding([.leading, .trailing])
            .frame(height: 50)
            .background(Color(red: 0.9, green: 0.9, blue: 0.9, opacity:
0.8))
        }
      }
   }
}
```

Listing 18-27: Playing and pausing the video

The toolbar contains a button and a `Rectangle` view representing the progress bar. The button's label depends on the value of the `playing` property. When the video is playing, the text "Pause" is displayed, and when it is paused, the text "Play" is shown instead. To calculate the size of the `Rectangle` view that represents the progress bar, we embed the view in a `GeometryReader` and then multiply its width by the value of the `progress` property. Since this property contains a value between 0.0 and 1.0, the operation returns the value we need to set the width of the bar and display the progress on the screen.

 Do It Yourself: Update the model with the code in Listing 18-26 and the `ContentView` view with the code in Listing 18-27. Run the application. You should see the video player illustrated in Figure 18-12.

The observer added with the `addPeriodicTimeObserver()` method is not the only way to get information from the player. The `AVPlayerItem` class also defines several notifications to report events that occur during media playback. For example, we can listen to the `AVPlayerItemDidPlayToEndTime` notification to know when the video has finished playing. For this purpose, we need to define a method in the model that listens and responds to the notification, and a task that calls this method once the representable view is created. The following are the changes we need to introduce to the `ApplicationData` class.

```
@Observable class ApplicationData: @unchecked Sendable {
   var playing: Bool = false
   var progress: CGFloat = 0
   @ObservationIgnored var customVideoView: PlayerView!
   @ObservationIgnored var viewData: ViewData

   static let shared: ApplicationData = ApplicationData()
   private init() {
      customVideoView = PlayerView()
      viewData = ViewData()

      let bundle = Bundle.main
      let videoURL = bundle.url(forResource: "videotrees", withExtension:
"mp4")
      let asset = AVURLAsset(url: videoURL!)
      viewData.playerItem = AVPlayerItem(asset: asset)
      viewData.player = AVPlayer(playerItem: viewData.playerItem)
```

```
            Task {
                await MainActor.run {
                    viewData.playerLayer = customVideoView.view.layer as?
AVPlayerLayer
                    viewData.playerLayer?.player = viewData.player
                }
                let interval = CMTime(value: 1, timescale: 2)
                viewData.player?.addPeriodicTimeObserver(forInterval: interval,
queue: DispatchQueue.main, using: { time in
                    if let duration = self.viewData.playerItem?.duration {
                        let position = time.seconds / duration.seconds
                        self.progress = CGFloat(position)
                    }
                })
                await rewindVideo()
            }
        }
        func rewindVideo() async {
            let center = NotificationCenter.default
            let name = NSNotification.Name.AVPlayerItemDidPlayToEndTime
            for await _ in center.notifications(named: name, object: nil) {
                if let finished = await viewData.playerItem?.seek(to:
CMTime.zero), finished {
                    await MainActor.run {
                        playing = false
                        progress = 0
                    }
                }
            }
        }
        func playVideo() {
            if viewData.playerItem?.status == .readyToPlay {
                if playing {
                    viewData.player?.pause()
                    playing = false
                } else {
                    viewData.player?.play()
                    playing = true
                }
            }
        }
    }
```

Listing 18-28: *Executing an asynchronous method to detect the end of the video*

In the `rewindVideo()` method, we must listen to the `AVPlayerItemDidPlayToEndTime`
notification and prepare the video to be played again. For this purpose, the `AVPlayerItem` class
provides the `seek()` method. This method moves the playback to the time specified by the
argument and executes a closure after the process is complete. In this case, we use a `CMTime`
value of 0 to move the player to the beginning of the video and then reset the `playing` and
`progress` properties to allow the user to replay the video.

 Do It Yourself: Update the `ApplicationData` class with the code in Listing
18-28. Run the application. Press play and wait until the video is over. The
player should reset itself and you should be able to play the video again.

If we want to play multiple videos in sequence, we could use the `AVPlayerItemDidPlay-`
`ToEndTime` notification to assign a new asset to the `AVPlayer` object, but the framework offers
a subclass of the `AVPlayer` class called `AVQueuePlayer` designed specifically to manage a list of
videos. The class creates a playlist from an array of `AVPlayerItem` objects. The following are the
initializer and some of its methods.

- ▷ **AVQueuePlayer(items:** [AVPlayerItem])—This initializer creates a play list with the items specified by the **items** argument.
- ▷ **advanceToNextItem()**—This method advances the playback to the next item on the list.
- ▷ **insert(**AVPlayerItem, **after:** AVPlayerItem?**)**—This method inserts a new item on the list.
- ▷ **remove(**AVPlayerItem**)**—This method removes an item from the list.

An **AVQueuePlayer** object replaces the **AVPlayer** object used to represent the media. All we have to do to play a sequence of videos is to create the **AVPlayerItem** object for each video and an **AVQueuePlayer** object to replace the **AVPlayer** object we have used so far, as in the following example.

```
import SwiftUI
import Observation
import AVFoundation

class ViewData: NSObject, @unchecked Sendable {
    var playerItem1: AVPlayerItem!
    var playerItem2: AVPlayerItem!
    var player: AVQueuePlayer!
    var playerLayer: AVPlayerLayer?
    var playerObservation: NSKeyValueObservation?

    func setObserver() {
        playerObservation = playerItem1?.observe(\.status, options: .new,
changeHandler: { item, value in
            if item.status == .readyToPlay {
                self.player?.play()
            }
        })
    }
}
@Observable class ApplicationData: @unchecked Sendable {
    var playing: Bool = false
    var progress: CGFloat = 0
    @ObservationIgnored var customVideoView: PlayerView!
    @ObservationIgnored var viewData: ViewData

    static let shared: ApplicationData = ApplicationData()
    private init() {
        customVideoView = PlayerView()
        viewData = ViewData()

        let bundle = Bundle.main
        let videoURL1 = bundle.url(forResource: "videotrees",
withExtension: "mp4")
        let videoURL2 = bundle.url(forResource: "videobeaches",
withExtension: "mp4")

        let asset1 = AVURLAsset(url: videoURL1!)
        let asset2 = AVURLAsset(url: videoURL2!)
        viewData.playerItem1 = AVPlayerItem(asset: asset1)
        viewData.playerItem2 = AVPlayerItem(asset: asset2)
        viewData.player = AVQueuePlayer(items: [viewData.playerItem1,
viewData.playerItem2])
```

```
        Task {
            await MainActor.run {
                viewData.playerLayer = customVideoView.view.layer as?
AVPlayerLayer
                viewData.playerLayer?.player = viewData.player
                viewData.setObserver()
            }
        }
    }
}
```

Listing 18-29: Playing a list of videos

In this example, we assume that we are using the `ContentView` view defined in Listing 18-25. The code loads two videos, videotrees.mp4 and videobeaches.mp4, and then creates two `AVURLAsset` objects and two `AVPlayerItem` objects to represent them. The `AVQueuePlayer` object is defined next to play both videos in sequence. Note that because the interface we are using for this example does not include a button to play the videos, we add an observer to the first video and call the `play()` method when it is ready.

 Do It Yourself: Update the ApplicationData.swift file with the code in Listing 18-29. This example is designed to work with the `ContentView` view defined in Listing 18-25. Download the videobeaches.mp4 and videotrees.mp4 videos from our website and add them to your project. (Remember to select the target.) Run the application. The videos should be played one after another.

(Basic) 18.3 Color Picker

SwiftUI includes the `ColorPicker` view to allow the user to pick a color. The view creates a button that opens a predefined interface with tools to select and configure a color. The following is the view's initializer.

▷ **ColorPicker(String, selection: Binding, supportsOpacity: Bool)**—This initializer creates a color picker. The first argument provides the label to show next to the button, the **selection** argument is a binding property that stores a `Color` view with the color selected by the user, and the `supportsOpacity` argument determines whether the user will be allowed to set the color's opacity. The value by default is `true`.

The implementation of the color picker is simple. We define a `@State` property with a `Color` view and then use it to initialize the `ColorPicker` view so that each time the user selects a color, it is stored in that property and we can use it to modify other views. In the following example, we use the value of the property to change the background color of the interface.

```
struct ContentView: View {
    @State private var selectedColor: Color = .white

    var body: some View {
        VStack {
            ColorPicker("Select a Color", selection: $selectedColor)
                .padding()
            Spacer()
        }.background(selectedColor)
    }
}
```

Listing 18-30: Showing a color picker

The `ColorPicker` view shows a button that opens an interface for the user to select a color. Once the user makes the selection, the color is automatically assigned to the `@State` property. This means that the user can change the selection as many times as he or she wants, but only the last color selected will be preserved in the property.

Figure 18-13: Color picker

 Do It Yourself: Create a Multiplatform project. Update the `ContentView` view with the code in Listing 18-30. Run the application and press the color picker button. Select a color. You should see the color of the interface change, as shown in Figure 18-13.

(Basic) 19.1 Mac Apps

SwiftUI is available for every Apple platform. With SwiftUI we can program applications for iPhones, iPads, Mac computers, the Apple Watch, Apple TV and Vision Pro. However, this does not mean that we can use the same code. The system for iPhones and iPads is the same, but Mac computers, the Apple Watch, Apple TV and Vision Pro require their own set of frameworks. The good news is that Xcode is able to compile the same application for multiple devices. All we need to do is create the Swift files, as we have done so far, and then declare platform-specific code.

The first step is to configure the target to tell Xcode which platforms our app supports. When we build our project using the Multiplatform App template, it will be configured to work for iPhones, iPads, Macs, and Apple Vision.

⌄ **Supported Destinations**

Destination	SDK
📱 iPhone	iOS
📱 iPad	iOS
🖥 Mac	macOS
🥽 Apple Vision	visionOS

+ —

Figure 19-1: Supported platforms

The panel includes a + button at the bottom to add more platforms and configurations. For instance, to create applications for Mac computers, we have three options available: Mac, Mac Catalyst, and Designed for iPad.

Figure 19-2: Mac destinations

With the Mac option, we can create a Mac application using SwiftUI and have access to all the macOS exclusive features. This is the default option and the one recommended for new applications. The Mac Catalyst option can adapt an iPad app to the Mac and is therefore recommended to quickly convert our existing iPad apps to Mac apps. And the Designed for iPad option allows us to run our iPad apps on Macs without any changes (not recommended).

As mentioned in Chapter 5, Xcode includes toolbar buttons that let you choose the app's scheme and target, including simulators, real devices, and options for running the app on the Mac (My Mac).

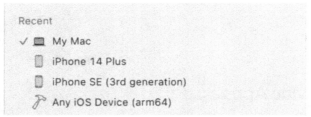
Figure 19-3: My Mac option

Xcode also allows us to provide images for each platform. The options are available in the Attributes Inspector panel when we select a set in the Asset Catalog. For example, if we select an image set and enable the Mac option in that panel (Figure 19-4, number 1), the set will contain placeholders to add images that will be available only when the app is running on the Mac.

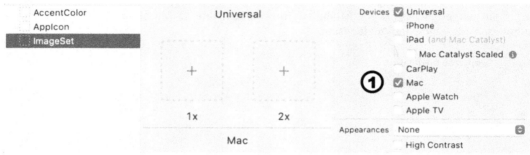
Figure 19-4: Mac images

(Basic) **Conditional Code**

Although the system can automatically build the application for each platform, it is our responsibility to define platform-specific code. An alternative is to use conditional compilation. These conditionals are checked before the code is compiled, and therefore we can use them to select the code we want to implement according to the target platform.

Conditional compilation in Swift is done using the **#if**, **#else**, **#elseif** and **#endif** keywords. The **#if**, **#else** and **#elseif** keywords work like the Swift conditionals **if else**, but because the statements are not delimited by a block, the **#endif** keyword is required to signal the end of the block.

There are several parameters we can use to set the condition. For example, we can use the statement **targetEnvironment()** to tell the compiler to run the code only on a specific environment. The values available are **simulator** and **macCatalyst**. Another useful statement is **os()**. With this statement, we can tell the compiler to run the code only on a specific system. The values available are **macOS**, **iOS**, **watchOS**, **tvOS**, **visionOS**, **Linux**, and **Windows**. In the following example, we use the value **macOS** to show a **Text** view only when the application is running on a Mac.

```
import SwiftUI

struct ContentView: View {
    var body: some View {
        VStack {
            #if os(macOS)
                Text("Mac Application")
            #else
                Text("Mobile Application")
            #endif
```

Chapter 19 - Multiplatform Applications

```
        }.frame(width: 500, height: 350)
    }
}
```

Listing 19-1: Detecting the platform before compiling

This is a very simple example, but it illustrates how to work with these types of conditionals. When we run this project on a mobile device, we get the message "Mobile Application", but on the Mac, we get a window with a size of 500 by 350 points and the message "Mac Application".

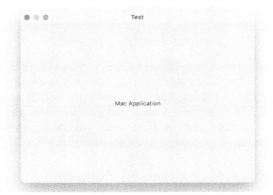

Figure 19-5: Mac application

 Do It Yourself: Create a Multiplatform project. Update the `ContentView` view with the code in Listing 19-1. From the Xcode's toolbar, click on the My Mac option (Figure 19-3). Press the Play button to run the application. You should see a window with a message at the center, as illustrated in Figure 19-5.

In the previous example, we applied the `frame()` modifier to all platforms, but we can use the `#if` `#else` keywords to select any code we want, including views and modifiers. In the following example, we apply different colors to a `Text` view depending on the platform.

```
struct ContentView: View {
    var body: some View {
        VStack {
            Text("My Application")
            #if os(macOS)
                .foregroundColor(.red)
            #else
                .foregroundColor(.green)
            #endif
        }.frame(width: 500, height: 350)
    }
}
```

Listing 19-2: Applying different modifiers to each platform

If the differences between platforms are significant, instead of selecting individual views or modifiers, we can load entire views designed specifically for iOS, macOS or visionOS. SwiftUI files are created as always and we can use conditional compilation to load them, but to avoid Xcode reporting other errors, we need to declare that the files should only be compiled for a specific platform. This is done in the Build Phases panel in settings. There is a section called Compile Sources where we can select a file and check the system for which we want to compile it.

Name	Filters	Compiler Flags
ContentView.swift ...in Test	Always Used	
MacDetailView.swift ...in Test	Always Used	
MenuView.swift ...in Test	Always Used	
MobileDetailView.swift ...in Test		Any Supported Platform
PlaceholderView.swift ...in Test		iOS
TestApp.swift ...in Test		☑ macOS
		visionOS

Figure 19-6: Platform selection

In this example, we have a view called `MobileDetailView` that is meant to be displayed on any platform, and another view called `MacDetailView` that is designed specifically for Macs. After telling Xcode to compile the `MacDetailView` view for macOS only (see Figure 19-6), we must tell the compiler which view to implement in the interface with `#if #else` statements. For example, the following application defines a universal interface with two columns, but loads different views in the second column depending on the platform.

```
struct ContentView: View {
    @State private var visibility: NavigationSplitViewVisibility
= .automatic

    var body: some View {
        NavigationSplitView(columnVisibility: $visibility, sidebar: {
            MenuView()
        }, detail: {
            #if os(macOS)
                MacDetailView()
            #else
                MobileDetailView()
            #endif
        })
    }
}
```

Listing 19-3: Defining a multiplatform interface

When we open this application on an iPad or a Mac, the system first loads the `ContentView` view and then creates two columns. The content of the left column is defined by the `MenuView` view, but the content of the right column depends on the platform. If the app is compiled for Mac computers, the system displays the `MacDetailView`, but if it is compiled for iPhones and iPads, the system loads the `MobileDetailView` instead.

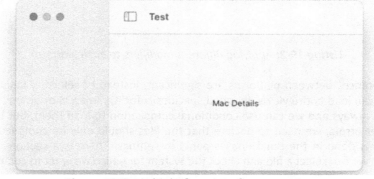

Figure 19-7: Multiplatform interface on a Mac

Chapter 19 - Multiplatform Applications

We can also compile code specific for a version of an operating system. To specify the minimum required version of a system to run the code, Swift includes the `#available()` statement. This statement is checked by the compiler but the condition is determined by Swift, so we must use it with `if else` statements. In the following example, we show the first `Text` view when the app is running on devices with iOS 18 and macOS 14 or newer, and the second `Text` view is shown in older systems.

```
struct ContentView: View {
    var body: some View {
        VStack {
            if #available(iOS 18, macOS 14, *) {
                Text("New Version")
            } else {
                Text("Old Version")
            }
        }.frame(width: 500, height: 350)
    }
}
```

Listing 19-4: Detecting the version of the operating system

Basic Menu

Mac applications include a menu bar that appears at the top of the screen to provide easy access to the application's main features.

Figure 19-8: Standard menu

The options included in the menu are predefined by the system and provide basic functionality for the app. To make changes and add custom features, SwiftUI includes the following modifiers.

▷ **commands(content:** Closure)—This modifier modifies the Scene to include the menus and options defined by the closure assigned to the **content** argument.

▷ **commandsRemoved()**—This modifier removes the standard menu option created by the system to create new windows.

The `commands()` modifier is applied to the Scene (the `WindowGroup` structure in the `App` structure) and returns a new Scene with the menu bar configured by the closure. To define the menus and the options from this closure, SwiftUI includes the `CommandMenu` and `CommandGroup` structures. The `CommandMenu` structure is used to create new menus. The following is the structure's initializer.

▷ **CommandMenu(**String, **content:** Closure)—This structure creates a menu to add to the menu bar. The first argument specifies the menu's title, and the closure assigned to the **content** argument defines the menu's option. The new menu is inserted between the View and Window menus.

To modify the options of standard menus, we can use the `CommandGroup` structure instead. The following are the structure's initializers.

- ▷ **CommandGroup(after:** CommandGroupPlacement, **addition:** Closure)— This structure defines a menu option. The **after** argument is a structure that specifies the option after which the new option will be added. The option is defined by the closure assigned to the **addition** argument.
- ▷ **CommandGroup(before:** CommandGroupPlacement, **addition:** Closure) —This structure defines a menu option. The **before** argument is a structure that specifies the option before which the new option will be added. The option is defined by the closure assigned to the **addition** argument.
- ▷ **CommandGroup(replacing:** CommandGroupPlacement, **addition:** Closure)—This structure defines a menu option. The **replacing** argument is a structure that specifies the option that will be replaced by the new option. The option is defined by the closure assigned to the **addition** argument.

The `CommandGroup` structure determines the position of the new option based on the position of a standard option. The standard options are represented by a `CommandGroup-Placement` structure. The structure includes type properties to return instances that represent all the standard options available. The properties are `appInfo`, `appSettings`, `appTermination`, `appVisibility`, `systemServices`, `importExport`, `newItem`, `printItem`, `saveItem`, `pasteboard`, `textEditing`, `textFormatting`, `undoRedo`, `sidebar`, `toolbar`, `singleWindowList`, `windowArrangement`, `windowList`, `windowSize`, and `help`.

Because the `commands()` modifier applies to the Scene, we can only implement it in the `App` structure. For instance, in the following example we use it to add a new menu to the menu bar.

```
import SwiftUI
@main
struct TestApp: App {
   var body: some Scene {
      WindowGroup {
         ContentView()
      }
      #if os(macOS)
      .commands {
         CommandMenu("Options") {
            Button("Option 1") {
               print("This is the option 1")
            }
            Button("Option 2") {
               print("This is the option 2")
            }
         }
      }
      #endif
   }
}
```

Listing 19-5: *Adding a menu to the menu bar*

Menu options are created with `Button` views. In this example, we include two: Option 1 and Option 2. The new menu is inserted between the View and Window menus, as shown below.

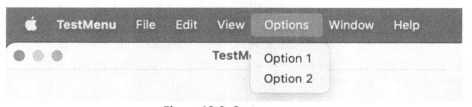

Figure 19-9: *Custom menu*

Do It Yourself: Create a Multiplatform project. Update the **App** structure with the code in Listing 19-5. Run the application on the Mac. You should see the Options menu in the menu bar with two options. When selected, these options print a message on the console, but you can use them for anything you want, such as modifying observable properties to update the interface or executing a method in the model, as we will see later.

Menu options can be associated with keys on the keyboard so that when the keys are pressed, the action assigned to the option is performed. SwiftUI provides the following modifiers to create these keyboard shortcuts.

▷ **keyboardShortcut(**KeyEquivalent, **modifiers:** EventModifiers**)**—This modifier assigns a keyboard shortcut to a menu option. The first argument can be a string representation of the key (e.g., "A") or a function key represented by a **KeyEquivalent** structure. The **modifiers** argument is an array of key modifiers that must be pressed along with the main key to perform the action. The structure includes type properties to return instances for every modifier key available. The properties are **all, capsLock, command, control, numericPad, option**, and **shift**.

▷ **modifierKeyAlternate(**EventModifiers, Closure**)**—This modifier offers an alternate menu option when a modifier key is pressed. The first argument is a structure that represents the key that must be pressed to activate the alternate option. The structure includes type properties to return instances for every modifier key available. The properties are **all, capsLock, command, control, numericPad, option** and **shift**. The second argument is the closure that provides the **Button** view that represents the alternate option.

The **KeyEquivalent** structure used by the **keyboardShortcut()** modifier to identify the key can be represented by a string (a letter, a number, or a punctuation character) or by type properties that return instances of the structure that represent function keys. The properties available are **upArrow, downArrow, leftArrow, rightArrow, clear, delete, delete-Forward, end, escape, home, pageDown, pageUp, return, space**, and **tab**.

In the following example, we use the **keyboardShortcut()** modifier to create a shortcut for the second option with the A and Shift keys, and use the **modifierKeyAlternate()** modifier as well to provide an alternate option when the Option key is pressed.

```
.commands {
   CommandMenu("Options") {
      Button("Option 1") {
         print("This is the option 1")
      }
      Button("Option 2") {
         print("This is the option 2")
      }
      .keyboardShortcut("A", modifiers: [.shift])
      .modifierKeyAlternate(.option, {
         Button("Option 3") {
            print("Alternate Option 3")
         }
      })
   }
}
```

Listing 19-6: Assigning a keyboard shortcut to a menu option

Do It Yourself: Update the `commands()` modifier with the code in Listing 19-6. Run the application on the Mac. Press the Shift + A keys. You should see the message produced by Option 2 on the console. Open the Options menu and press the Option key. Option 2 should be replaced by Option 3.

 IMPORTANT: You can add all the options you want to a menu. If you need to separate the options in groups, use a `Divider` view between `Button` views to draw a line.

In addition to our own menus, we can also add options to the standard menus or replace the options provided by the system with the `CommandGroup` structure. This structure defines three initializers that we can use to insert a new option before or after a system option, and also replace an existing one. For instance, the system includes an option in the File menu called New Window. This option is represented by the `newItem` property defined by the `CommandGroup-Placement` structure. The following example shows how to use this property to add an option to the File menu after the New Window option.

```
.commands {
    CommandGroup(after: .newItem, addition: {
        Button("Option 1") {
            print("This is option 1")
        }
    })
}
```

Listing 19-7: Adding options to a standard menu

Figure 19-10: Custom option added to a standard menu

If instead of adding an option we want to remove one, we just need to assign an empty closure to the **addition** argument. For instance, the following example adds a new option after the `newItem` option and removes that option from the menu. (Note that the removal must be done first.)

```
.commands {
    CommandGroup(replacing: .newItem, addition: {})
    CommandGroup(after: .newItem, addition: {
        Button("Option 1") {
            print("This is option 1")
        }
    })
}
```

Listing 19-8: Removing options

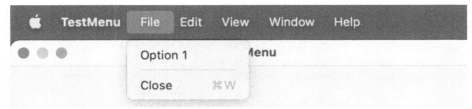

Figure 19-11: Standard option removed

We can also add submenus to a menu by using a `Picker` view instead of a `Button` view. For this purpose, we need a property in the model to store the current state.

```
import SwiftUI
import Observation

@Observable class ApplicationData: @unchecked Sendable {
   var selectedOption: Int = 1

   static let shared: ApplicationData = ApplicationData()
   private init() { }
}
```

Listing 19-9: Defining a property in the model to store the index of the selected option

The observable property in this model stores an integer value that we will use to identify the options in the picker with a `tag()` modifier. When an option is selected, the value in the `tag()` modifier is assigned to the observable property in the model, so views know which option is currently selected.

```
import SwiftUI

@main
struct TestApp: App {
   @State private var appData = ApplicationData.shared

   var body: some Scene {
      WindowGroup {
         ContentView()
            .environment(appData)
      }
      #if os(macOS)
      .commands {
         CommandGroup(after: .newItem, addition: {
            Picker("Options", selection: $appData.selectedOption) {
               Text("Option 1").tag(1)
               Text("Option 2").tag(2)
               Text("Option 3").tag(3)
            }
         })
      }
      #endif
   }
}
```

Listing 19-10: Adding a submenu

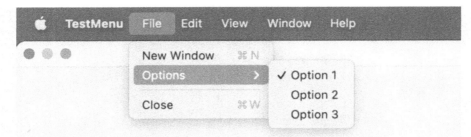

Figure 19-12: Submenu

 Do It Yourself: Create a Swift file called ApplicationData.swift for the model in Listing 19-9. Update the **App** structure with the code in Listing 19-10. Run the application on the Mac. Open the File menu and select an option. The option should remain selected.

SwiftUI includes structures that add predefined commands to the menu bar. The currently available are `SidebarCommands`, `TextEditingCommands`, `TextFormattingCommands`, `ToolbarCommands`, and `ImportFromDevicesCommands`. Probably the most interesting is `ImportFromDevicesCommands`, which adds a submenu that allows the user to import resources from nearby devices. For example, we can load and process an image taken by an iPhone's camera in our Mac application.

The option is added by the structure, but to process the data, we must apply the following modifier to a view.

▷ **importableFromServices(for:** Type, **action:** Closure)—This modifier imports data of the type specified by the first argument. The **action** argument provides a closure to process the data.

To add one of these options to the menu, we simply need to include an instance of the structure in the closure assigned to the `commands()` modifier. The following example adds the option to import resources from external devices.

```
.commands {
    ImportFromDevicesCommands()
}
```

Listing 19-11: Adding predefined options to import resources

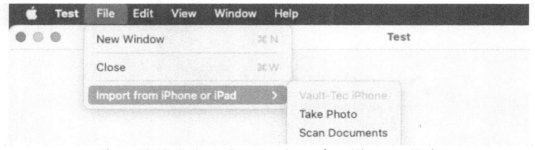

Figure 19-13: Option to import an image from iPhones or iPads

The process for receiving the data is similar to the one we used earlier to process drag-and-drop operations (see Drag and Drop Gesture in Chapter 12). We need to apply the modifier, specify a data type that conforms to the `Transferable` protocol to determine the type of data we want to accept, and then use the value received by the closure to process the data. However, since the devices send the images in JPEG format, we cannot implement standard types such as

Image or **Data**. Instead, we must create a custom structure that conforms to the **Transferable** protocol and is configured to import data with a JPEG content type. In our example, we call it **ImageRepresentation**.

```
import SwiftUI
#if os(macOS)
struct ImageRepresentation: Transferable {
    let image: NSImage

    static var transferRepresentation: some TransferRepresentation {
        DataRepresentation(importedContentType: .jpeg, importing: { data in
            if let newImage = NSImage(data: data) {
                return ImageRepresentation(image: newImage)
            } else {
                return ImageRepresentation(image: NSImage(named:
"nopicture")!)
            }
        })
    }
}
#endif

struct ContentView: View {
    @State private var MyPicture = Image(.nopicture)

    var body: some View {
        VStack {
            MyPicture
                .resizable()
                .scaledToFit()
        }.frame(width: 500, height: 350)
        #if os(macOS)
        .importableFromServices(for: ImageRepresentation.self, action:
{ elements in
            if let value = elements.first {
                MyPicture = Image(nsImage: value.image)
                return true
            }
            return false
        })
        #endif
    }
}
```

Listing 19-12: *Importing an image form an external device*

The macOS system does not implement the **UIImage** class for storing images, but the **NSImage** class. Therefore, the **ImageRepresentation** structure includes a property to store a value of this type with the image received from the device. When a value is received, the **importableFromServices()** modifier reads this property, creates an **Image** view with the value, and assigns it to a **@State** property to show the image on the screen.

 Do It Yourself: Update the **commands()** modifier in the **App** structure with the code in Listing 19-11 and the ContentView.swift file with the code in Listing 19-12. Run the application on the Mac. In the File menu, you should see the option Import from iPhone or iPad (Figure 19-13). Select the option Take Photo. Your cellphone should automatically open the camera. Take a picture. The image should appear on the screen. For more information on the **Transferable** protocol, see Drag and Drop Gesture in Chapter 12.

The options in a menu can be disabled. To disable an option, we just need to apply the `disabled()` modifier to the **Button** view that represents the option, and connect it with a state in the model that we can use to enable or disable the option when a condition is met. For example, we can disable the option if no text has been entered into a **TextField** view. To manage the value, we need an observable property in the model.

```
@Observable class ApplicationData: @unchecked Sendable {
   var inputMessage: String = ""

   static let shared: ApplicationData = ApplicationData()
   private init() { }
}
```

Listing 19-13: *Defining a state to enable and disable a menu option*

Now we can disable the option in the menu when this property is empty.

```
.commands {
   CommandGroup(after: .newItem, addition: {
      Button("Option 1") {
         print("This is option 1")
      }.disabled(appData.inputMessage.isEmpty)
   })
}
```

Listing 19-14: *Enabling and disabling a menu option*

To complete the example, we need to include a **TextField** view in our view that works with the observable property in the model.

```
struct ContentView: View {
   @Environment(ApplicationData.self) private var appData

   var body: some View {
      @Bindable var appData = appData

      VStack {
         TextField("Insert your Name", text: $appData.inputMessage)
         Spacer()
      }.padding()
      .frame(width: 500, height: 350)
   }
}
```

Listing 19-15: *Defining a* TextField *view to enable and disable the option*

When the user inserts a value in the text field, the option is enabled, but it is immediately disabled when the field is empty.

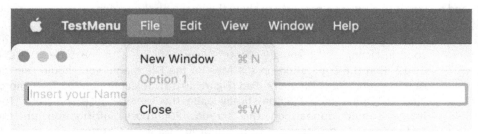

Figure 19-14: *Option disabled*

Do It Yourself: Update the `ApplicationData` class with the code in Listing 19-13, the `commands()` modifier in the `App` structure with the code in Listing 19-14, and the `ContentView` view with the code in Listing 19-15. Run the application on the Mac. Open the File menu. The option should be disabled. Insert a text in the text field and open the menu again. Now the option should be enabled.

In the last example, the option is disabled if a condition is not met, but often options are enabled or disabled depending on which element is focused on the interface. For example, we can have two `TextField` views, but the action can only be performed when the user is working on one of them (the text field is focused). In Chapter 6 we learned how to handle focus changes in a view, but to pass the focus state from one view to another, or as in this case from one view to the menu bar, we need to implement a structure called `FocusedValues`. This structure is a collection of values managed by the system that contains the state of the focused view. Each state is identified by a structure that conforms to the `FocusedValueKey` protocol. The only requirements of this protocol is a typealias named `Value` and the data type of the value managed by the view being monitored. Once we have this structure, we need to add a property of this type to the `FocusedValues` structure with an extension, as in the following example.

```
import SwiftUI
import Observation
struct AddressKey : FocusedValueKey {
   typealias Value = String
}
extension FocusedValues {
   var address: AddressKey.Value? {
      get { self[AddressKey.self] }
      set { self[AddressKey.self] = newValue }
   }
}
@Observable class ApplicationData: @unchecked Sendable {
   var inputMessage: String = ""
   var inputAddress: String = ""
   static let shared: ApplicationData = ApplicationData()
   private init() { }
}
```

Listing 19-16: Storing a focus state in the `FocusedValues` *structure*

In this example, we define a structure called `AddressKey` that conforms to the `FocusedValueKey` protocol with a typealias of `String` called `Value`, so we can store the values managed by the `TextField` view. Next, we define an extension of the `FocusedValues` structure to include our own property. We call this property `address`. The data type is the `Value` type defined in the previous structure, but set as an optional. This allows the system to assign the value `nil` to the property when the view is not focused. The property includes a setter and a getter to set and return the value in the collection with our structure as the key.

Now we need to set and read this focus state from the view and the `App` structure. To set the focus state, SwiftUI includes the following modifier.

▷ **focusedValue(**WritableKeyPath, Value)—This modifier stores a value in the `FocusedValues` structure. The first argument is the key path of the property in the `FocusedValues` structure we want to use to store the value, and the second argument is the value we want to store (usually the view's state).

To observe the value from the focused view, SwiftUI includes the `@FocusedValue` property wrapper. This property wrapper is created from the `FocusedValue` structure, which includes the following initializer.

> **FocusedValue**(KeyPath)—This initializer creates a structure to observe the values from a focused view. The argument is the key path of the property in the `FocusedValues` structure that stores the state we want to observe.

To store the focus state of a view in the `FocusedValues` structure, all we need to do is to apply the `focusedValue()` modifier to the view. In the following example, we do it to the `TextField` view that allows the user to insert an address.

```
struct ContentView: View {
    @Environment(ApplicationData.self) private var appData

    var body: some View {
        @Bindable var appData = appData

        VStack {
            TextField("Insert your Name", text: $appData.inputMessage)
                .padding()
            TextField("Insert Address", text: $appData.inputAddress)
                .padding([.leading, .trailing])
                .focusedValue(\.address, appData.inputAddress)
            Spacer()
        }.padding()
        .frame(width: 500, height: 350)
    }
}
```

Listing 19-17: Passing the focus state to the `FocusedValues` *structure*

When the second `TextField` view is focused, the `focusedValue()` modifier assigns the value of the `inputAddress` property to the `address` property of the `FocusedValues` structure, so the value is available for other views. Now we can observe this value from the **App** structure with the `@FocusedValue` property wrapper.

```
import SwiftUI

@main
struct TestApp: App {
    @State private var appData = ApplicationData.shared
    @FocusedValue(\.address) var addressValue: String?

    var body: some Scene {
        WindowGroup {
            ContentView()
                .environment(appData)
        }
        #if os(macOS)
        .commands {
            CommandGroup(after: .newItem, addition: {
                Button("Option 1") {
                    print("This is option 1")
                }.disabled(addressValue == nil)
            })
        }
        #endif
    }
}
```

Listing 19-18: Disabling a menu option according to the focus state of a view

The view defines a property called `addressValue`, which contains the value of the address property of the `FocusedValues` structure. If the `TextField` view that allows the user to insert an address is focused (the user is typing on it), this property contains the value inserted by the user, otherwise, the property returns `nil`, so we can enable or disable the menu option accordingly.

 Do It Yourself: Update the ApplicationData.swift file with the code in Listing 19-16, the `ContentView` view with the code in Listing 19-17, and the `App` structure with the code in Listing 19-18. Run the application on the Mac. Click on the first text field. Open the File menu. The option should be disabled. Click on the second text field to select it. Now the option should be enabled.

 IMPORTANT: SwiftUI also includes the `@FocusedBinding` property wrapper to observe the value of a binding property. This is useful when we need to change the state of a view from the menu. There is also a modifier called `focusedSceneValue()` to store the focus of a Scene instead of a single view. For more information, visit our website and follow the links for this chapter.

(Basic) **Toolbar**

Instead of navigation bars, Mac applications contain a toolbar at the top of the window where we can add all the items we need. The toolbar is added to the top of the right column in a two-column design created with a `NavigationSplitView` view. This means that we can use the `navigationTitle()` modifier to display a title, but SwiftUI also allows us to add a subtitle for macOS applications with the following modifier.

▷ **navigationSubtitle(**String**)**—This modifier adds a subtitle to the toolbar of a Mac application. The argument is the text we want to assign to the subtitle.

Like the navigation bar, the toolbar in a Mac application can contain buttons. The buttons are included with the `toolbar()` modifier used for iOS applications (see Chapter 8, Listing 8-3). For example, the following application defines a `NavigationSplitView` view with two views, one to create the content for the left column and another for the right column.

```
struct ContentView: View {
    var body: some View {
        NavigationSplitView(sidebar: {
            MenuView()
        }, detail: {
            DetailView()
        })
    }
}
```

Listing 19-19: Defining a two-column interface

The `MenuView` view defines the left column and doesn't require any special content for this example. The `DetailView` view, on the other hand, displays the toolbar, and here is where we should define the toolbar items, as in the following example.

```
import SwiftUI
struct DetailView: View {
    var body: some View {
        VStack {
            Text("Details")
        }
        .toolbar {
            ToolbarItem(placement: .automatic) {
                Button(action: {
```

```
                print("Adding Book")
            }, label: {
                Label("Add Book", systemImage: "plus")
            })
        }
    }
    .navigationTitle("My Title")
    #if os(macOS)
    .navigationSubtitle("My Subtitle")
    #endif
    }
}
```

Listing 19-20: Adding items to the toolbar for a Mac application

This view defines the title and subtitle and adds a button with an SF Symbol to the bar. We use the value **automatic** for placement, which positions the button on the right, but we could also have applied the value **principal**, which positions the buttons at the center.

Figure 19-15: Mac toolbar

If we don't want to show the toolbar, we can remove the title and make it transparent with the **toolbar(removing:)** and **toolbarBackgroundVisibility()** modifiers introduced in Chapter 8.

```
struct DetailView: View {
    var body: some View {
        VStack {
            Text("Details")
            Spacer()
        }
        .toolbar(removing: .title)
        .toolbarBackgroundVisibility(.hidden, for: .windowToolbar)
    }
}
```

Listing 19-21: Hiding the toolbar

Do It Yourself: Create a Multiplatform project. Update the **ContentView** view with the code in Listing 19-19. Create two SwiftUI files called MenuView.swift and DetailView.swift. Leave the **MenuView** view with a single **Text** view, but modify the **DetailView** view with the code in Listing 19-20. Run the application on the Mac. You should see a toolbar with a title and a subtitle, as illustrated in Figure 19-15. Update the **DetailView** view with the code in Listing 19-21. Run the application again. The toolbar should be invisible.

SwiftUI defines some modifiers that are exclusive to Mac applications. The following are the most frequently used.

▷ **help(**String**)**—This modifier creates a tooltip. (A tooltip is a message that appears next to the view when the mouse is positioned on top of it for a few seconds.)

▷ **pointerStyle(**PointerStyle**)**—This modifier changes the style of the mouse's pointer. The argument is a structure with properties and methods to define the style. The most useful are `columnResize`, `default`, `grabActive`, `grabIdle`, `horizontalText`, `link`, `rectSelection`, `rowResize`, `verticalText`, `zoomIn` and `zoomOut`.

▷ **pointerVisibility(**Visibility**)**—This modifier determines whether the mouse's pointer is visible or not. The argument is an enumeration with the values `automatic`, `visible` and `hidden`.

▷ **textInputSuggestions(**Closure**)**—This modifier creates a list of suggestions for a `TextField` view. The argument is the closure that provides the list of `Text` views with the suggestions. This modifier works along with the `textInputCompletion-`(`String`) modifier to specify the value to assign to the text field when an option is selected.

▷ **alternatingRowBackgrounds(**AlternatingRowBackgroundBehavior**)**—This modifier displays the views in a list or a table with alternative backgrounds. The argument is a structure that enables or disables the feature. The structure includes the properties `automatic`, `enabled` (default) and `disabled`.

Applying some of this modifiers is straightforward. In the following example, we show how to use the `help()` modifier to show a message to the user when the mouse is over a view and the `pointerStyle()` modifier to change the style of the pointer.

```
struct DetailView: View {
   var body: some View {
      VStack {
         Text("Details")
      }
      .toolbar {
         ToolbarItem(placement: .automatic) {
            Button(action: {
               print("Adding Book")
            }, label: {
               Label("Add Book", systemImage: "plus")
            })
            .help("Press this button to add a book")
            .pointerStyle(.link)
         }
      }
      .navigationTitle("My Title")
   }
}
```

Listing 19-22: Showing a tooltip for a button

If we position the mouse over the button, we can see the pointer changing into a hand and a message appearing after a few seconds.

Press this button to add a book

Figure 19-16: Tooltip

A more useful modifier is `textInputSuggestions()`. With this modifier we can show suggestions for a text field. The suggestions are created with `Text` views that can be declared as static or dynamic with a `ForEach` loop, as in the following example.

```
struct DetailView: View {
   @State private var text = ""
   let listSuggestions = ["Red", "Green", "Blue"]

   var body: some View {
      VStack {
         TextField("Insert Text", text: $text)
            .textInputSuggestions({
               ForEach(listSuggestions, id: \.self) { suggestion in
                  Text(suggestion)
                     .textInputCompletion(suggestion)
               }
            })
      }.padding()
   }
}
```

Listing 19-23: Showing suggestions for a text field

In this case, we use a simple array to provide the values, but because the text showed to the user may not be the one we need to insert in the field, we must apply the `textInputCompletion()` modifier to each view with the text to show in the field. The result is shown below.

Figure 19-17: Suggestions

The `alternatingRowBackgrounds()` modifier highlights alternate rows so they can be easily identified. The following example includes a model with a list of values to show how this modifier works.

```
import SwiftUI
import Observation

@Observable class ApplicationData: @unchecked Sendable {
   var foodList: [String]

   static let shared: ApplicationData = ApplicationData()
   private init() {
```

```
        foodList = ["bagels", "brownies", "butter", "cheese", "coffee",
"cookies", "donuts", "granola", "juice", "lemonade", "lettuce", "milk",
"oatmeal", "potato", "tomato", "yogurt"]
   }
}
```

Listing 19-24: Defining a model to test alternate backgrounds

The following are the changes we need to introduce to the `DetailView` view to display a list with alternate backgrounds.

```
struct DetailView: View {
    @Environment(ApplicationData.self) private var appData

    var body: some View {
        List {
            ForEach(appData.foodList, id: \.self) { item in
                Text(item)
            }
        }
        .navigationTitle("Food List")
        #if os(macOS)
        .alternatingRowBackgrounds()
        #endif
    }
}
```

Listing 19-25: Creating a list with alternate background

Food List

bagels
brownies
butter
cheese
coffee
cookies
donuts
granola

Menu

Figure 19-18: Highlighted rows

 Do It Yourself: Add to the previous project a Swift file called ApplicationData.swift for the model in Listing 19-24. Update the `DetailView` view with the code in Listing 19-25. Remember to inject the `Application-Data` object into the environment for the app and the previews (Chapter 7, Listing 7-4). Run the application on the Mac. You should see something like Figure 19-18.

Basic   Scenes

As explained in Chapter 5, to create an application, we must first define a Scene. SwiftUI includes several structures to create standard Scenes for every system. For Multiplatform applications, we used the `WindowGroup` structure, which is capable of managing one or more instances of our application on all Apple platforms. In Chapter 10, we introduced the `DocumentGroup` structure to create an application to manage internal and external documents. But there are more. For example, the framework includes the `Window` structure to create a Scene with only one window.

▷ **Window**(String, **id:** String, **content:** Closure)—This structure creates a Scene to present a single window. The first argument defines the window's title, the **id** argument defines the window's identifier, and the **content** argument is a closure that provides the view for the Scene.

The `Window` structure creates a single independent scene and is therefore useful for applications that cannot allow the user to open multiple windows, such as video games, but can also be composed·with other Scenes to present an auxiliary window, as in the following example.

```
import SwiftUI

@main
struct TestApp: App {
    var body: some Scene {
        WindowGroup {
            ContentView()
        }
        #if os(macOS)
        Window("My Window", id: "mywindow") {
            AuxiliaryView()
        }
        #endif
    }
}
```

Listing 19-26: Opening an auxiliary window

To create an auxiliary window, the `Window` structure is applied along with the `WindowGroup` structure, so the app's main window is created as always, but now we have an option in the Window menu to open the auxiliary window.

Figure 19-19: Option to open an auxiliary window

 Do It Yourself: Create a Multiplatform project. Update the `App` structure with the code in Listing 19-26. Create a new SwiftUI file called AuxiliaryView.swift with a single `Text` view. Run the application on the Mac. Open the Window menu. You should see an option with the name of the window, as shown in Figure 19-19 (My Window).

The menu option is automatically added to the Window menu when we add a `Window` Scene to the `App` structure, but most users don't know that the option even exists. To provide a better alternative, the Environment includes the following properties to open and close windows.

▷ **openWindow**—This property creates an action that presents a window. The property contains an instance of the `OpenWindowAction` structure that exposes a handler we can call to perform the action. There are two options available: we can call it with the **id** argument to open a window with a specific identifier (`openWindow(id: String)`), or with the **value** argument to open a window presented by the `WindowGroup` structure that can process that value type (`openWindow(value: Value)`).

▷ **dismissWindow**—This property creates an action that dismisses a window. The property contains an instance of the `DismissWindowAction` structure that exposes a handler we can call to perform the action. There are two options available: we can call it with the **id** argument to close a window with a specific identifier (`dismissWindow(id: String)`), or with the **value** argument to close a window presented by the `WindowGroup` structure that can process that value type (`dismissWindow(value: Value)`).

Just as with other Environment properties, such as `dismiss` and `dismissSearch`, we need to define an `@Environment` property and then call the handler to perform the action. Below you can see the `ContentView` view that we need to open the auxiliary view created in the previous example.

```
struct ContentView: View {
    @Environment(\.openWindow) var openWindow

    var body: some View {
        VStack {
            Text("Hello, world!")
            Button("Open Auxiliary Window") {
                openWindow(id: "mywindow")
            }
        }.frame(minWidth: 500, maxWidth: .infinity, minHeight: 300,
maxHeight: .infinity)
    }
}
```

Listing 19-27: *Opening a window programmatically*

The interface includes a `Button` view to open the auxiliary window. When the button is pressed, we perform the action with the **id** argument to open the window identified with the string "mywindow". We can add a similar button in the `AuxiliaryView` view to dismiss it.

```
import SwiftUI

struct AuxiliaryView: View {
    @Environment(\.dismissWindow) var dismissWindow

    var body: some View {
        VStack {
            Text("Auxiliary View")
                .padding()
            Button("Close Window") {
                dismissWindow(id: "mywindow")
            }
        }.frame(minWidth: 300, maxWidth: .infinity, minHeight: 200,
maxHeight: .infinity)
    }
}
```

Listing 19-28: *Closing a window programmatically*

When we press the button in the `ContentView` view, the window with the "mywindow" identifier is opened, and if we press the button in the `AuxiliaryView` view, the same window is closed.

Figure 19-20: Second window

In the previous example, we used the `frame()` modifier to set a minimum size for the views. The maximum size was declared with the value `infinity`, which means that the views will always take up the size of the window. This is the recommended approach, but it may not be suitable for our application. For example, if we set a maximum size for the view, this determines how large the view can be, but does not stop the user from expanding the window further. By default, the minimum size of the view determines the minimum size of the window, but users can expand the window as they wish, no matter the maximum size we set for the views. There are many ways to change this behavior. One alternative is to set the size of the window according to the size of the content with the following modifier.

▷ **windowResizability(**WindowResizability)—This modifier determines the strategy followed by the system to resize the window. The argument is a structure with the properties `automatic`, `contentMinSize` and `contentSize`.

By default, the behavior is set to `automatic`, which means that the window is going to respect the minimum size of the view but ignore the maximum size. If we want the window to respect these values, we can set the behavior to `contentSize` (the window determines its size according to the content).

```
import SwiftUI

@main
struct TestApp: App {
   var body: some Scene {
      WindowGroup {
         ContentView()
      }
      #if os(macOS)
      Window("My Window", id: "mywindow") {
         AuxiliaryView()
      }
      .windowResizability(.contentSize)
      #endif
   }
}
```

Listing 19-29: Configuring the window to adopt the size of the content

Now we can give the `AuxiliaryView` view a minimum and maximum size or a fixed size, as in the following example.

```
struct AuxiliaryView: View {
   @Environment(\.dismissWindow) var dismissWindow

   var body: some View {
      VStack {
         Text("Auxiliary View")
            .padding()
         Button("Close Window") {
            dismissWindow(id: "mywindow")
         }
      }
      .frame(width: 300, height: 200)
   }
}
```

Listing 19-30: *Giving the view a fixed size*

The `AuxiliaryView` view now has a fixed size of 300 x 200 points, and because we applied the `windowResizability()` modifier, the window adopts the same size and the user can't change it.

 Do It Yourself: Update the `App` structure with the code in Listing 19-29 and the `AuxiliaryView` view with the code in Listing 19-30. Run the application on the Mac. Click the button to open the `AuxiliaryView` view. The window should be of a size of 300 x 200 points and you shouldn't be able to resize it.

Unless we specify otherwise, the initial position and size of the windows are determined by the system. If we want to change these values, we can apply the following modifiers.

▷ **defaultPosition(**UnitPoint**)**—This modifier specifies the window's initial position relative to the screen. The argument is a structure with the type properties `topLeading`, `top`, `topTrailing`, `leading`, `center`, `trailing`, `bottomLeading`, `bottom`, and `bottomTrailing`.

▷ **defaultSize(width:** CGFloat, **height:** CGFloat**)**—This modifier specifies the window's size by default. The arguments determine the width and height.

Regardless of the position and size we choose, these values can be changed by the user. This means that we can only determine the position and size of a window when it is opened for the first time, but from that moment on the system will use the values selected by the user. If we want the window to always have the same initial position and size when the app is launched, we can use the following modifiers.

▷ **restorationBehavior(**SceneRestorationBehavior**)**—This modifier determines how the system restores previous opened windows. The argument is a structure with the properties `automatic` and `disabled`.

▷ **defaultLaunchBehavior(**SceneLaunchBehavior**)**—This modifier determines the window to be opened when the application is launched for the first time. The argument is a structure with the properties `automatic`, `presented` and `suppressed`.

In the following example, we ask the system to position the window for the `AuxiliaryView` view at the bottom-left corner of the screen, and to ignore any changes performed by the user every time the app is launched.

```
#if os(macOS)
Window("My Window", id: "mywindow") {
   AuxiliaryView()
}
```

```
.windowResizability(.contentSize)
.defaultPosition(.bottomLeading)
.restorationBehavior(.disabled)
#endif
```

Listing 19-31: Assigning a position by default

 Do It Yourself: Update the `Window` structure with the code in Listing 19-31. Run the application on the Mac. Click on the button to open the `AuxiliaryView` view. The window should appear at the bottom-left corner of the screen.

Other than specifying a standard position and default size for the window, we can calculate them dynamically with the following modifiers.

▷ **defaultWindowPlacement(**Closure**)**—This modifier runs a closure that we can use to calculate the position and size of the window. The closure receives two values: a `WindowLayoutRoot` structure that represents the content of the window, and a `WindowPlacementContext` structure that provides information about the screen and the windows.

▷ **windowIdealPlacement(**Closure**)**—This modifier runs a closure that we can use to calculate the position and size of the window when it is zoomed in. The closure receives two values: a `WindowLayoutRoot` structure that represents the content of the window, and a `WindowPlacementContext` structure that provides information about the screen and the windows.

The closures assigned to these modifiers must return a `WindowPlacement` structure with the new position and size of the window. The following is one of the structure's initializers.

▷ **WindowPlacement(**CGPoint, **size:** CGSize**)**—This initializer creates a structure that represents the position and size of a window. The first argument determines the window's preferred position, and the **size** argument its size.

To calculate the position and size of the window, the `WindowLayoutRoot` structure includes the `sizeThatFits()` method that returns a `CGSize` value with the width and height of the window's content, and the `WindowPlacementContext` structure includes the `defaultDisplay` property to return information about the screen. This property stores a `DisplayProxy` structure, which in turn includes the properties `bounds` to return a `CGRect` value with the dimensions of the screen, the `safeAreaInsets` property to return an `Edge-Insets` value with the safe area insets, and the `visibleRect` property to return a `CGRect` value with the dimensions of the portion of the screen where it is safe to place the window.

In the following example, we position the window for the `AuxiliaryView` view 100 points from the upper-left corner of the screen and give it a size half the width and height of the screen.

```
#if os(macOS)
Window("My Window", id: "mywindow") {
   AuxiliaryView()
}
.defaultWindowPlacement { content, context in
   let bounds = context.defaultDisplay.bounds
   let position = CGPoint(x: 100, y: 100)
   let size = CGSize(width: bounds.width / 2, height: bounds.height / 2)
   return WindowPlacement(position, size: size)
}
.restorationBehavior(.disabled)
#endif
```

Listing 19-32: Defining a custom position and size for the window

So far, we have opened the windows with a default configuration, but we can specify some attributes by applying the following modifiers to the views.

▷ **windowMinimizeBehavior(**WindowInteractionBehavior**)**—This modifier enables or disables the window's minimize functionality. The argument is a structure with the properties `automatic`, `disabled` and `enabled`.

▷ **windowDismissBehavior(**WindowInteractionBehavior**)**—This modifier enables or disables the window's dismiss functionality. The argument is a structure with the properties `automatic`, `disabled` and `enabled`.

▷ **windowFullScreenBehavior(**WindowInteractionBehavior**)**—This modifier enables or disables the window's full screen mode. The argument is a structure with the properties `automatic`, `disabled` and `enabled`.

▷ **windowResizeBehavior(**WindowInteractionBehavior**)**—This modifier enables or disables the window's resizing capabilities. The argument is a structure with the properties `automatic`, `disabled` and `enabled`.

▷ **windowBackgroundDragBehavior(**WindowInteractionBehavior**)**—This modifier enables or disables the possibility of dragging the window by the background. The argument is a structure with the properties `automatic`, `disabled` and `enabled`.

This modifiers are applied to the views, except for the `windowBackgroundDrag-Behavior()` modifier that is applied to the window. In the following example, we use the `windowResizeBehavior()` and `windowMinimizeBehavior()` modifiers with the `AuxiliaryView` view, so the only thing the user can do with this window is to close it.

```
#if os(macOS)
Window("My Window", id: "mywindow") {
   AuxiliaryView()
       .windowResizeBehavior(.disabled)
       .windowMinimizeBehavior(.disabled)
}
#endif
```

Listing 19-33: Disabling window controls

The windows we have used so far are presented with the design provided by the operating system, but SwiftUI offers modifiers to change the window's aspect and style. The following are the most frequently used.

▷ **windowStyle(**WindowStyle**)**—This modifier changes the window's style. The argument is a protocol with properties that determine the type of window to create. The properties available are `automatic` (default), `hiddenTitleBar`, `plain`, `titleBar` and `volumetric`.

▷ **windowLevel(**WindowLevel**)**—This modifier determines if the window is going to be shown on top or behind other windows. The argument is a structure with the properties `automatic`, `desktop`, `floating` and `normal`.

▷ **containerBackground(**Style, **for:** ContainerBackgroundPlacement**)**—This modifier defines the background style for the container. It works with many containers, including `NavigationStack` views, `NavigationSplitView` views, `TabView` views and windows. The first argument is the style to apply to the background, and the **for** argument is a structure that determines the container to be affected. Some of the properties provided by the structure are `navigation`, `tabView`, `widget`, `navigationSplitView` and `window`.

The two styles used in macOS to create the entire window are `automatic` and `plain`. The `automatic` style creates a standard view, while the `plain` style removes control bars, buttons and borders. The latter is the one used when we want to provide our own design, as in the following example.

```
#if os(macOS)
Window("My Window", id: "mywindow") {
   AuxiliaryView()
      .background(.yellow)
}
.windowStyle(.plain)
#endif
```

Listing 19-34: Applying a custom design to a window

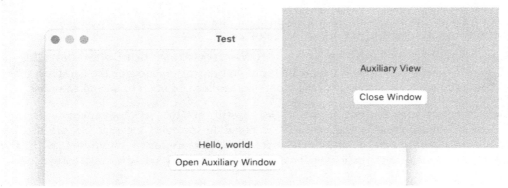

Figure 19-21: Custom window

A `plain` window doesn't include a navigation or a title bar and therefore it is not possible for the user to drag it or change its size. For a normal window, we can use the `windowBackground-DragBehavior()` modifier to allow the user to drag the window by positioning the mouse over the background, but because the plain style also removes the window's background, we need to apply the gesture to the view. SwiftUI includes the following structure for this purpose.

▷ **WindowDragGesture()**—This initializer creates a gesture recognizer to allow the user to drag a view.

Because we have already assigned a yellow background to the `AuxiliaryView` view in our previous example, all we need to do to allow the user to drag it is to apply the `gesture()` modifier with a `WindowDragGesture` structure, as we did in Chapter 12.

```
#if os(macOS)
Window("My Window", id: "mywindow") {
   AuxiliaryView()
      .background(.yellow)
      .gesture(WindowDragGesture())
}
.windowStyle(.plain)
#endif
```

Listing 19-35: Dragging a view

Another structure provided by SwiftUI for creating a Scene for macOS applications is `Settings`. This structure creates a Scene that provides the user with an interface to change the app's settings. Like the rest, the Scene is declared in the `App` structure along with the `WindowGroup` Scene, but it is displayed on the screen when the user selects the Settings option from the menu.

▷ **Settings(content:** Closure)—This structure creates a Scene to present the app's settings. The **content** argument is a closure with the views that render the Scene.

In the following example, we create a simple `Settings` Scene with a `Stepper` view for the user to set a value, and a `Text` view to show the current value on the screen. The value is stored in the App Storage system with the `@AppStorage` property wrapper, so we can read it later from the views to configure the interface.

```
import SwiftUI

@main
struct TestApp: App {
    @AppStorage("totalItems") var totalItems: Int = 0

    var body: some Scene {
        WindowGroup {
            ContentView()
        }
        #if os(macOS)
        Settings {
            HStack {
                Stepper("Total Items", value: $totalItems)
                Text(String(totalItems))
                    .font(.title.bold())
            }.frame(width: 200, height: 150)
        }
        #endif
    }
}
```

Listing 19-36: Defining a `Settings` *Scene*

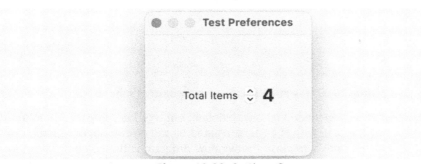

Figure 19-22: Settings Scene

 Do It Yourself: Create a Multiplatform project. Update the **App** structure with the code in Listing 19-36. Run the application on the Mac. Open the app's menu and click on the Settings option. You should see a small window appear on the screen, as shown in Figure 19-22.

Finally, there is one more structure for creating a Scene for macOS applications called **MenuBarExtra**. This structure creates a Scene that adds a control to the system's menu bar (an icon in the menu bar that provides additional functionality).

▷ **MenuBarExtra(**String, **systemImage:** String, **isInserted:** Binding, **content:** Closure)—This structure creates a Scene that adds a control to the system's menu bar. The first argument is the control's title, the **systemImage** argument is the SF Symbol we want to use to represent the control, the **isInserted** argument is a Boolean binding property that determines if the control is displayed or not, and the **content** argument is the closure that defines the menu or the view to show when the control is selected.

There are two different styles for the control. We can open a menu with options created by `Button` views, or a view with a custom interface. To select the style, the framework includes the following modifier.

▶ **menuBarExtraStyle(MenuBarExtraStyle)**—This modifier specifies the style of the content shown by the control. The argument is a structure that conforms to the `MenuBarExtraStyle` protocol. The framework includes three structures to define the styles. These structures include the type properties `automatic`, `menu`, and `window`.

By default, the style is set to `automatic`, which means the control will open a menu. To define the options for the menu, we can include `Button` and `Divider` views, as shown below.

```
import SwiftUI
@main
struct TestApp: App {
    var body: some Scene {
        WindowGroup {
            ContentView()
        }
        #if os(macOS)
        MenuBarExtra("My Control", systemImage: "phone") {
            Button("Option 1") {
                print("Option 1")
            }
            Button("Option 2") {
                print("Option 2")
            }
            Divider()
            Button("Quit") {
                NSApplication.shared.terminate(nil)
            }
        }
        #endif
    }
}
```

Listing 19-37: Inserting a control in the system's menu bar

Most Scenes contain a predefined menu with default options, including an option to close the application. This is not the case with the Scene created by the `MenuBarExtra` structure. In this case, we need to add the option to close the window programmatically. Applications in macOS are managed by an instance of the `NSApplication` class. The class includes a type property called `shared` to return this instance, and the instance includes the `terminate()` method to close the application. And that's all we need to create our own option to allow the user to terminate the app. The result is shown below.

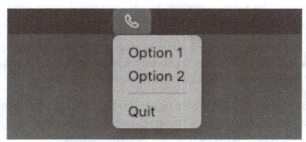

Figure 19-23: Control with a menu

To show a view instead of a menu, we must apply the `menuBarExtraStyle()` modifier with the `window` value and replace the buttons with a single view and its content.

```
MenuBarExtra("My Menu", systemImage: "phone") {
   VStack {
      HStack {
         Spacer()
         Button(action: {
            NSApplication.shared.terminate(nil)
         }, label: {
            Image(systemName: "xmark.circle")
         })
      }.padding()
      Button("Option 1") {
         print("Option 1")
      }.buttonStyle(.borderedProminent)
      Button("Option 2") {
         print("Option 2")
      }.buttonStyle(.borderedProminent)
      Spacer()
   }.frame(width: 200, height: 180)
}.menuBarExtraStyle(.window)
```

Listing 19-38: *Defining a control to open a view*

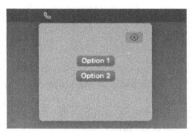

Figure 19-24: *Control with a view*

(Basic) Scene Storage

iPads and Mac computers can open multiple instances of an application in separate windows (Scenes). iPads offer several alternatives to open the application in a new window. The easiest is to split the screen from the bottoms at the top and reopen the application (see Chapter 12, Figure 12-4). On the Mac it is even easier, the option is available in the File menu.

Figure 19-25: *Option to create a new window*

When we open a new instance of our application (a new window), the `WindowGroup` structure creates a new Scene. Each Scene implements the same views and works with the same model. This means that all the Scenes will present the same values and have the same initial state. However, this is not always useful. Users often expect the window to be in the state it was before the application was closed, or for each window to manage its own data. To store information related to a Scene, SwiftUI includes the `@SceneStorage` property wrapper. This is equivalent to the `@AppStorage` property wrapper, but instead of storing values for the app, it stores values for the Scene.

In the following example, we create an application that allows the user to select a picture. The index of the selected picture is permanently stored in a `@SceneStorage` property, so the value is restored when the app is launched again.

To provide the data, we will use the model defined in Listing 19-24. The interface must include a **Picker** view to select the image and an **Image** view to display the selected image on the screen, as shown below.

```
struct ContentView: View {
    @Environment(ApplicationData.self) private var appData
    @SceneStorage("selection") var selection: Int = 0

    var body: some View {
        VStack {
            HStack(alignment: .top, spacing: 20) {
                Picker("Select", selection: $selection) {
                    ForEach(appData.foodList.indices, id: \.self) { index in
                        Button(appData.foodList[index].capitalized, action: {
                            selection = index
                        }).tag(index)
                    }
                }.frame(width: 200, height: 150, alignment: .top)
                Image(appData.foodList[selection])
                    .resizable()
                    .scaledToFit()
                    .frame(width: 200, height: 150)
            }
        }.padding(20)
    }
}
```

Listing 19-39: Storing the state of the Scene

Each time the user selects a different value, the **Picker** view saves that value in the **selection** property so it is preserved. When we close and reopen the application, the initial value is the one selected before. And since we use the **@SceneStorage** property to set the **Picker** view, the selection is unique for each Scene.

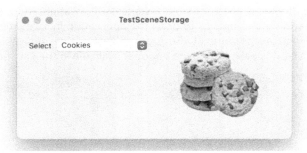

Figure 19-26: Scene with custom values

Do It Yourself: Create a Multiplatform project. Download the thumbnails from our website and add them to the Asset Catalog. Create a Swift file called ApplicationData.swift for the model in Listing 19-24. Update the **ContentView** view with the code in Listing 19-39. Remember to inject the **ApplicationData** object into the environment for the app and the previews (Chapter 7, Listing 7-4). Run the application on the Mac. Select a picture. You should see the selected picture on the screen. Stop the app from Xcode and run it again. The selected picture should be shown on the screen again. Open the File menu and click on the New Window option to open a new window. You should be able to select different pictures from each window.

Chapter 20
Internationalization

Basic **20.1 Localization**

Apple is present in more than a hundred countries, and apps are distributed in dozens of languages and dialects, but we can only create one version of our app, so we have to adapt it to each market. This includes not only translations, but also the arrangement of elements on the user interface, the formatting of numbers, and much more. This customization process is called localization. In SwiftUI, most of the localization process is done automatically. For example, the content of SwiftUI views is aligned using leading and trailing constraints that represent the left or right side depending on the language direction (right-to-left or left-to-right), and values, such as dates and units of measure, are automatically formatted according to the locale (see Chapter 4, Listing 4-32). But we still need to translate the text. For this purpose, Xcode provides String Catalogs.

Basic **String Catalogs**

String Catalogs are a tool provided by Xcode that allows us to translate text and adapt it to any language we want. The system tracks all the localizable text in the code and creates a file that we can edit or send to professional translators. The file is created like any other from the File from Template option in the File menu. The option is located under the Resource section.

Figure 20-1: String Catalog file

We can give the file any name we want, and it will be added to the project as always.

Figure 20-2: String Catalog file added to the project

Every time the application is run or built, the system tracks the views and updates the contents of this file. To test this, we can use a simple view.

```
import SwiftUI

struct ContentView: View {
    var body: some View {
        VStack {
            Text("Hello World!")
                .padding()
            Spacer()
        }
    }
}
```

Listing 20-1: *Testing String Catalogs*

This view contains only a `Text` view with the text "Hello World!". When we run or build the application (Command + B), this text is included in the String Catalog file, as shown below.

Figure 20-3: *String Catalog file updated*

When we select the String Catalog file, Xcode displays an interface for editing its contents. The interface includes a panel on the left with the available languages and another on the right to provide translations and adaptations for each language.

The file is created with the default language only (in our example, this is English). To add a new language, the panel includes a + button in the lower-left corner. When we click on this button, a popup menu appears with the list of languages we can add.

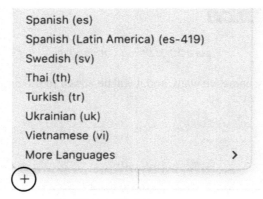

Figure 20-4: *Languages*

Once a language is added, we can click on it and enter the translation for each text. In the following example, we add Spanish and translate the text.

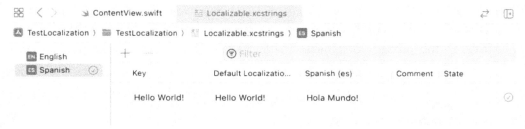

Figure 20-5: Translation to Spanish

 Do It Yourself: Create a Multiplatform project. Update the `ContentView` view with the code in Listing 20-1. Open the File menu, select the options New/File from Template, and create a String Catalog file (Figure 20-1). Run the application in the simulator or press Command + B to build it. Open the String Catalog file. You should see the text "Hello World!" in the list. Add the Spanish language, as shown in Figure 20-4. Use this project to test the rest of the examples in this chapter.

The localization is ready. Now, when our app is opened in a Spanish-speaking country, the `Text` view will display the text "Hola Mundo!". This works automatically on the user's device, but to test it in Xcode we need to change the scheme or configure the previews. By changing the scheme, we can test the localization in the simulator or a device. To edit the scheme, we must click on the scheme in the Xcode toolbar and select the Edit Scheme option.

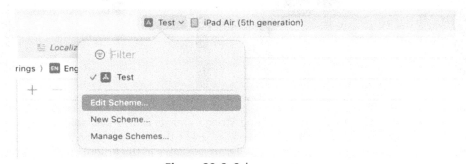

Figure 20-6: Scheme menu

The Edit Scheme option opens a window with all the options for configuring the project. To change the language, we must click Run, open the Options panel, and select the language from the App Language option (Figure 20-7, number 1).

Figure 20-7: App Language option

After we configure the scheme with the language we want to see, the previews, simulators and devices will run the app with that configuration. If we only want to test the localization in the previews, we can implement the following Environment properties instead.

- ▷ **layoutDirection**—This property determines the direction of the text. It is a **LayoutDirection** enumeration with the values **leftToRight** and **rightToLeft**.

- ▷ **locale**—This property determines the locale the views should use. It is a **Locale** structure.

To modify these properties, we must apply the **environment()** modifier to the preview, as we did in Chapter 5 (see Listing 5-94). For example, we can create two previews, one for the default language and another for Spanish.

```
#Preview {
    ContentView()
}
#Preview {
    ContentView()
        .environment(\.locale, Locale(identifier: "es"))
}
```

Listing 20-2: Selecting the language for the previews

Now we have two previews on the canvas, one with the text in English ("Hello World!") and another in Spanish ("Hola Mundo!").

Hello World!

Hola Mundo!

Figure 20-8: Previews in multiple languages

The interface provided by Xcode for editing String Catalogs is only available to developers. If we are working with third-party translators, we can export the files and then import them when we get them back from the translator. The options are available in the Product menu (Figure 20-9, number 1).

Figure 20-9: Export/Import options

When we send the localization files to a translator, it is recommended to include comments that can help the translator to achieve the most accurate result. For this purpose, the **Text** view includes the following initializer.

- ▷ **Text**(String, **comment:** StaticString?)—This initializer creates a **Text** view with the text specified by the first argument and the comment specified by the **comment** argument. The **StaticString** structure is designed to represent text that will not change after the application is compiled.

We can use this initializer to create all the **Text** views in our interface. In the following example, we add a comment to our **Text** view so that the translator knows what the purpose of the text is.

```
struct ContentView: View {
    var body: some View {
        VStack {
            Text("Hello World!", comment: "This is a welcome message")
                .padding()
            Spacer()
        }
    }
}
```

Listing 20-3: Including comments for the translator

The system tracks the views to find localizable text that can be included in the String Catalog. If the text is stored in properties or generated by external processes, we must declare it as localizable so that the system can find it. The **String** structure includes the following initializer for this purpose.

▷ **String(localized:** String)—This initializer creates a **String** structure with a localized string.

With this initializer, we can localize any text that our interface needs to display to the user. For example, we can add a button to our view that changes the text of a **Text** view when pressed, and localize both the original text and the new one assigned by the button.

```
struct ContentView: View {
    @State private var mytext = String(localized: "Hello World!")

    var body: some View {
        VStack {
            Text(mytext)
                .padding()
            Button("Change Text") {
                mytext = String(localized: "Goodbye World!")
            }
            Spacer()
        }
    }
}
```

Listing 20-4: Localizing strings

When the application is built, the system tracks the views, finds the text in the **Button** view, and then checks the code to find more localizable text. In this example we declare two localizable **String** structures, one to set the initial text for the **Text** view, and another to be assigned to that view later when the button is pressed. The String Catalog now includes three texts for translation.

Key	Default Localization (en)	Spanish (es)
Change Text	Change Text	Cambiar Texto
Goodbye World!	Goodbye World!	Hasta Luego Mundo!
Hello World!	Hello World!	Hola Mundo!

Figure 20-10: Localizable texts to be translated

If we receive normal strings from a process, we can tell the system that the strings are localizable by defining properties of type **LocalizedStringResource**. This structure includes the following initializer to specify a string and, if necessary, a comment.

▷ **LocalizedStringResource(**String, **comment:** StaticString?**)**—This initializer creates a structure to represent a localizable string that is received from another process.

We can use this structure, for example, when we know that the view will receive normal strings, but we want those strings to be localized.

```
struct ContentView: View {
    var body: some View {
        VStack {
            MyView(mytext: "Hello World!")
            Spacer()
        }
    }
}
struct MyView: View {
    let mytext: LocalizedStringResource

    var body: some View {
        Text(mytext)
            .padding()
    }
}
```

Listing 20-5: Localizing values

In addition to translations, String Catalogs also allow us to specify the singular and plural versions of a text. If the text contains a value, the system automatically selects the correct text to display to the user. For example, the following view includes a **@State** property to store an integer and a **Text** view to display it on the screen. Each time a button is pressed, the value is incremented by one.

```
struct ContentView: View {
    @State private var counter = 1

    var body: some View {
        VStack {
            Text("\(counter) Item")
                .padding()
            Button("Add Unit") {
                counter += 1
            }
            Spacer()
        }
    }
}
```

Listing 20-6: Specifying singular and plural versions of the text

Along with the value of the **counter** property, the **Text** view also displays the word "Item". The problem is that the text should read "Items" if the value is greater than 1. To set the two versions of this text, we can open the String Catalog, hold down the Control key and click on the word. This opens a menu with options to set versions for specific devices and also for singular and plural text.

Chapter 20 - Internationalization

Figure 20-11: Version menu

If we select the option Vary by Plural, the system creates two new fields for each case.

Figure 20-12: Singular and plural versions

In our example, we specify the word "Item" for the singular and "Items" for the plural version. Now the text that is displayed to the user depends on the value of the **counter** property.

Figure 20-13: The text depends on the value of the property

Basic # 21.1 Publishing

At the beginning of this book, we talked about Apple's tight control over the applications users can access. Applications for Mac computers can be sold separately, but mobile applications can only be sold through the App Store. The tools to submit our application to the App Store are provided by Xcode, but there are a number of requirements that we must meet in order for our application to be published and be available to users.

- We need an Apple Developer Program membership.
- We need a Distribution Certificate.
- We need a Provisioning Profile for distribution.
- We need an App ID to identify the application.
- We must register the app in the App Store Connect website.
- We must create an archive with our app for each platform to send to Apple servers.
- We must upload the archive to App Store Connect for review.

Basic ## Apple Developer Program

Developing and testing can be done with a free account, but publishing our app requires a membership in the Apple Developer Program. The option to sign up for this program is available on the **developer.apple.com** website. Click on the "Discover" option at the top of the screen, click on the "Program" option, click the "Enroll" option, and follow the instructions to register an account for an individual or organization. At the time of writing, the membership costs USD 99 per year.

Basic ## Certificates, Provisioning Profiles, and Identifiers

Apple wants to ensure that only authorized apps run on its devices, so it requires developers to add a cryptographic signature to each app. There are three values we need to authorize the app: Certificates, Provisioning Profiles, and Identifiers. Basically, a certificate identifies the developer who publishes the app, the provisioning profile identifies the device on which the app is allowed to run, and an identifier, called App ID, identifies the app. These values are packaged with the app's files so that Apple always knows who developed the app, who is authorized to run it, and on what devices.

Xcode automatically generates these values for us, so we do not have to worry about it, but Apple provides a control panel in our developer account in case we need to do it manually (the option is not available for free members). Figure 21-1 shows the menu we see when we go to developer.apple.com, click Account, and click Certificates in the section Certificates, IDs & Profiles.

Certificates, Identifiers & Profiles

Certificates	**Certificates** ⊕			Q All Types ˅
Identifiers				
	NAME	TYPE	PLATFORM CREATED BY	EXPIRATION
Devices				
Profiles				
Keys				

Figure 21-1: Web page to manage certificates, provisioning profiles, and identifiers

On this page we can create, edit or remove certificates, provisioning profiles and identifiers. The page contains two sections. The left pane provides a list of options to select the type of values we want to work with, and the right pane shows the list of available values and buttons to create new ones. When a value is selected, a new window opens with tools for editing the value.

(Basic) Icons

Before we submit the app to the App Store, we need to provide the resources that Apple requires to make our app available to the public. One important resource we must include in our project is the app's icons. Icons are the small images that users tap or click on to launch the app. By default, the Asset Catalog contains a set called AppIcon to manage the icons for the application. The set includes placeholders for every icon we need and for all available sizes and devices.

The icons can be created with any image editing software available on the market. A file must be created for each size required, but there are different options available. For iOS devices (iPhones and iPads) we can provide a single image of 1024x1024 pixels and the system takes care of creating the rest, but we can also provide an image for each size and device. The options are available from the Attributes Inspector panel on the right.

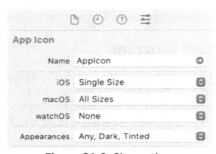

Figure 21-2: Size options

If the Single Size option for iOS is selected, we only need to provide a 1024x1024 pixel image, but three versions are required, one for any appearance, another for dark mode, and another for tinted interfaces. For the light and dark modes, we can specify the colors we want, but the tinted version must be provided in grayscale, as shown in Figure 21-3 below. The system will take care of converting the grayscale to the color tone selected by the user.

Figure 21-3: AppIcon set with the icons for iPhones and iPads

(Basic) Launch Screen

The launch screen is the first screen the user sees when the application is launched. Regardless of their size, applications always take a few seconds to load. The launch screen is required to give the user the impression that the app is responsive.

We can define two aspects of the launch screen: the background color and an image. The values are set via the Info panel in the app's settings. The option is called Launch Screen. When we press the + button on this key, Xcode shows a list of options from which we can choose.

Figure 21-4: Launch Screen options

Two options are available to specify the content and four to configure the screen. The Background color option specifies the name of the Color Set in the Asset Catalog that will be used to define the background color of the screen, and the Image Name option specifies the name of the Image Set that contains the image to be displayed. For configuration, there is the Image respects safe area insets option to specify the behavior of the image with respect to the safe area, and the Show Navigation bar, Show Tab bar, and Show Toolbar options to specify whether these bars should be displayed when the app is launched.

The following example shows what happens when we add a background color and an image. In this case, we use an Image Set called launchLogo and a Color Set called launchColor.

Launch Screen		Dictionary	(2 items)
Image Name		String	launchLogo
Background color		String	launchColor

Figure 21-5: Launch Screen configuration

Apple's guidelines recommend creating a launch screen that closely resembles your app's first screen. For example, if the background of the user interface is yellow, we should assign a yellow background to the launch screen as well. In our example, we define two sets in the Asset Catalog. The launchLogo set contains a PNG image with a logo, and the launchColor set defines a yellow color for the light and dark appearance. The result is shown below.

Figure 21-6: Launch screen for our app

App Store Connect

The first step we need to take to submit our application is to create a record on Apple's servers. Apple has set up a website for this purpose, which can be found at **appstoreconnect.apple.com**. To log in, we must use the same Apple ID and password that we use to access our account at developer.apple.com. Figure 21-7 shows the options available after logging in.

Figure 21-7: App Store Connect menu

In this section we can enter our financial information (Agreements, Tax, and Banking), publish our apps (My Apps), and see how the business is doing (Sales and Trends). The first step is to create a record for the app we want to publish in My Apps. When we click on this icon, a new window will open with a list of our apps and a + button at the top to add more.

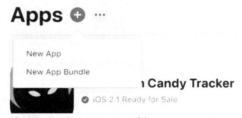

Figure 21-8: Menu to add apps to our account

To add a new app, we must select the New App option and enter the app's information. The first window asks for the platform for which we developed the app (in our case iOS and macOS), the name of the app, the main language, the bundle ID, and a custom ID (SKU) that we can use later to identify the app. The name and language are values we already have, and the SKU is a custom string, but the Bundle ID is an Xcode-generated value. Xcode creates a Bundle ID and sends it to the Apple servers when we enable services from the Capabilities panel. If our app does not use any of these services, we can register a new Bundle ID from developer.apple.com.

Figure 21-9: Bundle ID and SKU identifier

After these values are entered, we can click the Create button and complete the rest of the information. This includes the description of the app, screenshots, and personal information. Also, we need to select the Pricing and Availability option on the left to set the price and the locations where the app will be available. Once all the information is provided, we can click the Save button and go back to Xcode to upload the files.

Basic Submitting the Application

The application and resources must be compiled into a single archive for each platform and then submitted to App Store Connect. We need to create one archive for iOS devices and another for macOS. The option is available in the Product menu, but it is enabled only when the corresponding device is selected in the Scheme. We can select a real device connected to the computer, or we can use the Any iOS Device option for iOS apps or the Any Mac option for macOS (Figure 21-10, number 1).

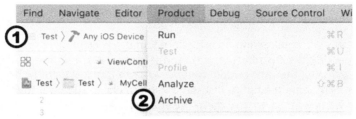

Figure 21-10: *Archive option*

After we click the Archive option (Figure 21-10, number 2), Xcode compiles the application and creates the archive. The next window displays the archive and offers buttons to validate and submit the application.

Figure 21-11: *List of archives created for our app*

Figure 21-11 shows an archive created for an application called Test (number 1). The item representing the archive includes the date it was created, the app's version, and the number of the build. (We can send multiple builds to App Store Connect and later decide which one we want Apple to review.)

 IMPORTANT: The app's version and the number of the build (archive) are determined from the app's settings (by default, both values are set to 1.0). If we want to specify a different version, we must declare the numbers separated by one or two periods (e.g., 1.0 or 1.2.5). The values represent different revisions of our app, with the order of relevance from left to right. The values are arbitrary, but we are required to change them every time an update is published to the App Store to reflect how big the update is.

Although it is not required, we should always validate the archive before submitting the app. This process allows Xcode to detect errors and make suggestions on how to fix them. To start the validation process, we can click the Validate App button (Figure 21-11, number 3). The first window displays icons for selecting the validation method. There is an option for automatic validation called Validate and another one to customize the process.

Select a method for validation:

Validate   Custom

Figure 21-12: *Options for validation*

When this process is complete and no errors are found, we can finally submit our app to the Apple servers by clicking the Distribute App button (Figure 21-11, number 2). The first window displays icons for selecting the distribution method. We can use TestFlight to submit the app for testing to other users or team members, distribute it internally, or submit it to the App Store. The latter is the option we need to choose to make the app available to the public.

Select a method for distribution:

TestFlight & App Store   TestFlight Internal Only   Release Testing   Enterprise

Debugging   Custom

Figure 21-13: *Options for distribution*

As mentioned earlier, we can submit multiple archives to the server (builds). For this reason, we need to return to the App Store Connect website, open the description of our application, and select the archive we just uploaded (it may take a few minutes for it to become available). Figure 21-14 below shows what we see in the Build section.

Build

BUILD	VERSION	HAS APP CLIP
1	3.3	NO

Figure 21-14: *Selecting the build to send to the App Store*

After the archive is selected, we can click on the Save button to save the description of the app. If all the required information has been provided, we can click on the Submit for Review button at the top of the page to submit the application. The system will ask some questions and then the application will be sent to Apple for review (the message Waiting for Review will be displayed under the app's title).

The process takes a few days. If the app is approved, Apple sends us an email to let us know that the app is available in the App Store.

Index